EXPOSITORY
OUTLINES
~~ on the
Whole Bible

EXPOSITORY OUTLINES
on the
WHOLE BIBLE

CHARLES SIMEON

EXPOSITORY OUTLINES

~~ on the
Whole Bible

by CHARLES *Simeon*

✝
✝

VOLUME 7

PROVERBS
through
ISAIAH 26

ZONDERVAN PUBLISHING HOUSE
Grand Rapids 1956 Michigan

EXPOSITORY OUTLINES ON THE WHOLE BIBLE

was formerly published as "Horae Homileticae." This reprint edition was made from the 8th edition published by Henry G. Bolm, Publishers, London in 1847. It has been reproduced by the photo offset process.

Printed in the United States of America

CONTENTS TO VOL. VII.

Dick Mills Purchase 1989 N.L.

PROVERBS.

OUTLINE NO. 753

THE NEED OF ATTENDING TO GOD'S GRACIOUS INVITATIONS.

Prov. i. 20—31. Wisdom crieth without; she uttereth her voice in the streets: she crieth in the chief place of concourse, in the openings of the gates: in the city she uttereth her words, saying, How long, ye simple ones, will ye love simplicity? and the scorners delight in their scorning, and fools hate knowledge? Turn you at my reproof: behold, I will pour out my spirit unto you, I will make known my words unto you. Because I have called, and ye refused; I have stretched out my hand, and no man regarded; but ye have set at nought all my counsel, and would none of my reproof: I also will laugh at your calamity; I will mock when your fear cometh; when your fear cometh as desolation, and your destruction cometh as a whirlwind; when distress and anguish cometh upon you. Then shall they call upon me, but I will not answer; they shall seek me early, but they shall not find me: for that they hated knowledge, and did not choose the fear of the Lord: they would none of my counsel: they despised all my reproof. Therefore shall they eat of the fruit of their own way, and be filled with their own devices.

TO expostulate with men respecting their evil ways, to point out the consequences of persisting in them, to urge the necessity of a speedy and thorough conversion to God, and to enforce the address with affectionate entreaties and encouraging assurances, is stigmatized as the effervescence of a heated imagination, the offspring of a weak enthusiastic mind. But, however it be foolishness with men, it is wisdom in the sight of God. No expostulations, entreaties, promises, or threatenings can be delivered with greater

energy or affection than those in the text; yet God
calls them the voice, not of folly and enthusiasm, but
of " wisdom;" and, whatever we may think of them,
they will be found to be " the words of truth and
soberness." We are now " in the chief place of concourse," and it is wisdom itself, or God under the
name of Wisdom, that now addresses us. The substance of the address may be comprehended under
two general observations :

I. To those who receive his invitations, God will be
    exceeding gracious—

Nothing can be more tender than the expostulation
before us—

[The words are addressed not merely to the " simple," but
to those who " love simplicity;" not only to the ignorant, but
to them that " hate knowledge;" not only to those who are
destitute of religion, but who "delight to scoff" at it. What
can we suppose that God should say to such daring transgressors? What, but to denounce the heaviest judgments?
But " he is God and not man," and therefore he speaks to
them as God, in terms of inconceivable love and mercy; "How
long will ye love your evil and destructive ways?" Will not
" the past time suffice to have followed" them? Have they
been so pleasant or profitable that ye will forego all the happiness of heaven for them? or, if ye intend to turn away from
them, have ye fixed the period of your conversion? "How
long" do you intend to persist? Till the time of sickness, and
the hour of death? or till some more convenient season?
Ah! "turn you at my reproof;" let the words of a Father
and a Friend prevail with you: do not attempt to justify
your actions; or to extenuate your guilt: you see clearly
enough that your conduct is indefensible: turn, turn from it
without delay—]

The promises, with which the expostulation is
enforced, add greatly to its weight—

[A consciousness both of weakness and of ignorance often
contributes to keep men under the power of their sins—A
thought arises in their minds, ' I know not how to turn;
I know not how to obtain either the pardon of my sins, or
victory over my lusts.' But God obviates at once all such
discouraging reflections. He says in effect, 'Are your corruptions insuperable by any efforts of your own? "I will pour
out my Spirit" to sanctify you throughout. Are you at a loss

how to obtain my favour? "I will make known to you the words of life;" I will reveal my Son in your heart; I will shew you the efficacy of his atonement, and make you wise unto salvation through faith in him.' Thus does he silence their objections, and dissipate their fears: "Behold, what manner of love" is this! surely we should not hear of it but with wonder; we should not receive its overtures, but with grateful adoration—]

But "God will not always strive with man." On the contrary,

II. They, who despise his invitations, shall be given up to final impenitence and ruin—

The contempt too generally poured upon the mercy of God, is awful in the extreme—

[One would suppose that such invitations and promises could not fail of producing the desired effect. But, alas, the reception they meet with is such as God himself represents it: men " refuse to obey his calls; when he stretches out his hands to them with parental tenderness and importunate entreaties, they will not regard him; they set at nought his counsel; they despise his reproof; they hate even to hear of their duty, and determine, whatever be the consequence, that they will not perform it." The zeal and earnestness of his ministers are made a subject of profane ridicule; and the dictates of wisdom are laughed at as the effusions of folly and fanaticism. We appeal to the consciences of all respecting these things. Who that has made any observations on the world around him, or on what passes in his own heart, must not attest that these things are so? Yes; we are all guilty: "This has been our manner from our youth." Some have been more open and notorious, and others more secret and reserved, in their oppositions to God's will; but all have opposed it, and, if divine grace have not slain our enmity, we are opposing it still: the deliberate sentiment of every unregenerate man is like theirs of old, " As for the word which thou hast spoken unto us in the name of the Lord, we will not hearken unto thee[a]".]

But such conduct, if persisted in, will one day meet a suitable reward—

[As God cannot be deceived, so neither will he be mocked: if he have a day of grace, so has he also a day of vengeance; and that day is hastening on apace. However secure the sinner may think himself, there is an hour of " desolation, and of consequent distress and anguish coming upon him." Perhaps

[a] Jer. xliv. 16.

it may come in this life; on a dying bed he may be filled with terror and remorse; and though, like Judas, he may confess his sin, or, like Esau, pray for a revocation of his sentence, his prayers may be cast out, and God laugh at his calamity. Often does God threaten this, and often has he executed his threatening; "Go to your gods whom ye have chosen," said he to his people of old; let them deliver you; for I will deliver you no more[b]." So now does he often suggest to the mind of an awakened, but unconverted sinner, 'What will the world do for you now? What will your pleasures, your riches, or your honours profit you in this day of my wrath? What do you think of the seed which you have been sowing, now you begin to reap the fruit thereof?' But if God deal not with us thus in this world, most assuredly he will in the world to come. That will indeed be an hour of distress and anguish when these despisers of mercy shall stand at the tribunal of their Judge: and oh! how will HE then "laugh at their calamity! how will he mock at all their fear" and terror! 'You would not believe my word: now see whether it be true or not. You would not be persuaded that I would ever vindicate my insulted Majesty: What do you think of that matter now? You despised me, and said, "Depart from me; I desire not the knowledge of thy ways!" You shall have your request: I will depart from you; and you too shall depart from me: depart, accursed, into everlasting fire: and though you should pray to all eternity for a mitigation of your pain, you shall never have so much as a drop of water to cool your tongue.'

Would to God that men would realize these things, and be persuaded to believe that God is true! But whether they will hear, or whether they will forbear, we must declare what God has spoken: and, however an ignorant world may deride it as folly, we will aver it to be the "counsel of true wisdom," and the declaration of an unerring God.]

APPLICATION—

1. Let all adore the divine goodness—

[Which of us must not plead guilty to the charge of despising God? Which of us has not persevered in a course of disobedience to him in spite of all his messages of mercy; and *that* too, not for days merely, but for months and years? Yet has God exercised forbearance towards us; and at this very instant renews to us his gracious invitations. Let us consider how many thousands have been cut off in their sins, while we are yet spared to hear the tidings of salvation: and "let the patience and long-suffering of God lead us to repentance."

[b] He has threatened it, Mic. iii. 4. Jer. ii. 27, 28; and he has executed it, Zech. vii. 11—13. Judg. x. 13, 14.

Let us magnify him for such distinguished favours; and turn to him " to-day, while it is called to-day, lest he swear in his wrath that we shall never enter into his rest."]

2. Let all tremble at the divine justice—

[Though God be so full of compassion, "not willing that any should perish, but that all should come to repentance and live," yet is he a just and sin-avenging God: " he will by no means clear the guilty[c]." He sometimes " repays the wicked to their face" even in this life; but there is a day which he has appointed for the full display of his own righteousness ; a day, wherein he will render to every man according to his deeds ; to those, who have sought for immortality, eternal life; but to the despisers of his truth, indignation and wrath, tribulation and anguish[d]. Let us then get our minds impressed with this thought, that it is a fearful thing to fall into the hands of the living God[e]: and let us instantly comply with his invitations here, that we may be partakers of his promises in a better world.]

c Exod. xxxiv. 7. 	d Rom. ii. 6—9. 	e Heb. x. 31.

OUTLINE NO. 754

THE WAY OF ATTAINING DIVINE KNOWLEDGE.

Prov. ii. 1—6. *My son, if thou wilt receive my words, and hide my commandments with thee; so that thou incline thine ear unto wisdom, and apply thine heart to understanding ; yea, if thou criest after knowledge, and liftest up thy voice for understanding; if thou seekest her as silver, and searchest for her as for hid treasures ; then shalt thou understand the fear of the Lord, and find the knowledge of God. For the Lord giveth wisdom ; out of his mouth cometh knowledge and understanding.*

WISDOM is justly considered as the first of human attainments. It is that which elevates us in the scale of being, and to it we are indebted for all the most refined comforts of civilized society. But there is a spiritual wisdom totally distinct from that which is merely intellectual, and as much superior to it both in its qualities and effects, as reason is superior to instinct. What this is, and how it is to be attained, we are informed by Solomon in the words before us.

Let us then consider,

I. Wherein true wisdom consists—

The nature of true wisdom is plainly the text—

[That which in one verse is called, " Wisdom," and " Understanding," in a subsequent verse is called, " The fear of the Lord," and " The knowledge of God." The wisdom which unregenerate men possess, resides only in the head; but that of which the text speaks is seated in the heart. The former consists merely in a knowledge of men and things, with a faculty of applying that knowledge to present circumstances: but the latter consists in a knowledge of God as reconciled to us in Christ Jesus, together with a correspondent fear and love of his name. The former enlarges the mind, and directs the conduct in things relating to time: the latter informs and regulates the soul in reference to eternity.]

This description is just and accurate—

[We confess that the knowledge and fear of God is not so reputed by the world: on the contrary, it is stigmatized as folly and madness. But that which arrogates to itself an exclusive title to the appellation of wisdom, is by no means so deserving of it as this: because, whatever excellencies it possesses, its operations are weak, uncertain, transient: whereas " the wisdom that is from above" brings into subjection every rebellious passion, and progressively prepares us for the enjoyment of our God. It was with this wisdom that the Messiah himself was endued[a]. And it is of this that Solomon speaks, when he declares that nothing else is worthy the name of wisdom[b].]

Respecting wisdom the text further informs us,

II. By what means it is to be attained—

The wisdom of this world may be gained by study only: but spiritual wisdom requires,

1. Sincerity—

[If a man have not a disposition to obey the word of God, he will find occasion of cavil and dispute in the plainest expressions. The Pharisees of old, though conversant with the sacred writings, and instructed by our Lord himself, remained ignorant of the truth, because " they loved darkness rather than light." Thus it will be with *us*. However good the seed that is sown may be, it will never bring forth fruit to perfection, unless it be " received into an honest and good heart." If we would be truly wise, we must imitate the docility of Cornelius[c]; or, in the language of the text, we must " receive God's word, and hide his commandments with us," as an inestimable jewel which we are solicitous to possess and keep.]

2. Diligence—

[a] Isai. xi. 2, 3.   [b] Prov. ix. 10.   [c] Acts x. 33.

[This idea is strongly inculcated in the words before us:
" we should incline our ear, and apply our heart to understanding, and seek it as silver, and search for it as for hid
treasures." We should consider the inspired volume as an
inexhaustible mine, which yields nothing to a superficial
observer, but will richly repay those who explore its inmost
recesses. To this effect was the direction given to Joshua[d];
and if we follow that advice, we shall succeed like the Be-
reans of old[e]. It is the diligent hand, and that only, that
can ever make us rich.]

3. Prayer—

[Nothing will succeed without prayer. A man might
commit to memory the whole Bible, and yet not understand
one spiritual truth contained it, if he trusted in his own
powers, instead of looking up to God for the teaching of his
Spirit. Our blessed Lord assures us, that none knoweth the
Father, but he to whom the Son shall reveal him[f]. And this
also is intimated in the repeated direction given us in the text,
to " cry after knowledge, and lift up our voice for understanding." The Apostles themselves needed to have " their
understandings opened, before they could understand the
Scriptures[g]." Yea, established Christians still need "a spirit
of wisdom and revelation to be given" to them, in order to
their obtaining a juster view of revealed truths[h]. All of us
therefore, if we would be taught of God, must cry with David,
" Open thou mine eyes, that I may behold wondrous things
out of thy law[i]."]

For the encouragement of all, Solomon further
declares,

III. The certain issue of those means—

God is the source and giver of all spiritual knowledge—

[Nothing can be more positive than the assertion before
us, That " God giveth wisdom, and that out of his mouth
cometh knowledge and understanding." It is in this view that
he is called, "The Father of lights[k];" because as that bright
luminary, the sun, was the work of his hands, so all light, intellectual or spiritual, is derived from him. Human learning
gives a man no advantage towards the attainment of true
wisdom. All, under God, depends on the state of mind with
which men seek divine knowledge: if they be willing to "learn
of the Father[l]," he will teach them: if they be too proud to

[d] Josh. i. 8.　　[e] Acts xvii. 11.　　[f] Matt. xi. 27.
[g] Luke xxiv. 45.　[h] Eph. i. 17, 18.　[i] Ps. cxix. 18.
[k] Jam. i. 17.　　[l] John vi. 45.

submit to his instructions, he will leave them to wander further and further from the right way. He will " take the wise in their own craftiness[m]," and " reveal to babes what he hides from the wise and prudent[n]."]

Nor will he suffer us to use the appointed means in vain—

[Frequent are the assurances which God has given us respecting this[o]. And he has made distinct promises to each of the foregoing means. Are we sincere? he will open our eyes[p]. Are we diligent? he will reveal himself to us[q]. Are we importunate in prayer? he will give us liberally, and without upbraiding[r]. No want of learning, no weakness of intellect, shall be any obstacle to him, or deprive us of the benefits which we seek[s]. On the contrary, he will make use of the weakest and most contemptible of men to confound the wise and mighty[t].]

INFER—

1. How highly should we value a preached Gospel!

[Men spend much time and money in acquiring human knowledge, and are glad to avail themselves of all lectures, public or private, whereby they may gain instruction. But a frequent ministration of divine ordinances, and a faithful dispensation of God's word, are deemed worthy of censure rather than of approbation; and the very persons for whose benefit the word is preached, can scarcely be prevailed upon to lend an ear to the instruction that is freely offered. Little do they think what it is that they thus despise. The ordinances are appointed of God for the express purpose of " converting souls, and making wise the simple[u]." How many are there now in heaven, who would have " perished for lack of knowledge," if the voice of God in his ministers had not reached their hearts, and " brought them out of darkness into marvellous light[x]!" Let all then improve the ordinances with diligence, and pray that by means of them they may be " made wise unto salvation[y]."]

2. How precious should the Scriptures be in our sight!

[It is only at certain seasons that we can attend on public ordinances: but the Scriptures we may read at all times. In them is contained all that we need to know. And the Holy Spirit is promised us, to guide us into all truth[z]. Let the

---

[m] 1 Cor. i. 19. and iii. 19.   [n] Matt. xi. 25.
[o] Ps. xxv. 9, 12, 14.   [p] John vii. 17.   [q] Prov. viii. 17.
[r] Jam. i. 5.   [s] Isai. xxxv. 8.   [t] 1 Cor. i. 27, 28.
[u] Job xxiii. 12. Ps. xix. 7.   [x] 1 Pet. ii. 9.
[y] 1 Pet. ii. 2. Heb. ii. 1.   [z] John xvi. 13. 1 John ii. 20, 27.

sacred volume then be our delight, and our meditation all the day[a]. Let us not cavil at any part of it, or say, This is a hard saying[b]; but let us receive it with meekness, knowing that, if it be engrafted in our hearts, it is able, and shall be effectual, to save our souls[c].]

[a] Ps. i. 2.   [b] John vi. 60.   [c] Jam. i. 21.

OUTLINE NO. 755

PIETY A PRESERVATIVE FROM EVIL.

Prov. ii. 10, 11. *When wisdom entereth into thine heart, and knowledge is pleasant unto thy soul, discretion shall preserve thee, understanding shall keep thee.*

PIETY, more than any other thing whatever, is regarded with jealousy and suspicion: and it is no uncommon thing for parents to guard their children against its advocates and professors, as they would against persons infected with a contagious disease. What the fruit of this folly, both in parents and children, too generally is, may be easily conceived: the children, taught to dread piety, which alone could preserve them from evil, become the victims of temptation, and fall into every species of iniquity; and the parents not unfrequently are bowed down by the misconduct of their children, till their grey hairs are brought with sorrow to the grave. Men vainly hope to effect that by moral suasion, which nothing but the grace of God can produce: they would have fruit without a root, and blamelessness without any fixed principle of piety in the soul. But the only way in which any man can be kept in one uniform path of goodness and of honour, is, by submitting his soul to the influence of true religion, and surrendering himself up unreservedly to God. This at least was the conviction of Solomon's mind: " When wisdom entereth into thine heart, and knowledge is pleasant to thy soul, discretion shall preserve thee, understanding shall keep thee." By "wisdom and knowledge" we are not to understand *worldly* wisdom: for a proficiency in *that*, however great it may be, is no pledge of morality, no preservative from sin. These terms are used in Scripture to express real piety; and

it is that alone which will prove a sufficient antidote
to temptation, or become a perennial source of holiness in the life.

In confirmation of this sentiment, I will shew,

I. What reception divine truth should meet with—

The heart is the proper seat of divine knowledge—

[Other knowledge is seated in the *head :* it is acquired
only by deep study, and by force of intellect : nor, in whatever degree it be attained, does it at all sanctify and renew
the soul. But the truth of God " enters into the *heart :*" *there*
is that " incorruptible seed " deposited ; and from thence is it
brought forth into life and action. I mean not to say, that
the understanding is not to be exercised, or exercised deeply,
in relation to divine truth ; for, beyond all doubt, every truth
must so far approve itself to our judgment, as evidently to
appear worthy of God, and suited to our condition : nor should
any man give an unrestrained scope to his imagination or
affections : for, if he were implicitly to follow them, he would
of necessity be led away from the solid maxims of the Gospel :
but when once he is convinced of any truth of God, then is he
to deliver up his affections to be moulded and directed by it.

To make this clear, let me state what I mean by divine
knowledge. The word of God teaches us that sin is an evil
of extreme malignity ; that, to every soul in which it reigns,
it is defiling, debasing, damning. It teaches us that we are
altogether incapable of cancelling its guilt, or of subduing its
power ; and that if we find not a Saviour who is able to effect
these things for us, we must inevitably and eternally perish.
It teaches us yet further, that the Lord Jesus Christ is precisely
such a Saviour as we want, and that he is both " able and
willing to save to the uttermost all who come unto God by him."
Still further, it teaches us the beauty of holiness, and the
blessedness of serving and enjoying God. But of what use are
these things, as *a mere theory?* It is only by their being
actually experienced in the soul that they can be productive of
any solid benefit. But, when truly received into the heart,
they set in motion all the affections of the soul, and call into
activity our fears and our hopes, our sorrows and our joys.]

It should be received there with supreme delight—

[Truth of any kind is pleasing to the mind, as all who are
accustomed to the investigations of science can attest. But
divine truth should generate the sublimest joy ; or, as my text
expresses it, should be " pleasant to the soul." It should be
to us what light is to the wandering and benighted traveller :
he pants for it ; and congratulates himself on the very first
appearance of its orient dawn. To him it comes as a remedy

that is suited to his most urgent necessities. Conceive of the Israelites, when pressed with hunger, or perishing with thirst; with what interest must they have beheld the manna that was showered about their tents! and with what avidity must they have bowed down to drink of the streams that issued from the rock! Or, if it be said that these things are objects of *sense*, and therefore inapplicable to the point in hand, take the instance of the brazen serpent, which was exhibited to their *faith*. They felt themselves dying of the wounds which had been inflicted by the fiery serpents: they were perfectly conscious that no physician on earth could help them: and they were informed, that, by God's appointment, a brazen serpent had been erected, in order that, by looking to that, they might be restored to health. Would they hear of that with sceptical indifference, or behold it with an uninterested curiosity? No: it would be to them a matter of life and death: the very first tidings of such an instrument would make them eager for the exposure of it to their view; and when they saw or heard others attesting its efficacy, they would look to it with a desire to experience in themselves its healing power. Now this is the way in which divine truth should be viewed by us. To the ungodly world it is most unwelcome, because it bears testimony against them, and against all their ways: hence " they hate the light, and will not come to it, lest their deeds should be reproved." But to *us* it should be an object of ardent desire and supreme delight. We should look to it, not for the purpose of critical discussion, but of grateful application to the soul. Our spirit should be precisely that of the blind man whom Jesus had healed. Our Lord put the question to him, " Dost thou believe on the Son of God?" To which he replied, " Who is he, Lord, that I might believe on him [a]?" Here he finds no disposition to speculate upon the subject, as on a matter of mere critical inquiry; but shews a readiness to admit the truth the moment it should be revealed to him, and to embrace it as the one ground of all his future conduct. Such should be the disposition of our minds also. And when we have attained clearer views of divine truth, we should " rejoice as one that findeth great spoil [b]."]

That we may be stirred up to seek divine truth in this way, let us consider,

II. Its salutary influence when duly received—

" Discretion will preserve us, and understanding will keep us." This is the testimony of God himself. But it may be asked, ' If common knowledge be not effectual to keep us, or even divine knowledge when

---

[a] John ix. 35, 36.   [b] Ps. cxix. 162.

received only into the head, how can the circumstance of receiving knowledge into the heart be productive of any such effect?' I answer, 'It is this very circumstance which makes all the difference: divine knowledge, when it resides merely in the head, is speculative only; whereas, when it enters into the heart, it becomes practical.

1. It rectifies the judgment—

[On every subject connected with the soul, the judgment of mankind is in direct opposition to the mind of God. In their eyes, the things of time and sense are of the first importance; but in the sight of God they are all lighter than vanity itself: in his eyes, the concerns of the soul and of eternity are alone worthy of the care of an immortal Being. To the ungodly, even the Gospel itself, that unrivalled production of divine wisdom, is "foolishness;" but to an enlightened mind, it is "the power of God and the wisdom of God." To the stout-hearted infidel, to follow the commands of God is to "be righteous over-much:" but to one who is taught of God, obedience to God's commands appears his highest honour and felicity. But the truth is, he once was in darkness, but is now "brought into marvellous light:" he once saw only through the distorting medium of sense; he now beholds with the eye of faith, which brings him within the vail of the sanctuary, and discovers every thing as it is beheld by God himself. Nor should this appear strange to us. The difference made in the aspect of any object by its being viewed through glasses of different construction, may easily convince us how different an appearance every object must assume, according as it is viewed through the medium of sense, or by the penetrating eye of faith. The person who turns to God has the very law of God written in his heart; and needs only to look within, and he will see the correspondence between the divine records and his own actual experience: so that he does not merely *believe* the divine testimonies to be true and good, but "*has within himself a witness*" of their transcendent excellence: or, as it is said in the verse before our text, "he understands righteousness, and judgment, and equity, yea, every good path."]

2. It infuses sensibility into the conscience—

[The conscience of an unenlightened man is blind, partial, and in many respects seared; since, in relation to the dispositions of the soul towards God, which is of far greater importance than any thing else, it never reproves at all. But when divine wisdom has entered into his soul, a man will not be satisfied with a freedom from great and flagrant transgressions: he will examine his duties towards God as well as those towards man: he will mark his defects, no less than his excesses: he will observe his thoughts, yea, and " the very imaginations of his thoughts;" and will be more grieved for an evil propensity or *desire*, than the world at large are for an evil *act*. He endeavours to have his conscience as much alive to the least evils, as to the greatest; and to keep it tender, as the apple of his eye: and if but a mote assail it, he will take no rest, till he has wept it out with tears of penitence and contrition. See this in the Apostle Paul. Before his conversion, he could find no evil in himself, though he was " a blasphemer, and a persecutor, and injurious;" but after his conversion, he did but utter a disrespectful word to a judge who was violating the plainest rules of justice, and he made it a matter of humiliation in the presence of the whole court.]

3. It instils a watchfulness against the occasions of evil—

[Those who are destitute of vital godliness will venture themselves any where, without fear and without remorse: but a man of real piety will be afraid to expose himself where the objects around him present only what has a tendency to vitiate his mind: he prays to God " not to lead him into temptation;" and therefore he will not voluntarily run into it; he will select his associates from amongst the excellent of the earth, who will forward, rather than retard, the growth of holy affections within him; and, as far as his situation will admit of it, he will " come out from the ungodly world, and be separate, and not even touch an unclean thing," lest he be defiled, and have " his good manners corrupted by evil communications." This is very particularly insisted on in the following context, in reference both to evil *men* and evil *women*. It is said, " Discretion shall preserve thee, understanding shall keep thee; to deliver thee from the way of the *evil man*, from the man that speaketh froward things; who leave the paths of uprightness to walk in the ways of darkness; who rejoice to do evil, and delight in the frowardness of the wicked; whose ways are crooked, and they froward in their paths: to deliver thee also from *the strange woman*, even from the stranger who flattereth with her words; who forsaketh the guide of her youth, and forgetteth the covenant of her God: for her house inclineth unto death, and her paths unto the dead: none that go unto her return again, neither take they hold of the paths of life: That thou mayest *walk in the way of good men*, and keep the paths of the righteous[c]." Here the conduct of *evil men* is drawn to the very life, as is the character of the *evil woman* also, against both of whom the man of piety will be

[c] ver. 11—20.

strictly on his guard, proposing to himself the example of *the godly*, and availing himself of their aid in his walk before God. He knows, that " he cannot take fire in his bosom, and not be burned;" and therefore he will use the utmost possible circumspection in the whole of his deportment. The books, the company, the conversation that would defile his mind, he carefully avoids; and, like the Jews at the time of the Passover, he searches the most secret recesses of his soul, to sweep from it the leaven that would offend his God.]

4. It leads us continually to God for direction and support—

[Without divine aid all human efforts are vain. But the word of God clearly, fully, constantly directs us to look to him; and an experience of it in our own souls will convince us of the necessity of crying to him continually, " Hold thou me up, and I shall be safe." It is in this way chiefly that divine wisdom preserves us. The soundness of our principles may prescribe what is right; and our love to those principles may incline us to the performance of it: but divine grace alone can ever prove effectual for us. No " power, but that which raised Jesus Christ himself from the dead," will be sufficient to carry on within us the work that has been begun. On the other hand, if we really trust in the Lord Jesus Christ, we shall, " through his strength, be able to do all things," " nor shall any thing ever prevail to separate us from his love."]

Having illustrated the great truth in our text, we would further IMPROVE it, by suggesting,

1. In what spirit we should hear the word—

[We should not come to the house of God in a mere customary manner, for example sake, or to perform a duty, and still less to be amused with what we hear: but, as Cornelius and his friends, when Peter came to minister unto them, said, " Now are we all here before God, to hear all things that are commanded thee of God;" so should we come up to the house of God to " hear what the Lord our God shall say concerning us." We should come to learn our duty, in order that we may practise it. We should bless our God that so sublime a privilege is accorded to us. We should come as a patient to receive the counsels of his physician, with a determination of heart to follow his prescriptions. A mariner, if amongst shoals and quicksands, does not consult his chart and compass for amusement, or with a disposition to dispute their testimony, but with a desire to have every mistake rectified, and to navigate his ship through the dangerous passage, agreeably to their direction. O! when will Christian assemblies meet in this frame? When will God's ordinances be thus improved for their proper end? Brethren, only reflect on the office of true wisdom, as delineated in the passage before us, and you will never want either a direction or a motive for a profitable attendance on the means of grace.]

2. With what care we should improve it—

[The word we hear will judge us in the last day: and if we do not take occasion from it to follow the counsels of the Most High, we shall greatly aggravate our guilt before God. The word we hear, if it prove not " a savour of life unto life, will become to us a savour of death unto death." The lessons of wisdom had better never have been delivered to us, than be suffered to pass away without a suitable improvement of them. Our blessed Lord told his hearers, that if he had not come and spoken unto them, they had not had sin; but that now they had no cloak for their sin. And so must I also say unto you. All that you have heard respecting the evil of sin, the sufficiency of Christ, the beauty of holiness, of what use will it be to you, if it do not humble you as sinners, encourage you as penitents, and animate you as believers? I pray you, neglect not the day of your visitation, nor " hold the truth in unrighteousness;" but receive the truth in the love of it; and deliver your souls into it as a mould, that it may fashion you after the image of your God. And never imagine that you have got above the use of ordinances, or that it is of no profit to attend upon them: they are the golden pipes through which, to your latest hour, you must receive the golden oil into your lamps; and through the supplies of the Spirit which you may receive by them, you may hope that your path shall shine brighter and brighter unto the perfect day."]

OUTLINE NO. 756
BENEFITS OF TRUE WISDOM.

Prov. ii. 10—22. *When wisdom entereth into thine heart, and knowledge is pleasant unto thy soul, discretion shall preserve thee, understanding shall keep thee; to deliver thee from the way of the evil man, from the man that speaketh froward things: who leave the paths of uprightness, to walk in the ways of darkness; who rejoice to do evil, and delight in the frowardness of the wicked; whose ways are crooked, and they froward in their paths: to deliver thee from the strange woman, even from the stranger which flattereth with her words; which forsaketh the guide of her youth, and forgetteth the covenant of her God: for her house inclineth unto death, and her paths unto the dead. None that go unto her return again, neither take they hold of the paths of life; that thou mayest walk in the way of good men, and keep the paths of the righteous. For the upright shall dwell in the land, and the perfect shall remain in it: but the wicked shall be cut off from the earth, and the transgressors shall be rooted out of it.*

WHETHER we regard Solomon as a saint walking with his God, or as a backslider restored to God, we must consider him as pre-eminently qualified to give advice for the regulation of our conduct: for, as a saint, he was endued with wisdom above all the children of men ; and, as a backslider, he had a wider range for his wickedness, and a deeper experience of its folly, than any other person ever possessed.

Under the character of "wisdom," he here speaks of true religion; which he recommends to all, but especially to persons in early life; and, in order to impress his advice the more deeply on our minds, he sets before us,

I. The benefits derived from true wisdom—

When once religion is deeply rooted in the heart, it will render us the most essential services—

1. It will keep us from the society of ungodly men—

[There are many whose delight is in wickedness: they have departed from God themselves, and have "made crooked paths for themselves;" in which they proceed with all imaginable "frowardness" and perverseness. Disdaining to receive any light from God or his word, they "walk in utter darkness, not at all knowing whither they go[a]." And not content with casting off all restraint themselves, and walking after their own lusts in all manner of uncleanness, they wish to draw all they can along with them: they deride all serious piety, and labour to the uttermost to turn aside from the way of godliness any who may be inclined to it[b]— — — "They rejoice to do evil:" and, if they can but succeed in their efforts to ensnare a person who has been fleeing from sin, and to divert him from following after God, not even Satan himself will exult more than they— — —

Now from such companions true religion will preserve us. We shall see at once how far they are from God, and how impossible it is to be happy in their society : "for what fellowship can righteousness have with unrighteousness; or light with darkness; or Christ with Belial; or he that believeth with an unbeliever[c]?" Instead of seeking their society, therefore, we

a ver. 13. with 1 John ii. 11.   b 1 Pet. iv. 4.
c 2 Cor. vi. 14, 15.

shall come out from among them, and be separate[d];" and not have any fellowship with the unfruitful works of darkness, but rather reprove them[e]" — — —]

2. It will keep us from the snares also of ungodly women—

[It is lamentable to think how degraded human nature is, and how assimilated to the very beasts multitudes are, who were originally formed in the image of their God. Females, married, as well as unmarried, "forsaking the guide of their youth and the covenant of their God," will abandon themselves to the most vicious courses, soliciting the embrace of men to whom they are utter "strangers," and practising every species of artifice, to ensnare and vitiate all who come in their way — — —

And such is their influence over those whom they have once ensnared, that it is a miracle almost if even one is recovered to a sense of his duty, and is brought back again in penitential sorrow to his God[f]. Truly their ways lead down to death and to hell[g]: for not only do they draw men from all thoughtfulness about their souls, but they bring them into extravagances and crimes, which not unfrequently issue in suicide, or death by the hands of the public executioner.

But from these also will vital piety preserve us. It will lead us to use all the precautions against them, that a prudent government employs against the infection of the plague. We shall have no communication with persons, whose very presence will endanger the life of our souls. We shall not go near their houses, or the places of their resort[h]. We shall not parley with temptation when it comes in our way; but shall flee from it, as Joseph did, saying, "How shall I do this great wickedness, and sin against God[i]?" — — —]

3. It will guide us in the paths of righteousness and peace—

[When once true religion enters into the soul, we shall take the Scriptures for our guide, and endeavour to walk in the paths which all the holy men of old have trod before us[k]. We shall not be satisfied with following the customs of those around us, or with conforming to the standard of duty which the world approves; we shall desire to be "holy, as God is holy;" and shall determine through grace to "perfect holiness in the fear of God" — — —]

Such being the effects of true wisdom, I will proceed to point out to you,

[d] 2 Cor. vi. 17.   [e] Eph. v. 11.   [f] ver. 19.
[g] Prov. v. 3—5. and vii. 26, 27.   [h] Prov. v. 8.
[i] Gen. xxxix. 9.   [k] ver. 20.

II. The vast importance of seeking after it—

Both the promises and threatenings of the Mosaic law were chiefly of a temporal nature; the people who served God faithfully being encouraged to expect peace and plenty in the land of Canaan; whilst those who were disobedient to his laws were to be visited with war, famine, pestilence, and ultimately to be driven out of that land, as the Canaanites had been before them. But under these figures truths of far higher moment were veiled : and the present and eternal states of men were shadowed forth as indissolubly connected with their moral and religious character. Hence the contrast drawn between the sentence accorded to "the upright" and "the wicked" in the concluding verses of our text, must be understood as referring to their respective states,

1. In this world—

["Godliness is profitable unto all things, having the promise of the life that now is, and of that which is to come[1]." Certainly *in this world* there is an immense "difference between those who serve God, and those who serve him not[m]." We readily grant that the ungodly and profane may prosper in respect of outward things, and that the saints may be in a state of degradation and oppression[n]: but there is no comparison between the real happiness of the one and of the other : the ungodly are "like the troubled sea, whose waters cast up mire and dirt[o]:" they are agitated by many ungovernable and conflicting passions: their tempers are a source of continual disquietude[p]: and they have no inward resources to calm the tumult of their minds ——— But the godly have consolations peculiar to themselves, and abundantly sufficient to counterbalance their afflictions. They have a God to go unto ; a God, who says, "Cast thy burthen on the Lord, and he will sustain thee." The very tribulations which they endure for righteousness sake, are to them a ground of glorying[q]: and the light of God's countenance lifted up upon them fills their souls with joy and peace, even with "a joy that is unspeakable," and "a peace that passeth all understanding."

If then we look no further than to this present life, we do not hesitate to declare, that "the fear of the Lord, that is wisdom ; and to depart from evil, that is understanding[r]."]

[1] 1 Tim. iv. 8.   [m] Mal. iii. 18.   [n] Ps. lxxiii. 3—10.
[o] Isai. lvii. 20, 21.   [p] Rom. iii. 16, 17.   [q] Rom. v. 3.
[r] Job xxviii. 28.

2. In the world to come—

["There is a rest which remaineth for the people of God[s];" a rest, into which the true Joshua shall introduce them, as soon as ever they shall have completed the period fixed for their abode in this dreary wilderness: and there shall they "remain" for ever: there shall they be as "pillars in the temple of their God, and shall go no more out[t]." But how shall I represent their happiness in that place where there will be no remains of those evils which they experienced in this world[u]; and where every blessing which they here sought for, shall be imparted to the utmost extent of their desires, and of their capacities for enjoyment[x]— — —

On the other hand, there is a day of retribution for the ungodly, when they shall not only be "convinced of all their ungodly deeds which they have ungodlily committed, and of all their hard speeches which they have spoken against the Lord and his ways, but will have judgment executed upon them" by the Judge of quick and dead[y]. And what words can ever suffice to give an adequate idea of their misery, when, driven from the presence of their God, and from the congregation of his saints[z], they shall be consigned to those regions of misery, where they will take their portion in "the lake that burneth with fire and brimstone," and "dwell for ever with everlasting burnings?"— — —

If men would but reflect one moment on these consequences of their impiety, there would be no longer any occasion to descant on the wisdom of seeking after God, or the folly of provoking his displeasure by a life of sin.]

Let us LEARN then,

1. To form a right estimate of religion—

[Religion is wisdom, even though the whole world should combine to call it folly— — —]

2. To seek it in due measure—

[To receive it into *the head* is to little purpose: the proper seat of it is *the heart*. Nor is it sufficient that we yield a constrained obedience to it: its service should in our estimation be accounted perfect freedom. It is only "when wisdom *enters into our heart*, and knowledge *is pleasant to our soul*," that we can be said to have received the grace of God in truth. The worldly man is at home in the world: it is his element wherein he moves. And such must religion be to the child of God, his rest, his element, his delight— — —]

3. To let it have its full operation on our souls—

[s] Heb. iv. 9.   [t] ver. 21. with Rev. iii. 12.   [u] Rev. xxi. 4.
[x] Psal. xvi. 11.   [y] Jude, ver. 15.   [z] Ps. i. 5. Luke xiii. 28.

[Wherever true wisdom is, there will be " *discretion* to preserve us, and *understanding* to keep us[a]." *We conceive this observation to be deserving of peculiar attention;* because the indiscretions of religious people are rarely traced to their proper source, a want of right dispositions in the heart. Where meekness, and modesty, and diffidence, and humility reside in the heart, there will be a corresponding propriety of conduct in the life; but where pride, and conceit, and forwardness, and self-will are predominant, there will the deportment savour of these hateful qualities in all our intercourse with mankind. There is this remarkable difference between human wisdom and that which is divine: human wisdom leaves the heart untouched, or even administers fuel to its corruptions: but divine wisdom " pours the very soul into the mould of the Gospel[b]," and assimilates all its dispositions to the image of God himself. It was not Paul's eminence in intellectual attainments that made him so eminent in Christian tempers: it was the abundance of God's grace that rendered him so fruitful in every good word and work: and, if the grace of God abound in us, we also shall proportionably adorn the Gospel in the whole of our life and conversation. Let that then be remembered which Solomon has told us, " I Wisdom dwell with Prudence[c]:" and let us be careful that we do not by any indiscreet conduct give " occasion to the adversary to speak reproachfully." Our determination, through grace, must be, to cut off from the world all unnecessary occasion of offence. We must not imagine that our separation from an ungodly world gives us a licence to violate either the duties or the charities of life; but, whilst we " abstain from all appearance of evil," we must cultivate to the uttermost not only " whatsoever things are true, and honest, and just, and pure, but whatsoever things are lovely and of good report[d]." We must labour to " behave ourselves wisely in a perfect way[e]."]

[a] Prov. ii. 11.   [b] Rom. vi. 17. The Greek.
[c] Prov. viii. 12.   [d] Phil. iv. 8.   [e] Ps. ci. 2.

OUTLINE NO. 757

CONFIDENCE IN GOD ENCOURAGED.

Prov. iii. 5, 6. *Trust in the Lord with all thine heart; and lean not unto thine own understanding. In all thy ways acknowledge him; and he shall direct thy paths.*

THE book of Proverbs is not so much designed to open to us the way of salvation, as it is to regulate our conduct after we have attained the knowledge of the truth. It abounds with maxims admirably calculated to assist us in our intercourse with men, and with instructions also relative to our walk before God. Of this latter kind is the advice given us in the words which we have just read; wherein we see,

I. The confidence which God requires of us—

As creatures, we are of necessity dependent on Him who first gave us our existence; for in him we live, and move, and have our being. But it is by no means sufficient for us to acknowledge this as a truth which we cannot controvert: we must acquiesce in it as a state that we approve, and glory in it as our highest privilege. Our confidence in God must be co-extensive with our necessities: it must be—

1. Entire—

[We must trust in the Lord "with all our heart." There must be no aversion to such an appointment as unnecessary, no distrust of it as insufficient. We should view ourselves as utterly incapable of ensuring our own happiness; and we should regard God as engaged to order every thing for our good. We should not for a moment doubt his wisdom to discern what shall eventually prove best for us, nor his power to execute it, however great or numerous the difficulties may be which appear to obstruct its accomplishment. Nay, we must be persuaded, that his love delights in caring for us, and that his truth and faithfulness will perform all that in his unbounded mercy he has undertaken in our behalf. From this conviction we must commit all our concerns to him, to be ordered and overruled as he in his infinite wisdom shall see best. There must be an actual transfer of them (if we may so speak) into his hands, and a full conviction of mind that he is able to keep, and will assuredly keep, what we have so committed to him, so as to bring all our affairs to a blessed and successful issue[a].]

2. Exclusive—

[We must "not lean to our own understanding," so as to rely on it for any thing. We are to *use* our understanding indeed, but not to transfer to it any measure of that dependence which should be placed on God only. We know not what would be the ultimate issue of any one thing. We are ready to suppose, that whatever obstructs our wishes for a time, will endanger their final accomplishment: whereas God often makes those very events subservient to his own gracious

---

[a] Ps. xxxvii. 5. with 2 Tim. i. 12.

purposes, and uses them as means whereby his ends shall be fulfilled. This was remarkably the case with Joseph, in all his trials: and there is no true believer who will not acknowledge, that in his own experience many things which have been desired by him would have proved injurious, and many things which have been deprecated by him have been overruled for his welfare. From a full conviction that " a man's way is not in himself, and that it is not in man that walketh to direct his steps [b]," we must renounce all idea of planning for ourselves, any further than in an entire dependence on the divine guidance and direction. We are doubtless to use all proper means for attaining what on the whole appears most desirable: but *the relying on* our own devices, as calculated of themselves to ensure success, is the thing which God has marked with his strongest disapprobation [c] — — — The doing of this demonstrates our folly [d], and exposes us to the heaviest curse [e]. We must therefore altogether " cease from our own wisdom [f]."]

3. Uniform—

[" In all our ways we must acknowledge him;" not in those only which seem to be of greater importance, but in all without exception. It is not in the rise and fall of empires only that God's hand is to be viewed, but in the falling of a sparrow, or in any event equally insignificant. We are apt to consider some things as important, and others as unimportant; but the truth is, that in God's sight nothing is important (except as it may advance his glory); nor is there any thing unimportant as it relates to us. Many things which in their effects and consequences have been of the greatest imaginable importance, may in their origin be traced to the slightest possible occurrence. If we look into the book of Esther, we shall see this observation confirmed in its utmost extent. Nor is God to be acknowledged only in those events which would be deemed small, but in those also which are casual, or, as we call them, accidental: " the lot (than which nothing is more casual) is cast into the lap, but the whole disposal thereof is of the Lord." In every thing therefore, whether great or small, painful or pleasant, concerted or fortuitous, God must be acknowledged as having sent it, if past, and as having the entire disposal of it, if future.]

To place this entire confidence in God will be found our truest wisdom, if we consider,

II. The encouragement he gives us to trust in him—

---

[b] Jer. x. 23.
[c] Isai. xxii. 8—11. See also Isai. xxx. 1—3. and xxxi. 1—3.
[d] Prov. xxviii. 26.   [e] Jer. xvii. 5, 6.   [f] Prov. xxiii. 4.

Wonderful is the promise here given for our encouragement; "He will direct our paths." But how will he direct us? Will he speak to us in dreams, or visions, or by Urim and Thummim, or by an audible voice? Or will he go before us in the pillar and the cloud, as he did before his people in the wilderness; or answer us, as he did David, in reference to the men of Keilah, and the Amalekites[g]? No: we are not authorized to expect any thing of the kind: yet will he direct us sufficiently to preserve us from any material error,

1. By his Spirit—

[To "open the eyes of our understanding" is one of the most important offices of the Spirit: and, in doing this, he will purge away from our eyes that film which obstructs our sight. Pride, passion, interest, and a thousand other things, incapacitate us for a clear and perfect discovery of our duty: and, till these be mortified, we are constantly exposed to the most awful delusions: we are ready at all times to "call good evil, and evil good; to put darkness for light, and light for darkness." But, when our minds are duly enlightened, we see things in their proper colours. On different occasions, when the apostles would have called fire from heaven to consume a Samaritan village, and when they contended with each other who should be the greatest, our blessed Lord instructed them better: and so will he do with us, bringing to our remembrance some portion of God's word which bears upon the point in hand. Thus he fulfils that blessed promise, "that we shall hear a word behind us, saying, This is the way, walk ye in it; when we should otherwise have turned either to the right hand or to the left[h]." We say not, that the Holy Spirit does not sometimes effect this *without the word:* we are inclined to think he does; and *that* too by a kind of impression on the mind deterring us from evil and guiding us to good[i]: but he never does it *contrary to the word.* Suffice it to say, that whether with or without the word, he will guide us into all truth, so far as shall be necessary for the rectifying of our views, and the regulating of our conduct.]

2. By his Providence—

[God often interposes for men in a most wonderful manner, to preserve them from evil, and to guide them into that which is good. Even a wicked Balaam was obstructed in his way by God's appointment, in order to awaken him to a just

[g] 1 Sam. xxiii. 4, 11, 12. and xxx. 8.   [h] Isai. xxx. 21.
[i] Ps. lxxiii. 24. 1 John ii. 20, 27.

sense of his duty. A remarkable instance of such an interposition occurs in the life of David. He, being incensed against Nabal for the contemptuous manner in which he had treated his messengers, and for his ungrateful refusal to administer to his necessities[k], had determined to avenge himself upon him and all that belonged to him. But God put it into the heart of Abigail to go to meet him, and by mild representations to pacify his wrath[l]. Thus were the greatest impieties prevented through the intervention of this prudent female[m]. And in this way God often directs the ways of his people, either sending a friend perhaps, or a minister, to suggest such considerations as shall influence their minds: or by some particular occurrence " raising, as it were, a hedge, or building a wall," to keep them in the path of duty[n]. It may be, that the occurrence may occasion much grief at the time: but God knows how to accomplish his own purposes, and will constrain us all in due time to acknowledge that " he doeth all things well."]

We will ADD a few words,

1. To direct your exertions—

[Do not imagine that confidence in God is to supersede your own personal exertions. You are to labour, as much as if every thing depended on yourselves; and then to trust in God, as if nothing had been done by you. You must also expressly commit your concerns to God in fervent and continual prayer. The Psalmist particularly combines this with confidence in God: " Trust in God at all times, ye people; pour out your hearts before him[o]." The confidence that is unaccompanied with prayer and diligence is mere presumption. We have a beautiful pattern in Jacob, when he was about to meet his brother Esau. He disposed every thing in a way most suited to pacify his brother's anger, or, in the event of not succeeding in that attempt, to secure that part of his family who were most dear to him: but, whilst he acted thus, he committed himself wholly to the Lord, and looked for success from him alone[p]. Thus let there be no want of prudence or of diligence on your part; and then you may be assured that God will not suffer you to be disappointed of your hope.]

2. To regulate your expectations—

[Though God promises to direct your paths, he will not so direct you as to keep you from every degree of error. The apostles themselves, though in what they declared to be the will of God they were inspired to utter nothing but what was true, were not infallible in their own personal conduct. Peter

---

[k] 1 Sam. xxv. 4—11.   [l] 1 Sam. xxv. 18—31.
[m] 1 Sam. xxv. 32—34.   [n] Hos. ii. 6, 7.
[o] Ps. lxii. 8.   [p] Gen. xxxii. 9—32.

greatly erred on one occasion, in his conduct towards the
Gentiles; as Paul also did in reviling God's high priest. You
must not therefore conceive that you are *certainly* and *altogether*
right, because you have prayed to God for direction: God may
have many wise and gracious purposes to answer by leaving
you still under some measure of darkness and ignorance : if it
be only to humble you still more, and to shew you the blindness of your minds and the deceitfulness of your hearts, it is a
good and gracious end, for which you will in the issue see
reason to be thankful.   Be modest then, and diffident in your
conclusions: and instead of assuming infallibility to yourselves,
be always ready to suspect that your way is still far from perfect; and to the latest hour of your lives be praying to God
to lead you in a right path, and to fulfil to you that gracious
promise, " The meek he will guide in judgment ; the meek he
will teach his way."]

OUTLINE NO. 758

THE REWARD OF CHARITY.

Prov. iii. 9, 10. *Honour the Lord with thy substance, and with
the first-fruits of all thine increase : so shall thy barns be filled
with plenty, and thy presses shall burst out with new wine.*

TO instruct men how to ensure success in their
agricultural pursuits or commercial speculations, is
no part of a minister's office. Were we able sub-
stantially to benefit mankind in those particulars,
there would be no want of hearers, nor any complaint
that we laboured too zealously in our vocation : on
the contrary, the more successful we were in effecting
our wishes, the more gratefully should we be acknowledged as public benefactors. Shall I then, for once,
exceed, as it were, the commission given me, and attempt to teach you how to thrive in this world ? Yes;
suffer me for once to usurp this office ; and to assure
the most unlearned person amongst you, that by
acting on the principles which I will set before him
this day, he shall be as sure to prosper in his business, as if he were ever so conversant with the arts of
trade. I mean not indeed to say, that a person going
out of his own proper line shall be enabled to prosecute that line to advantage; but that, whilst proceeding prudently in his proper vocation, he shall
succeed more certainly, and to a greater extent, than

on other principles he can expect to do. And I say
this the more confidently, because the directions
which I shall give are not the results of fallible reasonings or of uncertain conjectures, but the plain
unequivocal declarations of Heaven: "Honour the
Lord with thy substance, and with the first-fruits of
all thine increase: so shall thy barns be filled with
plenty, and thy presses shall burst out with new wine."

In these words we see,

I. Our duty—

We must "honour the Lord with our substance"—

[All that we have is the Lord's. "Our very bodies and
souls are his;" and much more the property which he has
committed to our care. With the whole of that he is to be
honoured; and in the disposal of it, respect must be had to his
will, his interests, his glory. We are to consider every thing
that we possess, not as given to us, but merely as *confided* to
us, to be improved for him; and we must so employ the whole,
as to meet his approbation in the day that we shall give up our
account, and to be acknowledged by him as good and faithful
stewards.]

We must honour him, also, "with the first-fruits
of all our increase"—

[The first-fruits under the Law were claimed by God as
his, and they were to be presented to him as his peculiar property: "Thou shalt take of the first of *all* the fruit of the earth,
which thou shalt bring, of the land which the Lord thy God
giveth thee, and shalt put it in a basket, and shalt go unto the
place which the Lord thy God shall choose to place his name
there[a]." Besides these, was the tithe of all their increase to be
offered to him every third year: "At the end of three years
thou shalt bring all the tithe of thine increase the same year,
and shalt lay it up within thy gates. And the Levite, because
he hath no part nor inheritance with thee, and the stranger,
and the fatherless, and the widow, which are within thy gates,
shall come, and shall eat and be satisfied; that the Lord thy
God may bless thee in all the work of thine hand, which thou
doest[b]." Under the Gospel, the *letter* of this law is abolished;
but the *spirit* of it yet remains in force: for the express command of God to *us* is, "On the first day of the week let every
one of you lay by him in store as God has prospered him[c]."
We are not to wait for the gathering in of our harvest; and
then give a portion to the Lord after our own interests are

[a] Deut. xxvi. 2.   [b] Deut. xiv. 28, 29.   [c] 1 Cor. xvi. 2.

secured : but rather to honour the Lord first, as the real pro-
prietor of all ; and then, trusting him for a supply of our own
wants, to employ for ourselves what he shall graciously bestow
upon us.]

This duty will not appear hard, if we consider
what God has spoken for,

II. Our encouragement—

It should seem as if the giving of our substance
were the way to diminish it; and the devoting of our
first-fruits to him, the way to endanger our own provision through the year : but God has declared the
very reverse, and has pledged himself that he will
amply make up to us all that we part with for his sake.

This, under the Law, he did, visibly, *according to
the letter*—

[Under that dispensation, a present and visible retribution
marked, for the most part, the approbation or displeasure of
God. When the people delayed to build his temple, he chastised them with famine, and referred to that visitation as a
judgment inflicted on them for their sin: " Ye looked for much,
and, lo! it came to little ; and when ye brought it home, I did
blow upon it. Why? saith the Lord of Hosts. Because of
mine house that is waste, and ye run every man to his own
house. Therefore the heaven over you is stayed from dew, and
the earth is stayed from her fruit[d]." And when they were
stirred up to begin the work, he not only assured them of his
blessing on their temporal concerns, but bade them note down
the day that the foundation of his temple was laid, and see
whether their blessings were not augmented from that very
hour: " Consider now, from this day and upward, from the
four-and-twentieth day of the ninth month, even from the day
that the foundation of the Lord's temple was laid, consider it:
from this day will I bless you[e]." He bids them even to prove
him in relation to this matter, and to see whether his bounty
would not keep pace with their piety: " Bring ye all the tithes
into the storehouse, that there may be meat in mine house:
and prove me now herewith, saith the Lord of Hosts, if I will
not open the windows of heaven, and pour you out a blessing,
that there shall not be room enough to receive it[f]."]

Under the Gospel, also, he will do it, but invisibly,
and *according to the spirit*—

[*We* are not taught to look so much to temporal rewards,
as to those which are spiritual and eternal: though still we are

---

[d] Hagg. i. 9, 10.   [e] Hagg. ii. 18, 19.   [f] Mal. iii. 10.

told that " godliness has the promise of the life that now is, as
well as of that which is to come[g];" and that, if we " seek first
the kingdom of God and his righteousness, all needful things
shall be added unto us[h]." A *temporal* recompence for our
liberality we may not obtain: but a *spiritual* reward is sure.
For thus said the Lord: " If thou deal thy bread to the hungry,
and bring the poor that are cast out to thy house; if, when
thou seest the naked, thou cover him, and hide not thyself from
thine own flesh; then shall thy light break forth as the morning,
and thine health spring forth speedily: and thy righteousness
shall go before thee; the glory of the Lord shall be thy rereward.
If thou draw out thy soul to the hungry, and satisfy the afflicted
soul; then shall thy light rise in obscurity, and thy darkness
be as the noon-day: and the Lord shall guide thee continually,
and satisfy thy soul in drought, and make fat thy bones: and
thou shalt be like a watered garden, and like a spring of water,
whose waters fail not[i]." An *eternal* recompence will also most
assuredly await us: for our blessed Lord has expressly told us,
that if, instead of lavishing our money in feasting the rich, we
delight to expend it on the poor, " we shall be recompensed at
the resurrection of the just[k]." He has commanded us on this
account to " make friends to ourselves of the mammon of unrighteousness," in the full expectation that at our death " we
shall be received into everlasting habitations[l]." And St. Paul
speaks to the same effect, when he says, " Charge them that
are rich in this world, that they do good, that they be rich in
good works, ready to distribute, willing to communicate, laying
up in store for themselves a good foundation against the time
to come, that they may lay hold on eternal life[m]."

But, after all, we must not altogether put out of our consideration even a present reward in the precise sense spoken of
in our text: for it is beyond a doubt, that God does engage to
supply the necessities of those who honour him with their substance[n]: and we can appeal to many, and ask, whether they
have not seen, in relation to their temporal concerns, many
gracious interpositions of God in their behalf? But, independent of these, who does not know that liberality is the parent
of economy, and economy of wealth? A man desirous of
honouring God with his substance, is delivered at once from
all those vices and follies which ruin the estates of thousands.
Besides, who that delights in doing good has not found incomparably greater delight in self-denial for the benefit of others,
than the utmost latitude of self-indulgence could ever have
afforded him? Granting, then, that no addition is actually

[g] 1 Tim. iv. 8. [h] Matt. vi. 33. [i] Isai. lviii. 7—11.
[k] Luke xiv. 12—14. [l] Luke xvi. 9. [m] 1 Tim. vi. 17—19.
[n] Phil. iv. 18, 19.

made to our wealth; yet, if our desires are moderated, and our expenditure restrained, the same effect is ultimately produced: for we are not more truly enriched by the increase of our substance, than we are by the diminution of our wants and our consumption.]

Let me now point out THE BEARINGS of this subject,

1. On those who are engaged in visiting the sick[o]—

[Persons engaged in imparting instruction to the ignorant, and consolation to the afflicted, have yet, in a more eminent degree, the promise in our text fulfilled to them. Their light perhaps, at first, is but very imperfect; but by imparting it to others, their own views become enlarged, and their own experience of divine truth becomes deeper, from the very circumstance of their improving it for the benefit of others. Indeed, I can hardly suggest any better method for enlarging our own knowledge, than the making use of it for the instruction of our less enlightened brethren: for, besides the natural effect which may be expected from the communication of knowledge, we may expect a peculiar blessing from God whilst we are so employed. A remarkable instance of this may be found in Apollos: " He, when he knew only the baptism of John, spake and taught diligently the word of the Lord." " Aquila and Priscilla hearing him in the synagogue, took him, and expounded unto him the way of God more perfectly." And then, going forth with his augmented light, he prospered far more in his labours of love, not only " convincing the Jews that Jesus was the Christ, but helping them much who had believed through grace[p]." This example is most encouraging to all, to improve for God the light which they possess: for, whatever we do for God, is regarded by him as a loan which he will repay[q]: and in every instance shall it be found, that " he who watereth others, shall be watered also himself[r]."]

2. On those who contribute for the support of the charity—

[On these, the subject bears to its full extent; and we are warranted to affirm, that men shall "reap either sparingly or bountifully, according as they sow[s]." But there is one point of view in which they pre-eminently " honour God," and with peculiar advantage secure their reward. They honour God particularly, not merely by the distribution of their alms, but by employing and calling forth into activity the piety of others,

---

[o] This part must be varied, according to *the occasion*. It was preached in behalf of a Visiting Society; but it may easily be accommodated to a *Spital* Sermon, or any other Charitable Institution.

[p] Acts xviii. 24—28.   [q] Prov. xix. 17.
[r] Prov. xi. 25.   [s] 2 Cor. ix. 6.

for the benefit of their fellow-creatures. It is obvious that individuals of small property could not, without assistance from others, relieve the necessities of the poor to any great extent: and if they could not administer *some* temporal relief, they could not find easy access to the chambers of the sick. But being furnished with the means of easy access, they can pour the light of instruction and the balm of consolation into the souls of the afflicted to great advantage; and the persons so instructed and comforted, not only abound in thanksgivings to God for the benefits received, but in prayers to God in behalf of their benefactors. This St. Paul speaks of, as ennobling charity far beyond the mere conveyance of temporal relief[t] —— Now, then, let me ask, How can you *honour God* more, than in causing thanksgivings to arise to him from the altars of many hearts? and, What compensation under heaven can equal the prayers and intercessions of saints in your behalf? Put your alms in one scale, and the prayers offered to a *prayer-hearing* God in the other, and say whether your recompence be not very abundant, or whether it is possible to lay out money in any other way to such advantage? Let all of you, then, according to your power, "abound in this heavenly grace" of charity, after the example of your blessed Lord; "who, though he was rich, yet for your sakes became poor, that ye through his poverty might be rich[u]." Only get a sense of his love upon your souls, and a " sincere love to him" in return, and we shall have no occasion to entreat liberality from you; for " you yourselves will be willing of your own accord, and will be ready to pray us, with much entreaty, that we will take upon ourselves the office of ministering to the saints" as your stewards[x].]

[t] 2 Cor. ix. 12, 13. *Cite the words*, and mark what is said of their *thanksgivings* and *prayers*.
[u] 2 Cor. viii. 9.   [x] 2 Cor. viii. 3—8.

OUTLINE NO. 759

THE PLEASANTNESS OF RELIGION.

Prov. iii. 17. *Her ways are ways of pleasantness, and all her paths are peace.*

TO be sincerely and eminently religious is considered by the world as a symptom of weakness and folly. But the Scriptures represent such a life as characteristic of true wisdom. Upon such " wisdom" Solomon bestows the highest commendations[a]: he

[a] ver. 13—16. That this is the true meaning of "wisdom" and " understanding," is evident from Job xxviii. 28.

speaks of it as incomparably more precious than gold,
or rubies, or any earthly good whatever : he paints
her as a queen disposing of riches, honour, and lon-
gevity to all her subjects : and, because we are more
captivated by the idea of pleasure than of any thing
else, he commends her to us in the text as productive
of it in the highest possible degree.

We are naturally led to shew from the words before us, that the duties of religion are,

I. Pleasant in their exercise—

In confirmation of this truth, let us consider religion,

1. In a general and comprehensive view—

[Religion, as our Lord informs us, is comprehended in two
things; the love of God, and the love of our neighbour.

Let us then inquire into the love of God. Suppose a person
filled with admiration of the divine perfections as exhibited in
the works of creation, must not that be a *pleasant* exercise of
mind? Suppose him rising yet higher to the works of redemption, and contemplating the justice and the mercy, the truth
and the love, the wisdom and the goodness of the Deity, as
united, and harmonizing, and glorified in the cross of Christ;
suppose him, I say, contemplating these with rapture, till he
burst forth in songs of praise similar to those uttered by the
angels at the birth of Christ, or those which are now sung
around the throne of God; would there be no *pleasure* in such
an employment? Suppose him yet further meditating upon the
mercies of God vouchsafed to himself in particular, and adoring
the triune God for all the wonders of electing, redeeming,
sanctifying grace; must not such a frame be *pleasant?*

Inquire, next, into the love of our neighbour: suppose one
to be exercising all those dispositions towards him which his
relation to us or his situation demand: suppose one to be
rejoicing with him in his prosperity, or to be weeping over his
adversity in tender sympathy; suppose one to be stretching out
the hand of charity for his relief, or administering consolation
for his support;—is there no *pleasure* in all this? Surely he
has not the heart of a man, who can question this obvious,
indubitable truth.]

2. In its most difficult and painful duties—

[*Repentance* is a principal duty of religion: but can we
find, it may be asked, any pleasure in that? We answer, Yes:
only view repentance in its proper light, and we will affirm that
it is pleasant. Suppose that one of us had by mistake swallowed
somewhat that was poisonous; that we felt the deadly venom
preying on our vitals; and that our medical attendant informed

us, that, unless removed from our stomach, the poison would destroy us in a few hours; should we deem the exertions necessary for the removal of it a painful task? Should we not gladly renew them, till we had accomplished our end? Should we not, instead of regretting the pain occasioned by them, feel thankful that we had an opportunity to use them? And would not the success that accompanied our efforts turn our pain into a pleasure? Such then is repentance; it is a painful exertion to get rid of sin, which, if not expelled from our hearts, will utterly and eternally destroy us: and, though we do not say that pain can ever be pleasure, yet we affirm, that the very pangs of contrition, *considered in a complex view*, as consonant with our wishes and conducive to our good, are really pleasant: and for the truth of our assertion we will appeal to all who ever experienced those pangs: we will ask whether the seasons of their deepest humiliation have not been the sweetest seasons of their lives? We fear no contradiction upon this point, unless from those who are wholly ignorant of the matter.

Self-denial is another, and a very important, duty. But this, it should seem, precludes, in the very nature of it, the idea of pleasure, because it is a thwarting our own inclinations. We must however include this also among the ways that are ways of pleasantness. That the gratifying of a corrupt inclination is pleasant to flesh and blood, we cannot deny: but that the mortifying of it is abundantly more pleasant, we do not hesitate to affirm. Suppose a person tempted to yield to the solicitations of lust, or to gratify a no less keen appetite for revenge; would not a victory over his evil passions afford him more pleasure than a compliance with them? would not the mortifying of an unchaste desire be attended with a pleasure more pure and refined than could be attained by the indulgence of it? And, granting that the overcoming of evil with evil would be pleasant, (for revenge, they say, is sweet,) would not the " overcoming it with good" afford him incomparably sublimer happiness[b]? Let us illustrate each of these positions by an example. Joseph, we know, resisted the importunity of his mistress: but were his sensations less pleasing when he had got out of the reach of temptation, than they would have been if he had consented to her wishes? David, when enraged at the ingratitude and insolence of Nabal, went to avenge himself by his destruction: but when stopped and pacified by Abigail, did he regret the loss of any satisfaction which he would have felt in executing his cruel designs? No: he blessed her, and blessed God for her; and found infinitely more delight in the exercise of a forgiving spirit than the completest revenge could ever have afforded him[c]. We maintain it then,

---

[b] Rom. xii. 21.　　　　[c] 1 Sam. xxv. 31—33

that the self-denial which religion calls for, is a source of real pleasure to the soul.

The bearing of the cross is another duty inculcated on all the followers of Christ[d]. And can this be pleasant? Yes, we must affirm that this also is a source of pleasure to the true Christian. Doubtless the contempt and hatred which we must expect from an ungodly world are not pleasant *in themselves :* to be shut up in prison, and scourged, and put to a cruel and lingering death, are not pleasant *in themselves :* but, *as endured for the sake of Christ,* they are pleasant. To ascertain this, inquire of those "who took joyfully the spoiling of their goods[e];" or those who, with their feet in the stocks and their backs torn with scourges, "sang praises to God at midnight[f];" or those who, after their imprisonment, "rejoiced that they were counted worthy to suffer shame for the sake of Christ[g]." Ask what our Lord meant, when he taught his followers to "rejoice and be exceeding glad," whenever they should be called to suffer[h]? and inquire of all the primitive saints who had learned, through grace, to "glory in tribulation[i]." Inquire of him, who suffered more than any other of the Apostles, and who, speaking of his expected martyrdom, exults in it as a matter of the warmest congratulation[k]. The experience of all true Christians is the same at this day : they "count themselves happy when they are called to endure[l];" and look upon it as a special honour conferred upon them, when "it is given them to suffer any thing for their Redeemer's sake[m]." In a word, religion raises us so much above earthly pains and pleasures, as to render us altogether independent on them for our happiness[n].

Seeing then that even the most painful duties of religion are sources of pleasure, we may confidently affirm the same respecting "*all*" her ways.]

To this blessed account of wisdom's ways, we may add, that they are,

II. Peaceful in their issue—

Mark the influences of religion on all who walk in her ways : mark them,

1. In life—

[None know any thing of "peace," except the true Christian. As God has said, so experience proves, that "there is no peace to the wicked[o]." The cisterns to which they go for refreshment, are polluted; or rather, they are

---

[d] Luke ix. 23. 2 Tim. iii. 12.   [e] Heb. x. 34.
[f] Acts xvi. 23—25.   [g] Acts v. 41.   [h] Matt. v. 11, 12.
[i] Rom. v. 3.   [k] Phil. ii. 17, 18.   [l] Jam. i. 2. and v. 11.
[m] Phil. i. 29.   [n] Hab. iii. 17, 18.   [o] Isai. lvii. 21.

" broken cisterns that can hold no water[p]." All that they possess is mere " vanity and vexation of spirit." " Even in laughter their heart is sorrowful ; and the end of their mirth is heaviness[q]." But is it thus with the true Christian? Has not he peace in his soul, and " joys, with which the stranger intermeddleth not[r]?" Yes, he " has already entered into rest[s]:" he has a tranquillity arising from the subjugation of his passions : he has a holy composure of mind springing from the testimony of a good conscience[t]: he has many sweet manifestations of God's love to his soul : he has that within him which mitigates every sorrow, enhances every enjoyment, and supplies his every want. In a word, from committing his soul, and all his concerns, to God, he has " a peace that passeth all understanding." This peace, we say, flows from the very exercises of religion, and is, more or less, an inseparable attendant on them. To this effect the inspired writers uniformly speak. The Psalmist observes, " Great peace have they that love thy law, and nothing shall offend them[u]." To the same purpose Isaiah also says, " The work of righteousness is peace, and the effect of righteousness is quietness and assurance for ever[x]:" and St. Paul confirms their testimony, saying, " To be carnally-minded is death ; but to be spiritually-minded is life and peace[y]."]

2. In death—

[Even in the time of health the ungodly cannot bear to think of death : conversation upon that awful subject is irksome and disgusting to them : they avoid it, because it makes them melancholy. If they be attacked with any fatal disease, their friends do all that they can to abate their fears, and to hide from them the real state of their disorder. When at last they come to feel their danger, then they are full of alarm and terror ; and, however much they despised the duties of religion before, will then begin to pay attention to them. There are some indeed so blinded by their own delusions, that they believe themselves safe ; while others are so callous as to be altogether insensible of their awful condition. But if men are not wholly blinded by conceit, or hardened by wickedness, they cannot but tremble at the approach of death : and then the hopes which they once fondly entertained, give way to painful forebodings, even to " a fearful looking-for of judgment and fiery indignation." On the contrary, he who hath walked in wisdom's ways, is enabled in the midst of life to look forward to death, (like a bridegroom to his approaching nuptials,) as to the period, when all his desires shall be fulfilled, and his joys consummated. As

p Jer. ii. 13.   q Eccl. ii. 2. Prov. xiv. 13.   r Prov. xiv. 10.
s Heb. iv. 3.   t 2 Cor. i. 12.   u Ps. cxix. 165.
x Isai. xxxii. 17.   y Rom. viii. 6.

he beholds death approaching, he rather chides its tardiness, than deprecates its advent. He " knows in whom he has believed;" and, in the hour of his departure, commits his soul with confidence into the hands of his ever-living and adorable Redeemer. Thus Stephen[z], thus Paul[a], and innumerable others, have died; and David tells us, that it is the privilege of all true believers to expect and enjoy such a death as this: " Mark the perfect man, and behold the upright; for the end of that man is peace[b]."]

3. In eternity—

[As soon as the ungodly enter into the eternal world, whether they were conceited or callous, whether confident or trembling, they know the truth of all that God's word has declared. The Rich Man that fared sumptuously no sooner breathed out his soul, than he understood and felt the evil of neglecting his eternal interests; he then found his misery irremediable, and incapable of the smallest alleviation. He knew his five surviving brethren were living in the same thoughtless way, and hastening to the same fatal end; and wished that they might be apprised of their danger, ere it were too late: he knew by bitter experience that to those who lived and died in sin, nothing remained but unintermitted everlasting misery; " they drink of the wine of the wrath of God, which is poured out without mixture into the cup of his indignation; and the smoke of their torment ascendeth up for ever and ever; and they have *no rest* day nor night[c]." How different is the state of true Christians! They enjoy " the rest which here remained for them;" they rest in the bosom of their Saviour, free from all sin and temptation, from pain and weariness. The peace which they enjoyed in this world, was but a taste of that banquet on which they feast continually, a drop of " those rivers of pleasure which are at God's right hand for evermore."]

ADDRESS—

1. The votaries of pleasure—

[There are two fatal mistakes under which you labour: the one is, that you think religion (according to the Scriptural representation of it), will afford nothing but pain; the other is, that it will consist with an enjoyment of all the pleasures of the world. With respect to the former of these, we hope that nothing need be added to what has been already spoken: we hope that religion, if it have a dark and gloomy side, has also, like the pillar and cloud, a bright and cheering aspect: it is only on God's enemies that it casts a gloom: to his friends it affords a reviving light, a refreshing shade, a sure and safe

---

[z] Acts vii. 59, 60.   [a] 2 Tim. iv. 6—8.
[b] Ps. xxxvii. 37.   [c] Rev. xiv. 10, 11

directory to heaven.   With respect to the latter idea, namely,
that of its countenancing worldly pleasures, surely no one can
deliberately put such a construction on our text.   If Religion's
ways be pleasant, must therefore Pleasure's ways be religion?
If so, what can be meant by St. Paul, when he says, " She that
liveth in pleasure is dead while she liveth[d]?"   What could St.
John mean, when he said, " If any man love the world, the love
of the Father is not in him[e]?"   And what could our Lord mean,
when he said, " They are not of the world, even as I am not of
the world[f]?"   Be not deceived, as though carnal and worldly
pleasures were the only sources of enjoyment; but be assured,
that the renunciation of them will contribute more to your
happiness than the indulgence ; and that real pleasure is to be
found in God alone.]

2. The disciples of Christ—

[The wicked know that you profess to find more pleasure
in religion than they can obtain in the world : give them not
then any reason to think that you are disappointed in your expectations.   If they see you lukewarm in religion, will they
not conclude that it has not charms sufficient to allure you, or
benefits sufficient to reward your labour?   And if they see you
joining in their company and vain pursuits, will they not, however they may encourage you in such a conduct, suppose that
religion is not able to make you happy, and that you are forced,
after all your professions, to come and borrow of their carnal
pleasures, in order to eke out the scanty pittance that religion
has bestowed?   O bring not such disgrace upon your holy
profession.   Shew that you despise the vanities of this world,
and that you have no appetite for husks after living upon " the
bread that is in your Father's house."   Our Lord has said,
" My yoke is easy, and my burthen is light;" shew therefore
that you feel it so; and let it be seen by your zeal in religious
duties, that they are not a weariness to you, but a delight.   Thus
will you recommend to others the paths you tread, and prove to
them that " your feet are guided into the way of peace."]

[d] 1 Tim. v. 6.   [e] 1 John iii. 15, 16.   John xvii. 16.

OUTLINE NO. 760

TRUE RELIGION DELINEATED.

Prov. iii. 21—24.   *My son, let not them depart from thine
eyes: keep sound wisdom and discretion: so shall they be
life unto thy soul, and grace to thy neck.   Then shalt thou
walk in thy way safely, and thy foot shall not stumble.   When
thou liest down, thou shalt not be afraid ; yea, thou shalt lie
down, and thy sleep shall be sweet.*

IN the book of Proverbs, "wisdom" is generally put for religion : in some places, perhaps, it may be interpreted as representing Christ himself, who is " the wisdom of God and the power of God :" but in our text there can be no doubt of its importing piety, or the influence of true religion in the soul. And though in the Book of Proverbs the *doctrines* of religion are not very distinctly specified, the general *character* of it is developed with peculiar richness and beauty : and this gives to the Proverbs of Solomon an importance far beyond what would belong to a mere collection of moral lessons. We have, in the passage before us, what I might almost call a full-length picture of religion, both in its character and effects : and in these two points of view, we shall, in conformity with our text, proceed to consider it,

I. In its true and proper character—

Doubtless religion admits of an infinite diversity of description. But in no place can we find a juster representation of it than in that before us. It is,

1. " Wisdom" in the heart—

[Were we to define " wisdom," we should say, It is the seeking of the best ends by the fittest means. And were we to declare what true religion is, we should say, It is the seeking of the salvation of the soul through the mediation and intercession of Jesus Christ.

Now, then, I would ask, What end is there for us to propose to ourselves, that can be compared with the everlasting salvation of our souls ? The pursuit of crowns and kingdoms would be unworthy of an effort in comparison of this ——— Truly it is " the one thing needful."

Again I would ask, What means are there fitted for the attainment of this end in comparison of those which are proposed to us in the gospel of Christ ? There we find a Saviour precisely suited to our necessities ; One who has made an atonement for all our sins ; One who " ever liveth to make intercession for us " in heaven ; and One who, as the Head of all vital influence, is " able to save to the uttermost all who come unto God by him." By the simple exercise of faith in him, we become partakers of all his blessings : and, therefore, it is our one aim from day to day to " live by faith upon him," and to " receive out of his fulness " all the blessings which we stand in need of.

Now, compare with this any other mode of salvation that can
be devised; and its wisdom will shine forth as the sun, which
eclipses, and, as it were, blots from the firmament, all the lights
of heaven ———]

2. Discretion in the life—

[When once religion occupies the soul, it implants a
principle there which thenceforth regulates the whole man.
No longer does an anxiety about earthly things distract the
mind. Pleasure, riches, and honour, are all subordinated to the
welfare of the soul; and the will of God is the one only rule
of conduct to him. A regard for God's honour, too, will then
operate, so as to give to all circumstances, whether of time or
place, their legitimate influence, and to secure to him who is
under its influence the approbation of the wise and good. He
illustrates in his life that saying of Solomon, "I, Wisdom, dwell
with Prudence." In a word, to approve himself to God is the
one object of his life : and that one object being ever before
his eyes, he is kept from every corrupt bias, and from the incon-
sistencies which an unhallowed principle would produce.

Of course, it must not be supposed that a person, naturally
weak and foolish, will pass in a moment to a comprehensiveness of mind and soundness of judgment: *that* is not to be
expected: on the contrary, inasmuch as a principle of piety
infinitely outweighs every earthly object, it may be expected,
that, on its first entrance into the soul, it will operate rather
in a way of extravagance, and cause a person to overlook the
minor considerations of prudence and discretion. But this must
be imputed not to religion itself, but to the weakness of him in
whom it dwells: and the effect of religion will be to correct his
errors, and to induce habits of wisdom, which no other principle would ever have been able to form within him.]

Let us now proceed to consider it,

II. In its just and necessary effects—

Religion is not a mere *principle;* nor does it consist in any peculiar *practice* without a principle: it is
an *operative principle,* producing,

1. Life in the soul—

[I cannot give any juster view of religion, than by saying,
It is *that* in the soul which the soul is in the body. Without
the soul, the body is dead; and without religion, the soul is
dead. By the soul the body is animated, and performs all the
functions of the animal life; by religion the soul is quickened,
and performs all the functions of the spiritual life. By the
union of the soul with the body, all the powers, both of body
and mind, are called into activity; and by the operation of

religion in the soul, the understanding, the will, the affections, the memory, the conscience, perform their respective offices, in subserviency to God, for the promotion of a man's spiritual and eternal good. The soul, pervading the whole body, acts with ease and regularity, and with so little ostentation, that its operations, though effectual, attract no notice : and so it is with religion in the soul : it brings into easy and harmonious use all its different faculties and powers, governing the whole man, and subjecting even the thoughts themselves to the obedience of Christ. In a word, it is, as my text has said, " life to the soul." If we were to understand by this expression, that it tends to lengthen out the existence of man on earth, it would be true, and an important truth : but we cannot so contract the sense, or comprehend less in these words than what we have expressed. Religion makes a man a new creature : " old things pass away, and all things become new."]

2. Gracefulness in the deportment—

[Well is it said by the Apostle, that " a meek and quiet spirit is, in the sight of God himself, an ornament of great price." Through the operation of divine grace upon the soul, all the tempers and dispositions will be kept in order; so that none shall prevail to the injury of other men, or to the dishonour of the man himself. The discipline of religion is not unlike that which prevails in reference to the body amongst the higher ranks of society. In persons untaught, there is an awkwardness, as it were, apparent in their whole gait; whilst those who have mixed in polished society have a comparative ease and elegance in all their motions. So, if you see a person uninstructed in religion engaged in religious exercises, he is not at home in any of them : his occupation sits not easy upon him : and if he attempt to assume the posture of real piety, he betrays his want of true feeling by the very motions in which he attempts to express it. But let a contrite and devout soul draw nigh to God, and there is a correspondence between his looks and attitude, his words and professions. His every motion is such as befits the employment in which he is engaged : yea, there is a symmetry in every part of the spiritual man, so that his whole demeanour is simple, uniform, becoming. He exemplifies in his life that expression of the Psalmist, " I will beautify the meek with salvation :" and he shews in his deportment what that inspired writer meant by that petition, " Let the beauty of the Lord our God be upon us." The more of real piety any man possesses, the more of this image will be stamped upon him; and the more he communes with his God, the more will a divine glory surround his head, and beam forth from his countenance in the sight of all who behold him.]

3. Stability in the walk—

[The man of sound wisdom takes heed to his ways: he desires to see his path clear before him: if he be in doubt, he will take " the word of God as a light to his feet, and a lantern to his paths." If his path be slippery, he will cry unto his God, " Hold thou up my goings in thy paths, that my footsteps slip not!" And in answer to his prayer, " God will give his angels charge over him, to keep him in all his ways, that he dash not his foot against a stone." Of these advantages the unconverted man has no experience. He ventures into scenes of temptation, without being aware of his danger: nor has he any guidance or strength but his own. What wonder, then, if *he* fall? But the man who, with wisdom in his heart, and discretion in his life, " suffers not these" guardian angels, as it were, " to depart from his eyes," will be kept amidst all the most trying scenes in which he can be engaged, and " will be preserved blameless unto the kingdom of his God." " The Law of God is in his heart, and therefore his footsteps do not slide[a]."]

4. Peace in the heart—

[" What man is he that feareth the Lord? His soul," says the Psalmist, " shall dwell at ease." A man without religion may pass through the day with some degree of comfort, because of the variety of occupations that engage his thoughts. But when he comes to lie down at night, and he has time for reflection, some painful occurrence will dwell upon his mind, and agitate his spirits, and disturb his rest: and when he wakes in the morning, the same unpleasant feelings will haunt him, and destroy that serenity which sleep was calculated to convey. Or, if nothing particular have occurred to distress him, he lies down and rises up without any other feeling than that which he possesses in common with the beasts. But not so the truly religious man. He, when retiring to rest, calls to remembrance the mercies with which he has been encompassed during the day, and renders thanks for them to his heavenly Benefactor; to whom also he commends himself for protection during the defenceless hours of the night. Shall I speak too strongly if I say, that he lies down, as it were, in the bosom of his God, saying, " I will lay me down in peace, and sleep; for thou, Lord, only makest me to dwell in safety?" In the morning, too, when he awakes, he finds that " his sleep has been sweet unto him;" not to his body merely, but to his soul; for his soul, at the first resuming of its powers, finds God present with it, in a way which the merely natural man has no conception of: so true is that expression of the Psalmist, " When I awake, I am still with thee." So true, also, is that encouraging promise of Solomom, " Bind the commandment upon thine heart, and tie it about thy neck: when thou goest, it shall lead thee;

[a] See Ps. xxxvii. 31. and Prov. iv. 11—13.

when thou sleepest, it shall keep thee; and when thou awakest, it shall walk with thee."]

APPLICATION—

1. Are there now any present, who are *prejudiced against religion?*

[Know what true religion is. It is not by any means that thing which prejudiced persons are ready to imagine. "It is wisdom, sound wisdom, and discretion." There are doubtless in the Gospel many things which surpass our comprehension. But so there are also in all the other works of God, whether of creation or providence. But if there are truths at which a proud man will stumble, there is not one which will not commend itself to an humble and childlike spirit. And as far as it operates upon the soul, it induces discretion in every part of a man's conduct, and assimilates him to the very image of his God. Who amongst us will say that the Saviour's example was not good? Yet his enemies condemned it, and accounted him worthy to be crucified as the vilest malefactor. And may there not be a measure of the same prejudice in you, a prejudice that blinds your eyes, and makes you to hate those whom you should love and honour? But, at all events, know this: whatever corresponds not with religion, as described in our text, we disclaim. If there be folly and indiscretion in any who profess the Gospel, let *them* bear the blame, and not religion. But if you will condemn the care of the soul as a needless preciseness, and a cleaving unto the Saviour as an enthusiastic and vain conceit, you shall bear the burthen; for, blame these things as ye may, know that "Wisdom will be justified of all her children."]

2. Are there those here who *profess to love religion?*

[Beware, lest by any thing imprudent ye "cause the way of truth to be evil spoken of:" yea, seek rather to the utmost of your power to "adorn the doctrine of God our Saviour in all things." On your conduct much depends. Men will not judge of religion so much by what *we say*, as by what *we do*. In vain shall Solomon himself describe it as forming such lovely characters, if you contradict his statements in your life and conversation. However we may expose the folly of so doing, men will identify religion with the conduct of its professors; and will take occasion, from any thing that is unbecoming in you, to cast reflections upon religion for your sake. But, knowing this propensity in them, you should be doubly careful not to cast a stumbling-block in their way. See to it, then, that ye "walk worthy of your high calling." If ye be children of the light, let it be seen by the holiness of your conversation: and, wherever ye go, be ye epistles of Christ, known and read of all

men; so that all who behold you may be constrained to say,
" We will go with you; for we see that God is with you of
a truth."]

OUTLINE NO. 761

THE REWARDS OF WISDOM AND OF FOLLY.

Prov. iii. 35.   *The wise shall inherit glory ; but shame shall be
the promotion of fools.*

A DESIRE of distinction and a fear of shame are
powerful incentives to the human mind, and produce,
in every department of life, exertions far beyond
those to which mere natural inclination would prompt
us.   The soldier on the field of battle finds those
principles stronger than the fear of death : nor is the
student insensible of their influence upon his mind :
on the contrary, the nearer the time approaches for
a judgment to be passed upon him, the greater are his
anxieties respecting it[a].   Now, these feelings being
founded in nature itself, God is pleased to call them
into action in reference to things of far higher moment
than those which too generally engross them.   Disgrace or honour are awarded to men, even in the
present life, on moral and religious grounds, and
much more will they in the life to come : and I wish
that a due concern may be felt in reference to them,
whilst I point out the influence of wisdom,

I. On our present state—

Wisdom may fitly be described as a conformity to
the mind of God ; and folly, as any aberration from
it.   But it is the Gospel alone that places these in
their true light.   Let us,

1. Distinguish the two characters—

[The Gospel is a proclamation of mercy to perishing sinners, through the blood and righteousness of the Lord Jesus
Christ; nor is there any way of salvation for fallen man, except
that which is there revealed.   All who are not interested in that
Saviour must perish under the guilt of their sins — — —

---

[a] Preached a little previous to the Degree time at Cambridge ; a
time of extreme anxiety to the young men preparing for the Examinations.

Now, who is wise, but he who labours to secure that salvation? or who is a fool, but he who neglects it? Suppose that means of escape from a sinking vessel, or a house in flames, were offered to one in danger of instantaneous destruction; would any person in the universe hesitate to assign the proper and distinctive epithets to him who availed himself of them, and to him who disregarded them? Yet would their conduct but very faintly shadow forth that which is exhibited under the Gospel dispensation; and the terms used to designate that conduct would very faintly describe its appropriate character. Let the two characters, then, be properly distinguished. Where is the man who, with all humility of mind and entire devotion of soul, seeks an interest in the Saviour? ——— Him we may safely designate as " wise." Where, on the other hand, is the man who neglects the Saviour? ——— Whatever excuses he may allege in vindication of his conduct, we need not hesitate to assign to him the humiliating appellation of a " fool."]

2. Declare their proper award—

[" The wise" shall even here " inherit glory." Every one, whatever his own practice may be, has within his own bosom a witness in favour of those who are religious, provided their conduct be uniform and consistent. In outward profession, I grant, the world may brand religion with the name of folly: but their consciences in secret give a very different testimony: nor is there any man, however ungodly, so wicked, but that he reverences in his heart a pious character, and wishes, if it were possible, to be found in his place at the day of judgment. Herod, in the midst of all his impiety, " feared John, because he knew him to be a just and holy man." And so it is with the ungodly world; they venerate the very man whom for his piety they hate and persecute. On the other hand, vain and thoughtless as are the world at large, and interested in upholding each other in their various pursuits, there is not one among them, who, in his moments of reflection, does not see the emptiness and vanity of worldly things; and who would not regard it as an inconsistency in a religious character, if he should betray an eagerness in the prosecution of them. The truth of these observations will be manifest beyond either contradiction or doubt, if only we bear in mind the conduct of the Scribes and Pharisees of old, who, whilst persecuting our blessed Lord even unto death, " built the tombs of the prophets, and garnished the sepulchres of the righteous," whom their forefathers had put to death[b]. Precisely thus we also at this time honour the memory of the Apostles, and of our own reformers too, (for who does not honour the names of Cranmer, and Latimer, and Ridley?) whilst we hate, revile, and persecute the living saints, who walk

---

[b] Matt. xxiii. 29—31.

in their steps: and the names of the Scribes and Pharisees of old are odious to us, whilst we pay respect to those who sustain the same character amongst ourselves. All this clearly shews, that whatever our *outward* behaviour may be towards the two different parties, both of them have an *inward* witness in our own bosoms; " the wise inheriting the glory" that is due to them, whilst "shame is the only promotion of fools."]

But still more effect will wisdom have,

II. On our condition in the eternal world—

There the conduct of all will be rightly appreciated—

[In this world there are many things which obscure the wisdom of the wise, and which serve to palliate the folly of fools. The weaknesses of many good men excite a prejudice against their sentiments and conduct, and do really cast an air of folly over their very profession. This is deeply to be lamented: but, whilst there is so much folly bound up in the heart of man, and in many the seed of Divine Grace is but as a grain of mustard-seed, it is not to be wondered at that such stumbling-blocks should occur: indeed, unless a miracle were wrought to turn babes at once into young men and fathers, it is scarcely possible that offences of some kind should not arise from the injudicious deportment of weaker brethren. On the other hand, amongst those who are not devoted to the Saviour, there are many eminent for their attainments in science, and abounding in every species of worldly wisdom; and amidst so much that is amiable and good, it is difficult to mark with becoming severity the folly of which they are guilty. But God will judge righteous judgment: he will distinguish infallibly between the errors of the judgment and the bias of the heart: and to those who sought him, though in much weakness, he will give a testimony of applause; but on those who sought him not he will denounce his sentence of eternal condemnation.]

Then will wisdom and folly appear in their true light—

[Behold the saint approved of his God, and seated on a throne of glory! Will any one think he sacrificed too much for this, or laboured too hard for this? Will there be any difference of opinion respecting him, amongst the hosts of heaven, or even in the regions of hell? No; there will be but one testimony respecting him. Every creature in the universe will pronounce him wise. See, on the other hand, the most successful and distinguished of the human race banished from the presence of that Saviour whom he would not seek, and of that God whom he refused to serve! Will there be any difference of opinion respecting his folly? Nay, will not he himself be the very first to accuse himself, and to curse the folly which once he so fondly cherished? Yes: we are told that, in hell, men will "weep, and wail, and gnash their teeth" with anguish: and I cannot doubt but that their self-reproach will be one of the bitterest ingredients in the cup which will there be given them to drink. When they see in what their love of "promotion" has issued, and that it has brought nothing but a pre-eminence in "shame" and sorrow, they will set their seal to that once-despised truth, that "wisdom excelleth folly, as much as light excelleth darkness."]

Permit me now to RECOMMEND to every one amongst you,

1. A retrospect of your past lives—

[What is your estimate now of your past life? Is there one amongst you who would not rather that it should have been under the influence of wisdom, than that it should have been so devoted to folly, as in the great majority of cases it has been? I suppose there is scarcely any one that has not, at some season or other, had moments of reflection, and formed some faint purposes of amendment. Let the humiliation then experienced have been ever so transient, do you not at this time look back upon it as the best hour of your lives? and do you not regret that it so speedily passed away? And, however deeply you may have drunk of the cup of pleasure, do you not now feel that it is all vanity, and that nothing of it remains but the dregs, which have a bitter taste? Where is there one amongst you, who, if he should hear a dying man glorying in having lived altogether to the flesh and to the world, would not be shocked at it as an excess of impiety and folly? Or who, if he were himself in dying circumstances, would not wish for a far different frame of mind to prepare him for his great account? I make this appeal with confidence, and am content to rest the whole of what I have said on the testimony of your own consciences. Yes, beloved Brethren, you shall be constituted judges in your own case; and I will abide by the decision which you yourselves shall give. Let your convictions, then, be now realized; and let the Lord Jesus Christ be now sought by you without delay.]

2. A prospective view of futurity—

[Soon you will be convinced, at all events, whether you will listen to good instruction now, or not. Soon you will "see whose word shall stand—the world's, or God's." Depend upon it, God's word will not change. What he has designated as wisdom by the mouth of Prophets and Apostles, he will pronounce to have been so, when he shall sit on his throne of judgment. Why will ye not then anticipate that sentence? And why will ye not consider what your reflections

will be, when all your present opportunities of turning unto
God shall have passed away? This only do I ask of you:
' Act now, as you will then wish you had acted.' Methinks
this is a reasonable request: it is a request which every one
acknowledges to be good in reference to the things of time;
and surely it cannot be less good in reference to eternity.
May God enable all of you, then, to comply with it! and may
you all not only become wise, but be made wise unto salvation through faith in Christ Jesus!]

OUTLINE NO. 762

THE NATURE AND EXCELLENCE OF TRUE WISDOM.

Prov. iv. 7. *Wisdom is the principal thing: therefore get
wisdom; and with all thy getting, get understanding.*

THE inspired volume is no less useful in rectifying
the prejudices of education, than it is in restraining
the indulgence of forbidden appetites. As far as
relates to the grosser violations of moral duty, the
advice of parents and teachers is in unison with the
Holy Scriptures; but we are very rarely exhorted to
follow that which is the main end and purpose of life.
Get wealth, get honour, are the lessons inculcated on
all the rising generation. David however sets us a
better example: he earnestly entreated his son above
all things to cultivate true religion. And Solomon,
having reaped much advantage from those instructions, has left them on record for our benefit[a]. We
shall endeavour,

I. To shew the nature and excellence of true wisdom—

That which is usually termed wisdom is far from
being the object so extolled in the text—

[We mean not to depreciate the attainments of art or
science. They are valuable in themselves, and, if duly improved, may, like the Egyptian gold, enrich and beautify the
sanctuary of God. But the wisdom spoken of in the text, has
respect entirely to spiritual things.]

True wisdom is the proposing of the best ends and
prosecuting of them by the fittest means—

[There is no *end* so worthy to be pursued by a rational
creature, as the sanctification and salvation of his own soul.

[a] ver. 3—7.

Nor are there any *means* of attaining it so proper, as those prescribed in the Holy Scriptures. To repent of all our sins, to flee to Christ for the pardon of them, and to seek the renovation of our hearts by the Holy Spirit, are represented as the only effectual means of salvation. These things, it must be confessed, are often called folly; but they are called so only by those, who have never known them by experience. Not one among the holy angels would account it folly to love and serve God. None of the redeemed in heaven regret that they were once so strenuous in the exercises of religion. The saints on earth are precisely of the same mind with those in heaven. Hence conversion to a holy life is called " a turning of the hearts of the disobedient to the wisdom of the just[b]." Even devils and damned spirits would confess that devotedness of heart to God is the truest wisdom. Careless sinners are the only beings who dissent from this truth; and they in a little time will assuredly alter their opinion[c].]

Such wisdom is justly termed "the principal thing"—

[There are many other things which are important in their place; but this is far superior to them all. Riches cannot be put in competition with it[d]. Pleasure, honour, or even life itself, are not worthy to be compared with it[e]. It excels every thing else as much as light excelleth darkness[f]. This exclusively deserves the name of wisdom, God himself being witness[g]. It is " the good part;[h]" and he alone can be called truly wise, who, like Paul, accounts every thing but loss for that unspeakably excellent attainment[i].]

Its excellency being thus established, we may proceed,

II. To urge upon you the diligent pursuit of it—

In the text, with the preceding context, we may see the utmost fervour that language can express. May we be animated with the same, while we labour to impress the subject on your minds by the following considerations! Consider then,

1. This wisdom is both more easily, and more certainly, to be attained than any thing else—

[With respect to other things, every one has not a capacity for making great attainments; nor have all, who possess

[b] Luke i. 17.
[c] Wisdom v. 4. What do those rich men, Luke xii. 19, 20. and xvi. 19, 23. *now* think of their once envied state?
[d] Job xxviii. 12—19.   [e] Prov. iii. 13—18.   [f] Eccl. ii. 13.
[g] Job xxviii. 28.   [h] Luke x. 42.   [i] Phil. iii. 7, 8.

good abilities, an opportunity of cultivating them to advantage. Nor can great industry united with great talents, always ensure success[k]; but no man ever sought this in vain. The poor fishermen of Galilee were as capable of comprehending it, as the philosophers of Greece and Rome. We attain it, not by the mere exertion of our own powers, but by the teachings of God's Spirit[l]. Nor will he ever refuse that heavenly gift to any who seek it with a teachable and childlike disposition[m]. This thought may well encourage all. May *we* be stirred up by it to seek the unction that shall teach us all things[n]! Then will God bestow upon us his promised blessing[o]; and make us wise unto salvation through faith in Christ[p].]

2. There is nothing else which will so conduce to our *present* happiness—

[The creature is justly represented as a cistern that will hold no water[q]. All who seek happiness in it are disappointed. Even science itself, which is the most rational of all earthly pleasures, is often a source of sorrow and vexation[r]; but true wisdom is an overflowing fountain of joy. In prosperity, it adds a zest to all our comforts; and in adversity, a balm to all our sorrows. In a time of pain and trouble more especially its excellency appears. What can earthly things do to assuage our anguish or compose our minds[s]? But religion enables us to see the rod in our Father's hand, and to know that all is working for our good[t]. St. Paul found it to be wealth in poverty, joy in sorrow, life in death[u]. And such will every Christian experience it to be in the hour of trial[x]. Shall not this consideration then quicken our diligence in the pursuit of it?]

3. There is nothing besides this that can in the least promote our *eternal* welfare—

[Our duties, when performed with an eye to God, are a part of religion itself; but, independent of the respect which we have to him in the performance of them, they are of no value in his sight. A person may do many things that are beneficial to society, and yet be dead in trespasses and sins. But Solomon, specifying the supreme excellency of wisdom, affirms, that it giveth life to them that have it[y]. No man can perish that possesses wisdom; nor can any man be saved who is destitute of it[z]. Shall we not then be prevailed upon to seek it? Shall we disregard the commendations that David and Solomon have given of it? And shall their importunity be treated

[k] Eccl. ix. 11.	[l] John i. 13. and vi. 45.	[m] Jam. i. 5.
[n] 1 John ii. 20.	[o] Prov. ii. 1—6.	[p] 2 Tim. iii. 15.
[q] Jer. ii. 13.	[r] Eccl. i. 17, 18.	[s] Eccl. v. 17.
[t] Rom. viii. 28.	[u] 2 Cor. vi. 9, 10.	[x] Prov. iii. 21—26.
[y] Eccl. vii. 12.	[z] Rom. viii. 6, 13.	

by us with coldness and neglect? Surely such a conduct may well expose us to the most severe of all reflections[a].]

" Suffer then a word of EXHORTATION "—

[The wisdom here spoken of is not the *only* thing in the world that is desirable; nor the *only* thing that you may laudably pursue. There are innumerable other things which demand our attention; and which our several conditions in life render necessary. The text itself supposes, or rather enjoins, that we should labour to get other things; but wisdom is indisputably " the *principal* thing;" and " *with all our getting* we must be mindful to get understanding." Whatever else be neglected, this must not: it is " the one thing needful." Therefore, " get it, get it, get it, get it[b]." " Forsake it not, neither forget it; exalt it, love it, and embrace it; so shall it be an ornament of grace to your head, and a crown of glory to your soul." For whoso findeth it findeth life, and shall obtain favour of the Lord[c].][d]

[a] Prov. xvii. 16.   [b] Four times is this repeated, ver. 5, 7.
[c] Prov. viii. 35.
[d] If this were the subject of *a Commemoration Sermon*, the intention of the founder, and the obligations necessarily attaching to every member of the society, might be urged as a *fourth* and *more appropriate* consideration to enforce the royal precept given in the text.

OUTLINE NO. 763

THE CHRISTIAN'S PATH COMPARED TO THE LIGHT.

Prov. iv. 18. *The path of the just is as the shining light, that shineth more and more unto the perfect day.*

HABITS, of whatever kind, are strengthened by exercise; the more congenial they are with our natural feelings, the more easily are they confirmed. Hence the wicked, without any express purpose on their part, are daily more and more riveted to the world and sin. The righteous too increase in love to the ways of God in proportion as they endeavour to fulfil his will. They have indeed a bias, which, if they were left to themselves, would soon turn them aside. But God will not leave them destitute of needful succour: he pledges himself that their path shall resemble the shining light. This is found true by happy experience. Their path is,

I. Beautiful in its appearance—

The rising sun is as beautiful an object as any in the whole creation—

[At its first approach it tinges the distant clouds with light. On its first appearance it gilds the summits of the woods and mountains : then, dispelling all the shades of night, it illumines the whole horizon. How delightful is this to every one that beholds it[a] !]

Thus is the path of the righteous exceeding beautiful—

["The just" are they who are renewed and sanctified by the Spirit of God. Their path *in the very outset* is beautiful to behold. Their simplicity of mind, and teachableness of spirit, endear them to us; their lowliness and humility attract the notice of the very angels themselves[b]. The fervour of their love engages both our admiration and esteem. The very shades in their character serve as a contrast to shew the excellence of the change that has passed upon them. *As they proceed* their graces are more matured. Their course is justly described by the Apostle Paul[c]. Surely such a conduct must be beautiful in the eyes of God and man. They are justly spoken of as " beautified with salvation[d]: they even reflect a lustre upon the Gospel itself[e].]

While their path is so amiable, it resembles the light further, in that it is

II. Beneficial in its influence—

The sun does not shine with unproductive splendour—

[It enables the several orders of men to return to their respective callings. In the darkness they could not go without stumbling[f]; but now they follow their occupations without fear or difficulty. The productions of the earth also feel the genial influence of the sun, and are matured by means of its invigorating beams.]

Nor is the Christian unprofitable in his course—

[The wicked are stumbling on every side of him[g]; but the Christian affords a light to the benighted souls around him[h]. He shines in the midst of a crooked and perverse generation[i]: he is an epistle of Christ, known and read of all men[k]. The account given of Job, describes his course, as far as his situation and circumstances will allow[l]. Thus by his conduct he

[a] Eccl. xi. 7.	[b] Luke xv. 10.	[c] Phil. iv. 8.
[d] Ps. clxix. 4	[e] Tit. ii. 10.	[f] John xi. 9, 10.
[g] Prov. iv. 19.	[h] Matt. v. 14.	[i] Phil. ii. 15, 16.
[k] 2 Cor. iii. 2, 3.	[l] Job xxix. 11—16.	

puts to silence the ignorance of foolish men[m]. He even wins some, perhaps, whom the word alone would never have converted[n], and causes many to glorify his heavenly Father[o].]

The comparison yet further holds, in that the path of the just, like that of the sun, is,

III. Constant in its progress—

The sun invariably pursues its wonted course—

[From the instant it rises, it hastens toward the meridian. Sometimes indeed its splendour is intercepted by clouds, and sometimes it may be partially, or even totally eclipsed; still, however, it proceeds in its appointed path, and is sure to arrive at its meridian height.]

The Christian too goes forward towards perfection—

[He never rests as though he had attained the summit[p]. He determines to be ever pressing forward for higher attainments[q]. He may indeed for a season be involved in clouds: yea, perhaps, he may through the violence of temptation, suffer an eclipse; but, if he be really "just" and upright, his light shall break forth again. God has ensured this by a solemn promise[r]. Jeremiah illustrates it by the very allusion in the text[s]: nor is this progress the privilege of some only[t]. David speaks of it as belonging to Israel of old[u]. Paul represents it as enjoyed by every true Christian[x]; and Peter shews us whence this stability proceeds[y]. None indeed arrive at absolute perfection in this life[z]; but soon the just will be changed into Christ's perfect image[a], and shine above the sun in the firmament for ever and ever[b].]

IMPROVEMENT—

1. For conviction—

[We are in a world that lieth in darkness and the shadow of death; and, if we be Christians indeed, we are shining as lights in a dark place. Do our consciences testify that this is the case with us? Are we examples of holiness to those of our own age and rank? Do we reprove all works of darkness, instead of having fellowship with them[c]? If not, how can we ever be numbered among the just? Shall we say that we once were such, but are now under a cloud? Or that our light is at the present eclipsed? Let us beware lest we prove only as a

[m] 1 Pet. ii. 15. [n] 1 Pet. iii. 1, 2. [o] Matt. v. 16.
[p] Phil. iii. 12. [q] Phil. iii. 13, 14. [r] Job xvii. 9.
[s] Jer. xxxi. 33—37. [t] Phil. i. 6, 7. [u] Ps. lxxxiv. 7.
[x] 2 Cor. iii. 18. [y] 1 Pet. i. 5. [z] 1 Cor. xiii. 9, 10.
[a] 1 John iii. 2. Phil. iii. 21.
[b] Dan. xii. 3. and Matt. xiii. 43. [c] Eph. v. 11.

fleeting meteor. Our light must be steady and increasing, like
that of the sun. The tree is known by its fruit; and the just
by their light[d]; and a false profession will deceive us to our
eternal ruin[e].]

2. For consolation—

[There are many true Christians who do not enjoy much
comfort, and the darkness of their minds sometimes makes them
doubt whether they be upright before God; but they often
write bitter things against themselves without a cause. Distress, whether temporal or spiritual, argues nothing against our
integrity. Job never shone brighter than in his trouble; nor
Christ, than in the depths of his dereliction. Let him then that
is in darkness, stay himself upon his God[f]. It is to such persons
that God sends us with words of comfort[g]. To them in particular is that delightful declaration addressed[h]. Wait then the
Lord's leisure, ye afflicted souls, and trust in him. Soon shall
your "light rise in obscurity, and your darkness be as the
noon-day;" nor will God be glorified less in your patience,
than in more active services.]

[d] Eph. v. o.   [e] 1 John i. 6. and ii. 9, 11.
[f] Isai. l. 10.   [g] Isai. xxxv. 3, 4.   [h] Isai. liv. 7—10.

OUTLINE NO. 764

KEEPING THE HEART.

Prov. iv. 23. *Keep thy heart with all diligence; for out of it*
are the issues of life.

IT is certainly of infinite importance that we be
deeply convinced of our utter inability to do any
thing that is good, and of our entire dependence upon
God for the effectual aids of his Holy Spirit. But
we must not imagine, that, because we have no sufficiency of ourselves to do the will of God, we are not
bound in duty to do it, or not to be exhorted and
stimulated to the performance of it. Our duty is the
same, whatever be the circumstances to which we
have reduced ourselves; and it is *in*, and *by*, our
personal exertions, that God has promised to " work
all our works in us." Hence, in the Scriptures of
Truth, we are continually exhorted to serve our God
in the way of his commandments. It is obvious that
we cannot preserve the life of our bodies for one
single moment; yet God expects, that we keep

ourselves from those things which would destroy life, and use all proper means of preserving it: so neither can we, of ourselves, preserve the life of our souls; yet are we bound to "keep our heart with all diligence; since out of it are the issues of life."

It is indeed supposed here, that a new heart has been given to us; because from the unregenerated heart no good thing can issue: but inasmuch as even the renewed heart has still innumerable corruptions within it, we must keep it with all diligence.

To impress this duty on our minds, let us consider,

I. The duty enjoined—

"To keep the heart" is indeed an arduous task. To assist you in the performance of it, we will offer such suggestions as appear suitable to the occasion:

1. Fortify it with good principles—

[A city unfortified is open to assault on every side: and so is the heart, if not duly fortified by the principles of true religion. As a sinner redeemed by the precious blood of Christ, and sanctified by his Spirit, I am the Lord's peculiar property: I live by him; and I must live for him: " having been bought with a price, I am not my own, but his" who bought me: and I have nothing to do but to "glorify him with my body and my spirit, which are his." When therefore any thing attempts to gain possession of my heart, I must keep it for Him; for Him wholly; for Him alone. Nothing is to break in upon this principle. Let earth and hell assault me, I must oppose them in this impregnable bulwark; " Depart from me, ye evil-doers; I will keep the commandments of my God[a]." The Christian *is* furnished *by* God with armour for this contest[b]; and, clothed in this panoply, he must maintain the conflict even unto death[c].]

2. Watch all its most secret motions—

[A citadel, however strong, if filled with traitors waiting for an occasion to open it to the enemy, needs to be guarded with peculiar care: the professed defenders of it must themselves be watched. So it is with the heart, notwithstanding it be at present garrisoned for the Lord. It is inconceivably difficult in many instances to distinguish between the loyal and the treacherous. They are both habited in the same uniform; and both make the very same professions: both too appear actuated by the same holy zeal. The Apostles, when

[a] Ps. cxix. 115.　　[b] Eph. vi. 11—16.　　[c] Rev. ii. 10.

disputing with each other who should be the greatest, and forbidding others to cast out devils, because they followed not with them, and desiring to call fire from heaven to avenge their Master's cause, appeared as faithful as men could be[d]: yet were they in reality actuated by pride and envy, in the garb of zeal and love: and, had not these corrupt passions been checked at first, who can tell, "how great a matter this little fire might have kindled[e]?" There is not a motion of the heart but must be strictly marked: its associates must be carefully noticed; its tendencies examined; its professions scrutinized; lest Satan himself be found there, under the semblance of an angel of light[f].]

3. Combine all its energies in the service of your God—

[The Psalmist has a remarkable expression on this subject; "Unite my heart, O Lord, to fear thy name[g]." If the powers of the soul be scattered, they will be as inefficient as soldiers that are dispersed. It is by a combination of efforts for a preconcerted end, and by simultaneous movements for its accomplishment, that success is attained. The various powers of the soul must act in unison: the understanding, the will, the affections, the memory, the conscience, must all have the same object in view, each defending its proper post to the uttermost, and ready to succour the other with all its might. If, whilst the understanding is occupied about spiritual and heavenly things, the will and the affections are running after earthly and carnal things, what can be expected, but that the enemy shall soon gain undisguised and permanent possession of the soul? Every one knows, that " a house divided against itself, falleth;" and a divided heart must become a prey to the great adversary of God and man. All its powers must center in God, if God is to inhabit it as his temple, and to possess it as his inheritance.]

4. Call in for it the most effectual aid—

[Human efforts, unassisted by God, will be of little avail. Indeed we can do nothing but as we are assisted by "the Captain of our Salvation [h]." To him then must we look to "strengthen us with might by his Spirit in our inward man [i]:" we must go forth against our enemies, as David did against Goliath, not in dependence on an arm of flesh, but in the name of the Lord God of Israel: we must " be strong in *the Lord*, and in the power of *his* might [k]." Then we may defy all our adversaries: we may boldly ask the greatest amongst them; " Who art thou, O thou great Mountain? Before Zerubbabel

---

[d] Luke ix. 46, 49, 54. [e] Jam. iii. 5. [f] 2 Cor. xi. 13, 14.
[g] Ps. lxxxvi. 11. [h] John xv. 5. [i] Eph. iii. 16.
[k] Eph. vi. 10.

thou shalt become a plain." See how Paul taught the first Christians to triumph, whilst yet in the midst of all their conflicts : "Who shall separate us from the love of Christ? Shall tribulation, or distress, or persecution, or nakedness, or peril, or sword? No : in all these things we are more than conquerors [1]:" so then may the weakest of us triumph, if we call in our blessed Lord to our aid : for "through Christ strengthening us, we can do all things [m]."]

But to form a right judgment of our duty, we must yet more distinctly notice,

II. The particular instruction relating to it—

We must keep our heart "*with all diligence.*" Our attention to it must be,

1. Earnest—

[It is not a slight or superficial attention to it that will suffice. The work is too great to be effected in such a way. To keep the heart from sin amidst so many temptations on every side, and to keep it in the exercise of all holy and heavenly graces, from every one of which it is by nature alienated; *this* is a great work indeed, and requires the utmost possible exertion on our part. The metaphors by which the Christian's life is set forth, sufficiently shew what efforts are called for on our part. A race is not to be won without straining every nerve: an adversary, whether in fight or in wrestling, is not to be overcome without putting forth all our strength. Can we then suppose, that, when our contest is not with flesh and blood only, but with all the principalities and powers of hell, the victory can be gained without the most strenuous exertions? No; it cannot : and our Lord plainly tells us that it cannot : "*Strive,*" says he, "to enter in at the strait gate; for many shall *seek* to enter in, and not be able." Know then, that whatever you have to do in the keeping of your heart, you must "do it with all your might."]

2. Constant—

[The work which we have to do, is not like that of a painter or a statuary, who may leave his work for a time, and find it afterwards in the state in which he left it : it is rather like that of one who is rolling up hill a stone, which will return upon him, as soon as ever he intermits his labour. Our hearts of themselves are "bent to backslide from God," ever ready to "start aside as a deceitful bow :" and Satan is ever on the watch to draw us aside. If he intermit his labours, it is in appearance only, and not in reality : for he is ever "going about, as a

[1] Rom. viii. 35, 37.   [m] Phil. iv. 13.

roaring lion, seeking whom he may devour." His wiles and
devices are innumerable : and, if once he can find us off our
guard, he will assuredly avail himself of the occasion to deceive
and, if possible, to destroy us. We therefore must be always
" on our watch-tower," according to that direction of our
blessed Lord, " Watch and pray, lest ye enter into temptation :
and, what I say unto you, I say unto all, Watch."]

3. Persevering—

[There is no state at which we can arrive in this world that
supersedes the necessity of continued vigilance and care. Were
we as eminent as Paul himself, we must still, like him, " keep
our body under and bring it into subjection, lest by any means,
after having preached to others, we ourselves become cast-
aways." Let our circumstances be ever so favourable, we
know not but that we shall fall the very next moment. Hezekiah was but just recovered from a dangerous illness, and
that by miracle; yet when the Babylonish ambassadors came to
offer him their master's congratulations, he fell, and offended
God by "the pride of his heart[n]." Peter also was but just
descended from Mount Tabor, where he had beheld his Lord
transfigured, and shining forth in all his glory, when he acted
Satan's part in dissuading his Lord from completing the work
assigned him : so that he drew forth from his Divine Master that
just reprimand, " Get thee behind me, Satan[o]." We may add
too, that there is no wickedness so great, but we may be drawn
to the commission of it. Who can reflect on David's adultery
and murder, or on Peter's denial of his Lord with oaths and
curses, and not see reason to cry continually to God, " Hold
thou me up, and I shall be safe ! "

Thus then we see, it is not enough to keep our hearts, but
we must " keep them with all diligence," engaging in the work
with earnestness, and maintaining it with constancy and perseverance to the latest hour of our lives.]

Let us now attend to,

III. The reason with which both the one and the other are enforced—

The heart may in some respects be considered as
the seat of vitality in the human body, because from
thence issues the blood that circulates through the
whole frame. But still more may it be said of the
heart in a spiritual view, that out of it are the issues
of life. For,

1. It is the proper source of all evil—

[n] 2 Chron. xxxii. 24—26.   [o] Matt. xvi. 23, 24.

[There are many evils to which our corrupt nature is apt to yield; some are spiritual, and some are fleshly; but the womb where all are generated, and from whence they proceed, is the heart. Adultery, and murder, and theft, with many other evils, might be supposed to arise rather out of external circumstances connected with our outward man: but they are all traced by our blessed Lord to the heart: " From within, out of the heart of man, proceed evil thoughts, adulteries, fornications, murders, thefts, covetousness, wickedness, deceit, lasciviousness, an evil eye, blasphemy, pride, foolishness: all these things come from within[p]." Now, if the heart be the fruitful spring of such evils, ought it not to be watched? ought it not to be kept with all diligence? It is evident that, without continual care, the whole man would soon be inundated with evil: should we not then watch the sluices? should we not guard the banks, and keep them in good repair? In other words, should we not do all in our power to prevent such fatal effects? Let it never be forgotten, that the smallest breach in a bank will soon yield to the torrent, and, by its extension, bid defiance to any remedy that can be applied: consequently, if we would not be overrun with *all manner* of evil, we must guard against the irruption of *any*. " A little leaven will soon leaven the whole lump."]

2. It is the proper seat of all good—

[Grace is planted in *the heart :* it has no other residence : it may operate by the members; but its seat is in the heart. *Repentance* flows from thence, even from " the broken and contrite heart." *Faith* has there its first formation. " With the heart man believeth unto righteousness." *Love* combines and concentrates all its powers; " We are to love God with all the heart :" yea, " *Christ himself* dwells in our hearts by faith." Whatever then proceeds not from the heart, is of no value : all our best services for God are no other than hypocrisy, if the heart be far from him[q]. Must we not then keep the heart with all diligence, to see that it be duly influenced by divine grace, and that all which we do is the result of gracious principles implanted there? Truly, if " a man may give all his goods to feed the poor, and his body to be burned, and, after all, be no better than sounding brass or a tinkling cymbal," because his actions proceed not from a principle of love in the heart, we are called upon to watch over our hearts with all imaginable care, that they be duly stored with all that is good. This is the plain and obvious inference from what our Lord himself hath distinctly affirmed in those memorable words, " The evil man out of the evil treasure of his heart bringeth forth that which is evil; and the good man out of the good treasure of

[p] Mark vii. 21—23.   [q] Matt. xv. 7, 8.

his heart bringeth forth that which is good:" in both cases the produce is "from the abundance of the heart[r]:" and "the tree is known by its fruits."]

3. By it shall our state be determined in the last day—

[Even in courts of judicature amongst ourselves, it is not so much the *act*, as the *heart*, that is the object of investigation. Murder itself is not accounted murder, if it was not attended with a purpose of heart to injure and destroy. Much more therefore may it be expected that God will inquire into the designs and purposes of our hearts : "He looketh not on the outward appearance, but at the heart :" and "he searcheth the heart, and trieth the reins, on purpose to give to every man according to the fruit of his doings." For this end "he will bring to light the hidden things of darkness, and will make manifest the counsels of the heart." To our hearts then must we look, if ever we would give up our account with joy : for, as our hearts are, so shall we appear in his sight[s]. Let us then not only search and try ourselves, but beg of God also to "search and try us, and to see if there be any wicked way in us, and to lead us in the way everlasting."]

APPLICATION—

1. Grudge not your labour in the way to heaven—

[You cannot make any attainments in this life without labour : how then can you hope to attain without it the glory and felicity of heaven? True it is, that heaven is a gift of God ; a gift altogether of his free and sovereign grace : but it is also true, that we must labour for it, according to that direction of our Lord ; "Labour not for the meat that perisheth, but for that meat which endureth unto everlasting life, which the Son of man shall give unto you[t]." Labour then with all earnestness, and constancy, and perseverance. If you be frequently foiled, still return to your post, and increase your vigilance in proportion as you discover the deceitfulness and wickedness of your hearts : and be assured, that, however great your toil may be, heaven will be an abundant recompence for all.]

2. Doubt not but that your labour shall at last be crowned with success—

[Were your success dependent on an arm of flesh, you might well despond : but your God and Saviour is pledged to "carry on in you the work he has begun," and to "perfect that which concerneth you." Your enemies may renew their assaults as often as they will ; but they shall not prevail : for

[r] Luke vi. 45.   [s] Prov. xxiii. 7.   [t] John vi. 27.

God has said, that "No weapon that is formed against you shall prosper[u]:" and again, "The law of God is in his heart; his footsteps shall not slide[x]." Go on then: "watch ye; stand fast in the faith; quit you like men; be strong[y]:" and know for your comfort what the all-gracious and unchanging God hath spoken; "Be not weary in well-doing; for in due season ye shall reap, if ye faint not[z]."]

[u] Isai. liv. 17.   [x] Ps. xxxvii. 31.   [y] 1 Cor. xvi. 13.   [z] Gal. vi. 9.

OUTLINE NO. 765

SINNER'S RETROSPECT.

Prov. v. 12, 13. *How have I hated instruction, and my heart despised reproof; and have not obeyed the voice of my teachers, nor inclined mine ear to them that instructed me!*

A TIME of reflection must come to all: if men shake off all thought till the hour of death, they will not be able to do so when once the soul is separated from the body: their ways will *then* be brought to remembrance; and all the powers of their minds be fixed upon the contemplation of them. Happily, with many this season arrives before it is too late: and, not unfrequently, the very enormities which have been committed are the means of exciting in the soul a salutary remorse. Sometimes the present consequences of sin press heavily upon the mind, and awaken the energies of a sleepy conscience. Thus Solomon supposes many to be affected after they have brought trouble on themselves by their licentious courses: and he urges this very consideration as an argument for guarding against all temptations to sin, that, however pleasurable a life of sin may be, the retrospect will be painful in the extreme; and the now thoughtless debauchee "will mourn at the last," in the review of the mercies he has abused, and will say, "How have I hated instruction, and my heart despised reproof!"

We shall not confine our attention to the particular subject treated of in the context, though in every congregation, it is to be feared, there are but too many to whom it would be applicable; but shall rather take occasion from our text to set before you in a more enlarged view,

I. The sinner's retrospect—

That we may bring home the subject to every man's bosom, we shall consider men under two distinct classes;

1. Those who already feel some painful consequences of their past conduct—

[Amongst these we must first notice the persons more immediately referred to in our text, namely, those who have wasted their property, and injured their constitution, in habits of criminal indulgence[a]. What reason for regret have they! How glad would they now be, if they had restrained their appetites, and not purchased a momentary gratification at so high a price!——— Next to these we may mention the spendthrift, and the gamester, who through covetousness or the love of pleasure have dissipated their fortune, and involved themselves in ruin. How common is it for persons so circumstanced to destroy their own lives, and to seek in suicide a remedy for the evils they have entailed upon themselves!——— To these we may add the persons who by any disgraceful act have blasted their reputation, and rendered themselves obnoxious to just reproach: to such the seasons of reflection are bitter. They attempt perhaps to divert their thoughts by business or pleasure; but they can never cease to rue the day in which they brought upon themselves so heavy a calamity. There are times when all who have entailed misery on themselves will bring to mind the instructions given them in early youth; and then they will, inwardly at least, complain, "How have I hated instruction, and my heart despised reproof!"]

2. Those who, though they feel no present pain arising from their sins, are yet sensible that they have not answered the great ends of life—

[The necessity of turning unto God, and the means of acceptance with God through the atonement of Christ, have been distinctly set forth from time to time; so that, supposing persons to have diligently attended to the word that has been preached to them, and to have "mixed faith with it," it would have been impossible for them to have continued in the ways of sin and death. But how many are at this moment as far from God as they were years ago! How many have reason to regret that they have ever heard the Gospel, which, instead of being a savour of life to them, has, through their neglect of it, been made a savour of death unto death! Our blessed Lord told his hearers, that " if he had never come to instruct them, they would not, comparatively, have had sin; but that now they had no cloak for their sin." So must it be said to many amongst us; " that having been exalted to heaven" in their privileges, they have reason to expect that they shall, with Capernaum, " be cast the deeper into hell" for their abuse of them. It is a small matter that their sins have not been such as to expose them to shame and reproach among men: their neglect of Christ, their want of love to his name, and of zeal in his service, must be reckoned for at the last day, when he will say, " Bring hither those that were mine enemies, who would not that I should reign over them, and slay them before me." O painful retrospect! O afflictive prospect! Brethren, take a review of your past lives; and seek " the things belonging to your peace, before they be for ever hid from your eyes."]

What then remains to be done by these distinct, but perishing, classes? To both the one and the other we would say, Consider,

II. The sinner's alternative—

There is but one alternative for any child of man: we must either attend to the voice of instruction given us in the Gospel, or we must carry with us unchanging and unavailing remorse into the eternal world.

Are we willing to spend eternity in self-condemning reflections?

[They must follow us, if we die in our sins. God himself will remind us of the benefits which here we neglected to improve: " Son, remember, that thou in thy life-time hadst such and such advantages." What anguish of mind will be occasioned by such thoughts as these: ' I once had the same offers of salvation, as they had who are now before the throne of God: I enjoyed the same heavenly instruction as they; but I despised it, and would not hear the voice of the charmer, how wisely soever he endeavoured to charm me!' This will be the ground of our heavier " condemnation, that light came into the world, but that we loved darkness rather than light, because our deeds were evil:" and our reflections upon this will be " a never-dying worm," gnawing our conscience to all eternity. Whether our sins were more or less flagrant, this will be the source of our greatest torment, that we despised the instructions given us in the Gospel, and trampled under foot that very Son of God who came into the world to seek and save us.]

If we would not spend an eternity in these bitter

reflections, we must *now* attend to the things which are revealed to us in the Gospel—

[If our teachers speak out of their own minds, we may refuse to hearken to them: but, if they speak to us the very word of God, then it is at our peril to turn a deaf ear to their instructions. The word of God is sufficient to " make us wise unto salvation through faith in Christ." It bids us flee to Christ, as to a strong hold, where we shall be safe from the assaults of sin and Satan. It assures us, that " Christ is able to save to the uttermost all that come unto God by him;" that " his blood will cleanse us from all sin;" that " his grace is sufficient for us;" and that " he will cast out none who come unto him." Follow these directions, and you are safe: give yourselves up to him; live altogether by faith upon him; improve for his glory the grace which you receive out of his fulness; and you have nothing to fear. Instead of remorse and sorrow, you shall be filled with peace and joy. In the midst of life it shall be a matter of " rejoicing to you, that you have the testimony of a good conscience;" in a dying hour you shall look back with comfort in the thought of having " fought a good fight, and finished your course, and kept the faith;" and to all eternity shall you glory in the mercies and privileges which you here enjoyed [b].

Here then is your alternative: Despise this instruction, and you shall perish: Obey it, and you shall live for ever.]

ADVICE—

1. Endeavour to view every thing in the light of eternity—

[If you think of time only, the value of present enjoyments will be unduly magnified: but think of eternity, and nothing will be deemed important but the salvation of the soul — — —]

2. Endeavour so to spend each day, as you will wish you had spent it, when you shall be standing at the judgment-seat of Christ—

[We know what the wishes are of men who are condemned to death for their violations of the law: and we may be sure that such will be our wishes when we are summoned to meet our Judge: ' O that I had lived a very different life!' — — — Now then cleave unto Christ with full purpose of heart, and devote yourselves to him without reserve. So shall you behold his face in peace, and be partakers of his glory for evermore.]

[b] Rev. i. 5.

OUTLINE NO. 766

THE CAPTIVATING POWER OF SIN.

Prov. v. 22. *His own iniquities shall take the wicked himself, and he shall be holden with the cords of his sins.*

THE force of habit is well known : it operates as a second nature; so constant is it in its exercise, and so imperious in its demands. There is this difference however in habits of piety, and habits of sin; that the one are easily lost ; but the other are with great difficulty overcome. Nor is this difficult to be accounted for; seeing that the one is against the course of nature, and the other conformable to all its propensities : the motion of the one is a continual ascent ; the other is downward on a declivity. But it is not *merely* as a natural consequence that sin, when indulged, has so great a power : there is an additional influence given to it by God himself, as a judicial act, and as a just punishment for indulging it : so that in a judicial, no less than in a natural sense, our text is true : " His own iniquities shall take the wicked himself: and he shall be holden with the cords of his sins."

Let us consider,

I. The declaration itself—

In a two-fold view it may be noticed ;

1. As a judgment inflicted—

[It is inflicted on the whole human race. There is not a sinner in the universe who cannot from his own experience attest the truth of it. Every sin has a power to enslave the mind, and to lead captive him who has indulged it. But we will instance this in some particulars.

The man addicted to drinking previous to the formation of his habit, had perhaps no particular love to strong drink, or desire after it : but he has been drawn into company, he has there acquired a taste for conviviality, and at last, by repeated excesses, he has contracted such a thirst for intoxicating liquors, that he cannot deny himself the use of them, or use them in moderation. He can see his character sinking in the estimation of all the sober part of the community, his health impaired, his fortune injured, his family suffering, and his eternal interests sacrificed; and yet he cannot cast off the habit which he has contracted: his soul is bound with it as with a cord, and he cannot burst his bonds.

In a similar plight is he who has given himself up to the gratification of his lusts and passions. They, at least as far as the mind is concerned, are increased by indulgence, so that every object calls forth desire, and "the eyes of the libertine are full of adultery, and cannot cease from sin[a]." His very soul, as it were, is sensualized, and, whether sleeping or waking, his imagination roves after the gratification of his lawless appetites.

Nor must I omit to mention the gamester, in whom the text is most awfully verified. Nothing can induce him to abandon his ruinous pursuits. Domestic ties of wife and children have no influence at all. The ruin of himself and family are all suspended on a card or die. Not even the experience of ruin will reclaim him. *Let his losses* be repaired again and again, and again and again will he return to the fascinating object, like the moth, and hover round it, till he is consumed.

I have mentioned these instances, as being more obvious and acknowledged: but the declaration is equally verified in the gay, the worldly, the profane; yea, and in the superstitious and self-righteous also. They all "feed on ashes; and a deceived heart hath turned them aside, so that *they cannot deliver their souls,* nor say, Is there not a lie in my right hand[b]?"]

2. As a warning given—

[In this view more especially the declaration in our text is introduced, to guard young men against the temptations to which they are exposed[c]. And a most awful warning it is: it shews us how earnestly we should guard against our besetting sins. Every man has some "sin which more easily besets him[d]," and by which he is more in danger of being enslaved. Now every man should find out what this peculiar temptation is; and should watch and pray against it; lest, by yielding to it, he provoke "God to give him over to a reprobate mind[e]," and to say, "He is joined to idols; let him alone[f]." We should labour to say with David, "I have kept myself from my iniquity[g]:" and, with Job, "Thou knowest I am not wicked," not deliberately and habitually wicked[h]. We should dread lest that be inflicted on us which is spoken in the text; a judgment far heavier than any other that can be inflicted on us even by God himself, as long as we continue in this present life; because it is a certain prelude to everlasting misery, and the means of augmenting it every day and hour: for, if we are delivered over to our own lusts, we do nothing but "treasure

[a] 2 Pet. ii. 14.   [b] Isai. xliv. 20.   [c] ver. 20.
[d] Heb. xii. 1.   [e] Rom. i. 28.   [f] Hos. iv. 17.
[g] Ps. xviii. 23.   [h] Job x. 7.

up wrath against the day of wrath," and accumulate mountains
of guilt to sink us deeper and deeper into everlasting perdition[i].
Our employment will be like that of those mentioned by the
Prophet Isaiah, who " drew out iniquity with cords of vanity,
and sin as a cart-rope[k]:" for, as a rope is spun out continually
to an indefinite length by the constant addition of fresh mate-
rials, so will our sin be drawn out to an endless extent, till
death shall cut it short, and the deserved punishment be
awarded to it.]

It would be improper to pass over such a declaration as this without drawing your attention to,

II. The reflections which it naturally suggests—

1. How thankful should we be for the Gospel of
Christ !

[Heathens are in the bondage above described, and have
no conception of any way of deliverance from it. But in the
Gospel a Saviour is proclaimed; who came on purpose to
" preach deliverance to the captives, and the opening of the
prison to them that are bound[l]." His power no lusts can
withstand. As he delivered Peter from prison, causing his
chains to fall off, and the prison doors to open of their own
accord, so can he liberate the slaves of sin and Satan from their
bondage, and bring them forth into the glorious liberty of the
children of God. Diseases, devils, elements, all obeyed his
voice in the days of his flesh : and at his word the most deep-
rooted lusts shall be plucked up, and the most inveterate habits
changed. The day of Pentecost sufficiently attests the truth
of this assertion. The hands of the men who had crucified him
were yet reeking with his blood, yet in an instant were their
hearts renewed, and they became altogether new creatures,
" the wolf being as harmless as the sheep, and the lion as
gentle as the lamb[m]."

However inveterate then your habits may have been, despair
not: but look to "that Mighty One on whom your help is laid,"
and who is able to save " to the uttermost all who come unto
God by him."]

2. How watchful should we be against the first
incursions of sin !

[As we know not "how great a matter a little fire will
kindle," so we know not what evils one sin may introduce. Every
evil habit originated in one sin. Judas little thought in what
his first act of dishonesty would issue: and millions, who are
now gone beyond the hope of redemption, once thought as little
to what a state they should be ultimately brought, as we now

[i] Rom. ii. 5. [k] Isai. v. 18. [l] Luke iv. 18. [m] Isai. xi. 6.

do.   Say not, This angry temper is a light evil: It is murder
in the seed and embryo; and may terminate in the very act of
murder much sooner than you imagine.   Say not, This impure
thought or look is venial: it is constructive adultery; to which
it leads, and in which, ere you are aware of it, it may soon
issue.   The same I would say of envy, hatred, malice, covetousness, ambition, and the whole catalogue of spiritual lusts:
the admission of them into the heart is as a leak in a ship,
which will sink it ultimately, if it be not stopped in time.   A
mariner will not neglect that leak, though it be but small;
because he knows the consequences: he knows that if it be
neglected, his efforts to preserve the ship will ere long be vain
and ineffectual.   It is not possible to look around us without
seeing, in numberless instances, what dominion the evil tempers
of men have gained, and what misery they diffuse throughout
their respective families and spheres.   Had they been checked
in their commencement, how much sin and misery would have
been prevented!   If then we would not forge chains for our
own souls, let us guard against the first risings of sin: for,
whatever we may think, " we shall reap according to what we
sow: he that soweth to the flesh shall of the flesh reap corruption; but he that soweth to the Spirit, shall of the Spirit
reap life everlasting[n]."]

3. How constant should we be in waiting upon
the Lord Jesus Christ, both in his public ordinances,
and in secret prayer!

[None but Christ can afford us any effectual help: for
" without him we can do nothing[o]."   To him we must carry
our every trial, and every temptation: and we must plead with
him for help, as the Apostle did, till he answer us, and say,
" My grace is sufficient for thee[p]."   Let us never forget that
it is in vain to resist sin in our own strength.   None but God
himself can subdue it in us.   " Our sufficiency even to think
a good thought must be of him[q]."   If he help us, it is well:
" We can do all things through Christ who strengtheneth us[r]."
But if we address ourselves to the purifying of our hearts in
our own strength, we shall fail, as the Apostles did, when in
self-confidence they attempted to cast out a devil, which " could
only be ejected through the influence of prayer and fasting[s]."
Let us look simply to Christ to purge us both from the guilt
and power of our sins; and then we shall find, that " according
to our faith it shall be done unto us[t]."]

[n] Gal. vi. 7, 8.   [o] John xv. 5.   [p] 2 Cor. xii. 9.
[q] 2 Cor. v. 5.   [r] Phil. iv. 13.   [s] Matt. xvii. 21.
[t] Matt. ix. 29.

OUTLINE NO. 767

THE SLUGGARD REPROVED.

Prov. vi. 6—10. *Go to the ant, thou sluggard; consider her ways and be wise: which having no guide, overseer, or ruler, provideth her meat in the summer, and gathereth her food in the harvest. How long wilt thou sleep, O sluggard? when wilt thou arise out of thy sleep? Yet a little sleep, a little slumber, a little folding of the hands to sleep: so shall thy poverty come as one that travelleth, and thy want as an armed man.*

FORESIGHT in relation to temporal concerns, though not universally practised, is universally approved; and it is a ground of thankfulness that those classes of society who have hitherto scarcely known how to secure any little sums which they might save, have now, by the establishment of *Provident Banks*, encouragement to provide for themselves against the day of adversity[a]. Happy would it be if a similar zeal were now exerted in relation to the concerns of eternity. But here, alas! there is still a sad indifference amongst us. The wants which we are sure to feel in the eternal world are not anticipated; nor is the importance of providing for them generally felt. In relation to these things, all around us are cast, as it were, into a deep sleep, from which they need to be roused by the most solemn warnings. This address therefore of Solomon to the sluggards of his day may well serve us as a foundation for a similar remonstrance with those who are yet sleeping in security and sin.

Addressing ourselves to persons of this description, we will speak,

I. In a way of humiliating reproof—

Justly does Solomon observe, that " a sluggard is wiser in his own conceit, than seven men that can render a reason[b]." The more careless men are about their souls, the more confident they are of their future safety. But how confident soever they may be, they may go and learn wisdom of the meanest insect.

[a] Preached the week before the establishment of a *Provident Bank* at Cambridge.   [b] Prov. xxvi. 16.

There is scarcely any thing in the whole creation from which we may not derive the most valuable instruction.   The ox and the ass, the crane and the swallow, are brought forward by God himself to teach and reprove us[c] : and here we are referred for instruction to the ant.   She collects in summer the food that is necessary for her subsistence in the winter. She does it with incredible labour, dragging to her cell grains of corn, that one would scarcely conceive she should be able to move.   And this she does " without any guide" to direct her, or " overseer" to watch her, " or ruler" to call her to account.   And, that her labour may not ultimately prove vain, she bites off, we are told, the ends of every grain, to prevent it from vegetating in the ground.

Go now to the ant, thou sluggard, and consider her ways : consider,

1. Her wise foresight—

[Has she a time approaching, against which it is needful for her to provide ; and hast not thou ?   Is there not a time coming, when thou must stand in the presence of thy God, and give an account of every thing that thou hast done in the body, whether it be good or evil ?   And hast thou not now to provide a righteousness wherein to appear before God, even the righteousness of our Lord Jesus Christ, wherein alone thou canst ever stand in the presence of a holy God ?   Hast thou not a new nature also to obtain, in order to fit thee for the enjoyment of the heavenly world?——— And is not the present the only time when this provision can be made ?   If thou neglect the present opportunities, wilt thou find them in the eternal world? Is there " any work or device to be executed in the grave, whither thou goest[d] ?"——— If her work, which relates only to the short transient life of the body, is important, is not yours, which relates to the eternal interests of the soul, much more important?———Go then to the ant, and learn wisdom of her.]

2. Her voluntary labour—

[She has none to direct her : she is guided by instinct alone. But you have reason to guide you, and to assure you of the certainty and importance of those things which you have not yet seen with your eyes.   You have God himself also inspecting every thing that you do, and pledged to call you into judgment for it, and to assign you your everlasting portion according to

c Isai. i. 3. Jer. viii. 7.   d Eccl. ix. 10.

it. Should not you then exert yourselves with all diligence?
Are you not convinced, that to prepare for eternity is "a reasonable service," yea, that it is, in fact, "the one thing needful?"————Will you then grudge your labour? Will you
not put forth willingly and habitually all the powers of your
souls in this blessed work?———]

3. Her prudent care—

[Is *she* careful to prevent her labours from ever proving
abortive; and should not *you* prosecute your work to a successful issue? Yet Solomon justly observes, that "the slothful
man roasteth not that which he took in hunting[e];" yea, that
"his very desire killeth him, because his hands refuse to labour[f]."
Some kind of pains we all have taken in attending ordinances,
and in complying with outward forms; but there we have rested,
without any persevering efforts to render those means effectual
for the salvation of our souls. We feel somewhat of a general
desire after eternal happiness; and with that consciousness of
desire we are satisfied, without pressing forward for the attainment of the things desired: and thus is fulfilled in us another
declaration of Solomon, "The soul of the sluggard desireth,
and hath nothing[g]?" If good desires would suffice, the sluggard would get to heaven as well as others: but if great and
persevering exertions are necessary, he will rather forego the
prize, than use the diligence necessary for the attainment of
it. In a word, instead of "looking to himself that he lose not
the things that he has wrought, but that he receive a full reward[h]," he suffers Satan to take out of his heart the seed that
has been sown in it, and to keep him, like the foolish virgins,
from providing oil for himself, till it is too late. Say, thou
sluggard, whether these things be not true of thee, and whether
thou hast not need to go and learn wisdom of the diminutive
and despised ant?]

We will yet further prosecute our address,

II. In a way of solemn warning—

As a man who has no provision independent of his
labour, and no disposition to exert himself, must soon
feel the pressure of poverty and want, so, sluggard,
shalt thou feel these evils in relation to thy soul—

1. Reflect on the awfulness of thy state—

[The consequences of thy sloth are coming upon thee:
they are coming *gradually* indeed, but *irresistibly*. "A traveller" comes not to his journey's end all at once, but *gradually*,
and almost imperceptibly, by many successive steps. So neither
wilt thou find the fatal consequence of thy sloth all at once;

[e] Prov. xii. 27. [f] Prov. xxi. 25. [g] Prov. xiii. 4. [h] 2 John, ver. 8.

but every day and hour brings them nearer towards thee; and *that* too so clearly, that, if thou wouldst stop to examine, thou shouldst see evident symptoms of their approach. Who has not found, that the longer he lives in any sin, the more he becomes addicted to it, and enslaved by it? The truth is, that as a man by indulging sloth, whether of mind or body, becomes daily more unfitted for exertion, so the man who is remiss and negligent in his spiritual concerns becomes daily more alienated from God, and more averse to those efforts that are necessary for his salvation[i]. The curse which is denounced against him seems so distant, that it will never come: but it is advancing as fast as the wings of time can carry it; as St. Peter says, " Their judgment now of a long time lingereth not, and their damnation slumbereth not[k]." O sluggard! remember this: thou mayest "linger, like Lot in the plain;" but " thy judgment lingereth not; thou mayest slumber on yet a little while, but thy damnation slumbereth not:" the time is fast approaching when God will say to thee, as to him who hid his talent in a napkin, " Thou wicked and slothful servant!" and will give orders concerning thee, " Cast the unprofitable servant into outer darkness, where shall be weeping, and wailing, and gnashing of teeth[l]."

These judgments too shall come upon you *irresistibly*. You well know how entirely a man unarmed and sleeping is at the mercy of " an armed man" that seeks his life. And such will be your state, in the day that God shall deal with you, and visit you for your sins. You may call on the hills to fall upon you, and the rocks to cover you, from the wrath of your offended God; but they cannot perform for you this friendly office: no creature in the universe can help you: " though hand join in hand, you cannot pass unpunished." Reflect on this, thou sluggard! Now thou mayest "puff at God's judgments:" but ere long thou wilt bitterly regret that thou didst not improve the opportunities afforded thee to escape from them.]

2. Reflect also on the vanity of thine excuses—

[There are none so hardened as to avow a fixed determination never to seek after God: on the contrary, there is in almost all an indistinct purpose to turn unto the Lord at some more convenient season, which they hope is at no very great distance. Hence to those who would rouse them to exertion, they say, " A *little* more sleep, a *little* more slumber, a *little* more folding of the hands to sleep." They acknowledge in general terms the propriety, and even the necessity, of exertion; but they wish a little more time for indulgence to the flesh, before they set themselves in earnest to mortify and subdue it. But what has been the consequence of indulgence

---

[i] Prov. x. 4. and xix. 15.   [k] 2 Pet. ii. 3.   [l] Matt. xxv. 26, 30.

hitherto? Are you at all more disposed for exertion now, than you were when first you were bidden to arise? Is your ability for God's service at all increased by deferring your attempts to serve him? Have you not found, invariably, that procrastination has increased your difficulties, at the very time that it also enfeebled your powers? Say not then any longer, " There is a lion in the way," nor plead any longer for delay: but arise and call upon your God, if peradventure time may be yet afforded you to " work out your salvation," and to " flee from the wrath to come."]

ADDRESS—

1. Those who have never yet been awakened—

[Have you no work to do? or is it a matter of small importance whether it be done or not? Is not the present life the only time for doing it? " How long, then, wilt thou sleep, O sluggard? When wilt thou arise out of thy sleep?" Knowest thou not, that if thou sleepest on till this short life be past, thou wilt assuredly awake in hell? What then shall I say to thee? Shall I say to thee, as Christ did to his sleepy disciples, " Sleep on now, and take thy rest?" No: God forbid. Let me rather say, " Awake thou that sleepest, and arise from the dead, and Christ shall give thee light[m]." Verily, if thou wouldst now, even now, call upon his name, it should not be too late. Whatever thou wantest, it should be given thee: he would give thee the light of truth to shine into thy heart; the light of joy in his reconciled countenance; the light of holiness to attest thine acceptance with him; and the light of glory to perfect thy felicity. While ye have the light then, walk in the light, that ye may be the children of light.]

2. Those who, though in part awakened, are yet disposed to give way to slothful habits—

[This, alas! was the case both with the wise and foolish virgins; " they all slumbered and slept." But let me affectionately guard you against yielding to sloth. It is said, and the very best amongst us know the truth of it by bitter experience, that " the idle soul shall suffer hunger[n]." Who has not heard of the vineyard of the sluggard, where, through inattention, nothing was produced but nettles and thorns? To him is the same warning given as to the sluggard in the text[o]. Guard then against the excuses which ye are ready to make. See the excuses made by the Bride in the book of Canticles; how injurious to her welfare! how destructive of her peace[p]! " Watch ye then, and pray always." Had the disciples watched, when they were directed to do it by their Lord, they

---

[m] Eph. v. 14.　　　　[n] Prov. xix. 15.
[o] Prov. xxiv. 30—34.　　[p] Cant. v. 2—7.

would never have forsaken him as they did in the hour of his deepest trial.   But, if you do not watch and be sober, depend upon it that Satan will prevail against you, and " sift you as wheat."   " Be sober then, and vigilant."   Give not way to drowsiness in your spiritual calling: but " give all diligence to make your calling sure."   And, seeing that ye look for a period when God shall come to judge the world, be diligent that ye may be found of him in peace, without spot and blameless.   And " what I say unto one, I say unto all, Watch."]

OUTLINE NO. 768

LOVE TO THE HOLY SCRIPTURES INCULCATED.

Prov. vii. 1—4.   *My son, keep my words, and lay up my commandments with thee.   Keep my commandments, and live; and my law as the apple of thine eye.   Bind them upon thy fingers; write them upon the table of thine heart.   Say unto Wisdom, Thou art my sister; and call Understanding thy kinswoman.*

THROUGHOUT the book of Proverbs, we are strongly reminded of that expression of Paul to Philemon, " Though I might be much bold in Christ to enjoin thee that which is convenient, yet for love's sake I rather beseech thee."   There is an exquisite tenderness in the exhortations of Solomon, addressed as they are by a father to a son.   Not that we are to suppose that they were intended only for Rehoboam: they were intended for the Church of God, in all ages :   and to us, no less than to Rehoboam himself, is the affectionate language of our text addressed. But indeed a greater than Solomon is here.   Condescending as the expressions are, they are addressed to us by the Lord Jesus Christ himself, who is Wisdom itself incarnate[a]; and *his* are the counsels which we are so earnestly entreated to treasure up in our minds.

In discoursing on the words before us, we will shew,

I. The respect which we should pay to the counsels of Divine Wisdom—

By comparing our text with similar language in the New Testament, we see, that by the terms here used we have to understand, not the Decalogue only,

[a] See Prov. viii. 22—32.

but the whole revealed will of God. Now to whatever the counsels of the Deity relate,

1. They should be treasured up with diligence—

[Whatever is of more than ordinary value in our eyes, we
lay it up with care in a place of safety; and the more of it we
can amass, the richer we feel ourselves to be. Now there is
nothing in the whole universe to be compared with the Scriptures
of truth, nothing that will so enrich the mind, nothing that will
so benefit the soul. In the great mystery of redemption " are
hid all the treasures of wisdom and knowledge." The precepts
too, and the promises, and the histories, and the examples, O!
who can estimate them as they deserve? — — — To treasure
these up in our minds should be our daily and most delightful
employment. Not a day should pass without adding to this
blessed store. We should always furnish ourselves with some
fresh portion, on which to ruminate. Not that it is merely in
the *mind* and *memory* that we are to store up this wealth, but,
as Moses tells us, in our *heart* and in our *soul;* " Ye shall lay
up these my words in your heart and in your soul[b]:" this is
the proper seat of Divine knowledge; and here should we
endeavour to amass the only true wealth, " the unsearchable
riches of Christ."]

2. They should be watched over with care—

[Nature has made peculiar provision for the eye, so that,
by an involuntary and instantaneous motion of the eye-lid, it
is preserved from innumerable injuries which it must otherwise
sustain. Now with the same care that we guard " the apple
of our eye," we should watch over and preserve the treasures
of wisdom, which we have accumulated in our hearts. Satan is
ever labouring to " take out of our hearts the word of life," as
our Lord has told us in the parable of the Sower: and it
requires the utmost vigilance on our part to defeat his efforts.
Indeed the heart itself is but too prone to lose its riches through
any apertures by which the world has entered; so that we need
to " give the most earnest heed lest at any time we should let
them slip[c]." Besides, if we be not constantly on our guard
against " the cares of this world, and the deceitfulness of riches,"
and other foolish and hateful lusts, we shall find to our cost,
that these " weeds and thorns will choke all the good seed that
has been sown in our hearts, and will render it unfruitful."
Our care and watchfulness therefore should be incessant, that
nothing be permitted to rob us of our good principles, or to
weaken their influence on our souls. If, as we are told, God
" himself keeps his people as the apple of his eye[d]," surely we

b Deut. xi. 18.   c Heb. ii. 1.
d Deut. xxxii. 10. and Zech. ii. 8.

should exercise all possible vigilance to keep his counsels, and
preserve inviolate his holy commandments.]

3. They should be kept ready for use—

[It is not sufficient that we have reduced the counsels of
God, as it were, to certain heads, and made memorandums of
them in our books, so as to be able to refer to them when
occasion requires: we should have them " inscribed on the
tablet of our hearts," so that they may be always at hand,
ready to direct and regulate our ways. Conscience, by looking
inward, should be able to see them in an instant, and to suggest
the line of conduct conformable to them. Moreover, we should
have them " bound also upon our fingers," so as both to be
reminded of them at all times, and be ever ready to carry them
into execution. To this effect Solomon explains his meaning:
" Bind them continually upon thine heart, and tie them about
thy neck. When thou goest, it shall lead thee; when thou
sleepest, it shall keep thee; and when thou awakest, it shall
talk with thee: for the commandment is a lamp, and the law
is light: and reproofs of instruction are the way of life[e]."]

4. They should be guarded with the tenderest affection—

[With persons standing in near and dear relation to us,
we are accustomed to live in habits of intimacy, consulting
them on any occasions of difficulty, paying considerable deference to their judgment, and easily influenced by their opinions.
Now in this light we should view the counsels of our God: we
should be familiar with them; we should consult them on all
occasions, and yield them a willing ascendency over our hearts.
Instead of standing aloof from them as strangers, we should
claim, and glory in, our relation to them: we should " say
unto Wisdom, Thou art my sister; and call Understanding our kinswoman." We should, by our conformity to the
dictates of Wisdom, prove, and manifest, our relation to her;
and constrain all who behold us to acknowledge, that God is
our Father, and that Christ, " the Wonderful Counsellor," is
our Friend.]

To encourage this acquaintance with the Divine
counsels, we will proceed to state,

II. The benefits which we shall derive from a due attention to them—

In our text itself, the great benefit of complying
with the exhortation is stated, in short but comprehensive terms; " Keep my commandments, and live."
But in the verses following our text, a particular ad-

[e] Prov. vi. 20—23.

vantage is insisted on, namely, the being delivered from the snares and temptations to which we are exposed. That we may comprehend both, we would observe, that by our attention to the Divine counsels,

1. We shall be delivered from evil—

["From the way of the evil woman" is particularly noticed, both here and in the preceding chapter : and doubtless an attention to the counsels of Wisdom will eventually secure us against those temptations which lead captive so great a portion of mankind. But we need not confine our views to iniquities of one kind only : the advice here given is equally useful in preserving men from snares of every kind. From the inspired volume we learn the folly and malignity of every sin. The temptations of the world, the lusts of the flesh, and the devices of Satan, are all there exposed; and armour is laid up for us, that we may successfully maintain the combat against them. Our blessed Lord himself, in whom was no sin, drew from this armoury the arrows and the shield with which he vanquished the tempter in the wilderness : and from the same source must we also be furnished. Thus David tells us : "Wherewithal shall a young man cleanse his way? Even by taking heed thereto according to thy word :" and again, "Thy word have I hid within my heart, that I might not sin against thee." Would you then be kept from evil tempers, and evil passions, and evil habits of every kind? Study the sacred records : treasure up in your minds the terrors of God's wrath as there revealed, and the declarations of his mercy as there promulgated. There see the wonders of redeeming love unfolded to your view, and the blessedness of those who have been monuments of converting and saving grace. Let every part of God's word have its proper bearing on your hearts and consciences, and it shall be effectual for your salvation. Whatever lusts you have hitherto indulged, you shall, through the influence of the word, and by the power of the Holy Ghost, be sanctified; as our Lord has said; "Sanctify them through thy truth; thy word is truth :" and again, "Now are ye clean through the word that has been spoken unto you."]

2. We shall be carried forward in safety to everlasting life—

[So says our text; "Keep my commandments, and live." So also says our blessed Lord : "I know that thy commandment is life everlasting [f]." We must remember, that it is not of mere morality that we are now speaking, but an impartial attention to the whole revealed will of God. And where this

[f] John xii. 49, 50.

is, God will surely pour out upon the soul his richest blessings. Hear what our blessed Lord says respecting this : " He
that hath my commandments and keepeth them, he it is that
oveth me : and he that loveth me, shall be loved of my Father;
and I will love him, and will manifest myself to him : " yea,
" We will come to him, and make our abode with him g." What
unspeakable benefits are these ! Favoured with such communications, what can we want ? ——— But it is not in this
world only that such persons are blessed: for to them are
secured all the blessedness and glory of the world to come;
according as it is written, " Blessed are they that do his commandments, that they may have a right to eat of the tree of
life, and may enter in through the gates into the city h." This
right indeed is not founded on any merit of their own; but
solely on the promises of God made to them in Christ Jesus.
It is Christ who, by his obedience unto death, has purchased
these blessings for us : but it is to his obedient servants only
that these blessings shall ever be vouchsafed. They however
shall inherit them; nor shall all the powers of darkness be able
to rob them of their promised inheritance. Only " let the
word of Christ dwell in you richly in all wisdom i," and you
shall never be straitened k, " nor ever fall; but have an entrance
ministered unto you abundantly into the kingdom of our Lord
aud Saviour Jesus Christ l."]

g John xiv. 21, 23.   h Rev. xxii. 14.   i Col. iii. 16.
k Prov. iii. 21—23. and iv. 12   l 2 Pet. i. 10, 11.

OUTLINE NO. 769

ADDRESS PREPARATORY TO CONFIRMATION.

Prov. viii. 17. *I love them that love me ; and those that seek
me early, shall find me.*

THESE are the words of our blessed Lord[a], who,
under the name of Widom, addresses himself to the
children of men[b], and urges them to receive instruction from him[c]. But to the *young* they are more particularly directed : and it is for their encouragement
more especially that I have selected them for our
consideration at this time.

Two things they declare to us most explicitly ;

I. Who they are that already enjoy God's favour—

God in some respects may be said to love the
whole world, even in their present degenerate state

a ver. 22—31.   b ver. 4, 5.   c ver. 32, 33.

for " he so loved them, that he gave his only-begotten Son for them." But there are some who are more particularly the objects of his favour. Mark,

1. The description given of them—

[" They love the Lord Jesus Christ." They know his character, as set forth in the Holy Scriptures; they know him to be the only, and all-sufficient Saviour of fallen man — — — They have seen and felt their obligations to him, and have sought for redemption altogether through the blood of his cross — — — They live in daily habits of communion with him — — — They have a good hope of acceptance with God through him — — — And his very name " is precious to their souls" — — —]

2. The love he bears towards them—

[" He loves them," and looks with peculiar complacency upon them, " rejoicing over them with joy, and resting in his love, and joying over them with singing[d]." To them he delights to " manifest himself, as he does not unto the world[e]," even to " come and sup with them[f]," and " make his abode with them" — — — " He rejoices over them to do them good[g]," imparting all needful supplies of grace and strength to their souls[h], and ordering all things both in heaven and earth for the promotion of their welfare[i] — — — He accounts them " his jewels[k]" and " his peculiar treasure[l];" and esteems the salvation of their souls a rich recompence for all the sufferings he ever endured[m] — — — For them does he interest himself day and night in heaven; ever " making intercession for them" with his Father, and preparing kingdoms for them, which they in due season shall inherit, in glory and felicity similar to his own[n] — — —

O! who amongst you does not desire to partake of this blessedness? — — —]

But as amongst you there must be many who are not yet in this blessed state, and who yet desire to participate this happy lot, we proceed to shew,

II. Who they are that shall certainly obtain it—

In some respects it may be said, that " He is found of them that sought him not, and made known to them that inquired not after him." But no person is authorized to hope for an interest in his favour, unless he seek after it. The promise is, " Ask, and ye shall have; seek, and ye shall find." But

---

[d] Zeph. iii. 17.   [e] John xiv. 21—23.   [f] Rev. iii. 20.
[g] Jer. xxxii. 40, 41.   [h] John xv. 5, 7, 16.   [i] Rom. viii. 28.
[k] Mal. iii. 17.   [l] Exod. xix. 5.
[m] Heb. xii. 2. Isai. liii. 11.   [n] John xiv. 2. Rev. iii. 21.

The persons to whom the promise is more especially made, are " those who seek him early."

[Those who seek the Lord even " at the eleventh hour"
shall not be cast out°; but those who in the early dawn of their
day are found desirous of entering into the service of their Lord,
shall surely be employed by him. The very circumstance of
their seeking the Lord while yet they are free from the cares
of this life, and before their souls are vitiated with its sinful
pleasures, whilst their consciences are yet tender, and their
hearts open to every good impression, is a strong *presumption*
in their favour: we should be ready, without any express
promise from God, to say, that such persons " shall never seek
his face in vain." But we have an absolute *promise* in their
favour: we can assure them from God himself, that they " shall
never fail."]

" They," says our Lord, "shall find me"—

[Yes, he will delight to visit them: they are " the lambs
which he will carry in his bosom P;" " the little ones, whom he
will never suffer to perish q." Though they be weak both in
knowledge and in grace, " he will not despise the day of small
things r." He says, " Suffer the little children to come unto me,
and forbid them not: for of such is the kingdom of heaven."
And when he sees them flocking around him, he will " take
them up in his arms, and put his hands upon them, and bless
them s"——— When he saw only " *some* good thing towards
the Lord God of Israel" in the heart of young Abijah, he
noticed it with a distinguishing mark of his favour t: and how
much more will he, when he sees " the babes desiring the
sincere milk of the word, that they may grow thereby," and
actually growing in stature up to young men and fathers!———
Verily their hosannahs, however despised by men, shall enter
into his ears with acceptance, and their prayers shall return in
" showers of blessings" upon their souls u——— They shall
" find him" *here* an ever-present help, and *hereafter* their inestimable and everlasting portion————]

ADDRESS—

1. To the Young People here assembled—

[You are about to be confirmed. But do you know what
confirmation is? You were consecrated to the Lord in your
baptism; and a solemn engagement was then entered into in
your behalf, that you should love him, and surrender up yourselves entirely to his service. This vow you are now going to

° Matt. xx. 6, 7.   P Isai. xl. 11.
q Matt. xviii. 14. Luke xii. 32.   r Zech. iv. 10.
s Mark x. 14—16.   t 1 Kings xiv. 13.   u Luke xix. 40.

take upon yourselves. And tell me Whether in my text you
have not all the encouragement that your souls can desire?
Give yourselves to the world, and you will inherit only vanity:
but "seek to love the Lord, and you shall inherit substance[x]."
Think how happy you will be through life, when you are the
objects of the Saviour's care and love — — — and think how
happy you will be in death — — — O let me not plead with you
in vain! but "remember your Creator in the days of your youth,
before the evil days come, in which you shall say, you have no
pleasure in them[y]" — — — "Seek ye the Lord whilst he may
be found; call ye upon him whilst he is near[z]" — — —]

2. To Parents, and those who have an opportunity
of influencing the minds of young people—

[This is a favourable opportunity for you to exert yourselves, and to concur with your minister in his labours of love.
Be labourers together with him, with all your might — — —
But do not forget that the glorious truths in our text are to
be experienced by you also — — — And, if much of your day
is already past, be the more earnest now in "redeeming the
time" that yet remains to you — — —]

[x] ver. 21.　　[y] Eccl. xii. 1.　　[z] Isai. lv. 6.

OUTLINE NO. 770
WISDOM'S ADDRESS TO MEN.

Prov. viii. 29—32. *When he appointed the foundations of the
earth, then I was by him, as one brought up with him: and I
was daily his delight, rejoicing always before him: rejoicing
in the habitable part of his earth: and my delights were with
the sons of men. Now therefore hearken unto me, O ye
children! for blessed are they that keep my ways.*

THE Proverbs of Solomon are a rich compendium
of moral precepts, suited to men in all the various
situations of civil, social, and domestic life. Some
intimations indeed there are of Evangelical doctrines;
but they are neither numerous, nor distinct; the
scope and intent of the author having been, not so
much to enlighten the minds of men with respect to
principles of religion, as to supply them with a code
of sacred ethics, for the regulation of their conduct.
Yet, in the chapter before us, the language is so peculiar, as to have induced the most able commentators
to think, that there was in the author's mind an in-
tentional departure from his accustomed plan, and a

designed reference to Christ, the Saviour of the world.
It is not our object to decide this point, but, rather,
to exhibit the passage in such a view, as may render
it most conducive to our spiritual improvement.

Let us consider then,

I. What is that wisdom which here addresses us—

The two leading views of it will come under our
consideration, if we interpret it as importing,

1. Wisdom personified—

[It is evident that, throughout the whole chapter, Wisdom
is represented as *a person*, and it must be spoken of *as a
person*, in order to give scope for such a representation of it as
is contained in our text[a].

Wisdom was then ever "with God, as one brought up with
him." It is an essential perfection of his nature, attendant on
him on all occasions as a counsellor, without whose advice not
any thing was ever transacted from all eternity. God has never
done any thing from the mere impulse of his own sovereign will
and pleasure: whatever he has predestinated, has nevertheless
been "wrought according to the counsel of his own will[b].
Wisdom has presided in all his councils; nor has any thing
ever been carried into effect without having previously received
her sanction.

*Her deliberations have been very mainly conversant about the
affairs of men.* God foresaw that man would fall, and, if left
to himself, would perish like the fallen angels. But he greatly
desired to save man, if peradventure it might be accomplished
consistently with his own perfections. Every one of his attributes concurred in the wish; but with some of them there
seemed to be claims, which interfered with that object, and
which could not by any means be set aside. *Holiness* required,
that its hatred of sin should be fully known. *Justice* required
satisfaction for the violations of God's law, and could in no wise
be induced to relax its demands. *Truth* also desired, that its
honour should not be compromised. It had no objection to the
exercise of mercy, if only the sacred word of God might be kept
inviolate: but it could never consent, whatever object were to
be attained thereby, that the immutable God should be "made a
liar[c]." In this difficulty, all looked to Wisdom, to know, whether she could devise any way, whereby the exercise of mercy
might consist with the rights of all the other attributes of the

---

a We beg this to be particularly noticed; because it is *the sole
ground* of the following statement; which, if that circumstance were
overlooked, might appear fanciful.

b Eph. i. 5, 10.   c 1 John v. 10.

Deity. Wisdom intimated, that she had a plan to propose; a plan, whereby *Mercy* might have free scope for exercise, not only without invading or injuring the rights of any other attribute, but to the great advantage of them all, insomuch that all should be honoured to an infinitely greater extent than they ever could have been, if their demands had been satisfied through the destruction of the whole human race. It proposed, that the Son of God himself should take upon him the sins of the whole world, and suffer, as man's substitute, all that Truth and Holiness had denounced against him, and all that the most rigorous justice could require. *Such* a sacrifice made to law and justice, to truth and holiness, would put on all of them an honour, which they could never by any other means obtain — — —

Her proposal, made with infinite delight to herself, was heard with infinite delight by Almighty God. Whilst she was thus, by anticipation, " rejoicing in the habitable part of the earth, and her delights were with the sons of men, she was daily God's delight, and rejoiced always before him." We may be assisted in our meditations on this subject, by considering a philosopher occupied with the deepest investigations, and crowned with unexpected success: what joyous exultation fills his breast! how is he ready to proclaim to all the world, " I have found it! I have found it!" Or perhaps we shall approximate nearer to the point, if we conceive of a physician, on whose skill the life of thousands is depending, discovering an antidote that will arrest the progress of the plague, and a remedy that will restore to health all those who are already infected with it: what pure and holy joy will animate his soul! But the Scripture itself furnishes us with various illustrations of this important idea: the woman finding the piece of money which she had lost, and the shepherd his sheep that had strayed from the fold, are each represented as calling for the sympathetic joys of their friends and neighbours: and, as these are intended to elucidate the joy which our Redeemer feels in the successful execution of his office, they may well serve to illustrate the ineffable delight which the proposals of Wisdom are represented as exciting in her own bosom, and in the bosom of the Deity.

But we have said that Wisdom may also be interpreted as signifying,]

2. Wisdom incarnate—

[Most Commentators think that the expressions in our text refer to Christ, who is called " the Wisdom of God[d];" and who, as the *Logos* or *Word*, declares to men the hidden counsels of the Father.

Of him it is distinctly said, that *He " was with God*, and

[d] 1 Cor. i. 24.

was God[e];" that " He made all things; and that without him
nothing was made that was made." Here then we have the
precise language of our text applied to the Son of God, who
was from all eternity " in the bosom of the Father[f]," concur-
ring with him in all that ever he planned or executed[g].

How *he was occupied in the concerns of men,* is familiar to all
our minds. Truly " his delights were with the sons of men,"
whom he determined to rescue from perdition, and to " redeem
unto God by his own blood." This was " the joy that was set
before him, for which he engaged to endure the cross, and
despised all the shame that should ever be poured upon him[h]."
No sacrifice was too great for him to make. Was it necessary
that satisfaction should be made for all the breaches of God's
law; and that the very nature that had sinned should suffer?
He willingly engaged to lay aside his own glory, and to assume
our nature, in order that he might suffer, and, by suffering in
our stead, " make reconciliation for our iniquities."

*In understanding this mysterious office, he was filled, as his
Father also was, with ineffable delight.* What joy the thought
of ransoming our fallen race excited in his bosom, we are told
by the Psalmist: for when it was declared by the Father,
" with whom the council of peace was held[i]," that all creature-
sacrifices would be insufficient for the occasion, he instantly
replied, " Lo, I come; (I, thy co-equal, co-eternal Son, come:)
I delight to do thy will, O my God! yea, thy law is within
my heart[k]." A corresponding joy sprang up also in the
Father's breast; as the prophet Isaiah tells us; for in the contemplation of the future accomplishment of this mystery, the
Father, looking with infinite complacency on his Son who had
undertaken the office, and on his people as accepted in and
through him, said, " Behold my servant, whom I uphold;
mine elect, in whom my soul delighteth[l]!" And, at the time
when he bore an audible testimony to his Son from heaven,
it was in these words, " This is that my beloved Son, in
whom I am well pleased[m]." Thus, in reference to this great
event, it is said in our text, " I was daily his delight, rejoicing
always before him:" and in reference to the same we must
understand that declaration of our Lord himself, " Thou
lovedst me before the foundation of the world[n]."]

Thus, whether we understand the address as made
to us by *Wisdom personified,* or *Wisdom incarnate,* we
cannot but feel a deep interest in all that it has spoken
to us, and set ourselves carefully to ascertain,

[e] John i. 1—3. with Heb. i. 10.   [f] John i. 18.
[g] John v. 19. and x. 38.   [h] Heb. xii. 2.
[i] Zech. vi. 13.   [k] Ps. xl. 6—8. with Heb. x. 5—9.
[l] Isai. xlii. 1.   [m] Matt. iii. 17. See the Greek.   [n] John xvii. 24.

II. Our duty in reference to it—

Doubtless we should "hearken to its voice," and with child-like simplicity receive its loving instructions. We should,

1. Delight ourselves in the contemplation of wisdom—

[Wisdom generally, wisdom universally, should be the object of our continual pursuit: "through a desire of attaining it, we should separate ourselves, and seek, and intermeddle with all wisdom[o]." The works of creation should, as far as we have a capacity for such subjects, be investigated by us, in order to excite our admiration of that wisdom by which they were framed. The order and harmony of the heavenly bodies, the beauty and richness of this terraqueous globe, the exquisite workmanship of the human frame, together with the powers and faculties of our immortal souls, all open to us such inexhaustible stores of wisdom and knowledge, as, if duly explored, will strike with reverential awe the humble inquirer, and fill with devoutest gratitude the admiring soul. The works of Providence also, if once we are enabled to view them in their mutual relation and dependence, will transport the soul with wonder, and overwhelm it with the deepest sense of gratitude. No book in the universe, except the Bible, will convey half so much instruction to the mind, as may be gathered from a man's own experience of God's dealings with him, especially in the concurrence of his providence with the operations of his grace: and the man who has learned to read this book, and become conversant with its contents, has acquired "secrets of wisdom, which are double[p]," yea, which are tenfold greater than any which are known to the merely natural man. God has said, that "he has abounded towards his people in all wisdom and prudence[q]:" but "his secrets are with those alone who fear him[r]:" none others are at all able to appreciate his love: that "knowledge is plain only to him that understandeth[s]."

Our chief attention however must be directed to that adorable Saviour, who "spake as never man spake," and in whom his most inveterate enemies could not find a flaw[t]. In him we have such lessons of wisdom as the whole universe besides does not afford. In tracing all the circumstances of his life, we should do well at every step to inquire, What answer should *I* have given? what conduct should *I* have pursued? and, from such examinations frequently repeated, we shall learn at last, how far we are removed from true righteousness, and how much "folly is bound up in our hearts." In a word, we should sit

---

o Prov. xviii. 1.   p Job xi. 6.   q Eph. i. 8.
r Ps. xxv. 14. Hos. xiv. 9.   s ver. 9.   t John viii. 46.

at the feet of Jesus, as Mary did, drinking in, with insatiable avidity, the instructions of Wisdom, and applying our hearts to them as the clay to the seal. " In Him are hid all the treasures of wisdom and knowledge[u]." In Him is revealed to us " the mystery that was hid from ages and generations," and " which the angels themselves desire to look into[x];" and the mystery, at the first intimation of which, long " before the worlds were made, the morning stars sang together, and the sons of God, the holy angels, shouted aloud for joy[y]." No sooner was the commission given to make this known to men, than a host of the heavenly angels left their bright abodes, and came down to earth exulting, " Glory to God in the highest! and on earth peace; good will towards men[z]!"

These are contemplations worthy of our exalted powers, worthy of our high destinies: and to delight ourselves in them is the wisdom, and the happiness of man.]

2. Surrender up ourselves to its dictates—

[In every duty of life there is need of the suggestions of wisdom. Even good men often act a very foolish part, for want of a well-regulated mind. Many have no idea of that important truth, " I, Wisdom, dwell with Prudence[a]." To " walk in wisdom towards them that are without[b]," and to " give no offence either to the Jews, or to the Gentiles, or to the Church of God[c]," come not into the contemplation of many, any more than if no such things were required of us, and no such example had been ever set us. But our determination, through God's help, should be, under all circumstances, like that of David, " I will behave myself wisely in a perfect way[d]."

In fact, there is no true wisdom but that which is practical. The very end of knowledge is practice: and, however deep or exalted our speculations may be, " if we walk not circumspectly, we are fools[e]." But, in order to carry into effect the lessons of Wisdom, we must " watch daily at her gates, and wait at the posts of her doors[f]." We must bring our views, our desires, our motives, to the strictest scrutiny: we must apply to every thing " the line of judgment, and the plummet of righteousness:" and, above all, we must beg of God to give us " the Spirit of wisdom and understanding, the Spirit of counsel and of might, the Spirit of knowledge and of the fear of the Lord, and to make us quick of understanding in the fear of the Lord[g]." Without *this*, we shall continually err: without this, we shall inevitably fall.]

[u] Col. ii. 3.	[x] 1 Pet. i. 12.	[y] Job xxxviii. 6, 7.
[z] Luke ii. 13, 14.	[a] ver. 12.	[b] 1 Col. iv. 5.
[c] 1 Cor. x. 32.	[d] Ps. ci. 2.	[e] Eph. v. 15.
[f] ver. 34.	[g] Isai. xi. 2, 3.	

" Hear then the voice of Wisdom, O ye children !"
     Hear it,

1. Ye children in age—

[Ye can never begin too early to listen to the counsels of
Wisdom.   It is by them only that you can avoid the snares of
a corrupt heart, and of a deceitful world———O! think what
dangers are before you: see " what multitudes are walking in
the broad road that leadeth to destruction, and how few there
are that walk in the narrow path that leadeth unto life!" and
remember, that " you must reap according to what you sow :
if you sow to the flesh, you must of the flesh reap corruption; but if you sow to the Spirit, you shall of the Spirit
reap life everlasting[h]."   Say not, that you are too young to
receive her lessons : for she particularly encourages *you* by expressing a more than ordinary solicitude for your welfare : " I
love them that love me," says she; " and they that seek me
early, shall find me[i]."]

2. Ye children in understanding—

[The poor, whose intellectual powers have never been expanded by the aid of education, are ready to imagine that it
is in vain for them to explore the depths of heavenly wisdom.
But be it known to all, that divine wisdom enters, not by the
head, like earthly knowledge, but by the heart : be it known
also, that it is not acquired by deep laborious research, as
human sciences are, but by the teaching of the Holy Ghost ;
(for " the Lord *giveth* wisdom ; out of his mouth cometh knowledge and understanding[k]:") and so far are the poor from having
any reason to despair of attaining it, that they are by far the
most likely to obtain it, because they are more willing than
others to be taught of God.   Hence our Lord himself says,
" I thank thee, O Father, Lord of heaven and earth, because
thou hast hid these things from the wise and prudent, and hast
revealed them unto babes: even so, Father, for so it seemed
good in thy sight[l]."   Pray then to God to " give you the
Spirit of wisdom and revelation in the knowledge of him[m],"
and be assured " it shall be given you[n]," and you shall be made
" wise unto salvation through faith in Christ."]

3. Ye children in grace—

[You have begun to know the value of wisdom : you have
a little glimmering view of those great mysteries, of which we
have been speaking.   "The day-star has arisen in your hearts,"
and you have found " the ways of Wisdom to be ways of pleasantness and peace."   But you must " go on unto the perfect

---

[h] Gal. vi. 7, 8.   [i] ver. 17.   [k] Prov. ii. 6.
[l] Matt. xi. 25, 26.   [m] Eph. i. 17, 18.   [n] Jam. i. 5.

day," even till Christ himself, " the Sun of righteousness, arise
upon you with healing in his wings."   O seek to " grow in grace,
and in the knowledge of our Lord and Saviour Jesus Christ!"
Be constant in your attendance on the ordinances of God;
search the Scriptures, and treasure them up in your hearts; and,
above all, " be instant in prayer" for fresh supplies of the Spirit
of Christ : then shall you be guided into all truth ; and " the
light of the moon shall be as the light of the sun, and the light
of the sun seven-fold, as the light of seven days."]

OUTLINE NO. 771

THE VALUE OF TRUE WISDOM.

Prov. viii. 35, 36.   *Whoso findeth me, findeth life, and shall
obtain favour of the Lord.   But he that sinneth against me,
wrongeth his own soul : all they that hate me, love death.*

IT is common in the prophetic writings to find
expressions which really relate to the Messiah, while
they apparently speak only of some other person or
thing; and while other expressions in the same passage have no proper reference to him at all.   It is
impossible not to notice this in the 22d and 69th
Psalms, and in many other places which are quoted
in the New Testament as referring to him.   The
same mode of speaking, we apprehend, may be observed in the chapter before us.   In some parts of it,
true religion seems to be characterized under the
term " Wisdom ;" but in others, Christ himself.
From the 22d to the 31st verse, the language cannot
well be interpreted as designating religion, nor even
an attribute of the Deity : it can only be understood
of God's eternal Son, who lay in the bosom of the
Father, and before the foundation of the earth rejoiced in the prospect of becoming an inhabitant of
this globe, for the salvation of sinful man.   Yet, on
the whole, we apprehend, that the exhortation to
Wisdom at the beginning of the chapter speaks
rather of piety as the proper object of our pursuit.
We are sure that this is the general import of the
term throughout the book of Proverbs ; and that
piety, as personified under this name, frequently
addresses us.   We rather lean therefore to the safe

side in our interpretation of the text, than ground upon it any observations which may appear forced, or unwarranted by the text itself.

Two things then we shall be led to notice ;

I. The benefit of seeking true wisdom—

Wisdom, whether relating to temporal or eternal things, is never found by chance : it must be sought by persevering inquiries, and be obtained as the fruit of diligent research.   To those who do find it, it will be productive,

1. Of present happiness—

[By "life" we may understand *happiness ;* and then the first clause of our text will exactly correspond with what is more diffusely stated in the third chapter [a]. Till we have attained true wisdom, we know not what real happiness means: " There is no peace," saith God, "to the wicked." As for the mirth which the men of this world enjoy, it is only " like the crackling of thorns under a pot ;" it blazes for a moment, and then goes out in spleen and melancholy.   He who knows perfectly what is in man, says, " Even in mirth their heart is sorrowful, and the end of that mirth is heaviness [b]."   But when once they have just views of Christ, and are truly devoted to him, they are filled with " a peace that passeth all understanding," and, at times, with " joy unspeakable and glorified." Now they begin to know what life is: " they truly pass from death unto life."   Their former was little better than a state of mere animal existence ; but now they see the true end, and taste the true enjoyment, of life : they participate in a measure the blessedness of heaven itself.   We appeal to those who have ever known what it is to " live by faith on the Son of God," and to feel the constraining influence of his love, whether one hour of " fellowship with the Father and the Son" does not outweigh whole years of fellowship with sin and sinners.]

2. Of future happiness—

[" No favour can we find with God," till we are brought to the possession of true wisdom [c].   But, instantly on our embracing his dear Son as he is revealed in the Gospel, we are numbered amongst " his peculiar people," whom " he has set apart for himself," and esteems as " his jewels." *Then* there is no favour that he will not shew them : he will come down and " make his abode with them, and sup with them." He will

---

[a] Prov. iii. 13—18. In this sense the term occurs elsewhere. See Prov. xxii. 4. 1 Thess. iii. 8.

[b] Prov. xiv. 33.   [c] Isai. xxvii. 11.

" keep them with all the care and tenderness with which we keep the apple of our eye :" and he will administer to them, in every hour of trial, whatever shall be most suited to their necessities [d]. In the hour of death especially, "when they are going, as it were, through fire and water, he will be with them : " and, on the instant of their release from this mortal body, he will transport them on the wings of angels to his blest abode, there to behold and participate his glory to all eternity. But who can form any idea of the blessings he will *then* bestow. It is sufficient for us to know that his word is pledged, and that what he hath promised, he is able also to perform.]

If such be the value of true wisdom, what must be,

II. The folly of neglecting it—

Sin of every kind is an act of hostility against sound wisdom : and, if the sin be wilful, it is an evidence that our hostility proceeds from a rooted hatred of vital godliness. There is the same mutual opposition, and irreconcileable enmity, between sin and holiness, as between darkness and light : they cannot consist together, nor can the love of both find room to dwell in one bosom. If then we allowedly neglect true wisdom,

1. We " wrong our own souls"—

[The soul has strong and just claims, which every sinner resists. As being of a higher nature, and endued with larger capacities, than the body, it claims that the body *should submit to its authority*. As being the only seat of intelligence, it claims that the body *follow its guidance*. As being immortal, and doomed to spend an eternity in inconceivable happiness or misery, it claims that the body *consult its interests*. But when the voice of wisdom is silenced, and sin is permitted to rule in our mortal body, then is the soul wronged in every respect; its authority is slighted; its counsel rejected; its interest sacrificed: it is even made the drudge and slave of the body, to execute its devices and to gratify its lusts. Who does not see, that if any man, for the gratification of avarice, should resist the natural claims of the body for food and raiment, he would be justly and universally condemned? And does *he* act less foolishly, who, in the manner before mentioned, wrongs his soul? Yea rather, is not his folly greater in proportion as his soul is of greater value? Truly this is a just picture of one who sins against true wisdom.]

2. We " love death"—

[d] Ps. v. 12.

[Can any one, it may be asked, love death? We answer, No; *not for its own sake ;* but, *as connected with sin,* he may. There is an inseparable connexion between life and holiness on the one hand, and sin and death on the other. Could sin and heaven be allied, and enjoyed together, doubtless every sinner would prefer it. But that is impossible. A specific and unalterable option is given us: and every man is perfectly free to choose the one and refuse the other, to adhere to the one and renounce the other. The sinner determines for himself; and by his determination declares his preference: he practically says, " If I cannot have the gratifications of sin without death, welcome death, welcome damnation; for sin I will have, whatever be the consequence[e]." Now can one reflect a moment on such a choice as this, and not stand amazed at the folly that determines it? Will it bear an argument? Are not the excuses with which it is veiled, mere vain and empty delusions? And does not every one see the folly of them, the very moment he sets himself to serious consideration? Yet this is the conduct which men *call* wisdom; but which, if it obtained in relation to worldly affairs, they would call downright madness.]

" Suffer now, Brethren, a word of EXHORTATION," while I address myself,

1. To the despisers of true wisdom—

[Consider a little more attentively, what it is that you despise. The thing to which you are exhorted is, to seek acceptance with an offended God; to embrace the salvation which he offers us in the Son of his love; and to devote yourselves to him in a way of holy obedience — — — Is there any thing in this that merits hatred and contempt? any thing that should make a man choose damnation rather than submit to it? What if an ungodly world has agreed to call it folly; is it therefore folly? Has not God said, " The fear of the Lord, that is *wisdom ?*" Is there a saint in heaven, or on earth, that does not account it wisdom? Yea, is there a soul even in hell itself that is not now of the same mind? We go further still, and ask, Whether they who most deride religion now, will not be convinced of its excellence the very moment that their soul is required of them? " How long then, ye simple ones, will ye love simplicity?" " Turn you at my reproof," says God: "O ye simple, understand wisdom; and, ye fools, be of an understanding heart[f]" — — — Say not, " It is too soon for me to seek the Lord." It is never too soon to be wise: and they who seek the Lord in their youth, have peculiar encouragement from

[e] Mark strongly here God's own appeal, " Why *will* ye die? Ezek. xxxiii. 11. compared with Acts xiii. 46. and Prov. xv. 32.

[f] Prov. i. 22, 23. and viii. 5.

him to do so: " I love them that love me; and they that seek
me early, *shall* find me[g]."]

2. To those who profess to have found it—

[Men will judge of religion, not by what the Bible says
of it, but by what they see in those who profess it: and one
instance of folly in the Lord's people will do more to prejudice
them against religion, than a thousand good actions to recommend it.   I would therefore strongly urge those who profess
godliness, to bear in mind how much the interests of religion
depend on them.   Real piety consists not in talkativeness or
eccentricities of any kind, but in a devout regard to God's
honour and authority, and a wise, prudent, circumspect deportment before men.   It does not countenance us in an officious
assumption of the duties of others, but in a punctual performance of those which belong to our own place and station: " I,
Wisdom, dwell with Prudence[h]."   The not attending to this
declaration has caused much offence in the world: and it becomes us to be very careful of casting stumbling-blocks before
men, or " causing the way of truth to be evil spoken of."   Let
us then " walk in wisdom towards them that are without;"
" giving no occasion to the adversary to speak reproachfully."
And while we adopt the resolution of David, " I will behave
myself wisely in a perfect way[i]," let us remember by whose
strength alone we can effect this; and pray with him, " O give
me understanding in the way of godliness!"]

g ver. 17.   h ver. 12.   i Ps. ci. 2.

OUTLINE NO. 772

WISDOM'S FEAST.

Prov. ix 1—6. *Wisdom hath builded her house, she hath hewn
out her seven pillars: she hath killed her beasts; she hath
mingled her wine; she hath also furnished her table: she
hath sent forth her maidens: she crieth upon the highest
places of the city, Whoso is simple, let him turn in hither:
as for him that wanteth understanding, she saith to him,
Come, eat of my bread, and drink of the wine which I have
mingled: forsake the foolish, and live; and go in the way
of understanding.*

IN the New Testament, parables abound.   In the
Old Testament, they are comparatively rare.   But
this comes commended to us by peculiar authority,
in that our blessed Lord repeatedly borrowed it, if
I may so speak, and adopted it on different occasions, for the elucidating of the truths which he

wished to convey[a]. In order to unfold it to you, I
shall notice separately,

I. The feast prepared—

In the Holy Scriptures, the term " Wisdom" is
generally used to signify true religion : but sometimes it is a name given to the Lord Jesus Christ,
who is, with good reason, supposed to be characterized by it in the chapter that precedes my text[b],
and who, I think, is intended by it in the parable before us. He is " the Wisdom of God[c];" and " in him
are hid all the treasures of wisdom and knowledge[d]:"
and, beyond all doubt, he is the person who, in the
parables which he himself has founded on this, both
furnishes the feasts and sends forth the invitations[e].

By Wisdom,

1. The banqueting-house is built—

[Solomon elsewhere speaks of a " banqueting-house,"
where he had been wont to meet his Saviour[f]; and such
buildings have been raised by the great and opulent in all ages,
for the entertainment of their guests. This edifice, which was
built by Wisdom, was supported by " seven pillars; " which I
suppose to intimate, that it was constructed with *perfect stability,* and adorned with the *perfection of beauty.* And what
is this banqueting-house, but the ordinances of divine grace,
which are appointed altogether for the setting forth of this
feast, and for the accommodation of all who attend upon it?
In them there is room for all : and God will not fail, when
they are attended as they ought to be, to manifest himself in
the midst of them.]

2. The feast, too, is prepared—

[" The beasts," the sacrifices, " are killed ;" and " the
wine," for the purpose of rendering its flavour more exquisite,
is " mingled." The entertainment is, in reality, a feast upon
a sacrifice. And what is that sacrifice on which the whole
world may feast, but the sacrifice of Christ, " the Lamb slain
from the foundation of the world ? " Precisely such a feast
was the passover, which Hezekiah kept unto the Lord. He
kept it for the space of fourteen days; during which time not
less than two thousand bullocks and seventeen thousand sheep
were sacrificed, and all Judah were feasted[g]. But the Lord

a See Matt. xxii. 1—4. Luke xiv. 16, 17.   b Prov. viii. 1, 22—31.
c 1 Cor. i. 24.   d Col. ii. 3.   e See Note a.
f Cant. ii. 4.   g 2 Chron. xxx. 22—26.

Jesus Christ, the true Passover, is sacrificed for all, and will afford an ample feast for all, not for a limited time only, but through the endless ages of eternity. As for the wine, which is so essential to a feast, what is that but the consolations of the Spirit, of which all shall partake who eat of this divine repast? For "Christ's body is meat indeed, and his blood is drink indeed [h]:" and in the ordinances of divine grace, both the one and the other are offered to every child of man. In fact, this is the very feast which the Prophet Isaiah spoke of as to be established under the Christian dispensation: " In this mountain shall the Lord of Hosts make unto all people a feast of fat things, a feast of wines on the lees, of fat things full of marrow, of wines on the lees well refined [i]:" and in the ministration of the gospel is this now set forth more amply than if " all the beasts upon the mountains were slain for us, or the cattle upon a thousand hills."]

Let me, then, without further delay, announce to you,

II. The invitation given—

For the preserving of the propriety of the parable, Wisdom, as a Queen, is said to " send forth her maidens." But Christ, whom wisdom represents, sends forth his Ministers to call men to the feast.

The persons invited are, " the simple, and those who want understanding"—

[This, I grant, is a humiliating description; and it seems to designate the poor only and the ignorant. But, permit me to say, that it comprehends those also who stand the highest in their own estimation for wisdom and prudence. For who, in the whole universe, betray their folly more than those who " seek to fill their belly with the husks that the swine eat of, whilst in their Father's house they might find bread enough and to spare?" Yet this is the very state to which the learned, no less than the illiterate, reduce themselves, whilst seeking their happiness in the world rather than in God, and in the perishing vanities of time and sense rather than in the substantial blessings of eternity. I appeal to all of you, whether this be not the conduct of all by nature, and whether experience do not prove to all the folly of it? This is well represented in Scripture, as " filling our belly with the east wind [k]:" and I ask of all, whether such conduct do not merit the imputation cast upon it in my text? I ask, too, whether, to persons of this character, the invitation be not most fitly sent? You cannot but confess, however successful you may

[h] John vi. 55.　　[i] Isai. xxv. 6.　　[k] Job xv. 2.

have been in your pursuit of earthly objects, "in the fulness of
your sufficiency you have been in straits [1]."]

To you, then, is the invitation given—

[To you, says Wisdom, "Come and eat of my bread, and
drink of the wine which I have mingled." Your past conduct
has involved you in guilt and misery; both of which shall be
removed by partaking of the feast provided for you. The
sacrifice of Christ was expressly offered as an atonement for
your sins; and if you partake of it in faith, your iniquities
shall all be blotted out as a morning cloud. "Whoso eateth
my flesh and drinketh my blood," says our blessed Lord, "hath
eternal life [m]:" yes, he has both a title to it, and the very
beginning of it in his soul. As for "the wine that is mingled"
for you, not all "the wine in Lebanon" can afford you such
consolation and refreshment as the Holy Spirit will to those
who receive his gracious communications.

But, of course, you must forsake those habits which you
have hitherto indulged, and separate yourselves from those
associates who would divert you from Wisdom's ways. For,
"what fellowship can righteousness have with unrighteousness,
or what communion can light have with darkness? There is
a necessity for you to come out from the ungodly and be separate, if you would have God for your father, and enjoy the
privilege of his sons and daughters [n]." The whole course of
your life must be changed: you must not only "forsake the
foolish," but "go also in the way of understanding," approving
yourselves worthy disciples of our blessed Lord. In fact, your
whole *taste* must be changed: you cannot "savour the things
of the flesh and of the Spirit" too [o]: "you cannot serve God
and Mammon" too [p]; or "be the friends of the world and of
Jehovah" too [q]. If you come to the Gospel-feast, you must
"affect only the things which are above [r]," on which you shall
"feast in the presence of your God for ever and ever [s]."]

APPLICATION—

[Let me now address myself to you, my beloved Brethren.
I am sent as Wisdom's servant, as the minister of our Lord
and Saviour Jesus Christ, with a message of mercy to every
one of you. And let it not be offensive to you to be addressed
under the character of those who are here invited. You
surely will not deny, that you have sought your happiness in
the world, rather than in God. Even though you were the
greatest philosophers in the universe, this charge would be as

[1] Job xx. 22.   [m] John vi. 54.   [n] 2 Cor. vi. 14—18.
[o] Rom. viii. 5.   [p] Matt. vi. 24.   [q] Jam. iv. 4.
[r] Col. iii. 1, 2.   [s] Matt. xxvi. 29.

applicable to you as to the meanest of mankind. And, if at this present moment you feel averse to range yourselves under the humiliating term here accorded to you, be assured the time is not far distant when you will designate yourselves by this name with bitter emphasis, and, contrasting yourselves with the Lord's guests, will exclaim, " We fools, counted their life madness, and their end to be without honour : but how are they numbered with the children of God, and their lot is among the saints ! Therefore have we erred from the way of truth[t]." Let me entreat you now to humble yourselves before God, and to welcome, as especially suited to your state, the invitation which I now bring you. But that I may be sure to address you in Wisdom's own words, I will adopt the language of an inspired prophet : " Ho, every one that thirsteth, come ye to the waters, and he that hath no money ; come ye, buy, and eat ; yea, come, buy wine and milk, without money and without price. *Wherefore do ye spend money for that which is not bread, and your labour for that which satisfieth not?* (Here are proofs enough of your folly.) Hearken diligently unto me ; and eat ye that which is good ; and let your soul delight itself in fatness. Incline your ear, and come unto me : hear, and your soul shall live[u]." You will find, at the close of the chapter from whence my text is taken, that folly also has her messengers : A foolish and abandoned woman will cry, " Whoso is simple, let him turn in hither : for stolen waters are sweet, and bread eaten in secret is pleasant. But he knoweth not that the dead are there, and that her guests are in the depths of hell[x]." Yes, these invitations are soon and widely followed ; whilst the invitations of Wisdom are scornfully rejected. Truly this is greatly to be lamented ; and bitter will be the consequences to those who persist in their folly. Accept the invitations that are gratifying to flesh and blood, and nothing but everlasting destruction awaits you : but accept that which now in Wisdom's name I deliver, and you shall " *live :*" " forsake the foolish, and *live.*" Fain would I prevail with you, my Brethren, ere it be too late, and the door of her banqueting-house be shut against you. I have it in commission to " compel you to come in[y]." O, resist me not, but let me by holy importunity prevail ; that so the blessings of salvation may be yours, when the contemners of our message are wailing in everlasting darkness and despair.]

t Wisd. v. 4—6.   u Isai. lv. 1—3.
x ver. 13—18.   y Luke xiv. 23.

OUTLINE NO. 773

GOD'S CARE FOR THE RIGHTEOUS.

Prov. x. 3. *The Lord will not suffer the soul of the righteous to famish.*

GOD, who is the author and giver of all good, dispenses his blessings no less to the evil and unjust, than to the good and just. But he promises to those who seek first his kingdom and his righteousness, that all other things shall be added unto them. To this effect he speaks also in the passage before us. But though this be the primary import of the text, we must not exclude its relation also to the concerns of the soul.

To elucidate this blessed promise, we shall shew,

I. What reasons the righteous have to apprehend that their souls may famish—

A sense of weakness and of guilt may greatly discourage them: for,

1. They cannot secure provisions for themselves—

[The word of God, and Christ in the word, is the proper food of the soul: and, if a person can read, he need not be wholly destitute. But it is by the public ministration of the word that God principally confirms the souls of his people. Now in many places where Christ should be preached, his name is scarcely heard; and, instead of children's bread, little is dispensed besides the husks of heathen morality. Even where some attention is paid to Christian doctrines, there is often much chaff mixed with the wheat; and " the trumpet that is blown, gives but an uncertain sound." Those therefore who by reason of distance, or infirmity, or other insurmountable obstacles, cannot have access to the purer fountains of truth, have great reason to fear that their souls will famish.]

2. They cannot, of themselves, feed upon the provisions set before them—

[Where all the treasures of the Gospel are fully opened, it is God alone that can enrich any soul by means of them: even " Paul may plant, or Apollos may water, but it is God alone that can give the increase." The very same word is often made a peculiar blessing to one, that was altogether useless to another. God reserves the times and the seasons in his own hands; and " gives to every one severally as he will." When therefore the righteous hear of the effects wrought on others, and feel conscious that they themselves reaped no benefit from the word, they are ready to fear that their souls will famish even in the midst of plenty.]

3. They well know that they deserve to be utterly abandoned by their God—

[It is not only for their sins in general, that the righteous find occasion to humble themselves before God, but more particularly for their misimprovement of divine ordinances. Perhaps there is not any other more fruitful source of self-condemnation to the godly than this. When therefore they see how many opportunities of improvement they have lost, and how much guilt they have contracted by their deadness and formality in the worship of God, they are sensible that God may justly " remove their candlestick," and leave them to experience " a famine of the word."]

But lest a dread of famishing should oppress the minds of the righteous, we shall proceed to shew,

II. What grounds they have to hope, that God will never suffer such a melancholy event to happen—

However great the grounds of fear may be which the righteous feel within themselves, they have abundant reason to " encourage themselves in the Lord their God."

1. He has bountifully provided even for the ungodly—

[The Gospel is " a feast of fat things full of marrow, and of wines on the lees well refined ;" and God has " sent out into all the highways and hedges to invite the poor, the halt, the lame, and the blind," and has commissioned his servants to compel men, by dint of importunity, to accept his invitation. Now has he shewn such concern for the wicked, and will he disregard the righteous? Will he not rather " cause the manna to fall around their tents," and " the water to follow them" through all this dreary wilderness? Yes; he would rather send a raven to feed them, or sustain them by a continued miracle[a], than ever suffer their souls to famish.]

2. He is peculiarly interested in the welfare of the righteous—

[The righteous are God's " peculiar treasure above all people;" they are even " his sons and daughters." If they were left to perish, Jesus would lose the purchase of his blood, and the very members of his body. And can we imagine that

---

[a] 1 Kings xvii. 6, 14.

God will be so unmindful of them as utterly to forsake them? Did he not on many occasions vouchsafe mercy to his chosen people *for his own name sake,* when their backslidings had rendered them fit objects of his everlasting displeasure? Thus then will he still be actuated by a regard for his own honour, and " not forsake his people, because it hath pleased him to make them his people [b]."]

3. He has pledged his word that they shall never want any thing that is good—

[" Exceeding numerous, great, and precious are the promises which God has given to his people." He " will supply all their wants, according to his riches in glory by Christ Jesus: he will give them grace and glory; and will withhold no good thing:" their souls " shall be even as a well watered garden:" " bread shall be given them; and their water shall be sure." And will he violate his word? he may leave his people in straits, as he did the Israelites of old: but it shall be only for the more signal manifestation of his love and mercy towards them. Let them only trust in him, and he " will never leave them, never, never forsake them [c]."]

We shall CONCLUDE with a word—

1. Of reproof—

[It is certain that many do not " make their profiting to appear" as they ought. To such therefore we must say, " Wherefore art thou, being a king's son, lean from day to day [d]?" Why art thou crying continually, " Woe is me! my leanness! my leanness [e]!" when thou shouldest be " growing up as the calves of the stall [f]?" Some part of the blame perhaps may attach to him who dispenses the ordinances among you, as wanting more life and spirituality in his ministrations; yet even this would be no excuse to you, since if your hearts were more spiritual, God would render your mean fare as nutritious as the richest dainties [g]. If God should even " give you your desire, yet would he also send leanness into your souls [h]," while you continued to lothe the heavenly manna. Learn then to come with more eager appetite——— Be more careful to digest the word afterward by meditation and prayer——— And look, not so much to the manner in which the word is preached, as to Christ in the word; since HE is that bread of life which alone can nourish your souls; and which, if eaten by faith, will surely nourish them unto life eternal [i]———]

2. Of consolation—

---

[b] 1 Sam. xii. 22.   [c] Heb. xiii. 5. See the Greek.
[d] 2 Sam. xiii. 4.   [e] Isai. xxiv. 16.   [f] Mal. iv. 2.
[g] Dan. i. 12—15.   [h] Ps. cvi. 15.   [i] John vi. 51

[Some may put away from them this promise, under the idea that they are not of the character to whom it belongs. Now, though we would by no means encourage any to apply the promises to themselves in a presumptuous manner, and thereby to deceive their own souls with ungrounded expectations, yet we would not that any should refuse the consolation that properly belongs to them.   Suppose then that any cannot absolutely number themselves among the righteous, yet, " if they hunger and thirst after righteousness, they are blessed, and shall be filled[k]."   This is the word of God to their souls; and we would have them expect assuredly its accomplishment in due season — — — Let them " desire the sincere milk of the word, and they shall grow thereby[l]" — — —]

k Matt. v. 6.   l 1 Pet. ii. 2.

OUTLINE NO. 774

EFFECTS OF SLOTH AND DILIGENCE COMPARED.

Prov. x. 4. *He becometh poor that dealeth with a slack hand; but the hand of the diligent maketh rich.*

IT is certainly true, that men's circumstances in life depend on their own exertions, so far at least, as to justify the declaration in the text. Sometimes indeed God is pleased to raise men to opulence by labours not their own; and sometimes to withhold success from the industrious. But though this inequality is sometimes found in the dispensations of his Providence, we never see it in the dispensations of his grace. After the first communications of grace to the soul, men's progress or decay will always be proportioned to their own care and vigilance: the propositions in the text may be advanced without any exception;—

I. Remissness will impoverish the soul—

Many there are who " deal with a slack hand"—

[This may be said of men *when they improve not the means of spiritual advancement.* God has appointed reading[a], and meditation[b], and prayer[c], and self-examination[d], as means of furthering the welfare of the soul — — — But, if we be remiss in these, we resemble a man who neglects to cultivate his fields:

a Col. iii. 16.   b Ps. i. 2.   c 1 Thess. v. 17.
d Ps. iv. 4. and lxxvii. 6. and 2 Cor. xiii. 5.

nor can it be expected that we should ever prosper in our spiritual concerns.

It may also be said of them *when they shun not the occasions of spiritual decay*. God has mercifully guarded us against the cares[e], the pleasures[f], the company of the world[g]; and against the indulgence of any secret sin[h] —— — And it is of the utmost importance that we attend to these salutary cautions. But if we are unmindful of them, we certainly shew a very culpable remissness, and give advantage to our enemies to prevail against us.]

Under such circumstances they will infallibly " become poor"—

[They will lose *their joy and confidence*. Persons living in habitual watchfulness are often full of the most lively joy[i], and can look up to God as their Father[k], to Christ as their Saviour[l], and to heaven as their home[m]. But these divine impressions are tender plants, which, if not duly watered, will soon wither and decay[n] —— —]

2. They will also lose *their health and strength*—

[There is a health of the soul, as well as of the body: and as the one cannot be maintained in strength but by proper food and exercise, so neither can the other. The graces of the soul, if not duly cultivated, will soon languish. The faith will become weak, the hope faint, the love cold —— — and whatever good " things remain in us, they will be ready to die." So poor will every one become, who dealeth with a slack hand.]

While the soul is exposed to such evils from remissness, we are assured, on the contrary, that—

II. Diligence will enrich it—

Christian diligence comprehends far more than a mere attention to outward forms, however regular—

[It imports *a seasonable attention to all duties*. There are some duties which, in comparison of others, are easy : but Christian diligence makes no distinction on this account; nor does it make the observance of some an excuse for neglecting others ; but endeavours to do every work, whether public or private, civil or religious, in its season[o].

[e] Matt. xiii. 22. and vi. 21.   [f] 1 Tim. v. 6. and 2 Tim. iii
[g] 2 Cor. vi. 14—17.
[h] Prov. iv. 23. Heb. iii. 12. See the examples of Job, Job xxxi. 1
David, Ps. cxli. 3. and cxxxix. 23, 24.
[i] 1 Pet. i. 8.   [k] Rom. viii. 15.   [l] Gal. ii. 20.
[m] 2 Cor. v. 1.   [n] Gal. iv. 15.   [o] Ps. i. 3.

It includes also *a conscientious improvement of all talents.*
Various are the talents committed unto men. Time, money,
influence, together with every mental endowment, are among
those which a Christian will feel himself more especially bound
to improve. He considers them as given to him for the purpose of honouring God with them, and of rendering them
subservient to the good of men. He therefore will not wrap
any one of them in a napkin, but will so trade with them as
to deliver them up with interest whenever he may be called
to give up his account[p].]

Such diligence will infallibly enrich the soul—

[The exertion of our powers does not command success;
but God invariably puts honour upon it, and makes it both the
occasion and the means of communicating his blessings. Our
diligence in cultivating the land cannot ensure the crop: yet it
is by that, for the most part, that God replenishes our barns,
and supplies our returning wants. Thus the diligent hand
makes us rich in *grace,* in *peace,* in *holiness,* and in *glory.*

" To him that hath (that hath improved his talent) shall be
given; and he shall have abundance." Every grace is improved
by exercise[q]—from that improvement arises a " peace which
passeth all understanding[r]"—the whole man is thus progressively renewed after the divine image[s]—and an increased
weight of glory is treasured up for the soul, when it shall receive its full reward[t]—]

INFER—

1. What a pitiable state are they in who never labour at all for the salvation of their souls!

[If remissness only will prove fatal, and that to persons
who were once diligent, surely they must be poor indeed who
have never entered on their work at all! Let the gay and
thoughtless well consider this: for every man shall receive
according to his own labour. Nor shall it be sufficient to say
at the last day, " I did no harm:" the question will be, " What
improvement didst thou make of thy talent?" And if we have
buried it in the earth, we shall be condemned as wicked and
slothful servants.]

2. What reason have all for humiliation and contrition!

[If we consider the greatness of our work, and how little
any of us have done in it, we shall find reason to blush and
be confounded before God. Yes; while the world condemn
us as " righteous overmuch," we should be condemning, and

---

p Matt. xxv. 15—18.   q Matt. xxv. 29.   r Isai. xxxii. 17.
s 2 Cor. iii. 18.   t 2 Cor. iv. 17. 2 John, ver. 8.

even lothing ourselves for doing so little. What might we
not have attained, if we had laboured from the beginning with
the same anxiety and diligence as others manifest in their temporal concerns? How low are the attainments of the best of
us, not only in comparison of what they might have been, but
of what we once expected they would be! Let us then trace
our poverty to its proper cause, our own remissness: and
" whatever our hand findeth to do, let us henceforth do it with
all our might."]

OUTLINE NO. 775

GOD'S BLESSING, THE GREATEST RICHES.

Prov. x. 22. *The blessing of the Lord, it maketh rich; and he
addeth no sorrow with it.*

AMIDST the lessons of practical wisdom which
we are taught in the Book of Proverbs, we find a
continual reference to God as the source and the end
of all. If we attempt to spiritualize the different moral
apophthegms, we in fact pervert them, and apply them
to a use for which they were never intended : if, on
the other hand, we regard them solely in a moral
view, without any relation to God, we fall exceedingly short of their true import. In explaining them,
therefore, a proper medium must be observed ; that
we neither strain their meaning, on the one hand;
nor enervate it, on the other.

To unfold to you the passage before us, I will shew,

I. In what respects " the blessing of God" may be
  said to " make us rich"—

This effect may well be ascribed to " the blessing
of God,"

1. Because it is in reality the only source of all
wealth—

[Men are apt to ascribe their success in life to their own
industry, and to the wisdom which they have exercised in the
management of their affairs. But this is to rob God altogether
of the glory due to him. The people of Israel were guarded
against it by God, who particularly cautioned them not, when
they should be established in Canaan, to arrogate any thing
to themselves; or to " say in their heart, My power and the
might of my hand hath gotten me this wealth :" for that " it
was God alone who had given them power to get wealth[a]."

[a] Deut. viii. 17, 18.

Who sees not how often men fail even in their best-concerted efforts? Success depends, in fact, on so many contingencies, which it is altogether beyond the power of man to control, that the wisest and most industrious of men must of necessity rely on God alone; even as the husbandman, who, though he can plough and sow his land, can command neither the clouds to water it, nor the sun to fructify it with his invigorating rays. No man therefore, however successful, should " sacrifice to his own net, or offer incense to his own drag[b];" but all must give glory to God alone, " who maketh poor, or maketh rich; and bringeth low, or lifteth up; who raiseth up the poor out of the dust, and lifteth up the beggar from the dunghill, to set them among princes, and to make them inherit a throne of glory[c]."]

2. Because it is itself the greatest of all wealth—

[What can be compared with the blessing of God upon the soul? If we succeed in life, it is *that* which constitutes our chief joy; or, if we fail in our earthly pursuits, it is *that* which will compensate for the loss of all. The poorest man in the universe is rich, if he have the presence of God with his soul: and the richest man in the universe is poor, miserably poor, if he be destitute of that great blessing. Behold Paul and Silas in prison, their feet fast in the stocks, and their backs torn with scourges; and yet singing praises to God at midnight! Were they poor? They were rich, truly rich; as were the Hebrew youths, when, in the fiery furnace, the Lord Jesus Christ came and walked with them[d]. To the eye of faith Lazarus was rich, though he subsisted only on the crumbs which fell from the rich man's table. And had he been offered an exchange of condition with his opulent benefactor, he would have disdained the offer, and called himself incomparably the richer man. So, in having God for our portion, *we* are truly rich. St. Paul, under such circumstances, accounted himself the richest man in the universe: and so he was; for, " though he had nothing, yet he possessed all things[e]." And in like manner of us also, even though we are at this moment destitute of bread for the morrow, it may with truth be said, that " all things are ours, if we are Christ's[f]." Thus, if we can say, " The Lord is the portion of my inheritance and my cup[g]," we may account ourselves richer than those who have crowns and kingdoms at their command.]

But we are especially informed by Solomon what is,
II. The peculiar happiness of the person so enriched—

With all other riches there is a mixture of sorrow to embitter them—

[As for riches obtained by iniquity, the curse of God is

---

[b] Hab. i. 16.   [c] 1 Sam. ii. 7, 8.   [d] Dan. iii. 25.
[e] 2 Cor. vi. 10.   [f] 1 Cor. iii. 22, 23.   [g] Ps. xvi. 5.

upon them[h]. But where there has been nothing of rapacity or dishonesty in acquiring them, yet, if the blessing of God be not upon the soul, there is much care in the preserving of them, much grief if they be lost, and little but disappointment and dissatisfaction in the use of them. In truth, they are entitled to no better name than " vanity and vexation of spirit[i]." Let the whole state of mankind be candidly surveyed, and it will be acknowledged that the most wealthy are far from being the happiest of men: for, partly from the tempers generated in their own bosoms, and partly from the collision into which they are continually brought with persons envious, or proud, or dishonest, or in some way disobliging, it may well be doubted whether the pain occasioned by their wealth do not far exceed any pleasure which they derive from it. It was a wise petition which was offered by Agur, " Give me neither poverty nor riches; but feed me with food convenient for me[k]."

But there is another view, in which riches are far from affording any solid satisfaction; and that is, on account of the responsibility attached to them. They are talents to be improved for God: and, whether wasted in extravagance, or hid in a napkin, they will bring down nothing but a curse in the day of judgment. " Go to now, ye rich men," says St. James, " weep and howl for your miseries that shall come upon you." To those who have amassed wealth, he says, " Your gold and silver is cankered; and the rust of them shall be a witness against you, and shall eat your flesh as it were fire: ye have heaped treasure together for the last days." To those, on the other hand, who have wasted their money on personal gratifications, he says, " Ye have lived in pleasure on the earth, and been wanton; ye have nourished your hearts, as in a day of slaughter[l]."]

But where God gives his blessing with wealth, " he addeth no sorrow with it."

[There is then no conscious guilt in the acquisition of it; no anxiety in the preservation; no disappointment in the use; no grief in the loss; no dread of the responsibility attached to it. On the contrary, " God has given to his people all things richly to enjoy[m]:" and they have a rich enjoyment of every thing, because they enjoy God in it. They receive it all as his gift: they taste his love in it. They consider it, also, as a means of honouring God, and of doing good to man. A benevolent steward, who should be sent by his master to dispense his bounties to a famished multitude, would feel great delight in all the comfort which he was thus empowered to bestow: he would view *his master* as *the author* of the benefits, and *himself* only as *the instrument;* but his pleasure would still be exquisite,

---

[h] Jer. xvii. 11. Hab. ii. 6—11. [i] Eccl. ii. 26.
[k] Prov. xxx. 8. [l] Jam. v. 1—5. [m] 1 Tim. vi. 17.

yea, and the more exquisite because his master was honoured in all the good that was done.   Such a steward the true Christian feels himself to be: and his final account, also, he contemplates with joy; assured that his stewardship shall be both approved and rewarded in that day.]

From this subject I would take occasion to suggest two important LESSONS—

Learn,

1. In what spirit to address yourselves to every duty in life—

[Be not contented to perform a duty; but look for the blessing of God upon every thing you do. Without his blessing you will have but little comfort in your own souls.   I will not hesitate to say, that in every line whatever, from the highest to the lowest, the man who acts *to* God and *for* God will be the happiest man.   Others, it is true, may exceed him in wealth; but he will have no reason to envy them; for they have sorrows which will not come near him[n]; and he will have " a joy with which the stranger intermeddleth not[o]."]

2. What to look for as your chief portion—

[Earthly things are not to be neglected. Your worldly calling, whatever it may be, should be diligently followed. But the blessing of God should be the one object to which all others should be subordinated. Nothing, either on earth or in heaven, should, in your estimation, bear any comparison with that[p]. If the question be put, " Who will shew us any good?" your unvaried answer should be, " Lord, lift thou up the light of thy countenance upon us[q]."   Then will you have " durable riches[r]."   And whilst those who seek any other portion will, "in the midst of their sufficiency, be in straits[s]," you, in whatever straits you are, will have a sufficiency for your support and comfort both in time and in eternity.]

n Ps. xci. 7.	o Prov. xiv. 10.	p Ps. lxxiii. 25.
q Ps. iv. 6.	r Prov. viii. 18.	s Job xx. 22.

OUTLINE NO. 776

PORTION OF THE WICKED AND THE RIGHTEOUS CONTRASTED.

Prov. xi. 18. *The wicked worketh a deceitful work: but to him that soweth righteousness shall be a sure reward.*

TO a superficial observer the wicked appear to have a far better portion than the righteous: for it is certain, that, in respect of earthly things, the wicked have the larger share; whilst the righteous, whether poor or not in this world's goods, are objects of general hatred and contempt. But, if we examine more attentively, we shall find that the advantage is decidedly and universally on the side of the righteous: for the wicked man, how prosperous soever he may be, "worketh a deceitful work," but to the righteous, however depressed he may be for a season, shall be a sure reward.

Let us notice the contrast which is here formed between the righteous and the wicked;

I. In their characters—

Though "the wicked" are not distinguished in this place by any appropriate description, yet they are sufficiently marked by standing in contrast with the righteous, whose characters are accurately defined. The one "sow righteousness," which the other neglect to sow.

1. Let us consider this distinction—

[The sowing of righteousness imports, that the person so engaged deliberately and with diligence endeavours to fulfil the will of God; and that he does so with a view to a future harvest. The great "commandment" under the Gospel being, "that we believe in the name of the only-begotten Son of God[a]," he makes that his first concern. He comes to Christ daily as a self-ruined sinner, and looks to him as the appointed Saviour of the world. He seeks to be washed in his blood from all his sins, and to be renewed by his Spirit after the Divine image. In a word, his daily consolation is, "In the Lord have I righteousness and strength[b]." The aim of his soul is also to "walk in all things as Christ walked;" to cultivate altogether "the mind that was in him;" and so to approve himself to God in the whole of his conduct, that in the last day that testimony may be given him from the lips of his applauding Judge, "Well done, good and faithful servant; enter thou into the joy of thy Lord."

"The wicked," on the contrary, has no such thoughts, no such desires. An interest in the Saviour is not of any great importance in his eyes, because he feels no need of it, and concludes of course that he possesses all that is requisite for his acceptance with God. As for "mortifying his earthly members," and "crucifying the flesh with the affections and lusts," that is a work to which he is utterly averse. He rather studies

[a] 1 John iii. 23. [b] Isai. xlv. 24.

to gratify himself, and to follow the bent of his own carnal inclinations. He may not indulge in gross sins: but he is altogether earthly: and whatever he may have of religion, it is a mere form, that engages not his heart, not is in any respect the delight of his soul.

In a word, the one looks forward to a future harvest, and sows with a view to that; the other looks no further than to this present world, and has all his desires bounded by the things of time and sense.]

2. Let us see how far this distinction is confirmed by the word of God—

[This is the very distinction which St. Paul himself makes between the carnal and the spiritual man; "They that are after the flesh do mind the things of the flesh; and they that are after the Spirit, the things of the Spirit[c]." The one " seeks his own things, and not the things that are Jesus Christ's[d]:" the other "lives not unto himself, but unto Him who died for him and rose again[e]."

It is here particularly to be noticed, that the Scriptures do not make the distinction to consist in outward acts, but in the inward habit of the mind: the wicked is not necessarily distinguished by open irregularities; but he makes *self* the end, and aim, and object of his life; whilst " the righteous liveth altogether for, and to, his God."]

A similar difference will be found between them,
II. In their end—

The wicked follows a mere shadow, which eludes his grasp—

[He seeks for happiness, and hopes to find it in the path which he has marked out for himself. But " he worketh a deceitful work," which invariably disappoints his hopes. Whatever be the gratification afforded him, it is transient, and brings no solid satisfaction with it. Whether his pursuit be more sensual, or more refined, it still leaves in the bosom an aching void, which the world can never fill. Solomon tried every thing that was within the reach of mortal man, intellectual as well as sensual; and, after a full experience of it all, declared it all to be " vanity and vexation of spirit." And, if there be a man in the universe who is able from experience to give any other testimony respecting it, we will be content that that man shall walk in his own ways, and not in the ways of God. But we have no fear that this concession will be productive of any evil; for there is not a man in the whole world that will presume to avail himself of it, since there is no man whose conscience does not tell him that the creature altogether is a broken

[c] Rom. viii. 5.   [d] Phil. ii. 21.   [e] Rom. xiv. 7, 8.

cistern, and that no true happiness can be found, but in Christ the fountain of living waters.]

The righteous, on the coutrary, have a sure reward—

[The seed he sows may lie a long time under the clods, and may seem as if it were buried for ever: but it shall spring up in due season, and bring with it a harvest of solid joy. The Scripture attests, that "the work of righteousness is peace[f]," and that "in keeping of God's commandments there is great reward[g]." And so it is invariably found. This "reward is *sure*" on two accounts: one is, that his success is independent of all casualties: and the other is, that it is secured to him by the promise of God himself. Happiness as arising from earthly things may be altogether destroyed by disease or accident, or pains either of body or mind: but spiritual happiness is independent of all these things, and often derives a zest from those very things which seem most calculated to subvert it.

If we look to a future state, where the wicked, notwithstanding all their neglect of heavenly things, hope to have a portion with the righteous, we shall see the text fulfilled in all its extent. What surprise and anguish will seize hold upon the wicked the very instant he opens his eyes in the eternal world! Conceive of "the Rich Man" summoned from his carnal indulgences into the presence of his God: how little did he imagine but a few days before in what such a life would issue[h]! How deceitful had his work been, and how delusive all his hopes! But the righteous is sure to find his hopes realized, and his highest expectations infinitely exceeded; for God's express determination is, that "whatsoever any man soweth, that shall he also reap: he that soweth to the flesh shall of the flesh reap corruption; and he who soweth to the Spirit shall of the Spirit reap life everlasting[i]."]

SEE then,

1. The wisdom of true piety—

[Wisdom consists in pursuing the best ends by the fittest means. Now I would ask, What end is to be compared with eternal life? And by what other means can it be sought, than by those mentioned in the text? Let me then entreat you to "walk, not as fools, but as wise, redeeming the time:" for now is the seed time; and you will to all eternity reap according to what you sow: "if you sow iniquity, you will reap vanity[k]:" "if you sow the wind, you will reap the whirlwind[l]:" but if you "plow up your fallow ground, and sow in righteousness, you shall reap in mercy," both in this world and the world to come[m].

[f] Isai. xxxii. 17.   [g] Ps. xix. 11.   [h] Luke xvi. 23.
[i] Gal. vi. 7, 8.   [k] Job iv. 8. Prov. xxii. 8.
[l] Hos. viii. 7.   [m] Hos. x. 12

Let me however add, that you must not be sparing of your seed: for, " if you sow sparingly, you will reap sparingly; but if you sow bountifully, you shall reap also bountifully[n]."]

2. The folly of neglecting the immortal soul—

[Men will deride piety, because it is cultivated by few; and applaud worldliness, because its advocates are many. But the broad road is not at all the safer because it is trodden by so many, nor the narrow way the less safe because it is trodden by so few. Each path will have its proper termination, and issue in the state that God has assigned to it[o]. Can any thing then be conceived more foolish than to put our eternal happiness on such an issue, that it cannot possibly be attained but at the expense of God's veracity? Truly if such conduct were pursued in reference to this world, it would be accounted not only folly, but madness itself. It is represented by Solomon as a " laying in wait for our own blood, and lurking privily for our own lives[p]," yea, and as a " being in love with death itself[q]. Let me then urge all of you now to seek " the one thing needful:" and let me encourage you to it by this consideration, that, " if you sow in tears, you shall reap in joy: and if you now go on your way weeping, bearing precious seed, you shall doubtless come again with rejoicing, bringing your sheaves with you[r]."]

[n] 2 Cor. ix. 6.   [o] Matt. vii. 13, 14.   [p] Prov. i. 18.
[q] Prov. viii. 36.   [r] Ps. cxxvi. 5, 6.

OUTLINE NO. 777

CHRISTIAN LIBERALITY ENCOURAGED.

Prov. xi. 25. *The liberal soul shall be made fat : and he that watereth shall be watered also himself.*

IF only we be careful to divest our statements of every thing which carries with it the idea of *merit*, it is scarcely possible to speak too strongly in praise of liberality, as lovely in itself, and as acceptable to God. To speak of it as contributing in any degree to justify the soul before God, would doubtless be a fatal error; but as rewardable, and certain to be rewarded both in this life and the life to come, we ought to speak of it: and the squeamish jealousy which is entertained on this head, and which fears to declare all that God's blessed word contains upon the subject, is, in my apprehension, extremely erroneous and unbecoming.

The words which I have just read will lead me to shew you,

I. The spirit we should possess—

In my text we see a spirit of liberality, and a spirit of benevolence; the one constituting an internal principle in the soul, the other displaying itself in active exertions towards all within our sphere. Let me call your attention, then, to,

1. A spirit of liberality—

[The liberal *hand* is good; but the liberal *soul* is far better: and this it is which every Christian should possess. We should consider all that we have as so many talents committed to us by our heavenly Master, to be improved for him. Our time, our property, our influence, should all be considered *his;* and nothing as really *ours,* but the honour and happiness of employing all for God. We can easily conceive what the feelings of an angel would be, if he were sent from heaven to dispense blessings of any kind: there would be no grudging of his time and labour, nor would there be any pride and self-complacency in his mind on account of his fidelity in the execution of his office. He would consider himself simply as God's servant; and find all his delight in doing the will of Him who sent him, and in being instrumental to the welfare of mankind. If this appear too strong an image, I must say, Instead of being too strong, it falls far short of the example which our blessed Lord has set before us: "Ye know the grace of our Lord Jesus Christ, who, though he was rich, yet for your sakes became poor, that ye through his poverty might be rich[a]." This is the true standard at which we should aim; even such a delight in advancing the welfare of others, as disposes us to encounter whatever self-denial may be requisite for the attainment of our end. *This* may properly be called "a liberal soul."]

2. A spirit of benevolence—

[Principles in the heart must shew themselves by actions in the life. To "water others" should be the employment of us all. The whole world is the garden of the Lord. All of us are his plants; and all of us his husbandmen, that should be occupied in watering the plants around us. Whether our capacity for exertion be greater or less, we should endeavour to improve it for God and man. If we have but one talent, we should not hide it in a napkin, but employ it for the Lord. We should consider what it is that every plant around us wants, in order that we may minister, as far as we are able, to its necessities. Does any need instruction, or comfort, or temporal relief? We should adapt our labours to his

[a] 2 Cor. viii. 9.

necessities, and look to God for his blessing on our endeavours. Day by day the earthly husbandman is so occupied; and it is an employment in which we should daily engage, and of which we never should be weary. At the close of every day we should have the same testimony from conscience as holy Job enjoyed : " When the ear heard me, then it blessed me ; and when the eye saw me, it gave witness to me : because I delivered the poor that cried, and the fatherless, and him that had none to help him. The blessing of him that was ready to perish came upon me; and I caused the widow's heart to sing for joy. I put on righteousness, and it clothed me : my judgment was as a robe and a diadem. I was eyes to the blind, and feet was I to the lame. I was a father to the poor; and the cause which I knew not, I searched out[b]."]

Such being the proper spirit of a Christian, let us consider,

II. The benefits that will accrue to the possessor of it—

However great may be the good which a person of this spirit may do, I hesitate not to say, that he will receive far greater benefits than he imparts : he will receive them,

1. From the very exercise of the principle itself—

[The high-priest within the vail, whilst offering incense before his God, was regaled with the odours of his own offering; a privilege which no other individual was permitted to enjoy. So the person who exercises love will derive from that very employment a blessedness of which no one else can form any just conception. Well is it said, in a foregoing verse of this chapter, " A merciful man *doeth good to his own soul*[c]." The exercise of liberality and benevolence tends exceedingly to the suppression of evil in the soul, and to the cultivation and establishment of every holy disposition[d] — — — And is it not a sweet evidence to the soul, that God has wrought a good work within it? No doubt it is: for if we " love, not in word and in tongue, but in deed and in truth," we may, from that very circumstance, " know that we are of the truth, and may assure our hearts before God[e]." Indeed this is no small part of the recompence which God will bestow on those who serve him with fidelity: he would even consider himself as unrighteous and unjust if he did not thus remember our work and labour of love, which we have shewed toward his name in ministering to his saints:" and on this very ground the Apostle

[b] Job xxix. 11—16.   [c] ver. 17.
[d] Mark the contrast which is drawn, 1 Tim. vi. 10, 11.
[e] 1 John iii. 18, 19.

says, " We desire that every one of you do shew the same diligence unto the full assurance of hope unto the end[f]."]

2. From the immediate agency of Almighty God—

[God has said, that "what we give to the poor, we lend unto *him*, and he will repay it again[g]." And this he will do both in this life and in the life to come. Very remarkable is his promise in relation to the present life : " Give, and it shall be given unto you : good measure, pressed down, and shaken together, and running over, shall men give into your bosom. For with what measure ye mete withal, it shall be measured to you again[h]." In a spiritual view, more especially, will God recompense his faithful people. Hear the words of the Prophet Isaiah, which remarkably accord with the expressions of our text : " If thou draw out *thy soul* (not thy *purse*, but thy *soul*) to the hungry, and satisfy the afflicted soul, then shall thy light rise in obscurity, and thy darkness be as the noon-day; and the Lord shall guide thee continually, and *make fat* thy bones; and thou shalt be like a *watered garden*, and *like a spring of water*, whose waters fail not[i]." Nor shall our labours of love be forgotten of Him in the eternal world. He holds forth this as an encouragement to us to exert ourselves in all the offices of love : " Charge them that are rich in this world, that they be rich in good works, ready to distribute, willing to communicate, laying up in store for themselves a good foundation against the time to come, that they may lay hold on eternal life[k]." And that no doubt may remain on this head, he tells us expressly, that such persons shall " be recompensed at the resurrection of the just;" and that to those who have administered to the relief of the poor and the distressed, he will say, " Come, ye blessed of my Father, inherit the kingdom prepared for you from the foundation of the world." Thus freely and thus richly shall " he who watereth be watered also himself;" yea, as the prophet says, "with showers of blessings shall he be blessed[l].]

We may clearly SEE from hence,

1. From whence proceeds that leanness, of which so many complain—

[Many complain, that, notwithstanding the Gospel is so rich in its blessings, they are not happy. But I believe it will be generally found, that they who complain thus live only for themselves. I think it *almost* impossible that they who live for God and for their fellow-creatures should not be happy. Such circumstances as Job's *may* exist, but they are rare; and

---

[f] Heb. vi. 10, 11.   [g] Prov. xix. 17.   [h] Luke vi. 38.
[i] Isai. lviii. 10, 11.   [k] 1 Tim. vi. 18, 19.   [l] Ezek. xxxiv. 26

even he himself endured them but for a time. Examine, then, your state as before God, and see whether you possess the dispositions of which my text speaks: for, if you do not, how is it possible that you should have any blessing from the Lord? Hear what Job would have thought of such a state as yours: "If I have withheld the poor from their desire, or have caused the eyes of the widow to fail; or have eaten my morsel alone, and the fatherless have not eaten thereof; if I have seen any perish for want of clothing, or any poor without covering; if his loins have not blessed me, and if he were not warmed with the fleece of my sheep; then let mine arm fall from the shoulder-blade, and mine arm be broken from the bone[m]." What you sow, you must expect to reap: and if you "sow but sparingly," in the way of love and mercy, "you shall reap but sparingly" of those blessings which the God of love and mercy will bestow.]

2. What encouragement we have to proceed in the work before us—

[The charity which I would propose to your support is worthy of all the aid which you can afford to give it[n] — — — And for your encouragement, I will appeal to all: Who amongst you ever abounded in liberality, without finding it a source of joy? or who ever watered others, without being himself watered of the Lord? — — — If I considered only the charity before us, I should urge you to be liberal: but I chiefly urge it because "I desire fruit that may abound to your account[o]."]

---

[m] Job xxxi. 16—22.
[n] Here enter into a description of the particular charity: and if it be a *Benevolent Society*, address separately the *Contributors* who "give," and the *Visitors* who "water."   [o] Phil. iv. 17.

OUTLINE NO. 778

THE WISDOM OF WINNING SOULS.

Prov. xi. 30.   *He that winneth souls, is wise.*

REAL piety is operative, and influential on the whole life; and discovers itself very principally in labours of love to those around us. "The fruit of the righteous is" very fitly compared to "a tree of life," which administers to the welfare of all who come under its benignant shade.   True, indeed, such persons are often regarded only as weak enthusiasts; and are despised in proportion as they exert themselves for the benefit of their fellow-creatures.   But they have a good report from God himself, who says concerning them, " He that winneth souls, is wise."

This sentence it shall be my endeavour to confirm : and confirmed it will be beyond all doubt, if we consider what may be justly said in vindication of every one who engages in this good work.

I. The object he proposes to himself is most excellent—

[What in the universe is there worthy to be compared with an immortal soul? — — · — And what work can be compared with that which is done for the soul, in its conversion to God? — — — Think of its being plucked as a brand out of the fire of hell itself — — — Think of its being restored to the favour of its offended God — — — Think of its being transformed into the divine image — — — Think of its being exalted to a participation of all the glory and felicity of heaven — — — Is there any object that can stand in competition with this? What is the acquisition of crowns and kingdoms in comparison of this? — — —]

Further,

II. The labour he bestows upon it is most beneficial,

1. To the soul he wins—

[Let the foregoing hints be duly contemplated ; and then say what a benefactor he is, " who turns a man from the error of his ways, and saves a soul alive[a]"— — —]

2. To the world around him—

[Man, in his unconverted state, is a snare to all around him. By his example at least, if not by any avowed declarations, he teaches men to think that the concerns of this world are most worthy of their attention, and that the concerns of the soul are only of secondary importance — — — But, when once he is truly turned to God, the honour of God is dear unto him, and the welfare of immortal souls lies near his heart — — — For the extension of the Redeemer's kingdom he prays in secret, and labours according to his ability in the sphere wherein he moves. " Thy kingdom come," is the language, not of his lips only, but of his heart also. He now lives, not for himself, as heretofore, but for God, for his Saviour, for his fellow-men ; and whatever he possesses he considers as a talent to be improved for them — — — Now, therefore, he becomes " a light in the world ; " and, from being an agent of Satan to advance the kingdom of darkness, he is a favoured instrument of Jehovah, to promote in every way the happiness and salvation

[a] Jam. v. 19, 20.

of the human race — — — Who can calculate the benefits accruing from such a change?]

3. To himself also—

[Who ever laboured for God without receiving in his own soul a rich reward [b]?" " Who ever watered others, and was not himself watered by the Lord [c]?" The very graces which a man exercises, in winning souls to God, diffuse a sweet serenity, a holy joy, over the whole man, and assimilate him to his Lord and Saviour, and render him meet for the inheritance that is reserved for him. I may add also, his very labour augments for him the weight of glory that is reserved for him in heaven: for God has said, in reference to this very thing, that " every man shall receive according to his own labour [d];" and that " they who turn many to righteousness shall shine as the stars, for ever and ever [e]."

Is not he " wise," then, who engages in such a work as this?]

In addition to all this I must say,

III. The end he accomplishes is most glorious—

[This is the end which God the Father had in view, when he delegated to his Son the office of redeeming man — — — This was the end for which our adorable Saviour " left the bosom of the Father," and assumed into union with himself our fallen nature, and led a life of sorrow upon earth, and at last died for us upon the cross. To this he looked forward, as " the joy that was set before him, for the which he endured the cross and despised the shame [f]. " And when he beholds this as the fruit of his sufferings, he is altogether " satisfied with the travail of his soul [g] "— — — The Holy Spirit also regards this as the end for which he performs his part in the economy of redemption. For what does he " strive with rebellious man [h]? " For what end does he enlighten, quicken, sanctify the souls of men, or refresh and invigorate them with his heavenly consolations? All of this is to " glorify Christ [i]," in the salvation of man. In truth, it is in this work that every person of the Godhead will be glorified to all eternity. What is it that illustrates in harmonious union all the perfections of the Deity?— — —What is it that is the one subject of praise and adoration amongst all the heavenly hosts? Is not this the song of all that have been redeemed? " To him that loved us, and washed us from our sins in his own blood, and hath made us kings and priests unto our God, to him be glory and dominion for ever and ever [k]." Even the angels, that never sinned, add

[b] Ps. xix. 11. [c] ver. 25. [d] 1 Cor. iii. 8.
[e] Dan. xii. 3. [f] Heb. xii. 2. [g] Isai. liii. 11.
[h] Gen. vi. 3. [i] John xvi. 14. [k] Rev. i. 5, 6.

their "Amen to this; and sing their praises unto God who sitteth upon the throne, and unto the Lamb for ever and ever[1]."

Compare with this work, then, " all the labour that is done under the sun," and it is no better than laborious folly. Not he that accumulates to himself wealth or honour, but " he that winneth souls, is wise."]

What, in CONCLUSION, shall I say? What?

1. Let every one seek the salvation of his own soul—

[Is it *wisdom* to *win* the souls of *others?* What *folly*, then, must it be to *lose our own?* — — — In this labour we have more abundant encouragement. We may seek to save others, and fail in our attempt: but who ever failed, that sought salvation for his own soul? Find, in the annals of the whole world, one who ever looked to Christ in vain? Who ever washed in the fountain of his blood in vain? or for whom did the grace of Christ ever prove inadequate and insufficient? Let the world deride this labour as folly, if they please : they will soon see who it is that is really wise ; and will soon condemn themselves, more bitterly than now the most envenomed amongst them condemn the righteous : " WE *fools* accounted their life madness, and their end to be without honour : but now we see how greatly we have erred from the way of truth[m]." — — — Who then is wise among you, let him " give himself wholly " to the concerns of his soul ; for " the wise shall inherit glory ; but shame shall be the promotion of fools[n]."]

2. Let every one seek also the salvation of others—

[There are many ways in which this may be done[o] — — — In particular, let every one attend to his own household. For these, in a more especial manner, is every one responsible — — — But in whatever way our exertions are called forth, let us remember that they must be used in a wise, discreet, *affectionate* manner. We must doubtless declare the whole counsel of God : but, if we would succeed in our labours, we must endeavour to " *win* souls" *by love*, and not drive them away by severity and terror — — —]

[1] Rev. v. 11—13.   [m] Wisd. v. 4—6.   [n] Prov. iii. 35.

[o] Here any particular means may be insisted on, according as the particular occasion may require : for instance, The Ministry — The Visiting of the Sick—The Instructing of Children—The Sending forth of the Holy Scriptures—The Support of Missions, &c. &c.

OUTLINE NO. 779

THE EXCELLENCY OF THE RIGHTEOUS.

Prov. xii. 26. *The righteous is more excellent than his neighbour.*

MEN in their external appearance are alike ; so far at least, that their moral character cannot with any accuracy be determined by it. But God, who searches the heart, sees an immense difference between different men ; such a difference as suffices to arrange them all under two great classes—the righteous and the wicked. In the righteous he finds an excellency which he in vain looks for in others ; and to point out this superior excellency is my object, in this discourse. But here it is proper to observe, that Solomon does not draw the comparison between a righteous and a *notoriously wicked* man ; but between a righteous man and "his neighbour," however excellent that neighbour may be : for, if there be in any man a want of positive and inherent righteousness, whatever else he may possess, he must be classed with the wicked : and with such only will my present comparison be instituted.

" The righteous man, then, is more excellent than his neighbour ;"

I. In his connexions—

A truly righteous man is born of God—

[This is frequently and fully declared in the Holy Scriptures[a] — — — — and though he be the poorest man upon earth, he is entitled to address his God under the endearing name of Father.]

He is united to Christ—

[He is united to him as a building to the foundation[b] ; as a wife to her husband[c] ; as a branch to the vine[d] ; as a member to the body[e]. There is no other union so close and intimate, except that which subsists between God the Father and the Lord Jesus[f] : for he is not only one body with him, but one spirit also[g] : for Christ lives in him[h], and is his very life[i].]

a John i. 12. and iii. 5. and 1 John iii. 1.	b 1 Pet. ii. 4, 5.
c Eph. v. 32. Rev. xxi. 9.	d John xv. 1.
e Eph. v. 30. f John xvii. 21, 23.	g 1 Cor. vi. 17.
h Gal. ii. 20. i Col. iii. 4.	

The Holy Ghost also dwells in him—

[He is a temple of the Holy Ghost[k], who abides in him more manifestly and more effectually than in the whole universe besides: and so desirable a residence is his heart accounted by the Holy Spirit, that, in comparison of it, the temple of Solomon itself was held in utter contempt[l].]

He is of the same family with all the glorified saints and angels—

[There is but one family, whether in heaven or earth, of which Christ is the head[m]: and so far is he from being disowned by them, that there is not an angel before the throne that does not account it an honour to wait upon him, and to minister unto him[n].]

What does any worldly man possess, that can be compared with this?

[Whose child is *he*? " A child of the wicked one[o]:" as our Lord has said, " Ye are of your father the devil[p]." True it is, that in the last day the holy angels will minister to them also; but it will only be to " gather them together" from every part of the universe, and to " bind them up in bundles," and to cast them headlong into the fire of hell[q]. Tell me, then, to which of these the superior excellency belongs?]

Let us trace this,

II. In his principles—

The righteous man is altogether under the influence of faith and love—

[He looks for salvation solely through the blood and righteousness of the Lord Jesus Christ. He has no hope whatever, but in the redemption that is in Christ Jesus. As for any righteousness of his own, he utterly disclaims it. He knows, that if he were judged by the best act he ever performed, he must for ever perish. The way which God himself has provided for the salvation of sinners is that which he affects, and in which he glories: the language of his inmost soul is this, " God forbid that I should glory, save in the cross of our Lord Jesus Christ, by whom (or by which) the world is crucified unto me, and I unto the world[r]."

At the same time that he looks thus to be saved *as a sinner*, he labours to walk *as a saint*, and to " adorn the doctrine of God his Saviour in all things." Nor is he impelled to this by any slavish fear of punishment: no: " the love of Christ

[k] 1 Cor. vi. 19.   [l] Isai. lxvi. 1, 2.   [m] Eph. iii. 15.
[n] Heb. i. 14.   [o] Matt. xiii. 38. 1 John iii. 10.
[p] John viii. 44.   [q] Matt. xiii. 30.   [r] Gal. vi. 14.

constrains him; because he thus judges, that if one died for all, then were all dead; and that he died for all, that they who live should not henceforth live unto themselves, but unto Him who died for them and rose again[s]." And as he serves his God from love, so is he actuated by the same principle in all his intercourse with men: " he walks in love, as Christ has loved him[t];" and he looks upon this as the best fruit of his faith[u], and as the surest evidence of his acceptance with God[x].]

How widely different from these are the principles of the wicked!

[Let it be remembered, that I am not speaking of those who indulge in gross wickedness, but of those only who are not positively righteous. Whatever they may possess in respect of outward morality, they are strangers to the true exercise both of faith and love. They do not fully enter into the great mystery of redemption: they feel not their need of such a Saviour as God has provided for them. That God himself should become a man, and die under the load of their sins, and work out a righteousness wherein they may stand accepted before him—they see no occasion for all this: they think they might be saved on easier terms, or, if I may so express it, at a cheaper rate. They cannot see why they should have so inestimable a price paid for them, when their own repentance and reformation might have well sufficed for all the demands which God had upon them. Nor do they feel their need of the Holy Spirit to teach and sanctify them, when their own wisdom and strength were, upon the whole, adequate to their necessities. At all events, if they assent to the Gospel salvation as true, they do not embrace it with their whole hearts, and rejoice in it as that which alone could give them a hope before God. So also in their obedience, all which they do is from constraint, rather than from love: as clearly appears from hence, that they are satisfied, upon the whole, with what they do; whereas, if they felt their obligations to God for the gift of his only Son to die for them, and of his Holy Spirit to renew them, they would feel nothing but dissatisfaction and grief on account of their short-comings and defects. In fact, all their works are done merely in conformity with the customs of the world, and for the purpose of forming a ground for self-estimation, and for the estimation of those around them.

What comparison, then, will these bear with the characters with which they are here contrasted? They are as inferior to the righteous " as dross is to the purest gold[y]."]

Let us trace the comparison yet further,

[s] 2 Cor. v. 14, 15. 　　[t] Eph. v. 2. 　　[u] Gal. v. 6.
[x] 1 John iii. 14, 19. and iv. 7, 17. 　　[y] Jer. vi. 30.

III. In his habits—

The righteous man lives altogether to his God—

[See him from day to day: his whole soul is *humbled* before God, under a sense of his own extreme unworthiness. Were you to behold him in his secret chamber, you would behold him more abased before his God for an evil thought or desire, than an ungodly man would be for the actual commission of the grossest sin. Oh! the sighs and groans which he involuntarily utters, under the load of that burthen, that body of sin and death, from which he cannot get free! and many are the tears which he sheds in secret, because he cannot attain that perfect holiness which his soul panteth after.

With his humiliation he breathes forth in devoutest accents his *prayers and praise.* His prayers are no formal service, but a holy wrestling with God; and his praises resemble those of heaven, that are accompanied with the devoutest prostration of soul.

A life of *self-denial,* too, characterizes his daily walk. He desires to " crucify the flesh, with its affections and lusts;" and it is his incessant labour to " mortify the whole body of sin." " Not a right hand, or right eye," would he willingly retain : he would gladly part with every thing, however dear to him, if only he may but enjoy the testimony of a good conscience, and approve himself faithful to the heart-searching God.

To *prepare for death and judgment* is his one concern. He lives as on the borders of eternity. He knows not at what hour the bridegroom may arrive; and therefore he " keeps his loins girt, and his lamp trimmed, that he may be ready to enter into the bride-chamber" with his beloved Lord.]

But how is it with the wicked in these respects ?

[Are they from day to day humbling themselves in the Divine presence ? What cares and sorrows they have are altogether of a worldly nature. To " abhor themselves," like Job, and " to repent in dust and ashes," unless for some wickedness that has exposed them to public hatred and contempt, is no part of their experience before God.

And what are their prayers and thanksgivings? Nothing but a mere lip-service, in which their hearts are not at all engaged.

As for self-denial, they know little about it. Their whole life is a system of self-indulgence. They may not run into gross sins on account of their regard for their character amongst men; but they pursue with unabated ardour those earthly vanities on which their hearts are set. Pleasure, or riches, or honour, occupy all their thoughts, and stimulate all their exertions. They live altogether for themselves, and not for God; for the body, and not for the soul; for time, and not for eternity.

Surely the further we compare the characters, the more will the superiority of the righteous appear.]

It remains that we yet further contemplate the righteous,

IV. In his end—

How blessed this will be, no words can adequately describe!

[Were you present with him in his dying hour, and God were to open your eyes, you would see angels attendant on him, to bear upon their wings his departing spirit into Abraham's bosom. Could you follow him, and witness his reception by the Most High God, what plaudits would you hear! "Well done, good and faithful servant, enter thou into the joy of thy Lord!" How would you, then, behold him graced with a crown of gold, seated upon a throne, invested with a kingdom, and shining forth with a glory that would eclipse the noon-day sun! To all eternity will he then live, in the immediate fruition of his God, holy as God himself is holy; and happy, according to his capacity, as God himself is happy.]

Alas! alas! here all comparison must for ever cease—

[The wicked, unhappy creatures! are dragged into the presence of an angry God, in vain "calling upon rocks and mountains to cover them from his wrath." From him they hear that terrific sentence, "Depart accursed, into everlasting fire, prepared for the devil and his angels!" and into that fire are they cast, even "that lake that burneth with fire and brimstone," from whence "the smoke of their torment will ascend for ever and ever." But this is too painful to reflect upon. O that the very mention of it may suffice to confirm the assertion in my text, and to convince you all wherein alone true excellency can be found!]

ADDRESS—

1. Those whom God has classed with "the wicked"—

[You will find, in the words following my text, that the persons contrasted with the righteous are so designated: and of them it is said, "The way of the wicked seduceth them." Now, it must be granted, that "their way" is *more easy*, and to flesh and blood *more pleasant*, and *more approved* by an ungodly world; and, therefore they imagine it to be, on the whole, preferable to the difficult and self-denying and despised path of the righteous. But they are "seduced" by these specious appearances; and "a deceived heart has turned them aside; so that they cannot deliver their soul, or say, Is there not a lie in my right hand[z]?" But be dispassionate, and judge as before the Lord. If you deceive yourselves, you cannot deceive him : he will judge, not according to your own erroneous estimate of yourselves, but according to truth, and to the real state of your souls. Yet methinks you cannot deceive even yourselves, if you will but reflect with any degree of candour upon the comparison that has been set before you. In truth, you have in your own bosoms a witness for God : for, whether your conduct be more or less moral, there is not one of you that does not say in his heart, especially in his more thoughtful moments, " Let me die the death of the righteous, and let my last end be like his."]

2. Those who are disposed to number themselves amongst " the righteous"—

[Many who claim this distinction prove themselves, by their habits, most unworthy of it. It is a melancholy truth, that many professors of religion, instead of being more excellent than their neighbour, are inferior to him in almost every thing that is amiable and praiseworthy. Such self-deceivers will have a fearful account to give at the last day. To every one, then, amongst you I would say, If you profess yourselves to be righteous, let it appear to all around that you are so by the superior excellence of your lives. Our Lord says to his disciples, " What do ye *more than others?*" More than others ye *ought* to do; inasmuch as your obligations and assistances are more than others are acquainted with. You are to " shine as lights in a dark world;" and in every relation of life to approve yourselves more excellent than your neighbour. Are you husbands or wives, parents or children, masters or servants, you should fill up your station in life more to the honour of God and the good of the community than any others around you. I conclude, then, with that direction which our blessed Lord has given you: " So let your light shine before men, that they may see your good works, and glorify your Father who is in heaven."]

[z] Isai. xliv. 20.

OUTLINE NO. 780

THE CHARACTER AND END OF THE WICKED.

Prov. xiii. 5. *A wicked man is lothesome, and cometh to shame.*

THE world in general uphold and countenance one another in their evil ways; some will even " make a mock at sin," and glory in it. But God's testimony respecting the wicked man is, that, whatever be his rank, or talents, or estimation among men, he is indeed " lothesome, and cometh to shame."

In these words we behold,

I. The character of the wicked—

The wicked comprehend all who are not righteous—

[There are but two classes of persons mentioned in the Scriptures; and to one or other of them we all belong. There is no intermediate character. We indeed cannot always determine to which of these classes men belong, because we cannot discern the heart; but God, to whom all things are naked and open, will distinguish them from each other as easily as we do sheep from the goats.

It is of infinite importance that we should have this truth impressed on our minds: for we are ready to rank among the wicked those only who are guilty of great enormities: whereas all are wicked who are not truly righteous; all, who are not converted to God, and renewed in the spirit of their minds.]

God's testimony respecting them is applicable to them all, whether they be more or less wicked in respect of gross sins—

[*The openly profane* are doubtless exceeding lothesome in the sight of God. Let any one but notice their conversation; how replete is it with lewdness and blasphemy! Let their tempers be marked; what evil dispositions do they manifest on all occasions! Let their conduct be scrutinized, their drunkenness, their whoredoms, and all their other abominations; and who must not confess the justice of that representation, which compares them to swine wallowing in the mire, and dogs devouring their own vomit [a]?

The more decent, it is true, are not so vile in the eyes of men, (yea, perhaps they are honoured and esteemed) but they also are lothesome in the sight of God. What monsters of ingratitude are the very best of unregenerate men! What mercies have they received from God; what inconceivable love has been shewn them by the Lord Jesus Christ; and yet they have never spent one hour in humble and grateful adorations. If they had laboured thus to win the affections of some worthless wretch, and after many years of unintermitted kindness were requited by him as they requite their God, would they not consider *him* as deserving of utter execration? How lothesome then must *they* be, whose obligations are infinitely greater, and whose conduct is inexpressibly more vile! Their actions, it is confessed, may have been fair and specious: but what have their hearts been? have they not been a very sink of iniquity [b]? Yes; so depraved

[a] 2 Pet. ii. 22. See also Job xv. 16. Ps. liii. 1—3.
[b] Jer xvii. 9. Gen. vi. 5.

are the very best of men, that there are few, if any, who would not rather die, than have all the secrets of their hearts known to men as they are known to God. What then are such persons, but whited sepulchres[c]? No wonder that, however they be esteemed among men, both their persons and services are an abomination to the Lord[d].]

Conformable to their character must surely be,

II. Their end—

Sin is in itself inconceivably vile, and will bring its votaries to shame,

1. In this world—

[How often are the fairest characters blasted by detection, and exposed to infamy! The deeds of darkness, when brought to light, often reflect such dishonour upon men, as to make them shun society, and put a period to their own existence. And how many are brought to die by the hands of a public executioner, and to entail disgrace on their latest posterity! Little do men think, when first they yield to temptation, whither sin will lead them. It is a principal device of Satan to conceal the consequences of sin, and to make men believe that they can recede from it whenever they please: but when he has once entangled their feet, they find to their cost, that they cannot escape from his net.]

2. In the world to come—

[There are many who pass honourably through life, and, for their conduct in society, deserve every token of our respect. But God will try the hearts of men in the last day; and "will bring to light every secret thing, whether it be good or evil." Then what shame will overwhelm the most specious moralist, whose heart was unrenewed by grace! A want of love to Christ now is thought but a light matter: but then it will appear in its true colours, as deserving of God's heaviest indignation[e]. Secret lusts too are overlooked, as though they did not at all defile the soul: but they will then be found to have made us altogether lothesome and odious to God[f]. Then will Christ[g] with all his saints[h] and angels[i] unite in expressing their abhorrence of these whited sepulchres; so fully shall that declaration be verified, They shall awake to shame and everlasting contempt[k].]

We cannot IMPROVE this subject better than by pointing out,

---

[c] Matt. xxiii. 27. [d] Luke xv. 16. Prov. xv. 8, 26. and xxviii. 9.
[e] 1 Cor. xvi. 22. [f] Ezek. xiv. 4, 7. [g] Matt. vii. 22, 23
[h] 1 Cor. vi. 2. [i] Matt. xiii. 41, 42. [k] Dan. xii. 2

1. What is that repentance which such persons need—

[It is by no means sufficient to confess that we are sinners: we should feel that we are indeed lothesome[1]; and should be filled with shame on account of the extreme vileness of our hearts[m]. Nothing less than this will constitute that "repentance which is not to be repented of[n]."]

2. How their character and end may be completely changed—

[Lothesome as we are we may be purified by the blood of Jesus, and be made without spot or blemish in the sight of God[o]. Our natures also may be changed by his Spirit, so that we shall possess a beauty that God himself shall admire[p]. Yea, instead of having shame for our portion, we shall be made to inherit " glory and honour and immortality." We shall be sons of the living God, and be seated with Christ on thrones of glory. Let us then seek this change, and rely on God's promises, that by means of them it may be accomplished in us[q].]

[1] Isai. lxiv. 6.
[m] Ezek. xxxvi. 31. and xvi. 63. and Rom. vi. 21.
[n] See Ezra ix. 6. Job xl. 4. and xlii. 6.
[o] Eph. v. 25—27.   [p] 1 Pet. iii. 4.   [q] 2 Cor. vii. 1.

OUTLINE NO. 781

THE WAY OF TRANSGRESSORS HARD.

Prov. xiii. 15.   *The way of transgressors is hard.*

THE Scriptures abound with weighty aphorisms, which deserve the deepest consideration. For the most part, they will be found directly opposed to the general opinions of mankind. The maxims of men are too often founded on the appearance of things, and on the respect they bear to our temporal advantage; but the declarations of God exhibit things as they really are, and as they will approve themselves to be, if we take into consideration their aspect on eternity. The transgressors of God's law account themselves happy in having cast off his yoke, and freed themselves from the restraints which his law would impose upon them. But the truth is, that he is under a most desperate delusion, and grievously deceives his own soul. " A good understanding," regulating the conduct agreeably to God's commands, "will ensure to a man favour" and comfort, both in this world and the next :" "but the way of transgressors is hard." Their whole life is a state,

I. Of bondage—

[Whatever be the besetting sin of the ungodly, it has within them the force of a law, to which alas! they yield a willing obedience[a]." As the ten tribes "ran willingly after the commandment" of Jeroboam to the commission of idolatry, to which they had an inward and almost invincible propensity[b]; so do the worldling, the sensualist, the drunkard, follow but too readily, the impulse of their own corrupt hearts. A spring will not more naturally rise, when the power which compressed it is removed, than their lusts will rise to demand their wonted gratification, when an opportunity for indulgence is afforded them. The poor infatuated agents will call this liberty[c]; but the whole Scriptures designate it bondage : " Know ye not, that to whom ye yield yourselves servants to obey, his servants ye are to whom ye obey[d]?" Yes, in yielding to temptation we are " the servants of sin[e];" and the servants of Satan also: for " he it is who worketh in all the children of disobedience[f]," and leads them captive at his will[g]." In fact, the whole Gospel takes this for granted: for Christ was sent on purpose to redeem us from this bondage[h], and to " make us free indeed[i]." But, whilst thus enslaved, are we not in a most pitiable condition? True, we may not be sensible of the bondage, because the service of sin and Satan is in accordance with our own corrupt inclinations: but we are, in fact, the more to be pitied, because of our insensibility: even as a maniac is, whose whole life is occupied in things which tend to the destruction of his own welfare. The transgressor's life is also a state,]

II. Of disquietude—

[The ungodly man, whatever be his pursuit, finds nothing in which his soul can rest. Possess what he may, "in the midst of his sufficiency he is in straits[k]." There is always a secret something unpossessed; some object which he thinks would make him happy, but which, even when in appearance almost attained, eludes his grasp : and after he has " hewn out to himself a cistern with great labour, he finds it only a broken cistern, that can hold no water[l]." His continual disappointments fill him with vexation ; so that he finds even the objects of his fondest hope prove, in the issue, to be " vanity and vexation of spirit." Not being devoted to his God, he wants

[a] Rom. vii. 21.   [b] Hos. v. 11.   [c] 2 Pet. ii. 19.
[d] Rom. vi. 16.   [e] Rom. vi. 17.   [f] Eph. ii. 2.
[g] 2 Tim. ii. 26.   [h] Luke iv. 18.   [i] John viii. 36
[k] Job xx. 22.   [l] Jer. ii. 13.

those enjoyments and those prospects which alone can afford
consolation to him under his trials ———To his other pains
are added those of a self-condemning conscience. He tries
indeed to stifle the voice of conscience; and betakes himself to
business, and pleasures, and company, in order to get rid of its
remonstrances: but there are times when it will speak, especially a time of sickness and approaching dissolution; and at
those seasons he feels regret that he has so long and so entirely
disregarded his eternal interests. Gladly at such a season
would he consent to have his miserable life protracted to an
indefinite period, yea, or to suffer annihilation; not because he
could contemplate either the one or the other with pleasure,
but because he dreads the judgment for which he has neglected
to prepare.

Say, Brethren, whether such a way be not hard and painful? Yet I appeal to the conscience of every man, whether
that declaration be not verified in his own experience; "The
wicked are like the troubled sea, when it cannot rest, whose
waters cast up mire and dirt. There is no peace, saith my God,
to the wicked[m]." Yes, verily, this testimony is incontrovertible;
and it proves beyond all doubt the truth in my text, that "the
way of transgressors is hard."

But all this is heightened by the consideration of the transgressors' way as a state,]

III. Of danger—

[In some respect it may be said of every man, that he is
exposed to danger, and that "we know not what a day or an
hour may bring forth." But, if we be servants of Christ, we
have nothing to fear; since He is pledged to preserve us from
every thing that shall be really evil, and to make "all things
work together for our good[n]." Even death itself is a blessing
to the pious man, who is privileged to count it amongst his
richest treasures[o]. Far different from this, however, is the
state of the ungodly man: he knows not but that the next
moment may precipitate him into the bottomless abyss of hell.
Death waits but for its commission from on high, and it will
in an instant transmit his soul to the bar of judgment, and to
the presence of his offended God. What a fearful thought!
With what terror would it inspire the unconverted man, if it
were contemplated aright! Could we but conceive a transgressor hurried to the tribunal of his Judge, to give up his
great account, and to receive his final doom, what a view should
we have of the folly of his ways! Oh! the anguish to which
he is now subjected under the wrath of an avenging God?

---

[m] Isai. lvii. 20, 21.   [n] Rom. viii. 28.   [o] 1 Cor. iii. 22.

what "weeping" under the load of his misery! what "wailing" on account of his folly, in having so wasted his day of grace! and what "gnashing of teeth," with unprofitable execrations against his avenging God! Such is the danger to which the unconverted man is every moment exposed. At his most joyous feasts, this sword is suspended over him by a single hair; which cut or rent asunder, he is instantly consigned to endless woe. Whether the transgressor think of it or not, this is his state; and a miserable state it is: and if he awake not out of it before death shall seize him, it were better for him that he had never been born.]

IMPROVEMENT—

1. How desirable is the conversion of the soul to God!

[Compare the state of a converted soul with that which has been before described. The saint, doubtless, has his trials, as well as the ungodly man: but in him, so far as it prevails, religion makes a most essential difference: "it frees him from the law of sin and death [p];" and he finds all its ways to be the ways of pleasantness and peace [q]." If men consulted only their happiness in this life, they would devote themselves to God, whose service is perfect freedom: but if they take eternity into the account, they will confess him to be the only happy man, who enjoys the Divine favour and looks forward with confidence to a participation of the Divine glory.]

2. How infatuated are they who delay to seek it!

[Truly, if men were conscious of their danger in an unconverted state, they could no more sleep than they could in a ship that was on fire, or on a rafter on which they were making their escape to land. I pray you, beloved, consider the shortness and uncertainty of time! Consider how every day's continuance in sin operates to grieve the Holy Spirit of God, to harden your own hearts, to confirm your evil habits, to accumulate your load of guilt, and to augment the misery that awaits you. O! will you delay to turn unto your God? Will you delay one single hour? What if your soul be required of you this very night, and your doom be fixed without a hope or possibility of change for ever? I beseech you, to-day, while it is called to-day, harden not your hearts; but "repent, and turn yourselves from all your transgressions; so iniquity shall not be your ruin."]

[p] Rom. viii. 2. [q] Prov. iii. 17.

OUTLINE NO. 782

THE FOLLY OF MAKING A MOCK AT SIN.

Prov. xiv. 9.   *Fools make a mock at sin.*

MAN in his first creation was formed after the
Divine image ; and there was not in his soul the least
inclination to evil of any kind.   But since his fall, he
is become in love with sin : sin is the very element
in which he lives : and so unconscious is he of its
malignity, that he makes a mock at it.   Doubtless all
do not carry their impiety to the same extent.   Some
are openly profane, and given up to all manner of
wickedness; not only not being ashamed of their
ways, but actually " glorying in their shame."

We must not however restrict to persons of this
description the declaration in our text.   The evil
that is there complained of is of far wider extent, it
more or less attaches to every unconverted man.
This will appear, whilst we open to you,

I. The conduct here reprobated—

Let us remember what sin is : " it is the transgression of the law[a]."   Whichever table of the law
be broken, or whatever command be violated, the
violation of it is sin : and to make light of that transgression, whether it be more or less heinous in itself,
is to make a mock at sin.   Bearing this in mind, we
say, that this evil is committed,

1. By those who live in sin themselves—

[Passing over the drunkard, who says to his companions,
" We will fill ourselves with strong drink ; and to-morrow
shall be as this day and much more abundant[b];" and the rob-
ber, who invites his fellows, " Come, let us lay wait for blood,
that we may fill our houses with spoil[c];" and the unhappy
prostitute, who " impudently" assaults with importunity the
unwary youth[d]; or a variety of other characters alike notorious and abandoned ;—passing by these, I say, (whom to have
named is quite sufficient,) let us look to the worldling, who,
though walking in a more sober way, lives altogether for himself; or look to the self-righteous, who though admired and

---

[a] 1 John iii. 4.   [b] Isai. lvi. 12.
[c] Prov. i. 11, 13.   [d] Prov. vii. 6—18.

applauded as characters of superior excellence, have no true
humiliation before God, no earnest desires after a Saviour, no
real delight in holy exercises, no fixedness of mind to glorify
their God. What shall I say of them all? Have they any
just views of sin? Have they any suitable apprehensions of the
state to which they have been brought by means of sin? Do
not their whole spirit and temper shew, that they think light
of it? and, if it were set before them in all its malignity and
ill desert, would they not say, that the representation was
exaggerated, and that the person who gave them the representation was deceived? They need not utter any words, to
betray the thoughts of their hearts: these are sufficiently evident by the absence of all those feelings which a just estimate
of sin would create: and exactly as those who imagine that
God will never punish sin, are said to " contemn God[e]," so
may those, who think that sin will not involve us in misery, be
justly said to contemn sin, and, in heart at least, if not in act,
to " make a mock at it."]

2. By those who discountenance piety in others—

[Though a form of godliness will gain us applause, no man
begins to experience the power of it without exposing himself
to the censure of an ungodly world. Let a person be really
broken-hearted and contrite, as every sinner ought to be; let
him be seeking the Lord Jesus Christ with his whole heart;
let him turn his back upon the vanities of the world, and separate himself from the society of those who would ensnare his soul;
let him give himself to reading the holy Scriptures, to devout
meditation, to fervent prayer, to a diligent use of all the appointed ordinances of religion; let him join himself to the Lord's
people, and choose the excellent of the earth for his companions; let him, in a word, be in earnest in fleeing from the
wrath to come, and in laying hold on eternal life; let him do
this, and his nearest friends will instantly dissuade him from
such a course: they will represent to him the inexpediency of
such extravagant measures; they will complain of him as enthusiastic and righteous over-much. They will impute the
change that has taken place in him to weakness, or vanity, or
perhaps to hypocrisy and a desire of human estimation. Now
then I ask, whence would such a disapprobation of his ways
arise? Are they not such ways as are marked out by God?
Are they not the very footsteps of the flock who have gone
before him? Is not this course precisely such as common sense
would dictate, and such as all mankind would approve, if the
bodily life were in danger? Who would complain of earnestness in a shipwrecked mariner? Who would deride the cries
and fears and efforts of a person endeavouring to escape from

[e] Ps. x. 13.

a house on fire? Yet in matters relating to the soul and to
eternity, no sooner is the importance of salvation felt, and manifested, as it ought to be, than all who have any influence
endeavour to quiet the fears, and to discourage the exertions,
of the awakened soul. Could this be, if sin were viewed by
them as God views it? No: the persons who thus discountenance fervent piety, declare, that they see no occasion for it;
that we may very well be saved without it; and that sin has no
such terrors but that a moderate degree of attention will not
suffice to escape from its threatened dangers. What is this,
but to "make a mock at sin?"]

That such conduct may appear in its true light, I
proceed to shew,

II. The folly of it—

However much we make a mock at sin,

1. We cannot alter the nature of it—

[Sin is "that abominable thing which God hates[f]:" he
cannot look upon it, or on those who commit it, without the
utmost abhorrence[g]. It is, whether we will believe it or not,
"exceeding sinful[h]." Now we are told by the prophet, that
many will "call evil good, and good evil; and will put darkness for light, and light for darkness; bitter for sweet, and
sweet for bitter[i]." But if the whole universe should do this,
would they alter the essential qualities of these things? Would
darkness cease to be darkness, and serve all the purposes of
light? or would bitter change its properties to sweetness? So,
whatever construction men may put upon sin, and however they
may palliate its enormity, it will ever remain immutably the
same; a defiling, debasing, damning evil; more to be dreaded
than death itself. We may call it innocent; but it will "bite
like a serpent, and sting like an adder[k]." We may roll it as a
sweet morsel "under our tongue; but it will be the gall of asps
within us[l]."]

2. We cannot avert its consequences—

[God has said, "The wicked shall be turned into hell,
and all the nations that forget God[m]." Now we may say to
sinners, as the serpent did to Eve, "Ye shall not surely die[n]:"
but we can never separate the penalty from the offence. We
may represent the transgression, whatever it may be, as small;
and may expatiate upon the goodness of God, and the impos-
sibility of his visiting such an offence with such a tremendous
punishment: but we shall not prevail on him to rescind his

f Jer. iv. 44.   g Hab. i. 13.   h Rom. vii. 13.
i Isai. v. 20.   k Prov. xxiii. 32.   l Job xx. 12—14.
m Ps. ix. 17.   n Gen. iii. 4.

decree, or to reverse his sentence. He has said, " The soul that sinneth, it shall die[o]:" and die it shall, even " the second death, in the lake that burneth with fire and brimstone:" nor if the whole universe should combine their efforts to avert the sentence, should they ever prevail in any single instance[p]. " The wrath of God is revealed against all ungodliness and unrighteousness of men[q]:" and sooner shall heaven and earth pass away, than one impenitent transgressor escape. How great then must be the folly of making a mock at sin! If we could prevail on God to accord with our views, and to concede that sin should pass unpunished, we might have some plea for our conduct: but if the effect of our representations be only to deceive our own souls, and to rivet the chains with which sin and Satan have already bound us, we must confess that Solomon's views of such conduct are just, and that they are " fools" who " make a mock at sin."]

To all of you then I would, in CONCLUSION, say,

1. Make not light of sin yourselves—

[Your souls, your immortal souls, are at stake. Were the consequences of your error only temporary, we might leave you to enjoy your own delusions: but they are eternal. There is no repentance in the grave. " As the tree falls, so it will lie." If you die under the guilt of sin, your doom is irreversible, your misery everlasting. How do millions that are now in the eternal world curse their folly for making light of sin, in direct opposition to all that God had spoken in his word respecting it! and in what accents would they speak, if they could now have access to you to warn you! I pray you then be wise in time; and seek without delay to obtain " the forgiveness of your sins through the redemption that is in Christ Jesus[r]" — — —]

2. Regard not the scoffs of those who do—

[Suppose it desirable to possess the good opinion of the world: yet surely to purchase it at the expense of your immortal soul is to pay too high a price for it: it is but for a moment at all events: and though it is valuable so far as it may give you an influence over them for their good, yet it cannot for one moment be put in competition with the testimony of a good conscience, and the approbation of your God. You are taught to expect, that if you will not countenance the world in their ways, they will do all they can to discountenance you in yours. You see that this has been the case from the beginning: from the time of Abel to this hour, " they who have been born after the flesh have persecuted those who

---

are born of the Spirit[s] :" and not even the Lord Jesus Christ himself could escape their reproaches. " If then they called the Master of the house Beelzebub," wonder not if his servants also be designated by reproachful names[t]. If these things come upon you for righteousness sake, receive them as a token for good[u], and bless God that you are " counted worthy to endure them[x]." God permits these things as trials of your faith and love ; and if they at any time appear grievous to you, then think of the plaudit of your Judge, and how speedily the very people who now condemn you will themselves " awake to shame and everlasting contempt[y]," and will be among the foremost to proclaim your praise[z]. " Be faithful unto death ; and God will give you a crown of life."]

3. Endeavour so to walk, that those who mock at sin may have no occasion given them to mock at righteousness also—

[Whilst you in departing from evil " condemn the world[a]," you may be well assured that they will be glad enough to find occasion against you, and to condemn religion on your account. Endeavour then to " walk wisely before God in a perfect way[b]." Let the world " have no fault to find in you, except concerning the law of your God[c]." Let not your regard for the duties of the first table lead you to neglect those of the second ; but be careful to fulfil the duty of your place and station towards man, as well as that which consists in the more immediate service of your God : and be careful to avoid all needless singularities, which in the sight of God make you neither better nor worse. As for preventing the world from taking offence, that is impossible. Darkness must of necessity " hate the light :" but take care that the light be that which proceeds from God, and not from any " sparks of your own kindling." " Walk in wisdom towards them that are without[d] :" " give them no occasion to speak reproachfully[e] :" but so cause " your light to shine before them, that they may be led to glorify your heavenly Father." Thus, though you should not " win them by your good conversation," you may at least hope " to put to silence the ignorance of foolish men[f] ;" and constrain them, in spite of all their mocking, to confess, that " the righteous is more excellent than his neighbour[g]."]

[s] Gal iv. 29.   [t] Matt. x. 25.
[u] Luke xxi. 13. " *Unto* you : not *against* you."
[x] Acts v. 41.   [y] Dan. xii. 2.   [z] Wisd. v. 1—6.
[a] Heb. xi. 7.   [b] Ps. ci. 2.   [c] Dan. vi. 5.
[d] Col. iv. 5.   [e] 1 Tim. v. 14.   [f] 1 Pet. ii. 15.
[g] Prov. xii. 26.

OUTLINE NO. 783

MAN'S EXPERIENCE KNOWN TO HIMSELF ALONE.

Prov. xiv. 10. *The heart knoweth his own bitterness; and a stranger doth not intermeddle with his joy.*

THE inward experience of men, any further than it is discovered by acts or other outward signs, must of necessity be known to themselves alone. St. Paul puts the question to us, " Who knoweth the things of a man, save the spirit of man which is in him[a]?" Whether a man be filled with sorrow or joy, he alone can be sensible of the measure and extent of his own feelings.

The assertions in my text will be found true,

I. In reference to the concerns of this world—

[Great are the troubles of many, as arising from their own unhappy tempers — — — from their connexions in life — — — or from circumstances of embarrassment in their affairs — — — And who but themselves can fully appreciate their sorrows ? — — — On the other hand, the comforts of many are considerable, as flowing from the exercise of benevolence and love — — — from the endearments of domestic life — — — and from that success in their affairs which enables them to supply with ease the wants of themselves and families — — — And of the satisfaction which they feel, a stranger would form a very inadequate conception — — —]

II. In reference to the concerns of the soul—

[In matters relating to the soul, the feelings are still more acute. None but the person feeling it can tell " the bitterness" which is occasioned by a sense of sin, with all its aggravations — — — by the prospect of death and judgment, whilst the soul is unprepared to meet its God — — — and by temptations to despondency, and perhaps to suicide itself — — — Job's friends could not at all appreciate his sorrows, as depicted by himself[b] — — — Nor can any, but the man whose " heart is thus broken," conceive fully what " a broken and contrite spirit is" — — —

On the other hand, there are in the heart of a true Christian " joys, with which a stranger intermeddleth not." The peace that is experienced by him, when God speaks peace to his soul " passeth all understanding[c]" — — — And " the joys" with which he is transported, in the views of his Redeemer's glory, in

a 1 Cor. ii. 11.   b Job vi. 2—4.   c Phil. iv. 7.

the experience of God's love shed abroad in his heart, and in the earnest and foretaste of his eternal inheritance, " are unspeakable and glorified[d]" — — — These joys are, " the white stone, with a new name written on it, which no man can read, saving he who has received it[e]" — — — Michal could not understand the exercises of David's mind[f] — — — Nor can any one fully estimate the blessedness of a soul, when thus admitted to close communion with its God — — —]

LEARN from hence—

[Contentment—(the very persons whom you envy, are perhaps even envying you — — —) charity—(we can see the outward act only, and can little tell what passes in the hearts of men, whether in a way of humiliation or desire — — —) and earnestness in the ways of God;—that you may attain the deepest measures of contrition, with the sublimest experience of joy. The lower we lay our foundation, the higher we may hope our superstructure shall be raised — — —]

[d] 1 Pet. i. 8. See also Rom. viii. 15, 16. and Eph. i. 13, 14. and iii. 18, 19.   [e] Rev. ii. 17.   [f] 2 Sam. vi. 16, 20—22.

OUTLINE NO. 784

MISCONCEPTIONS ABOUT THE WAY OF SALVATION.

Prov. xiv. 12. *There is a way which seemeth right unto a man, but the end thereof are the ways of death*[a].

ON no topic do men express a greater confidence than on the subject of religion; whilst that, of all subjects that can be offered to our consideration, requires most care in our inquiry, and most diffidence in our decision. All other subjects, as far as they can be determined at all, may be determined by reason; and in the investigation of them, reason is to a certain degree free, both in its deliberations and decisions. But spiritual things must be spiritually discerned: they are out of the reach of reason. Reason must judge whether the things which are presented to it are revealed: but, when that point is ascertained, they must be apprehended by faith alone. Reason can tell us nothing about the mystery of redemption: it is faith alone that can apprehend that,

[a] This was written a great many years after that on Prov. xvi. 25. without any consciousness that the subject had been treated by the author before: and, though it goes over some of the same ground, yet as it contains much new matter, he has here inserted it.

or any of the other mysteries connected with it. Moreover, whilst reason can do so little in favour of religion, all the prejudices, and passions, and interests of mankind are acting in full force against it. Faith and sense are always at variance with each other, and always striving for the mastery; and unless faith be in lively exercise, sense is sure to triumph. Hence the Church of God is inundated with errors of various kinds: and hence we need to have frequently inculcated upon our minds the truth contained in our text, " There is a way which seemeth right unto a man, but the end thereof are the ways of death."

In illustration of this truth, I will point out some of those ways, which, though right in the estimation of those who walk in them, will assuredly terminate in death. No other issue will there be to the way,

I. Of sceptical indifference—

[There is a great degree of scepticism prevailing, in reference both to the divine authority of the Holy Scriptures, and to all the principal doctrines contained in them: and men of considerable ability have laboured much to invalidate the former, and to explain away the latter. Hence many will say, ' How can I ascertain what is true, amidst such a conflict of opinions?' or, 'How can I depend on any thing, of which so many great and learned men have doubted? Is it reasonable to suppose that God will call us to an account for not admitting what has been so often controverted, and, in the opinion of some, so successfully refuted? Let us rather hope that God, as a God of mercy, will accept us all, though we do not all walk in that precise way, which those who profess a greater reverence for the Scriptures conceive to be right.'

But these hopes will be found fallacious at the last: for there is far more criminality in unbelief, than men in general are aware of. It does not proceed from any want of evidence in the Scriptures, but from an evil bias in the heart of man. There is " an evil heart of unbelief," which causes us to depart from the living God. Men will not submit to God, but will exalt themselves against him; and think themselves justified in rejecting whatever they, with the short line of their reason, are unable to fathom. What would a philosopher think of a peasant who should argue thus in reference to sciences which he was unable to comprehend? and in what light must God view us, when we presume to sit in judgment thus on the plainest declarations of his word?

But supposing that there were not so much criminality in unbelief, should we be at all the more justified in neglecting our eternal interests? Does not reason itself teach us, that we are amenable to God for our conduct; and that, whether our views of revelation be more or less clear, we should labour incessantly and with all our might to secure his favour? and should we not use all possible means, particularly such as he himself has prescribed, for the attaining of an insight into his revealed will?

However innocent we may imagine our scepticism to be, or however justifiable the indifference connected with it, this way will at last infallibly end in death. The Jews in the wilderness could not enter into the promised land because of their unbelief: and the same cause will operate also to the exclusion of our souls from heaven[b]. The people who denied the Messiahship of Jesus doubtless thought that they were justified in so doing by a want of evidence: but our Lord said to them, "If ye believe not that I am He, ye shall die in your sins[c]:" and in like manner he has commanded it to be proclaimed to every child of man, "He that believeth and is baptized, shall be saved; but he that believeth not, shall be damned[d]."]

II. Of proud formality—

[Multitudes there are, who, like the Pharisees of old, are extremely attentive to the established forms of religion, and are observant of morality also, as far as it is approved by the world. In relation to these things they may be said to be blameless: and so good is the opinion which they entertain of their own state, that they would, without any fear of being confounded, ask, "What lack I yet?" In this state they are approved and admired of men; and therefore they conclude, that they are equally acceptable in the sight of God also. Persons of this description scarcely ever entertain a doubt, or a fear, but that all will issue well with them at the last. But they will find themselves awfully mistaken as soon as ever they go hence. They will then discover, that their obedience was infinitely more defective than ever they conceived it to be: and that, if it had been as blameless as they imagined, it would still have afforded them no ground of hope before God. Had such attainments as these sufficed, St. Paul needed never to have embraced the Gospel at all: or had they been capable of adding any thing to the righteousness of Christ, he never would have desired to be found in Christ, not having his own righteousness which was of the law? How erroneous a way to life this is, will be seen at once in the parable of the Pharisee and the Publican. Few of the formalists of the present day can

[b] Heb. iii. 19. and iv. 1, 11.   [c] John viii. 24.   [d] Mark xvi. 16.

say so much in their own favour as he could : he could appeal
to God that he was not guilty of such sins as were common in
the world, and that, on the contrary, he was observant of many
religious duties, "fasting twice every week, and giving tithes
of all that he possessed." Yet, because he viewed his state
with self-confidence and self-complacency, he was dismissed
without any blessing; whilst the self-abasing Publican was par-
doned and justified from all his sins [e]. But thus it ever will
be : " God will fill the hungry with good things, but the rich
he will send empty away [f]: " he will resist the proud, but give
grace unto the humble [g]."]

III. Of intolerant bigotry—

[There are not wanting those who imagine that all religion
consists in zeal for their own particular sect or party in the
Church. Amongst the papists, this error prevails to an awful
extent: and happy would it be if it were confined to them ;
but it is found in protestants also, who are as bitter in pro-
scribing each other, as the papists are in anathematizing them.
At what a fearful distance are the churchmen and dissenters
separated from each other, from the mere circumstance of their
not adopting the same external form of Church government,
even whilst they are perfectly agreed in sentiment as to all the
fundamental doctrines of Christianity ! From the spirit with
which they view each other, one would be ready to think that
Christ did indeed come to introduce division, not accidentally,
but intentionally ; not by a separation of his people from the
world, but by an alienation of heart from each other. Who
has not seen and mourned over the mutual accusations of the
two parties, each rejoicing in any evil that can be found in the
other, and each wishing the conversion, perhaps I should rather
say, the extermination, of the other ? And as men hate each
other on account of outward forms, so no less are they embittered against each other by a difference in their internal
principles ; the Arminian hating Calvinists ; and the Calvinist
despising Arminians ! Need I say how much some persons
value themselves on the opposition they give to what they call
enthusiasm, but what, in fact, is " pure and undefiled religion?"
Verily, in persecuting the truth, they think that they do God
service : and well pleased they are to render him a service so
congenial with the malignity of their own hearts. St. Paul
before his conversion was of this very spirit : and our Lord has
told us, that in every age such would prove the persecutors and
tormentors of his Church [h]. But whoever may be wrong, it is
not possible for persons of this description to be right: the
very spirit which they breathe shews "whose they are, and

[e] Luke xviii. 11—14.   [f] Luke i. 53.
[g] 1 Pet. v. 5.   [h] John xvi. 2.

whom they serve," even him "who was a murderer from the beginning[i]," and who has been the great instigator of persecution from the time of Cain even to the present hour. Let such persons only see St. Paul's review of his own conduct in relation to this matter, and he cannot doubt one moment whither this path must lead[k]. Or if this convince him not, let him know, that if he possessed all the knowledge and faith and zeal of angels themselves, he would be only as "sounding brass, or a tinkling cymbal," because he is destitute of that prime grace which is essential to the very existence of true religion in the soul, the grace of love[l].]

IV. Of lukewarm attachment to the Gospel—

[Where the Gospel is preached with fidelity, it commends itself to many as true, whilst they yet experience not its saving power on their souls. Yet the very circumstance of their discerning and approving of it is to them in the place of vital godliness, and an evidence that they are in the way to heaven. But religion is not a mere matter of opinion: it is a principle that pervades the soul, and operates upon all its faculties and powers. See how it wrought in the converts on the day of Pentecost; what new creatures they immediately became! And such will all become, as soon as ever they receive the grace of God in truth. The metaphors by which the Christian life is designated in the Scriptures, sufficiently shew how mistaken *they* are who rest in a mere approbation of the Gospel without feeling its constraining influence upon their souls: if the running of a race, or wrestling for the mastery, or fighting for one's life, have any just signification as applied to the Christian's state, it is impossible for those to be in the way of life who bear no resemblance whatever to persons so engaged: and the total want of anxiety and of exertion which they betray, proves, beyond all doubt, that they are not in the narrow way which leadeth unto life, but in the broad road that leadeth to destruction.]

V. Of unsanctified profession—

[Amongst the little company of the Apostles themselves, there was a Judas: and in all the Apostolic Churches also there were some who "professed that they knew God, but in works denied him." It must not be wondered at therefore if such exist in the Church at this present day. Indeed the parable of the Sower, and that also of the Tares, teaches us to expect, than Satan will sow tares amongst the wheat, and that it is not possible for man to separate them the one from the other. Unhappily, the persons themselves who are unsound at heart

i John viii. 39—44.   1 John iii. 11, 12, 15.
k 1 Tim. i. 13.   l 1 Cor. xiii. 1—3.

are not conscious of it. Satan so blinds their eyes, that they cannot distinguish between the unallowed infirmities of their nature, and the indulged corruptions of their hearts. Their evil tempers which are unsubdued, are regarded as light and venial frailties: their carefulness about the things of this world is softened down to necessary prudence: and the reigning impurity of their hearts is cloked under the veil of temptation. Whatever be their besetting sins, they find some excuse for them; and, because they have a zeal for the Gospel and make some sacrifices for it, they conclude that all is well with them. Having "a name to live," they have no conception that they can be really "dead." But such persons need to be reminded of what our blessed Lord has so plainly and forcibly declared, namely, that one single lust retained in the soul, though dear as a right eye or necessary as a right hand, will infallibly plunge the soul into that lake of fire that never shall be quenched[m]. Our blessed Lord has warned us, that the "saying, Lord! Lord!" however confidently we may repeat it, will never avail us, whilst we do not the things which he says: and, that though we may have "cast out devils in his name," we shall find no acceptance with him in the day of judgment, if we have not really, and unreservedly, mortified the whole body of sin[n]. Let all professors of religion know assuredly, that "without holiness, real and universal holiness, no man shall see the Lord[o];" and that, whatever estimate they may form of their own state, "not he who commendeth himself shall be approved, but he whom the Lord commendeth[p]."]

Seeing then that so many mistake the way to heaven, I will ADD a few words,

1. To guard you against all erroneous ways—

[There is one great evil which more or less pervades all descriptions of men, and that is, an undue confidence in their own opinions. If they "think a thing to be right," they conclude that it is right, and will take no pains to ascertain the truth or falsehood of their judgment. They think not of the deceitfulness of sin, or of the blindness of their own hearts, or of the subtlety of Satan; but go on confidently, as if they were in no danger of self-deceit. But why has God so often repeated that admonition, "Be not deceived," if we are not in danger of being carried away by our own delusions? We are told of many whom a deceived heart hath turned aside, so that they cannot deliver their souls, or say, Is there not a lie in my right hand?" And why should not this be our state, as well as the state of others? We actually *see* it in others: why then should we not

[m] Mark xi. 43—48.   [n] Matt. vii. 21—23. Luke xiii. 26, 27
[o] Heb. xii. 14.   [p] 2 Cor. x. 18.

suspect it in ourselves? It is certain that a man may "seem to be religious, and yet deceive his own soul, and have all his religion vain," because of some *one* sin that is unsubdued, and unperceived within him[q]? I can never therefore too earnestly impress upon your minds the necessity of diffidence in all that relates to your souls. There is but one standard of truth: and by that must every opinion be tried. If the way which you think right will stand the trial of God's word, it is well: but, if it accord not with that, it will prove delusive in the end, and issue in the everlasting destruction of your souls. Be it ever so specious, it cannot deceive God. To all then I would say, Act in reference to your souls as the mariner does in navigating a dangerous sea: he consults his chart and his compass continually; and, not contented with *thinking* himself right, he puts his thoughts to the test, and seeks for evidence that he is right. Then may you hope to avoid the rocks and quicksands on which so many thousands perish; and to reach in safety the haven you desire.]

2. To point out the only true way—

[There is a way, which seemeth indeed wrong to the greater part of mankind, which, however, is surely right, and the end thereof are the ways of life. This is the way of faith in the Lord Jesus Christ; as Christ himself has told us; "I am the way, and the truth, and the life: no man cometh unto the Father but by me[r]." This indeed is not approved by the world at large: "to the Jews it is a stumbling-block, and to the Greeks foolishness[s]:" but it is "the good old way, wherein whosoever walks shall find rest unto his soul[t]." Let it not be any matter of astonishment that this way is not generally approved: for it is too humiliating for our proud hearts, and too self-denying for our low and grovelling spirits. Men do not love to renounce all self-dependence, and to have all their wisdom, all their righteousness, and all their strength treasured up in another for their use, to be received daily out of his fulness in answer to urgent and believing prayer. Nor do they like to have that high standard of holiness, which he gives to his disciples as the rule of their life, and the test of their attainments. But, beloved, this is the only true way to heaven: we must believe in Christ, and live altogether by faith in him, going forward in his strength, and "growing up into him in all things as our living head." Then, though regarded by men as self-deluding enthusiasts, we shall be approved of our God, and receive at last "the end of our faith, even the salvation of our souls."]

[q] Jam. i. 26.   [r] John xiv. 6.
[s] 1 Cor. i. 23.   [t] Jer. vi. 16. Matt. xi. 28, 29.

OUTLINE NO. 785

THE VANITY OF CARNAL MIRTH.

Prov. xiv. 13. *Even in laughter the heart is sorrowful; and the end of that mirth is heaviness.*

WE are apt to imagine, that whatever is sanctioned by the approbation and practice of the world at large, must be right: but we cannot have a more erroneous standard than popular opinion. This is sufficiently evident from the estimation in which mirth and laughter are generally held: they are supposed to constitute the chief happiness of man; whereas they are far from producing any solid happiness at all. To this mistake Solomon refers, in the words preceding the text; and in the text itself he confirms the truth of his own position.

We shall,

I. Demonstrate the vanity of carnal mirth—

We mean not to condemn all kinds and degrees of mirth: there certainly is a measure of it that is conducive to good, rather than to evil; "A merry heart maketh a cheerful countenance," and "doeth good like a medicine." But carnal mirth is distinct from cheerfulness of disposition; inasmuch as it argues a light frivolous state of mind, and indisposes us for serious and heavenly contemplations. Of *this* mirth we affirm, that it is,

1. Empty—

[Let us examine the mirth which we have at any time experienced; let us weigh it in a balance; let us compare it with that sobriety of mind which results from scenes of woe, and with that tenderness of spirit which is the offspring of sympathy and compassion; and we shall confess, with Solomon, that "it is better to go to the house of mourning than to the house of feasting[a]:" yea, the more we examine it, the more shall we be constrained, like him, to "say of laughter, It is mad; and of mirth, What doeth it[b]?" It may be justly called, "a filling of our belly with the east wind[c]."]

2. Fictitious—

[The gaiety which is exhibited in worldly company is often assumed, for the purpose of concealing the real feelings

a Eccl. vii. 1—3.   b Eccl. ii. 1, 2.   c Job xv. 2.

of the heart. They who appear so delighted to see each other, have frequently no mutual affection: even the nearest relatives, who seem to participate each other's joys, have so little real cordiality at home, that they can scarcely endure each other's conversation; and would be heartily glad, if the knot which binds them together could be dissolved. Truly " in their laughter their heart is sorrowful;" their pride, their envy, their jealousy, their private piques, their domestic troubles, or their worldly cares, make them inwardly sigh, so that they can with difficulty prevent the discovery of the imposture which they are practising. The very emptiness of their pleasure fills them often with disgust; and they are constrained to acknowledge, that " they are feeding on ashes, and that they have a lie in their right hand[d]."]

3. Transient—

[Suppose it to have been far more substantial than it has, yet how speedily has it vanished away! What trace of it remains? It is like a dream when one awaketh: in our dream we thought of satisfaction; but when we awoke, we found ourselves as unsatisfied as ever[e]. If we thought by repeated participation to protract the pleasure, we weakened the zest with which we had partaken of it; and thus diminished, rather than increased, the sum of our enjoyment.]

4. Delusive—

[We hoped that the ultimate effect of all our mirth would be an easy comfortable frame: but has it always been so? Has not the very reverse been often experienced by us? Has not " the end of our mirth been heaviness?" An excessive elevation of spirit is naturally calculated to produce depression. Besides, we cannot always shake off reflection: and the thought of having so foolishly wasted our time, instead of improving it in preparation for eternity, will sometimes produce very uneasy sensations. Such warnings as Solomon[f], and our Lord[g], have given us, will frequently obtrude themselves upon us, and make us almost weary of life, while at the same time we are afraid of death: so justly is this mirth compared to " the crackling of thorns under a pot[h];" the one, after an unprofitable blaze, terminating in smoke and darkness, the other, after a senseless noise, expiring in spleen and melancholy. In fact, there are no people more subject to lowness of spirits, than they who spend their time in vanity and dissipation.

What will be " the end of their mirth" when they come into the eternal world, is inexpressibly awful to consider. Fearful indeed will be the contrast between the festivities of their

[d] Isai. xliv. 20.　　[e] Isai. xxix. 8.　　[f] Eccl. xi. 9
[g] Luke vi. 25.　　[h] Eccl. vii. 6.

present, and the wailings of their eternal state[i]! Would to God that man would learn this from a parable[k]! but, if they will not, they must realize it in their own experience.]

That we may not appear as if we would deprive you of all happiness, we shall—

II. Shew how we may attain more solid mirth—

There is evidently a contrast intended in the text: for when it is said that " the end of *that* mirth is heaviness," it is implied, that there is another species of mirth that shall end in a very different manner.

The Gospel is a source of mirth to all who embrace it—

[The Gospel is called " glad tidings of great joy to all people." It proclaims salvation to a ruined world; nor can it fail of creating the liveliest emotions of joy wherever it is received[l]— — —]

And the mirth resulting from it, is the very reverse of carnal mirth—

[It is *solid*.—Behold the change wrought in the first converts! see them turned from darkness to light, and from the power of Satan unto God! see them enjoying peace with God and in their own consciences! see them filled with love to each other, and with admiring and adoring thoughts of their beloved Saviour! Can we wonder that they ate their bread with gladness and singleness of heart, blessing and praising God? Yet precisely the same grounds of joy has every one that truly believes in Christ[m]. The Prodigal *fancied* that he was in the road to joy, when he was wasting his substance in riotous living: but he never tasted real happiness till he returned to his father's house: then " he *began* to eat, and drink, and be merry."

It is *permanent*.—It will consist with trials and tribulations; yea, it will even arise out of them[n]; we may be " sorrowful, yet alway rejoicing[o]." And, as it is not interrupted by the occurrences of life, so neither will it be terminated by death: it will then be augmented a thousand-fold: and continue without interruption to all eternity — — —]

ADDRESS—

1. The young and gay—

[Follow your career of pleasure as long as you will, you will be constrained to say at last, with Solomon, not only that

---

[i] Amos vi. 1—6.   [k] Luke xvi. 19, 24, 25.
[l] Isai. li. 3, 11. and lxv. 18. and Jer. xxxi. 4. with Acts viii. 8, 39
[m] Jer. xxxi. 11—14.   [n] Rom. v. 3. Jam. i. 2.   [o] 2 Cor. vi. 10

it was all " vanity," but also " vexation of spirit." Yet think not, that in dissuading you from these lying vanities, we would deprive you of all happiness: we wish only that you should exchange that which is empty and delusive, for that which will afford you present and eternal satisfaction[p]. Even your past experience may suffice to shew you, that " in the fulness of your sufficiency you have been in straits[q]:" try now what the service and enjoyment of God can do for you; and you shall find that religion's " ways are indeed ways of pleasantness and peace."]

2. Those who profess godliness—

[In avoiding carnal mirth, you must be careful not to give occasion to the world to represent religion as sour and morose. There is a cheerfulness which recommends religion, and which it is both your duty and privilege to maintain. Yet, on the other hand, beware of levity. Live nigh to God, and you will easily find the proper medium. " God has certainly given you all things richly to enjoy[r]:" yet it is in himself alone, and in the light of his countenance, that you must seek your happiness. *There* you are sure to find it[s]; and while you find it in him, you will shine as lights in a dark world, and recommend the Gospel to all around you.]

[p] Isai. lv. 2.   [q] Job xx. 22.   [r] 1 Tim. vi. 17.   [s] Ps. iv. 6, 7.

OUTLINE NO. 786

THE DANGER OF BACKSLIDING.

Prov. xiv. 14. *The backslider in heart shall be filled with his own ways: and a good man shall be satisfied from himself.*

THOUGH God does not select those as objects of his mercy, who are most diligent in external duties, yet he increases his favours to those whom he has chosen, in proportion as they themselves are earnest in improving what he has already bestowed upon them. In the dispensations of his providence it is generally found, that " the diligent hand maketh rich :" but in the dispensations of his grace, this seems to be an unalterable rule of his procedure : " his ways with respect to these things are equal;" " whatsoever a man sows, that he may assuredly expect to reap ;" " to him that hath, shall be given, and he shall have abundance." To this effect are the declarations before us; in which we may observe,

I. The danger of backsliding—

Open apostasy is confessedly a certain road to destruction : but we may also perish by indulging the more specious and equally dangerous habit of secret declension. Not that every variation in our frame constitutes us backsliders in heart; (for who then could be saved ?) but,

We come under this description,

1. When we are habitually remiss in secret duties—

[It is possible we may once have run well, and enjoyed much blessedness in the service of our God; and yet have been so hindered in our course, as to have relapsed into a state of coldness and formality[a]. The word, which was once precious, may have lost its savour; and prayer, which was once delightful, may have become an irksome task. Both public and private ordinances may have degenerated into an empty form, in which God is not enjoyed, nor is any blessing received. Where this is the case the person must surely be denominated a " backslider in heart."]

2. When we habitually indulge any secret lusts—

[Whatever attainments a man may have made in religion, if his heart be not whole with God, he will sooner or later decline; and that which was his besetting sin in his state of ignorance, will regain its ascendency, and (as far at least as relates to its inward workings) recover its dominion over him. He may still, for his profession sake, restrain sin, in a measure, as to its outward exercise, while yet its inward power is unsubdued. Was he naturally addicted to pride, envy, malice, covetousness, lewdness, or any other sin? If he *allow* it to return upon him after he has been once purged from it[b], if he be averse to have the evil of it pointed out to him, if he justify it, or cover his fault with excuses, instead of endeavouring earnestly to amend it, he certainly is a backslider in heart—]

In either of these states we are exposed to the most imminent danger—

[There are a variety of ways in which God will punish sin, but none so terrible as that specified in the words before us. If God were to fill the backslider with acute and long-continued pain, or visit him with some other temporal affliction, it might work for good, and bring him to consideration and repentance: but if he give him up to his own heart's lusts, and leave him to be " filled with his own ways," nothing but a certain and

a Gal. i. 6. and v. 7. and iv. 15.
b 2 Pet. i. 9. and ii. 20. Gal. iv. 16.

aggravated condemnation can ensue. Was he far from God? he will be further still : was he addicted to any sin? he will be more and more enslaved by it : nor can there be a doubt, but that God *will* give us up to this judgment, if we "leave off to behave ourselves wisely," and return to the indulgence of wilful neglects and secret sins[c]— — —]

But we shall see a strong additional motive to persevere, if we consider,

II. The benefit of maintaining steadfastness in religion—

The " good man" is here put in contrast with the backslider—

[As every occasional declension does not denominate a man a wilful backslider, so neither does every transient inclination to virtue denominate a man good. To be truly good, he must set out well, and "hold on his way," causing his "light to shine more and more unto the perfect day[d]."]

Such an one shall find much satisfaction both *in* and *from* his way :

He shall have the comfort of seeing that he is advancing in religion—

[The testimony of a good conscience is one of the richest comforts we can enjoy[e]. Hezekiah pleaded it before God in a dying hour, not indeed as a ground of justification before him, but as a ground whereon he might hope for some favourable indulgence with respect to the continuance of this present life[f]. And Paul, in the near prospect of the eternal world, found it a source of unutterable joy[g]. Now this satisfaction every upright soul shall enjoy. If he cannot distinctly see the progressive steps of his advancement from day to day, he shall have a testimony in his own conscience that he is *on the whole* advancing : he shall feel himself more and more fixed in his " purpose to cleave unto the Lord," and increasingly desirous of approving himself faithful to his God and Saviour.]

He shall also enjoy more abundant manifestations of God's love—

[God will not leave his people without witness that he is pleased with their endeavours to serve and honour him. " He is a rewarder of them that diligently seek him." If he behold any persons striving to please him, " he will love them and come unto them, and sup with them, and manifest himself to

---

[c] Ps. lxxxi. 11, 12. Deut. xxxii. 15, 18, 19, 20. Prov. i. 30, 31.
[d] Prov. iv. 18.   [e] 2 Cor. i. 12.
[f] 2 Kings xx. 2, 3.   [g] 2 Tim. iv. 7, 8.

them as he does not unto the world[h]:" and the more diligent he sees them in doing his will, the more richly will he impart to them the tokens of his love, and the more abundantly communicate to them the blessings of grace and peace[i].]

His prospects, moreover, of the eternal world shall be more bright and glorious—

[To many does God vouchsafe, as to Moses from Mount Pisgah, delightful prospects of the heavenly Canaan. He draws aside the veil, and suffers them to enter into the holy of holies, that they may behold his glory, and receive a foretaste of the blessedness which they shall one day enjoy in his presence. But on whom are these special favours bestowed? on the slothful, the careless, the inconstant? No. It is "the faithful man that shall abound with these blessings;" it is "him that rejoiceth in working righteousness, that the Lord will meet" in this intimate and endearing manner[k].]

INFER—

1. How much more ready is God to shew mercy than to execute his judgments!

[Had God been extreme to mark what is done amiss, who is there amongst us, whom he would not often have abandoned in an hour of secret declension? But he is full of compassion; and "judgment is his strange work," to which he is greatly averse. At this very moment does he follow the backslider with the most earnest invitations, and most gracious promises, saying, "Return, ye backsliding children, and I will heal your backslidings, and love you freely[l]." Let us thankfully acknowledge his long-suffering and forbearance; and seek that happiness in the service of our God, which we shall in vain look for in any deviations from the path of duty.]

2. What need have we to watch over our own hearts!

[We are bidden to "keep our hearts with all diligence, because out of them are the issues of life and death[m]:" and indeed we have need to guard them well, because they are so "bent to backslide from God." It will be rarely, if ever, found, that the watchful Christian is left to fall into any gross sin. Men decline from God in secret, before he withdraws from them his restraining grace: they have chosen some evil "way of their own," and deliberately followed it in their hearts, before God leaves them to be "filled with it." If then we would not be swept away with a deluge of iniquity, let us be careful to

[h] John xiv. 21—23. Rev. iii. 20.   [i] Isai. xxxii. 17.
[k] Prov. xxviii. 20. Isai. xxxiii. 14—17. and lxiv. 5.
[l] Jer. iii. 22. Hos. xiv. 4.   [m] Prov. iv. 23.

stop the breach at first; for, if left a little time, it will widen,
till it defies our utmost exertions.   The present satisfaction,
as well as the future salvation, of our souls depends on a steadfast walk with God.   Let us then " hold fast the profession of
our faith, and the practice of our duty, without wavering :" and
" let us look to ourselves that we lose not the things which we
have wrought, but that we receive a full reward[n]."]

[n] 2 John, ver. 8.

<h2 style="text-align:center">OUTLINE NO. 787</h2>

THE FEAR OF THE LORD A SOURCE OF MUCH GOOD.

Prov. xiv. 26. *In the fear of the Lord is strong confidence; and
his children shall have a place of refuge.*

IN the Holy Scriptures there is often much contained in a small space.   Hence we read them frequently without discerning one half of their beauty
and importance — — — In the passage before us, we
have in a concentrated form the benefits arising from
the fear of God.   They are two:

I. Confidence—

Before we speak of the benefit itself, we must endeavour to attain accurate views of that from which
it flows.   By " the fear of the Lord," I understand
such a fear as brings us to his footstool; and such a
fear as stimulates us to an unreserved surrender of
ourselves to him.   It is clear that it must comprehend these, and cannot possibly exist without them[a]
— — — Now, wherever this is found, there is " a
strong confidence" of acceptance with God; a confidence founded,

1. On the general character of God—

[There is, in the mind of every one who has the least
knowledge of God, a persuasion that " he delights in mercy:"
and though this *of itself* is not sufficient to warrant a confidence
of our acceptance with him, it is *a strong confirmation of our
confidence*, when we have really come to him with a humble
believing, and obediential fear — — —]

2. On the Scripture account of him, as revealed to
us in Christ Jesus—

[a] Ps. cxii. 1.

[There we see his assumption of our nature, his death upon the cross as an atonement for our sins, his ascension to heaven, to govern all things for the good of his Church and people. O! what confidence must such wonders of love and mercy inspire! Can we turn to him in faith and fear, and doubt his willingness to receive us? Impossible. It cannot be but that our "confidence" in such a God must be "strong [b]" ————]

3. On the express promises which he has given us in his word—

[These are "exceeding great and precious," and fully commensurate with all our wants. There is no state in which we can be, that has not a promise especially adapted to it. Only let those be embraced, and the most desponding soul must be comforted [c] ————]

To them, under all circumstances, is afforded,
II. Safety—

They stand in the relation of "children" to God, who "is not ashamed to be called their God" and Father. And to them there is ever open "a place of refuge,"

1. From the calamities of life—

[True, the saints are exposed to calamities like other men; but they see that every thing, whoever be the instrument, proceeds in reality from their Father's hand, who sends it only for their good. Hence the very character of the visitation is changed; and instead of being an occasion for mourning, it is welcomed as a blessing in disguise [d] ————]

2. From the assaults of Satan—

[Doubtless Satan will exert himself to the uttermost to harass and destroy them [e]: but they are furnished with armour to withstand his fiercest assaults [f]; and they have an impregnable fortress ever open to them, even "the name of the Lord, which is to them as a strong tower, wherein they are safe [g]." And, after maintaining their conflict the appointed time, they are sure of beholding "him bruised under their feet [h]."]

3. From the fears of death—

[Death is still an enemy: but they triumph over him, saying, "O death, where is thy sting? O grave, where is thy victory?" They are enabled to number him amongst their friends and treasures [i]; and to long for his arrival, to introduce them into the more immediate presence of their God [k] ————]

[b] 2 Tim. i. 12.   [c] Heb. vi. 17, 18. 2 Cor. i. 20.
[d] Prov. xix. 23. Ps. xci. 9—12.   [e] 1 Pet. v. 8.
[f] Eph. vi. 12, 13.   [g] Prov. xviii. 10.
[h] Rom. xvi. 20.   [i] 1 Cor. iii. 23.   [k] Phil. i. 23.

4. From all the penal consequences of sin—

[At the very bar of judgment itself they stand with great boldness. The curses of the Law infuse no terror into their minds ; because they can point to " Him who has redeemed them from its curse, having himself become a curse for them[1]." " To them there is no condemnation[m] : " to them remains nothing but unbounded, everlasting bliss — — —]

ADDRESS—

1. Those who have confidence without fear—

[This is the state of the world at large — — — But such confidence is presumption[n] : it is " the broken and contrite soul, and that alone, which God will not despise ;" — — — To them, therefore, would I say, " Awake, and arise ; and Christ will give you light[o]."]

2. Those who have fear without confidence—

[Brethren, you should not so dishonour your Lord and Saviour. If only you have such a fear of God as humbles you before him, and makes you desire truly and unfeignedly to serve him, what reason have you to entertain any doubt of his willingness to save you ? Has God become a man for you, and died upon the cross for you ; and is he ordering every thing for you, both in heaven and earth ; and should you not trust in him ? Be ashamed of entertaining such unworthy thoughts of him, and cast yourselves altogether upon him both for time and for eternity — — —]

3. Those who have the happiness of uniting both—

[This is the state in which you should both live and die. It is the due mixture of fear and confidence which will bring you to that holy frame in which God most delights[p]. He would have you ever to " rejoice with trembling," and to tremble with rejoicing — — —]

[1] Gal. iii. 13.　　　　　　　　　[m] Rom. viii. 1.
[n] Deut. xxix. 19, 20. and 1 Thess. v. 3.　　[o] Eph. v. 14.
[p] Acts ix. 31. and Ps. cxv. 13.

OUTLINE NO. 788

THE OMNIPRESENCE OF GOD.

Prov. xv. 3. *The eyes of the Lord are in every place, beholding the evil and the good.*

THE omnipresence of the Deity is plain and obvious to all, who have learned to acknowledge the unity of God. The heathens indeed, who worshipped a multitude of gods, assigned to each his proper limits, conceiving that they who could exert their power in the hills, were destitute of power in the neighbouring valleys. But this absurd idea arose from their polytheism; and vanishes the very instant we confess the true God. The Scriptures place this matter beyond a doubt: every page of the inspired volume either expressly asserts the omnipresence of God, or takes it for granted as an unquestionable truth. In the words before us, Solomon not only affirms it, but declares, that God is actively employed throughout the whole universe in inspecting the ways of men.

In discoursing on his words we shall shew,

I. The truth of his assertion—

[One would suppose that reason itself might discern the point in question: for, if God be not every where present, how can he either govern, or judge, the world? His creatures, if removed from the sphere of his observation, would be independent of him; and, if withdrawn from his sight, would cease to feel any responsibility for their actions; since, being ignorant of what they did, he would be altogether unqualified to pass upon them any sentence of condemnation or acquittal.

But, to proceed on surer ground, let us notice *the declarations of holy men, and especially of God himself,* respecting this point.

If we look into the Old Testament, we shall find, that the testimony of all the prophets is in perfect correspondence with those words of David, " The Lord searcheth all hearts, and understandeth all the imaginations of the thoughts[a]." Sometimes they assert this matter as a thing *they know,* and are assured of; " I *know,*" says Job, " that no thought can be withholden from thee[b]." Sometimes, with yet greater energy, they make it *a subject of appeal* to the whole universe, defying any one to gainsay, or even to doubt, it; " Doth he not see my ways, and count all my steps[c]?" Sometimes they labour to convey this truth under the most impressive images; " His eyes behold, his *eye-lids try,* the children of men[d]."

In the New Testament, the same important truth is inculcated in terms equally clear and energetic. Not to mention mere assertions[e], or acknowledgments[f], that " God knoweth all things," the author of the Epistle to the Hebrews represents the perfect insight of the Deity into the hearts of men under the image of the sacrifices, which, when flayed and cut down the back-bone, were open to the minutest inspection of

---

[a] 1 Chron. xxviii. 9.   [b] Job xlii. 2.   [c] Job xxxi. 4.
[d] Ps. xi. 4.   [e] 1 John iii. 20.   [f] John xxi. 17.

the priests: " All things are naked and opened unto the eyes
of Him with whom we have to do[g]."

But let us now turn our attention to *God's own declarations*.
He is peculiarly jealous with respect to this attribute. In reference to " *places*" and " *persons*," he says, " Am I a God
at hand, and not a God afar off? Can any hide himself in
secret places that I shall not see him? saith the Lord: do not
I fill heaven and earth? saith the Lord[h]." Again, in reference to *things* that might be supposed most beyond his reach,
he says, " I know the things that come into your mind, every
one of them[i]." And when an atheistical world have entertained doubts respecting this, and said, " Thick clouds are a
covering to him[k];" " he cannot see, he will not regard us;"
he has risen with utter indignation to vindicate his injured
honour; " Understand ye brutish among the people; and, ye
fools, when will ye be wise? He that planted the ear, shall
he not hear? he that formed the eye, shall he not see[l]?"]

To multiply proofs of so plain a point is needless.
We shall therefore pass on to shew,
II. The concern we have in it—

[Here the text directs and limits our views. " The evil
and the good" are objects of his unwearied attention; and
consequently, both the one and the other are equally interested
in the subject before us.

Let " *the evil*" then consider their concern in this momentous
truth. God views them all, at all times, in all places, under
all circumstances. If they come up to worship in his *sanctuary*,
he sees their impious mockery, while " they draw nigh to him
with their lips, but are far from him in their hearts[m]." He
follows them to their *families*, and observes all their tempers,
dispositions, and conduct. He enters with them into their
shops: he inspects their weights and measures; he examines
their commodities; he hears their bargains: he marks their
deviations from truth and honesty[n]. He retires with them to
their *chambers*, and " compasseth about their beds," (for " the
darkness and light to him are both alike") and notices their
every thought[o]. If they were to go up to heaven, or down to
hell, they could not for one moment escape his all-seeing eye[p].

But *for what end* does he thus " behold" them? Is he a
mere curious or unconcerned spectator? no: " he pondereth
all their goings[q]," in order *to restrain* that excess of wickedness which would militate against his sovereign appointments[r];

g Heb. iv. 13. h Jer. xxiii. 23, 24.
i Ezek. xi. 5. Deut. xxxi. 21. k Job xxii. 13, 14.
l Ps. xciv. 7—9. m Matt. xv. 7, 8. n Mic. vi. 2, 10, 11, 12.
o Ps. cxxxix. 1—5. p Ps. cxxxix. 7—12.
q Prov. v. 21. r Gen. xx. 6. and xxxi. 24.

to confound their daring attempts against his church and people[s]; *to over-rule* for the accomplishment of his own purposes the voluntary exercise of their own inveterate corruptions[t]; and finally *to justify himself* in the eternal judgments, which he will hereafter inflict upon them[u].

O that the wicked would consider these things, and lay them to heart, while yet they might obtain mercy!

Next let "*the good*" consider their concern also in this truth. "God's eye is on them also; and his ear is open to their prayers[x]." He meets them in his house of prayer[y]: if there were but one broken-hearted sinner in the midst of a whole congregation, God would fix his eye in a more especial manner upon *him*[z]. When they go forth into the world, he follows them as closely as their shadow[a]. When they retire to their secret chamber, he "draws nigh to them[b]," and "manifests himself to them as he does not unto the world[c]."

And *wherefore is all this solicitude* about such unworthy creatures? *wherefore is all this attention* to their concerns? "Hear, O heavens; and be astonished, O earth." God has deigned to inform us on this subject, and to declare, that he "beholds the good," to *protect them in danger*[d]; to *comfort them in trouble*[e]; to *supply their wants*[f]; to *over-rule for good their multiplied afflictions*[g]; lastly, he notices them, to *observe the workings of his grace in them*[h], in order that he may *proclaim before the assembled universe* the secret exercises of piety in their hearts[i], and *give a lively demonstration* to all, that in exalting them to a participation of his glory, he acts agreeably to the immutable dictates *of justice and equity*[k].

Let the righteous then "set the Lord always before them[l]." Let them "walk *circumspectly*," that they may not grieve him[m]; and *actively*, that they may please him well in all things[n]: and, whatever difficulties they may have to contend with, let them proceed *boldly*, and "endure, as seeing him that is invisible[o]."]

---

[s] Exod. xiv. 24, 25. "*looked*," and Isai. xxxvii. 28, 29.

[t] Ps. ii. 1—6.   [u] Jer. xvii. 10. and xvi. 17, 18. and Ps. li. 4.

[x] Ps. xxxiv. 15.   [y] Isai. lxiv. 5. Matt. xviii. 20.

[z] Isai. lxvi. 2.   [a] Josh. i. 9. with Heb. xiii. 5, 6.

[b] Jam. iv. 8.   [c] John xiv. 22.

[d] 2 Chron. xvi. 9. Ps. cxxi. 5—7.   [e] Ps. xli. 1, 3.

[f] Ps. xxxiii. 18, 19. and xxxiv. 9, 10.

[g] Mal. iii. 3. "*as a refiner*." Job xxiii. 10. with John xv. 2.

[h] Hos. xiv. 8. Jer. xxxi. 18, 20.   [i] Matt. vi. 4, 6, 18.

[k] Rom. ii. 5—7. "*righteous* judgment."

[l] Ps. xvi. 8. See also Matt. xxv. 35, 36, 46.

[m] Exod. xxiii. 20, 21.   [n] Col. i. 10.

[o] Isai. xli. 10, 13, 14. Heb. xi. 27.

OUTLINE NO. 789

THE UPRIGHT ALONE ACCEPTABLE TO GOD.

Prov. xv. 8. *The sacrifice of the wicked is an abomination unto the Lord: but the prayer of the upright is his delight.*

THE language of Scripture is often extraordinarily emphatic. This not unfrequently arises from the strength of the metaphors that are used to express the mind of the writer: and frequently from his speaking of God in terms, which, in their strict sense, are applicable only to men. Of course, we are not to conceive of God as possessing either parts or passions; and when either the one or the other are ascribed to him, we must regard it only as a condescension to our weakness, which is incapable of comprehending any thing respecting God, except by a sort of comparison of him with man. Of all his natural perfections, such as immensity and eternity, we know nothing at all: that is to say, our knowledge is merely negative. And respecting his moral perfections, as justice, mercy, truth, we know as little, except as we transfer to him the notions which we have formed of such perfections as exist in the human mind. We associate very distinct ideas with those attributes as applied to man: and by the help of those terms we express what we conceive to regulate the actions of God in the moral government of the universe. In like manner, when we speak of any thing being " an abomination" or " a delight" to God, we mean only, that he will act in reference to that thing as we should towards any thing which excited such feelings in our minds. This is clearly understood by all. No man needs to be informed, that God is not susceptible of such feelings, or capable of those emotions which such feelings import: we therefore, in conformity with Scripture, shall proceed to speak of God in the same figurative language: and we pray God that your minds may be suitably impressed by it, whilst we consider,

I. The truths here asserted—

1. " The sacrifice of the wicked is an abomination to the Lord"—

[Where so strong an assertion is used in reference to any character, it is obvious, that we ought to understand, very clearly and distinctly, who they are that are designated by that character. For instance, suppose that under this general term, "the wicked," we were to comprehend those only who are grossly and openly immoral, we should release all others from any participation in the feelings which the assertion respecting them is intended to create. But this we cannot do: for Solomon himself has accurately defined the character which he is here speaking of; and after defining it, has annexed to that very definition the same declaration as occurs in my text: " *He that turneth away his ear from hearing the law,* even HIS prayer shall be abomination[a]." You will observe then, that the wicked is one who is inattentive to the commands of God in his word, and *averse to comply with the requisitions of his Law and of his Gospel*[b]— — —

Now such an one, even though he be guilty of no flagrant sins, is an abomination to the Lord. *The rebellious state of his mind* is most offensive to God: and therefore every thing that he does is hateful to him: " A high look, and a proud heart, and even the ploughing of *the wicked,* is sin[c]." No act can be more innocent than that of ploughing: but *the most innocent acts* of such a person participate in the guilt of his general state and habit of mind.

His most religious acts too are hateful to God: his very "sacrifices" are an abomination. In the first chapter of Isaiah's prophecies, the Jews are represented as bringing *the offerings appointed* by the Law, as bringing *the best* too, and *in great number*, and *at the seasons ordained* by God himself; and as accompanying those sacrifices with fervent prayer; and yet as being, at the same time, objects of God's utter abhorrence, because their conduct was altogether at variance with their professions[d]. In another chapter he speaks of them as " taking delight in approaching to God," and as abounding in the self-denying exercises of fasting and prayer ; and yet as altogether hateful in his sight[e]. The prophet Amos speaks strongly to the same effect[f]. To what an extent the services of such persons are abhorred, God himself has told us: " He that killeth an ox, is as if he slew a man : he that sacrificeth a

[a] Prov. xxviii. 9.
[b] This distinction should be more fully opened, in order that *all* may know how deeply they are interested in what follows.
[c] Prov. xxi. 4.   [d] Isai. i. 11—13.   [e] Isai. lviii. 2.
[f] Amos. v. 21—23. This and the two preceding quotations should be recited at full length, and with the emphasis due to them.

lamb, as if he cut off a dog's neck: he that offereth an obla-
tion, as if he offered swine's blood: he that burneth incense,
as if he blessed an idol." I pray you, Brethren, to mark these
expressions, and to apply them to yourselves whilst living in
an unhumbled and unconverted state: for, "whilst you regard
any iniquity in your heart, the Lord will not hear you[g]:" your
very prayers are turned into sin.]

2. " But the prayer of the upright is God's delight"—

["The upright" is he who truly and unfeignedly gives
himself up to God, to be saved in his appointed way, — — —
and to serve him with a pure heart and mind — — — Of such
an one God approves: and both his person and his services are
accepted of him: "The prayer of such an one is God's *delight*."
In itself it may be no more than a few broken accents, or a
desire expressed only in sighs and groans: but it enters into
the ears of the Lord of Hosts, and shall be answered by him
to the full extent of its import.   It is, in reality, the voice of
his own Spirit in the suppliant: and as " he knows the mind
of the Spirit," so he cannot but delight in every petition that
is dictated by him[h].   Besides, in the prayer of the upright
there are dispositions exercised, which are "in the sight of
God of great price[i]" The suppliant himself perhaps is mourning as though he could never hope for acceptance: but God
listens to him with unspeakable delight: he loves "the prayer
that goeth not out of feigned lips[k]:" above all, he delights in
the prayer of the upright, because it gives scope for the exercise of love and mercy towards the poor suppliant, and for a
rich communication of all spiritual blessings to his soul.   God
" will be inquired of by his people[l]," before he will impart to
them his promised blessings: and the moment they do pray to
him, he is like a mother that hears the cry of her beloved
infant, whom she instantly presses to her bosom, and in administering to whose necessities she finds relief, as it were, to her
own soul.   See this exemplified in his dealings with repenting
Ephraim: " Surely I have heard Ephraim bemoaning himself
thus: Thou hast chastised me, and I was chastised as a bullock
unaccustomed to the yoke: turn thou me and I shall be turned;
for thou art the Lord my God." " Is not Ephraim my dear
son? is he not a pleasant child? for since I spake against him,
I do earnestly remember him still: yea, my bowels are troubled
for him; I will surely have mercy upon him, saith the Lord[m]."
Here we see a true picture of what every upright soul shall
experience.   Let us only be " Israelites indeed, and without
guile, and our blessed Saviour will see us under the fig-

g Ps. lxvi. 18.   h Rom. viii. 26, 27.   i 1 Pet. iii. 4.
k Ps. xvii. 1.   l Ezek. xxxvi. 37.   m Jer. xxxi. 18, 20.

tree," or in our most secret retirements, and visit us in due
season with the most endearing expressions of his love. [n].]

Such are the truths asserted in our text. We now
proceed to suggest,

II. Some obvious deductions from them—

From these truths it is evident,

1. That God's views of sin are widely different from
those of men—

[Men, if free from gross sin, imagine, that they have little
cause for self-reproach. They see no evil in the general course
of this world: the pleasures, the gaieties, the amusements of
it, are all accounted innocent; and if a man perform res-
pectably the different offices of social life, they think he has
nothing to apprehend in the eternal world. But "God's thoughts
are widely different from theirs." We will suppose, for argument sake, that there is nothing flagrantly sinful in conviviality, and a round of pleasurable amusements; yet inasmuch
as such a state argues a departure of the soul from God, and
strengthens its habit of rebellion against him, it is highly sinful; and should be so esteemed by all who would not deceive
their own souls. For, if the very best actions of such persons
are hateful to God, if the very sacrifices with which they
attempt to honour him are an abomination in his sight, what
must those actions be which have no respect to him, but which
tend to banish him from their thoughts, and from the world?
I tell you, Brethren, that "to walk according to the course of
this world, is to walk according to the prince of the power of
the air, the spirit that now worketh in the children of disobedience [o]." You cannot be of the world and of Jesus Christ at
the same time [p]: "you cannot serve God and Mammon too [q]."
You may as well imagine light can have communion with
darkness, and Christ with Belial, as that a person truly "upright" and believing, can find pleasure in the society of "the
wicked" and unbelieving [r]. "The friendship of the world is"
essentially, as well as constructively, a state of enmity against
God [s]." Whatever therefore may be pleaded in extenuation
of those habits in which the more respectable part of the
world are living, they are all, whether social or personal, civil
or religious, one continued act of sin, as long as the soul continues alienated from God, and not altogether devoted to his
fear: and the man who thinks himself safe because he is in
a path frequented by the great mass of his fellow-creatures,

[n] John i. 47—51.   [o] Eph. ii. 2.   [p] John xvii. 14, 16.
[q] Matt. vi. 24.   [r] 2 Cor. vi. 14—16.
[s] Jam. iv. 4.

will find himself fearfully mistaken the moment he comes to the termination of it[t].]

2. That the provisions of the Gospel are admirably suited to our necessities—

[Here is " a wicked man:" he offers " a sacrifice" to his offended God: that very sacrifice is " an abomination to the Lord. Must the man then be left to perish? No: the Gospel reveals to him a sacrifice which is pleasing and acceptable to God, and which shall avail for the salvation of all who trust in it, even the sacrifice of the Lord Jesus, who " presented himself an offering and a sacrifice to God for a sweet smelling savour[u]." Again; Man, though originally made upright, has fallen[x], and become utterly averse to God and his law[y]. As for creating himself anew, he can no more do it than he could create himself at first. Shall *he* then perish? No: the Gospel proclaims to him a promise from almighty God, that " he will give him a new heart, and renew a right spirit within him[z];" so that, as the most guilty may be forgiven through the atonement that has been offered for him, so the most polluted may be " transformed into the very image of his God in righteousness and true holiness[a]." Thus may those who were odious as the fallen angels, become as accepted and as happy as the angels that have never sinned. O! Brethren, when will you study this blessed Gospel? when will you search into it, to find a remedy for your diseases, and a supply for your wants? Behold it is " a fountain opened," and ever flowing for the relief of sinful man: and every sinner in the universe is invited to " come and drink of it without money and without price[b]." I would that you should no longer be " an abomination" to your God! I would that he should look upon you with " delight," yea, that he should " rejoice over you with joy, and rest in his love, and joy over you with singing[c]!"]

3. That by the heart, and not by the mere acts, will God form his estimate of us in the last day—

[I know that our actions will be brought into judgment, and be adduced as evidences of our state before God, and as grounds of the sentence that shall be passed upon us. But it is not *merely* as acts that they will be either rewarded or punished; but as evidences of the real state of our souls. Even in human judicatories the object inquired into is, the intent of the mind. It is malice prepense that constitutes murder: where that did *not* exist, the act of killing is not accounted murder: but where that manifestly *did* exist, there the attempt

[t] Matt. vii. 13, 14.   [u] Eph. v. 2.   [x] Eccl. vii. 29.
[y] Rom. viii. 7.   [z] Ezek. xxxvi. 26, 27.   [a] Eph. iv. 24.
[b] Isai. lv. 1—3. John vii. 37—39.   [c] Zeph. iii. 17.

to kill, though unsuccessful, has the penalty of murder attached to it. Thus at the bar of judgment, the sacrifices of a wicked man, how numerous or costly soever they were, will be regarded as of no value: whilst the mere sighing of an upright soul shall not lose its reward. Let that then which is chiefly marked by God, be chiefly attended to by us. Let us endeavour to get our " hearts right before God." Let us remember, that, whether evidenced by overt acts or not, he can discern its real state: for " he searcheth the heart and trieth the reins[d]." " To him all things are naked and opened[e];" as the sacrifices of old, when flayed and cut open, were to the eye of the priest who inspected them. " Hell and destruction are before him : how much more then the hearts of the children of men[f]!" " He weigheth the spirits[g]," and discerns exactly how much there is of every different motive that may operate to the production of every act. Watch, therefore, and examine carefully the state of your own hearts : and as " he requireth truth in the inward parts[h]," cease not to pray day and night, that, being " perfect and upright before him," you may have light in darkness[i], peace in death[k], and glory in eternity[l].]

[d] Jer. xvii. 10.   [e] Heb. iv. 13.   [f] ver. 11.
[g] Prov. xvi. 2.   [h] Ps. li. 6.   [i] Ps. cxii. 4.
[k] Ps. xxxvii. 37.   [l] Ps. cxl. 13.

OUTLINE NO. 790

INSTRUCTION TO BE OBEYED.

Prov. xv. 32. He that refuseth instruction, despiseth his own soul.

THE Scriptures speak plainly, and represent things as they really are. Perhaps there is no man that would acknowledge he *despised* God : yet does God lay that sin to the charge of all who question his retributive justice : " Wherefore doth the wicked *contemn* God, while he doth say in his heart, Thou wilt not require it[a] ?" So none would confess that they " *despise* their own souls :" yet is that the real character of all who refuse the instruction which God sends to them by his written word, and by the ministration of his faithful servants. And this will appear, if we consider,

I. The need that every man has of divine instruction—

Much may be known to man from sensation and reflection : he may gather much from observation

[a] Ps. x. 13.

and experience, and the mere force of reasoning, without any revelation from heaven: but without divine instruction,

1. He can never know the extent of his wants—

[He cannot know his fall in Adam, or the depravity of his fallen nature, or his utter incapacity to restore himself to God's favour. If told that " his carnal mind is enmity against God," and that "without Christ he can do nothing," and that God alone can give him either to will or to do any thing agreeable to the divine command, he would think it all a libel upon human nature. It is revelation alone that can give him any just views on these subjects ————]

2. He can still less know how those wants are to be supplied—

[Who could ever have thought that God himself should become incarnate, and live and die for the express purpose of supplying the necessities of his fallen creatures? Who could ever have imagined that God's righteousness should be imputed to man? and that the Spirit of the living God should ever dwell in man, for the purpose of revealing the Saviour to him, and of imparting to him the divine image? A man not instructed in these things can know nothing about them. They are all matters of pure revelation, and directly contrary to those methods of salvation which uninstructed man would have adopted for himself ————]

3. He can never avail himself of those offers which God has made to him in the Gospel—

[In the Holy Scriptures are contained " exceeding great and precious promises," yea, promises confirmed by an oath, and ratified by an everlasting covenant. These promises relate to every want of fallen man, and make over to him a supply of every want by the simple exercise of faith on the part of man. How can the unenlightened man obtain an interest in these? How is it possible for him to lay hold of them, and rest upon them, and plead them before God, when he has never been instructed in relation to them? ———— It is obvious, that without divine instruction he must for ever lie under the guilt and power of his sins, and endure the punishment due to his unrepented and unpardoned transgressions.]

What then must be,

II. The light in which *he* must be viewed, who refuses instruction?

We use by no means too strong an expression, if we say, " He despises his own soul." For,

1. He grievously underrates its value—

[Who can estimate the value of an immortal soul, a soul capable of knowing, honouring, and enjoying, the Most High God; and actually assured of that honour, if only it obtain the knowledge of Christ, and repose all its confidence in him? But, to judge of its value aright, we must take into account the love that God has borne towards it, and the price which our adorable Lord and Saviour has paid for its redemption. Contemplate its nature and its capacity, its estimation by God, and its eternal destinies; and then say, Whether the man who refuses the instruction whereby he is to be made happy, does not altogether betray an ignorance of its true value? — — —]

2. He shamefully disregards its interests—

[Without an attention to the concerns of the soul, it is in vain to hope that it can ever be happy in the eternal world. The man that refuses divine instruction, does in reality inflict upon his soul the heaviest judgment that it can sustain in this life: he says, in fact, ' Let me alone, that I may go on to increase my guilt, and " treasure up for myself wrath against the day of wrath."' What would be thought of a man who should so trifle with his temporal interests? Would there be any term of reproach too harsh or too contemptuous whereby to designate so foolish a character? What, then, must we say of a man who so neglects the interests of his soul? — — —]

3. He casts it away for a thing of nought—

[Give to sensual gratifications all the importance you will, they are only as the small dust upon the balance when weighed against the soul. Yet for these does the man who refuses instruction sell his soul. Truly, if Esau " *despised* his birthright," when he " sold it for a mess of pottage[b]," much more do *they* pour contempt upon their own souls, who, for any consideration whatever, abandon all reasonable hopes of heaven, and subject themselves to the infliction of everlasting misery in hell — — —]

ADDRESS—

1. Avail yourselves now of the opportunities that are afforded you—

[There has been declared unto you from time to time, so far as I have been enabled to declare it, " the whole counsel of God." Think what improvement you have made of these instructions — — — and what will be your reflections in the eternal world, if you reject them[c] — — — Indeed, whilst disregarding the instructions given you, you greatly " wrong your own souls," and act as persons that are " in love with death[d]." O that ye may be wise ere it be too late! For, " if they

---

[b] Gen. xxv. 34.   [c] Prov. v. 12, 13.   [d] Prov. viii. 36

escaped not, who refused Moses who spake on earth, much more shall not ye escape, if ye turn away from him, even the Lord Jesus, who now speaketh to you from heaven[e]."]

2. " Be doers of the word, and not hearers only, deceiving your own selves[f]"—

[Instruction, if it abide in the understanding only, will be of no profit. To be really useful, it must descend into your hearts, and operate in your lives. Our blessed Lord's warning upon this subject deserves your deepest attention. I would have you not only wise, but " wise unto salvation." I would not that you should erect a house upon the sand; and that, after all your labour, it should fall upon your heads, and crush you; but rather, that you should build your house upon a rock, and find it able to shelter you from all the storms and tempests that ever can assault it[g]. This will shew that " you have real love to your soul[h];" and richly shall you " be recompensed at the resurrection of the just[i]."]

[e] Heb. xii. 25. [f] Jam. i. 22. [g] Matt. vii. 24—27.
[h] Prov. xix. 8. [i] Prov. viii. 33—35.

OUTLINE NO. 791

MAN'S ESTIMATE OF HIMSELF AND GOD'S CONTRASTED.

Prov. xvi. 2. *All the ways of a man are clean in his own eyes; but the Lord weigheth the spirits.*

AMONGST the purest joys of a Christian is " the testimony of a good conscience;" and all the labour that can possibly be bestowed on the attainment of it will be well repaid by the acquisition. But we must not forget, that man is a fallen creature, and that his mind and conscience partake of the defilement which sin has brought upon all the faculties of his soul[a]. Hence it is necessary to try even the verdict of conscience itself, and not to trust too implicitly to its representations. To " put evil for good, and good for evil; bitter for sweet, and sweet for bitter; darkness for light, and light for darkness;" is, alas! but too common, and more especially in forming an estimate of our own character and conduct. So has Solomon informed us in the words which we have just read: from which we shall take occasion to shew,

[a] Tit. i. 15.

I. Whence it is that men have such an over-weening
confidence respecting the rectitude of their own
ways—

We can know little of mankind, if we do not know
that men of every character and every class go forward in their respective ways with a considerable
measure of self-confidence, and self-approbation; and,
as Solomon elsewhere observes, that "every way of a
man is right in his own eyes[b]." Now whence does this
arise? How is it that all, notwithstanding the vast
difference there is in their habits and conduct, yet
think themselves right? We apprehend that it arises
from hence:

1. They judge themselves by a wrong standard—

[Every man has a standard of his own, suited to the views
and habits of the class among whom he moves. Some allow
themselves in a very great latitude, both of principle and practice; and never condemn themselves, unless they grossly violate
the code that is established amongst their own particular associates: they are "clean in their own eyes," as long as they keep
within the bounds of purity which their own friends prescribe.
Others are far more strict, as Paul in his unconverted state
was. "As touching the righteousness of the law, he was, in
his own estimation, blameless:" so blameless, as to be quite
sure of his acceptance before God: "I was alive without the
law once." His very zeal, which was so hateful in the sight
of God, and so directly pointed against the Lord Jesus Christ
himself, furnished him with an occasion for nothing but self-
applause. Though he did not altogether lay aside the law of
God in forming his estimate, he used it only to confirm his own
delusions, limiting its injunctions to the mere letter, instead of
entering into its spiritual import. None but the truly enlightened Christian brings himself fairly to the test of God's
holy law: all others have a defective standard; a standard of
their own, fitted for their own ways: and this is the first great
source of the delusion specified in our text.]

**2. They turn their eyes from things that have a
doubtful aspect—**

[Men, if they suspect that all is not right, are very averse
to a strict examination of their case: they content themselves
with looking at one side of the question only. Whatever tends
to justify their conduct, is dwelt upon with pleasure; but whatever tends to cast a shade upon it, is passed over in silence:

[b] Prov. xxi. 2.

" they hate the light, and will not come fairly to it, lest their
deeds should be reproved." This is very observable in the conduct of the Apostles, when our Lord touched upon their mutual
contentions about worldly preference and distinction: they instantly shifted off the blame, by turning the discourse to another
subject[c]. A true picture this of the generality of men, not
excepting those of whom better things might be hoped!]

3. They use all possible artifices to obtain a favour-
able testimony from their own conscience—

[Many are not ashamed to *justify what yet they know* in
their consciences *to be wrong :* " It was expedient: it was even
necessary under existing circumstances: they were constrained
to it, and could not do otherwise." It was in this way that Saul
justified his impious intrusion into the priestly office. He cast
the blame on Samuel, for not coming so early as he had expected;
and affirmed, that, however contrary to the divine law his conduct had been, it was expedient, and necessary, and good;
since the Philistines would otherwise have come upon him,
before he had sought by proper offerings the protection of
Heaven[d]. But notwithstanding all his specious arguments,
Samuel told him plainly, that he had " done foolishly," and
grievously provoked the Lord to anger[e].

If they proceed not in their self-vindication to this extent,
yet they will *excuse what they cannot justify.* ' True, it was
not altogether right; but they were compelled to do it; and
the fault was rather in others than in them. It was done in
haste, and without due consideration. It was a mistake; or
was done to prevent a greater evil; or to answer some valuable
end.' Here again we may see in the same unhappy monarch
the evil we are speaking of. He had spared Agag, and the best
of the flocks and herds, which he should have utterly destroyed:
yet, when he saw Samuel, he boasted that " he had fulfilled
the commandment of the Lord." But, on Samuel's inquiry
into the reasons of the flocks and herds being spared, he
excused himself by saying, that he had reserved them for
sacrifices: and, when further reproved, he cast the blame on
the people, asserting, that *they* had taken of the spoil without
his consent or privity[f].

When their conduct is too plainly reprehensible to admit of
such replies, they will then *palliate what they cannot excuse.*
Satan will never leave them at a loss for something whereby to
extenuate their faults, and to silence the reproaches of a guilty
conscience. 'It was not so bad as is represented: the intention
was good: it was done only once, and *that* under circumstances
that might well account for it.' But there is no end to the

---

c Luke ix. 46—49.   d 1 Sam. xiii. 8—12.
e 1 Sam. xiii. 13, 14.   f 1 Sam. xv. 13—21.

suggestions of self-love. There is not a man under heaven, except the broken-hearted penitent, that will acknowledge his faults in *all their real malignity*, and with *all their attendant aggravations*. All will cast some veil over their ways, to hide their deformity, and to make them appear " clean ;" and will put such a colour even on their basest actions, as to leave in them scarcely any criminality at all.]

But, whilst we thus varnish over our own ways, so as to make them clean in our own eyes, it is of infinite importance for us to know,

II. How God will form *his* estimate of them—

Certainly he will not judge as we do : he will scrutinize our actions more narrowly, and will weigh as in a balance every thing that pertains to them. He will weigh,

1. Our actions themselves—

[Every thing we do is put, as it were, into a balance, even " the balance of the sanctuary." God will examine with infallible accuracy what the motives were, and the principles by which we were actuated ; for by *these*, and not by the mere external appearance, must the quality of our actions be determined. He will examine how much there was of love to his name : how much of gratitude to the Lord Jesus Christ ; how much of humility, of self-denial, of love to our fellow-creatures ; and how much of zeal for the honour and glory of our God. Precisely according to the measure of these things will be his estimate of our actions : all else will be only as dross that is blended with the gold, and which the fire will consume.]

2. Our excuses—

[These, for the most part, when put into his scales are found lighter than the dust upon the balance. By means of them we impose upon ourselves, and upon our fellow-creatures; but we cannot impose on him ; " he cannot be deceived :" and the very excuses which we urge with such confidence, will be rejected by him with scorn. See how strongly he has cautioned us on this head. He supposes us to have made some rash vow, and then to excuse ourselves from performing it, by saying that we were under a mistake : " Suffer not thy mouth to cause thy flesh to sin; *neither say thou before the angel, that it was an error :* wherefore should God be angry at thy voice, and destroy the work of thine hands[g]?" It is on this account that we so often meet with this warning ; " Let no man deceive you with vain words;" " Be not deceived ; God is not mocked." In

g Eccl. v. 6.

truth, so far are we from satisfying him by our vain pleas, that
the more confident we are of the validity of our own excuses,
the more we provoke his wrath and indignation : "Thou sayest,
Because I am innocent, surely his anger shall turn from me :
behold, I will plead with thee, because thou sayest, I have not
sinned[h]."]

3. The disposition and habit of our minds—

[It is not so much the transient act that determines our
character, as the rooted habit of the mind. This *we* are apt
to overlook : and if we see not any glaring faults in our conduct, we think that all is well with us. But God views us as
creatures, who by the very law of our creation are bound
not to live to ourselves, but unto him. He views us too as
redeemed creatures, who, having been bought with the precious blood of his dear Son, are bound by this further tie to
" glorify him with our bodies and our spirits which are his."
By this test will he try us : and according to the result of this
scrutiny will he determine our eternal state. In particular, he
will mark, What degree of candour there is in us whilst examining our own ways ; and, Which is our predominant feeling,
a *partial* desire to think our " ways clean," or an *impartial*
desire to find out every atom of uncleanness that adheres to
them. He will further notice what means we are using to
ascertain the truth, and to escape from all kinds of self-delu-
sion ; whether we candidly consult others who are more impartial than we can be supposed to be ; and whether we are
crying mightily to Him to search and try us. Both these are
necessary ; because, whilst, on the one hand, we may too easily
rest in the favourable opinion of friends, we may, on the other
hand, be determinately holding fast our confidence against the
judgment of friends, even whilst we are pretending to ask
counsel of our God. Truly " the heart is deceitful above all
things, and desperately wicked ;" and one of the principal dispositions that God will expect to see in us is, a holy jealousy
over ourselves, and a willingness rather to die than be left under
a mistaken confidence of our own purity. Where this is wanting, there is a radical defect in the character ; a defect which,
if not rectified, will exclude us from the number of true Israelites, whose character is, that " they are without guile."]

ADDRESS—

1. The careless worldling—

[You will not believe that you are wrong. But consult
the Scriptures, and see. Find, if you can, one single word
that sanctions a life of carelessness and indifference. To what
purpose is it to be saying, " Peace, peace ! when there is no

[h] Jer. ii. 35.

peace?" Did you never hear what God replies to those who say, " I shall have peace, though I walk after the imaginations of my heart?" " The Lord, it is said, will not spare that man; but the anger of the Lord and his jealousy shall smoke against him; and all the curses that are written in this book shall lie upon him ; and the Lord shall blot out his name from under heaven[i]." Go on, if you are determined so to do; but know, that " whatsoever a man soweth, that shall he also reap: he that soweth to the flesh, shall of the flesh reap corruption ; and he that soweth to the Spirit, shall of the Spirit reap life everlasting[k]."]

2. The self-righteous moralist—

[Solomon justly observes, "There is a generation that are pure in their own eyes, but are not washed from their filthiness[l]." And such is the character of those whom we are now addressing. They are ready to say, " I have kept all the commandments from my youth up: and what lack 1 yet?" But, like that deluded Youth, they lack the one thing needful, namely, " to forsake all, and follow Christ." This they do not: this they will not do: they hold fast their own righteousness, and will not renounce it for an interest in his. Such was Paul in his unconverted state: but when his eyes were opened to see the plan of Salvation revealed in the Gospel, then " he counted all things but dung and dross that he might win Christ, and be found in him, not having his own righteousness, but Christ's." Know then, Brethren, that, if you trust in the law, you shall be tried by the law, and suffer all its penalties for your infractions of it : but if you will embrace the Gospel, and seek for acceptance solely through the Lord Jesus Christ, you shall find that " in him you shall be justified, and in him shall you glory."]

3. The professed believer—

[Much blindness yet remains within us after we have believed in Christ : and the most eminent believer still needs to maintain a godly jealousy over his own deceitful heart. The Apostles themselves at one time "knew not what manner of spirit they were of." But where shall we find any amongst ourselves that suspect this to be their own case? Alas! we all are more or less blinded by self-love : and, when most confident of our own integrity, we still need to say with Paul, " I know nothing by myself; yet am I not hereby justified; but he that judgeth me is the Lord[m]." We entreat you to guard with all possible care against the delusions of your own hearts; for they will assuredly, if persisted in, betray you to your everlasting ruin. The express declaration of God on this subject is, " If thou sayest, (in reference to any duty neglected, or sin

i Deut. xxix. 19, 20.   k Gal. vi. 7, 8.

l Prov. xxx. 12.   m 1 Cor. iv. 4.

committed,) Behold, we knew it not; doth not he that pondereth the heart consider it ? and He that keepeth thy soul, doth not he know it ? and shall not he render to every man according to his works[n] ?" Yes: His estimate will not be regulated by your opinion of yourselves, but by his perfect knowledge of your real character. May God enable us so to lay these things to heart, and so to act upon them, that "we may be found of him in that day without spot and blameless!"]

[n] Prov. xxiv. 11, 12.

OUTLINE NO. 792

TRUSTING IN GOD.

Prov. xvi. 3. *Commit thy works unto the Lord, and thy thoughts shall be established.*

WE all believe in the existence of a Supreme Being, and in a general way acknowledge his agency in the government of the world: but his particular care of us individually we find it extremely difficult to imagine. This, however, is most clearly revealed in the Holy Scriptures; and our duty is so to realize it, as, under all circumstances of trial and of difficulty, to look to him for his gracious interposition, and to expect from his hands whatever shall most conduce to our real benefit.

In the words before us we see,

1. A state supposed—

[It is here supposed that we may be in a state of great perplexity, so as not to know what to do for the best. This is often the case with nations, especially when menaced by a potent enemy[a] — — — Nor is there scarcely an individual to be found, who does not, at some time or other, experience an oppression of mind, arising out of difficulties with which he has to contend, and troubles which he knows not how to avert — — — Even in relation to men's spiritual concerns, the same trials are felt. Many, in a season of deep conviction, have poured out their complaints like Israel of old[b] — — — And many, under grievous temptation, have been reduced to the desponding frame of David[c] — — — At such times their thoughts are altogether distracted; and they are, like the persons so beautifully described in the 107th Psalm, brought, as it were, " to their wit's end."]

[a] Isai. vii. 2. and Joel ii. 6, 10.
[b] Isai. lix. from the middle of ver. 9. to 12.   Ps. lxxvii. 6—9.

But in all such cases there is abundant consolation, if only we use,

II. The remedy prescribed—

The remedy is both simple in itself, and invariably efficacious: " Commit your works unto the Lord"—

[Believing that God both knows your trials, and is willing to afford you the help you need, carry them to him, and spread them before him, as Hezekiah did the letter of blaspheming Rabshakeh[d]. Then plead his promises, which are so " exceeding great and precious;" and " roll on him[e]" your entire burthen, assured that " he will sustain you[f]," and accomplish your most enlarged desires[g]. This is the direction given to every living man[h]: and,]

In the performance of this duty you will find effectual relief—

[Nothing can be more fluctuating than the thoughts of men, especially in seasons of great embarrassment. But the very instant we commit our works to God, " our thoughts" become composed, and peaceful, and " established." God has taught us to expect this[i]: and to what an extent he fulfils his word, we may see in Hezekiah; who, from a state of the most extreme distress, was filled in an instant with the liveliest joy and most confident exultation[k] — — —]

OBSERVE, then, with humble and adoring gratitude,

1. How exalted are the privileges of the true Christian!

[It is your privilege, Brethren, to be " without carefulness[l]," both in relation to your temporal concerns[m], and even in respect to your immortal souls[n]. All your care, whether for the one and the other, should " be cast on God, who careth for you[o]." Then, though you will have many trials to bear, you shall be able to say with Paul, " We are troubled on every side, yet not distressed; we are perplexed, but not in despair; persecuted, but not forsaken; cast down, but not destroyed[p]." Be your trials what they may, " you shall be more than conquerors over all."]

---

[d] Isai. xxxvii. 14.　[e] See the marginal reading.　[f] Ps. lv. 22.
[g] Ps. lxxxi. 10.　[h] Ps. xxxvii. 5. and the margin there.
[i] Phil. iv. 6, 7. and Isai. xxvi. 3.
[k] Isai. xxxvii. 3, 22, 33. See also Ps. xl. 1—3.
[l] 1 Cor. vii. 32.　[m] Matt. vi. 25—34.　[n] 2 Tim. i. 12.
[o] 1 Pet. v. 7.　[p] 2 Cor. iv. 8, 9.

2. How marvellous is the condescension of our God!

[From low thoughts of God, we are apt to fear that he will not exert himself for *us*. But he will attend to *us*, if we trust in him, as much as if there were not another creature in heaven or on earth to attract his notice. Nor is it in great things only that he will interpose for us, but in the smallest that can possibly be imagined. In fact, there is nothing great or small with *him;* nor indeed is there any thing small as it respects *us*. Let any one see in Scripture what good arose from the accidental opening of some national records by King Ahasuerus, or what evil arose from David's accidental glance at Bathsheba, and we shall see that we need the divine care in every thing : and in every thing it shall be afforded us, if only we commit our ways to God, and place all our confidence in him. Not so much as a hair shall fall from the head of any of his saints, but according to his all-wise appointment ; nor any circumstance occur which shall not be overruled for their everlasting good q.]

q Rom. viii. 28.

OUTLINE NO. 793

THE BENEFIT OF EXPERIMENTAL RELIGION.

Prov. xvi. 23. *The heart of the wise teacheth his mouth, and addeth learning to his lips.*

THE depths of human science can be explored by few, because few have either leisure or ability for learned investigations. The same observation is true with respect to theology also, considered as a science : a very considerable knowledge both of history and ancient languages is required, in order to a full understanding of the various branches of sacred literature. But the spiritual and most essential parts of divine knowledge are totally distinct from these subjects ; nor is that species of erudition, which the learned only can possess, at all necessary for the obtaining of a clear and accurate acquaintance with them. There are two books, if we may so speak, and two alone, which we need to know ; and they are, the Bible and our own hearts. Till the latter be opened to our view, the former will be only "a sealed book :" but a discovery of our own hearts will throw an astonishing light upon the sacred oracles ; and make innumerable passages, which once seemed obscure and inexplicable, so plain,

that " he who runs may read" and understand them.
To this effect Solomon speaks in the words before us;
in elucidating which we shall inquire,

I. Who are here meant by " the wise ?"

Solomon certainly did not intend to limit his assertion
to those who were possessed of literary attainments—

[Human knowledge, when sanctified by grace, is a valuable instrument in the hands of its possessor, inasmuch as it will
qualify him for discharging many duties, which, without it, he
would not be able to fulfil. Moses, by being " learned in all
the wisdom of the Egyptians," was better fitted to stand forth
as the deliverer of Israel: and Paul, notwithstanding he
declined using " the words of man's wisdom," was the better
furnished for his work by his learned education, and his uncommon proficiency in the studies of his age and nation. Nevertheless it is not such learning that will form our minds to true
wisdom. On the contrary, if unsanctified, it will be as inimical
to religion as even the most inveterate lusts would be. The more
we have of it, the more will " the things of the spirit appear
foolishness unto us;" and the greater will be our backwardness
to seek that spiritual " discernment" which alone can qualify us
to judge of them aright[a]; and it is on this very account that
God so often pours contempt upon it and confounds it[b].]

Nor was it of persons eminent for worldly prudence
that Solomon spake—

[There can be no doubt but that true wisdom will make
us prudent, for the voice of inspiration says, " I, Wisdom,
dwell with Prudence[c]." But there are many who are " prudent in their own sight," and in the eyes of the world, who
are considered by God as altogether destitute of wisdom[d].
The Rich Man, who had so judiciously cultivated his grounds
as to obtain large crops, and who, to preserve the produce,
enlarged his storehouses, would have been accounted prudent
by the world; but God gave him most deservedly the appellation of a fool; " Thou fool, this night shall thy soul be required of thee[e]."]

The persons characterized in the text as wise, are
they who are endued with heavenly wisdom—

[Some there are, whose " eyes have been enlightened" by
the Spirit of God, and whose hearts are regulated by his lively
oracles. They have been taught of God to know their own
state, and have been formed to a disposition and temper suited

---

[a] 1 Cor. ii. 14.   [b] 1 Cor. i. 19, 20.   [c] Prov. viii. 12.
[d] Isai. v. 21.   [e] Luke xii. 20.

to their real character[f]. These are the wise, the only wise in the sight of God. And they are truly wise, even though they should be the most illiterate upon earth. We do not hesitate to say that the fishermen of Galilee possessed more true wisdom than all the heathen philosophers that ever existed.]

Their superiority to others will soon appear, if we inquire,

II. What are those subjects of which they are so well able to speak?

Their spiritual views do not at all qualify them to speak on matters of science and philosophy. But there are many things relating to Christian doctrine and experience, of which they can speak more truly, and more accurately, than any other people upon earth:

1. On the deceitfulness and depravity of the heart—

[This is a subject with which they are well acquainted; nor are they afraid of declaring it in its full extent. They have found on ten thousand occasions how fatally their heart has deceived them, what false glosses it puts upon any thing which it is desirous to retain, and what specious pretexts it will suggest for rejecting any thing that is distasteful to flesh and blood. They have seen the deep-rooted enmity of their hearts against God, their aversion to all holy exercises, and their proneness to do every thing that was evil. In speaking on these points, they speak not by hearsay, or according to a received system, but according to the word of God, confirmed as it has been by their own experience[g].]

2. On the suitableness and excellency of the salvation provided for us—

[They no more doubt that they need a Saviour, or that the Saviour provided for them is exactly such a one as they want, than they doubt their own existence. They know full well that they could not fulfil the law; they know also that Christ has satisfied all its demands by his obedience unto death; and that by believing in him they shall be interested in all that he has done and suffered. They perceive that in this way of salvation God gives all, and we receive all: and though the pride of their hearts formerly revolted at this, they are now disposed, not only to acquiesce in it, but to thank and adore God for so gracious a dispensation—]

3. On the way in which sinners are brought to the knowledge of Christ—

f Eph. i. 17, 18.   g Jer. xvii. 9.

[Here they can point out, as in a map, the country which they themselves have travelled over. They have been convinced of sin; they have seen the refuges of lies which they fled to in succession, one after another, till God sent home the law in all its spirituality to their hearts. They have thus been made to despair of saving themselves, and have, like the wounded Israelites, looked simply to him that was lifted up upon the cross. And though there is a great variety in the experience of different persons with respect to these things, yet these are the general outlines in which all true Christians are agreed; and therefore they can speak of them with truth and certainty.]

4. On the nature of the spiritual warfare—

[They are daily engaged in maintaining a conflict with sin and Satan. They have within them the two principles of flesh and spirit, which are continually struggling, as fire and water, to subdue each other[h]. They know the discouragements and fears with which the Christian is assailed, and the consolations and joys with which he is revived. Nor are they "ignorant of Satan's devices," having often "withstood his wiles," and "repelled his fiery darts." On these subjects their mouth is taught, and learning is added to their lips.]

The world are often struck with this fact, and ask with amazement,

III. Whence it is that they have attained this knowledge?

Experience, under God, is the best teacher; and it is from experience that they know these things—

[They derive not their knowledge from books: for many either cannot read, or never have studied the writings of men upon those subjects. Nor have they received their instructions from man: for though God taught them by man, yet God alone made the word effectual to open their eyes; and the very truths, perhaps, which they had heard frequently before without any profit, are suddenly applied to their souls, and made the power of God to their conviction and salvation. In short, it is not merely in their heads, but in their hearts that they know these things: and in speaking of them they can say with the apostle, "What our eyes have seen, and our ears have heard, and our hands have handled of the word of life, the same declare we unto you."]

Hence it is that *their* knowledge of these things is so superior to that of others—

[h] Gal. v. 17.

[Others cannot comprehend any one of the foregoing truths. If they should attempt to speak of them, they would only expose their own ignorance. Yea, though they may write well on the theory of religion, they are totally in the dark with respect to the nature of Christian experience. The poorest and meanest of God's people have incomparably greater penetration in these things than the wisest philosopher. This is plainly declared by the Apostle, " He that is spiritual judgeth all things; yet he himself is judged of no man[i]". It is confirmed also by that expression of Solomon, "The rich man is wise in his own conceit; but the poor man that hath understanding searcheth him out[k];" that is, discovers his ignorance, and is able to rectify his errors. As a man who has experienced any great pleasure or pain has a juster idea of what he has felt, than another has who only speaks of such things by hearsay; so, in a far higher degree, has the experienced Christian a clearer insight than others into divine truths, because he has the archetype and image of them in his own heart.]

APPLICATION—

1. Let none attempt to excuse their ignorance by saying that they are no scholars—

[Nothing is more common among the lower classes of mankind than to offer this as an excuse for their ignorance. But such excuses are vain : God has told us that he has chosen *them* in preference to the rich and learned[l], and that he has revealed to *them* what he has hid from the wise and prudent[m]. Let the blind then pray that they may receive their sight; so shall they "understand all things[n]," and be made " wise unto salvation[o]."]

2. Let us improve our conversation with each other for the purpose of spiritual edification—

[Too apt are we to trifle away our precious hours. But the tongue of the wise is justly compared to choice silver that enriches, and to a tree of life that nourishes us with its precious fruits[p]. Our words, if rightly ordered, might " administer grace" to each other. Let us then endeavour to obtain " the tongue of the learned, that can speak a word in season unto him that is weary[q]." Thus, we may " speak profitably out of the abundance of our hearts," and approve ourselves truly "wise by winning souls " to God[r].]

[i] 1 Cor. ii. 15.	[k] Prov. xxviii. 11.	[l] 1 Cor. i. 26—28.
[m] Matt. xi. 25.	[n] Prov. xxviii. 5.	[o] 2 Tim. iii. 15.
[p] Prov. x. 20.	[q] Isai. l. 4.	[r] Prov. xi. 30.

OUTLINE NO. 794

ERRONEOUS VIEWS OF RELIGION REFUTED.

Prov. xvi. 25. *There is a way that seemeth right unto a man; but the end thereof are the ways of death.*

THE testimony of an inspired prophet respecting the human heart is, that it " is deceitful above all things and desperately wicked." This testimony, as far as it respects the world at large, we all are ready to confirm. We see that in the great mass of mankind there is a propensity to deceive, not others only, but themselves also. They are often unconscious of principles by which they are manifestly actuated; and as often take credit to themselves for virtues which they do not really possess. Persons who have made considerable attainments in self-knowledge, are yet by no means free from this infirmity: the Apostles themselves, on more occasions than one, betrayed by their conduct, that " they knew not what spirit they were of." Nor does this proneness to self-deceit discover itself only in relation to individual acts, wherein men may be supposed to be biassed either by their interests or passions: it extends itself to men's whole character, and leads them to form a most erroneous judgment of their state: it leads them to " call evil good, and good evil; to put darkness for light, and light for darkness; to put bitter for sweet, and sweet for bitter." But it may be thought, that, if a man be deceived by his own heart, a less degree of criminality will attach to his actions, and he will have less reason to apprehend the displeasure of God. This however is not true: for we are responsible to God for the judgment we form of good and evil; and if we err, after all the means of information he has given us, we must be willingly deceived, and abide the consequences of our folly. To this effect Solomon speaks in the words before us: he concedes that " a way may appear right to a man;" but he tells us, nevertheless, that " the end thereof will be death."

This assertion of his is not to be understood of one particular way only: it is a general assertion, that

is applicable to a great variety of cases, or rather, I
hould say, to every kind of way that is followed by
man and condemned by God. Of course we cannot
enter into all the cases which might be specified: it
will be sufficient to notice two or three ways, which
are the most commonly followed, and most fatal
in their issue.

I. The *first* way to which we would call your
attention is that of *gay licentiousness.*

We cannot suppose any person so ignorant as really
to think that licentious gaiety is *right:* but there are
millions who do not think it materially wrong.   Criminal excesses and indulgences are palliated by the
mild appellations of conviviality and youthful indiscretion: and they are deemed necessary to the well-
being of society. They are even made subjects of
boasting; and persons who through age and infirmity
are disabled from pursuing their former courses, will
yet repeat them in effect, by glorying in the remembrance of them, and encouraging others in the same
career. So far from condemning these things in their
minds, the generality will laugh at those who are
scrupulous enough to doubt the lawfulness of such
courses: and if any one were bold enough to bear a
decisive testimony against them, he would instantly
be characterized by some opprobrious name. To
suppose that such indulgences, if restrained within
moderate bounds, would subject a man to the wrath
of Almighty God, would be considered as bordering on
insanity: and every one is encouraged to regard such
innocent liberties (as they are called) as perfectly
compatible with a well-grounded hope of salvation.

Let us then inquire what foundation there is for
such a confidence. Does God say nothing in his word
respecting the issue of such ways? or does he speak
of them in the same gentle terms? No: not a syllable
of this kind is to be found in all the sacred records.
A general caution is given us by Solomon in reference
to carnal indulgences of every kind: " Rejoice, O
young man, in thy youth, and let thy heart cheer

thee in the days of thy youth, and walk in the ways
of thine heart, and in the sight of thine eyes: but
know thou, that for all these things God will bring
thee into judgment[a]." The general warning given by
St. Paul is plainer still; "If ye live after the flesh,
ye shall die[b]." Lest we should mistake his meaning,
he frequently enumerates the works of the flesh:
"Adultery, fornication, uncleanness, lasciviousness,
hatred, variance, emulations, wrath, envyings, murders, drunkenness, revellings, and such like; these,"
says he, "are the sins, of the which I tell you before,
that they who do such things shall not inherit the
kingdom of God[c]." But because men are ready to
offer vain pleas and excuses for such things, he particularly guards us against laying the smallest stress
on any surmises of our own, or any suggestions of
others: "Let no man," says he, "deceive you with
vain words: for because of these things cometh the
wrath of God upon the children of disobedience[d]."
But Moses, and after him the Prophet Jeremiah,
meet the case in the most pointed terms: "It shall
come to pass," says Moses, "when a man shall hear
the words of this curse, and shall bless himself in his
heart, saying, I shall have peace though I walk in the
imagination of my heart; the Lord will not spare
him; but the anger of the Lord and his jealousy shall
smoke against that man; and all the curses that are
written in this book shall come upon him, and the
Lord shall blot out his name from under heaven[e]."

Now permit me to ask, For what end are these
things written? is it merely to alarm and terrify us?
Can we conceive that God would falsify, in order to
keep us within some decent bounds? Is there any
necessity for him to resort to such an expedient; or
could he do it in consistency with his own perfections?

Here then we are reduced to this dilemma; either
to believe that the word of God is full of the most
palpable falsehoods from one end to the other, or to
acknowledge that the confidence of ungodly men is

[a] Eccl. xi. 9. [b] Rom. viii. 13. [c] Gal. v. 19—21.
[d] Eph. v. 6. [e] Deut. xxix. 19.

unfounded, and their hope delusive. Choose ye the former alternative if ye please : but you must excuse me if I embrace the latter. Believing as I do the word of God to be true, I must believe, and must exhort you also to believe, that they who make light of sin "shall not inherit the kingdom of God." The drunkard, the swearer, the whoremonger, in short the careless sinner, may " think his ways right;" but, if there be any truth in the word of God, they shall end in death. The express declaration of God concerning them is, " The end of those things is death[f]."

II. The *next* way to which I would call your attention, is that of *proud unbelief.*

Associated with loose morality will be found, for the most part, a contemptuous disregard of the Gospel. Ungodly men feel no need of it; they see no excellency in it; they consider it as unworthy of their attention; and they leave it as a proper field for the discussion of angry disputants, or the contemplation of wild enthusiasts.

If any urge the necessity of faith in Christ, they either contend, that, having been educated in the belief of Christianity, they have all the faith that is necessary; or they cut the matter short, and tell us in a word, " His faith cannot be wrong, whose life is in the right." As to the idea of their salvation depending on the exercise of faith, they cannot for one moment endure it: nothing is too bad to be spoken of so preposterous an opinion : and all who maintain such a sentiment are set down as designing hypocrites, or as gloomy fanatics.

Thus confident are they that their way is right.

But what saith the Scripture to these things? Does God himself lay no stress on the exercise of faith? Does he leave us at liberty to embrace or reject his Gospel as we please ? Having given us his only-begotten Son to die for us, and set him forth to be a propitiation for sin through faith in his blood, does he attach no guilt to unbelief? Does he represent the

[f] Rom. vi. 21.

contemners of his Son as in the same predicament
with those who receive him? Nothing of this kind can
be found in all the book of God. It may be called
candour; but there is no such candour in the inspired
volume. *That* calls every thing by its proper name,
and assigns to every thing its proper character: and
the unbelief which is thought a matter of so much
indifference by the world at large, is declared to be
the infallible source of ruin to all who indulge it. But
let the Scriptures speak for themselves: " He that
believeth on Christ is not condemned; but he that
believeth not, is condemned already, because he hath
not believed in the name of the only-begotten Son of
God:" and again, " He that believeth on the Son,
hath everlasting life: but he that believeth not the
Son, shall not see life, but the wrath of God abideth
on him." In conformity with these declarations is
the whole tenour of sacred writ: " I am the way, the
truth, and the life," says our Lord; " no man cometh
unto the Father but by me." " Come unto me, all ye
that labour and are heavy laden! and I will give you
rest." " Ye will not come unto me, that ye might
have life." To the same effect is the testimony of
his Apostles; " Other foundation can no man lay
than that is laid, which is Jesus Christ." " There is
not salvation in any other: there is no other name
under heaven given among men whereby we can be
saved, but the name of Jesus Christ."

What now shall we say to these things? Is there
any difficulty in understanding these passages? I
know, it is fashionable with many to represent the
doctrines of the Gospel as so abstruse and intricate
that no one of common discernment can understand
them. But what intricacy is there here which the
most unlettered man in the universe may not understand? Men may invent subtleties on any subject;
and on this among the rest: but there is nothing here
which is not plain and easy to the most common
apprehension. Christ has made an atonement for our
sins: and he calls us to seek salvation through his
blood and righteousness. He tells us, that " having

no sin of his own, he was made sin for us, that we might be made the righteousness of God in him." And when he sent his disciples to go and preach this Gospel to every creature, he added, " He that believeth and is baptized shall be saved, and he that believeth not shall be damned."

What shall we say then? Shall we believe what the Lord Jesus Christ has so strongly affirmed? or shall we believe the surmises of ungodly men, and, as St. John expresses it, " make God a liar?" Even if there were no such strong assertions to guide us, our own reason might tell us, that God, after having given his only dear Son to die for us, would never leave it a matter of indifference whether we believed in him or not : but when we find the testimonies of Scripture so plain and so express on the subject, we must conclude, that the unbelief which men so proudly and impiously justify, will issue in the everlasting confusion of those who indulge it.

III. The *last* way to which we shall direct your attention, is that of *cold formality*.

Many who have respect for the Gospel as a system, content themselves with yielding to it a bare assent; and persuade themselves that they receive it aright, even though they never are stimulated by it to any extraordinary exertions. As for all that zeal and love and diligence in the service of the Lord Jesus which they behold in some few around them, they account it all a needless preciseness; and they impute it, for the most part, to ostentation or vanity in those who dare to maintain it. To be regular in their attendance on public worship, to fulfil the duties of their station, and to do unto others as they would be done unto, *this* is enough for them, and more than this they utterly despise. Speak not to them of loving God, of living by faith on the Lord Jesus, of maintaining fellowship with him in the exercise of prayer and praise : speak not to them of walking as Christ walked, of bearing the cross after him, and of rejoicing that they are counted worthy to suffer for him : speak

not to them of receiving out of his fulness, of living
to his glory, or of growing up into his image : such
ideas are quite foreign to their minds : they sound
only as the reveries of an over-heated imagination :
to aspire after such things would be to be righteous
over-much : if such exertions were necessary for the
attainment of heaven, what must become of all the
world ? Their religion lies in a much narrower space ;
they do as they would be done unto, and they mind
their proper business in life : if this will not save them,
nothing will : and they have no fear but that, when
they shall have finished their course, God will say to
them, " Well done, good and faithful servants ; enter
ye into the joy of your Lord."

But if these views of a Christian's duty be right,
whence is it that the Christian course is represented
in Scripture as so arduous, that the most " righteous
persons are scarcely saved," and with great difficulty ?
How comes it, that the divine life is compared to a
race, that calls for such exertion ; a wrestling, that
requires such skill ; a warfare, that is attended with
such labour and danger ? What is there, in the kind
of life which has been described, that at all corresponds with such images as these ? If the way to
heaven be so easy that people can walk in it without
any material difficulty, how comes it that our Lord
has represented the path of religion as strait and
unfrequented, and has bidden us to *strive* to enter in
at the strait gate, because many *seek* to enter in, and
are not able ? St. Paul, when enumerating many
classes of ungodly persons who should arise in the
latter days, mentions those who have " a form of
godliness without the power ;" and in those very
words describes the characters which we are now
considering. The persons of whom we are speaking,
particularly value themselves upon their moderation
in religion ; as though it were a virtue to love God
moderately ; to serve our Lord and Saviour moderately ; and to seek the salvation of our souls moderately. This was the religion of the Laodicean Church :
they determined to guard against all extremes : they

would not neglect the service of God altogether; nor would they, on the other hand, engage in it with all their might. And what says God unto them? Does he commend this boasted moderation? No: he says, " I know thy works, that thou art neither cold nor hot: I would thou wert cold or hot! So then because thou art lukewarm, and neither cold nor hot, I will spue thee out of my mouth."

Let me not be understood as though I would vindicate any thing that was really enthusiastic: God forbid! The only thing for which I am contending is, that God is to be served, not in a cold, lifeless, formal manner, but with unfeigned delight, and with all the powers and faculties of our souls. We must " yield ourselves living sacrifices to him:" we must endeavour to " walk worthy of him;" and strive to the uttermost to " glorify him with our bodies and our spirits, which are his." This is the holiness to which we are to attain; and " without this holiness no man shall see the Lord."

Having specified some of those ways which seem right to the generality of men, but will assuredly end in death, namely, the ways of *gay licentiousness, proud unbelief,* and *cold formality,* we would entreat you to contemplate the state of those who walk in them, at that period when they are about to be undeceived.

Whilst they are in health, and the world smiles upon them, their religion, such as it is, will suffice; and their confidence will bear them up. But when sickness comes, and they draw near to the chambers of death, a doubt will not unfrequently arise in their minds, whether they are prepared to meet their God. To dispel these thoughts, they betake themselves to business or pleasure or company, or perhaps to strong drink: but in spite of all the means used to allay their fears, their suspicions will recur with greater force, and excite a wish to know the opinion of some one better informed than themselves: but they are afraid to suggest their doubts, lest they should create an alarm in the minds of others, and impress them with an unfavourable apprehension of their state. The

recurrence of these thoughts makes them cling to
life : not that life is pleasant to them ; but they are
afraid to die. Compelled at last by inward uneasiness,
they perhaps put to some friend a question respecting
the evidences of our acceptance with God. They are
then answered in the most confident manner, that, as
they have done no harm, and have been very attentive
to their duties in life, they have no cause of fear.
The satisfaction founded on such an answer as this,
soon passes away ; and their former fears return.
Now perhaps they would be glad to see some person,
whose piety they have heretofore ridiculed as needless
preciseness : but they are afraid, lest a conversation
with him should confirm, rather than remove, their
doubts and fears. They wish, but cannot make up
their minds, to send for him. Perhaps they suggest
the idea to their attendant, but are dissuaded from
encouraging it : they are told with increasing confidence, that all is well with them. Perhaps they
persevere in their wishes, and a faithful monitor is
sent for. The servant of God deals tenderly with
them, but at the same time points out the errors they
have fallen into, and the importance of seeking salvation in another way. This disquiets them for a time,
and makes them doubly earnest about their souls.
The faithful monitor repeats his visit : but the officious
friends have barred the door against him ; or perhaps
have over-persuaded the dying man to decline all
further interviews, and to venture his soul upon his
own delusions. Any excuse is offered : the dying
man is asleep, or too ill to see any one ; and thus
the only remaining hope for the poor man is banished.
Such consolations as are founded on error and presumption are administered to the last : and at length
the disembodied spirit rushes unprepared into the
presence of its God.

But who can conceive the surprise and horror of the
soul at the instant of its separation from the body ?
Methinks it shrinks back, wishing if possible to hide
itself in its former tenement of clay. But the time is
come for it to be undeceived. Now it sees the weakness

and futility of all its former hopes.   Now it sees how
erroneous were its views of sin, and its conceptions of
true religion.   Now it sees that the representations
which God had given in his word were true.   The
self-deceiver now can no longer doubt to what an end
his former ways were leading, or whither they will
come who follow the paths he trod.   To indulge a
wish for another period of probation, or even for
the smallest mitigation of his misery, now were vain.
Gladly would he go back for a moment to the world
he has left, to warn his surviving friends, lest they
also come into the same place of torment : but that
cannot be admitted.   The sacred volume is given
them for their guide; and if they will follow their
own delusions in preference to it, they must abide the
consequences.   Now despair and anguish seize hold
upon him ; and he is delivered up a prey to all those
horrors, which once he ridiculed as idle tales.

Would we avoid this awful end, let us turn from
the paths that lead to it.   Let us remember, that the
assertions of men, however confident, are of no value,
any further than they are founded on the word of
God.   Let not their light thoughts of sin lead us to
tamper with it, or to doubt its issue.   Let not their
excuses for rejecting Christ prevail on us to neglect
his great salvation.   Rather, let us embrace him, and
glory in him, and cleave to him with full purpose of
heart.   Let not their standard of religion be ours :
let us go " unto the word and to the testimony :" let
us see how Christ and his Apostles walked: and though
we be ridiculed as precise and righteous over-much,
let us persevere in following the path of duty.   Let
us " stand," as the prophet speaks, " and ask for the
good old way, and walk therein."   Let us seek instruction wherever we can find it: and let us remember,
that the broad and frequented path is, according to
our Lord's express declaration, a way that leadeth to
destruction ; but that the path to life is narrow, difficult, and unfrequented ; for " few there be that find
it."   In short, let us look forward to the *end* of our
journey.   At *that* we shall soon arrive ; and then it

will be of no consequence whether we have been honoured for keeping the world in countenance, or despised for putting them to shame. The only thing that will then be of any consequence, will be, whether we be approved of our God. Let this end then be kept in view : let us regulate our ways in reference to it : and let us both by precept and example endeavour to undeceive the world around us. Then shall we be blessings to the generation in which we live, and shall attain that glory which ought to be the one object of our constant pursuit.

OUTLINE NO. 795

GOD IS THE DISPOSER OF ALL EVENTS.

Prov. xvi. 33. *The lot is cast into the lap; but the whole disposing thereof is of the Lord.*

THOUGH we would not be unnecessarily fastidious in condemning the use of any particular term, where we knew that in its popular sense it was not very exceptionable, yet we cannot altogether approve the use of such terms as 'luck,' and 'chance,' and 'fortune :' for though we know, that the persons who adopt those kind of expressions do not intend to deny *the doctrine* of a superintending Divine Providence, yet we cannot but think that such language tends exceedingly to weaken *a sense* of God's Providence upon the soul, inasmuch as it excludes his agency from the affairs of men, and regards them as left to mere and absolute contingency. With the Scriptures in our hands, we are perfectly assured, that all things, however casual or contingent with respect to man, are under the controul of a Superintending Providence ; or, as it is said in our text, that, "when a lot is cast into the lap, the whole disposal thereof is of the Lord."

In confirmation of this truth, we shall shew,

I. That God is the disposer of all events—

Events, of whatever kind they be, are equally under the direction of Almighty God. He disposes of,

1. The things which are most dependent on human agency—

[In the government of kingdoms all the powers of the human mind are called forth and concentrated: but the time for their commencement and continuance is altogether under the direction of a superior power[a]. The success of all human plans, whether relating to military enterprises[b], or commercial speculations[c], or agricultural pursuits[d], or matters of inferior moment and of daily occurrence[e], depends entirely on him — — — It was he who directed to Ahab's heart the bow drawn at a venture, and to Goliath's forehead the stone out of David's sling. In a word, he " worketh all things after the counsel of his own will[f];" and " his counsel shall stand, and he will do all his pleasure[g]."

2. The things that are most independent of human agency—

[Nothing has less dependence on human skill or foresight than a lot. As far as respects the determining of that, an idiot is on a par with the wisest man in the universe. But it is entirely at God's disposal; as all who acknowledge the existence of a Deity have confessed, by resorting to it on emergencies which nothing else could determine. Saul, and all the people of Israel, resorted to it, in order to learn from God who it was that had displeased him; and again, to determine the same matter between Saul and Jonathan his son[h]. In like manner the Apostles had recourse to it, in order to know whom God willed to be the successor of Judas in the Apostolic office[i]. Even the heathens themselves had a persuasion, that, when matters were solemnly referred to Him in a way of lot, he would make known to them the point which they wished to ascertain[k]. But as in these instances the event, though supposed to have been directed of God, might have been casual, since the chances against it were not very great, we will adduce one, which marks beyond all possibility of doubt the Divine interposition; since, in the language of chances, it was above a million to one that the lot did not fall on the person to whom God infallibly directed it[l]. Here is a striking illustration of that passage, " Evil shall *hunt* the wicked man to overthrow him[m]." The hounds see not their prey in the first instance, but trace it by its scent, and follow it with certainty in all its turnings, till at last they come in sight of it, and overtake it,

---

[a] Dan. iv. 17, 35.   [b] 1 Sam. xvii. 45—47. 2 Chron. xx. 17.
[c] Deut viii. 17, 18.   [d] Hagg. i. 6—11.
[e] Prov. xix. 21. 1 Sam. ii. 6—9.   [f] Eph. i. 11.
[g] Isai. xlvi. 10.   [h] 1 Sam. xiv. 40—42.
[i] Acts i. 23—26.   [k] Jonah i. 7.
[l] Josh. vii. 14—18. There were two millions of people: but in the last lot the *men* only were concerned.   [m] Ps. cxl. 11.

and destroy it. So it was in regard to this pursuit of the man who had troubled the camp of Israel: the lot fell on the right tribe, then on the right family of that tribe, then on the right household, and lastly on the right individual in that household:—and to every human being it speaks in this awful language, " Be sure your sin will find you out."]

That we may see how important a truth this is in a practical view, we shall proceed to shew,

II. That in this character he is constantly to be regarded by us—

His hand and his will we should trace,

1. In every thing that is past—

[Have we been loaded with benefits? they must be received as from Him, "from whom cometh every good and perfect gift." It matters nothing whether our blessings came to us by inheritance, or were the fruit of our own industry: to God, and to God alone, must they be referred, as their proper source[n]. Have we, on the other hand, been visited with afflictions? We should know, that " they did not spring out of the ground," but proceeded from his gracious hand; since "there is no evil in the city, but the Lord himself hath done it." Thus Job viewed all his diversified trials: he overlooked the second causes, and fixed his eyes on God alone: "The Lord gave, and the Lord hath taken away."

Now in all this we see the great importance of tracing every thing to the Lord; for by our blessings we are inflamed to gratitude, and by our troubles are softened to submission.]

2. In every thing that is future—

[If nothing can occur without his special appointment, how safely may we commit to him our every concern; and how confidently may we expect a happy issue of every occurrence! Can we do better than leave ourselves at his disposal? Were it possible that he should err, or that, having devised any thing, he should be unable to accomplish it; or that, having begun to accomplish it, he should, through versatility, change his purpose, and alter his dispensations; we might then not feel so well satisfied with having every thing subject to his disposal: but when infinite wisdom and goodness concur to direct all our concerns, and infinite power also engages to overrule every thing for our good, we may well dismiss every fear, saying with the Apostle, " I know whom I have believed, and that he is able to keep that which I have committed to him." We may be as composed as Hezekiah was when surrounded by Senna-

[n] 1 Chron. xxix. 14.

cherib's army[o], or as Elisha, when surrounded by the army of the king of Syria[p]. "Having God for us," we may rest assured, that "none can effectually be against us."]

Let us SEE from hence,

1. The excellency of faith—

[This is the principle which, far beyond any other, honours and glorifies God. By faith we are prepared to receive every thing as from him, and to say, "It is the Lord; let him do what seemeth him good." Mere reason, though it may acknowledge these truths, can never enable us to realize them: but "by faith we see Him that is invisible;" and learn to acknowledge him, as much "in the falling of a sparrow," as in the ruin of an empire. Seek then this blessed principle; yea, seek it in its highest and noblest exercises, that "being strong in faith, you may give glory to God."]

2. The blessedness of the true Believer—

[Whatever confederacies may be against you, it is your privilege to know, that "no weapon that has been formed against you can prosper." God has said, that "all things shall work together for your good:" and they shall do so, however much you may be at a loss to conceive in what way the good shall be elicited. Only take care that "Christ is yours;" and then you may be sure that all things else are yours[q]. If Christ is yours, all the perfections of God are so far yours, that they shall all be exercised for your good. Having "Christ for your sanctuary," you shall be inaccessible to the fiery darts of Satan: and having "your life hid with Christ in God, you shall, at his second coming, assuredly appear with him in glory[r]."]

o 2 Chron. xxxii. 7, 8.   p 2 Kings vi. 16, 17.
q 1 Cor. iii. 21—23.   r Col. iii. 3, 4.

OUTLINE NO. 796

THE NAME OF THE LORD A STRONG TOWER.

Prov. xviii. 10. *The name of the Lord is a strong tower: the righteous runneth into it, and is safe.*

IN the Proverbs of Solomon we must not expect to find long and accurate statements of Divine truth, nor elevated strains of devotion founded upon it: the scope of the book is rather by brief sentences to fix upon the mind truths already acknowledged, and to shew the excellency of them in their effects. The passage before us is very instructive in this view namely, as illustrating the blessedness attendant on true piety. But it commends itself to us yet more forcibly, by exhibiting a contrast between the dispositions and habits which religion inspires, and those which are indulged by the whole ungodly world. The text informs us what " the righteous man" does: the verse following our text informs us what the worldling does : the one makes God his refuge ; the other trusts in his wealth, or some other idol equally vain : the one founds all his hopes on God, as made known to us in the Scriptures of Truth ; the other, on some vanity, that has no title to confidence but " in his own conceit."

It was to mark this contrast that the blessedness mentioned in our text was confined to " the righteous." Solomon did not mean to intimate, that an unrighteous man, if he would flee to this tower, should be shut out : for the most unrighteous man in the universe is invited to come to it ; and, like the cities of refuge, its gates stand open day and night for the admission of all who desire to flee to it for refuge. But the truth is, that none but the righteous will run to it : none but they who are sensible of their guilt and danger, and are fleeing in earnest from the wrath to come, will enter in. All others deny the necessity of submitting to so humiliating a measure : they think they are safe enough without it. The believing penitent, on the contrary, is thankful for such a refuge, and is in the habit of running to it on every occasion : and therefore to him, and to him alone, is the security confined.

To elucidate the passage, we will endeavour to unfold,

I. The character of God—

By " the name of the Lord" we are not to understand the mere *word*, Jehovah, as though that would afford us any security. This is a vain and foolish superstition, that has no foundation whatever in the Oracles of God. But, by " the name of the Lord" we must understand his character ; as we learn from that expression of David, " They that know thy name," *i. e.* thy character, "will put their trust in thee[a]." Consider then the character of Jehovah,

1. As described by himself—

[God, in infinite condescension, was pleased to make himself known to Moses, and by an audible voice to "proclaim his name[b]:" "The Lord passed by and proclaimed, The Lord, the Lord God, merciful and gracious, long-suffering, and abundant in goodness and truth; keeping mercy for thousands, forgiving iniquity, transgression, and sin, and that will by no means clear the guilty[c]." Now we would ask the trembling sinner, What character he would wish Jehovah to bear? Would he wish God in no instance to testify his displeasure against sin, but to treat all men alike, putting no difference between "the guilty" who are going on in all manner of wickedness, and the penitent, who are turning from all iniquity? No: there is not a penitent in the universe that would wish God to act in a way so unworthy of his Divine Majesty. But if he desire to be assured of mercy to returning penitents, it is not possible that any words he could devise could more richly portray this attribute, than those which God himself has used. Consider them distinctly and separately, —— — and see how constantly they have been verified towards you hitherto, and how abundantly they contain all that you can desire.]

2. As revealed to us in Christ Jesus—

[The Lord Jesus Christ is "Emmanuel, God with us;" and he is particularly called, "The image of the invisible God." because in him the whole character of the Deity is made, as it were, visible to mortal men. He is "the brightness of his Father's glory, and the express image of his person;" and his whole character is marked in the name given him before he was conceived in the womb[d]. The name "Jesus" is the same with Joshua, or "Jehoshua," that is, Jah Hosea, Divine Saviour. What a glorious and comprehensive name is this! All that he has done and suffered for us, and all that he has promised to us, is contained in it; together with his perfect sufficiency for all that he has undertaken to effect. The trembling sinner finds in the very name of Jesus a pledge of all that he wants. Besides, whilst we contemplate him in the whole of his work and offices, we are expressly authorized to apply to ourselves the benefit of them all, and to call him, "The Lord our Righteousness[e]." Follow this idea in all its bearings, and what unsearchable mysteries of love and mercy will it unfold to our view!]

[a] Ps. ix. 10.   [b] Exod. xxxiv. 5.   [c] Exod. xxxiv. 6, 7.
[d] Matt. i. 21, 23.   [e] Jer. xxiii. 6.

Such being the name and character of God, let us contemplate,

II. The interest we have in it—

It is indeed " a strong tower"—

[Consider every perfection of the Deity : there is not one which is not " a chamber where we may hide ourselves till every calamity be overpast[f]."   The wisdom, the goodness, the love, the power, the faithfulness of Jehovah—who that is encompassed by them does not feel himself in an impregnable fortress? Truly they are not merely a wall, but " a wall of fire" round about the righteous ; of fire, which whilst it protects the fugitive, will devour the assailant. ———What a tower too is the Lord Jesus Christ in the whole of his work and offices ! Well is he said to be " a strength to the poor, a strength to the needy in his distress, a refuge from the storm, a shadow from the heat, when the blast of the terrible ones is as a storm against the wall[g]."   Yes, " the man" Christ Jesus, in his Mediatorial character, is such " a hiding-place[h]," where no adversary shall " ever penetrate."]

All who run to it shall " be safe"—

[Who shall ever approach " to harm" those who are thus protected[i]?   Surely " they shall be kept in perfect peace." They are " safe :" safe from the curses of the broken law ; for " there is no condemnation to them that are *in Christ Jesus*[k]" ———They are safe too from the assaults of Satan ; for " their lives are hid with Christ in God," where Satan can never come[l]———In a word, they are safe from every kind of evil ; for God has said of those who make the Most High their habitation, that " no evil shall befall them[m]"———The persecutor may touch their body, but cannot reach their soul[n] : they shall sooner be fed with ravens, than be suffered to " want any manner of thing that is good[o]."   And if any thing occur that has the semblance of evil, they may be assured that it shall work for their present and eternal good[p].   Like Elisha, they are surrounded with horses of fire and chariots of fire[q] ; and any assaults made upon them shall only terminate as in Elijah's case, with the confusion and ruin of their enemies[r].]

" Suffer now a word of EXHORTATION"—

1. Study much the character of God—

[f] Isai. xxvi. 20.   [g] Isai. xxvi. 4.   [h] Isai. xxxii. 2.
[i] 1 Pet. iii. 13.   [k] Rom. viii. 1.   [l] Col. iii. 3, 4.
[m] Ps. xci. 9, 10.   [n] Luke xii. 4, 5.   [o] Ps. xxxiv. 9, 10.
[p] Rom. viii. 28. 2 Cor. iv. 17, 18.
[q] 2 Kings vi. 14—17.   [r] 2 Kings i. 9—14.

["To know God, and Jesus Christ whom he hath sent, is," as our Lord informs us, "eternal life." All other knowledge is mere vanity in comparison of this. Without this we have nothing to warrant our hopes, or to dissipate our fears — — — "Acquaint then yourselves with God, and be at peace" — — —]

2. Maintain constant and intimate communion with him—

[You know how a child runs to his parent on every occasion: do ye in like manner run unto your God. This is the very character of the true Christian; "The righteous runneth unto God as his strong tower." Get to him under every fear, and every want, and every distress: and "cast your care on Him who careth for you" — — —]

3. Assure yourselves of the safety which you are privileged to enjoy—

[Well may you say, "If God be for me, who can be against me?" See how David exulted in his security[s]! — — — and learn like him to glory in your God: for it is God's desire that you should enjoy all possible consolation[t]. Your Saviour has assured you, that "none shall pluck you out of his hands:" lie there then in peace and safety, "knowing in whom you have believed, and that he is able to keep that which you have committed to him" — — — —When he has lost his power to save, then, and not till then, shall any enemy prevail against you.]

[s] Ps. xviii. 1, 2. and xxvii. 1.   [t] Heb. vi. 18.

OUTLINE NO. 797

A WOUNDED SPIRIT.

Prov. xviii. 14. *The spirit of a man will sustain his infirmity: but a wounded spirit who can bear?*

MAN being placed in a world where troubles of various kinds continually await him, he is endued with a firmness of mind suited to the occasion, so that he is enabled to bear them with a considerable measure of composure and ease. Previously to the arrival of afflictions, they appear more formidable than they really are. We should suppose that poverty, and sickness, and pain, and losses of friends and relatives, would produce a permanent depressure of mind: but this is not found to be the case: time soon heals the wounds that are inflicted by them; and habit soon reconciles men to the burthens which they are called to sustain. Where piety is superadded to natural fortitude, and the grace of God is in full activity, a man can support any load, however heavy. What an accumulated weight of afflictions came on Job! yet he not only blessed God for them, but, when his wife urged him to renounce his allegiance to God on account of these visitations, he, with wonderful composure, answered, "Shall we receive good at the Lord's hands, and shall we not receive evil?"

Yet there are bounds beyond which a man cannot go, without almost miraculous assistance. The spirit, like the body, may be borne down by a weight beyond its strength : and when the spirit, which ought to support a man under all his other trials, is itself broken, he must fall of course.

Now there are many things which inflict so deep a wound upon the spirit, as to destroy all its energy, and incapacitate it for its proper office : and that we may provide an antidote against them, and afford some consolation under them, we will,

I. Consider the case of a wounded spirit—

A spirit may be deeply wounded,

1. By nervous disorders—

[The mind may be disordered, as well as the body, and indeed through the medium of the body : and it is certain that there are disorders which so operate upon the nerves as to weaken and depress the animal spirits, and to sink a man into the very depths of despondency. This is often mistaken for religious melancholy : but it frequently has nothing to do with religion : it is found in persons who never turned their minds at all to the subject of religion : and, as it comes with, and by, a bodily disease, so it ceases with the removal of that disease. But in its effect it is inexpressibly painful, unfitting persons for every duty, indisposing them for all the proper means of relief, and leading them to put away from themselves all manner of consolation. They constrain their kindest friends to apply to themselves that proverb, "As vinegar upon nitre, so is he that singeth songs to a heavy heart[a]."]

2. By great and long-continued afflictions—

[Job himself, who had so nobly sustained all his complicated afflictions, sank at last, and cursed the day of his birth.

---

[a] Prov. xxv. 20.

Nor is it at all uncommon for men of the greatest fortitude thus
to sink. To produce this, is the tendency of calamities of any
kind, *personal, domestic,* or *public.* See the Apostle's caution
to the Church of Corinth respecting their conduct towards a
member whom they had excommunicated from among them.
As they had been formerly too backward to punish his offence,
so now they were too backward to restore him; on which occasion St. Paul says to them, " Ye ought rather to forgive him,
and to comfort him, lest perhaps such an one should be swallowed up with over-much sorrow[b]." Here the grief was purely
personal: but in Jacob it was of a *domestic* nature. He had,
in his own apprehension, lost his favourite son, Joseph; and now
he was afraid of losing Benjamin also: *that,* he said, would fill
up the number of his sorrows, and " bring down his grey hairs
with sorrow to the grave[c]." How many at this day have ground
to adopt this complaint, in reference to their children! *Public*
calamities, it is true, do not so often press with an unsupport-
able weight upon the mind: yet have we several instances of
their depressing, almost to the lowest ebb of sorrow, persons of
the strongest and the holiest minds. How were Moses and Joshua
discouraged, when unexpected circumstances arose to render
doubtful the ultimate success of their mission[d]! Nor was it a
love of life, or a fear of death, that made Hezekiah so extremely
dejected at the prospect of his approaching dissolution, but an
apprehension of the evils that would accrue to his country in
the event of his removal; and that one consideration reduced
him to such a state of grief as would in any other view have
been utterly unworthy of him as a saint of God[e].]

3. By guilt upon the conscience—

[What terrible effects did this produce on the mind of the
traitor Judas! He could not retain the wages of his iniquity,
nor bear his own existence; but sought in suicide a termination
of the sorrows he could no longer endure[f]. Nor is it at all uncommon for persons who once " made a mock of sin," to feel
so bitterly the torments of an accusing conscience, as to be
driven by them to habits of intoxication, and even to death
itself, as a refuge. Even good men, previous to their having
received a renewed sense of God's pardoning love upon their
souls, have been brought to such terrors and despondency, as to
find within their own souls a foretaste of hell itself. David's
experience in this particular is a just, but lamentable, exhibition of this painful truth[g] — — —]

4. By violent temptations—

[b] 2 Cor. ii. 7.   [c] Gen. xlii. 38. and xliv. 31.
[d] Exod. v. 22, 23. Josh. vii. 7, 8.   [e] Isai. xxxviii. 13, 14.
[f] Matt. xxvii. 3—5.
[g] Ps. xxxi. 9, 10. and xxxviii. 1—8. and xl. 12.

[Satan, though he can no longer possess the bodies of men as formerly he did, has yet great power over their souls. "His fiery darts" can inflict the deadliest wound. Paul himself was not able to endure " the buffetings " of that malignant enemy, till, by repeated cries to his Divine Master, he had obtained from him augmented supplies of grace and strength[h]. As for Job, though he was a perfect man, yet he sank entirely under the assaults of this great adversary[i] — — — Even the Lord of Glory himself, when he had assumed our feeble nature, was so exhausted in his first conflicts with Satan, that he needed to have " angels sent from heaven to strengthen him[k]." And in his last hours, when all the powers of darkness made their united assault upon him, he was constrained to say, " My soul is exceeding sorrowful, even unto death." What wonder then if Christians of ordinary stature be on some occasions unable to bear up under the wounds which he inflicts upon them?]

5. By spiritual desertion—

[This, after all, is the most overwhelming to a pious soul. With the presence of his God a man may bear any thing: but when " God hides his face from him, he must of necessity be troubled[l]." In this respect also David shews us what an insupportable affliction this is, and how impossible it is for the strongest or most pious mind to endure it[m] — — — But in our blessed Lord himself we see the most awful exemplification of this truth: for when all his other afflictions together had not been able to extort from him one complaint, this forced from him that heart-rending cry, " My God! my God! why hast thou forsaken me[n]?"]

Seeing then that many may be fainting under the agonies of " a wounded spirit," we will,

II. Administer some balm for its relief—

There is no wound that can be inflicted on the soul in this life, which may not, by an application of the proper remedies, be healed. Consider then,

1. There is no affliction which is not sent by God for our good—

[Afflictions, of whatever kind they be, " spring not out of the ground:" they are all appointed by God, in number, weight, and measure, and duration. If it be disease of body, it is he that inflicts the wound: if the trial come from any other quarter,

[h] 2 Cor. xii. 7, 9.   [i] Job vi. 2—4. and vii. 2—4, 13—16.
[k] Matt. iv. 11.   [l] Ps. xxx. 6, 7.
[m] Ps. lxxvii. 2—4. and lxxxviii. 3—7, 14—16.
[n] Matt. xxvii. 46.

it still is his chastening rod that strikes us, with a view to our spiritual good, "that we may be made partakers of his holiness." Convictions of sin are the work of his Spirit, to prepare us for the final restoration of his favour: and Satan himself, as in the case of Job and of Peter, is restrained by God, so as ultimately to display the triumphs of divine grace, and to benefit the souls which he endeavours to destroy: and God himself, in the hidings of his face, seeks only so to humble and purify our souls as to prepare us for the fuller manifestations of his love and mercy[o]————

Now it must be granted, " that afflictions are not for the present joyous, but grievous: nevertheless, afterwards they work the peaceable fruits of righteousness unto them that are exercised thereby." " If we be in heaviness through manifold temptations," God sees that there is " a needs be" for them[p]; and that by putting us into the furnace, we shall be purged from our dross, and come out of it as vessels better fitted for his service[q]. Well therefore may the consideration of the end for which they are sent, and of the benefit to be derived from them, reconcile us to the pressure of them, and dispose us patiently to wait for the removal of them. Could Job have foreseen the issue of his troubles, they would have been deprived of more than half their weight.]

2. Our afflictions, of whatever kind they be, will endure but a little time—

[The Apostle speaks of all, even the heaviest afflictions, as light and momentary[r]. Even life itself is but as a shadow that declineth; or a weaver's shuttle, which soon finishes the piece that is to be severed from the loom. And when once this frail life is ended, there is an everlasting termination of all our sorrows. If only we have believed in Christ, and sought an interest in him, we enter immediately into " his presence, where is fulness of joy for evermore." Into that blissful world nothing that is afflictive can ever enter to disturb their peace: " all tears are wiped away from their eyes; and there shall be no more death, neither sorrow, nor crying, neither shall there be any more pain: for the former things are passed away[s]." And, as no created evil can then impair their bliss, so no created good can add to it: " The city has no need of the sun, neither of the moon to lighten it; for the glory of God does lighten it, and the Lamb is the light thereof[t]." How little will the transient clouds that once occasioned a momentary gloom be remembered, when our dwelling is for ever fixed in the full splendour of the Sun of Righteousness. Surely we need not

[o] Isai. liv. 7, 8.   [p] 1 Pet. i. 6.   [q] Mal. iii. 2, 3.
[r] 2 Cor. iv. 17.   [s] Rev. xxi. 4.   [t] Rev. xxii 23.

be much cast down at trials, however painful to flesh and blood, when we consider that their duration is but as the twinkling of an eye, and that they will so soon terminate in inconceivable and everlasting felicity.]

3. There is in Christ a full sufficiency for every wound—

[We need not go to the eternal world for consolation; for we may find it here. What says the Prophet Jeremiah? "Is there no balm in Gilead? Is there no Physician there? Why then is not the health of the daughter of my people recovered[u]?" Did we but cry to Jesus, as Paul did, we should find " his grace abundantly sufficient for us." " If we cast our burthen upon him, he would sustain us." See the experiment tried by David, and the account which he gives of the result: how soon was he " taken out of the horrible pit, out of the miry clay, and a new song was put into his mouth, even praise unto our God[x]!" The very office which our blessed Lord undertook, was that, not of a Redeemer only, but of a Comforter; " to comfort them that mourn in Zion, to give them beauty for ashes, the oil of joy for mourning, and the garment of praise for *the spirit of heaviness*[y]." Let all then look unto him, whatever their afflic- tion now be: even though, like David, they were under the depths of dereliction, they shall soon, with him, have occasion to say, " Thou hast turned my mourning into dancing; thou hast put off my sackcloth, and girded me with gladness[z]."

The Lord Jesus " will not break a bruised reed, or quench the smoking flax, but will bring forth judgment unto victory:" and, if we confide in him, " our heaviness may indeed continue for a night, but joy shall come in the morning."]

[u] Jer. viii. 22.   [x] Ps. xl. 2, 3.   [y] Isai. lxi. 2, 3.   [z] Ps. xxx. 11.

OUTLINE NO. 798

DIVINE KNOWLEDGE MOST DESIRABLE.

Prov. xix. 2. *That the soul be without knowledge, it is not good.*

THERE is nothing so highly prized as knowledge. No pains are deemed too great for the acquirement of it; no expense too large ——— It is that which, more than any thing else, raises a man in public estima- tion, and gives him influence in the world[a] ——— There is, however, a knowledge which is far from

[a] If this were a subject for a COMMEMORATION SERMON, before a Learned Body, the use and excellency of Learning should be largely opened, and form the first head of the Discourse. The second head would be, The superior importance of divine knowledge.

being duly appreciated; I mean, that which relates
to the concerns of the soul. Yet is this, beyond all
comparison, more important than the other. For this,
St. Paul counted all things but as dross and dung.
Without the attainment of human sciences, a man
may be both holy and happy; but without divine
knowledge he can have

I. No directory for his ways—

[Reason is very inadequate to guide our steps. We know
not of ourselves how to walk and to please God. The wisest
of heathen philosophers were but blind conductors in the paths
of real holiness: they understood not what holiness was. Of
humility, which is the very foundation of holiness, they had no
just ideas. So it is with unenlightened Christians. They see
little beyond forms and external duties. The exercise of
spiritual affections is beyond their attainment or their aim.
Of an entire superiority to the world, and a total surrender of
themselves to God, they have no conception; unless, indeed,
it be in a way of monastic institutions, where the duties of
social life are overlooked, and form is substituted in the place
of vital power. Of a life of faith in particular, a person uninstructed in the Gospel can have no proper views. Being
ignorant of Christ, he cannot see what a fulness there is in him
of wisdom and righteousness, and sanctification and redemption; or what necessity there is for the sinner to receive supplies from it, by the daily exercises of faith and prayer. In a
word, from a man ignorant of the Gospel, every thing that
constitutes vital godliness is concealed. He has no higher
principle than that of fear; no better *standard* than that of
heathen morals; no nobler *end* than that of saving his own
soul. As for being constrained by the love of God, or aspiring
to a full conformity to the divine image, or living altogether for
the glory of God's name, he knows it not; yea, he regards it
rather as fanciful, enthusiastic, impracticable, and absurd. Not
feeling his obligations to his Redeemer, he wants the entire
spring of vital godliness, and can rise no higher than to the
low attainment of heathen morals. Tell me then whether he
be not in a truly pitiable state.]

II. No remedy for his sins—

[Every man feels himself to be a sinner, and to stand in
need of forgiveness with God. But a man ignorant of the
Gospel, seeks remission only in a round of duties, or in mortifications of human origin. He sees not his need of a Mediator, through whose obedience unto death he is to obtain
acceptance with God. He knows not of " the fountain which

was opened for sin" upon the cross; and therefore he cannot wash in it. He knows not of a righteousness wrought out for him; and therefore he cannot clothe himself with it. The great and precious promises which God has given us in his word, have, in his mind, but little weight, little reality. His repentances, his reformations, his alms-deeds and works of charity, these form his chief dependence, and these administer to him his principal consolation. Hence he never acquires any solid peace. He always has a secret misgiving that he has not obtained peace with God; and he has no conception of what is meant by " the joy of faith." The true Believer "rejoices in the Lord with joy unspeakable and full of glory." But to this the poor blind moralist can never attain; and therefore he can never enter into " the glorious liberty of the children of God." In what a lamentable condition then is he!]

III. No support in his troubles—

["Man is born to trouble, as the sparks fly upward." But to those who have received the Gospel, there are consolations that bear them up above all their afflictions. They know from whence all their trials spring, even from the hand of God himself. They see them to be the fruit of a Father's love, sent for the production of the most gracious ends. They feel within themselves their humbling, sanctifying efficacy. They perceive that they are instrumental to the carrying on of God's work within them, and to the augmenting of that weight of glory which shall be accorded to them at the last day. But of all this the man who is uninstructed in the Gospel is altogether ignorant. He has little except the principles of philosophy for his support. He feels that he cannot ward off affliction; and that to repine under it, is only to augment its pressure: and that, consequently, patience is his truest wisdom. But to " glory in tribulation," and be thankful for it, and " take pleasure in it," are attainments of which he has no conception. Truly "to be thus ignorant, it is not good."]

IV. No strength for his duties—

[An unenlightened man, of necessity, engages in duty depending only on his own strength. He knows not what union with Christ is; or what is that vital energy which is derived from him, as from a vine to its branches, or from the head to the members of a body. Nor is he acquainted with the operations of the Holy Spirit, so as to be "strengthened with all might by the Spirit in his inward man." In consequence of this, if he go forth to mortify sin, or conflict with Satan, or engage in any spiritual duty, he fails, and is ready to consider success as utterly unattainable. Being a stranger to " the mighty working of God's power, which wrought in Christ

to raise him from the dead, and to set him above all the principalities and powers whether of heaven or hell," he conceives
that similar conquests are not to be expected by mortal man ;
and that to rise thus superior to sin and Satan, is an object to
be desired rather than attained. Hence he satisfies himself
with the poor performances of outward duty ; and never dreams
of being " changed into the image of the Lord Jesus, from
glory to glory, by the Spirit of his God." " Through the
strength of Christ he might do all things :" but, being ignorant
of Christ, he is left to his own resources, and " can do nothing."
Say, Brethren, whether in this view also he does not fearfully illustrate the truth contained in my text.]

V. No hope in his end—

[At the approach of death, an unenlightened man is in a
truly pitiable state. He has no other hope but what is founded
on the uncovenanted mercies of his God, and a persuasion that
he has done his duty to the utmost of his power. As for an
assurance of faith, or a spirit of adoption enabling him to cry
Abba, Father, he knows not of it ; nor can imagine how it is
that some attain such joy in the prospect of eternity. Of the
covenant of grace, and of all its blessed provisions, he, alas !
is ignorant. He cannot take hold of the promises of the Gospel, or rely on the faithfulness of God. He sees not how a title
to heaven may be attained, or with what confidence it may be
pleaded at the throne of grace. He sees not Christ as his forerunner, that is gone to prepare a place for him, and has engaged
to come and take him to himself. Hence he clings to life even
to the last ; and never reckons death amongst his treasures, or
accounts it gain to die. St. Paul well describes the state of such
an one ; that being ignorant of God's righteousness, and going
about to establish his own righteousness, and not submitting
himself to the righteousness of God, he perishes at last under
the guilt of all his sins. Whatever his exertions be in the pursuit of righteousness, he fails, " because he seeks it by works,
and not by faith only ; for he stumbles at that stumbling-
stone [b] ;" and thus, as God has said, " he is destroyed for lack
of knowledge [c]." The unhappy man living all his days " without
Christ," dies at last " without hope [d]." Who will doubt now
the truth of Solomon's assertion, that for the soul to be without knowledge is the greatest calamity that can befall a man on
this side the grave ?]

And now, Brethren, what shall I say unto you ? O,
LEARN,

1. To pity those who are in ignorance of the truth
of Christ—

b Rom. ix. 30—33. and x. 2, 3.   c Hos. iv. 6.   d Eph. ii. 12.

[You would surely pity your friends and relatives, if you saw them destitute of the common faculties of men: but, believe me, they are still greater objects of pity, if, possessing all the faculties of men, they are ignorant of the Gospel. In what an awful state are they who have no directory for their ways, no remedy for their sins, no support in their troubles, no strength for their duties, and no hope in their end! Yet is this, indeed, the condition of all who are ignorant of Christ. They may be endued with human wisdom, and may be placed on the highest pinnacle of human glory; but yet a poor Lazarus, that is destitute of all that man values, is happier than they. Consider this, I pray you, and exert yourselves to the utmost of your power for the bringing of their souls to God ————— and pity the heathen world, who are yet sitting in darkness and in the shadow of death. Pity also God's ancient people, who have yet a veil upon their hearts, and who still reject that Saviour whom their fathers crucified. Concur in all the methods that are used for the enlightening of this benighted world: and if you see, indeed, that " for immortal souls to be without knowledge is not good," address yourselves with all energy to the dispelling of the darkness that reigns throughout the world, and to the " turning of men universally from darkness unto light, and from the power of Satan unto God."]

2. To improve the means of grace which are afforded you—

[Permit me to say, that you have the light set before you, and " the whole counsel of God faithfully declared unto you." Do not then trifle with the opportunities which you enjoy. They are sent of God to " make you wise unto salvation;" and, if they be disregarded, they will greatly augment both your guilt and condemnation. In truth, if you had not such instructions, your guilt would be comparatively light, and your condemnation tolerable: but, with your advantages, your state will be worse than that of Sodom and Gomorrha, if you make not a suitable improvement of them. In attending on divine ordinances, learn to regard them as Bethesda's Pool, where, unless the waters be stirred, you will attend in vain; and beg of God to accompany them with power from on high, and to give them a saving efficacy to your souls.]

3. To make a good use of the knowledge which you possess—

[Be careful that you do not " hold the truth in unrighteousness." The servant who knew his Lord's will, and did it not, was beaten with more and heavier stripes than he who erred through ignorance. And you may be sure, that if the Lord Jesus Christ will be revealed at last in flaming fire, to

take vengeance on them that *knew not* God, and obeyed not
the Gospel; much more will he take vengeance on those who
have trodden under foot his blood, and done despite to his
Spirit of grace. If God have shined into your hearts, to give
you the light of his Gospel, you must walk as children of the
light and of the day. It is in this way only that you can shew
the excellency of the Gospel, or convince the world that the
knowledge you possess is of any real value. But, to make
this improvement of the Gospel, much consideration will be
necessary. The word of Christ must be treasured up in your
minds, and must "dwell in you richly in all wisdom." A mariner
who will not consult his compass will derive no benefit from it:
nor will you, if you do not take " the word as a light unto your
feet and a lantern to your paths." Solomon, in the words
following my text, justly says, " He that hasteth with his feet,
sinneth:" and so I say to you; If you will have your way acceptable unto God, you must apply to him constantly for fresh
supplies of his grace, and must "take heed unto your ways
according to his word."]

OUTLINE NO. 799

THE SINFULNESS OF MURMURING AGAINST GOD.

Prov. xix. 3. *The foolishness of man perverteth his way, and
his heart fretteth against the Lord.*

THE wickedness of the heart is deep and unsearchable. They who do not watch its motions,
have no idea of its depravity; but they who diligently examine it may discover many evils, and by
the light of God's word attain considerable knowledge. The disposition mentioned in the text deserves special attention. We will,

I. Illustrate the disposition here spoken of—

The careless and ungodly world are ever ready to
cast blame on God,

1. On account of their sins—

[They give the rein to every evil thought and desire; they
expose themselves to every kind of temptation; they lay innumerable stumbling-blocks in their own way; and thus become
enslaved by vicious lusts and appetites: against these iniquities
God denounces his judgment: but the slaves of sin continue
hardened in their evil ways; they condemn even God himself
as the author of their sins. This was the conduct of Adam

immediately after the fall[a], and is it too often imitated by his guilty descendants —]

2. On account of their sorrows—

[Sorrow is entailed on all as the punishment of the first transgression: but most of the afflictions which men suffer are brought on them by their own folly. Some involve themselves in distress through sloth or intemperance; others ruin themselves by imprudence and extravagance. Others bring themselves into difficulties by the tempers which they exercise, and the habits which they form: but all under their calamities " fret against the Lord." They are full of invectives against those that have been the more immediate occasions of their trouble[b]; they consider their lot as hard and severe; and thus do they reflect on Providence rather than on themselves. Cain, the first-born of Adam, indulged this malignant spirit[c]; nor are there any sons of sorrow who do not more or less follow his example.]

Nor are believers themselves wholly free from this disposition—

[They watch and pray against their besetting sin, yet are sometimes brought under the power of it. On these occasions they are tempted to fret against the Lord; they are ready to expostulate with him like those of old[d]; they forget how justly they might have been eternally forsaken; and that the remaining power of their sins is the consequence both of former habits, and of present neglects. Under afflictions also they feel too much proneness to murmur. What sinful impatience did the holy Elijah manifest[e]! Even Job himself preserved not wholly a becoming temper[f].]

This disposition however is most hateful in the sight of God.

II. Point out the evil of it—

It betrays the most *deplorable ignorance*—

[God is not, nor can be, the author of sin. He maintains in all things the character given of him[g]: hence St. James shews the folly of casting blame on God[h]; nor can God punish any of us more than our iniquities deserve: hence the expostulation of the prophet is unanswerable[i]. Besides, to fret against God is not the way to interest him in our behalf, nor

[a] Gen. iii. 12. He obliquely condemns God for giving the woman to him.

[b] Numb. xvi. 11, 41.   [c] Gen. iv. 13, 14.   [d] Isai. lviii. 3.
[e] 1 Kings xix. 4.   [f] Job vii. 15, 16.   [g] Deut. xxxii. 4.
[h] Jam. i. 13, 14.   [i] Lam. iii. 39.

will it tend to the peace and composure of our own spirits. It is as unprofitable to us as it is unjust towards him. True wisdom would teach us to humble ourselves in his presence, and to renew our supplications with greater earnestness. This conduct is as sure to succeed, as the other is to fail of success[k].]

It manifests the most *obstinate impenitence*—

[Both sins and sorrows ought to produce humility. When they increase our rebellion, our state is almost desperate[l]. How awfully does such a temper characterize God's enemies[m]! and make us resemble those that are consigned over to perdition[n]! Surely nothing more heinous can be laid to our charge, nor any thing more speedily fit us for destruction.]

It evinces the most *consummate arrogance*—

[To fret and murmur is, in fact, to reprove God. God himself considers it as a direct attack upon him[o]; and can any thing be more presumptuous in such worms as we? St. Paul reprobates this impiety with holy indignation[p], and every one who allows himself in it, must answer it at his peril[q].]

We conclude with suitable ADVICE—

1. Let us search into the occasions of our sins and sorrows—

[We may be surprised into sin by a sudden temptation, but may trace our fall to preceding unwatchfulness; nor can we expect God to keep us, if we neglect to keep ourselves. We are rarely earnest enough in using the means of safety. We are too backward to meditation, prayer, and fasting. Our afflictions also may have come without any misconduct on our part: but who has not merited them by his sins? Men should only be considered as instruments in God's hands[r]: and the consideration of his will should silence every murmur[s].]

2. Let us always be careful to justify God—

[We may not always be able to account for his dispensations, but we should not on that account doubt the equity of them: whatever we suffer, we should not "charge God foolishly." Under the darkest dispensations we should say as the Psalmist[t]. If we wait we shall see the wisdom of many things which now seem utterly inexplicable; we may rest assured that David's assertion shall be verified[u].]

3. Let us see what improvement may be made of our troubles—

[k] Prov. xxviii. 13.	[l] Isai. i. 5.	[m] Rev. xvi. 9.
[n] Matt. viii. 12.	[o] Mal. iii. 13, 14.	[p] Rom. ix. 20.
[q] Job xl. 2.	[r] Ps. xvii. 13, 14.	[s] 2 Sam. xvi. 10.
[t] Ps. xxii. 2, 3.	[u] Ps. li. 4.	

[There is no rod which has not a voice to us. Our very sins may be permitted, in order to humble us, and to make us more thankfully cleave to the Saviour. Our trials, of whatever kind, are to purge away our dross, and to fit us for our eternal rest. To view them in this light will greatly compose our minds; instead of fretting against the Lord, we shall be thankful to him; and instead of increasing our misery, we shall make it a source of joy.]

OUTLINE NO. 800

THE CONSEQUENCE OF SLOTH.

Prov. xx. 4. *The sluggard will not plow by reason of the cold; therefore shall he beg in harvest, and have nothing.*

ARGUMENTS from analogy, when the analogy itself is just, are easy of apprehension, and well calculated to convince the mind: and one distinguished excellence of the Book of Proverbs is, that it abounds with such arguments; and without any formal statement of premises and conclusions, presents the truth to us in short, sententious aphorisms, that are plain, obvious, incontrovertible. Whoever has made the least observation on human affairs, must have seen the evil consequences of neglecting our proper business in life, whether in husbandry, or trade, or any other line: and it is easy to infer from thence, that similar consequences must attend a neglect of our Christian duties. Nor is it necessary that this analogy should be always pointed out to us: the whole scope of that divinely inspired book naturally leads us to make a spiritual improvement of the hints, which, in their literal sense, apply only to the things of this life.

Let us then in this view consider,

I. The sluggard's conduct—

The duties both of the husbandman and the Christian require industry—

[It was a part of the curse introduced by sin, that man should obtain his bread by the sweat of his brow: nor will the earth yield us any thing but briers and thorns, unless we bestow much pains in the cultivation of it. Our attention to it must be unremitted: it is not the labour of a month or a year that will suffice: we must repeat again and again the same processes, in order to guard against the noxious weeds that would overrun

it, and cherish the good seed, which we want it to produce.
Thus also must the Christian exert himself in order to bring
forth the fruits of righteousness.   His heart is prolific in what
is evil, but barren in what is good: he must therefore daily
counteract its natural propensities, and foster the holy desires
that have been sown in it.   The same work of repentance and
faith must be continually renewed, till the Lord himself shall
come to gather in his harvest.]

Yet are we ever ready to neglect our work on frivolous pretences—

[A regard to temporal interest will often overcome men's
natural sloth, and excite them to diligence in their several voca-
tions.   Yet are there many instances, where the indulgence
of sloth makes men blind to their own happiness, and deaf to
the cries of their distressed families.   With respect to spiritual
concerns, an indisposition to labour universally prevails.   The
work of the soul is irksome and difficult; and every one either
deems it altogether unnecessary, or desires to defer it as long
as possible.   But it is observable that the sluggard does not
absolutely say, " I hate my work, and therefore will not do
it;" much less does he say, " I am determined never to plough
at all:" but he finds some excuse for neglecting what he is
averse to perform; and fixes on some plea, which, *in certain
circumstances* and *to a certain extent*, might be sufficient.
Thus the Christian does not say, " I hate repentance and faith
in Christ; much less does he resolve never to repent and believe: but he always has some reason at hand for deferring
this unpleasant work, and promises himself a more convenient
season, before the time for ploughing be entirely passed away.
He has the cares of a family, or a pressure of business, or something that serves him for an excuse: but, upon examination, it
will either be found a mere excuse, or a reason, on which he
lays a very improper stress; making use of it to justify a total
and habitual neglect, when, at the most, it would only account
for a partial and occasional omission.   But as a husbandman
who should yield to such a disposition, is denominated by God
himself, " a sluggard," so we are sure, that he, who on such
frivolous pretexts intermits his Christian duties, will receive
no better appellation at the day of judgment than that of a
" wicked and slothful servant."]

But in whomsoever such conduct is found, he will
at last have reason to deplore,
II. The consequences of it—

As industry and wealth, so idleness and want, are
very closely connected—

[Circumstances occur in this world to interrupt the natural operation of causes and effects: but *in general*, where any man's subsistence depends upon his labour, the consequences of sloth or activity will be such as might be expected. In spiritual things the rule is absolute and invariable. Every man's progress will be according to his labour. Some indeed may enjoy more of comfort than others, from other causes than their own diligence: but every person's real proficiency in grace will be proportioned to the improvement he makes of the talents committed to him: without detracting at all from the grace of God, we may safely affirm, that the difference between one Christian and another in respect of victory over sin, and happiness in the divine life, must be traced in a very great measure to their different degrees of watchfulness in secret duties.]

This truth however will not appear in its full extent till the day of judgment—

[At the time of harvest the care or negligence of the husbandman will very clearly appear; and, if we should suppose a man to have wholly neglected the cultivation of his fields, he would find himself destitute, while others were satiated with abundance; nor, if he were reduced to beggary, would he find any one to pity his forlorn condition. But his situation, deplorable as it would be, is not to be compared with that of a negligent Christian in the day of judgment. *He* will see others reaping a glorious harvest, while he is not permitted even to glean an ear: he will behold others " crowned with glory and honour and immortality," while nothing remains for him but " indignation and wrath, tribulation and anguish." The foolish virgins, who slept while they should have been procuring oil for their lamps, came and pleaded in vain for admittance, when the door was once shut against them: none but the wise virgins were suffered to participate the nuptial feast. In the same manner, the Rich Man, who lived only to the flesh, sought in vain for one drop of water to mitigate his anguish, while Lazarus, who had lived to nobler purposes, had a fulness of joy in Abraham's bosom. Thus also will it be with all, when the great harvest shall arrive: they, who had improved their season of grace, will be partakers of glory; while they, who had wasted it in sloth and self-indulgence, will reap the fruits of their folly, in deserved shame, in perpetual want, in unalleviated, unpitied, everlasting misery.]

APPLICATION—

1. Let us, in the view of this subject, take shame to ourselves—

[How long has our season of grace been protracted; and

what little improvement have we made of it! How apt are
we to yield to sloth, and to defer the most important of all
duties on slight and frivolous pretences, which we know beforehand will never satisfy our Judge! But what can ever equal
this folly? A sluggard in temporal things may find some one
to pity his distress; and may learn from his experience to
amend. But who will ever pity the self-ruined sinner? Or
what further opportunity for amendment will be afforded him?
Let us then begin, and prosecute without remission, the work
of our souls. Let us " plow up the fallow ground, and sow in
righteousness," knowing assuredly, that " the diligent hand
shall make us rich," and that, " if we sow in tears we shall
reap in joy."]

2. Let us look forward with earnestness to the
future harvest—

[The husbandman waits with patience, in expectation that
the harvest will compensate his labours. And will not our
harvest repay all the exertions we can use, and all the self-denial
we can exercise? Let us then put forth all the energies of our
souls in preparing for that day. Let us not suffer any difficulties or discouragements to abate our ardour; but " whatever our
our hand findeth to do, let us do it with our might," " and so
much the more as we see the day approaching."]

OUTLINE NO. 801

TRUE PIETY IS RARE.

Prov. xx. 6. *Most men will proclaim every one his own good-*
ness; but a faithful man who can find?

IF we were to apply to every individual of mankind for his own character, and to form our estimate
of the world from the aggregate report, we should
soon find, that self-knowledge is a rare attainment,
and that men are but partial judges in their own
cause. Hence it is, that the more intercourse we
have with the world, the more we learn to distrust
the professions of men, and to suspend our judgment
of them, till we have more substantial ground whereon
to form it. Some indeed, from seeing unsuspecting
youth so often become a prey to designing men,
and frankness and candour so often fall a sacrifice to
deceit and treachery, have been led almost to expel
charity from their hearts, and practically to reverse
its most established laws. Charity would require that

we believe every man honest, till we have evidence to the contrary : but they exempt no man from their suspicions, till a full experience of his integrity has constrained them to revere his character. But between the extremes of blind confidence and uncharitable suspicion, there is a medium, a cautious reserve, which prudence dictates, and religion approves. Such a reserve seems naturally, and as it were necessarily, to result from the observation in our text ; an observation humiliating indeed to our proud nature, but justified by the actual state of mankind in all ages ; and fitly calculated to guard us against an undue confidence either in ourselves or others.

This observation we shall confirm, by shewing,

I. That a profession of goodness is common—

The virtues of truth, honour, integrity, benevolence, friendship, liberality, are claimed by every one as the inherent and characteristic qualities of his heart : and even piety itself is, if men's opinions of themselves be true, an inmate of every bosom. " Goodness" is not only approved by all, but claimed as the property of all :

1. Of the profane—

[They do not indeed boast of their goodness ; they will say, as hypocrites do, that ' they are as good as their neighbours. It is true, they are not always quite so correct in their conduct as they might be ; yea, they are sometimes betrayed into follies which they cannot justify ; but they mean no harm ; they injure nobody ; they have good intentions, good dispositions, good hearts' ———— The fruit is bad, they acknowledge : but they will have it, that the tree is good.]

2. Of the moral—

[These have some more pretensions to goodness, it may be thought : but their estimate of their own character is scarcely less erroneous than the judgment of the profane. They are observant of many duties ; and oftentimes are really eminent for honour and integrity in their dealings. But they omit from their catalogue of duties all that pertains to the spiritual life, and content themselves with a system of heathen ethics. Humility and contrition, faith and love, heavenly-mindedness, and communion with God, are scarcely considered by them as forming any part of true goodness : on the contrary, they allow themselves in self-esteem, self-preference, self-righteousness, and self-dependence; and, when full of these hateful dispositions, they will be " thanking God (with the Pharisee) that they are not as other men[a]," and will, in the habit of their minds at least, say to a repenting publican, " Stand off; come not near to me; I am holier than thou[b]." Of these St. Paul says, that " they have the form of godliness, but deny the power thereof[c]."]

3. Of the unsound professor—

[No one stands higher in his own conceit, than the person who has learned to talk about the Gospel, but not to practise its precepts. Because he has a zeal for some religious tenets, or for his own particular party in the Church, he is ready to conclude himself a true, perhaps an eminent, Christian; though his religion is seated altogether in his head, and has never descended to his heart. He never stops to inquire into his spirit and conduct, or to examine whether his tempers and dispositions accord with those of Christ. It is highly probable that he is guilty of very shameful neglect in many of his social and domestic duties: as a master he is proud and imperious; as a servant, inattentive and impatient of rebuke; as a parent, remiss in the instruction of his family; as a child, wilful and disobedient to his parents; in conversation, censorious; in dealings, unfaithful; and in the whole of his demeanor, conceited, forward, petulant, morose. Yet behold, this man, because he can *talk* about religion, arrogates to himself the title of good. Truly this man, whatever he may think of himself, belongs to " the generation that are pure in their own eyes, but are not washed from their filthiness[d]." He " professes to know God; but in works denies him[e]."]

But however common a profession of goodness may be, it must be confessed,

II. That a life suited to this profession is very rare—

We have seen what opinion we should form of the world, if we implicitly received men's record of themselves. But, if we apply to those who have been most conversant with the world, what shall we think of it then? Will they not tell us, that scarce any man is at all to be trusted, where his own interests are at stake: that it is scarcely possible to have dealings in any branch of commerce without meeting with numberless frauds and impositions: and that, if you rely on men's professions of disinterestedness

[a] Luke xviii. 11.　　　[b] Isai. lxv. 5.　　　[c] 2 Tim. ii. 5.
[d] Prov. xxx. 12.　　　[e] Tit. i. 16.

and friendship, you will, as soon as you come into
any great trouble, find yourself in the predicament
of one, "who has a broken tooth, or a foot out of
joint[f];" being not only deceived in your expectations
of succour, but deriving great pain from your endeavours to obtain it ?

Even in reference to these virtues to which all lay
claim, and to be destitute of which they would account it the greatest disgrace, we may apply that
humiliating question, "A faithful man who can find ?"
We must not indeed understand this question as importing that no such person can be found; but only,
that there are very few. But we must not limit the
question to mere heathen virtues: we must extend
it to all the obligations, which, as Christians, we
acknowledge. Who then is faithful,

1. To his principles ?

[As Christians, we profess to lie low before God, to live
by faith on his dear Son, to devote ourselves unreservedly to
his service, and to seek our happiness in communion with God.
But where are they whose lives correspond with these professions? Are they not so few, that they are even "signs and
wonders upon earth ?" — — — As for the generality, they will
commend departed saints, but revile and persecute the living
ones: they will applaud goodness *in general*, but decry and
discourage it *in* its most exalted *particulars*.]

2. To his promises ?

[In our baptism we all promised to "renounce the devil
and all his works, the pomps and vanities of this wicked world,
and all the sinful lusts of the flesh." When we were confirmed,
we renewed these promises, and confirmed, by our own personal
consent, the engagements that had been before made in our
behalf. If we have attended at the Lord's Supper, we there
also solemnly dedicated unto God ourselves, our souls and
bodies, to be a reasonable, holy, and lively sacrifice to him; to
be employed in his service, and, if he see fit, to be consumed
for his glory. And how have we fulfilled these promises? Has
the world been under our feet? Have all the desires of the
flesh been mortified? Have the service and enjoyment of God
been the one business of our lives? — — —]

3. To his convictions ?

[There is no one so thoughtless or obdurate, but he has
at some times a conviction arising in his mind, that he ought

[f] Prov. xxv. 19.

to repent, and turn to God, and to stand ready for death and judgment. Even the most advanced Christians feel many secret reproofs in their consciences, and are constrained to acknowledge, that they should be more meek and humble, more earnest and vigilant, more pure and spiritual. But who is faithful to his convictions? Who makes the advances that he *ought*, or the advances that he *might?* — — —]

Let us LEARN then from this subject,

1. To be jealous over ourselves—

[If there be so much self-deceit in the world, who are *we*, that we should be altogether free from it? Have not *we* a great measure of self-love within us, as well as others? Are not *we* liable to be biassed in our judgment by passion and interest? and is not *our* heart, no less than the hearts of others, "deceitful above all things and desperately wicked?" Surely we have need to tremble, when we hear God saying to us, "There is a way *that seemeth right* unto a man, and the end thereof are the ways of death [g]:" and again, "That which is highly esteemed among men, is an abomination in the sight of God [h]." Let us then be on our guard against the overweening conceit of our own goodness: let us bring ourselves to the touchstone of God's word: and let us beg of God to " search and try us, to see if there be any wicked way in us; and to lead us in the way everlasting [i]." " Not he that commendeth himself is approved, but he whom the Lord commendeth [k]."]

2. To seek the influences of God's grace—

[It is no easy matter to be a Christian *indeed*, " an Israelite without guile." We may be free from gross sin, and yet far enough from that state in which we ought to be. Our own efforts (so to speak) may suffice to " keep the outside clean;" but who, except God, can cleanse the heart? None, but he who formed the universe at first, can create our souls anew: nor unless " chosen and called by him," shall we ever be found " faithful" in the last day [l]. Let us, under a full conviction of our own insufficiency, cry mightily unto him; that he would " put a new spirit within us, and *cause* us to keep his statutes and his commandments, to do them [m]." It is " he who must work all our works in us;" it is he alone that can make us " sincere and without offence until the day of Christ!"]

3. To value and trust in the righteousness of Christ—

[Who amongst us would dare to found his hopes of salvation on his own faithfulness? Who is not sensible that he

---

[g] Prov. xiv. 12.   [h] Luke xvi. 15.   [i] Ps. cxxxix. 23, 24.
[k] 2 Cor. x. 18.   [l] Rev. xvii. 14.   [m] Ezek. xxxvi. 26, 27.

has, in instances without number, been unfaithful to his principles, his promises, and his convictions? If we presumed to
stand on that ground, God would say, "Out of thine own
mouth will I judge thee, thou wicked servant." But, if we
were not conscious of any unfaithfulness, we still could not
venture to make *that* the foundation of our hopes; because
we are so ignorant of ourselves, and so prone to self-deceit.
We could even then only say with the Apostle, "I know nothing by myself, yet am I not hereby justified: but he that
judgeth me is the Lord:" yes, we must then cast ourselves
altogether on the mercy of God in Christ Jesus. Let this then
be done by every one of us: and, instead of proclaiming every
one his own goodness, let us all humble ourselves before God
in dust and ashes, and say with the Church of old, "In the
Lord alone have I righteousness and strength[n]."]

[n] Isai. xlv. 24.

OUTLINE NO. 802

NO ABSOLUTE PERFECTION HERE BELOW.

Prov. xx. 9. *Who can say, I have made my heart clean, I am
pure from my sin?*

THE great characteristic of the Proverbs is wisdom; as that of the Psalms is piety. They were
the result of much thought and observation: and the
instructions contained in them were such as a father
might be supposed to give to his children. Occasionally, however, according as his mind had been
occupied, the tenour of his observations was varied;
and they assumed, what may be rather called, a vein
of piety. We suppose, that, when he penned the
passage before us, he had been led into some unexpected discovery of the corruptions of his own heart;
and from thence had been drawn to contemplate in a
more extended view the general depravity of human
nature, not merely as evinced by the ungodly, but
as manifested by the remains of sin in the most eminent saints. However this may be, his observation
is deep, and of singular importance. It is a challenge
to the whole world, to find, if they can, a perfect
man. Let us consider,

I. The truth that is here intimated—

There have been, and yet are, persons in the
Church of Christ who boast of sinless perfection.
But they are awfully deluded. In order to maintain
their favourite system, they reduce exceedingly the
requirements of God's law; they deny many things to
be sin, which most assuredly are sin ; and, after all,
they shut their eyes against many things which they
know to be sinful in their own hearts and lives, but
which they will not acknowledge to be sinful, lest
they should overturn the system which they are
anxious to defend. But it is a certain truth, that no
man is sinless in this world. And this appears,

1. From express declarations of Holy Writ—

[Both the Old Testament and the New concur to establish
this truth. Solomon, at his dedication of the temple, expressly
asserted, that " there was no man that lived and sinned not[a]:"
and more strongly does he elsewhere affirm, that " there is not
a just man upon earth, that doeth good, and sinneth not[b]."
To this agree also the testimonies of the inspired Apostles :
St. John says, that "if we say we have no sin, we deceive ourselves, and the truth is not in us[c]:" and St. James says, that
" in many things we offend all[d]." The whole Scripture uniformly attests this awful truth.]

2. From such instances as are undeniable—

[Among the most distinguished of God's people, were
Abraham, and Moses, and Hezekiah, and Paul: yet all of
these, even when they had arrived at the summit of human
excellence, fell into sin. Abraham, purely through fear, twice
denied his own wife, and thereby subjected her and others to
temptations, which might have issued in the everlasting destruction of their souls. Moses, the meekest man upon the face of
the earth, gave way to wrath, whereby he provoked God to
exclude him from the earthly Canaan. Hezekiah, than whom
no man upon the whole ever more honoured God, yet yielded
to pride and creature-confidence, when he shewed all his treasures to the ambassadors of the king of Babylon. And Paul,
after he had preached for twenty years, and attained an eminence in the divine life, not inferior to that of any of the children
of men, was so carried away by his own spirit under a sudden
trial and temptation, that he reviled God's High Priest, which
he himself acknowledged to be a violation of an express command. Who then, after viewing these, will " say, that he is
pure from sin ?"]

[a] 1 Kings viii. 46.   [b] Eccl. vii. 20.
[c] 1 John i. 8—10.   [d] Jam. iii. 2.

3. From the confessions of God's most eminent saints—

[Job, previous to his trials, was pronounced by God " a perfect man ;" yet, after his trials, confessed, " Behold, I am vile !" Paul occupies a whole chapter in his epistle to the Romans in describing the internal conflicts of his mind; sin and grace mutually striving to overpower each other, and disabling him from fully vanquishing the one, or carrying into effect the dictates of the other. " In his flesh," he says, " dwelt no good thing :" but there was, notwithstanding all the attainments of his renewed mind, " a law in his members warring against the law of his mind, and bringing him into captivity to the law of sin which was in his members." Will any other then of the children of men say, " I am pure from all sin?" From the *dominion* of sin every saint may affirm that he is freed ; yea, and from the *wilful and allowed* indulgence of any. David justly appeals to God respecting his perfect freedom from sin, as to any *intention and purpose* to commit it[e]; as Job also does respecting the extinction of its reigning power: "Thou knowest, that I am not wicked[f]." But, if any man should go farther, and say, that sin was not still living within him, and operating occasionally to the polluting of his soul, he must stand self-convicted, and self-condemned ; just as Job has said, " If I justify myself, mine own mouth shall condemn me : if I say, I am perfect, it shall also prove me perverse[g]."]

Such being the state of our fallen nature, it becomes us to consider,

II. The improvement we should make of it—

This truth should never be lost sight of for one moment : it should regulate every feeling of the heart: it should never cease to call forth and to augment,

1. Our humiliation—

[We are sinful creatures at the best ; and are in the situation of wretched captives, who, having a dead body fastened to them, were compelled to drag it about, till they themselves were destroyed by its pestilential vapours[h] — — — This, it must be acknowledged, is a most humiliating truth, and not unfitly expressed in the general Confession of our Liturgy, " There is no health in us." Hence, when we are taught to " lothe ourselves for our iniquities and our abominations," we must remember that it is not for the actions only that are long

---

[e] Ps. xvii. 3.   [f] Job x. 7.   [g] Job ix. 20, 30, 31.
[h] See what is said of Mezentius in Virgil ; Æn. lib. viii. l. 485—488.

since past, but for the taint also which they have left behind them, that this self-abasement is necessary. So Job thought[i], and so Isaiah[k], and so Paul[l]: and, if we know ourselves aright, we shall find no terms more suited to express our real state, than those in which the prophet Isaiah described the Jews of his day; " The whole head is sick, and the whole heart faint: from the sole of the foot even to the head, there is no soundness in us, but wounds, and bruises, and putrifying sores[m]."]

2. Our watchfulness—

[A magazine wherein there was a large store of combustible matter that might produce extensive injury by an explosion, would be guarded with all possible care: and can any care be too great, when we consider how many thousand things there are on every side ready to kindle a destructive flame in our hearts, and how incessantly our great adversary is striving to make use of them for our destruction? We know not what a day or an hour may bring forth. We may be as far from thinking of evil as at any moment of our lives, and yet evil may arise from some unexpected quarter, and produce upon us the most painful consequences. We are never safe for one moment, but whilst we are upheld in the arms of our Almighty Friend. We should therefore be continually crying to him, " Hold up my goings in thy paths, that my footsteps slip not!" at the same time that we should be striving continually to " put off the old man, and to put on the new." This is the advice given us by our Lord himself; " Watch, and pray, that ye enter not into temptation:" for however " willing the spirit be" to approve itself to God, " the flesh is weak."]

3. Our gratitude—

[What a miracle of mercy is it, that, with so much corruption about us, we are preserved in any measure from dishonouring our holy profession! The wonder is not that any fall, but that any are " kept from falling." And to whom is it owing that any of us are enabled to maintain our steadfastness in the divine life? is it to ourselves? No: Peter shews us, what we should soon be, if left to ourselves: Satan would soon " sift us all as wheat," if our blessed Saviour did not intercede for us, and give us fresh supplies of grace and strength[n]. Let us then be sensible of our great and unbounded obligations to Him, who has said, that " he keepeth the feet of his saints." Let us bear in mind to whom it is owing, that, notwithstanding the bush is ever burning, it is yet unconsumed: and let us give all the glory of our stability to God, saying with David, " My foot standeth in an even place; in the congregations will I bless the Lord[o]."]

i Job xlii. 6.　　　k Isai. vi. 5.　　　l Rom. vii. 24.
m Isai. i. 5, 6.　　　n Luke xxii. 31, 32.　　　o Ps. xxvi. 12.

4. Our love to Christ—

[Notwithstanding in ourselves we are so corrupt, in Christ we are accepted, and beloved of the Lord. Washed in his blood, and clothed in his righteousness, we are presented unto the Father " without spot or wrinkle, or any such thing; yea, holy, and without blemish." O! how " precious" ought this Saviour to be to all our souls! How continually should we go to him, and plunge beneath " the fountain of his blood, which was opened for sin and for uncleanness," and which is able to " cleanse us from all sin!" How should we delight ourselves in him, and " cleave to him," and " glory in him," and devote ourselves to him! Yes, Brethren, this is the tribute which we owe to our blessed Lord. We must " not continue in sin, that grace may abound," but turn from sin because grace has abounded; and, " because He has bought us with the inestimable price of his own blood, we should strive to glorify him with our bodies and our spirits, which are his[p]."]

p 1 Cor. vi. 20.

OUTLINE NO. 803

DESIRE IS NOTHING WITHOUT LABOUR.

Prov. xxi. 25. *The desire of the slothful killeth him; for his hands refuse to labour.*

IT is the duty of a minister to " comfort the Lord's people," and on no account to " make the heart of the righteous sad." Our blessed Lord " brake not the bruised reed, nor quenched the smoking flax :" and in this respect all who minister in his name must follow his example, never " despising the day of small things," but " carrying the lambs in their bosom, and gently leading them that are with young." But there are occasions whereon they " must change their voice, especially when they stand in doubt of any," or judge it necessary to give a salutary warning to their flocks. Now there is an error against which I would wish affectionately to guard you, and that is, the laying of an undue stress upon good desires without pressing forward for the attainment of the object desired. To this line of instruction I am led by the passage before us ; from which I will take occasion,

I. To shew you the influence of good desires.

It is plain that, in Solomon's opinion, good desires, which when duly cherished and improved, will be productive of the happiest effects, may through sloth and indolence issue in self-deception and ruin. That we may have a just view of this important subject, I will mark the influence of good desires,

1. In the bosoms of the diligent—

[This, though not expressly mentioned, is evidently implied, since it is in the slothful only that good desires can have a fatal issue.

Now we need only see how desire operates in diligent men, whatever their vocation be, whether in trade, or agriculture, or science; and that will shew us how it will operate in reference to religion: it will stimulate men to such exertions as are necessary to the acquisition of the object desired[a] — — — For the attainment of heaven, we must exert ourselves in a way of "repentance towards God, and faith in our Lord Jesus Christ:" and, if our desires after heaven be sincere, they will render us earnest and laborious in the pursuit of these, and never suffer us to pause till we have actually attained them — — — Thus accompanied with diligence, they will bring us to the enjoyment of peace and holiness and glory — — —]

2. In the bosoms of the slothful—

[In *them* good desires may justly be said to occasion death. They do so *indirectly*, because they are not productive of suitable exertions. It is said, "The slothful man roasteth not that which he took in hunting[b]." And this is precisely the case with those whose conduct we are considering. They have, in consequence of their good desires, pursued and obtained the knowledge of religious truth; but in consequence of their sloth they have neglected to follow their advantages, and to improve their attainments for the benefit of their souls. Hence "their vineyard is overgrown with thorns, and the stone wall thereof is fallen down; yea, and poverty comes upon them (*gradually*) like one that travelleth, and want (*irresistibly*) like an armed man[c]:" so true is that declaration of Solomon, "He that is slothful in his work is brother to him that is a great waster[d]."

But this is by no means the full sense of our text. It is not in an indirect way only that in the slothful man good desires operate to the production of death: no; they have a *direct* influence towards the destruction of his soul. The man in whose bosom good desires arise, is conscious of them; and

---

[a] Point out this in reference to the fore-mentioned pursuits.
[b] Prov. xii. 27.   [c] Prov. xxiv. 30—34.   [d] Prov. xviii. 9.

takes occasion from them to entertain a good opinion of his state before God. *He puts them in the place of good attainments;* and, because he hopes that they shall at some future period accomplish their proper work, he overlooks the necessity of immediately experiencing that work, and conceives, that God will, if I may so speak, accept the will for the deed. To countenance this delusion, he applies to himself such promises as these; "The Lord will fulfil the desire of them that fear him [e]:" "The desire of the righteous shall be granted [f]." He forgets that the end is connected with the means; and that, however we may acknowledge our obligations to God for ability to *will* what is good, we can have no hope of acceptance with him, unless we exert ourselves with all diligence to *do* it, and to "work out our salvation with fear and trembling [g]." Hence he is a living witness of that melancholy fact, "The soul of the sluggard desireth, and hath nothing, whilst the soul of the diligent is made fat [h]." Yes, to all eternity will he be a monument of that mysterious truth. "The desire of the slothful killeth him."]

Having marked the operation of good desires, I now proceed,

II. To offer some salutary counsel in relation to them—

Doubtless good desires must take the lead, yea, and must move us, in the whole of our Christian course : but, as "faith itself is dead without works," so are good desires of no value any farther than they are productive of holy lives. I say then, if God have given to any of you good desires, see to it that those desires be,

1. Abiding—

[There are few persons so depraved but they have felt on some particular occasion the risings of good desire. But to what purpose are such emotions in the soul, if they "pass away like the morning cloud, or as the early dew [i]?" To know what is good, and not to do it, involves us in the heavier guilt [k], and will prove a ground of heavier condemnation to the soul; as God has said, "This is the condemnation, that light is come into the world, and men have loved darkness rather than light, because their deeds are evil [l]." If then you would derive real benefit from the desires which God has mercifully implanted in you, see that they take root within you, and become living and active principles in your souls.]

[e] Ps. cxlv. 19.   [f] Prov. x. 24.   [g] Phil. ii. 12, 13.
[h] Prov. xiii. 4.   [i] Hos. vi. 4.   [k] Jam. iv. 17.
[l] John iii. 19.

2. Operative—

[You desire to obtain salvation. It is well: but to what
purpose will this desire be, if it do not stimulate you to action?
Will a desire of knowledge render any one a philosopher, if he
neglect his studies? Will a desire of a harvest enrich a man,
if he neglect to cultivate his land? How then can you hope
that a desire of heaven will ever bring you thither, if you
neglect the concerns of your souls? You must read the Holy
Scriptures with meditation and prayer: you must search out
your sins, and mourn over them before God: you must get
views of Christ as the only Saviour of the world, and must go
to him continually that you may receive out of his fulness the
grace that shall be sufficient for you. You must be gaining
an increasing victory over the world, and the flesh, and the
devil, and be growing more and more like unto your God and
Saviour in righteousness and true holiness. You must be
living more for God in the midst of this corrupt world, and be
bringing glory to his name by your exertions in his sacred
cause. It is in this way that your good desires must work, if
you would have them productive of any saving benefit to your
souls. The stony-ground hearers, whose desires were only
temporary, perished, notwithstanding the fair appearances
which for a season they assumed; as did the thorny-ground
hearers also, because they " brought forth no fruit to perfection." And you also must not only begin well, but " endure
unto the end," and " be faithful unto death," if ever you would
be saved in the great day of the Lord Jesus. The " slothful,"
be they who they may, shall be condemned in that day as
" wicked[m]."]

3. Supreme—

[" You cannot serve God and mammon." The world may
have your hands; but God must have your heart, your whole
heart[n]. He will not accept a divided heart[o]. " The world
must become crucified to you, and you unto the world[p]."
" Your affections must be set on things above, and not on
things below[q]:" and " your conversation must be altogether in
heaven[r]." " There must be nothing either in heaven or earth
that you desire besides God[s]."

You must resemble David, who says, " This one thing have
I *desired*[t]," and St. Paul, who says, " This one thing I *do*[u]."
Then shall God fully answer you in the desires of your heart,
and your efforts be crowned with glorious success.]

[m] Matt. xxv. 26.   [n] Prov. xxiii. 26.   [o] Hos. x. 2.
[p] Gal. vi. 14.   [q] Col. iii. 1.   [r] Phil. iii. 20.
[s] Ps. lxxiii. 25.   [t] Ps. xxvii. 4.   [u] Phil. iii. 13.

OUTLINE NO. 804

THE FEAR OF GOD ALL THE DAY.

Prov. xxiii. 17, 18. *Be thou in the fear of the Lord all the day long: for surely there is an end; and thine expectation shall not be cut off.*

THE men of this world, feeling but little restraint from the voice of conscience or the fear of God, gratify, each in his own way, their natural inclinations; and therefore they appear happy: and the people of God, especially under troubles and persecutions for righteousness sake, are almost ready to look upon them with an eye of envy: and, if this world only were considered, and temporal enjoyments were the proper standard of happiness, perhaps they might on the whole be congratulated as possessing a happy and an enviable lot[a]. But the righteous, under whatever disadvantages they may lie, have no just cause to "envy sinners;" seeing that nothing but disappointment awaits the children of this world; whilst the servants of God, who look forward to heavenly bliss, can never be disappointed of their hope. On this assurance the exhortation in my text is founded; and for the fuller elucidation of the subject, I will set before you,

I. The duty inculcated—

"The fear of the Lord" is, especially in the Old Testament, a common expression, comprehending in its import the whole of practical religion. And when we are bidden to live under its influence "all the day long," we must understand the precept as enjoining us to maintain, throughout the whole course of our lives,

1. A sense of love to God, as our Father—

[Jehovah, as reconciled to us through the Son of his love, stands in the relation of a Father to us; for all, the very instant they believe in Christ, have "the privilege of becoming the Sons of God[b]." Till we come to God by Christ, we have no *filial* fear of him in our hearts. A *slavish* fear of him we may

<hr>

a Ps. lxxiii. 3—5.   b John i. 12.

have; but we neither have, nor can have, " a Spirit of adoption, emboldening us to call him Father:" for "the Holy Spirit
can never bear witness with our spirit, that we are the Lord's[c],"
till we are made his by faith in Christ Jesus[d]. But when we
are become his children, then we must go in and out before
him with holy confidence, exactly as duteous children before
a loving parent — — — To walk thus before him was the
perfection of Abraham's attainments[e]; and it is that which is
held forth to us also as the summit of a Christian's duty and
privilege[f] — — —]

2. A sense of duty to him, as our Master—

[This is united with the former by God himself: " A son
honoureth his father, and a servant his master: if, then, I be a
father, where is mine honour? and if I be a master, where is
my fear[g]?" Now, what is the conduct of a good servant?
When he rises in the morning, he asks himself, ' What have I
to do for my master?' and through every part of the day, even
to the close of it, the same question recurs to his mind, and
calls forth suitable exertions for the discharge of the duties
required of him. And if, when engaged in executing his master's commands, he were solicited by any one to embark in
some other pursuit, he would immediately reply, as our blessed
Saviour did, " I must be about my Father's business:" nor
could any consideration tempt him to neglect his duty. He
would, under all circumstances, regard his master's work as
claiming a just preference at his hands, and his master's approbation as that which, above all, he was anxious to obtain. Let
it be thus, then, with you in every situation of life; and make
it your one business to approve yourselves good servants of
Jesus Christ.]

3. A sense of responsibility to him as our Judge—

[Never are you to lose a sense of this. It is quite a mistake to call this _legal_. St. Paul, and all the Apostles, acted
with a direct reference to the future judgment; and sought so
to demean themselves that they might welcome the second
coming of their Lord, and stand with boldness before him at
that awful day[h]. This will secure the obedience of the _heart:_
for in that day shall " the secrets of men's hearts be disclosed,"
and, " their inmost counsels be made manifest:" and, to secure
his approbation _then_, you must be upright, and without any
allowed guile. Let every place then bear, as it were, this inscription, " Thou, God, seest me;" and take heed to your

[c] Rom. viii. 15, 16.   [d] Gal. iii. 26.   [e] Gen. xvii. 1.
[f] Eph. v. 1.   [g] Mal. i. 6.
[h] 1 Cor. ix. 26, 27.   2 Cor. v. 9, 10.   Jam. v. 8, 9.   1 Pet. v. 1—4.

thoughts, no less than to your actions, that so you may be found " sincere and without offence until the day of Christ[i]."]

And, lest such a constant attention to duty should appear irksome to you, let me shew you,

II. The encouragement given us to the performance of it—

The whole Scripture declares, that, " verily, there is a reward for the righteous[k];" and this, I conceive, is the true import of my text[l]. The ungodly expect to find happiness in their ways of sin; but they pursue a phantom, and embrace a shadow. But not so they who fear the Lord: *they* shall " have a sure reward;" as God hath said, " The hope of the righteous shall be gladness; but the expectation of the wicked shall perish[m]." What, then, my Brethren, do ye expect? Do you expect pardon of sin?

[This shall surely be accorded to you: for " in the fear of the Lord there is strong confidence; and his children shall have a place of refuge[n]." Yes, verily, however numerous your sins may have been, " they shall all be blotted out, even as a morning cloud." Will God cast out one who comes to him in his Son's name? Will he spurn from his footstool one humble suppliant? No: " to this man will he look, even to him that is poor and of a contrite spirit, and that trembleth at his word[o];" and " to him will he give beauty for ashes, the oil of joy for mourning, and the garment of praise for the spirit of heaviness[p]."]

Peace of conscience?

[This also shall you possess. Hear what David says: " What man is he that feareth the Lord? Him shall the Lord teach in the way that he shall choose; and his soul shall dwell at ease[q]." Peace is the legacy which Jesus has bequeathed to all his redeemed people, saying, " Peace I leave with you; my peace I give unto you[r]." " To the wicked there is no peace[s]:" but for you is there " a peace that passeth all understanding."]

Strength for duty?

[Doubtless you may have many difficulties to encounter:

---

[i] Phil. i. 10.   [k] Ps. lviii. 11.
[l] See the marginal reading, and compare it with ch. xxiv. 14.
[m] Prov. x. 28. with xi. 18.   [n] Prov. xiv. 26.
[o] Isai. lxvi. 2.   [p] Ps. lxi. 1—3.   [q] Ps. xxv. 12, 13.
[r] John xiv. 27.   [s] Isai. lvii. 21.

but God himself promises that "your strength shall be according to your day." His very covenant with his people is, " He will put his fear in their hearts, that they shall not depart from him [t]." This is a principle which cannot but operate, and cannot but be effectual for the mortification of all sin, and for the performance of all duty. See its operation in the Apostle Paul. Under trials as severe as man could well be called to endure, he said, " I know that this shall turn to my salvation, through your prayer, and the supply of the Spirit of Jesus Christ, according to my earnest expectation and my hope, that in nothing I shall be ashamed, but that with all boldness, as always, so now also, Christ shall be magnified in my body, whether it be by life or by death [u]." Thus you may encounter all difficulties without fear; and, knowing in whom you have believed, may assure yourselves that no enemy whatever shall be able to prevail against you [x].]

Comfort in death?

[This also is secured to you: " Mark the perfect man, and behold the upright; for the end of that man is peace [y]." I say not that you shall have *joy:* for there may be in the very nature of your disorder much to prevent that buoyancy of mind which is a necessary attendant on joy: but *peace* shall assuredly be your portion, if only you trust in God: for God has said, " I will keep him in perfect peace whose mind is stayed on me, because he trusteth in me [z]."]

Glory in eternity?

[This also shall be yours. Your expectations cannot be too enlarged, if you walk in the fear of God as you are here enjoined: " I know the thoughts that I think towards you, saith the Lord; thoughts of good, and not of evil, to give you an expected end [a]. " And in this you differ widely from the sinner, who casts off the fear of God. To persons of this latter description God says, " What fruit had ye then of those things whereof ye are now ashamed? for the end of those things is death. But now, being made free from sin, and become servants to God, ye have your fruit unto holiness and your end everlasting life [b]."

Tell me now, Brethren, whether ye have not encouragement to fear the Lord? — — — and whether there be any sinner in the universe whose portion can be compared with yours? — — —]

APPLICATION—

[t] Jer. xxxii. 40.   [u] Phil. i. 19, 20.   [x] Rom. viii. 35—39.
[y] Ps. xxxvii. 37.   [z] Isai. xxvi. 3.   [a] Jer. xxix. 11.
[b] Rom. vi. 21, 22.

[As for *you who fear not God*, whatever ye may possess of this world, or whatever gratifications ye may enjoy, ye have a miserable portion indeed: and though ye abounded with every thing, like the Rich Man in the Gospel, yet were a pious Lazarus, that was destitute of all things, or even a martyr at the stake, in a preferable state to yours: and well may *ye envy* the poorest, the meanest saint on earth. Where will ye look for pardon, for peace, for strength, for comfort in a dying hour, and for glory in eternity? Think ye of your misery ere it be too late; and beg of God to implant in your hearts that fear of his name, which is the certain and the only prelude to his final approbation.]

OUTLINE NO. 805

BUYING THE TRUTH.

Prov. xxiii. 23. *Buy the truth; and sell it not.*

THE rich variety of metaphors contained in the Holy Scriptures gives an endless diversity to the most simple truths: and the commonness of those metaphors brings home to our minds the deepest truths, with a clearness that cannot be misinterpreted, and a force that cannot be withstood. The idea of buying and selling is familiar to every mind; so familiar, that many would be offended at the application of it to the concerns of the soul. But we should not affect a squeamishness which the Inspired Writers did not feel; except, indeed, in reference to subjects which, though not offensive to Jewish ears, the refinement of modern ages has justly deemed indelicate. Permit me then, without offence, to shew you,

I. What it is that is here commended to us—

Truth, abstractedly considered, is of great value; and the acquisition of it in science and philosophy is counted worthy of the most laborious researches. In astronomy, for instance, the ascertaining of the motion and mutual relation of the heavenly bodies is justly regarded as a rich recompence for a whole life of labour. But this is not the truth of which my text speaks: for *that*, once gained, remains with us: whereas the truth which is here commended to us may be sold as well as bought.

"The truth" here referred to is the Gospel—

[The Gospel was revealed to Abraham, as well as unto us: and it was made yet more fully known to Moses and the Israelites; though, from their "not mixing faith with it, it did not profit them." On us it shines in its meridian splendour: it exhibits to us a Saviour, even our incarnate God, living and dying for sinful men; and marks our path to heaven so plainly, that "a way-faring man, though a fool, cannot err therein" — — —]

This truth is of incalculable importance to every child of man—

[There is much truth which the philosopher alone can appreciate or understand. But "the truth, as it is in Jesus," may be understood by all. It is not by strength of intellect that its wonders are discerned, but by a spiritual perception, which God alone can impart[a]; and which he often does impart to "babes and sucklings, whilst he withholds it from the wise and prudent[b]." And to every human being it is of equal importance: none can be saved without it, and by it every creature in the universe may be saved. Our blessed Lord has assured us of this: "Ye shall know *the truth;* and *the truth* shall make you free[c]." Nothing but that will impart freedom: but that will make us free indeed; delivering us from all the guilt we have ever contracted, and from all the bondage under which we have groaned. Let us only "receive the truth in the love of it," and we shall be brought by it into the "glorious liberty of the children of God."]

This view of the truth may prepare us for,

II. The advice given us in relation to it—

"Buy the truth"—

[It must be purchased: freely as it is given, I say again, it must be purchased: it must be bought with labour, and with the sacrifice of every thing that can stand in competition with it. The fruits of the earth, though given us entirely by God through the genial influence of the heavens, must be sought and laboured for: nor can we hope to obtain "the fruits of the Spirit" without similar exertions. Solomon tells us, that, notwithstanding it is "the Lord who *giveth* knowledge," "we must cry after it, and lift up our voice for it, and seek it as silver, and search for it as for hid treasures: and that *then only* can we understand the fear of the Lord, and find the knowledge of God[d]."

Nor is it less necessary that we be ready to part with all earthly interests in order to secure it. Our Lord compares the Gospel salvation to "a treasure hid in a field," and to "a pearl

[a] 1 Cor. ii. 14. [b] Matt. xi. 25, 26. [c] John viii. 32.
[d] Prov. ii. 3—6.

of preat price: which whosoever finds, should go and sell all that he has and purchase it[e]." If, like the Rich Youth in the Gospel, we refuse to part with all, we never can possess the salvation of God. St. Paul is our pattern in this respect. He possessed more of what was really valuable than any unconverted man ever did before him: but " what things were gain to me," says he, " those I counted loss for Christ: yea, doubtless, and I count all things but loss for the excellency of the knowledge of Christ Jesus my Lord." Nor does he give this as a sentiment which he was *ready to maintain*, but as one which he had already carried into effect: " for whom," adds he, " I *have suffered* the loss of all things, and *do count* them but dung that I may win Christ[f]." And it is worthy of observation, that amongst the things which he despised thus, are to be reckoned, not his temporal interests only, but his own carnal wisdom and his legal righteousness[g]; which, to a man of Pharisaic habits, are far more dear than all the world besides. After his example, then, we must renounce all that is pleasing to flesh and blood, and take " Christ for our Wisdom, our Righteousness, our Sanctification, and our complete Redemption."]

2. " Sell it not"—

[We shall be continually tempted to part with it: but we must " hold fast what we have, that no man may take our crown." We must " never, after having once put our hand to the plough, look back again." In seasons of prosperity we may be lulled asleep; and Satan may rob us of our prize. And in times of persecution we may be intimidated, and draw back through fear. But " nothing," however terrible, " should move us." We should " be ready, not only to be bound, but also to die, at any time, and in any manner, for the name of the Lord Jesus." If called to suffer for his sake, we must " rejoice that we are counted worthy" of so high an honour: yea, we must even " leap for joy," because we are thereby rendered conformable to Christ, and because " God is glorified in us." We must " be faithful unto death, if ever we would obtain a crown of life."]

ADDRESS—

1. Examine whether you have " the truth" set before you—

[In purchasing any commodity, you endeavour to ascertain that it is good and genuine. And so must you do in relation to the Gospel. You must not take any thing for granted. You have a touchstone, by which you must try whatever is offered to you for sale. St. Paul speaks of a false Gospel, as finding an extensive currency in the Galatian Church[h]; and

---

[e] Matt. xiii. 44—46.   [f] Phil. iii. 7, 8.   [g] Phil. iii. 9.   [h] Gal. i. 6, 7.

such a Gospel is but too often commended to us at this day. Examine, then, what ye hear; and bring it all to the test of God's blessed word. The salvation which we offer you, is that which Christ purchased for us on the cross; a salvation altogether *by grace* and *through faith* in Christ. It is *that*, and that only, that we call on you to buy. And our counsel is that which is given to every one of you by our Lord himself: " I counsel thee to buy of me gold tried in the fire, that thou mayest be rich; and white raiment, that thou mayest be clothed, and that the shame of thy nakedness do not appear; and anoint thine eyes with eye-salve, that thou mayest see[i]." Ascertain, I say, that this is the very truth of God; and then hesitate not to buy it, though at the price of all that you possess.]

2. Inquire whether any who have bought it ever repented of their purchase—

[I know, indeed, that you may find stony-ground hearers in every place where the Gospel is preached; yea, and many a Demas too. But the former are persons who never had the root of grace within them; and the latter carry back with them into the world a self-condemning conscience, that will embitter their whole lives. Could you ask of Moses, whether he now regrets, or ever did regret, the having sacrificed all the treasures of Egypt for that apparently worthless portion, the reproach of Christ; or, could you consult the myriads who " came out of great tribulation," and who "loved not their lives unto death;" would you find one amongst them all that thought he had ever paid too dear for this heavenly prize? No: there is no such thought in heaven; nor is there any such feeling upon earth amongst the faithful followers of the Lamb. Be not ye afraid, then, to pay the price demanded of you: for, as " the gain of the whole world would be a poor matter in exchange for the soul;" so the sacrifice of life itself will be found to have been unworthy of a thought, when the glory purchased by it shall have been accorded to you.]

3. Lose not the opportunity that is now afforded you—

[What would millions that are now in the eternal world give, if they could have but one more offer of that salvation which they once despised? And soon you yourselves also will be filled with bitter regret, if you close not with the offer now made to you —— Say not that you are poor, and cannot pay the price: for you are invited " to *buy* it *without money and without price*[k]." O that I might but prevail upon you, ere it be too late! Refuse not, with Herod, to give up your

i Rev. iii. 18. k Isai. lv. 1.

Herodias; nor, with Agrippa, to become altogether Christians: but now forsake all for Christ; and expect, both in this world and the next, a rich and glorious equivalent[1].]

[1] Luke xviii. 28—30.

OUTLINE NO. 806

THE DUTY OF GIVING THE HEART TO GOD.

Prov. xxiii. 26. *My Son, give me thy heart.*

THIS address, however it may be considered in some respect as delivered by Solomon to his son, must certainly be understood as proceeding from Him who is Wisdom in the abstract, Wisdom personified, even from the Lord Jesus Christ[a]; and as directed generally to all the children of men, but especially to those who regard him as their Sovereign Lord. And though the more immediate object of the address may seem scarcely suited to this view of it, (because those who are possessed even of incipient piety may seem less likely to fall into the snare which is there spoken of,) yet the caution is necessary for youth of all descriptions; and, as a general lesson, it teaches us, that there is no snare whatever into which we may not fall, if our hearts be not given up to God; and that the only sure way of being kept from sin of every kind, is, to give the heart to God.

Taking the words then as addressed by the Lord Jesus Christ to all who acknowledge his paternal authority, we will proceed to mark *the extent and reasonableness of this command.*

I. The extent of it—

To give our heart to God, implies that we give him,

1. The affections of the soul—

[These should all center in him, and in him alone. Him we should desire as our supreme good, and in him should we delight as our chief joy — — — We should be able to say with David, "Whom have I in heaven but Thee? and there is none upon earth that I desire besides thee[b]."]

2. The confidence of the mind—

[a] Prov. viii. 1, 22—32.   [b] Ps. lxxiii. 25.

[If there be any thing besides God in the whole universe, on which we rely, we do not really give our heart to him. To trust, though in ever so small a degree, in an arm of flesh, argues a departure of heart from God[c]. We should confide altogether in his wisdom to guide, and his power to uphold us, in his goodness to supply our wants, and his truth to fulfil to us the promises of his word. We should "trust in him with all our heart, and not lean either to our own understanding" or strength: we should consider him as alone able to help us, and as all-sufficient for our utmost necessities.]

3. The service of the life—

[Without this, all else is vain. Obedience is the certain fruit of love to God[d]; yea, it is altogether identified with it: "This is the love of God, that ye keep his commandments[e]." To the man that has given his heart to God, no commandment can be grievous[f].]

The extent of the command being ascertained, we proceed to shew,

II. The reasonableness of it—

To surrender up our whole selves to God, is called by St. Paul, "a reasonable service[g]." And reasonable indeed it is;

1. Because of his right over us as our Creator—

[God "made all things for himself: all that we are, and all that we have, was given us by him, to be improved for his glory. How then can we with propriety alienate any thing from him? A potter feels himself entitled to the use of the vessel which his own hands have made: and has not God a right to all the services that we can render him? Of all that have truly given their hearts to God, it may be said, "No man liveth to himself; and no man dieth unto himself: but whether we live, we live unto the Lord; and whether we die, we die unto the Lord: whether we live therefore or die, we are the Lord's[h]."]

2. Because of his mercies towards us, as our Redeemer—

[The Lord Jesus Christ has "redeemed us to God by his own blood;" and by this has acquired a new right over us. To this effect the Apostle says, "Ye are not your own; ye are bought with a price: therefore glorify God with your bodies and your spirits, which are his[i]." And in another place he

---

[c] Jer. xvii. 5. [d] John xiv. 15, 21. [e] 1 John ii. 3—5.
[f] 1 John v. 3. [g] Rom. xii. 1. [h] Rom. xiv. 7, 8.
[i] 1 Cor. vi. 19, 20.

gives this as the duty of every man according to the dictates of his most deliberate judgment: "The love of Christ constraineth us, because we thus judge, that if one died for all, then were all dead; and that he died for all, that they who live should not henceforth live unto themselves, but unto him who died for them, and rose again[k]." Was he mistaken in his judgment? and are we at liberty to alienate from him what he has purchased at so great a price?]

3. Because of his relation to us, as our Father—

[If we profess to have been born again, and begotten to God by his word and Spirit, then are we yet further bound to him by the relation he sustains towards us: "What manner of love is this, wherewith the Father hath loved us, that we should be called the sons of God!" Can we have learned to cry, "Abba, Father!" and doubt whether the giving of our hearts to him be a reasonable service? The utmost then we can do to serve and honour him is no more than our bounden duty.]

4. Because of the utter worthlessness of all his competitors—

[What is there worthy to be compared with him? The whole creation is but as "a broken cistern that can hold no water." Shall we then, "for any thing that is in it, forsake the Fountain of living waters?" Survey the choicest blessings that the world affords; and they are all "vanity and vexation of spirit." Are these then to stand in competition with him who is the unfailing and only source of all blessedness? The more we see the vanity of all created good, the more we shall see the reasonableness of giving our hearts to God alone. We must not only not love our father or mother more than him, but must "*hate* every earthly relative, yea, and our own lives also, *in comparison* of him[l]."]

ADDRESS—

1. In a way of affectionate invitation—

[In this view we may take the words of our text, even as an invitation to us from the Lord Jesus Christ to set our affections on him alone. And how astonishing is it that he will accept such hearts as ours! If we of ourselves had presumed to offer them to him, how justly might he have rejected and despised the offering! Yet behold, he solicits it at our hands! And what can such an offering add to him? Does he need any thing from us? or can we add any thing to him? O then admire and adore this astonishing condescension; and let him not woo your souls in vain.]

2. In a way of authoritative injunction—

[k] 2 Cor. v. 14, 15.   [l] Luke xiv. 26.

[This command of Almighty God is not to be trifled with. Let none presume to withstand it, or to delay their obedience to it: for if we obey it not, we never can behold his face in peace[m]. Attend to it then; and see that ye obey it in truth. Give not to your God and Saviour a divided heart; for such an offering he will not accept: but give yourselves *wholly* to him; and so shall that promise be fulfilled to you; " I will be a Father unto you, and ye shall be my sons and daughters, saith the Lord Almighty."]

[m] 1 Cor. xvi. 22.

OUTLINE NO. 807

THE FOLLY OF VAIN EXCUSES.

Prov. xxiv. 11, 12. *If thou forbear to deliver them that are drawn unto death, and those that are ready to be slain; if thou sayest, Behold, we knew it not; doth not he that pondereth the heart consider it? and he that keepeth thy soul, doth not he know it? And shall not he render to every man according to his works?*

OFFICIAL influence is a valuable talent: but to use it aright is often very difficult, and painful to the feelings. Hence those who are possessed of it, are apt to shrink back, when the exercise of it is likely to involve them in much trouble; and they will connive at abuses, which they cannot easily prevent. For such connivance they have excuses ever ready at hand; " They were not aware of the circumstances;" or, " They thought their interposition would be to no purpose." But power and responsibility are inseparable: and the magistrate who neglects his duty, must give an account of such neglect to God, and have his excuses weighed in the balance of the sanctuary. To succour the needy, and to relieve the oppressed, is a sacred duty, which no man can neglect, but at the peril of his soul: and to deceive ourselves with vain excuses is folly in the extreme.

We shall not however limit our views of this subject to magistrates, but shall extend them generally to all those excuses which men make for their neglect of acknowledged duties; and shall consider,

I. The excuses by which men deceive their own souls—

None are so hardy as to deny their obligation to serve God : yet the great mass of mankind will plead excuses for their neglect,

1. Of religious duties—

["They have not time to attend to their spiritual concerns." Not time ? For what then is their time given them? and what other business have they in comparison of this? But, if they would speak the truth, is not their disregard of religion to be traced rather to their want of inclination to spiritual things———their want of faith in the divine records——— their want of all fear of God, and all concern about their souls? ——— How vain then their plea of want of time, when their neglect arises from a total alienation of their hearts from God!]

2. Of moral duties—

[The duties of sympathy, of compassion, of activity in succouring the distressed, are mentioned in our text. Now for the neglect of these duties, such as the visiting of the sick, the instructing of the ignorant, the relieving of the needy, and the comforting of the afflicted, men will plead ignorance, inadvertence, forgetfulness, inability. But is there not a great degree of criminality attaching to us, if we do not search out the poor and afflicted, on purpose to alleviate their distresses? ——— and is not the true cause of our supineness, that we have no love to our fellow-creatures, no zeal for God, no gratitude for redeeming love? ———It is in vain to think that our neglects are venial under any circumstances, and more especially when they originate in cowardice, and sloth, and selfishness.]

Seeing then that such excuses are vain, let us mark,

II. The folly of resting in them—

Were there no God to call us into judgment, our delusions would be of less consequence : but there is a God by whom all our excuses will be weighed ; and he,

1. Will judge with truth—

[He looketh not at the outward appearance; "He searcheth the heart and tries the reins," and is privy to the most secret workings of our minds. We may easily deceive ourselves ; but him we cannot deceive. See how forcible is the appeal made to us in our text. Can we have any doubt whether he sees our conduct, or forms a correct estimate of it? Let us remember, that " he will bring to light the hidden things of darkness, and make manifest the counsels of the heart;" and that, whatever our judgment be, his will be according to truth.]

2. Will award with equity—

[Here again the appeal is strong, and carries conviction with it. We are sure that "God will judge the world in righteousness," and " give to every man according to his works." " Whatsoever we have sowed, that shall we also reap: if we have sowed to the flesh, we shall of the flesh reap corruption ; but if we have sowed to the Spirit, we shall of the Spirit reap life everlasting."]

Let this subject TEACH us,

1. To be jealous over ourselves with a godly jealousy—

[We are apt to think that conscience is a safe guide, and that we may rest satisfied with its testimony. But conscience is corrupted by the Fall, as well as all the other faculties of the soul. It is blinded, bribed, partial, and in many instances " seared as with an hot iron." Hence it is that " every man's way is right in his own eyes." Paul thought he ought to do many things contrary to the name of Jesus ; and was applauded by his own conscience, whilst he was sinning against God with all his might. Be not therefore satisfied merely because you feel no condemnation in your own minds ; but beg of God to enlighten your conscience, that it may guide you aright, and keep you from those delusions which would involve you in everlasting ruin.]

2. To live in daily expectation of the future judgment—

[Ask yourselves, not merely, What do *I* think of this or that conduct? but, What would God say to it, if I were instantly summoned to his tribunal? Such a question as this would often lead you to a very different estimate of yourselves from that which you have formed ; and the consideration of his recording every thing in order to a future judgment would tend to keep you vigilant in all your conduct. Walk then as in his sight, and be satisfied with nothing which you are not well assured will satisfy him.]

OUTLINE NO. 808

THE SLUGGARD'S VINEYARD.

Prov. xxiv. 30—34. *I went by the field of the slothful, and by the vineyard of the man void of understanding : and, lo, it was all grown over with thorns, and nettles had covered the face thereof, and the stone wall thereof was broken down. Then I saw, and considered it well : I looked upon it, and received instruction. Yet a little sleep, a little slumber, a little folding of the hands to sleep: so shall thy poverty come as one that travelleth, and thy want as an armed man.*

IF we have an observant eye, and a mind open to receive instruction, there is not any thing in the creation which may not afford us some useful lessons. We may learn as much from what we see, as what we hear; and as much from what is evil, as from what is good. Indeed it is a mark of true wisdom to exact a tribute, as it were, from every thing which comes within our reach, and to suffer nothing to pass without contributing its quota to our stock of useful knowledge. Solomon has set us a good example in this respect: he saw a vineyard that had been shamefully neglected: and instead of turning away from it, as incapable of affording either pleasure or profit to his mind, he set himself to "consider it well, and to derive instruction from it." Surely then we cannot be unprofitably employed while we consider,

I. The sight which he observed—

It is not uncommon to see ground ill cultivated, or business neglected; but as persons reprehensible for inattention to their worldly concerns are comparatively few, we apprehend that the remedying of the evils arising from it comes rather within the province of private admonition than of public discussion. We shall therefore take occasion from the text to speak of a vineyard which all ought to cultivate, but which all are too prone to neglect. This vineyard is the soul; which, with the generality, lies,

1. Uncultivated—

[A man possessed of a common vineyard, ought to procure good plants for it, and to water it regularly, and to weed it carefully, in order that it may yield him its fruits of increase[a]. And we have the same labour to perform for our souls. We ought to get it filled with the choicest graces from heaven. We should water it with prayers and tears, and seek to have it nourished with the influences of the Holy Ghost, which when duly sought, will descend on it as the dew, and distil upon it as rain upon the new-mown grass. We should be daily occupied in pulling up the thorns and nettles that spontaneously

[a] Matt. xxi. 33.

rise, and which, if suffered to remain, will materially impede
the growth of every good plant. But is there not reason to
fear that the greater part of us have shewn ourselves " slothful,
and void of understanding? Have we not been shamefully
remiss in our attention to these great concerns? Have not the
fruits produced by us, been " grapes of Sodom, and clusters of
Gomorrha?" Have not unbelief and impenitence, pride and
anger, envy and malice, covetousness and impurity, with ten
thousand other noxious weeds, been suffered to spring up and
grow within us, till they have even " covered the face of the
ground?" Alas! the proofs of spiritual sloth are but too
evident in us all.]

2. Unprotected—

[Whatever care a man should take of his vineyard, he
would lose his labour, if he should forget to fence it in; " the
wild beast of the field would soon root it up and devour it."
What then can be expected to spring up in our souls, when
they are left at the mercy of every enemy that chooses to tread
them down? We should long since have fortified them *with
holy purposes and resolutions*. These, it is true, can avail
nothing, if made in our own strength; but, if made in reliance
upon God, they will be no slight barrier against the invading
foe. Joshua[b], David[c], Nehemiah[d], Paul[e], found them useful
and effectual for their preservation. We should also have had
our souls strengthened *by the grace of Christ*. That would
have proved " sufficient for us:" it would have been even as a
wall, yea, " as a wall of fire, round about us." Above all, we
should have taken care to have them encompassed *by God's holy
covenant*, " which is ordered in all things and sure." Inclosed
by that, we might defy all the assaults of earth and hell.

But have we been careful thus to protect our souls? Have
we not rather left them open to the incursion of our enemies,
the sport of every temptation, the prey of every lust?]

Such a melancholy sight should make us doubly
attentive to,

II. His reflections upon it—

Solomon was more desirous to benefit himself,
than to criminate others, even though their conduct
was justly reprehensible. His reflections therefore
on the sight which he beheld, were of a general nature respecting the evil and danger of sloth. The
state of our souls may well lead us to similar reflections, and convince us that sloth is,

[b] Josh. xxiv. 15   [c] Ps. cxix. 106.
Neh. vi. 11.   [e] Acts xxi. 13.

1. Deceitful—

[The slothful man does not intend to involve himself in
ruin: he only pleads for *a little* more indulgence of his indo-
lent habits: but, alas! His "*little* slumber" insensibly becomes
a great deal: his time passes away, and his work is left undone.
The rest which he takes, instead of refreshing him, enfeebles all
his powers, and indisposes him for action; so that, though he
never *intends* to plunge himself into difficulties, he does it most
effectually.　And how lamentably does an indisposition to spiritual labour deceive us!　No man *intends* to destroy his own
soul: he only pleads for *a little* more delay, *a little* more
slumber: he thinks he shall awake time enough to do all that
is necessary.　Thus, while he sleeps, the thorns and nettles
grow, and seed, and multiply, and take such deep root, that
they can scarcely ever be eradicated: in the mean time, every
good desire that may at any time have sprung up within him,
is choked; and the decaying wall that should protect him falls
to the ground.　Ah! how many thousands have perished, like
Felix, while they were waiting for "a more convenient season!"
There has always been some " lion in the way[f]," whenever the
time came for labour and exertion; and thus they have lost the
only season which the great Husbandman had allotted for the
performance of their work.]

2. Ruinous—

[The ruin of a man who neglects his farm or merchandize
is *gradual* and *irresistible:* his circumstances become more and
more embarrassed; and at last he is apprehended for debt,
immured in a prison, and reduced to utter "poverty and want."
What a picture does this exhibit of a man who neglects his
soul! He does not feel the consequences all at once; but "his
poverty comes as one that travelleth:" it proceeds *gradually*
step by step: it is not one hour, or day, that makes a very
great difference to a man that is travelling many hundred miles
on foot; but every step in reality brings him nearer to his
journey's end: and so it is with the man that indulges spiritual
sloth; his ruin approaches, though imperceptibly, every day
and hour: but though it comes insensibly, yet it will seize
upon him *irresistibly*, even " as an armed man."　How glad
would many be in their dying hours, if a portion of the time
which they have wasted, could be restored to them! How glad
would they be if they could recover the seasons they have lost!
But death waits not their leisure: when sent, he executes his
office, and transmits them, however reluctant, to the tribunal
of their Judge.　O that we would endeavour to realize these
reflections in our minds, that we may not learn the truth and
awfulness of them by bitter experience!]

[f] Prov. xxvi. 13—15

By way of IMPROVING this subject, we will entreat you all,

1. To inquire into the state of your vineyard—

[Look well, and compare your ground with that of others; not of sluggards like yourselves, but of the Apostles and primitive Christians. And do not mistake, as, alas! too many do, weeds for plants (worldliness for prudence, levity for cheerfulness, formality for devotion, or pride and hypocrisy for zeal and piety;) but consult those who are able to instruct you, and be willing to have your vineyard weeded, your plants pruned, your wall reared, and your habits of indolence subdued and rectified.]

2. To cultivate it with speed and diligence—

[Had we improved our past time with diligence, how different would have been the state of our souls! O think of the time that is irretrievably lost; and the probable shortness of that which remains! Let not sloth deceive you any more. There is not one amongst us who may not see in his own soul what advances it has made, and what an increase of work it has occasioned. Let us be thankful that the period for cultivation is not yet ended: and let us henceforth "walk, not as fools, but as wise, redeeming the time, because the days are evil."]

OUTLINE NO. 809

RETURNING GOOD FOR EVIL.

Prov. xxv. 21, 22. *If thine enemy be hungry, give him bread to eat; and if he be thirsty, give him water to drink: for thou shalt heap coals of fire upon his head; and the Lord shall reward thee.*

THE morality both of the Old and New Testament is the same. Some have imagined, that, because our blessed Lord said, "A new Commandment give I unto you," he has in his Gospel enlarged the duties of his followers beyond what was required by the moral law. But no command of his was new *in itself,* but only in *its circumstances;* as being enjoined from new principles, and illustrated by new examples. Morality does not depend on any arbitrary appointment: it arises out of the relation which we bear to God as our common Parent, and to each other as Brethren: and, irrespective of any express revelation of it, "To love God with all our heart and mind

and soul and strength, and our neighbour as ourselves," must of necessity be the duty of every child
of man.   Had our blessed Lord increased the demands of the moral law, either the Law must have
demanded too little of us, or the Gospel must demand too much.   But neither of these is the case :
the requirements both of the one and of the other are
the same, as far as morals are concerned.   Love is
acknowledged to be the fulfilling of the Law, and the
great commandment of the Gospel also.   But to love
our enemies is the utmost extent to which this duty
is carried, either in the Law or Gospel: yet is this
enjoined, as we see, under the Mosaic dispensation ;
which is a clear proof, that it is not, as many erro-
neously suppose, a requirement peculiar to the
Christian code.   The very words of our text are
cited by the Apostle Paul, as inculcating all that
Christianity itself requires on this head[a]: only there
is one point in our text which adds greatly to its
interest, and which has determined us to select the
original words for our consideration, rather than the
Apostle's citation of them.

From the words before us we shall be led to consider,

I. The duty inculcated—

Certainly the love of enemies was never regarded
as a duty by any of the heathen philosophers.   Whatever might be occasionally spoken by them in praise
of magnanimity, the love of enemies, and the rendering of good for evil under all circumstances, was
never admitted by them as a proper principle and
rule of conduct.   Such a principle is directly contrary to all our natural sentiments and feelings.

By nature we all are inclined to render *evil* for evil—
[There is not a child that does not manifest this disposition, as soon as it begins to act : nor is there any one whose
own experience will not furnish him with unnumbered proofs,
that this is the natural bent of his own heart.   Circumstances
may indeed prevent us from retaliating injuries in an open
way : the person that has inflicted the injuries may be out of

[a] Rom. xii. 19, 20.

our reach ; or be too powerful for us to contend with ; or be
so low, as to be deemed unworthy of our notice. But in our
hearts we shall find the vindictive principle strongly operative,
disposing us to take pleasure in any evil that may have befallen
our enemy, and to decline yielding him any service, which,
under the influence of a better principle, we might have rendered him. The man under the workings of hatred scarcely
thinks of his enemy but with pain, and with a direct reference
to the injuries received from him : and though from want of
opportunity he may not retaliate, he has in him the spark,
which might soon, by a concurrence of circumstances, break
forth into a flame. In proof of this we need only see how this
spirit has operated in others ; sometimes rankling for years, till
an opportunity to gratify itself should offer ; and sometimes
bursting forth at once into furious resentment. The sons of
Jacob, Simeon, and Levi, full of indignation against Shechem
for defiling their sister Dinah, formed a plan to murder, not
Shechem only, but every male of the city in which he dwelt :
and, to put them off their guard, and disable them for resistance, they devised a scheme the most hypocritical, and most
infernal that could enter into the heart of man ; having succeeded in which, they executed their bloody purpose without
pity and without remorse [b]. In Absalom's bosom the determination to avenge the wrongs which his sister Tamar had
sustained, and to expiate them by the blood of Amnon, her
offending brother, rankled two full years ; till by artifice he was
enabled to effect his murderous design [c]. More rapid, but not
less cruel, was the vindictive wrath of David, when Nabal had
refused to recompense his services in the way he desired : he
instantly hasted with an armed force to cut off Nabal, and
every male belonging to his numerous household [d]. Alas! alas!
what is man, when left to the workings of his own corrupt
nature? His every thought accords with that Pharisaic principle, " Thou shalt love thy friend and hate thine enemy."]

But religion requires us to render *good* for evil—

[Every species of revenge it absolutely forbids, even in
thought. " Say not, I will do so to him, as he has done to me ;
I will render to the man according to his work [e]." To this
effect were those ordinances of Moses: " Thou shalt not avenge,
nor bear any grudge against the children of thy people : but
thou shalt love thy neighbour as thyself [f]." And, " If thou
meet thine enemy's ox or his ass going astray, thou must surely
bring it back again to him : and if thou seest his ass lying under
his burthen, and wouldst forbear to help him, thou shalt surely

[b] Gen. xxxiv. 13—15, 25.   [c] 2 Sam. xiii. 15, 28.
[d] 1 Sam. xxv. 21, 22.   [e] Prov. xxiv. 29.
[f] Lev. xix. 18.

help him [g]." Thus by the law of Moses the secret alienation of heart was to be counteracted by the exercise of actual kindness and benevolence. But the words of our text are stronger still, and especially as they are cited by the Apostle Paul. The idea conveyed by him is, that we must not merely give our enemy bread and water when he needs it, but must *feed him with the tenderness of a mother towards her little infant* [h]. O what a victory does this suppose over all the vindictive feelings of our hearts!

We have a beautiful instance of this recorded in the history of Elisha. The prophet was surrounded by an army of Syrians, determined to apprehend and destroy him. By a power communicated to him from above, he smote them all with blindness, and then conducted them into the heart of Samaria. The king of Israel having gained this advantage over them, would have slain them: but the prophet said, "Thou shalt not smite them; but shalt set bread and water before them, that they may eat and drink, and go to their master [i]." Such is the disposition which we also are called to exercise towards our most inveterate enemies. We must "bless them that curse us, do good to them that hate us, and pray for them that despitefully use us and persecute us [k]." If they should have offended against us ever so often, even seventy times seven, we are still to retain the same disposition towards them, and to manifest it the very instant they express regret for the unkindness they have shewn us [l]. Nor are there to be any other bounds to our forgiveness, than those which the Lord Jesus Christ has affixed to his: we are to forgive others "even as Christ has forgiven us [m]:" and, if we refuse to do so, our doom is sealed: "So also shall the Lord do unto you, if ye from your hearts forgive not every one his brother their trespasses [n]."]

Such is the duty which we are called to perform: but, that we may not be deterred by the arduousness of it, let us consider,

II. The encouragement given us to perform it—

If we act thus, we have reason to hope,

1. That we shall overcome the hatred of our enemy—

[Certain it is, that no enemy was ever yet won by a vindictive conduct. We may, it is true, silence him by power; but we never can gain his affections by any thing but love. And this will, if not always, yet sometimes, prevail; as St. Paul

---

[g] Exod. xxiii. 4, 5.   [h] Ψώμιζε αὐτόν. Rom. xii. 20.
[i] 2 Kings vi. 21, 22.   [k] Matt. v. 44.   [l] Matt. xviii. 22
[m] Eph. iv. 32.   [n] Matt. xviii. 35.

intimates, when he says, "Be not overcome of evil; but overcome evil with good[o]." Indeed, where there is a spark of ingenuousness left, we cannot but hope that such benevolence as this will at last prevail. We have some remarkable instances of this in the life of David. Saul had persecuted him with most relentless and bitter animosity: yet, when David twice had him in his power, and could easily have destroyed him, he spared his life; and by this generosity constrained his persecutor to confess his own extreme injustice, and to take shame to himself for his own malignant and cruel proceedings[p]——— Such effects we also may hope to see produced on our enemies. It is well known that metals are fused, not by putting fire under them, but by heaping also coals of fire upon them: and thus shall the hard hearts of our enemies be melted by accumulated instances of undeserved love. True, we cannot convert their souls by this; for nothing but omnipotence can effect so great a work as the conversion of a soul: but we may reasonably expect to appease their wrath, perhaps also to slay their enmity against us: and one such victory will be a rich recompence for all the forbearance we have ever exercised, and all the love we have ever displayed.]

2. That we shall be rewarded by our God—

[This is plainly asserted in our text; and to all who conform themselves to the direction before us shall the promise be assuredly fulfilled.

It shall be fulfilled *here:* for such conduct will bring unspeakable peace into the soul. It is said, that revenge is sweet: but with infinitely greater propriety may it be said, that the returning of good for evil is sweet. The one is a malignant pleasure, such as we may suppose Satan himself felt, when he had prevailed, as he thought, against the Lord of life and glory: but the other is such a sacred pleasure as Christ himself felt, when he prayed, "Father, forgive them; for they know not what they do." What satisfaction did David experience, when, in consequence of Abigail's interposition, he had changed his mind in relation to Nabal, and sacrificed his resentment to a sense of duty! Again and again did he bless her for diverting him from his purpose[q]. And we also, whenever love rises superior to resentment, and enables us to render good for evil, shall find unspeakable comfort springing up in our souls.

But the promise shall be yet more fully accomplished *hereafter.* Every act of patient self-denial and of generous love will be noticed by God with special approbation; and, if a cup of cold water given to *a disciple* for Christ's sake shall in no

o Rom. xii. 21.

p 1 Sam. xxiv. 4, 11, 16—19. and xxvi. 12, 21, 25.

q 1 Sam. xxv. 32, 33.

wise lose its reward, much less shall services rendered to *an enemy* for his sake pass unnoticed. St. Peter tells us, that we are called to such trials, and carried through them in a triumphant manner, on purpose " that we may inherit a blessing[r]." But the point is repeatedly asserted by our Lord himself: "Blessed are the merciful; for they shall obtain mercy:" " Forgive, and ye shall be forgiven[s]." Let this thought occupy the mind; and the performance of the duty will be a delightful task.]

ADDRESS—

1. Guard against those reasonings which favour the indulgence of a vindictive spirit—

[You will be sometimes inclined to think that the exercise of resentment is necessary; and that if some displeasure be not manifested, your enemies will be emboldened to proceed to still further outrages. But look at the command of God; and, if this be clearly on the side of forbearance and love, say to every contrary suggestion, " Get thee behind me, Satan; thou art an offence unto me."]

2. Set the Lord Jesus Christ before you as your example—

[There are many passages in the Psalms which seem to breathe a spirit of revenge[t]: but these are frequently only prophecies, which might properly have been translated in the future tense; and when they are clearly imprecations, as sometimes they doubtless are, they are spoken in the person of the Messiah, who had a right either to denounce or imprecate judgments on those who obstinately rejected all the offers of his grace. David, when speaking in his own person, manifested the same spirit that becomes us[u]. But David was a fallible man, like unto us; as we have seen in the case of Nabal. Look therefore to the Lord Jesus Christ himself, in whom was no sin. When you were enemies, He left the bosom of his Father for you: yea, " when you were yet enemies, he died for you" — — — I need say no more. Set him before you, and your way will be clear: and, if you look to him for all needful succour, his " grace shall be sufficient for you," and you shall be able to do all things through the strength he will impart.]

[r] 1 Pet. iii. 9.　　　　　　　　[s] Luke vi. 37.
[t] Particularly Ps. cix. throughout.　[u] Ps. xxxv. 13, 14.

OUTLINE NO. 810

THE DANGER OF CONCEIT.

Prov. xxvi. 12. *Seest thou a man wise in his own conceit? there is more hope of a fool, than of him.*

THE Scripture seeks not to please the fastidious ear of man, but calls both persons and things by their appropriate names.   Sin is declared to be the extremest folly; and those who commit it, are proclaimed fools.   In the eleven verses preceding our text, the folly of fools is mentioned *no less than ten times:* and from this humiliating picture our text derives a force and emphasis which no single expression could give.   The import of the text, as connected with the context, is this: The condition of a fool is, as you have seen, awful in the extreme: but " seest thou a man wise in his own conceit? there is more hope of a fool than of him."   This is a solemn delaration, and worthy of the deepest attention.   Let us consider it,

I. As a general truth—

Here we may distinctly notice,

1. The character described—

[There is in man a strange conceit, and a proneness to take very undue credit to himself for his abilities and attainments. Some are so confident in their own wisdom, that they seem to think they cannot err; and they would have it supposed that they possess, almost by intuition, what others have attained only by laborious investigation.   Persons of this description will not condescend to examine their sentiments by any test; nor will they listen to any statements that are opposed to them. Confidence is to them in the place of proof; and any attempt to controvert their opinions excites only their indignation or contempt.]

2. His hopeless condition—

[Truly pitiable is the condition of " a fool." He is ignorant of all that constitutes true wisdom: he is also, in a great measure, incapable of receiving instruction; and the instruction he does receive, he is incapable of turning to a good account, or of making a suitable improvement of it.   Of such a one there certainly is but little hope: yet is the conceited person in a more hopeless state than he.   If in respect of capacity he have the advantage, he labours under a tenfold disadvantage, by reason of his precipitancy, his confidence, his pertinacity.   The endeavours used to convince him of his errors do but rivet him the more firmly in them; and opposition to him serves but to increase his obstinacy.   Thus, whilst the conceit of his mind indisposes him for the proper exercise of his judgment in relation to truth. it unfits him for the reception of any benefit from the wisdom of others: so that to bring him to sound wisdom and discretion is indeed a hopeless task. If he will not deliberate and weigh matters for himself, or listen to instruction and advice from others; and if the means used to rectify his views do but confirm him the more in his delusions, there is indeed no hope of him: and " you may even bray him in a mortar, and he will remain the same; his conceit and folly will not depart from him[a]."]

The declaration in our text will be found still more weighty, if considered,

II. With a more especial reference to religion—

A man that carries his conceit into religion is indeed in a most deplorable state—

[Truth, in general, is too pure and refined to obtain ready admittance into such a mind as his; but religious truth is altogether folly in his eyes. " The natural man," even though not blinded by that measure of conceit of which we have been speaking, " receiveth not the things of the Spirit of God; for they are foolishness unto him; neither can he know them, because they are spiritually discerned[b]." But where, in addition to the natural blindness of the human mind, there is a large measure of overweening conceit, the state of that man is bad indeed; because every truth of the Gospel not only offends him, but offends him in proportion to its sublimity and importance. The total corruption of our nature, the necessity of a new birth by the operation of the Spirit of God, justification by faith in the Lord Jesus, and an entire dedication of the soul to God, all appear to him extravagant and absurd: he sees no occasion for such humiliating and self-denying doctrines; nor will he believe them, whatever testimony be adduced from the Holy Scriptures in support of them. In vain are God's express declarations brought before him: he believes his own conceits in preference to them: and every person that would persuade him to examine with candour, he regards as a weak visionary, and a deluded fanatic. Such a person, therefore, is never likely to come to the knowledge of the truth.

But, besides the obstacles which he meets with from the sublimity of the truths, and the blindness of his own mind, he has another source of blindness peculiar to himself: for God is particularly offended by such conduct, in reference to his revealed will; and he will " give such an one up to his own delusions, to believe a lie[c]," and to harden himself in his impenitence and unbelief: and if once a man have provoked God so to withdraw his Holy Spirit from him, and to surrender him up to the power

[a] Prov. xxvii. 22.   [b] 1 Cor. ii. 14.   [c] 2 Thess. ii. 11, 12.

of sin and Satan, he will never be undeceived, till he shall open his eyes in the eternal world.]

The fool then, I say, is in a more hopeful state than he—

[The fool, notwithstanding his ignorance, *may* learn: and if he will only submit himself to divine teaching, he *shall* learn; nor shall his weakness be any bar to his instruction: for God has said, that " What he has hid from the wise and prudent, he has, of his own good pleasure, revealed unto babes[d]:" and so plain shall his ways be made to them, that " a wayfaring man, though a fool, shall not err therein[e]." Of him, then, we may have a hope, because he will use the appointed means of instruction, and will embrace truth as far as he discerns it; whilst the conceited man will not condescend to be " taught of God," and therefore must continue ignorant even to the end, and " perish at last for lack of knowledge."]

On this subject I would found A GENERAL EX- HORTATION—

[Conceit, when strongly manifested in relation to earthly things, generally excites pity and contempt; but when exercised in reference to spiritual things, is deemed oracular and wise. But I entreat all to be on their guard against it. It is most dangerous, and fatal to the soul. Humility is at the very root of divine knowledge; nor can any saving acquaintance with the Gospel spring up without it. This, then, I say to all:

Be sensible, that, instead of being " rich and increased with goods, and in need of nothing," as too many suppose themselves to be, you are in yourselves wretched, and miserable, and poor, and blind, and naked[f]"— — —

Bear in mind, that the Scriptures alone are the fountain and standard of truth. Every thing must be brought " to the Law and to the testimony:" and " whoever speaks not according to the written word, he has no light in him[g]"— — —

Remember, too, that it is by divine teaching only that we can understand the Scriptures. If the eyes of our understanding be not enlightened by the Spirit of God, notwithstanding the light that shines around us, we shall go on still in darkness, even as Paul did, in his unconverted state; and as the twelve Apostles did, in the midst of all their Master's instructions, till after the resurrection of their Lord[h]— — —

And forget not, that this instruction must be sought by earnest prayer. God alone can give it; and it is only in answer to prayer that he will impart it to us[i]— — —

Moreover, after you have been guided into truth, you must

[d] Matt. xi. 25, 26.   [e] Isai. xxxv. 8.   [f] Rev. iii. 17.
[g] Isai. viii. 20.   [h] Eph. i. 18. Luke xxiv. 45.   [i] Prov. ii. 1—6.

still be on your guard against the same propensity which acts so powerfully in the unconverted mind. Many, after all their partial illumination, are drawn aside after "philosophy and vain deceit[k]." If you would be preserved in the right way, you must not only "be converted, and become as little children," but retain a childlike simplicity even to the end. To your latest hour you need to be reminded of that counsel given to the Christians at Rome, "Be not wise in your own conceits[l]." You need to be guarded against "thinking that you know any thing" perfectly; for, whilst you are under such an impression, "you know nothing yet as you ought to know[m]." "If you will be truly wise, it is by becoming fools in your own estimation, that you are to be made wise[n]."———If you will not follow this counsel, "God will take you in your own craftiness[o]"———

I must then, as God's ambassador to you, call your attention to the warning which he has given you by the prophet Isaiah: "Woe unto them that are wise in their own eyes, and prudent in their own sight[p]!" And to all I must recommend those petitions of God's most favoured saints, "Open thou mine eyes, that I may behold wondrous things out of thy Law[q]:" and, "What I see not, Teach thou me[r]."]

[k] Col. ii. 8.   [l] Rom. xii. 16.   [m] 1 Cor. viii. 2.
[n] 1 Cor. iii. 18.   [o] 1 Cor. iii. 19, 20.   [p] Isai. v. 21.
[q] Ps. cxix. 18.   [r] Job xxxiv. 32.

OUTLINE NO. 811

A CAUTION AGAINST DEPENDING UPON FUTURE TIME.

Prov. xxvii. 1. *Boast not thyself of to-morrow: for thou knowest not what a day may bring forth.*

THE opinions of men are not less opposite to the mind of God in what relates to practice, than in the most mysterious doctrines of our holy religion. We are told, that "the things of the Spirit are esteemed as foolishness by the natural man:" and to what an extent they are so, is visible in the commendation universally given to a worldly spirit, and in the contempt poured upon heavenly-mindedness, as though it were the offspring of folly and enthusiasm. But in the judgment of God there is no truer mark of wisdom than to consider earthly things as transient and worthless, and to place one's-self continually as on the brink and precipice of eternity. To this effect Solomon speaks in the passage before us: in discoursing on which, we shall,

I. Explain the caution here given—

It is of great importance to distinguish between *providing for* to-morrow, and *presuming upon* to-morrow: the former is necessary for our very existence, since without it, the whole world would be in a state of stagnation: but the acting as if we were certain of another day, is the error against which we are cautioned. Now we do this,

1. When our affections are inordinately moved by present things—

[If we feel eager *desires* after any earthly thing, so as to envy the possessors of it, and account the attainment of it necessary to our happiness; or, if we take such *delight* in what we do possess, as to forget that this world is not our rest, and that infinitely higher joys are prepared for us above; or if we *grieve* exceedingly on account of some loss we have sustained; we manifest that we have been promising ourselves many days, and even years to come: for, would a person be very solicitous about a vanity that he thought might very probably last but a day? Or would he so congratulate himself on a possession which he apprehended to be of such short continuance? or would he lay so much to heart the loss of any thing which he had expected to enjoy but a little time? We cannot but see that in proportion as he was impressed with a sense of the shortness and uncertainty of time, and its nothingness in comparison of eternity, his affections would be moderated towards every object of time and sense: he would "rejoice as though he rejoiced not, and weep as though he wept not, and use every thing as not abusing it."]

2. When we are but little interested about eternal things—

[Every one knows that sin must be repented of; and that, if the guilt of it be imputed to us, we must perish. But this is not all; we must be born again and be made new creatures in Christ Jesus: and though this be not generally understood, every one has an idea that he must become religious before he die, if he would find acceptance with God in the world to come. Now if persons be deferring the great work of religion, whence can that delay arise but from their expectation of some more convenient season, when they shall execute their purposes of reformation and amendment? Or if they commit sin, whence can they be emboldened to do so, but from a secret confidence that they shall live to repent of it; and to rectify what they know to be amiss? Would any man deliberately do what he knows *must* be undone, or leave undone what he knows he *must* do in order to his eternal salvation, if he were *assured* that he had not one day more to live? And would not the *probable* nearness of death influence him in like manner *in proportion as it was felt?*]

The whole world standing greatly in need of this caution, we proceed to,

II. Enforce it—

The reason urged by Solomon commends itself immediately to our hearts and consciences:

1. We know not what shall be on the morrow—

[We are to-day perhaps enjoying all that our hearts can wish; our bodies are vigorous, our spirits gay, our friends numerous, our means of gratification greatly diversified, and accessible at all times. To-morrow we may be cast down from our pinnacle of happiness; our honour may be laid in the dust; we may be languishing on a bed of sickness; and deprived of all the comforts of life; and our reverse of fortune may be yet further aggravated by the loss of all our friends. The case of Job, if more recent instances were wanting, would sufficiently shew what may happen to us all[a]. Shall we then be promising ourselves years of happiness in the enjoyment of earthly things, when we consider how unstable they are? Again: to-day we are sinning in expectation that we shall, at some future period, repent. To-morrow possibly we may, like Nebuchadnezzar, be deprived of reason; or, like Pharaoh, be sealed up by God under final impenitence. Now is it not madness to risk the salvation of our souls upon the hope of having every thing that can conduce to our eternal welfare continued to us to the latest period of our lives? Should we not rather set ourselves to redeem the present time, and to "work while it is day, lest the night should come wherein no man can work[b]?"]

2. We know not whether we shall even live to see the morrow—

[What man is there that has "made a covenant with death, and an agreement with the grave" so as to be assured he shall live another day? Has he this assurance *from within himself,* or *from those around him,* or *from God?* Not from within himself, since neither youth nor health is any security against the stroke of death: not from others, since physicians, however useful in their place, can afford us no help, when God shall call away our souls: not from God; for though he promised to protract Hezekiah's life for fifteen years, he has not engaged to preserve ours so many minutes. If, with the Rich

[a] Job i. See, in spiritual concerns, the case of David, Ps. xxx. 6, 7.
[b] Eph. v. 16. John ix. 4.

Man in the Gospel we are saying, " Soul, thou hast much goods laid up for many years," God may say to us, "Thou fool, *this night* shall thy soul be required of thee[c]." Who then, that knows the uncertainty of life, will presume upon its continuance? Let us look at the many thousands who, though but lately they seemed as likely to live as ourselves, are gone into eternity, gone too, before they had prepared to give up their account to God; and surely we shall cry with the Psalmist, " Lord, so teach us to number our days, that we may instantly apply our hearts unto wisdom[d]?"]

This subject naturally leads us to ADDRESS,

1. The careless—

[Is it not sufficient that God has exercised such long-suffering towards you, but will you still continue to provoke him[e]? " O be wise, and consider your latter end." "To-day, while it is called to-day, harden not your hearts;" lest while you are saying, Peace and safety, sudden destruction come upon you[f].]

2. The lukewarm—

[Lukewarmness in religion is as odious to God as an utter neglect of it[g]. It is not by a round of formal duties, but a strenuous exertion of all your powers that you are to obtain the prize: for though heaven is the *gift* of God through Christ, it is bestowed on those only who labour for it[h]. Whatever then your hand findeth to do, do it with all your might[i].]

3. The zealous—

[Endeavour to realize more and more the uncertainty of life, that, like the Apostle, you may " die daily." And, as you know not but that on the morrow you may be numbered with the saints in glory, let nothing be deferred till to-morrow, which you can do for God to-day. Thus will death, however sudden, be welcome to you.]

[c] Luke xii. 19, 20. [d] Ps. xc. 12. [e] Jam. iv. 13—16.
[f] Heb. iii. 7, 8, 13. 1 Thess. v. 3. [g] Rev. iii. 15, 16.
[h] John vi. 27. [i] Eccl. ix. 10.

OUTLINE NO. 812

ENVY.

Prov. xxvii. 4. *Who is able to stand before envy?*

MAN is an enemy to his fellow man: nor is there any one who does not on some occasion experience reason for this complaint. But, if some find means of aggression, others obtain means of defence; some in their own powers; others in the assistance of friends; others in the arm of the law: others, where all these powers fail them, derive a measure of consolation from submission or flight. The most " cruel wrath, and most outrageous anger," may, by one or other of these means, be withstood, or tolerated, or escaped. But there is one weapon from which there is no flight, and against which there is no protection; and *that* is, envy: " Wrath is cruel, and anger is outrageous; but who can stand before envy ?"

In order to bring the subject of envy fully before you, I will shew,

I. What an odious principle it is—

1. Consider what envy is—

[Envy, as existing in the soul, is a sense of pain arising from the real or supposed excellence of another, accompanied with a desire to deprive him of it, and to possess it ourselves. The excellence may be either natural or acquired. Any faculty of body or mind which renders a man estimable in the world is a proper object for envy to fix upon, and against which to direct its shafts. So, in like manner, any attainment of wealth or honour will call forth its malignant efforts against the person in whom such a distinction has been found, especially if the distinction so obtained has been an object of desire to the person beholding it, and apparently within his reach: for envy finds scope for operation only between persons amongst whom some kind of rivalry exists. A peasant does not envy either a king or a philosopher; because the dignity of the one, and the wisdom of the other, are altogether beyond a hope, I had almost said a possibility, of his attainment. Envy includes in it a desire of the distinction that calls it forth, and a pain of seeing it possessed by another, when by possibility it might have been possessed by one's-self.]

2. Next mark its odiousness—

[Nothing excites it but what is either really, or in the person's estimation, good: nor does it ever exert itself, but for the destruction of the happiness of him in whom that good is found. It is the happiness of another that gives pain to the envious man; and the destruction of that happiness is the great object that would afford him pleasure. Its actings, indeed, are not open, like those of wrath and anger: on the contrary, they are as secret as possible; and they put on, as far as possible, a specious garb, a garb of candour and of equity. But its

inseparable attendants are of the same odious character with
itself: namely, " debates, wraths, strifes, backbitings, whisper-
ings, swellings, tumults[a]."   Indeed, it is very nearly allied to
murder: for, as it is invariably connected with anger, it is
murder in embryo[b]: and hence in the Scriptures it is generally
associated with murder: " The works of the flesh," says the
Apostle, are hatred, variance, emulations, wrath, strife, sedi-
tions, heresies, *envyings*, *murders*[c]:" and in another place he
says of unconverted men, that they are " full of *envy*, *murder*,
debate, deceit, malignity, whisperers, backbiters," and so on[d].
It indeed may appear harsh to load this principle with such horrid
accusations; but they are true, and all verified by experience.
Wherefore did Cain slay his brother ? it was because he saw
his brother receiving from God tokens of approbation which
were denied to him[e].   And whence was it that Joseph's
brethren took counsel to slay him ? it was on account of his
enjoying higher favour with his father than they, and his receiving more remarkable communications from God[f].   But,
in truth, we do not view this principle aright, unless we see in
it the very image of the devil himself.   No other principle in
the heart of man bears so strong a resemblance of the devil as
this.   See our first parents in Paradise, as happy as it was
possible for creatures in a state of probation to be.   The devil
saw and envied them their bliss, and never rested till he had
robbed them of it[g].   Nor does he behold one of their descendants turning to the Lord, without using every effort in his power
to divert them from their purpose, and to destroy their souls[h].
And what does he gain by this ?   Is he himself rendered happier by depriving others of their bliss ?   No: he only augments
his own guilt and misery ; and yet such is the malignity of his
disposition, that he can find no employment to his mind but
this: and, so far as he is capable of a momentary mitigation of
his pains, he finds it only in robbing man of his happiness,
and God of his glory.   This is the very character of the envious
man, whose " wisdom," as St. James says, " is not from above,
but is earthly, sensual, *devilish*[i]."

The fact is, that so odious is this principle in the estimation of
the whole world, that there is not to be found on earth a person
who will acknowledge himself to be actuated by it : though the
real truth is, that there is not an unconverted man in the whole
universe who is not, as I shall have presently to shew, under its
baneful influence.   But the very circumstance of all persons
disavowing it, whilst they will readily acknowledge that they
are led captive by pride, or anger, or impurity, is sufficient to

a 2 Cor. xii. 20.   b 1 John iii. 15.   c Gal. v. 20, 21.
d Rom. i. 29, 30.   e Gal. iv. 5, 8.   f Gen. xxxvii. 11, 18—20.
g 2 Cor. xi. 3.   h 1 Pet. v. 8.   i Jam. iii. 14—16.

shew how odious it is in itself, and how despicable in the eyes
of every living man.]

The evil of envy will yet more strongly appear,
whilst I shew,

II. What a destructive principle it is—

There is not a person in the universe able to stand
before it.   Its workings are inconceivably subtle—

[Persons are not always aware what principle it is which
stirs within them, when they are under its influence.   Joshua
conceived that he was only shewing a commendable regard for
the honour of Moses, when he desired that Eldad and Medad,
who were prophesying in the camp, should be silenced.   But
Moses reproved him, saying, "Enviest thou for my sake?
Would to God that all the Lord's people were prophets[k]!"
And doubtless those who, in order to grieve the Apostle Paul,
preached Christ of envy and strife[l], gave themselves credit for
a purer motive in their performance of that duty.   There are
a variety of ways by which men contrive to hide it from themselves.   They see some evil in the conduct which they blame:
or, if it was not evil in itself, it was faulty in the *time*, or *manner*, or *measure*, in which it was done: or, if no fault attach to
it in any of those respects, it was from an improper motive.
In short, *something* shall be found in every thing that a person
does, either to make it appear blame-worthy, or, at all events,
to abate its excellence: and the person judging of these things
will not openly condemn them, but only utter praise in a fainter
tone, and in more qualified terms, that so the measure of praise
accorded to the agent may be diminished, and his merits be
comparatively obscured.   *This*, to the person forming the
judgment, shall appear only strict justice: but God, who sees
the heart, will designate it envy.]

It finds an advocate in every bosom—

[There is in all a wish to be exalted among their equals:
and if there be any who have raised themselves by their own
merits above the common standard, every mind will be gratified
with hearing of something which shall divest them of their imputed excellence, and reduce them to their former level.   Hence
the envious man finds an ally in every bosom, and a readiness
in all around him to listen to any representation that is of an
unfavourable nature; because every one seems to himself
elevated in proportion as others are depressed.   The means of
misrepresentation are infinite in number: and if every statement were carefully investigated before it was received, a man

k Numb. xi. 29.   l Phil. i. 15.

of wisdom and discretion might defy them all : but when every misrepresentation that envy can suggest is listened to with pleasure, and received without inquiry, who must not fall before it?]

The more excellent any conduct is, the more obnoxious it is to its assaults—

[Even piety itself is not beyond its reach : for Solomon speaks of it as a peculiar vanity and source of vexation, that " for every right work a man is envied of his neighbour[m]." To say the truth, piety is more the object of envy than any thing else; not because others affect it for themselves, but because, in the common sentiments of mankind, it gives to its possessor a transcendent excellence, and raises him almost into a higher order of beings.   This was a peculiar source of Cain's resentment against his brother Abel[n]; as it was of Saul's against David[o]; and of the Jews against Christ himself[p].   Take an act of Christ's, the restoring of Lazarus from the grave; a more benevolent act could not be conceived, nor one which more strongly carried its evidence of a divine mission along with it. Was it possible for envy or enmity to be provoked by *that*? Yes: the very act instantly produced a conspiracy against the life of Jesus;—against the life, too, of the man who had been raised by him[q].   Was it so, then, that all the wisdom, or piety, or benevolence of our blessed Saviour himself could not elude this detestable enemy of God and man?   No: not even he could stand before it; but, as the Evangelist informs us, he fell a prey to its insatiate rage[r].   Against all his disciples, too, it raged in like manner[s] : and it is in vain for any one, who will serve God with fidelity, to hope for an escape from its virulent assaults[t].]

Methinks you are now prepared to hear,

III. What a damning principle it is—

God has marked his indignation against it even *here*—

[Greatly does this principle embitter the life of him in whom it dwells.   Its operation is not momentary, like that of anger : it lurks in the bosom ; it corrodes the mind; it makes a man completely miserable.   We may see its operation in Saul.   Saul heard the women, out of all the cities of Israel, celebrating the praises of himself and of David ; saying, " Saul has slain his thousands, and David his ten thousands.   And Saul was very wroth, and the saying displeased him ; and he

[m] Eccl. iv. 4.   [n] 1 John iii. 12.   [o] Ps. xxxviii. 20.
[p] John viii. 45—48.   [q] John ix. 45—48, 53. and xii. 10, 11.
[r] Matt. xxvii. 18, 20.   [s] Acts xiii. 44, 45. and xvii. 4, 5, 10—14.
[t] 2 Tim. iii. 12.

said, They have ascribed unto David ten thousands, and to me
they have ascribed but thousands: and what can he have more,
but the kingdom? *And Saul eyed David from that day and
forward.* And on the very next day did Saul *cast his javelin
at David twice,* in order to kill him;" and throughout all the
remainder of his life used every possible effort to destroy him[u].
This may enable us to understand what Solomon meant, when
he called " envy, the rottenness of the bones[x]." For as the
corporeal system must be altogether enfeebled and destroyed
when the bones are rotten; so the moral constitution of the
soul is rendered one entire mass of corruption, when a man lies
under the dominion of this hateful principle. He is, in fact, as
near to the consummation of his misery in hell as the other is
to the termination of his life on earth.]

But who can tell with what judgments it shall be
visited in the eternal world?

[It is not possible that a person under the dominion of it
should ever behold the face of God in peace. " God is love:"
love is his very nature and essence: but envy is hatred in its
most hateful form, as terminating upon an object, not for any
evil that is in him, but for the good which he manifests, and
for the success he meets with in the exercise of what is good.
How can two such opposites meet together? As well might
light and darkness coalesce, as God and an envious man delight in each other in heaven. It is said in God's blessed word,
that " without charity, whatever we *possess,* or *do,* or *suffer* for
God, we are only as sounding brass or a tinkling cymbal[y]."
But in that very place we are told, that " charity envieth not[z]."
What, then, are we to infer from this, but that, as envy proves
an entire want of charity, so it proves, equally and unquestionably, a state of mind that is wholly incompatible with the
favour of God and the felicity of heaven. But, that we may
be assured of God's indignation against it, let us see what God
said to Edom by the Prophet Ezekiel: " As I live, saith the
Lord God, I will even do according to thine anger, and according to thine envy which thou hast used out of thy hatred
against them: I will make myself known amongst them, when
I have judged thee[a]." True indeed it is, that in this passage
God is only denouncing temporal judgments; but it amply
shews what are his sentiments respecting the principle which
we are speaking of, and what will be his judgment upon it in
the day that he shall judge the world.]

Having thus exposed, in some measure, the true

[u] 1 Sam. xviii. 7—12.   [x] Prov. xiv. 30.   [y] 1 Cor. xiii. 1—3
[z] 1 Cor. xiii. 4.   [a] Ezek. xxxv. 11.

character of envy, I beg leave to suggest to you some cautions in relation to it. Be careful,

1. Not needlessly to excite it—

[Knowing, as you do, how common an evil it is, and how deeply rooted in the heart of man, you should guard against every thing which may call it into action. Whatever you possess, either of natural or acquired excellence, make not an ostentatious display of it; but rather put a veil over it, as it were, that its radiance may not offend the eyes of those who behold you. The less value you appear to put upon your attainments, and the less you arrogate to yourselves on account of them, the less will others be disposed to grudge you the enjoyment of them, and to despoil you of the honour due to them. It was unwise in Jacob to mark his partiality towards his son Joseph, by "a coat of many colours;" and he paid dearly for it by the sufferings it entailed. For your own sakes therefore, as well as for the sake of others, it will be wise in you to bear your honours meekly, and to shew that you are "little in your own eyes."]

2. Not wickedly to indulge it—

[Envy is a principle in our fallen nature far more powerful than men in general are apt to imagine. "Do you think that the Scripture saith in vain, The spirit that dwelleth in us lusteth to envy[b]?" If you will watch the motions of your own hearts, you will find a sad propensity to it, whenever a powerful occasion arises to call it forth. Suppose a person, whom you have regarded as inferior to yourself in industry and talent, has got before you, and attained a higher eminence than you in *your own peculiar line;* are you not ready to ascribe his success to chance, or to the partiality of friends, rather than to his own intrinsic merit? and would it not be gratifying to you to hear a similar judgment passed on him by others? Suppose he were by any means to fall from his eminence; would not his degradation give you pleasure? If you praise him, is it with the same decisive tone as you would have wished for, if the praise had been conferred on you? It is when your own honour or interest comes in competition with that of another, that envy betrays its power over you: and if you have been observant of the workings of your own mind, you will be no strangers to the operation of this principle within you. But remember what has been said of its odiousness and enormity; and cry mightily to God to deliver you from its baneful influence. Remember how transitory is all distinction here; and content yourselves with the honour which cometh from God, and will endure for ever.]

[b] Jam. iv. 5. See also Tit. iii. 3.

3. Not basely to fear it—

[Though you are not to make an ostentatious display of any excellence you may possess, and especially of piety, you are not to put your light under a bushel, through the fear of any hostility which a discovery of it may provoke. Whatsoever your duty is, whether to God or man, *that* you are to do ; and to leave all consequences to the disposal of an all-wise Providence. It should be in your mind " a very small matter to be judged of man's judgment[c]." If you have " the testimony of your own conscience that you are serving God in simplicity and godly sincerity," *that* should bear you up against all the obloquy that the envy or malignity of others can heap upon you. You must expect that " they who render evil for good will be against you, if you follow the thing that is good ;" and you must commit yourself to Him who judgeth right, and who will, in due season, both vindicate your character, and make your righteousness to shine forth as the noon-day.]

4. Not angrily to resent it—

[Supposing you to be traduced and injured in a variety of ways; " what temptation has befallen you but that which is common to men ?" Instead of grieving that you are persecuted for righteousness sake, you should rather regard the hatred of men as a homage paid to your virtue and should " rejoice that you are counted worthy to suffer shame for Christ's sake." You will remember the prayer of our blessed Lord for his murderers : " Father, forgive them ; for they know not what they do." This is the pattern which it becomes you to follow. Your envious neighbours really do not know what they do : they are not aware by what spirit they are actuated, or what evil they commit. Instead, therefore, of being angry with them for the evil they do you, you should rather pity them for the evil they do to themselves. This was the way in which David requited Saul, sparing him when he had him in his power, and mourning for him when he was removed to another world[d]. Your rule, under all circumstances, must be this ; " Not to be overcome of evil, but to overcome evil with good."]

[c] 1 Cor. iv. 3.
[d] 1 Sam. xxiv. 9—11. 16—18. and 2 Sam. i. 17, 24—27.

OUTLINE NO. 813

THE HEARTS OF MEN ALIKE.

Prov. xxvii. 19. *As in water face answereth to face, so the heart of man to man.*

THERE are many things which are justly considered as axioms, of the truth of which we are fully convinced, because they are the result of observation and experience : yet, being declared also by the voice of inspiration, they come to our minds with authority, and demand from us an unhesitating acquiescence. Such is the truth which we have just read from the Book of Proverbs. Any man conversant with the world, knows that human nature is, to a certain degree, the same in every age and in every place. But there are, amongst men, so many discrepancies arising out of incidental circumstances, and so many changes too in the same persons, that if the heart-searching God himself had not determined the point, we should scarcely have ventured to speak respecting it in terms so strong and unqualified as Solomon has used in the passage before us. His words, beyond all doubt, are true: but yet, if not well understood, they are capable of much misapprehension and perversion. In discoursing upon them, I will,

I. Explain his assertion—

It needs explanation : for if we were to take it as importing that all men in all circumstances manifest the same dispositions and desires, it would be the very reverse of what we see and know to be true. It is evident, that, though Solomon does not make any distinction, he does not intend to confound all persons in one common mass, and to affirm that, under all their diversified conditions, they are all alike : he sup-poses, that, amongst the persons so compared, there exists a parity, which may render them proper objects of comparison. He takes for granted, that there is in them a parity,

1. Of age—

[If we take men in the various stages of human existence, from infancy to old age, we know that there exists in them a vast diversity of sentiment. To imagine that amongst them all there should be found the same views, desires, and pursuits, would be to betray an ignorance and folly bordering on fatuity. Old men and children can no more be supposed to accord with each other in such respects, than light and darkness. Children must be compared with children ; young men with youths; and old men with those that are advanced in years.]

2. In character—

[There is in the natural *constitution* of men a great difference. Infants at their mother's breast display an astonishing variety of character; some being mild, gentle, placid; others, on the contrary, being filled with the most violent and hateful dispositions. *Education,* too, will operate very forcibly on men, and lead them to habits widely different from each other. One who is brought up in the unrestrained indulgence of every vicious appetite, cannot be supposed to resemble one who has been well instructed in all virtuous principles, and subjected to all salutary restraints. Still less can the godly and the ungodly be supposed to agree. Divine *grace* puts men far asunder, and induces sentiments and conduct widely different from any that are found in unconverted men. In comparing these different persons, a due respect must be had to their several characters; or else our judgment concerning them will be extremely erroneous.]

3. In condition—

[What community of sentiment, generally speaking, can there be between a prince and a peasant? or what between an unlettered countryman and a sage philosopher? Take a man under the pressure of disease, poverty, disgrace; and what will you expect to find in him that accords with the feelings of one who is living in the fullest enjoyment of ease, and opulence, and honour? Look at even the same person, when, either in a way of elevation or depression, he is changed from the one condition to the other; and you will find in him, for the most part, a corresponding change of views and habits.

I say then, that, to apprehend our text aright, we must consider it as declaring, *not* that all persons, whatever their circumstances may be, are alike; *but* that all persons *under the same circumstances*, due allowance being made for any difference existing from constitution, age, education, habit and grace, will be found to bear a very strong resemblance to each other.]

Taking the assertion of Solomon in this qualified sense, I proceed to,

II. Confirm it—

The reflection of a countenance from water will bear a strict resemblance to him whose countenance it is. And a similar correspondence will be found between the hearts of men, who, according to the foregoing limitations, are fit objects of comparison. It will be found in all,

1. Whilst in an unenlightened state—

[All unenlightened men agree in this; they affect supremely
the things of time and sense. In this also they agree; they dis-
affect things spiritual and eternal. Here we may range through
all the gradations of men, from the prince to the peasant; and
through all their ages, from infancy to old age; yea, and through
all the different periods of time, from the beginning of the world
to the present hour; and we shall not find so much as one differing from the rest, unless indeed a very few, who have been sanctified from the womb. The testimony of Almighty God is this:
" They that are after the flesh do mind the things of the flesh;
and they that are after the Spirit, the things of the Spirit. The
carnal mind is enmity against God: for it is not subject to the
Law of God, neither indeed can be[a]." Here both of these
points are asserted, with equal clearness, and with unquestionable authority. If the point be doubted, look for a person who,
from his youth up, has shewn a superiority to the pleasures,
honours, interests of this world, and sought his happiness in
communion with God, and in the exercises of prayer and praise.
Alas! not one such person will you find: the hearts of all have
been in perfect agreement with each other, even as the face that
is reflected, with the face that inspects the mirror.]

2. When awakened to a sense of their perishing condition—

[Let but the eyes of any one be opened to see his real
state, and he will begin immediately to tremble before God.
No sense of earthly dignity will uphold a man at that hour.
Felix on the throne of judgment, and Belshazzar in his drunken
carousals, become weak as other men; and betray the convictions of their mind, that " it is a fearful thing to fall into the
hands of the living God." Not the most obdurate sinners in
the universe can any longer defy the arm of justice: the very
instant they see themselves obnoxious to its stroke, their spirits
sink within them. Even the murderers of our blessed Lord,
whilst yet their hands were reeking with his blood, cry out in
agony of mind, " Men and brethren, what shall we do[b]?"
In another thing, too, they all agree: they all, without exception, seek, in the first instance, to conciliate God's favour
by some works of their own. They will repent; they will reform
their lives; they will perform the duties which they have hitherto
neglected; they will exercise benevolence to the utmost of their
power: they will do any thing, if by any means they may recommend themselves to God as objects of his mercy. Those
amongst them who have been somewhat better instructed will
allow to Jesus Christ the honour of saving them; but still they
must do something to entitle them to come to him, and to

---

[a] Rom. viii. 5, 7.   [b] Acts ii. 37.

warrant their hope in him. None, in the first instance, see, nor, if they were instructed, would they approve, the Gospel method of salvation, simply by faith in Christ. To renounce every kind and degree of hope in themselves is, to their proud hearts, an act of humiliation, to which they cannot submit. They think, so entirely to set aside good works, is to disparage them, and to countenance a neglect of them; and therefore they cannot cast themselves wholly and entirely on the merits of a crucified Redeemer. This reluctance to glorify Christ is, indeed, overcome sooner in some than in others: and in this respect " the publicans and harlots for the most part enter into the kingdom sooner than the Scribes and Pharisees[c]," because they are sooner convinced that they have nothing of their own to rely upon: but in all is there the same tendency to establish a righteousness of their own, and a difficulty in being brought to " submit to the righteousness of Christ[d]."]

3. When truly converted to the faith of Christ—

[To every one, without exception, " is Christ precious," even preciousness itself[e]. Find one to whom he is not " fairer than ten thousand, and altogether lovely[f]." You might as well look for one in heaven itself, as on earth. It is not possible to have " tasted how gracious He is," and not love him, and serve him, and glory in him. Equally characteristic also of the believer is the love of holiness. Sin is no longer that pleasant morsel which they would roll under their tongue: it is hateful and abominable in their eyes; and they would gladly have it crucified within them. The divine image is that which they now affect; and after which they pant, as the hart after the water-brooks. In all, indeed, these marks are not alike visible, because all are not alike gracious; but in all, according to their measure of the gift of Christ, is this grace found: and if there be a professor of religion in whom it is not found, I hesitate not to say, that he belongs not to the class of whom I am speaking, but must take both his name and portion with the hypocrites. Of course, when I speak of the love of holiness, I comprehend it in all its parts, and consider it as extending equally to both the tables of the Law The man who has a scriptural hope in the Lord Jesus Christ will not fail to " purify himself, even as Christ is pure[g]."]

Now this subject is not one of curious speculation; but of real use, of most important USE,

1. For our humiliation—

[See the portrait of human nature as drawn in the first chapter of the Epistle to the Romans. See it as again

---

[c] Matt. xxi. 31.   [d] Rom. ix. 30—33. and x. 1—3.
[e] 1 Pet. ii. 7. τιμή.   [f] Cant. v. 10, 16.   [g] 1 John iii. 3.

exhibited in the third chapter : " There is none righteous, no, not one : there is none that understandeth, there is none that seeketh after God. They are all gone out of the way; they are together become unprofitable : there is none that doeth good; no, not one. Their throat is an open sepulchre ; with their tongues they have used deceit; the poison of asps is under their lips : whose mouth is full of cursing and bitterness : their feet are swift to shed blood : destruction and misery are in their ways : and the way of peace have they not known : there is no fear of God before their eyes." But it may be asked, What can these passages have to do with the more moral part of the community ? I answer, that " whatsoever things the Law saith, it saith to them who are under the Law; (as every child of man is;) that *every* mouth may be stopped, and *all the world* become guilty before God[h]." Take this glass then, Brethren, and behold your own faces in it; and say, whether you have any reason for self-admiration and self-complacency ? The true character of your hearts is this : " They are deceitful above all things, and desperately wicked[i]:" and, if there be any superiority in the conduct of any, you owe it, not to the superior quality of your hearts, but to the preventing and assisting grace of God. And the best amongst you may look upon the vilest of the human race and say, 'Such an one might I have been, but for the grace of God !']

2. For our consolation—

[When under peculiar temptations, we are ready to think that there is no one like us, and that no one was ever tempted as we are. But "there has no temptation taken any one of us, but what is common to man[k]." And when we know this, it is a rich source of consolation to us. Not that the trials of others can do us any good : every man must bear his own burthen, whether it be greater or less : but, when a man supposes that he alone is subjected to any peculiar trouble, he is ready to imagine that he is an outcast from the Lord, and that there is no hope for him in God. The removal of this painful apprehension, however, raises him from his dejection, and emboldens him to maintain the conflict with all the enemies of his salvation. He will then chide himself, and say, "Why art thou cast down, O my soul? and why art thou disquieted within me? Hope thou in God: for I shall yet praise Him, who is the health of my countenance, and my God[l]."]

3. For our encouragement—

[If in the Scriptures we see what human nature is, we see also what divine grace is, and what it can effect in the heart of

h Rom. iii. 10—19.   i Jer. xvii. 9.
k 1 Cor. x. 13.   l Ps. xlii. 11.

man. After a most horrible description given by the Apostle, of persons who were to be excluded from the kingdom of heaven, he says to the Corinthians, " And such were some of you : but ye are washed, but ye are sanctified, but ye are justified in the name of the Lord Jesus, and by the Spirit of our God[m]." And the change wrought, on the day of Pentecost, on the murderers of our Lord, abundantly shews what may be expected by all who believe on him. The same holy joy shall animate their souls ; and the same Almighty power renovate them after the divine image. It was to Christians scattered throughout the world that Peter said, " Through believing in Christ, they rejoiced with joy unspeakable and full of glory ; receiving even now the end of their faith, even the salvation of their souls[n]." What, then, may not we also expect, if we truly believe in Christ ? Verily, as in water face answereth to face, so shall our hearts respond to the hearts of the primitive saints, in all that is good and great. Our victories shall be the same as theirs, as shall also be our triumphs and our joys. Let this encourage us to go forward in our heavenly way, expecting assuredly that we in due time shall " see the good of God's chosen, and rejoice in the gladness of his nation, and glory with his inheritance[o]."]

[m] 1 Cor. vi. 10, 11.   [n] 1 Pet. i. 8, 9.   [o] Ps. cvi. 5.

OUTLINE NO. 814

THE EFFECTS OF PIETY AND IMPIETY IN THE WORLD.

Prov. xxviii. 4. *They that forsake the Law, praise the wicked ; but such as keep the Law, contend with them.*

MAN, as a social being, has an influence on those around him : and his actions should be considered, not merely as they affect himself, but, in their social aspect, as tending to make an impression upon the minds of others. In this point of view, a great measure of responsibility attaches to us, far beyond what, at first sight, we should be ready to imagine. Our good or evil conduct operates as an example, and countenances a similar conduct in others : so that, in our daily actions, we, though unconscious of it, are doing good or evil to an unknown extent. This is proclaimed in the words before us : " They that forsake the Law, praise the wicked ; but such as keep the Law, contend with them."

From these words I shall be led to shew the effects
of piety and impiety on the surrounding world. And,
I. Of impiety—

Whatever be men's line of conduct, they must, of
necessity, " have pleasure in those who pursue the
same[a]." Those they will of course choose for their
companions; and if for no other reason, yet in their
own vindication they will approve of and applaud their
ways. The proud will commend the proud, and " call
them happy[b];" as will the worldling also " bless the
covetous, whom God abhorreth[c]." Indeed, it may be
laid down as a general rule, that if only you " do well
to yourself," by studying your own ease, interest, and
honour, " all men will praise you," as men that are
wise, and worthy of imitation[d]. It is a matter of
course that " the world will love its own[e]." This,
however, is a very partial view of our text; the true
sense of which lies much deeper. The praise which
an ungodly man will give to those who are like himself, is bestowed not only occasionally with the lips,
but uniformly and without intermission in the life. A
man who refuses submission to the will of God, and
" forsakes his Law," does by that very act tacitly,
though most intelligibly, declare to all around him,

1. That obedience to God's Law is unnecessary—

[He will acknowledge the Scriptures to be a revelation
from God; and would be greatly offended, if his belief in that
revelation were questioned. But his faith in it is nothing more
than a speculative assent: he regards not the authority of God
in it; and by his contempt of that authority he says, in fact,
that a submission to it is unnecessary. The language of the
heart and of the life is interpreted in this way by God himself: " Ye have said, It is vain to serve God: and what profit
is it that we have kept his ordinance, and that we have walked
mournfully before the Lord of Hosts[f]?" And this construction
is just; for what a man avows to be unnecessary for himself,
he must be understood as maintaining to be unnecessary for
others.]

2. That not even the Gospel itself entails any obligation upon us—

a Rom. i. 32.   b Mal. iii. 15.   c Ps. x. 3.
d Ps. xlix. 18.   e John xv. 19.   f Mal. iii. 14.

[Many who profess to believe the Gospel, and to make it the ground of their hope towards God, yet feel no constraining influence from all its wonders of love and mercy. They practically say, 'True, the Lord Jesus Christ came into the world, and "died the just for the unjust, that he might bring us to God[g]." But what has this to do with the regulation of our lives? We need not be "brought to God" in this world: it will be quite sufficient to be brought to him in the world to come: and we may be sure, even from this very mercy vouchsafed unto us, that God will accept us, even though no change shall have taken place in our hearts and lives. He has sent his Son indeed, as we are told, " to bless us, in turning every one of us from our iniquities[h]:" but we need not be anxious about experiencing any such effect of the Redeemer's mission: we may live to ourselves, and obtain his favour, as effectually and as certainly as if we lived to him.']

3. That the way of wickedness is preferable as it respects this present world—

[Finding pleasure only in the things of time and sense himself, he encourages the same taste in others. For, for what end " has God given us all things richly to enjoy," if we are not to enjoy them? As for a compliance with the precepts of the Law, it is obvious that it must require continual self-denial: and what happiness can there be in that? It must detach us, also, from those who are most able and willing to administer to our happiness: and how can that operate, but to our disadvantage? As for repentance, and holy exercises of every kind, they may be very good in a dying hour; but to a person in health they can be a source of nothing but gloom and melancholy. Thus he sanctions the ungodly in the whole of their conduct, and encourages them in all the delusions by which they are misled.]

4. That no evil is to be apprehended from it in the world to come—

[This necessarily follows from all the rest: for, if he really thought that God would execute his threatenings against the violators of the Law, he would be more attentive to his own ways. But he persuades himself, that God is too merciful to punish any one in the eternal world, or, at all events, for such slight offences as he commits: and, by his open contempt of God's threatened judgments, he says to all around him, that they have nothing to fear, since " the Lord will do neither good nor evil[i]." The exact description of these persons is given by the Psalmist, when he says, " The wicked, through the pride of his countenance, will not seek after God: God is not in all his thoughts. His ways are always grievous: thy

[g] 1 Pet. iii. 18.   [h] Acts iii. 26.   [i] Zeph. i. 12.

judgments are far above out of his sight: and *as for all his enemies, he puffeth at them*[k]."]

The very reverse of this is the influence,

II. Of piety—

The man who forsakes the Law, praises the wicked; but the man who keeps the Law, contends with them. He does this,

1. By the silent testimony of his life—

[A godly man is like " a light shining in a dark place." However unobtrusive his conduct may be, it forms a contrast with that of all around him, and especially with that of those who move in his sphere of life. If he be young, his sobriety is a reproach to all the giddiness and folly of his youthful acquaintance. If he be of a more advanced age, his zeal for God reproves the worldliness and indifference even of his most respected neighbours. Whether we view his abstinence from sin, or his practice of holiness, he equally casts reflections on the great mass of mankind. " *They* are of the world, and speak of the world : *he* is of God, and both speaks and acts for God[l]." " He is not conformed to the world " in any of its vanities[m] : " he comes out from the world, and is separate; and will not so much as touch the unclean thing[n]." He endeavours so to walk in the world, as to " keep his garments clean[o]," and undefiled with any of its abominations. He is even " crucified to the world, and regards it as a man would who was suspended on a cross, and looking for a speedy dissolution[p]." At the same time he gives himself to holy exercises ; and determines, with God's help, to fulfil every duty, as in the presence of his God. He shews that he has other views, other desires, other pursuits, than the world has any conception of; that he belongs to another world ; that his conversation is in heaven[q];" and that, "though in the world, he is not of the world, even as the Lord Jesus Christ was not of the world[r]."

Now all this, of necessity, attracts notice, and constrains all who behold him to say, " If he is right, we must be wrong." The effect of his conduct is precisely like that of Noah's, when he built the ark. It is said of Noah, that " being moved with fear, he prepared an ark to the saving of his house ; *by the which he condemned the world*[s]." How did this act of his *condemn the world?* He was, it is true, " a preacher of righteousness;" but it was not so much his preaching, as his practice, which was here said to condemn the world. His faith condemned

k Ps. x. 4, 5.   l 1 John iv. 5, 6.   m Rom. xii. 2.
n 2 Cor. vi. 17.   o Rev. xvi. 15.   p Gal. vi. 14.
q Phil. iii. 20.   r John xvii. 16.   s Heb. xi. 7.

their unbelief; his fear, their security; his obedience, their disobedience. He needed not to *say* any thing: his conduct spake sufficiently; and the consciences of the beholders made the application. Thus it is, in a measure, with every godly man; he is "an epistle of Christ, known and read of all men[t]." The ungodly world may shut their eyes against the light of God's written word; but *him* they are forced to see, whether they will or not: and in him they see what is the line of conduct which God requires, and how far they are from walking according to it.

That the world consider themselves as condemned by the godly, is evident, from the indignation which they manifest when the light of God's truth is made to shine before them. They instantly endeavour, by every possible means, to extinguish the light, or at all events to induce the godly to put their light under a bushel, and to hide it from their eyes[u]. They will *profess* to reprobate the *sentiments* of the godly: but they would never concern themselves about the *sentiments* of the godly, if they could but induce them to alter their *conduct*. It is their *conduct* that reproaches them, and that forms the real ground of their indignation against them. "If ye were of the world," says our Lord, "the world (whatever your sentiments might be) would love its own: but *because ye are not of the world,* but I have chosen you out of the world, *therefore* the world hateth you[x]." Let piety enter into any family amongst us, and we shall see a fulfilment of that word, "Think you that I came to send peace on earth? I came not to send peace, but a sword[y]."]

2. By the open avowal of his sentiments—

[A faithful servant of God, in whatever line he move, will not be ashamed of Christ, but will "confess him openly before men[z]." *This* he feels to be a bounden duty. He does not wish to make a parade of his religion: but he is commanded to "let his light shine before men[a];" and not only "not to have fellowship with the unfruitful works of darkness, but, when opportunity occurs, to reprove them[b]." Hence, though he is cautious, "not to cast pearls before swine, who would only trample them under their feet[c]," he is "ready to give to every inquirer a reason of the hope that is in him with meekness and fear[d]." Nor will he be afraid to reprove sin, where he has any hope that his admonitions will be well received. If he be a minister, he will be "bold in the Lord to speak the Gospel of God with much contention[e];" not fearing the face of man, but

---

[t] 2 Cor. iii. 3. [u] John iii. 19, 20. [x] John xv. 19.
[y] Matt. x. 34—36. [z] Matt. x. 32. [a] Matt. v. 16.
[b] Eph. v. 11. [c] Matt. vii. 6. [d] 1 Pet. iii. 15.
[e] 1 Thess. ii. 2.

declaring, before all, and without reserve, " the whole counsel
of God[f]." Nor, though he move in a private sphere, will he
be backward to exert his influence, so far as it extends, for the
suppression of evil, and for the diffusion of piety through the
world. This indeed will raise up enemies against him: for
men will " hate him that reproveth in the gate[g]." They hated
our blessed Lord principally on this account; as he himself
told them: " You, (who countenance its proceedings,) the
world cannot hate ; but me it hateth, because I testify of it
that the works thereof are evil[h]." It was this that incensed
Ahab against Micaiah : " I hate Micaiah because he doth not
speak good concerning me, but evil[i]. And it was the faithfulness of John, in reproving Herod's unlawful commerce with his
brother Philip's wife, that brought down the vengeance of that
prince upon him[k]. But, notwithstanding all the odium that
such fidelity will bring upon him, the true Christian will exercise it as occasion serves, declaring candidly his conviction, that
" the broad road of the world leadeth to destruction, and that
the narrow way alone will issue in eternal life[l]."]

From this subject we may clearly SEE,

1. How much guilt attaches to us all—

[I will not now speak of those who have lived in open and
flagrant sin ; though, of course, all that I shall say will apply
with double force to them; but I will speak of those who,
though moral and discreet, have not given up themselves unfeignedly to God ; or who grew up to maturity before they
fully embraced the Gospel. Look back to your early child-
hood : your example even at that time had an influence on
your youthful companions; and said to them, in language
which they clearly understood, that there was no occasion for
them to seek after God. As you grew up towards manhood,
your influence became proportionably extended, and proportionably more injurious also. Go now to your different companions, and to the thousands who, unknown to you, derived
from your example encouragement in sin: go, tell them how
you regret the injuries you have done, and how anxious you
are to repair the evil, by making known to them the way of
life and salvation. Thousands, alas! are gone beyond the
reach of any effort, and are already enduring in hell the
miseries which you contributed to heap upon them. But of
those to whom you may gain access, how many, do you suppose, would listen to your advice? there would scarcely be
found one amongst them all that would not laugh in your face,
and account you either a fool or mad. King Manasseh, by his

[f] Acts xx. 27.   [g] Isai. xxix. 21.   [h] John vii. 7.
[i] 1 Kings xxii. 8.   [k] Mark vi. 25—27.   [l] Matt. vii. 13. 14.

influence and example, did evil to as great an extent as any creature that ever lived: but when he exerted his royal influence to reclaim the persons he had seduced to sin, he could not prevail: they would still, notwithstanding all his edicts, and all his example too, continue to " offer sacrifices on their high-places," instead of conforming themselves to the commandments of their God[m]. Thus, even supposing that we are now walking in the ways of God, the influence of our former lives will continue to operate to the ruin of many souls, and to the unspeakable augmentation of our own guilt. Contemplate this, I pray you, my Brethren; and remember, that though you may never have committed one single sin that should expose you to shame before men, you are guilty in the sight of God, to an extent that no language can paint, no imagination can conceive. Nay, strange as it may seem, the very blamelessness of your conduct before men, inasmuch as it has attracted a greater measure of their admiration, has unhappily contributed, even beyond the example of the generality, to deceive their minds, and to ruin their souls. I must then say to every one amongst you, that the injury which in your days of thoughtlessness you have unconsciously done to the souls of men, should be a ground of the deepest humiliation to you, to the latest hour of your lives.]

2. What a pre-eminent measure of guilt is contracted by the backsliding professor—

[Whilst others, by their ungodly lives, encourage sin in all around them, *you* do it with far greater effect. For *you* are understood as speaking *from experience;* whilst others deliver only, as it were, a hasty and ill-formed *opinion. You* are considered as proclaiming that there is no excellency, no reality, in religion; that the ways of the world, from which for a season you had departed, are not either so dangerous or so sinful as you had ignorantly supposed; that, in fact, there is no sincerity in those who profess godliness; and that, if all were as honest as you, they would, like you, throw off the mask at once. Ah! think what a stumbling-block *you* lay in the way of others; how you " crucify the Son of God afresh;" and what cause multitudes will have to curse your very name for ever, whilst they call for vengeance on your souls for contributing so largely to their ruin!

And here let me speak to those who do not indeed draw back to open sin, but only so far as to conceal their principles in compliment to the world. You may account this prudence: but God will account it treason; and the Saviour, whom " you thus refuse to confess, will refuse to acknowledge you in the presence of his Father[n]." Consider this; and know assuredly

[m] 2 Chron. xxxiii. 15—17.   [n] Matt. x. 32, 33.

on what terms your sentence shall be passed in the last day:
" If you suffer with Christ, you shall also reign with him; but
if you deny him, he will deny you. If ye believe not his testimony, yet he abideth faithful; he cannot deny himself[o];"
but will assuredly execute judgment, in perfect conformity to
this rule.]

3. What an incentive we have to cultivate piety in
the highest possible degree—

[The more our light shines before men, the more shall we
put to shame the wickedness of the ungodly, and encourage the
exercise of all that is good in the world. And who can tell
how far our influence may extend? If we be the means of
leading one sinner to repentance, " we save a soul from death,
and hide a multitude of sins[p]." And what may be the ultimate effects on that person's family, or even on his remotest
posterity, who can tell? Let this then operate as an inducement with us to " shine as lights in the world[q]." I say not but
that the saving of our own souls should be our first motive:
nevertheless, a strong additional motive we may find in the
subject before us. Nor ought it to have light weight on our
minds: for, whilst we benefit the world, we greatly honour our
God; who is most glorified in those who most reflect his image,
and most advance his kingdom in the world.]

[o] 2 Tim. ii. 12, 13.   [p] Jam. v. 19, 20.   [q] Phil. ii. 15, 16.

OUTLINE NO. 815

THE LIGHT ENJOYED BY THE GODLY.

Prov. xxviii. 5. *They that seek the Lord understand all things.*

THERE are, in the Holy Scriptures, broad, and, if
I may so call them, sweeping expressions, which, if
taken in their strict and literal sense, have not so
much as even the semblance of truth. Yet are they
not liable to be misunderstood, because every candid
reader will of necessity supply the restrictions which
are necessary for a just interpretation of them. For
instance: no one who should read the words which
we have just heard, would suppose that Solomon ever
intended to assert that all who sought the Lord were
at once brought to the knowledge of all arts and
sciences, and to an acquaintance with all the languages
of the earth. Every expression must of necessity be
restricted either by the subject of which it treats, or

by the context in which it stands. The words before us are used in a way of contrast with those which precede them. The writer has just said, that " evil men understand not judgment;" that is, they understand not what they are doing, or what they ought to do, or the true end and scope of God's dealings with them. But they who seek the Lord are well instructed in *these* things : they may be as ignorant of worldly things as any other people ; but of things relating to their spiritual and eternal welfare they have a discernment which no ungodly man either does, or can, possess. Taking the words with this restriction, I shall,

I. Confirm the sentiment—

Here I might enumerate a great variety of particulars, such as the evil of sin, the beauty of holiness, the glory of Christ, which a spiritual man alone can truly apprehend : but, as the expression is broad and comprehensive, so shall my illustration of it be ; that so the contrast between the spiritual and carnal man may more forcibly appear. Of those, therefore, who seek the Lord, I will say, they understand,

1. The true state and character of the world around them—

[That every thing bears the appearance of some great change that has been wrought upon it, is obvious to all. The very elements bear this stamp upon them; as does also the whole creation, animate and inanimate, rational and irrational. No one can conceive of the world, or any thing in it, as having preserved that degree of perfection in which it was originally created. The ungodly therefore, as well as others, are sensible that there is a great deal of disorder in the world. But the godly man alone sees this in any degree according to its real extent. He sees that the whole universe is up in arms against Almighty God, under the command of that wicked fiend, who, having himself rebelled against his Maker, is labouring to bring every creature into a participation of his crime ; and who, having succeeded in this enterprise, is justly called, " the god of this world." He sees that this contest is carried on, not by those only who are sunk in open profligacy, but by the most moral and sober of mankind; who, in fact, are as much " alienated from the life of God" as others, and have their own " minds as much at enmity with him" as any other people upon earth. He sees, in a measure, what men ought to be, and what they are; and that all, without exception, are "living to themselves, and not unto their God." The different orders of men are, in his eyes, only like different parts of one great army; differently habited indeed, and differently employed; some under the very garb of friends, whilst others are arrayed as open and determined foes: but all are acting, in their respective places, for the establishment of Satan's kingdom, rather than of Christ's. This, I say, the godly man sees, in perfect correspondence with what St. Paul has declared: "There is none righteous, no, not one; there is none that understandeth; there is none that seeketh after God: they are all gone out of the way, they are together become unprofitable: there is none that doeth good, no, not one a."]

2. The real happiness of man—

[The world at large conceive of this as consisting in temporal enjoyment. Pleasure, riches, honour, are looked upon as the great sources from whence happiness must flow: and where these are not eagerly coveted, there is something of a temporal nature substituted in their place: some fond conceit, or a mere state of carnal ease, devoid either of any strong emotions, whether of pain or pleasure. But the godly man knows that there is no happiness but in God—in a sense of his favour, in a performance of his will, in a prospect of his glory. There is in his views, and those of an ungodly man, a most perfect contrast with respect to this matter; each coveting what the other despises, and each regarding as contemptible what the other desires. Our blessed Lord's words will put this matter in the clearest light b——— The rich, the gay, the honoured, are by the one regarded with admiration and envy; by the other, with pity and compassion. The poor weeping and persecuted saint, on the contrary, is by the one despised; whilst the other affects the experience of such an one with the fondest delight. In a word, whilst to the inquiry, "Who will shew us any good?" the ungodly man says, ' Give me a supply of corn, and wine, and oil;' the godly man pours out his soul in that petition of the Psalmist, "Lord, lift thou up the light of thy countenance upon me c."]

3. The proper tendency of all that God is doing in the world—

[God is seen both in his word and works; and both in the one and in the other does he appear, to an ungodly world, to obstruct, rather than to advance, the happiness of his creatures. The word is too strict in its requirements to suit our fallen state; and the dispensations of his Providence are calculated only to embitter life by continual troubles or

a Rom. iii. 10—12.   b See Luke vi. 20—26.   c Ps. iv. 6.

bereavements. Far different from these, however, are the sentiments of a godly man. The whole inspired volume, whether it promise or threaten, prohibit or enjoin, is in his eyes a fountain of good, springing up to everlasting life — — — And all the diversified afflictions which arise, are regarded by him as blessings in disguise; as messengers sent to " humble us, and to do us good at our latter end," by weaning us from things visible and temporal, and stimulating us to lay hold on those which are invisible and eternal.

An ignorant novice may dread a cross wind, as calculated only to retard the vessel in which he is embarked: but the experienced mariner will welcome it, as filling all his sails better than a wind that is the most direct; and thus, whilst the ungodly man views afflictions only as calamities which he would most avoid, the godly man welcomes them from God's hands, in the assured hope that " his light and momentary afflictions will work out for him a far more exceeding and eternal weight of glory d."]

Thus, to go no further, it sufficiently appears how much clearer insight the godly man has into God's word and works, than the ungodly man can pretend to. And now let us,

II. Account for the fact—

I readily concede, that, in point of natural talent or acquired learning, the godly man may be inferior to others; but in spiritual discernment he is superior to the wisest philosopher on earth. Does any one inquire how this should be? I answer,

1. He has God himself for his teacher—

[All God's people " are taught of him;" and it is in consequence of their " having heard and learned of the Father," that they attain to a knowledge which no other person can possess e. Were I to say that " the Spirit of God opens the eyes of their understanding," and " brings them out of darkness into marvellous light," I should say enough to justify all the assertions which I have made: nor would any one have a right to ask from me an explanation of the process by which this mysterious work is accomplished. Yet I think that the mode of divine teaching may be in some little measure comprehended by means of a suitable and familiar illustration. There are different ways in which an object which is obscure may be rendered visible: one way is, by bringing it nearer to us; another is, by removing intervening obstacles; another, by reflecting stronger light upon

d 2 Cor. iv. 17.　　　　　e John vi. 45.

it; and another, by strengthening the organs of vision to behold it. Now, without entering into a minute consideration of all these particulars, we may observe, in general, that God's methods of instructing us by his Spirit are somewhat analogous to these; in that he brings home with power to our souls the truths which we hear, and inclines our hearts to embrace them. The telescope, which brings distant objects to our view, and the microscope, which enables us to discern things which are too small to be seen by the naked eye, make no difference whatever either in the objects themselves or in the organs whereby we perceive them: the things themselves, and our faculties also, all remain the same, whether the instruments be used by us or not. So there is no difference in the truths which are heard by different persons, or in the capacity of those by whom they are perceived: the difference is in the manner in which the truths are presented to the mind: and if we, by instruments of human contrivance, are able thus to bring to the sight of men things that are invisible to the naked eye, we may well suppose that God is able to bring home to the souls of men truths which the unassisted mind is unable to apprehend. But I think we may get a juster view of this, by considering how it is that the imperfections of our sight are remedied in common life. When we have an indistinct vision of objects before us, it is for the most part owing to this: through an excess or defect of convexity in our eye, the object before us either falls short of the retina, or goes beyond it: and the use of glasses is, by a suitable medium to bring the object on the retina, that so it may be distinctly impressed thereon, in all its just symmetry and proportions. Now the Spirit of God, by giving to us " an honest and a good heart," imprints upon the tablet of our souls the truths, of which, without his aid, we could have no just perception: and thus we are enabled to understand what others are not able to discern. And thus is fulfilled what St. John has said: " The spiritual man judgeth all things; yet he himself is judged of no man: for who hath known the mind of the Lord, that he may instruct him? But we have the mind of Christ," and therefore are qualified to judge both ourselves and others[f]. Now, I the rather dwell on this, in order to remove from the minds of objectors the idea that we lay claim to any thing like miraculous inspiration. We do indeed say, that God alone can enable us to discern the things of the Spirit[g]; but we say, also, that he does this through the use of our own faculties, under the direction and influence of his good Spirit: and thus " he reveals to babes and sucklings the things which he has hid from the wise and prudent[h]."]

[f] 1 Cor. ii. 15, 16.   [g] 1 Cor. ii. 12.
[h] Matt. xi. 25.

2. He has an inward experience of the things which he knows—

[St. John affirms this very thing: "He that believeth on the Son of God hath the witness in himself[i];" that is, he has in his soul a distinct perception of those truths which he has received through the medium of his understanding. And this also, I think, may, through a familiar illustration, be made perfectly intelligible to our minds. We know that our senses are given us for the purpose of discerning the distinctive excellencies of every thing around us. It is not sufficient that one faculty alone be brought to bear upon the object that is set before us: we must exercise upon every thing that very faculty which is pre-eminently formed to discover and appreciate its excellence. Suppose we see, for instance, the sun, without *feeling* its beams; or a flower, without having our *smell* regaled by its odours; or honey, without *tasting* its sweetness; or a singing bird, without *hearing* his melodious notes; it is obvious that we can form but a very inadequate notion of these things, for want of an acquaintance with their chief excellencies: and, in like manner, we can ill judge of a diamond by the touch, when its brilliancy has never been submitted to our *sight*. It is through the apprehending of every thing by its appropriate sense, that we attain just and adequate perceptions of it. Now the Apostle tells us, that the godly man "has all his senses exercised to discern good and evil[k]:" and hence it is, that having within himself a perception of them which no other man can enjoy, he possesses also an evidence which no other man can attain. Now this test may be applied to every thing that is of a spiritual nature; and the perception arising from it is fitly called "a spiritual discernment[l]:" and by this, I say again, "we understand all things;" as St. John also has told us; "Ye have an unction of the Holy One, and ye know all things[m]." Here is contained all that I have spoken; namely, the extent of the knowledge possessed by God's people, and the means by which they are enabled to attain it: "We know all things," because God himself is our teacher; and by the unction poured out, that is, by the "eye-salve which he puts upon our eyes," he gives us the actual perception of every thing in our own souls[n], and, consequently, the clear and proper understanding of it.]

Methinks you are now ready to INQUIRE,

1. How shall I attain this understanding?

[I answer, Not by mere study, even of the Scriptures themselves; but rather by "seeking after God" in spirit and in truth. This is the particular point suggested in my text:

[i] 1 John v. 10, [k] Heb. v. 14. [l] 1 Cor. ii. 14.
[m] 1 John ii. 20, 27. [n] Rev. iii. 18.

" They that seek the Lord understand all things." You will remember what our Lord has said: " If any man will do his will, he shall know of the doctrine, whether it be of God[o]." This is that which I have spoken of before : it supposes that there is in us that "honest and good heart," which alone receives the word aright, and alone enables us to "bring forth fruit with patience[p]." I would not depreciate books of human composition, and still less the Scriptures of truth: but we must never forget, that "though Paul should plant, and Apollos water, it is God alone that can give the increase[q]." In fact, this is the reason why many hear the Gospel for years without any saving benefit to their souls: they will not humble themselves before God, and seek for mercy through Christ, and give themselves up unreservedly to God; and therefore they remain for ever without any true understanding of the word, and any sweet experience of its power. You must first be melted by it ; and then you will be "poured into its mould," and attain, by means of it, that knowledge of God which is life eternal.]

2. How shall I manifest it to the world?

[If "God have given you an understanding to know him[r]," shew it, not by a fond conceit of your own attainments, or a contemptuous spurning of others as blind and carnal — — — but by a holy life and conversation, such as none but those who are taught of God can maintain. If you *know* more than others, you should be prepared to answer that question, " What *do* ye more than others[s]?" "The tree must be known by its fruit :" and, if you have received a superior illumination in your mind, you must "walk worthy of that high distinction," and "shine as lights in a dark world." If the Lord, by his Spirit, have written his law upon your hearts, then must you shew forth that law in your lives, and be in the world as "epistles of Christ, known and read of all men[t]."]

[o] John vii. 17.	[p] Luke viii. 15.	[q] 1 Cor. iii. 5—7.
[r] 1 John v. 20.	[s] Matt. v. 47.	[t] 2 Cor. iii. 2.

OUTLINE NO. 816

ADVANTAGES OF THE RICH AND OF THE POOR COMPARED.

Prov. xxviii. 11. *The rich man is wise in his own conceit; but the poor that hath understanding searcheth him out.*

PROVERBS are, for the most part, very obscure: they are intended to convey an abundance of instruction in a small space : and the truths contained in them are almost always such as escape the observation of unthinking men, and such as militate against their most received opinions. That the rich have greatly the advantage of the poor in reference to knowledge in general, must be confessed: for they have leisure, which the poor cannot command; and instruction, which the poor cannot obtain. Hence it is generally supposed that the rich have the same advantage in reference to divine knowledge. But this is by no means true. On the contrary, the poor have, in reference to divine knowledge, the advantage of them. And this is what Solomon affirms, in the words before us: " The rich man is wise in his own conceit; but the poor that hath understanding searcheth him out."

In support of Solomon's assertion, I will shew,

I. That the poor have really the advantage of the rich in reference to divine knowledge—

Elihu, intending to criminate Job, observed, " Great men are not always wise[a]." And if this be true in relation to the affairs of this world, much more is it so in reference to the concerns of eternity. Nor indeed are the poor always wise in this respect; yet have they, on the whole, the advantage of the rich.

1. They had the advantage in the days of old—

[Look at those who received the testimony of our blessed Lord. It was said with a kind of triumph, " Have any of the rulers and of the Pharisees believed on him[b]?" Whereas we are told, on the other hand, that " the common people heard him gladly[c]." And such was also the experience of the Apostles: it was chiefly amongst the poor that their ministry was attended with success; as St. Paul observes: " Ye see your calling, brethren, how that not many wise men after the flesh, not many mighty, not many noble, are called: but God hath chosen the foolish things of the world to confound the things which are mighty; and base things of the world, and things which are despised, hath God chosen, yea, and things which are not, to bring to nought things that are; that no flesh should glory in his presence[d]."]

2. They have also the advantage at this day—

[It was to be one mark of the Messiah's advent, that " to the poor the Gospel should be preached[e]." By them, too, was

[a] Job xxxii. 9.   [b] John vii. 48.   [c] Mark xii. 37.
[d] 1 Cor. i. 26—29.   [e] Matt. xi. 5.

the Gospel to be received, whilst by the rich it should be rejected and despised.   Nor did our blessed Lord merely affirm this, but he accounted it a fit subject of praise and thanksgiving: " I thank thee, O Father, Lord of heaven and earth, because thou hast hid these things from the wise and prudent, and hast revealed them unto babes[f]!"   And now look around, and see if it be not thus at this day.   Who are they that value the Gospel?   Who are they that attend it, wherever it is preached with effect?   *Some,* indeed, there are of the wise and rich; but very few in comparison; so few, that if a man of wealth and learning shew a decided love to the Gospel, he is regarded almost as a phenomenon; and *that,* too, no less by the Church than by the world itself.   The great mass of religious people are of the poorer class; so that at this day, no less than in the apostolic age, when that appeal of the Apostle James is made to us, " Hearken, my beloved brethren, hath not God chosen the poor of this world to be rich in faith, and heirs of the kingdom which he has promised to them that love him[g]?" there is but one answer that can be given to it: we must say, It is even so; it is from among the poor, and not from amongst the rich, that God has formed his Church: it is " of unhewn stones that his altar is made[h];" and " of these very stones that he has raised up children to Abraham[i]."]

Seeing, then, that what we have asserted is an unquestionable fact, let us,

II. Account for it—

We might be satisfied with referring it, as our blessed Lord does, to the sovereign will of God: "Even so, Father, for so it seemed good in thy sight[k]," should be quite sufficient for us.   But we may trace the fact to natural causes.   The rich, from the very circumstance of their elevation in society, are under considerable disadvantages, beyond what are experienced by the poor:

1. They are more blinded by prejudice—

[Into the minds of the higher orders of society prejudices are instilled from their earliest infancy. Religious people are kept at a distance from them; religious books are taken out of their hands; and religious sentiments are branded with every epithet that can render them odious. For one word that would lead them to God, a hundred are spoken to draw them from him.   Let them betray a love to earthly things, and no one will offer a sentiment to turn them from such an evil way: but

f Matt. xi. 25, 26.   g Jam. ii. 5.   h Exod. xx. 25.
i Matt. iii. 9.   k Matt. xi. 26.

let them betray a decided love to heavenly things, and multitudes will exert themselves in every possible way to divert them from so dangerous a path. Hence their prejudices are all on the side of evil and of the world. And how great the effect of prejudice is, may be seen in the adherents both of Judaism and Popery. One would imagine that the superstitions both of the one and of the other must give way before the light of the New Testament: but prejudice, as has been said, has neither eyes nor ears. Truth has no force, and argument no power, when set before one whose mind is pre-occupied with statements of an adverse nature. The Apostle says of the Jews, that " to this day a veil is upon their hearts; so that, when Moses is read to them, they cannot see the true scope of his instructions[1]." And precisely thus it is also with the rich, when the Gospel is preached to them: " Their eyes are blinded; and they cannot discern" the truth of those things which are proposed to their consideration[m]. But the poor are, comparatively, but little subjected to this influence. People take not so much pains to prejudice their minds; and they are left more to think and act for themselves. Hence, when truth is proposed to them, they are more open to conviction, and more easily brought under its power. And this is one reason why even the " publicans and harlots enter into the kingdom before the Scribes and Pharisees."]

2. They are more enslaved by custom—

[The rich, amidst all their boasted liberty, are the veriest bond-slaves that the world contains. If negroes are afraid of the scourge of their masters, so are the rich afraid lest they should be subjected to the lash of censure amongst their equals. Let an opportunity of spiritual instruction be afforded them, they would be afraid to avail themselves of it, if it were offered at a place not frequented by the rich, or by a person not approved amongst them. Even though in their hearts they would be glad to hear the instruction, they dare not go over the line prescribed by custom and fashion, lest they should bring upon themselves some reproach. They would be ashamed to be found reading the Bible; and would be in perfect horrors if they were discovered weeping for their sins. True, a rich Papist would not blush at being known to follow the superstitious usages of his Church, because other rich persons both approve and follow the same superstitions: but a rich Protestant would not dare to spend a day in fasting and prayer, because the rich of his own community pour contempt on piety, and on the means by which piety is advanced in the soul. But the poor are more free to follow the dictates of

---

[1] 2 Cor. iii. 14, 15.   [m] 2 Cor. iv. 4

their conscience: and when they "have a spiritual under-standing," they will follow them: they will not be content to "continue in the broad road, because the many walk there; or to desert the narrow path, because there be but few who find it[n]:" they are more independent of the opinions of the world; and are prepared to say with Joshua, "Let others think or act as they please, I will serve the Lord[o]."]

3. They are more deluded by conceit—

[The rich, on account of their wealth and influence, have great deference paid to their opinions. The flattery which they receive is extremely grateful to them; and they soon begin to think that they are indeed as wise as fawning sycophants re-present them to be. Hence they become very confident in their own opinions, and can ill brook contradiction upon any sub-ject. They suppose, too, that they are as competent to judge of religion as of any other subject; and will lay down the law upon the subject of divine truth as confidently as if they had the wisdom of Daniel or St. Paul. But the poor man, that has been taught of God, sees at once how ignorant these per-sons are on those subjects on which they presume to dogmatize with such unblushing confidence. The rich conceited man will tell us how erroneous it is to represent our fallen nature as so depraved; and what a licentious doctrine that of salvation by faith alone is; and that a life of entire devotedness to God is no better than wild fanaticism or puritanical hypocrisy. But "the poor man, that hath understanding, *searcheth him out:*" he has within himself the evidence of those truths which the conceited man decries. St. John says, "He that believeth on the Son of God hath the witness in himself[p]:" and this internal evidence is more to him than all the assertions which conceit can dictate or arrogance maintain. He knows his own depra-vity: he feels his need of a Saviour: he tastes the sweetness of pure and undefiled religion; and from God he inherits a blessing[q], whilst the rich contemner of his faith receives nothing but woes at the hand of his offended God[r].]

IMPROVEMENT—

1. Envy not those who are rich in this world—

[Truly they are encompassed with snares, and exposed to great dangers. The advantages which they possess are very trivial: (what has the richest man beyond food and raiment, which the poor possess as well as they?) but their disadvan-tages are very great; so great, that "it is easier for a camel to go through the eye of a needle, than for a rich man to enter into the kingdom of heaven." Remarkable, *in this view*, is

[n] Matt. vii. 13, 14.   [o] Josh. xxiv. 15.   [p] 1 John v. 10.
[q] Matt. v. 3.   [r] Isai. v. 21.

that advice of Solomon; " Labour not to *be rich : cease from thine own wisdom*[s]." The errors here pointed at are almost inseparable from each other ; and every one that is truly wise will be on his guard against them both.]

2. Seek to be " rich towards God"—

[That is true wisdom: and the more you possess of spiritual riches, the more truly humble will you be before God. Indeed, *a poor pious man* is, in God's estimation, as high a character as exists on earth. When God's only-begotten Son became incarnate, *this was the character he assumed.* Seek to be conformed to him, and you need not desire any thing beyond. Nothing is of any value without piety ; nor can any thing add to piety, when it fully occupies the soul[t].]

[s] Prov. xxiii. 4.   [t] Phil. iii. 7, 8.

OUTLINE NO. 817

TRUE REPENTANCE RECOMMENDED.

Prov. xxviii. 13.   *He that covereth his sins shall not prosper : but whoso confesseth and forsaketh them shall have mercy.*

THE subject of repentance offers nothing for the gratification of " itching ears." But it must not on that account be overlooked; since, if less interesting than some other subjects on the score of novelty, it yields to none in point of importance. It is the first act whereby a sinner returns unto his God: and it is an act for which the most eminent saint has occasion from day to day ; insomuch that in him it assumes rather the character of a habit than an act. In the more grown Christian, it is the warp, whilst every other grace is the woof : whether the colours interwoven with it be grave or gay, this pervades the whole piece, and is, as it were, the foundation of all the rest.

For the advancing of this work in all our souls, I will shew,

I. The folly of covering our sins—

To conceal our sins from the all-seeing eye of God is impossible : yet

There are various ways in which men attempt to cover them—

[Sin, though it cannot be hidden from God, may be covered from ourselves, by *denial,* by *extenuation,* by *forgetfulness.*

Many, though walking in the habitual violation of the plainest duties, will *deny* that they commit any sin at all. As " the adulterous woman," of whom Solomon speaks, " eateth, and wipeth her mouth, and saith, I have done no wickedness[a] ; " so these, in gratifying their sensual appetites, think that they commit no more evil than if they had merely satisfied the demands of hunger and thirst: and, in *their* minds, one sinful indulgence is but a prelude to another, whenever opportunity and inclination concur to call for it. Persons of this description, if they receive only a distant intimation of their state, are ready to reply, even against God himself, just as Cain did, after murdering his brother Abel : " Where is thy brother Abel ? " " I know not : am I my brother's keeper[b] ? " Thus, rather than they will humble themselves before God, they will deny their accountability to him, saying, " Our lips are our own : who is Lord over us[c] ? " But this denial of their guilt will avail them nothing. God will reprove them as he did Israel of old[d] ; and will surely visit them with his heaviest indignation[e].

Others cover their sins by endeavouring to *extenuate* the guilt of them. Thus did Adam and Eve in Paradise. Thus also did Saul, after sparing the king of the Amalekites, and the spoil which he had taken, instead of destroying them utterly according to the direction which he had received from the Lord. He first of all asserted that he had executed the divine command ; and that being disproved by the lowing of the oxen, he vindicated himself, asserting, that, in as far as he was implicated in the affair, he had acted under the influence of the people, whom he could not restrain, and dared not to resist[f]. Thus it is also that the generality are acting all around us. They cannot actually deny that what they are doing is contrary to God's revealed will ; but they are so circumstanced, that they cannot on the whole act otherwise than they do : the current of the world is so strong against them, that they cannot resist it ; and, if they err, the fault is rather in those who have led the way, than in themselves, who have only gone with the stream.

But perhaps the most common way of covering sins is by letting them pass altogether unnoticed. Many are not altogether satisfied that their ways are right : but they go on without much thought, and presently *forget* any thing which may have made a slight impression on their minds. Forgetting

a Prov. xxx. 20.   b Gen. iv. 9.   c Ps. xii. 4.

d Jer. ii. 23, 24. This is a fine image to illustrate the insatiable avidity with which the wicked follow their own lusts and passions.

e Jer. ii. 31, 35.   f 1 Sam. xv. 13—15, 20, 21, 24.

their sins, they suppose that God has forgotten them also. Of such persons God complains; " They consider not in their hearts, that I remember all their wickedness[g]." Very beautiful is the description which God gives of such persons, by the Prophet Jeremiah: " I hearkened and heard, but they spake not aright: no man repented of his wickedness, saying, What have I done? Every one turned to his course, as the horse rusheth into the battle[h]." The horse is unconscious of his danger; and so are the mass of ungodly men: " it is a sport to them to commit iniquity;" and, provided it be not of such a heinous nature as to violate the usages of the place wherein they live, they say, " No evil will come unto us[i]."]

But all who thus attempt to cover their sins are guilty of the extremest folly—

[They " can never prosper." Temporal prosperity they may have as much as others: but in their souls they cannot prosper[k].

They cannot *in this world.* They can have no peace with God or in their own consciences; for God has said, " There is no peace to the wicked." They can have no victory over sin: for God will not interpose to deliver them from bonds, which they themselves are pleased with. They can have no delight in holy ordinances, either in the public assembly, or in their secret chamber. They may, like Ezekiel's hearers, be pleased with hearing a man that can play well upon an instrument[l]; but they can have no fellowship with God: for " what fellowship hath righteousness with unrighteousness, or light with darkness[m]?" They can have no bright and cheering prospects of the eternal world: for they have no evidence within themselves of their acceptance with God, nor any " meetness for the inheritance of the saints in light."

Much less can they prosper *in the world to come.* There the impenitent and unbelieving will meet their deserved recompence. No joy awaits them there. They sought not mercy; and therefore they find it not: they came not weary and heavy laden unto Christ; and therefore they have no part in the rest which he alone can give: they humbled not themselves; and therefore they can never be exalted.]

Let us now contemplate, on the other hand,

II. The benefit of true penitence—

True repentance consists of two parts; a confessing, and forsaking, of our sins—

[Confession is of absolute and indispensable necessity. We never can humble ourselves aright without it. Nor ought

---

[g] Hos. vii. 2. [h] Jer. viii. 6. [i] Jer. v. 12. [k] Job xxxi. 33
[l] Ezek. xxxiii. 31, 32. [m] 2 Cor. vi. 14.

we to rest in mere general acknowledgments : we should search out our sins : we should say, " Thus and thus have I done." We should go farther, and enter into the particular aggravations of our sins, in order the more deeply to affect our own hearts, and to fill our minds with self-lothing and self-abhorrence. Not that God needs to be informed : he knows all our iniquities, and all the circumstances with which they have been attended. But by spreading them all before God, we give the more glory to him as a God of infinite mercy and compassion ; at the same time that we prepare our own minds for a due reception of mercy at his hands.

But, besides this, we must forsake our sins. If we hold them fast, it is a clear proof that our repentance is not genuine. Nor must we forsake them *merely* as a man parts with a limb, which, if not amputated, would destroy his life : we may indeed take into our consideration the danger arising from them, as our Lord tells us in the case of " a right hand or right eye," which, if retained, would plunge us into everlasting perdition : but we must regard them as odious, and hateful, and abominable ; and long for deliverance from them as we would for deliverance from the most lothsome disorder.

These two, a confessing, and forsaking of sin, must go together. Supposing we could put away our sins for the future, it would still become us to bewail those which are past : and, if we bewail them ever so bitterly, still must we not rest without gaining the victory over them , it is the union of them both that marks true penitence ; and]

Where such repentance is, there God will bestow his richest blessings—

[It is said in a subsequent part of this chapter, that " a faithful man shall abound with blessings." And this is true of all who deal faithfully with their own souls and with their God, in bewailing and mortifying their most secret corruptions. This is strongly asserted by all the inspired writers. " Let the wicked forsake his way, and the unrighteous man his thoughts, and let him return unto the Lord, and he will have mercy upon him, and to our God, for he will abundantly pardon[n]." To such both the faithfulness and the justice of God assure a perfect remission of all sin[o]. Nor will God delay to manifest his love, when once he sees our souls truly humbled for sin. The self-condemning publican was justified even before he left the spot where his confessions were made[p]. And David speaks of the same truth as realized also in his experience. Whilst he forbore to humble himself, he was kept in a state of darkness

[n] Isai. lv. 7.   [o] 1 John. i. 9, 10.   [p] Luke xviii. 14.

and misery: but " as soon as he began to confess his sins unto the Lord, the Lord forgave the iniquity of his sin q."

And need we say what " mercy" God will vouchsafe to penitents in the last day? Surely all the manifestations of his love which he gives to them in this world, are but as a twinkling star compared with that full splendour of the Sun of Righteousness, which in that day every contrite soul shall enjoy. The joy of the Father over the returning prodigal, with all the music, and feasting, and dancing, are but faint images of what shall be realized in heaven over every true penitent through all eternity.]

From hence we may LEARN,

1. Whence it is that men know so little of spiritual prosperity—

[Repentance is a work to which we are very averse. If we did but occasionally set apart a day for solemn fasting and prayer, and set ourselves more diligently to the great duty of humiliation before God, we should have more delightful visits from him, and richer communications of his grace to our souls — — —]

2. How painful will be the self-condemnation of all who perish!

[The promise in our text will then be remembered with unutterable shame and sorrow. What a reflection will it be, " I might have obtained mercy, but would not seek it:" God said to me, " Only acknowledge thine iniquity r;" but I would not deign to acknowledge it. Verily the easy terms on which salvation might have been obtained, will form the bitterest ingredient of that bitter cup which the impenitent soul will have to drink to all eternity.]

3. What obligations do we owe to the Lord Jesus Christ!

[It is through him, and through him alone, that repentance is of any avail. There is nothing in repentance that can merit forgiveness: all the merit is in Christ Jesus, even in his obedience unto death: it is that which cancels all our guilt; it is that which purchases our title to the heavenly inheritance. Whilst therefore we confess and forsake our sins, let our eyes be directed to Him as our only hope, even to him, " in whom all the seed of Israel shall be justified, and in whom they shall glory."]

q Ps. xxxii. 3—5.　　　r Jer. iii. 12, 13.

OUTLINE NO. 818

THE PORTION OF THE FAITHFUL MAN.

Prov. xxviii. 20.   *A faithful man shall abound with blessings.*

ST. PAUL has told us, that " the love of money
is the root of all evil : and that many, whilst coveting
after it, have pierced themselves through with many
sorrows[a]." In truth, the effects of this principle on
the persons in whom it dwells, and on all connected
with them, are beyond all conception bitter and injurious. On the other hand, a superiority to the love
of money greatly elevates and ennobles those in whom
it is found ; and conduces, in a very eminent degree,
to their happiness both in this world and the next.

This appears to be the precise import of our text,
as it stands connected with the words which follow it.
But we need not so limit its use. It contains a
general truth, which will afford us much profitable
instruction. Taking it in this more enlarged sense,
I will endeavour to shew,

I. Who are they that answer the description here
given us—

Nehemiah, speaking of his brother Hanani, says,
" He was a faithful man, and feared God above
many :" and he assigns this as his reason for appointing him to superintend the repairs of the city
of Jerusalem ; since he might be fully depended on
for a conscientious discharge of his high office[b].
From hence, then, we see who they are that are entitled to the character of " faithful men." They are
those who are,

1. Faithful to their convictions in things relating
to God—

[There is in every man, under the Christian dispensation,
a conviction that he is a sinner who stands in need of mercy ;
that God has revealed to us in his Gospel the way in which
alone he will dispense mercy ; and that, as responsible beings,
who shall soon stand at the judgment-seat of Christ in order to
be judged according to our works, it is our duty and our happiness to be seeking for mercy in God's appointed way. Now,

[a] 1 Tim. vi. 10.   [b] Neh. vii. 2.

if a man be faithful to his convictions respecting these things, we may justly call him a faithful man; but, if he neglect God, and pour contempt upon the Lord Jesus, and disregard his eternal interests, and labour in every possible way to silence the remonstrances of his own conscience, is he faithful? No, indeed; he is a traitor to God and to his own soul. If he be truly upright before God, he will give to the concerns of his soul and of eternity the attention they demand ———]

2. Faithful to their engagements in things relating to man—

[Without supposing any express compact voluntarily entered into between man and man, there is of necessity a mutual obligation lying upon every man to perform the duties of his place and station. As husbands or wives, parents or children, masters or servants, magistrates or subjects, all of us have some line of conduct prescribed to us; and, as members of one great body, are bound to perform our proper office for the benefit of the whole. Every person feels this in relation to others; and would account himself very injuriously treated, if any should violate towards him the duties of their station: and, consequently, every one must owe to others the treatment which he himself claims at their hands. Now, a faithful man considers this, and will labour to do unto others as he, in a change of circumstances, would think it right that they should do unto him. But if a man consult nothing but his own interests and inclinations, and make his own will the only rule of his conduct, can he be called " faithful?" Is he not as much bound to observe the commandments of the second table as those of the first? His obligation to both the one and the other of them is unalterable; nor can either the one or the other in any wise be dispensed with. Religion and morality must go hand in hand. Neither of them can supersede the other; nor can either of them exist without the other: and he who is faithful in one, must of necessity be faithful in both.]

For the encouragement of such characters, I will proceed to state,

II. What are the peculiar blessings reserved for them—

Truly " the faithful man shall abound with blessings"—

[I might here enumerate thousands of blessings, if time would admit of it; but I will specify only three: the approbation of God; the testimony of a good conscience; and a blessed hope of immortality and glory ——— But how shall

I describe these blessings? " In God's favour is life; and his loving-kindness is better than life itself[c]" — — — As for the testimony of our own conscience, and the witness of God's Spirit with ours, that we are upright before him, man can have no greater joy on earth than that[d] — — — And who can adequately declare the blessedness of a soul that apprehends God himself as his portion, and all the glory of heaven as his inheritance? — — —]

But it is the peculiarity and exclusiveness of this portion which we are chiefly called to notice—

[To the faithful man these blessings are accorded; but to him also are they limited: for they are peculiar to him; " and a stranger intermeddleth not with his joy[e]." Let the man who is unfaithful to his convictions or to his engagements say what he knows of these blessings? If he speak the truth before God, he has no experience of them whatever in his own soul. Indeed, it is impossible that he should have any sense of them as already imparted to him; since, if God be true, no one of them belongs to him; " he has no part or lot in any one of them:" they belong to the faithful man, and to him alone — — —]

SEE, then,

1. What is the proper scope and tendency of the Gospel—

[It is doubtless intended to effect a change, yea, an exceeding great change, both in the characters and states of men. But what does it effect in their character? Does it make them hypocrites? No; but faithful both to God and man. And what does it effect in their states? Does it deprive them of comforts, and make them melancholy? No; but it makes them to abound with blessings, both in time and in eternity. O that you could be prevailed upon to view the Gospel in its true light, and to embrace it with your whole hearts!]

2. What bitter self-condemnation awaits the impenitent and unbelieving soul—

[You have now the blessings of time and sense. But what are they, in comparison of those that await the faithful man? Even here your portion is far inferior to his: but what will they be in *the eternal world?* Truly, you will all find, ere long, that to gain the whole world with the loss of your own souls was a sad exchange. May God make you wise in time, that you may not have to deplore your folly to all eternity!]

[c] Ps. xxx. 5. and lxiii. 3.   [d] 2 Cor. i. 12. Rom. viii. 16.
[e] Prov. xiv. 10.

OUTLINE NO. 819

SELF-CONFIDENCE REPROVED.

Prov. xxviii. 26. *He that trusteth in his own heart is a fool.*

THE Holy Scriptures speak plainly, and without reserve : they know nothing of that squeamish delicacy that keeps men from designating things by their appropriate names : they declare sin to be sin, and folly to be folly, without considering what the pride of man will say to the fidelity that is expressed. Now this gives an exceeding great advantage to ministers : for though it does not sanction rudeness, or indelicacy, or inattention to the feelings of mankind, it does authorize a " great plainness of speech" in all who deliver the messages of God to a sinful and self-deceiving world. Indeed, by universal consent, a greater freedom of speech is admitted, even by the most fastidious in our public addresses, than would be palatable in private converse : nor will any be offended with us, if we declare authoritatively, and without any palliating modifications, what God has said, and what we know to be true, and what therefore we must affirm, that " he who trusteth in his own heart is a fool."

In confirmation of this plain and solemn truth, I will shew,

I. What is the conduct here reprobated—

Man, when he fell from God, renounced not only his allegiance to him as his Maker, but his affiance in him as his God. Since that time, man affects to be a god unto himself, and places his reliance rather on his own inherent powers than on the Majesty of heaven. He relies on,

1. His own wisdom and understanding—

[This is true, especially in reference to all that concerns the soul. Every one conceives that he knows what religion is, and how he is to obtain favour at the hands of God. The most careless of men stand, in this respect, on a footing with the most thoughtful and sedate : every one is alike confident that his opinions are just ; and he holds them fast, with a degree of assurance which the most studious habits would scarcely warrant.

Some, however, will admit the Scriptures to be the only true standard of religious sentiment : but then they suppose themselves to be perfectly equal to the task of extracting from them the mind of God. They feel no need of divine teaching : they are unconscious of the blindness of their minds, and of the bias that is upon their hearts on the side of error. Hence they will take some few particular passages which favour the prejudices they have imbibed ; and on them they will build, as securely as if it was impossible for them to err.]

2. His own purposes and resolutions—

[Every one has, at some time or other, thought with himself, that it was desirable for him to be prepared for death and judgment : and most persons have formed some faint purposes at least, if not a fixed resolution, that they will amend their lives, and prepare for their great account. In some imminent danger, or under some distressing occurrence, the purpose may have been formed with a view to a speedy change : but, in general, the convenient season is looked for at somewhat of a distant period. But the power to turn to God is doubted by none. The sufficiency of man to execute his own purposes and resolutions is never questioned. Every one supposes that he shall be able to effect whatever his judgment shall direct, and his necessities require. As for any need of divine assistance for these things, men have no idea of it. Their own strength is equal to the performance of all that they judge necessary for their salvation; and therefore they may safely defer the great work of their souls to any period which it may suit them to assign.]

That I may dissuade you from such vain confidence, I proceed to state,

II. The folly of it—

Even in relation to earthly things an overweening confidence in our own judgment and strength is a mark of folly : but in reference to the concerns of the soul it is folly in the extreme. For,

1. It robs us of the benefit we might receive from trusting in God—

[This is particularly intimated in the words immediately connected with my text: "He that trusteth in his own heart is a fool; but whoso walketh wisely shall be delivered." Now here the "walking wisely" is put for trusting in God, rather than in ourselves : and the person who so conducts himself, "shall be delivered" from those evils into which the self-confident must fall. Indeed the very honour of God is concerned to leave us, that we may reap the bitter fruits of our own folly.

If we succeeded in effecting our own deliverance, we should "burn incense to our own net," and ascribe all the glory to ourselves. But God has warned us, that, if we provoke him thus to jealousy, we shall lose the benefits which, by trusting in him, we might have obtained; and bring on ourselves the very evils which, by trusting in him, we might have escaped:— "Thus saith the Lord: Cursed be the man that trusteth in man, and maketh flesh his arm, and whose heart departeth from the Lord: (where you will see, that to trust in ourselves is a departure of heart from God:) for he shall be like the heath in the desert; and shall not see when good cometh; but shall inhabit the parched places in the wilderness, in a salt land, and not inhabited. But blessed is the man that trusteth in the Lord, and whose hope the Lord is: for he shall be as a tree planted by the waters, and that spreadeth out her roots by the river; and shall not see when heat cometh; but her leaf shall be green, and shall not be careful in the year of drought, neither shall cease from yielding fruit[a]."]

2. It ensures, beyond all doubt, our ultimate disappointment—

[If ever any man was authorized to trust in himself, methinks Peter and the other Apostles were, in relation to their desertion of their Lord, in his lowest extremity. In the fulness of his own sufficiency, Peter said, " Though I should die with thee, I will not deny thee. And *so likewise said they all.*" Yet, behold, no sooner was their Master apprehended, than " *they all forsook him and fled.*" And Peter, the most self-confident of them all, denied him with oaths and curses. And thus will it be with all of us: however firm our resolutions be, they will prove only as tow before the fire, if they be made in our own strength. We need, indeed, only look back and see what has become of the resolutions we have already made. ' We would turn from this or that sin: we would mortify this or that propensity: we would give up ourselves to God in newness of life.' Alas! alas! how have these purposes vanished, as smoke before the whirlwind! And though we may think to profit by experience, and to become more steadfast in consequence of our former disappointments, we shall only live to prove with still greater evidence the folly of our own ways, and the truth of that inspired declaration, that " the heart is deceitful above all things, and desperately wicked: who can know it?"]

3. It will keep us from discovering our error, till it is past a remedy—

[Tell persons what God says of their ways, and they will not believe it. Every one thinks himself safe; and holds fast

[a] Jer. xvii. 5—8.

his persuasion, in spite of all the admonitions that can be given him. The Rich Man, who was clothed in purple and fine linen, and fared sumptuously every day, would have deemed any one very uncharitable who should have warned him of his approaching end. He would have found an abundance to allege in his own defence; and would not have believed that so inoffensive a life as his could ever issue in such misery as was denounced against him. His five brethren, who succeeded to his wealth, and followed him in what they esteemed so becoming their situation in life, were equally secure in their own minds, and equally averse to think themselves obnoxious to God's displeasure: nay, so averse were they to admit such an idea, that, if their deceased brother's wish had been granted, and one had been sent from the dead to warn them of their danger, they would not have believed his report. Hence, like him who had gone before them, they held fast their delusions, till, one after another, they all came into the same place of torment. Each, at the instant of his own departure, saw the danger of those who were left behind: for, as they would not believe Moses and the Prophets, their ruin was inevitable, and their misery sure. Precisely such is our state and conduct. We will trust in our own hearts, and deny the necessity for trusting only in the Lord; and the probability is, that we shall never be undeceived, till we come to experience what now we will not believe. And are not they who pursue such a course justly denominated fools? If a man would not be persuaded that the leaping down from a lofty precipice would hurt him, and should desperately put it to the trial, and break all his bones, would any one be at a loss to assign an appropriate name to him? Yet would he be wise, in comparison of one who, in defiance of all the warnings of Holy Writ, will trust in himself rather than in God.]

SEE, then, from hence,

1. How desirable is self-knowledge—

[Respecting gross offences, men cannot be ignorant of their condition before God: but respecting the state and habit of their minds, especially in relation to the object of their trust and confidence, they are almost as ignorant as new-born babes. People will not inquire; they will not examine; they will not even suspect that they may be wrong. In truth, they will not believe that their self-confidence is so criminal as the Scriptures represent it, or that any danger can await them on account of it. But, my dear Brethren, I beg you to remember, that the declaration in my text is the word of the living God, and shall surely be found true in the end. I charge you, therefore, to examine carefully into this matter. See whether you have just views of the deceitfulness of the heart. See whether you feel so fearful of its delusions, that you determine never to take its report of any thing without comparing it with the sacred records, and imploring direction from God that you may not err. And be assured, that, till you are brought to renounce all dependence on yourselves, and to depend only on the Lord, you are not, you cannot be, in a state of acceptance with God: for, if he pronounces you fools, he will surely deal with you according to your proper character.]

2. How necessary is the knowledge of Christ—

[Till we come to know what provision God has made for us in the Son of his love, we shall of necessity continue guilty of the folly which is here reprobated. But when once we are assured that there is another in whom we may trust, and who possesses in himself all the fulness of the Godhead, we are encouraged to look beyond ourselves, and to place our confidence in him. Now the Lord Jesus Christ is that person, who is sent of God for that very end, and " is of God made unto us wisdom, and righteousness, and sanctification, and redemption." Here, then, we have all that our necessities can require. By this, all temptation to creature-confidence is cut off: for who would lean upon a reed, that has Omnipotence for his support? or who would build upon the sand, that can have for his foundation " the Rock of ages?" Seek, then, I pray you, the knowledge of this Saviour; and beg of God to shew you what an inexhaustible fulness is treasured up for you in him; and how impossible it is that you should ever fail, if only you trust in him. Once begin in truth to " live by faith in the Son of God," and you " shall not be ashamed or confounded world without end.]

OUTLINE NO. 820

DANGER OF OBSTINACY IN SIN.

Prov. xxix. 1. *He that being often reproved, hardeneth his neck, shall suddenly be destroyed, and that without remedy.*

AWFUL, most awful, is this declaration; yet is it most salutary, and worthy of the deepest attention. Many indeed imagine that it is suited only to the dispensation of the Law: but it is no less suited to us under the Gospel. The Gospel does not consist of promises only, but of threatenings also: and St. Paul himself tells us, that " the day of the Lord will so come as a thief in the night; and that when men are saying, Peace and safety, then will sudden destruction come upon them as travail upon a woman with child, and they shall not escape[a]."

But in discoursing on such a subject, we would exercise all imaginable tenderness: and we entreat all who are here present to lift up their hearts to God, and to implore the effectual assistance of his good Spirit, that they may be enabled to " tremble at his word," and to " receive it with meekness, as an engrafted word, which is able to save their souls."

There are two things here to which we would draw your attention;

I. The character described—

God, with much patience and long-suffering, reproves the sinners of mankind—

[In a variety of ways he administers reproof. At all times he speaks, silently indeed, but powerfully, to men in *his word*. Every sin is there depicted in its proper colours, and marked as an object of his righteous indignation. There especially we hear him denouncing his judgments against impenitence and unbelief: " Except ye repent, ye shall all perish:" " He that believeth not, shall not see life; but the wrath of God abideth on him ." There too do we find him requiring of us, that we become "new creatures in Christ Jesus;" and declaring, that " except a man be born again, he cannot see the kingdom of God." In short, every thing that is necessary for us either to know or do, is there revealed — — —and in every part of it God himself is addressing us day and night — — —

He reproves us also by *his Providence*. Every one of his dispensations towards us has a voice, to which we should give heed, and from which we may gain the most valuable instruction. Does he summon to his tribunal a neighbour, a friend, a relative? He says to the survivors, " Prepare to meet your God." Does he make a severer inroad on your domestic circle, by cutting off the olive branches that were round about your table, or by "taking away the desire of your eyes with a stroke?" He bids you to seek all your happiness in him alone. By every change of whatever kind, he tells you that " this is not your rest." Nor does he speak less by mercies than by judgments. Every gift is sent to draw you to him as the Donor; and every instance of " his goodness and long-suffering and forbearance is intended to lead you to repentance."

Further, he reproves us also by *his Spirit*. Who amongst us has not often heard his still small voice, saying to us,

a 1 Thess. v. 2, 3.

"Repent?" Who has not felt many checks of conscience, when
he was tempted to commit iniquity? These have been no other
than the motions of God's Holy Spirit within us, testifying
against sin, and inviting us to serve our God[b].]

But against his reproofs how often have we " hardened our necks!"

[Many will not endure reproof at all: and, if the word
which is ministered to them by the servants of God disquiet
their minds, and especially if it strike at their besetting sin,
they will vent their indignation against the faithful Messenger
who thus disturbs their slumbers. The reproof given to Ama-
ziah was so reasonable, that one would imagine it could not
possibly give offence: yet behold, what resentment it kindled
in the infatuated monarch! " Art thou made of the king's
counsel? Forbear. Why shouldest thou be smitten[c]?"———
Nothing could be more just than the reproof which Jeremiah
was ordered to administer to the Jewish people: yet the only
effect it produced was, to excite their wrath, and to make them
threaten him with instant death: " When Jeremiah had made
an end of speaking all that the Lord had commanded him to
speak unto all the people, then the priests, and the prophets,
and all the people, took him, saying, Thou shalt surely die[d] "
———Herod went further still, and actually put the greatest
of all the Prophets to death, for no other fault than that of
telling him that he should not persevere in his adulterous commerce with his brother Philip's wife[e]. Thus it is at this day.
Men indeed cannot proceed to such extremities against their
reprovers now as they did in former times: but the world's enmity is the same against all who " testify of it that the works
thereof are evil;" and it is owing to the protection of the laws,
rather than to any diminution of men's hatred against the
truth, that contempt only, and not death, is the portion of
God's faithful servants.

But it is not only in a way of outward opposition that men
manifest their obduracy. Many who externally approve of the
faithful ministry of the word, are in reality as averse to it in
their hearts. They hear the word perhaps even with pleasure,
as Ezekiel's hearers did; but they will not do it[f]. Say whether
this be not the case with many amongst you: you have had the
whole counsel of God declared unto you; but have you complied with it? Are you truly brought to the foot of cross, in
deep humiliation, in earnest prayer, and in a simple reliance
on the blood of Jesus as your only hope?——— Have you
also taken his yoke upon you, so that you are daily and hourly
fulfilling his will, and regarding his service as perfect freedom?

[b] Gen. vi. 3.   [c] 2 Chron. xxv. 15, 16.   [d] Jer. xxvi. 2—8.
[e] Matt. xiv. 3—10.   [f] Ezek. xxxiii. 31, 32.

Are you dying daily to the world, and living altogether as pilgrims and sojourners here, having your conversation in heaven, and looking forward to the second advent of your Lord as the consummation and completion of your bliss? If you be not thus brought to live unto your God, you have not yet complied with his reproofs: and if you are speaking peace to yourselves in such a state, then are you hardening your necks against him. In words indeed you call him Lord, Lord: but whilst you do not the things which he says, you are still among the number of those to whom he will say, "Depart from me; I never knew you, ye workers of iniquity " — — —]

Having then seen the character that is described in our text, let us consider,

II. The judgment denounced against him—

What but destruction can await such a character, even " destruction from the presence of the Lord, and from the glory of his power?" Yes, this is the judgment denounced against him; and his destruction, whenever it shall arrive, shall be,

1. Sudden—

[Not unfrequently does God mark by some signal judgment those who have obstinately withstood his warnings and invitations. The Ante-diluvian infidels, who would not be reclaimed by the ministry of Noah, were swept away, as soon as ever their day of grace was ended; as were Pharaoh also, and all his host, when they proudly set themselves in array against the Majesty of heaven. Ananias and Sapphira were also made examples of God's indignation against wilful and deliberate sin.

But though death should come upon us gradually, as it respects the body, it may, as far as it respects our preparation for it, be altogether instantaneous. The effect of wilful sin is, to harden the heart, and to render us more and more indisposed for repentance. It also grieves the Holy Spirit of God, and provokes him to withdraw those gracious influences which he has hitherto vouchsafed. When delaying our repentance, we are apt to fancy that we shall in a time of sickness have such a favourable opportunity for spiritual exercises, as will abundantly make up for all the time that we have lost: but when sickness comes, we find that we cannot realize all our fond expectations: the state of our bodies perhaps unfits us for exertion: and the indisposition of our mind for holy things is become more deeply rooted, so that we cannot relent, or humble ourselves before God. The word of God, when we look into it, is only as a sealed book. The instructions we receive, produce no effect. Even during their full enjoyment of bodily health many are given over to final impenitence, so that the ministry of the word serves only to harden them, and the Gospel itself becomes to them only "a savour of death[g]"——— God gives them over to judicial blindness, and leaves them to harden themselves in order to their more aggravated condemnation. Thus he dealt with the sons of Eli[h]; and thus he has declared he will deal with us, if we wilfully reject his tender solicitations[i]——— Thus may death come in its most gradual and protracted form, and yet, as far as respects our souls, be as sudden, as if it visited us like a thief in the night.]

2. Irremediable—

[If once God say to his Holy Spirit, " Strive no longer with that man : he is joined to idols: let him alone[k];" the man is in fact left to irremediable destruction. He will live only to "fill up the measure of his iniquities," and to "treasure up wrath against the day of wrath." But at all events, the very instant that death arrests us, our day of grace is terminated : there is no repentance in the grave ; no possibility of passing the gulf that is fixed between heaven and hell: the worm that gnaweth the conscience will never die ; the fire that torments the body will never be quenched: the wrath to come will ever be the wrath to come.

What a fearful thought is it, that of those to whom the word of salvation is now preached, many will "come at last into that place of torment," and many, who, like the Foolish Virgins, once had the lamp of outward profession, and associated with the wise virgins, will, instead of being admitted to the marriage supper of their Lord, be "cast into outer darkness, where is weeping, and wailing, and gnashing of teeth!" The Lord grant that none of you may ever experience this doom! yet it is certain, that if you harden your necks against either the precepts of the Law or the promises of the Gospel, this will be your state for ever.

To put you more effectually on your guard, let me]

ADDRESS—

1. Those who are indisposed to submit to God's reproofs—

[The word delivered to you, so far as it accords with God's revealed will, is God's, and not ours. We are his ambassadors; and it is He who speaks to you by our mouth. Indeed, whoever he be that gives you the counsels of true wisdom, he is God's representative to you. Think then, ye who have rejected

[g] See Isai. vi. 9, 10. which is quoted six times in the New Testament. See also Jer. vii. 23—27.

[h] 1 Sam. ii. 25. [i] Prov. i. 24—31. [k] Hos. iv. 17.

the counsels of your friends, and the admonitions of your ministers, what will be your reflections in the last day: when you call to mind the instructions once given by your parents, the advice offered by some pious friend or relative, the warnings delivered by God's servants in the public assembly, how distressing will it be to see that they were only the means of aggravating your eternal condemnation! Oh! let me prevail with you, ere it be too late. Consider, I pray you, " Who ever hardened himself against God, and prospered?" To-day then, while it is called to-day, harden not your hearts, lest you provoke God to swear in his wrath, that you shall never enter into his rest.]

2. Those who are inclined to obey his will—

[Truly this disposition is of the Lord: " it is he that has given you either to will or do." Bless him, then, that the destruction which has come suddenly and irremediably on so many millions of mankind, was not permitted to come on you in your unawakened state. And now let your hearts be right with him: let every word of his sink down into your ears, and be obeyed without reserve. Seek an entire conformity to his mind and will. " Forget all that is behind, and reach forward constantly to that which is before." Seek to " grow up in all things into Christ, your living Head." Make more and more use of that remedy which is in your hands. Apply the precious blood of Christ more and more to your souls, to purge you from your sins; and seek more abundant supplies of the Spirit of grace, to transform you into the Divine image: so shall you be happy now in the prospect of your inheritance, and be progressively rendered meet for your full possession of it.]

OUTLINE NO. 821

THE IMPORTANCE OF GOSPEL MINISTRATIONS.

Prov. xxix. 18. *Where there is no vision, the people perish: but he that keepeth the Law, happy is he* [a].

THROUGHOUT the whole Scriptures, we have one unvaried testimony respecting man. We see, in every part,

I. The deplorable state of those who know not the Gospel—

Revelations to the prophets were often made in visions: and hence the subject-matter of the revelation

[a] This brief sketch is given as an useful subject for a *Mission* Sermon. The contrast between Heathens in an ignorant and in a converted state would be very striking.

was called their " vision." Now, where no revelation is, or where, though given, it is not attended to, " the people perish"—

[This is the unhappy state of *the heathen world*, who are constantly represented as dead in trespasses and sins, and as under the dominion of Satan [b]———— Still more is this the state of *God's ancient people*, whilst they reject the Messiah[c] ———— But far worse is the state of *those who hear, without obeying, the Gospel* [d]———]

II. The blessedness of those who hear and obey it—

Our Lord pronounces them supremely blessed[e]. And there is somewhat very emphatical in the declaration of it contained in our text—

[Those who truly believe in Christ, and live altogether by faith on him, " are happy." They are so, as *restored to God's favour* [f] ———— as *enjoying his presence* [g] ———— as *inheriting his glory* [h] ———]

OBSERVE from hence—

1. The importance of missionary exertions[i]————
2. The importance of improving our present privileges—

[On the due improvement of them depends both our *present*[k] and *eternal* happiness ———]

[b] Eph. ii. 1, 2, 11—13. Rom. iii. 19. 1 John v. 19. We have *no authority* to depart from the plain declarations of Holy Writ.
[c] Isai. xxvii. 11. Hos. iv. 6. John viii. 24.
[d] John xv. 22. 2 Cor. iv. 3, 4. 2 Thess. i. 7, 8. Heb. ii. 3. 1 Pet. iv. 17.
[e] Luke xi. 28.　　　[f] Rom. v. 1.　　　[g] Ps. lxxxix. 5.
[h] Rev. xxii. 14.　　　[i] Rom. x. 13—15, 17.
[k] Mark the latter clause of the text.

OUTLINE NO. 822

THE FEAR OF MAN.

Prov. xxix. 25. *The fear of man bringeth a snare; but whoso putteth his trust in the Lord shall be safe.*

OUR blessed Lord, at the very first introduction of his religion into the world, told his followers, that he was not come to send peace on earth, but a sword, and to set at variance with each other the nearest and dearest relatives. We are not however to suppose that this was the proper *end* of his religion: it was

not the end, but *the effect :* and it is, and must be, the
effect, as long as there shall be a carnal and unregenerate man upon earth.   What, then, must be done
by the followers of Christ?   Must they draw back,
because their carnal friends forbid them to proceed?
or must they put their light under a bushel, lest it
should offend the eyes of those who behold it?   No:
they must dismiss from their minds all fear of men,
and be faithful to their God at all events : for " the
fear of man bringeth a snare;" which they can only
avoid by giving themselves up faithfully to their God.

From the words before us, we learn,

I. Our great danger—

The fear of man is far more general than we are at
all aware of—

[*Ungodly men,* who, in relation to all other things, set at
defiance the whole world, are yet, almost as much as others,
in bondage, in reference to religion.   They can set at nought
all religion, without any fear at all : but, to shew respect for
it, and especially a desire to become acquainted with it, they
dare not.   They see that there are persons whose ministry
would prove instructive ; but they fear to avail themselves of
such a ministry, lest a suspicion should attach to them as
leaning towards a religious life, and as inclined to sentiments
which are generally decried.   And, as for cultivating an acquaintance with one of strict piety, however much they may
wish, they dare not do it, lest they incur ridicule from their
ungodly companions.

Persons who begin to feel any concern about their souls are
immediately beset with this evil principle.   They are conscious
that the change which is taking place in them will, of necessity,
offend their former companions ; and therefore they desire to
conceal their feelings, and to avoid the rupture which they foresee.   Hence they make many compliances contrary to the convictions of their own conscience ; and expose themselves to many
temptations, which their better judgment would have taught
them to avoid.   So common is this bondage, that scarcely one,
at the earlier period of his conversion, is free from it.   Whatever be men's rank in life, they are still in subjection to their
fellows : yea, the higher their station, the greater, for the most
part, is their cowardice.

Nor are *established believers* free from this thraldom.   They
do indeed disregard the world; but they are as much enslaved
by the maxims and habits of their associates in the church,
as ever they were by the world around them.   They dare **not**

think for themselves, or act for themselves, according to the convictions of their own minds. They take not their faith and practice from the Scriptures of Truth, but from a standard which obtains among them, and from which they are afraid to deviate. Who would think that Peter himself, bold and intrepid as he was by nature, and still more fortified by grace, should yet yield so far to the prejudice of his Judaizing brethren, as even to endanger the utter subversion of the Gospel, which he had been the honoured instrument of first opening both to the Jewish and Gentile world? Yet so he did, through fear of their displeasure. Who, then, has not cause to acknowledge himself in danger of erring, through the operation of this evil principle?]

To all who yield to its influence, it brings a fatal snare—

[Thousands it keeps from coming within the reach of spiritual instruction. The fear of that expostulation, "He hath a devil and is mad; why hear ye him[a]?" is quite sufficient to intimidate the generality of men, whom curiosity at least might otherwise bring within the sphere of spiritual instruction. And in those of whom better things might have been hoped, it has wrought, in unnumbered instances, to the production of the most tremendous evils, moral, spiritual, eternal. Behold in Peter a dissimulation, which led even Barnabas astray. They, through mercy, were recovered: but many it has led to utter apostasy, and involved in everlasting ruin. In the days of our blessed Lord many were "afraid to confess him, because they loved the praise of men more than the honour that cometh of God;" and many who had followed him "went back, and walked no more with him:" and so in every age, even to the present hour, have many been turned aside by the dread of persecution[b], and have "made shipwreck of their faith." And what the issue of this is to their souls, we are told: for "the fearful and unbelieving," no less than "murderers and whoremongers, have their portion in the lake that burneth with fire and brimstone, which is the second death[c]." In truth, our adorable Saviour warned his hearers respecting this, from the very beginning; declaring to them at all times, that they who should be ashamed of him, and should deny him, would assuredly find him ashamed of them, and would be ultimately denied by him in the presence of his Father and of the whole assembled universe.]

Seeing, then, that we are all exposed to this danger, it will be expedient that I point out to you,

II. Its proper and only effectual antidote—

---

[a] John x. 20.   [b] Matt. xiii. 21.   [c] Rev. xxi. 8.

There is nothing but a regard to God himself that
can ever overcome the fear of man: on which account
our blessed Lord says, " Fear not man, who can only
kill the body, and after that hath no more that he can
do; but fear him who can destroy both body and soul
in hell[d]." The same truth is suggested in my text,
only in somewhat of a more gentle form: " Whoso
putteth his trust in the Lord, shall be safe."

Would we then be delivered from the foregoing
snare, let us put our trust in God,

1. For happiness—

[A man who is dependent on the world for his happiness,
must of necessity be in bondage to its maxims, its habits, its
votaries. But one whose heart is fixed upon God, and who
looks up to God as his portion, feels himself at liberty. It is
to him a small matter whether the world frown or smile. All
that he is anxious about, is, to retain the favour of God, and to
have the light of his countenance lifted up upon him. His interest, his reputation, his life may be endangered; but he smiles
at the vain attempts of his enemies. They may shut him up
from all access of earthly friends; but they cannot deprive him
of communion with God: on the contrary, his communications
from God are, for the most part, enlarged, in proportion as
man's efforts to distress him are increased. And " when God
giveth quietness, who then can make trouble[e]?"]

2. For support—

[A man, when menaced by earthly enemies, is driven to
the Lord for succour: and, O! what strength does he find
communicated to him in the hour of need! Assured of strength
according to his day, the believer disregards the utmost efforts
of his persecutors. The furnace may be heated seven times
more than usual, or the lions have their appetites whetted for
their prey; but his mind is in peace, because he " knows in
whom he has believed, and that God is able to keep that which
has been committed to him." Whether he shall be delivered
by God from his trials, or be supported under them, he knows
not: but he is assured, that whatever be done by his enemies,
shall " work together for his good;" and that, in the issue, he
shall " prove more than conqueror, through Him who loved him."]

3. For recompence—

[To heaven the believer looks, as his final rest: and in
the prospect of that, all the transitory events of time become
of no account in his estimation. The crown of victory and of

d Matt. x. 28.   e Job xxxiv. 29.

glory is ever in his view; and he knows the condition on which alone it will be bestowed: we must "be faithful unto death, if ever we would obtain a crown of life." Hence he finds no difficulty in renouncing all that the world can give, and in enduring all that the most bitter persecutors can inflict; because, like Moses, he "looks unto the recompence of the reward;" and, like the "women who refused to accept deliverance from their tortures, he expects a better resurrection." Whatever tribulations he may pass through in his way to glory, he feels no doubt but that the glory which awaits him will amply make amends for all [f].]

For an IMPROVEMENT of this subject, I will add,

1. A word of caution—

[The foregoing sentiments, if not received with a becoming spirit, are liable to abuse. Indeed we have often seen, in young and inexperienced persons especially, conceit and self-will assuming the garb of religion; and exerting themselves, without controul, in opposition to all sound advice, and in defiance of all legitimate authority. Let me, therefore, be well understood in this matter. Though we are to be on our guard against the fear of man, we are not to set at nought the counsels of the wise, nor the injunctions of those who are over us in the Lord. In matters of indifference, it is well to consult the judgment and the wishes of those who are in authority over us. It is only when the counsels and commands of men go counter to the commands of God, that we are authorized to set them at nought: and even then we must conduct ourselves with meekness and modesty, and must not give way to a rude, unmannered, refractory spirit. This is of exceeding great importance. We cannot too strictly watch against the indulgence of any unhallowed temper under the pretext of religion: and if at any time we are constrained to oppose the wishes of our friends, we must order ourselves with such kindness and love, as may leave them in no doubt but that our perseverance is the fruit of real piety, and not the offspring of obstinate conceit.]

2. A word of encouragement—

[However careful we be, we must expect to incur the displeasure of those who wish to retain us in bondage to the world. But if, as we have reason to expect, our greatest foes be those of our own household, let us consider how much better it is to have the frowns of men and the approbation of God, than the smiles of men and the displeasure of God. If all the men in the universe were to applaud us, it would be a poor recompence for the loss of a good conscience, whose testimony in our behalf would repay us for the loss of the whole world. In fact, if we

[f] Rom. viii. 18.

inquire into the state of those who uphold each other in iniquity, we shall find that no one of them has peace in his own soul : for, how should they have peace who seek their happiness in the world rather than in God? Compare, then, your state with theirs; and you will have reason to bless God, even though the whole world be against you. For them nothing remains but "a certain fearful looking-for of judgment and fiery indignation:" for you is prepared an eternal weight of glory, which will be augmented in proportion to the trials which you sustained for God, and the services you rendered to him. Be of good cheer, then : for your trials do, in fact, " turn *unto* you for a testimony ; " and " if you suffer with Christ," you are assured, by the voice of Inspiration, that " you shall also be glorified together."]

OUTLINE NO. 823

A SAINT'S VIEWS OF HIMSELF.

Prov. xxx. 1, 2. *The words of Agur the son of Jakeh, even the prophecy : the man spake unto Ithiel, even unto Ithiel and Ucal, Surely I am more brutish than any man, and have not the understanding of a man.*

THE sayings of the wise and good have in all ages been regarded with veneration, and been treasured up in the minds of men as a kind of sacred deposit, for the enriching and instructing of future generations. We have here a very remarkable saying of Agur the son of Jakeh ; to which I would now call your attention. It does indeed, we must confess, appear, at first sight, a rash expression, savouring rather of intemperance than of sound discretion. But as it was delivered to " Ithiel and Ucal," who were probably his disciples; and as it was introduced with the word, " Surely," which marks it as the result of his deliberate judgment ; and, above all, it being called " a prophecy," which determines it to have been inspired of God; we should calmly inquire into it, and examine its import. That such an expression may be uttered by persons widely differing from each other in their moral and religious habits, I readily admit: and therefore, in order to prevent any misapprehension, I shall consider the text,

I. As the language of passion—

Sin, however fondly cherished in the heart of fallen man, is no other than folly and madness. So it is described by Solomon, in the Book of Ecclesiastes: " I applied mine heart to know and to search, and to seek out wisdom and the reason of things; and to know the wickedness of folly, even of *foolishness and madness*[a]." And again: " The heart of the sons of men is full of evil; *madness* is in their heart while they live; and after that they go to the dead[b]." When a person, who has been led captive by it, comes to discern somewhat of its true character, he is apt to feel indignation against himself, and to reproach himself in strong terms for the folly he has committed. We may well conceive of him as saying, in the language of our text, " Surely I am more brutish than any man, and have not the understanding of a man." But this indignation against himself may be the mere language of passion, and not of genuine humiliation: and it may be distinguished from that which is the fruit of piety,

1. In its object—

[An ungodly man may feel strongly, whilst he has no real humility: he may hate his actions and himself on account of them. But it is not *sin* that he hates, so much as *the consequences* of his sin. Nor does he hate *all* its consequences: he hates it not as defiling to his soul, as offensive to his God, as injurious to his eternal interests; but as destructive of his peace, as degrading him in the eyes of his fellow-men, and as ruinous to his present welfare. A gamester, who has staked his all upon the cast of a die, and has thereby reduced himself and his family from affluence to want, curses his folly with the most indignant feelings; and so hates himself for it, that he can scarcely endure his very existence. But, if his money were restored, he would do the same again: or, if taught wisdom by experience, he would not refrain from his former habits on account of any regard for God or his own soul, but only on account of the injury that was likely to accrue from them in a temporal view. The same may be said respecting the votaries of dissipation. When their fortune is wasted by extravagance, and their constitution ruined by excess, they may be strongly impressed with the folly and madness of their past ways; whilst, if they could be restored to their former affluence and vigour, they would run the very same career again. Under all the

[a] Eccl. vii. 25.   [b] Eccl. ix. 3.

painful consequences of his licentious habits, the libertine can scarcely avoid those reflections which Solomon represents as arising in his mind: " Thou wilt mourn at the last, when thy flesh and thy body are consumed, and say, How have I hated instruction, and my heart despised reproof; and have not obeyed the voice of my teachers, nor inclined mine ear to them that instructed me! I was almost in all evil in the midst of the congregation and assembly[c]." Nor can we doubt, but that in hell those reflections will be both universal and exceeding bitter: for the " wailing and gnashing of teeth" which will be there experienced, will arise, in no small degree, from the consideration of the opportunities once enjoyed, but now irrecoverably and for ever lost[d].]

2. In its operation—

[The indignation of an ungodly man is sudden and transient; and is always accompanied with a crimination of those who have been in any measure accessary to the evils that have come upon him. But, in a man of piety, they are the fruit of deep reflection, dwelling habitually in the mind, and always attended with self-reproach. We may see in the Prodigal Son a just exhibition of that which arises from genuine repentance. He does not, under the pressure of his distress, cry out with vehement exclamations, designating his conduct by every term that an embittered spirit can suggest; but he adopts a resolution to return to his father's house, and there, in measured and contrite language, confesses, " I have sinned against heaven and before thee; and am no more worthy to be called thy son." Generally speaking, the more violent the expressions are, the less genuine is the contrition from which they flow. The exercise of deep and just feeling is rather in a way of temperate meiosis, than of vehement and fluent exaggeration. The two kinds of indignation may be easily distinguished by their attendant feelings: the one is the fruit of wounded pride, and the root of every thing that is unhallowed, whether in word or deed; the other is the offspring of deep contrition; and either the parent or the child of genuine conversion to God.]

Having discriminated, we hope, sufficiently between the expressions of our text as used by persons of opposite characters, and shewn how to distinguish them when uttered as the language of passion, we proceed to notice them,

II. As the language of piety—

We know assuredly that indignation is a fruit of godly sorrow: for St. Paul says to the Corinthians,

[c] Prov. v. 11—14.   [d] Matt. xiii. 42.

" Behold this self-same thing, that ye sorrowed after
a godly sort, what carefulness it wrought in you, yea,
what clearing of yourselves, yea, what *indignation*,
yea, what fear, yea, what vehement desire, yea, what
zeal, yea, what revenge[e]!" And we have seen it
operate precisely as in the text, when, according to
common apprehension, there would appear to be but
little occasion for it. David, seeing the prosperity
of the wicked, and not duly adverting to their end,
had envied them: and in the review of his conduct
he exclaims, " So foolish was I, and ignorant; I was
even as a beast before thee[f]." Nor are such views
uncommon to the saints: or rather, I should say, there
is no true saint who does not on some occasions
apply them to himself.

If it be asked, ' How can such expressions fall from
the lips of a real saint?' I answer, they necessarily
spring,

1. From a view of the law under which we live—

[Whilst ignorant of the spirituality and extent of God's
Law, we take credit to ourselves for our external conformity
to its precepts; and are ready to imagine, that, " touching the
righteousness of the Law we are blameless[g]." But when we
come to see how " broad the commandment is[h]," that it reaches
to the inmost thoughts of the soul, prohibiting even so much
as an inordinate desire, and requiring us to " love and serve our
God with *all* our heart, and mind, and soul, and strength," we
are struck dumb; our towering " imaginations are cast down;"
and, like the Apostle Paul, we feel the sentence of death gone
forth against us[i], and attaching to us no less for our best deeds,
than for the most sinful action of our lives[k]." Then we become
observant of our *defects:* and, O! how lothesome are we then
in our own eyes[l], in the view of that very obedience of which
we once thought so highly! It is no wonder, if, with this
augmented view of his own deformity, the saint speak of himself in very humiliating and degrading terms. A person coming
into a room at night with a lighted taper, would see but little:
if he returned at the dawn of day, he would have a clearer view
of all the objects that before were scarcely visible: but, if he
entered when the sun was shining forth in its strength, he
would discern the smallest specks of dirt, and even the very

---

[e] 2 Cor. vii. 11.   [f] Ps. lxxiii. 3, 17, 22.   [g] Phil. iii. 6.
[h] Ps. cxix. 96.   [i] Rom. vii. 9.   [k] Job ix. 2, 3
[l] Ezek. xxxvi. 31.

motes in the air. But would he then conclude that all the
dust and dirt which he now beheld had been cast in since his
first entrance? No: he would know to what he must ascribe
the change in his views, even to the increased light by which
he was enabled to take the survey. And so a clearer view of
God's holy Law will give us a deeper insight into our own
deformity, and turn the gloryings of self-esteem into the mourn-
ings of humiliation and contrition.]

2. From a view of that God against whom we have sinned—

[The least knowledge of God is sufficient to abase us before
him: but the more we behold his glorious perfections, the more
shall we stand amazed at the coldness of our love to him, and
our want of zeal in his service. Job, previous to his troubles,
was considered as " a perfect man" even by God himself. But
when God had revealed himself more fully to his soul, how base
did this holy man appear in his own eyes! " Behold, I am vile!"
says he. " I have heard of thee by the hearing of the ear; but
now mine eye seeth thee. Wherefore I abhor myself, and repent
in dust and ashes[m]." This will be the effect of all God's manifestations of himself, whether in a way of providence or of grace.
It is impossible to behold his goodness, his patience, his forbearance, and not stand amazed at our own insensibility. "The
ox and the ass" do not appear so brutish as we[n]; nor "the stork
or crane or swallow" so unobservant of the things which we are
most concerned to notice[o]: and our only wonder is, that it should
be possible for God to endure with such long-suffering our great
and multiplied iniquities.]

3. From a view of the obligations we lie under—

[Our Lord has said, that our love to God will bear proportion to the sense we have of the extent of his mercy towards
us in forgiveness[p]. But, when we reflect on the means he has
used, in order to open a way for the exercise of his mercy
towards us, what shall we not account his due? When we
consider that he has "not spared even his own Son, but delivered HIM up for us all," what bounds will there be to our
gratitude; or rather, what bounds will there be to our humiliation for the want of gratitude? It will be impossible for
us then ever to satisfy our own desires: if we had a thousand
lives, we would devote them all to him, and at his call be ready
to sacrifice them all for him. The services which we once
thought sufficient will then appear little better than a solemn
mockery; so entirely will our souls be absorbed in wonder at
the thought of an incarnate God, a crucified Redeemer.]

m Job xl. 4. and xlii. 5, 6.   n Isai. i. 3.
o Jer. viii. 7.   p Luke vii. 47.

4. From a view of the interests we have at stake—

[If only the life or death of our bodies were at stake, we should feel deeply interested in the event: but, when heaven and all its glory, or hell and all its misery, are the alternatives before us, one would suppose that every temporal consideration should be swallowed up, and vanish as the light of a star before the meridian sun. But the saint is not always so indifferent to the things of time and sense as he would wish to be. There are times, when every thing below the sun is in his eyes lighter than vanity itself: but there are, also, times when he finds his heart yet cleaving to the dust, and when his progress heavenward is slow and imperceptible. On such occasions he he is amazed at himself: he can scarcely conceive it possible that, with such prospects before him, he should be so stupid and brutish as he feels himself to be. Truly, at these seasons the language of our text will be often in his heart, and in his mouth too, especially if he find an Ithiel, or an Ucal, that is capable of understanding it.]

After viewing this subject, we shall be at no loss to
UNDERSTAND,

1. Whence it is that saints are often dejected in their minds—

[None are at all times alike joyful. St. Paul says, that " they who have the first-fruits of the Spirit," no less than others, sometimes "groan within themselves, being burthened[q]." And so it ought to be. In the review of their past lives they should be humbled, even as Paul was, when he designated himself as " a blasphemer, and injurious, and a persecutor, and the very chief of sinners[r]." And under a sense of their remaining infirmities, it becomes them to lie low before God. Behold St. Paul, when he had preached the Gospel above twenty years, yet felt so much corruption within him, that he cried out, "O wretched man that I am! who shall deliver me[s]?" The image which he here uses is that which has often been realized. He refers to a punishment sometimes inflicted on criminals, by chaining them to a dead corpse, and constraining them to bear it about with them, till they died through the offensiveness of its noxious odours. Such was his in-dwelling corruption to him, even at that advanced period of his life: and such it should be felt by every saint on earth. In truth, there should not enter so much as a ray of comfort into the soul, but from a view of the Sun of Righteousness. It is He alone that can, or ought, to " arise upon us with healing in his wings.'

q Rom. viii. 23. 2 Cor. v. 4.   r 1 Tim. i. 13, 15.
s Rom. vii. 24.

And therefore the Apostle, after the lamentation just mentioned, adds, " I thank God, through Jesus Christ our Lord[t]."
Let not this, then, prove a stumbling-block to any : nor let it
be supposed, that, because a pious person uses, in reference to
himself, terms which a worldly person would not deign to use, he
must of necessity have committed any greater sin than others.
His humiliation, as we have seen, arises out of the views which
he has obtained of holy things : and the nearer his intercourse
with heaven is, the more ready will he be to exclaim with the
Prophet, " Woe is me, I am undone! ' I am a man of unclean
lips, dwelling in the midst of a people of unclean lips;" that
is, *a leper*, in the midst of a *leprous* and ungodly world[u].]

2. How far they are from piety who are filled with
self-complacent thoughts—

[Persons who have been exemplary in their conduct, and
punctual in their religious observances, are, for the most part,
filled with a conceit of their own goodness, and confident of
their acceptance with God on account of it. But little do they
know how odious they are in the sight of God, whilst they are
righteous in their own eyes. It is the Publican, and not the
Pharisee, that will be justified before God : and " the sick, not
the whole," that will experience " the Physician's" aid. Christianity is *not a remedial law*, lowered to the standard of our
weakness; but *a remedy*, by which the soul that is sick unto
death may be effectually healed. Christ is a Saviour; but he
is so to those only who feel themselves lost, and renounce every
other hope but him. Bear this, then, in remembrance. Bear
in remembrance, that there are no terms too humiliating to
express the real state of your souls before God. You have
lived as without God in the world, unconscious of his eye upon
you; and his address to you is, "Understand ye brutish among
the people; and ye fools, when will ye be wise[x]?" This may
be offensive to our proud hearts; but it is such an address as
we merit, and such a one as it becomes an holy God to deliver.
The particular ground of Agur's self-abasement was, that "he
had not learned wisdom, or attained the knowledge of the Holy
One[y]." And have not many amongst you the same ground for
self-abasement? Yes, "There are many amongst you who
have not the knowledge of God. I speak this to your shame[z]."
Many amongst you have never yet walked in the ways of true
wisdom. Humble yourselves, therefore, for your more than
brutish stupidity : and now, as the Psalmist says, " Kiss the
Son, lest he be angry, and ye perish from the way, when his
wrath is kindled but a little. Blessed are all they that put their
trust in him[a]."]

---

[t] Rom. vii. 25.   [u] Isai. vi. 5.   [x] Ps. xciv. 8.
[y] ver. 3.   [z] 1 Cor. xv. 34.   [a] Ps. ii. 12

OUTLINE NO. 824

AGUR'S WISH.

Prov. xxx. 7—9. *Two things have I required of thee; deny me them not before I die: Remove far from me vanity and lies; give me neither poverty nor riches; feed me with food convenient for me: lest I be full, and deny thee, and say, Who is the Lord? or lest I be poor, and steal, and take the name of my God in vain.*

IT is the privilege of man to make known his requests to God in prayer, and to solicit from him whatever may conduce to his real good. Even temporal things may be asked, provided it be in subserviency to our spiritual interests, and with entire submission to the Divine will. Who Agur was, we cannot certainly determine; but he was evidently an inspired person[a]; and his prayer in reference to his condition in this world is an excellent pattern for our imitation. He entreated the Lord with very great earnestness; yet he considered his condition in this world as altogether subordinate to his eternal welfare; and therefore in what he asked for his body, he consulted only the good of his soul.

We propose to consider,

I. His request—

Some interpret the former of his petitions as expressing a wish to be kept from error and delusion in spiritual matters; but we apprehend that the things which he requested were,

1. A removal from the temptations of an exalted state—

[He justly characterizes the pomp and splendour of the world as " vanity and lies;" " vanity," because they are empty and unsatisfying; and " lies," because they promise happiness to their possessors, but invariably disappoint them. In this light they are frequently represented in Scripture[b]; and they who have been most competent to judge respecting them, have been most forward to declare them mere vanity and vexation of spirit[c].

---

[a] His words are called " prophecies," ver. 1.
[b] Ps. cxix. 37. and lxii. 9.　　[c] Eccl. ii. 11.

Agur doubtless beheld them in this view, and therefore rather deprecated them as evils, than desired them as objects of his ambition.]

2. A mediocrity of state and condition—

[He did not, through a dread of wealth, desire to be reduced to poverty: he wished rather to stand at an equal distance from each extreme; and to enjoy that only which God should judge "convenient for him." It is not easy for us to say precisely what a competency is; because it must vary according to men's education and habits; that being poverty to one, which would be riches to another: yet the line drawn by Agur, seems to mark the limits most agreeably to the mind of God, because it exactly corresponds with the views of patriarchs[d], of prophets[e], of Apostles[f], and particularly with the prayer which our blessed Lord himself has taught all his followers to use[g].]

In urging his request, Agur manifested great zeal and earnestness: his whole soul appeared to be engaged in it: we are therefore interested in inquiring into,

II. The reasons with which he enforced it—

He was not actuated by any carnal motives, though he was praying about carnal things. It was not the incumbrances of wealth, or the hardships of poverty that he dreaded; he considered only the aspect of the different states upon his spiritual advancement; and deprecated them equally on account of the temptations incident to both.

1. On account of the snares of wealth—

[Riches foster the pride of the human heart, and engender a haughty and independent spirit. This was the effect of opulence on God's people of old[h]; and the same baneful influence is observable in our day. The great consider it almost as an act of condescension to acknowledge God. Scarcely one of them in a thousand will endure to hear his name mentioned in private, or his will propounded as the proper rule of his conduct. The atheistical expressions in the text are indeed the language of his conduct, if not also of his lips[i]. It is on this, as well as other accounts, that our Lord has spoken of riches as rendering our salvation difficult, yea impossible, without some

---

d Gen. xxviii. 20.   e Jer. xlv. 5.   f 1 Tim. vi. 8—10.

g Matt. vi. 11. and the first clause of ver. 13. between which and Agur's prayer there is a remarkable agreement.

h Deut. xxxii. 15. Hos. xiii. 6.   i See Exod. v. 2. Ps. xii. 4.

signal interposition of divine grace[k]. And therefore every one
who values his soul may well deprecate an exalted state.]

2. On account of the snares of poverty—

[Poverty has its snares no less than wealth: where its
pressure is felt, the temptations to dishonesty are exceeding
great. Even those who are in ease and affluence are too easily
induced to deviate from the paths of strict integrity, especially
when there appears but little probability of detection: how
much more strongly then may a dishonest principle be supposed
to operate, when called forth by necessity and distress! God
appointed that a person suspected of theft should clear himself
by an oath before a magistrate[l]; but this was a feeble barrier
against dishonesty; for he that will cheat, will lie; and, if
urged to it, will rather perjure himself to conceal his crime,
than expose himself to shame by confessing it. Thus one sin
leads to another; and a soul, that is of more value than ten
thousand worlds, is bartered for some worthless commodity.
Justly then may that state also be deprecated, which exposes
us to such tremendous evils.]

This subject may TEACH US,

1. Contentment with our lot—

[Whatever be the means used, it is God alone that fixes
our condition in the world: and, if we be Christians indeed,
we may be sure that our lot is that which, all things considered,
is most for the good of our souls. If any variations in it have
taken place, such changes have been sent to teach us that con-
tentment, which St. Paul so richly experienced, and which it
is no less our privilege than our duty to learn[m]. If we have
that which is best for our souls, then we have that which is
really best.]

2. Watchfulness against our besetting sins—

[Every situation of life has its peculiar temptations. Youth
or age, health or sickness, riches or poverty have their respective snares. It is our wisdom to stand on our guard against
the difficulties to which we are more immediately exposed[n];
and rather to seek for grace that we may approve ourselves
to God in the station to which he has called us, than to desire
a change of circumstances, which will change indeed, but not
remove, our trials.]

3. Solicitude for spiritual advancement—

[It was sin, and sin only, that Agur feared: and doubtless
sin is the greatest of all evils. Let the same mind then be
in us that was in him. Whether we have poverty or riches, or

k Matt. xix. 23—26.   l Exod. xxii. 7—12. and 1 Kings viii. 31
m Phil. iv. 11, 12.   n 2 Sam. xxii. 24.

whether we be equally removed from both, let us endeavour to improve in spirituality and holiness. Then will the wisdom of God, in appointing such a variety of states, be made manifest: and the collective virtues of the different classes will then shine with combined lustre, and, like the rays of the sun, display the glory of Him from whom they sprang.]

OUTLINE NO. 825

THE SELF-DECEIVER EXPOSED.

Prov. xxx. 12. *There is a generation that are pure in their own eyes, and yet is not washed from their filthiness.*

MEN of themselves are very backward to form an unfavourable estimate of their own character. Hence arises the necessity of accurate discrimination and undaunted fidelity in ministers, whose office is to " separate the precious from the vile," and to give to every one his portion in due season. The Scriptures draw a broad line of distinction between the righteous and the wicked; and *this,* not in their actions only, but in their dispositions and habits; by which the different characters may be as clearly discerned as by their outward conduct. The generation of self-deceivers is very numerous: multitudes there are who stand high in their own estimation, whilst in God's eyes they are as sounding brass or a tinkling cymbal. Amongst these we must number,

I. The decent formalist—

He is " pure in his own eyes"—

[He is punctual in the observance of outward duties, both civil and religious. He will attend constantly at the house of God, and even at the table of the Lord: he will also establish worship in his family: and in respect of his dealings with men, he will be all that is amiable and lovely: he will be honest, sober, just, temperate, benevolent: as far as the letter of the law goes, he may be blameless.

In such a state, what wonder is it if he be pure in his own eyes? He understands not the spirituality of the law, and can judge of himself only by the defective standard of heathen morality. By the world he is admired, and held up as a pattern of all excellence: and seeing that he stands high in the esteem of others, he almost of necessity entertains a high opinion of himself.]

But he " is not washed from his filthiness"—

[Much filthiness there is in the heart of every man by nature; and there is a filthiness which every person may properly
call *his own,* as being congenial with his own feelings, and
particularly connected with his own character. With the
character before us there is a very abundant measure of pride,
venting itself in a constant habit of self-confidence and self-
complacency. Combined with this are impenitence and unbelief: for how is it possible that he should repent and believe,
when he knows not the extent of his guilt and danger? " Being whole, he feels no need of a physician" — — — He is
altogether under the dominion also of worldly-mindedness.
When he has performed his religious duties, he goes to worldly
company, without feeling any want, or being sensible of any
danger. The friendship of the world is what he delights in as
his chief good, never once suspecting, that this very disposition
proves and constitutes him an enemy of God[a]. Thus, though
there is nothing in him that the world disapproves, and nothing
that seems to call for self-reproach, he is under the habitual
and allowed dominion of evils, which render him abominable
in the sight of God[b]. He has somewhat of " the form of godliness, but none at all of its power[c]" — — —]

Amongst this generation we must also number,

II. The almost Christian—

He goes much farther than the decent formalist—

[He is convinced of the truth and excellence of Christianity, and wishes to be a partaker of its benefits. He will
vindicate the faithful servants of God against the accusations
brought against them by the ungodly world; and will actually
comply with many things which the Gospel requires — — —
From this partial change in himself he begins to think that
he is a Christian indeed. His constrained approbation of the
Gospel appears to him to be a cordial acceptance of it : and
his slender performances of its duties are in his estimation like
an unreserved obedience.]

But, like him, he deceives his own soul—

[He will not renounce all for Christ. When our Lord
says, " Go, sell all that thou hast, and give to the poor, and
come and follow me," he departs sorrowful, like the Rich
Youth, and chooses the world in preference to Christ. He
draws back also from the cross, which he will not bear. He
is ashamed of Christ, even at the very time that he shews
some regard both for his word and ministers. He will not
" come out from the world and be separate ;" but still remains

---

[a] Jam. iv. 4. [b] Luke xvi. 15. [c] 2 Tim. iii. 5.

conformed to it, to its maxims, its habits, its spirit, and its company. Of the *true* Christian, our Lord says, " Ye are not of this world, even as I am not of the world :" but of the *almost* Christian, the very reverse is true : he strives to reconcile the inconsistent services of God and Mammon : and if this cannot be done, he will forego his eternal interests, rather than sacrifice his worldly interests, and subject himself to the scorn and hatred of the ungodly.

Thus, though pure in his own eyes, he is yet in bondage to the fear of man ; and gives a decided preference to this world, before the preservation of a good conscience, and the approbation of his God.]

To the same class belongs also,

III. The inconsistent professor—

Who more confident of the goodness of his state, than he who professes to believe in Christ?

[The man who has felt some conviction of sin, and some hope in Christ, and has been hailed by others as a sound convert to the Christian faith, is ready to conclude that all is well : his successive emotions of hope and fear, of joy and sorrow, are to him a sufficient evidence, that his conversion is unquestionable. If he have some ability to talk about the Gospel, and some gift in prayer, he is still further confirmed in his persuasion, that there exists in him no ground for doubt or fear. More especially, if he have views of the Covenant of grace, as " ordered in all things and sure," and have adopted a crude system of religion that favours a blind confidence, he concludes at once that he is, and must be, a child of God.]

But who more open to self-deception?

[Professors of the Gospel are very apt to forget that rule of judging which our Lord himself has prescribed, " By their fruits ye shall know them[d]." But this is the only safe criterion whereby to judge of our state before God. Yet, when brought to this test, how low do many religious professors appear! They can talk of the Gospel fluently ; but, if their spirit and temper be inquired into, they are found to be under the habitual dominion of some besetting sin, as they were before they ever thought of religion. It is lamentable to think what " filthiness there is both of flesh and spirit," from which many who profess the Gospel have never yet been " washed[e]:" yet an inspired Apostle declares, that " if a man seem to be religious and bridleth not his tongue, he deceiveth himself, and his religion is vain[f]." What then must be the state of those who yet remain proud and passionate, worldly-minded and covetous,

d Matt. vii. 16.   e Tit. i. 16.   f Jam. i. 26.

false and dishonest, impure and sensual, yea, and grossly defective in all the duties of their place and station? Truly, of all the people belonging to the generation spoken of in our text, these are in the greatest danger, because their confidence is founded in the idea, that they have already bathed in the fountain which alone is able to cleanse them from their sin.]

ADDRESS,

1. Those who, *though pure* in their own eyes, *are not washed*—

[Happy would it be if men would relax the confidence which they are ever ready to maintain of the safety of their state before God. Every one conceives, that whatever others may do, *he* deceives not his own soul: yet behold so great is the number of self-deceivers, that they constitute " a generation!" Beloved, learn to try yourselves by the only true test, your conformity to the will of God, and to the example of Christ————It is in the balance of the sanctuary, and not in your own balance, that you are to weigh yourselves; for in that shall you be weighed at the last day; and if you are found wanting in that, the measure of your deficiency will be the measure of your condemnation————]

2. Those who, *though not pure* in their own eyes, *are really washed* from their filthiness—

[Blessed be God! there is a generation of these also. Many who once wallowed in all manner of filthiness, are now washed from it, even as the Corinthian converts were [g]. Yet they are not pure in their own eyes: on the contrary, they are of all people most ready to suspect themselves[h], and to " lothe themselves" for their remaining imperfections. See how strikingly this is exemplified in the very chapter before us: Agur was a man of unquestionable piety: yet, under a sense of his great unworthiness, he complained, " Surely I am more brutish than any man, and have not the understanding of a man[i]." This may appear to many to be extravagant: but it is the real feeling of many a child of God; I may add too, it is their frequent complaint before God. Such were the feelings of Job, of Isaiah, and of Paul[k]———— If it be asked, Whence arises this, that such holy and heavenly persons should be so far from being pure in their own eyes? the reason is, that they try themselves by a more perfect standard, and from their clearer discoveries of the path of duty are more deeply conscious of their aberrations from it. Their love of holiness also makes them now to abhor themselves more for their want of conformity

[g] 1 Cor. vi. 9—11.   [h] Matt. xxvi. 21, 22.   [i] ver. 2.
[k] Job xl. 4. and xlii. 6.   Isai. vi. 5.   Rom. vii. 18, 24.

to the Divine image, than they once did even for the grossest sins. To you then, dearly Beloved, I would address myself in the language of consolation and encouragement. It is well that you see and lament your vileness, provided you make it only an occasion of humiliation, and not of despondency. The more lowly you are in your own eyes, the more exalted you are in God's, who has said, that " he who humbleth himself shall be exalted." Let your sense of your remaining imperfections make you plead more earnestly with your God that reviving promise, " From all your filthiness, and from all your idols, I will cleanse you[1]." And remember, that you are not to wash yourselves first, and then to lay hold on the promises, but to embrace the promises first, and then by means of them to cleanse yourselves from the defilements you lament. This is the order prescribed in the Gospel[m]; and, if you will adhere to it, you shall have increasing evidence that it is the destined path of purity and peace.]

[1] Ezek. xxxvi. 25.   1 John i. 9.   [m] 2 Cor. vii. 1.

OUTLINE NO. 826

USEFULNESS OF SCHOOLS OF INDUSTRY.

Prov. xxxi. 10. *Who can find a virtuous woman? for her price is far above rubies.*

WHILE we rejoice in the progress of civilization, we cannot but regret the loss of primitive simplicity. In former days, women of the highest rank did not disdain to employ themselves in the most common offices of life[a]. King Lemuel, supposed by some to be Solomon himself, was exhorted by his inspired mother to select for his wife a woman who was not ashamed to occupy herself in domestic duties. The description here given of a queen, is, alas! but ill suited to the refinement of the present age. It is rather calculated for the lower classes of the community. With a more immediate view therefore to *their* benefit, we shall consider it, and shew,

I. The character of a virtuous woman—

There is no other character so fully drawn in Scripture as this. She is described by,

1. Her industry—

[a] Gen. xviii. 6.

[She rises early[b] : and when occasion requires, goes late to rest[c]. She encourages industry in her dependents [d], and sets them an example of it herself[e], willingly[f], regularly [g], without regarding fatigue[h].]

2. Her prudence—

[She sells the produce of her labour[i], and lays out her money with judgment for the *permanent* benefit of her family[k]. She provides comfortably for her family in respect of food[l] and clothing [m]. She guards against all waste of her husband's property[n]. She employs her leisure in improving her mind[o] ; and conducts herself with love and kindness towards all[p].]

3. Her piety—

[She is not satisfied with performing her duties towards man, but endeavours to serve God also [q]. She accounts "the fear of God" to be the one thing needful. She labours above all things to cultivate this divine principle : she makes it the source and motive, the rule and measure, the scope and end, of all her actions ; and, while she serves her God, she delights also to benefit the poor[r].]

Of such a character it is not easy to estimate,

II. The worth—

Rubies are accounted valuable among earthly treasures : but the worth of such a woman is infinitely above them—she is,

1. An ornament to her sex—

[However highly beauty is prized among men, the endowments before mentioned render their possessor incomparably more lovely [s]. The person possessing them must be admired in any station in life ; but her excellence is then most conspicuous and most valuable, when she sustains the relations of a wife and a mother [t]. It is to be lamented that such characters are rarely " found[u] :" but the more scarce they are, the more worthy are they of our esteem.]

2. A blessing to her family—

[Of whatever rank they be, they cannot fail to reap much benefit from her prudent management, and pious example. If they be poor, especially, the good arising to them will be incalculable. They will enjoy a thousand comforts, of which others

[b] ver. 15.   [c] ver. 18.   [d] ver. 15.   [e] ver. 19.   [f] ver. 13.
[g] ver. 27.   [h] ver. 17.   [i] ver. 24.   [k] ver. 16.   [l] ver. 15.
[m] ver. 21. In the margin it is " with *double garments*."
[n] ver. 11, 12.   [o] ver. 26.   [p] ver. 26.   [q] ver. 30
[r] ver. 20.   [s] ver. 30.   [t] ver. 29.   [u] *The text*

of their class are destitute.   Their decent appearance will procure them respect, and redound to her praise [x].   Her children
will love and honour her, and bless God on her account [y].   Her
husband will delight in her himself, and make his boast of her
to others [z].   They will all esteem her as a rich and continued
source of domestic felicity.]

3. A comfort to all around her—

[The rich will be glad to aid her by their wealth and
influence.   The poor will find in her a friend, to counsel them
in difficulty, and relieve them in distress.   All who behold her,
will be constrained to applaud her conduct [a], and many will be
excited to follow her example.]

We may now hope for a favourable attention, while
we set before you,

III. The tendency of this institution to increase their number—

Though piety is as common among the poor as
among any class of the community, yet it is very rare
indeed that we can find among them a combination
of the qualities before insisted on.

[From want of education they know not how to manage
their affairs — — — And from habits of inattention, they are
indisposed to learn — — —]

But to the rising generation much good will arise
from a school of industry—

[The instruction which they gain in common schools, is very
confined; but in this they will be taught all that can qualify
them for usefulness in this world, or happiness in the next.
To read the Bible, and to fear God, will be proposed as the
first objects of their attention.   To qualify them for service,
and to fit them to manage their own families at some future
period, is the next concern we wish to promote.   To call forth
their own exertions, and stimulate a desire to excel, every
encouragement will be afforded them.   Thus habits of industry,
of economy, of subordination to men, and of piety to God,
being formed, they will fill up their future stations in life with
far greater advantage to themselves, and benefit to society.]

We will now consider SOME OBJECTIONS that may be
made—

1. Among the rich—

[Some think *it better that the poor should be kept in ignorance.*   But these are themselves ignorant, unfeeling, and

[x] ver. 23.   [y] ver. 28.   [z] ver. 28.   [a] ver. 31.

ungodly.   Some have a fear that *persons may be wanted for agricultural work;* but there will always be found many who stand in need of employment.]

2. Among the poor—

[These are *unwilling to forego the immediate earnings of their children.*   But in a little time they will earn much more than they now do.   They will sooner find situations where they will live at free cost.   They will probably be able at a future period to aid their parents, instead of being a grief, and perhaps a burthen, to them.   They will have a far better prospect of heaven, by having their minds instructed, and their conduct regulated, than they would have had, if brought up in ignorance and sin.]

We conclude with recommending the institution to your support—

[If self-interest alone were consulted, the rich should help forward such institutions: for, if extensively promoted, they would soon lower the rates.   But if benevolence be allowed to operate, it has unbounded scope for exercise in such institutions as these; since they render the lower orders of people more intelligent, more useful, more properous, and more happy.]

ECCLESIASTES.

OUTLINE NO. 827

THE VANITY OF THE CREATURE.

Eccl. i. 2. *Vanity of vanities, saith the Preacher, vanity of vanities; all is vanity.*

IF experience entitles a man to credit, and gives weight to his testimony, we derive great advantage as to the credibility of the inspired writings: for respecting much of which the Prophets and Apostles wrote, they could say, " What mine eyes have seen, mine ears have heard, and my hands have handled of the word of life, that same declare I unto you." And if this be an advantage in reference to the excellency of religion, it may well be regarded as of some importance in reference also to the vanity of all earthly pursuits. That there should have been a man possessed of such abundant means of gratification as Solomon was, and so ardent in the pursuit of it in every possible line, and at the same time so faithful in declaring his own experience in relation to it all, must be considered as an advantage to all subsequent generations, who should hear and receive his testimony respecting the things which he had so fully tried, and so invariably proved to be vanity itself. The words before us express a conviction that admitted not of doubt, and a decision that left no room for controversy. " The Preacher" who uttered them was inspired of God, at the same time that he recorded what, from personal knowledge, he was qualified to declare. And in considering his testimony, I shall,

I. Confirm it—

The things of which he spake were, all that the world contains; its grosser and more common pursuits of pleasure, riches, and honour, as also its more refined attainments of wisdom and knowledge.   And all of them, without exception, are vanity;

1. In their acquisition—

[It is not without great labour and toil that earthly distinctions are obtained.   The merchant, the warrior, the philosopher will bear record, that in their respective pursuits they have endured much fatigue, and many disappointments; insomuch that to one whose taste was different from theirs, they would appear to have paid too dear a price for all that they have gained.]

2. In their use—

[Suppose that the labours of any person have been crowned with success; What, after all, has he gained?   He thought he was following something substantial; but, to his mortification, he finds that he has grasped a shadow.   He has "hewn out cisterns" for himself, indeed, with great labour; but he finds, after all, that they are "broken cisterns, which can hold no water."   At the first moment, whilst the charm of novelty is upon them, the various objects we have attained afford a pleasing gratification to the mind: but scarcely have they been enjoyed a few days, before they lose their sweetness, and descend into the common routine of earthly comforts.   The man who rolls in wealth, and he who is dignified with high-sounding titles, is soon brought to a level with his inferiors in point of actual enjoyment: and even he who has acquired knowledge, finds, that, "in having increased knowledge, he has also increased sorrow[a];" because of the envy which his eminence has excited, and the uncertainty of much which he thinks he has attained.]

3. In their continuance—

[What is there of which a man may not be despoiled? Pleasure may, in a very little time, be turned into pain: honour may speedily be blasted by some unforeseen event: "riches make themselves wings, and fly away:" and through disease or accident, even reason itself, with all its highest attainments, may sink into more than infantine weakness and infirmity.   But grant to these things all that the most sanguine imagination can impute, how soon do they vanish away!   Even life itself is but as a hand-breadth, or as a shadow that declineth: and the moment that death comes, "all our thoughts perish," and we "go out of the world as naked and as destitute as we came into it."]

4. In their issue—

[a] ver. 18.

[Here it is that the vanity of earthly things pre-eminently appears. For in what respect can they advance our eternal happiness? Would to God that they did not so generally and so fatally obstruct it! Truly, " neither riches nor honours can profit us in the day of wrath." With our holy and heavenly Judge " there is no respect of persons." The rich and the poor will be dealt with according to one equal law : only the rich, and the great, and the learned, will be called to a more severe account in proportion to the influence they possessed, and the advantages they neglected to improve.]

But as the testimony is unquestionably strong, I shall,
II. Qualify it—

Beyond all doubt, the Scriptures generally contain the same language : " Surely men of low degree are vanity, and men of high degree are a lie : to be laid in the balance, they are altogether lighter than vanity[b]." But stronger still is the language of the Psalmist in another place, where he says, " Verily every man, at his best estate, is altogether vanity[c]." Consider how *strong* and how *unqualified* these expressions are, and you will not expect me to say much in mitigation of them. Yet I must say, that the vanity of the creature, though *the same in itself*, is differently *felt*,

1. According to our mode of acting in reference to it—

[If we give ourselves up to creature comforts, we shall be dreadfully disappointed — — — But if we enjoy them in subserviency to God, and in subordination to higher pursuits, we shall not find them so empty as may be imagined. For God has " given to his people all things richly to enjoy :" and provided only we enjoy God in them, they are both a legitimate and an abundant spring of pure delight. For, whilst we derive from them the happiness which they are calculated to impart, we taste not the bitterness which is infused into the cup of the mere worldling. Our enjoyments are elevated and sanctified; our pains, moderated and changed into an occasion of praise and thanksgiving. Only let them be sought in their proper place, and they are comforts in the way to heaven, though they can never stand to us in the place of heaven.]

2. According to the degree in which we blend religion with it—

[Religion raises us above the creature altogether. If we have much of this world, we shall have a high enjoyment of it,

---

[b] Ps. lxii. 9.   [c] Ps. xxxix. 5.

because we shall make it the means of benefiting our fellow-creatures, and of honouring our God. If, on the other hand, we have little of this world, we shall still be happy; because, in having God for our portion, we can lack nothing. There are but two lessons for the Christian to learn: the one is, to enjoy God in every thing; the other is, to enjoy every thing in God. The one ennobles the rich; the other elevates the poor: and all who have learned these lessons are, and must be, happy.

Whilst, therefore, I grant the general position, that the creature is vanity, I must say, that the experience of its vanity, depends altogether on our undue pursuit of it and expectations from it. Let us only take it in the manner that God approves, and for the ends for which he has sent it, and we shall still find it, like Jacob's ladder, unsubstantial indeed it itself, but still a medium of communication between heaven and earth; a medium of God's descent to us, and of our ascent to him.]

But, in our consideration of this testimony, let us further,

III. Improve it—

Much, very much, may it teach us. We may learn from it to be,

1. Moderate in our expectations—

[If we will foolishly look for that in the creature which God never designed to be put into it, we may well expect disappointment. Even in Paradise it was not intended to stand in the place of God, or to be to us any source of solid satisfaction: how much less, then, can it be so, when sin has infused a curse into it; agreeably to what is written, "Cursed is the ground for thy sake." Let us estimate it aright, and expect from it no more than God has ordained it to impart; and we shall prove but little of its emptiness, whilst we have a rich and becoming enjoyment of it. The direction of St. Paul is that which comes immediately to the point, and exactly suits the present occasion: "The time is short. It remaineth that both they that have wives be as though they had none; and they that weep, as though they wept not; and they that rejoice, as though they rejoice not; and they that buy, as though they possessed not; and they that use this world, as not abusing it. For the fashion of this world passeth away[d]." Only use the creature in this way, and you will find it no injury to your souls.]

2. Patient in our trials—

[Trials of different kinds must come: for "the whole creation has, through the sin of man, become subject to vanity."

[d] 1 Cor. vii. 29—31.

But, in our present state, this is in reality a benefit; for, if it were not so, we should be ready to take up our rest in this world, instead of seeking "that which remaineth for us" in the world to come. Troubles serve to bring us nigh to God for the supports and consolations which we stand in need of. And shall we complain of that which brings us near to him, and proves an occasion of richer communications from him? No, verily: we should taste love, and love only, in our diversified afflictions; and look to God as sending them "for our profit, that by means of them we may be made partakers of his holiness," and meet for his glory.]

3. Diligent in our pursuit of better things—

[In heavenly things there are no drawbacks, except those which are caused by our own defects in seeking after them. There is no vanity in love to God, or love to man: and the more we labour after them, and delight ourselves in them, the happier we shall be. Could we but give ourselves wholly to these things, we should find in them a very heaven upon earth. To every one of you, then, I would recommend that prayer of David, "Turn away mine eyes from beholding vanity, and quicken thou me in thy way[e]."]

e Ps. cxix. 37.

OUTLINE NO. 828

THE CREATURE IS VANITY AND VEXATION.

Eccl. i. 14, 15. *I have seen all the works which are done under the sun; and behold, all is vanity and vexation of spirit. That which is crooked cannot be made straight; and that which is wanting, cannot be numbered.*

THE Book of Ecclesiastes is generally supposed to have been written by Solomon, after he had repented of his manifold transgressions: and it is pleasing to view it in this light: for, if it be not so, we have no record whatever of his penitence. But in this view its declarations are doubly interesting: as inspired by God, they are of Divine authority; and, as resulting from actual experience, they carry a much deeper conviction with them to our minds. Had one of the fishermen of Galilee spoken so strongly respecting the vanity of the world, we might have said that he had never had any opportunity of knowing experimentally what attractions the world possessed: but Solomon had an ampler range for enjoyment than

any other human being. As a king, he had the wealth
of a nation at his command. As endued with a greater
measure of wisdom than all other men, he could combine all kinds of intellectual pleasure with that which
was merely sensual. As having a peaceful reign, he
was free from all the alarms and disquietudes of war,
and able to prosecute pleasure as the one object of
his life. Every species of gratification being thus
easily within his reach, he was amply qualified to
judge of what the world could give: and yet, after
having made the experiment, and " seen all the works
that are done under the sun," he pronounced them all
to be " vanity and vexation of spirit."

Two things in our text are to be noticed;

I. The general assertion—

Never was any truth more capable of demonstration
than this, that the world, and every thing in it, is,

1. Vanity—

[If we view the creature in itself, what a poor worthless
thing is it! Take gold, for instance : much as it is in request,
it has in itself no value : the value put on it is merely arbitrary,
arising not so much from its usefulness to us, as from the scar-
city of it. Iron is of infinitely greater service to mankind than
gold : and would be more valued by us, if it did not happen
that it is to be found in much larger quantities than gold. So
it is with jewels: the value of them is quite ideal : in themselves
they are of no more use than common pebbles ; and he who
possesses them in the greatest abundance, is in reality no richer
than if he possessed so much gravel out of the pit.

Nor is any thing that wealth can purchase, or any thing that
is associated with it, worthy of any better name than vanity.
What are high-sounding titles, but a mere sound that has its
value only in the estimation of men ; and that, by a change of
its acceptation (such as not uncommonly takes place in language, as, for instance, in the term Despot), may convey the
most painful feelings, instead of such as are agreeable to the
mind ? We may ask the same in reference to pleasure : What
is it ? Let but a very small change take place in the circumstances of the person, and the pleasure shall become a pain.
Or let it be enjoyed in all its fulness ; whom did it ever satisfy?
To whom did it ever impart any permanent delight ? The more
exquisite it is, the sooner does it cloy ; insomuch that we are
soon forced to flee from it through very lassitude and disgust.
And a recurrence to the same sources of gratification is far

from producing the same emotions in the soul: by use and habit we become indifferent to the very things which once we most ardently affected: so poor, so empty, so transient is all that passes under the semblance and the name of pleasure.

We may say therefore of "all that is in the world, the lust of the flesh, the lust of the eye, and the pride of life," that it is not only vain, but " vanity" in the abstract: " Vanity of vanities, saith the preacher, vanity of vanities, all is vanity[a]."]

2. Vexation of spirit—

[So far is the creature from affording any real happiness, that it is an occasion of constant vexation to the mind. The pursuit of earthly things is attended with much labour, and with much uncertainty also as to the attainment of them. When attained, they excite nothing but envy in others, and disquietude in ourselves. By reason of the casualties to which the possession of them exposes us, we are filled with care; insomuch, that those who only behold our acquisitions, often derive more pleasure from them than we who are the owners of them. Besides, the more we have attained, the more our desires are enlarged after something unpossessed; so that our labours are never at an end: and the pain issuing from a single disappointment frequently outweighs the pleasure arising from manifold successes. Indeed, the things from which we promise ourselves most pleasure, generally become, by some means or other, the sources of our keenest anguish; and our most sanguine expectations usually terminate in the bitterest disappointment: yea, it not unfrequently happens, that after having attained the object of our wishes, we welcome the period of our separation from it, and bless ourselves more in the loss of it, than ever we did in the acquisition.

Say then whether Solomon's testimony be not strictly true. Young people, when they hear such a sentiment avowed, are ready to think it an effusion of spleen, and a libel on the whole creation: but this testimony is the very truth of God, and shall sooner or later be found true in the experience of every living man: the world, and every thing in it, is a broken cistern, that disappoints the hopes of the thirsty traveller, and becomes to him, not only vanity, but " vexation of spirit:" and he that has most sought to satisfy himself with it, finds after all his labours, that he has only "filled his belly with the east wind[b]."]

Such is the import of the general assertion. We now proceed to notice,

II. The particular confirmation of it—

Two things are here specified by Solomon, as

strongly illustrating the foregoing truth; namely, that, however much we may exert ourselves,

1. We cannot alter that which is unfavourable—

[Every man, by the very constitution of his nature, is dependent on his fellow-man for the greater portion of his happiness. The welfare of a whole empire depends on the wisdom and prudence of the prince; as the prince's prosperity and comfort do on the industry, the fortitude, the loyalty of his people. So it is through all ranks and orders of society; all are deeply affected by the conduct of those around them. In the domestic circle, how impossible is it for the husband or wife, the parent or child, the master or servant, to be happy, if those with whom he is more immediately connected be perverse and obstinate in an evil way! Yet all come more or less in contact with unreasonable men: and, however much they may strive to rectify the views, or reform the habits, of such people, they find it altogether beyond their power: they can as easily change the leopard's spots or the Ethiopian's complexion, as they can prevail on persons to change those habits which are productive of so much uneasiness to their minds. Hence, though they form the wisest and most benevolent plans, they cannot carry them into execution, because of the blindness and perverseness of those whose concurrence is necessary for the accomplishment of them[c].

In like manner, there is often an untowardness in events as well as in men. The seasons will not consult us; nor will the elements obey us. Accidents utterly unforeseen will occur, and cannot be prevented by human foresight. Hence uncertainty attends our best concerted plans, and failure often disappoints our most laborious exertions. But these are " crooked things which no man can make straight:" no human wisdom or power can control them. We have a large and abundant harvest in prospect: but, behold, storms and tempests, or blasting and mildew, or insects of some kind, destroy the whole crop. We have gathered the harvest into our granaries, and a fire consumes it; or an enemy overruns the land, and devours it. We have attained the greatest felicity of which we suppose ourselves capable, by a connexion the most desirable, or by the acquisition of a first-born son: but how soon does death invade our dwelling, and blast all our promised joys! These are but a few of the evils to which we are exposed in this vain world; and they stamp " vanity and vexation" upon all that we possess.]

2. We cannot supply that which is defective—

[c] This may be noticed especially in the opposition made to the diffusion of the Scriptures, which persons of benevolence and piety labour to circulate through the world.

[The rich, the poor, the old, the young, the learned, the unlearned, all without exception, find that there is much lacking, to render them completely happy. Of those who possess most of this world's good, it must be said, " In the fulness of their sufficiency they are in straits [d]." Solomon is a remarkable example of this. He had formed, if not a wise, yet an honourable, connexion with Pharaoh's daughter. Not satisfied, he sought happiness in a plurality of wives. Still not having attained happiness, he multiplied his wives and concubines to the number of one thousand; and found himself, after all, as far from happiness as ever. Every other thing which he thought could contribute to his happiness he sought with insatiable avidity: but, after he had attained all his objects, he found, that " the things which were wanting could not be numbered." And so shall we find it to the latest hour of our lives. We may fancy that this or that will make us happy; but, when we have gained it, we have only followed a shadow that eludes our grasp. The truth is, that God never designed the creature to be a satisfying portion to man : not even Paradise itself could satisfy Adam : no, nor could the partner which he gave him : he must taste the forbidden fruit: he could not be content without an accession of wisdom, which God did not ever intend him to possess. Thus, even in man's state of innocence, nothing but God could satisfy his soul : nor can any thing, short of God himself, ever be a satisfying portion to any child of man.]

ADDRESS—

1. Set not your affections on things below—

[How happy would it be for us, if we could be content to receive the foregoing truths on the testimony of Solomon, instead of determining to learn them by our own experience! How much vexation and misery should we avoid! But, in spite of the united acknowledgments of all that have gone before us, we still think that we shall find something besides God to make us happy. This however we cannot do, even though we should possess all that Solomon ever enjoyed. We may continue our pursuit as long as we will; but we must come at last to the same conclusion as he, and give the same testimony as to the result of our experience. Be persuaded, Brethren, to credit the Divine testimony, and to spare yourselves all the pain and disappointment which you must otherwise encounter. We mean not that you should renounce the *pursuit* of earthly things; for you cannot do that without abandoning the duties which you owe to your families and to society at large; but *the expectation of happiness from them* you may, and must, renounce. You must never forget, that the creature without God is nothing; and that happiness is to be found in God alone.]

[d] Job xx. 22.

2. Seek the Lord Jesus Christ with your whole hearts—

[He is a portion in which you will never find any lack: in him is a fulness sufficient to fill all the capacities, and satisfy all the desires of the whole universe. Millions and millions of immortal souls may go to that fountain, and never diminish his exhaustless store. To the possession of him too no disappointment can attach, nor from the enjoyment of him can any vexation ensue. In him all " crooked things are made straight;" and where he is, no want can possibly exist. If you ask of the creature to heal the wounds of sin, to give peace to a guilty conscience, to subdue in us our corruptions, or to cheer us with hopes of immortality, it cannot do any one of these things: no, not even for the body can the creature do any thing to heal its sickness, to assuage its anguish, or to prolong its existence. But the Lord Jesus Christ can do every thing, both for the body and the soul, both for time and for eternity. Seek him, then, Beloved; and seek him with your whole hearts. In seeking him, your exertions cannot be too earnest, nor can your expectations be too enlarged. If he give you his flesh to eat, and his blood to drink, you will never hunger, never thirst again, either in this world or in the world to come. Only be able to say, " My Beloved is mine, and I am his," and then all, as well on heaven as in earth, is yours; according as it is written, " All things are yours; and ye are in Christ's; and Christ is God's."]

OUTLINE NO. 829

THE EMPTINESS OF WORLDLY MIRTH.

Eccl. ii. 2.   *I said of laughter, It is mad: and of mirth, What doeth it?*

WHO is it that has ventured to speak thus respecting that which constitutes, in the world's estimation, the great happiness of life? Was he an ignorant man? or one who from envy decried a thing which he was not able to attain? or an inexperienced man, who had no just means of forming a judgment? or an irritated man, who vented thus his spleen against an object that had disappointed him? Or was he one whose authority in this matter we are at liberty to question? No: it was the wisest of the human race, who had more ample means of judging than any other of the children of men, and had tried the matter to the

uttermost: it was Solomon himself, under the influence of the Spirit of God, recording this, not only
as the result of his own experience, but as the declaration of Jehovah, by him, for the instruction of the
world in all future ages. He had been left by God to
try the vain experiment, whether happiness was to be
found in any thing but God. He tried it, first, in the
pursuit of knowledge; which, to a person of his
enlarged mind, certainly promised most fair to yield
him the satisfaction which he sought. But partly
from the labour requisite for the attainment of knowledge; partly from discovering how little could be
known by persons of our finite capacity; partly also
from the insufficiency of knowledge to satisfy the
innumerable wants of man; and partly from the disgust which had been created in his mind by the insight
which his wisdom gave him into the ignorance and
folly of the rest of mankind; he left it upon record,
as his deliberate judgment, that " in much wisdom is
much grief; and that he who increaseth knowledge,
increaseth sorrow[a]." He then turned to pleasure, as
the most probable source of happiness: " I said in
my heart, Go to now, I will prove thee with mirth:
therefore enjoy pleasure." But being equally disappointed in that, he adds, " Behold, this also is vanity[b]."
Then, in the words of my text, he further adds, " I
said of laughter, It is mad: and of mirth, What doeth it?"

In discoursing on this subject, I shall,

I. Shew what that is which he here pronounces to be
　　" vanity"—

It becomes us, in considering such weighty declarations as that before us, to attain the most precise
and accurate views of the terms employed; neither
attenuating the import of them on the one hand, nor
exaggerating it on the other.

We are not, then, to understand the text as decry-
ing all cheerfulness—

[The Christian, above all people upon earth, has reason
to be cheerful. And religion in no way tends to destroy the

---

[a] Eccles. i. 18.　　　　　[b] ver. 1.

gaiety of the human mind, but only to direct it towards proper
objects, and to restrain it within proper bounds. The ways of
religion are represented as "ways of pleasantness and peace."
And "the fruits of the Spirit are, love, joy, peace;" all of which
suppose a measure of hilarity, and the innocence of that hilarity,
when arising from a becoming source, and kept within the
limits of sobriety and sound wisdom. Doubtless that tumultuous
kind of joy which is generally denominated mirth, and which
vents itself in immoderate laughter, is altogether vain and bad:
but a placidity of mind, exercising itself in a way of brotherly
love and of cheerful benevolence, can never be censured as
unprofitable, much less can it be condemned as verging towards
insanity.]

Neither, on the other hand, are we to restrict the
text to licentious and profane mirth—

[That needed not to be stigmatized in so peculiar a manner; because the folly of such mirth carries its own evidence
along with it. We need only to see it in others; and if we
ourselves are not partakers of it, we shall not hesitate to characterize it by some opprobrious or contemptuous name. We
need neither the wisdom of Solomon, nor his experience, to pass
upon it the judgment it deserves.]

The conduct reprobated in our text is, *the seeking
of our happiness in carnal mirth*—

[Solomon particularly specifies this : "I said in my heart,
Go to now, I will prove thee with mirth," I will see whether
that will afford me the happiness which I am in pursuit of.
And we may suppose, that, in the prosecution of this object,
he summoned around him all that was gay and lively in his
court, and all that could contribute towards the attainment of
it. We may take a survey of the state of society in what may
be called the fashionable world, and see how the votaries of
pleasure spend their time. They go from one vanity to another, hoping that in a succession of amusements they shall find
a satisfaction which nothing else can impart. Plays, balls,
concerts, routs, the pleasures of the field, of the race-course, of
the card-table, form a certain round of employment, which those
who travel in it expect to find productive of happiness, of such
happiness at least as they affect. And this, I conceive, is what
Solomon intended particularly to reprobate as folly and madness. Of course, we must include also in the same description
the more vulgar amusements to which the lower classes resort.
All, according to their taste, or the means afforded them for
enjoyment, whilst they pursue the same object, are obnoxious
to the same censure. The degree of refinement which may be
in their pursuits makes no difference in this matter. Whatever

it be which calls forth their mirth and laughter, it is equally unprofitable and equally insane. So Solomon judged; and]

We now proceed—

II. To confirm his testimony—

Let us take a candid view of this matter: let us consider pleasure in its true light: let us consider its aspect on us,

1. As men—

[As men, we possess faculties of a very high order, which we ought to cultivate, and which, when duly improved, exalt and dignify our nature. But behold the votaries of pleasure; how low do they sink themselves by the depravity of their taste, and the emptiness of their occupations! A man devoid of wisdom may abound in mirth and laughter as well as he: and there will be found very little difference in their feelings; except, as the more enlarged men's capacities are for higher objects, the keener sense will they have of the emptiness of their vain pursuits. In truth, we may appeal even to themselves in confirmation of what Solomon has said: for there are no persons more convinced of the unsatisfying nature of such pursuits, than those who follow them with the greatest avidity. But let Scripture speak: " She that liveth in pleasure is dead whilst she liveth[c]." It is the fool alone that can say, " Let us eat, drink, and be merry[d]."]

2. As sinners—

[As sinners we have a great work to do; even to call to mind, and to mourn over, the sins of our whole lives, and to seek reconciliation with our offended God — — — The time, too, which is afforded us for this is very short and very uncertain — — — And, oh! what an issue awaits our present exertions; even heaven with all its glory, or hell with all its inconceivable and everlasting terrors! Have persons so circumstanced any time for mirth, or any disposition to waste their precious hours in laughter? Is it not much more suitable to them to be engaged according to the direction of St. James, " Be afflicted, and mourn, and weep; let *your laughter be turned to mourning*, and your joy to heaviness; humble yourselves in the sight of the Lord, and he shall lift you up[e]?" — — —]

3. As the redeemed of the Lord—

[What redeemed soul can contemplate the price paid for his redemption, and laugh? Go, my Brother, to Gethsemane, and see thy Saviour bathed in a bloody sweat. Go to Calvary, and behold him stretched upon the cross. Hear his heart-

[c] 1 Tim. v. 6.   [d] Luke xii. 19.   [e] Jam. iv. 9, 10.

rending cry, " My God! my God! why hast thou forsaken me?"
See the sun himself veiling his face in darkness, and the Lord
of glory bowing his head in death : and then tell me, whether
you feel much disposition for mirth and laughter? or whether
such a state of mind would become you? Methinks, I need
add no more. Your own consciences will attest the justice of
Solomon's remarks. But if there be an advocate for mirth yet
unconvinced, then I put it to him to answer that significant
question in my text, " What doeth it?"]

APPLICATION—

1. Are any disposed to complain that I make religion gloomy?

[Remember, it is of carnal mirth that I have spoken; and
of that, not in its occasional sallies, from a buoyancy of spirit,
and in combination with love, but of its being regarded as a
source of happiness, and of its constituting, as it were, a portion
of our daily employment. And if I wrest this from you, do I
leave you a prey to melancholy? Go to religion ; and see whether that do not furnish you with mirth and laughter of a purer
kind: with mirth that is not unprofitable, with laughter that
is not mad? The very end of the Gospel is, to "give you beauty
for ashes, the oil of joy for mourning, and the garment of praise
for the spirit of heaviness :" and if you believe in Christ, it is
not merely your privilege, but your duty to rejoice in him, yea,
to "rejoice in him with joy unspeakable and glorified." If the
Church, on account of temporal deliverances, could say, "Then
was our mouth filled with laughter, and our tongue with singing [f];" much more may you, on account of the salvation which
has been vouchsafed to you. Only, therefore, let the grounds
of your joy be right, and we consent that "your mourning be
turned into dancing, and that to the latest hour of your lives
you put off your sackcloth and gird you with gladness [g]."
Instead of pronouncing such mirth madness, we will declare it
to be your truest wisdom.]

2. Are there those amongst you who accord with
Solomon?

[Remember, then, to seek those as your associates who
are like-minded with you in this respect. Affect not the company of those who delight in laughter, and in carnal mirth;
for they will only draw you from God, and rob you of the
happiness which you might otherwise enjoy. If they appear
happy, remember that " their mirth is like the crackling of
thorns under a pot [h] :" it may make a blaze for a moment; but
it soon expires in spleen and melancholy. Be careful, too, to

[f] Ps. cxxvi. 1, 2.   [g] Ps. xxx. 11.   [h] Eccl. vii. 6.

live nigh to God, and in sweet communion with your Lord
and Saviour: for if you draw back from God in secret, you
will, in respect of happiness, be in a worse condition than the
world themselves: for whilst you deny yourselves the pleasure
which you might have in carnal things, you will have no real
pleasure in spiritual exercises. But be true to your principles,
and you never need envy the poor worldlings their vain enjoyments. They drink of a polluted cistern, that contains nothing
but what is insipid and injurious, and will prove fatal to their
souls; but you draw from the fountain of living waters, which
whosoever drinks of, shall live for ever.]

OUTLINE NO. 830

THE EXCELLENCY OF WISDOM.

Eccl. ii. 13. *Then I saw, that wisdom excelleth folly, as far as
light excelleth darkness.*

THE more exact is our scrutiny into the things
of this world, the more decided will be our judgment
respecting them. If persons ever think highly of
them, it is because they have never set down seriously
to examine their true character, or laboured to form
a right estimate respecting them. Solomon possessed
means of ascertaining their real value beyond any
other person that ever existed: for, possessing wisdom
above any other of the sons of men, he had a greater
capacity to extract all the sweetness that was in them;
and, being a monarch, he could command all things
through the whole range of nature, to present to
him their tribute of gratification according to their
respective abilities. But, after a minute examination
of every thing, he was constrained to give this, at
last, as the result of his experience: "Then I saw
that wisdom excelleth folly, as far as light excelleth
darkness."

Now this, I conceive, refers in part to *human* wisdom, as occupied in intellectual pursuits. For it is
certain, that amongst objects that relate only to this
present life, there is nothing to be compared with
this. Intellect is that which distinguishes man from
the brute creation; and the enlargement of it with
arts and sciences is that which elevates man above

his fellows. The cultivation of it is more suited to the dignity of man than the gratification of his sensual appetites; in all of which the beasts have as large a capacity of enjoyment as he. The pleasures arising from it are also less apt to cloy; and will endure, when a taste for other enjoyments is passed away. It will gratify, also, when it is not the object of immediate pursuit; because it will supply in reflection much of what it conferred in the actual acquisition. It is also of great use, and qualifies a man for conferring extensive benefits on the world; at the same time that it opens to him a thousand channels of pleasure which are utterly unknown to the unfurnished mind. A person habituated only to bodily exertion has no conception what a fund of satisfaction the exercises of the mind supply, or what delight attaches to the investigation of science and the discovery of truth. Corporeal indulgences, indeed, strike more strongly upon the senses; and therefore, to a carnal mind, seem to furnish a greater measure of delight. But the more eagerly they are sought, the less pleasure they afford; and they bring with them, for the most part, many painful consequences : so that, in comparison of intellectual pursuits, they deserve the name of " folly;" whilst the prosecution of *the other* may properly be called " wisdom." Yet it must be confessed, that there is much truth in that observation of Solomon, " In much wisdom is much grief : and he that increaseth knowledge increaseth sorrow[a]." For " much study is undoubtedly a weariness to the flesh[b]." and it is often followed by painful disappointment. I conceive, therefore, that we are by no means to limit the import of our text to *human* wisdom; but must extend it to that which is *divine :* in reference to which we may say, without any limitation or exception, " It excelleth folly, as far as light excelleth darkness."

Of this therefore, even of spiritual wisdom, I will now proceed to speak; and its transcendent excellence I will point out in reference to,

[a] Eccl. i. 18.   [b] Eccl. xii. 12.

Its own proper character—

"Wisdom" is another word for piety—

[Piety in the Scriptures is frequently called by this name. Job says, " The fear of the Lord *that* is wisdom[c]." And Moses prays, "So teach us to number our days, that we may apply our hearts unto wisdom[d]."

But, not to rest in a mere general definition of the term, I shall consider it as embracing these two points, *The receiving of the Gospel, as sinners ;* and *the adorning of it, as saints.*

The very first part of wisdom is to receive the Gospel of salvation into our hearts. We all need it; nor can any human being be saved without it; and God offers to us all the blessings of it, freely, without money and without price. Were we under a sentence of death from a human tribunal, and were offered mercy by the Prince, it would be accounted wisdom to accept the offer, and folly to reject it. How much more is it our wisdom to accept a deliverance from eternal death, together with all the glory and felicity of heaven! *This* must commend itself to every man who reflects but for a moment: and to despise these proffered benefits must, of necessity, be regarded as folly, bordering upon madness

The next part of wisdom must be, to adorn that Gospel by a holy life and conversation; since it cannot otherwise be ultimately of any avail for our acceptance with God. The very intent of the Gospel is to transform man into the Divine image, and thereby to prepare him for the enjoyment of his God; and if this be not attained, heaven itself would be no place of happiness to him. Indeed, if a man profess to embrace the Gospel, and yet continue to walk unworthy of it, he dishonours God far more than he could do whilst he made no such profession: for he " tramples under foot the Son of God, and counts the blood of the covenant an unholy thing, and does despite unto the Spirit of Grace[e];" yea, he crucifies the Son of God afresh, and puts him to an open shame[f]." I think, therefore, that the pursuit of holiness in all its branches, with an uniform endeavour to glorify our God, must commend itself to every considerate mind, as true " wisdom."]

And this far excelleth " folly"—

[I will not go into particulars to characterize "folly:" it shall suffice to take the most lenient view of it that can be imagined: I will comprehend under it no positive vice, nothing that can render it odious in the eyes of men: I will take it only in a negative view, as importing a neglect of the two foregoing dictates of sound wisdom. And now I will ask, Who does not see the superiority of wisdom; and that " it excelleth folly as

c Job xxviii. 28.   d Ps. xc. 12.   e Heb. x. 29.   f Heb. vi. 6.

far as light excelleth darkness?" "Darkness" hath nothing whatever to commend it: it is utterly destitute of every good quality: whereas "light is sweet, and a pleasant thing it is for the eyes to behold the sun[g]." And precisely thus does piety approve itself to every beholder; whilst a neglect of God presents nothing but gloom, the end of which no human imagination can reach.]

Let us view wisdom next,

II. In its influence on this present life—

There is not a moment of our lives over which it does not cast a benign influence—

[In bringing us to the foot of the Cross, it is the means of effecting our reconciliation with God, and of filling the soul with peace and joy——— In stirring us up to mortify our corruptions, it keeps us from innumerable snares to which others are exposed, and from troubles in which others are involved. *This* seems to have been particularly in Solomon's mind, when he penned the words of my text: for he adds immediately, "The wise man's eyes are in his head; but the fool walketh in darkness[h]." It conduces also most essentially to the benefit of all around us. It tends to check vice and wickedness in the world, and to promote virtue in every possible way. It calls forth all the acts and offices of love, both in the professor himself, and in all who come within the sphere of its influence. It greatly honours God too, and tends to the advancement of his kingdom upon earth. There is no end to the benefits of true wisdom: for, so far as it prevails and operates, it repairs the ruins of the Fall; and changes this wretched, miserable world into a very Paradise.]

In this respect, how widely different is "folly!"—

[See the world as it is, and then you will see what "folly" has done. Enter into the bosoms of men, and see how full they are of all hateful tempers and dispositions, and how utterly destitute of every thing like solid peace. See what jarrings it has introduced into society, insomuch that there is scarcely to be found a single family which is not more or less torn with disputes and disagreements. See what evils it diffuses on every side; and then say in what light it appears as compared with wisdom. I boldly ask, Does not wisdom excel it "as far as light excelleth darkness?" Darkness is suited to nothing but the deeds of darkness, and the sanguinary excursions of beasts of prey: whereas light administers to the welfare of all, and enables every member of society to execute his functions for the good of the whole: so that in this respect, also, the comparison is fitly made.]

[g] Eccl. xi. 7.　　　　[h] ver. 14.

But let us trace " wisdom" yet further,

III. In its effects upon the eternal world—

[It is here that the great excellence of wisdom will be chiefly found. If there were no future state, folly might, with some *semblance* of truth, compete with wisdom, because its gratifications are so strong to the organs of sense. But, when we view the aspect of wisdom upon eternity, and reflect that every one of its dictates has a direct tendency to fit the soul for heaven and to augment its eternal bliss, whilst the operations of folly have a directly opposite bearing, all competition between them vanishes; since heaven and hell might as well bear a comparison as they. In truth, the light of heaven and its glory afford a just illustration of the one; whilst " the blackness of darkness " in the regions of hell gives but too just a portrait of the other. The one brings us to the divine image; the other reduces us to the likeness of beasts and devils: the one ensures to us the everlasting fruition of our God; the other entails upon us his everlasting displeasure. In requiring you, therefore, to receive the declaration of my text, that " Wisdom excelleth folly as far as light excelleth darkness," I do nothing but what every conscience must assent to, and every judgment approve.]

Permit me, then, in conclusion to ASK,

1. What is the judgment you have already formed?

[I know that in theory you will all accede to this statement. But what has been your *practical* judgment? If we look at your lives, what will *they* attest to have been your views of this subject? Has wisdom *there* shone, and folly been put to shame? Have you really been living with a view to the eternal world, embracing the Gospel thankfully as sinners, and adorning it as saints. I ask not what *"you have said"* with your lips, but what *" you have said"* in your lives. It is not by your professions, but by your practice, that God will judge you; and therefore it is by that standard that you must judge yourselves — — —]

2. What is the conduct you intend hereafter to pursue ?

[The world, I acknowledge, gives its voice in direct opposition to the foregoing statement. It represents religion as folly, and the prosecution of carnal enjoyments as wisdom. But its " calling good evil, and evil good," will not change their respective natures: nor, if the whole world should unite in putting darkness for light, or light for darkness, will either of them lose its own qualities, and assume those of the other. " Sweet" will be sweet, and " bitter" bitter, whether men will believe it or not[i]. Will you then go contrary to the convictions of your own minds, in compliment to an ungodly world? Or will you, for fear of offending them, sacrifice the interests of your immortal souls? I call upon you to seek " wisdom, which is more to be chosen than fine gold[k]." Let your whole life declare its value, and be a standing testimony against the folly of the ungodly. So shall you have in this world a sweet experience of my text, and enjoy an ample confirmation of it in the world above.]

[i] Isai. v. 20.   [k] Prov. xvi. 16.

OUTLINE NO. 831

THE DIFFERENT PORTIONS OF THE RIGHTEOUS AND WICKED.

Eccl. ii. 26. *God giveth to a man that is good in his sight, wisdom, and knowledge, and joy : but to the sinner he giveth travail.*

IN relation to earthly things, men run into two opposite extremes: some seeking their happiness altogether in the enjoyment of them; and others denying themselves the proper and legitimate use of them, in order that they may amass wealth for some future possessor. But both of these classes are unwise: the former, in that they look for that in the creature which is not to be found in it ; and the latter, in that, without any adequate reason, they deprive themselves of comforts which God has designed them to enjoy. A temperate use of the good things of this life is no where forbidden : on the contrary, " there is," as Solomon informs us, " nothing better for a man, than that he should eat and drink, and that he should make his soul enjoy good in his labour." Doubtless this concession must be taken with certain restrictions ; for we are not to spend all our substance on ourselves, but to be doing good with it to others : nor are we to suppose that our life consists in the abundance of the things that we possess, but to be seeking our happiness in God. That which alone will impart solid happiness, is religion : for to the good man God giveth what shall render him truly blessed ; namely, " wisdom, and knowledge, and joy : but to the sinner he giveth travail."

From these words I shall take occasion to shew you,

I. The different portions of the righteous and the wicked—

The world may be divided into two denominations; the righteous, and the wicked.

" To the righteous, God gives wisdom, and knowledge, and joy"—

[As to carnal wisdom, I am not sure that the wicked have not in general the advantage; as it is said, " The children of this world are in their generation wiser than the children of light[a]." But the godly have a discernment of earthly things, or, as my text expresses it, a " wisdom and knowledge" in relation to them, which no ungodly man has ever attained. The godly see the true use of worldly things; and how they may be rendered conducive to the honour of God, and the good of the soul. As instruments for advancing the welfare of mankind, they may be desired and employed to good effect: and in this mode of using them God will confer real and abiding " joy." Even the portion of them which is consumed upon ourselves will be relished with a richer zest; for " God has given us all things richly to enjoy:" but the thought of honouring God with them, and benefiting mankind, will give to them a kind of sanctified enjoyment, of such as was received from the harvest of which the first-fruits had been duly consecrated to the Lord[b]. The good man does not merely enjoy the things themselves: he enjoys God in them; and, in so doing, has the " testimony of his own conscience that he pleases God." Nor is he unconscious that he is laying up treasure in heaven, even " bags which wax not old, and a treasure which never faileth[c]."]

" To the sinner," on the other hand, " he giveth travail"—

[A man who neglects his God, can find no happiness in earthly things: in his pursuit of them, he is filled with care, which robs him of all real comfort[d]: in his enjoyment of them, they prove empty and cloying, " his very laughter being only as the crackling of thorns under a pot:" and, his mind being alienated from God, he has no source of peace from religion. Truly " the way of transgressors is hard[e];" or rather I must say, as the Scripture does, " Destruction and misery are in their ways[f]." Remarkable is that declaration of Zophar, " In the midst of their sufficiency they are in straits[g]." And if this be their state in the midst of life and health, what must it be in a time of sickness and death? Most true is that declaration of Solomon: " What profit hath he that hath laboured for the

---

[a] Luke xvi. 18.   [b] Luke xi. 41.
[c] Luke xii. 33, 34.   1 Tim. vi. 19.   [d] See ver. 22, 23.
[e] Prov. xiii. 15.   [f] Rom. iii. 16, 17.   [g] Job xx. 22.

wind? All his days he eateth in darkness, and he hath much sorrow and wrath with his sickness[h]."

Thus, whilst the blessing of the Lord is upon the righteous, seeing that, whatever he bestow, " he addeth no sorrow with it[i];" he mixes gall and wormwood with the sinner's cup, and " infuses a curse into his choicest blessings."]

Let us now notice,

II. The hand of God, as displayed in them—

It is said in relation to both the righteous and the wicked, that " *God giveth* to them" their respective portions: both the one and the other are " *from the hand of God*[k]." In them we see,

1. The true nature of his moral government—

[Even now is there far more of equity in the dispensations of God than a superficial observer would imagine. Doubtless there is a great difference in the states of different men; but the rich and great have troubles of which the poor and destitute have very little conception. The very state of mind fostered by their distinctions is by no means favourable to their happiness; and the habits of the poor so inure them to privations, that they feel much less trouble from them than one would imagine. But let piety enter into any soul; and we hesitate not to declare, that though he were a Lazarus at the Rich Man's gate, he were happier far than the man of opulence by whose crumbs he was fed. Peace of mind, arising from a sense of reconciliation with God, and a hope of final acceptance with him, is sufficient to weigh down all that an ungodly man ever did, or could, possess. And " the poorest man, if rich in faith and an heir of God's kingdom," is more to be envied than the greatest monarch upon earth, who possesses not real piety.

But with equity, goodness also is observable in all the dispensations of Providence. That God is good to the great and opulent, will be readily acknowledged: but he is so to the sinner, whom he leaves to experience the most painful disappointments. If a mother embitter to her child the breast on which he would fondly live, it is that he may learn to affect a more substantial diet: and if God, after all the labour which men put forth to render the creature a source of comfort, cause it to become to them only as " a broken cistern that can hold no water," it is only that they may the more readily turn to him, and seek him, as " the fountain of living waters."]

2. The certain issue of his future judgment—

[Is there, even in this world, " a difference put between him who serveth God, and him who serveth him not?" Much

[h] Eccl. v. 16, 17.   [i] Prov. x. 22.   [k] ver. 24.

more shall that be found in the day which is especially set apart for the display of God's righteous judgments. The Prophet Isaiah, as God's herald, received this awful commission: " Say ye to the righteous, that it shall be well with him: for they shall eat the fruit of their doings. But woe unto the wicked! it shall be ill with him: for the reward of his deeds shall be given him[1]." And this do we also proclaim. For the righteous is reserved a state of unutterable joy; but for the wicked, a state of utter exclusion from the realms of bliss, " in the lake that burneth with fire and brimstone," " where is weeping, and wailing, and gnashing of teeth." If the present inequalities of his dispensations lead us to expect this, much more does that previous distribution of good and evil which is even now accorded to men in correspondence with their moral habits. What is at this moment felt in the minds of the different characters, may well teach us what to expect in the day of judgment; even a separation of the righteous and the wicked; the one to everlasting fire; and the other to everlasting life, and blessedness, and glory.]

Let me now, from this subject, RECOMMEND,

1. Religion in general—

[It is this which makes the chief difference between different men. The prince on his throne, and the beggar on the dunghill, are but little apart in comparison of " the good" and " the sinner." Piety sets men asunder, as far as light from darkness, heaven from hell. Let those then amongst you, who would be happy either here or hereafter, give yourselves up to God, and approve yourselves to him. Only be " good in his sight," and happiness will be yours, both in time and in eternity.]

2. A due improvement of all that you possess—

[To squander it away in self-indulgence, or to hoard it for some future possessor, will be alike foolish and vain. Neither of these modes of employing wealth can ever make you happy. The serving of God, and the benefiting of your fellow-creatures, will, on the contrary, bring peace and joy into the soul: for " the work of righteousness is peace, and the effect of righteousness is quietness and assurance for ever." Not that any liberality of yours can ever form a ground of hope before God in a way of *merit:* all that you have is the Lord's: and it is only of *his own* that you give him: but if you are seeking righteousness and salvation by Christ alone, then will your works be accepted for Christ's sake: and whatever you dispose of for the advancement of his glory, he will acknowledge it as " lent to him, and he will pay you again." The talents that are improved for him, shall receive, in due proportion, a recompence at his hands.]

[1] Isai. iii. 10, 11.

OUTLINE NO. 832

DUTY OF PAYING OUR VOWS.

Eccl. v. 4, 5, *When thou vowest a vow unto God, defer not to pay it; for he hath no pleasure in fools: pay that which thou hast vowed. Better is it that thou shouldest not vow, than that thou shouldest vow and not pay.*

THE offering of vows was extremely common under the Mosaic dispensation; and many laws were instituted in relation to them. By them persons bound themselves to the performance of certain things which were not specifically appointed of God. Some were conditional, and depended on some mercy which should be previously bestowed by God[a]: and others were absolute, and to be performed by the persons at all events. Respecting vows made by persons who were under the government of others, especial provision was made, under what circumstances, and to what extent, they should be binding[b]. In cases where the vows themselves were not lawful, the person sinned, whether he performed them or not[c]; and in some cases at least, the violation of them was less criminal than the observance[d]: but where they were not in themselves contrary to any command of God, there they were to be punctually fulfilled, and without delay.

We propose, on the present occasion, to consider,

I. The vows which you have made[e]—

These are doubtless very comprehensive—

[The things promised *for* us in our baptism, are contained under the following heads: first, that we should "renounce the devil and all his works, the pomps and vanities of this wicked world, and all the sinful lusts of the flesh: next, that we should believe all the articles of the Christian faith: and lastly, that we should keep God's holy will and commandments, and walk in the same all the days of our life." In our confirmation we take these vows upon ourselves. Let us consider them distinctly———Let us often revolve them in our minds, and cry

---

[a] Gen. xxviii. 20—22. 1 Sam. i. 11.   [b] Numb. xxx. 3—15.
[c] ver. 6.   [d] Matt. xiv. 6—10. Acts xxiii. 12.
[e] This is intended for an Address *after* Confirmation; but may be easily changed to a Preparatory Address.

mightily to God for grace to assist us in the performance of them: for "who is sufficient for these things f?" — — —]

But the duties to which they bind us are highly reasonable—

[We universally consider children as bound to obey their parents, and servants their masters: but what parent has such a claim upon us as God, since from him we derive our whole existence and support? "in him we live and move and have our being:" or what master is entitled to such an unreserved compliance with his will, as God, whom all the angels in heaven obey? God himself founds his claim to our allegiance upon these very principles; "A son honoureth his father, and a servant his master: if I then be a Father, where is mine honour? and if I be a Master, where is my fear? saith the Lord of Hosts g." And indeed the most unrestricted devotion of all our faculties to his service is expressly called by him, not only an acceptable, but a *reasonable* service h.]

These duties are binding upon us independently of any vows which we may make respecting them—

[They arise from our very relation to God as his creatures, and more especially as his redeemed people. The potter is undoubtedly entitled to the use of the vessels which his own hands have formed. Even if our services were ever so painful, we should have no right to complain: "the thing formed could not, under any circumstances, presume to say to him that formed it, Why hast thou made me thus i?" But, as we have before observed, the whole of what we have taken upon ourselves is a truly reasonable service: and therefore it would be the height of impiety to hesitate for a moment in giving up ourselves unreservedly to God.

But God has redeemed us also, and that too by the blood of his only dear Son; "We are not our own; we are bought with a price; and therefore we are bound from this considera-tion also to glorify God with our bodies and our spirits, which are his." It is not optional with us, whether we will surrender to him what he has so dearly purchased: we cannot alienate it, we cannot withhold it; whether we make any vow respecting it, or not, we are equally bound to employ all our faculties for God: and the only reason we wish you to take these vows upon you is, not to increase your obligations to serve him, much less

f It would be easy to divide this subject into three or four; closing the first at this place; making the remaining part of this head into a second; forming the second head into a third sermon; and the concluding address into a fourth.

g Mal. i. 6.   h Rom. xii. 1.   i Rom. ix. 20.

to create obligations which did not exist before, but to impress your own minds with a sense of those duties which are indissolubly connected with every child of man.]

But to bind ourselves to these things by solemn vows is a duty truly and properly evangelical—

[Some would imagine this to be a *legal* act: and if we were to engage in it with a view to establish a righteousness of our own, or with an idea of performing our duties in our own strength, it would then indeed be *legal:* but if, in humble dependence on divine aid, we devote ourselves to God, it is no other act than that which God himself has specified as characterizing his people under the Gospel dispensation[k]. The very manner in which this act shall be performed is also specified; and it is particularly foretold, that all who are duly influenced by Gospel principles shall animate one another to the performance of it[l].]

Such then are the vows which we have made : they are comprehensive indeed, but highly reasonable, and relating only to things which are in themselves necessary; and the making of which is as much a duty under the Gospel dispensation, as ever it was under the Law.

We now proceed to notice,

II. The importance of performing them—

But how shall this be painted in any adequate terms ? In it is bound up,

1. Our comfort in life—

[Many foolishly imagine, that a life devoted unto God must be one continued scene of melancholy. But is not the very reverse declared in Scripture ? " The work of righteousness is peace," says the prophet: and "the effect of righteousness is quietness and assurance for ever." Yes, " Godliness has the promise of the life that now is, as well as of that which is to come: and we will venture to appeal to the consciences of all, whether even the greatest despisers of religion do not think that truly pious people are happier than they ? In the very nature of things it must be, that they who are delivered from the tyranny of their lusts are happier than those who are yet bond-slaves of sin and Satan : their minds must be more tranquil, and their consciences more serene. But if we take into the account, that God "will manifest himself to his faithful servants as he does not unto the world," and " shed abroad his love in

[k] Isai. xix. 21.   [l] Jer. l. 4, 5.

their hearts," and " fill them with a peace that passeth understanding, and joy that is unspeakable," we can have no doubt
but that religion's ways are ways of pleasantness," and that
" *in* keeping God's commandments there is great reward."   In
proof of this, we need only see with what delight David contemplated the paying of his vows to God[m]: and the more we
resemble him in the ardour of his piety, the more shall we
resemble him also in the sublimity of his joys.]

2. Our hope in death—

[What must be the prospects of an ungodly man in his
dying hour?   When he looks back upon all his duties neglected, all his vows broken, and his eternal interests sacrificed
to the things of time and sense, what must he think of the
state to which he is hastening?   He may try to comfort himself with his own vain delusions; but he will feel a secret
consciousness that he is building on the sand.   Hence it is,
that those who will not give themselves up to God, are so
averse to hear of death and judgment: they know that, if the
Scriptures be true, and God be such a God as he is there
represented, they have nothing to expect but wrath and fiery
indignation.   It is the godly only who can feel composed and
happy in the near approach of death: they, when the time of
their departure is at hand, can look forward with joy to " that
crown of glory which the Lord, the righteous Judge, shall give
them."   " Mark the perfect man, and behold the upright; for
the end of that man is peace."]

3. Our welfare in eternity—

[" God will surely put a difference between those who
served him here, and those who served him not."   Hear what
Solomon says to us in the text: "When thou vowest a vow
unto God, defer not to pay it: for *God hath no pleasure in
fools*."   No indeed; God can have no pleasure in those who
never delighted themselves in him.   How is it possible that he
should receive to his bosom those who spent their whole lives
in rebellion against him?   He shews his abhorrence of them
by the very name whereby he designates them in the words
before us: he calls them "fools," and will leave them to reap
the bitter fruits of their folly.   We may see how indignant
God was against Zedekiah for violating a covenant whereby he
had engaged to hold the kingdom of Judah as tributary to the
king of Babylon[n].   What indignation then must he feel against
those who have violated all their engagements with *him!*   If
the neglect of vows made by compulsion to an oppressive enemy
be so criminal, what must be the neglect of vows voluntarily

---

[m] Ps. xxii. 25. and lxvi. 13, 14.
[n] Ezek. xvii. 11—21.   Cite the whole of this.

made to the Most High God! But we need not collect this in a way of inference; for God himself has expressly told us, that we *must* pay our vows to him; that we must do it *without delay;* that if we defer to pay them, it will be imputed to us as a most heinous *sin;* and that *he will surely require* it at our hands [o]. And in the text itself he tells us, that however criminal it must be to feel such alienation of heart from God as not to vow any vow to him, "it were better for us never to vow at all than to vow and not pay."]

ADDRESS—

1. The young who have been just confirmed—

[Remember, I beseech you, that "the vows of God are upon you." And now hear what Almighty God says unto you: "If a man vow a vow unto the Lord, or swear an oath to bind his soul with a bond, he shall not break his word; he shall do according to all that proceedeth out of his mouth [p]." Now you, my Beloved, have "bound your souls with a bond;" you have "sworn unto the Lord, and cannot go back:" remember then that you "must not break your word;" you *must,* you "*shall* do according to *all* that has proceeded out of your mouths." O bear in mind the particular vows which you have made [q], and set yourselves diligently to the performance of them. See how determined David was, under your circumstances [r]; and make him the model of your conduct. And begin now without delay to prepare for attending on the Lord's Supper. *Your Confirmation is but a step to something beyond,* even to a dedication of yourselves to God at the table of the Lord. I mean not that you are to be hasty in taking this further step; because you ought doubtless to be well instructed in the nature of that ordinance before you partake of it; and to be fully determined through grace to live, not unto yourselves, but unto Him who died for you. But that you should keep this in view, and with all convenient speed renew at the Lord's table the vows which you have now made, the holy Psalmist informs you [s]: and his resolutions on the subject I earnestly recommend for your adoption.]

2. The elder part of this audience—

[To you the younger will look for instruction and encouragement in the ways of God. But many who desire to have their children confirmed, would actually oppose them if they should begin to execute their vows. If a young person should begin to renounce the world, to mortify the flesh, and to live by faith on the Son of God, the generality of persons

[o] Deut. xxiii. 21—23.　　[p] Numb. xxx. 2.
[q] See the Catechism.　　[r] Ps. cxix. 106.
[s] Ps. cxvi. 12—14, 16—19. Particularly notice ver. 16.

would rather be alarmed than comforted, and would exert
their influence to divert his thoughts from such ways. But
beware how any of you put a stumbling-block in the way of
your children, either by your influence or example. Beware
how, after having instigated them to vow unto the Lord, you
tempt them to forget and violate their vows. Rather take
occasion from the confirmation of your children to look back
upon your own conduct, and to see how you have kept your
own vows. Do not imagine that a lapse of years can make
any difference in your obligations to serve the Lord, or that,
because you have forgotten your vows, God has forgot them
too : they are all written in the book of his remembrance ; and
every word which we have addressed to the young people in
reference to this matter, is applicable to you ; yea, to you it
applies with double force, because your more advanced age
qualifies you so much better to see and follow the path of
duty. I call upon you then to watch over your children, and
to promote, by every possible means, their progress in the
divine life. Encourage them to read the Scriptures diligently,
to give themselves much to meditation and prayer, and to
commence in earnest that race, which must be run by all
who would obtain the prize.]

OUTLINE NO. 833

THE HOUSE OF MOURNING TO BE PREFERRED.

Eccl. vii. 4. *The heart of the wise is in the house of mourning;
but the heart of fools is in the house of mirth.*

IN order to learn what loss we have sustained in
our intellectual powers through the introduction of sin
into the world, it is not necessary for us to investigate
the *mysteries* of our holy religion, which exceed the
comprehension of any finite intelligence : we need
only look to the *ethics* that are revealed to us in God's
blessed word; and we shall see, even in them, that
darkness has veiled the human mind, and there is an
utter contrariety between the sentiments of fallen man
and the plainest declarations of Almighty God. Take,
for instance, the declarations which precede my text:
" The day of death is better than the day of one's
birth. It is better to go to the house of mourning,
than to go to the house of feasting :" and " sorrow is
better than laughter." Will any one say that these
apophthegms are agreeable to the general appre-

hension of mankind? Is there not, on the contrary, something in them extremely paradoxical, and, at first sight, almost absurd? Yet are these sentiments unquestionably true, as are those also which my text records: "The heart of the wise is in the house of mourning; but the heart of fools is in the house of mirth."

It shall be my endeavour,

I. To confirm these different positions—

It is not Solomon's intention to say, that a wise man can never go to the house of mirth, any more than that a fool may not sometimes go to the house of mourning. The question is not, To which of the places these different characters may occasionally go; but, *To which of them their " hearts" are inclined.* Let us then inquire,

1. Where is the heart of the wise?

[We hesitate not to say, that a man who is taught of God, and made wise unto salvation, has "his heart in the house of mourning;" and *that* for the following reasons:

First, because *he there learns the most invaluable lessons.* There he sees what is the lot of fallen man; "He is born to trouble, as the sparks fly upward." He sees, also, what may speedily become his own lot; for "he knows not what a day or an hour may bring forth." He sees how vain and empty are all earthly things; in that not all the wealth or honour that ever was possessed by man can either avert calamity, or assuage the pain arising from it. Above all, he sees the excellence of true religion, which can apply a balm to every wound, and turn tribulation itself into an occasion for joy[a].

Next, his heart is in the house of mourning, because *there he has scope for the exercise of the finest feelings of his soul.* There is compassion excited towards his suffering fellow-creature, and sympathy with him in his afflictions. True, these feelings are in some respects painful: but there is in them something so exquisite and refined, that they afford, if I may so speak, the sublimest pleasure of which the human mind is capable; and assimilate us, in a very eminent degree, to our God and Saviour, who "is touched with the feeling of our infirmities[b]," and "in all our afflictions is himself afflicted[c]." Nor can the sufferings of a fellow-creature be seen without exciting in our bosoms thanksgivings to God, who has been pleased to withhold

---

[a] Rom. v. 3.   [b] Heb. iv. 15.   [c] Isai. lxiii. 9.

his chastening rod from us, and to make us his honoured instruments of imparting comfort to our afflicted brethren. This also, though not attended with any ebullition of joy, is a very sublime and delightful feeling; not unlike to that of Joseph, when his bowels yearned upon his brother Benjamin, and a prospect was opened to him of making his own advancement an occasion of benefit to his whole family: "He made haste, and sought where to weep; and entered into his chamber, and wept there[d]."

A still further reason why his heart is in the house of mourning is, that *there he meets, and enjoys, and honours God.* God has said, that "he meeteth those who rejoice in working righteousness[e]." And, truly, he fulfils this word in a more especial manner to those who abound in works of mercy, because he considers himself as the object of that love, wherever it be exercised, and in whatsoever it be employed[f]. I will appeal to those who have frequented the house of mourning, whether they have not often found God more present with them there, than even in their own chamber. In truth, God is honoured there with more than common tributes of acknowledgment. There is he referred to as the All-wise Disposer of all events, and as the gracious Father that corrects only in love and for his people's good. There, too, is he set forth in all his glorious perfections, and especially in all the wonders of redeeming love: and there is he invariably set forth as the author of the very good which is at that hour dispensed to the troubled soul; so that the creature, his instrument, is overlooked, and he alone is glorified.

Say then, Brethren, whether here be not ample reason for the preference shewn to "the house of mourning:" and whether he be not truly wise, whose heart has dictated such a choice as this?

In contrast with this, we ask,]

2. Where is the heart of the fool?

[It is "in the house of mirth." And why? One reason is, that *there he is enabled to forget himself.* Men do not like to reflect upon their own state before God: and they account any thing desirable, which can dispel unwelcome thoughts, and furnish a pleasing occupation for their minds. Hence it is that all places of amusement are so thronged: and even the house of God is made to administer to our satisfaction; the irksomeness of prayer being rendered tolerable by the fascinations of music, and the charms of eloquence. Hence, too, every one who can devise a new expedient for preventing time from hanging heavy on our hands, will be sure to gain our patronage, and be welcomed and rewarded as a public benefactor.

[d] Gen. xliii. 29, 30.   [e] Isai. lxiv. 5.   [f] Matt. xxv. 35, 36.

Another reason is, that the fool *there finds what is most gra-tifying to his corrupt taste.* One has an appetite for conviviality and licentiousness: another affects the more decent gratifica-tions of music, and dancing, and such like: another, more elevated in the scale of being, desires rather the intellectual and refined pleasures of science and philosophy. But each is an epicure in his way; and, though their pursuits be different, each in his own line is as insatiable as the other. He is never weary of his favourite pursuit. He desires to be amused; and makes the gratification of his own particular taste the end of all his studies and pursuits. In a word, he lives only to have his own taste gratified, and to administer to the gratification of those who are like-minded with himself: and wherever he can attain these ends, there his heart is, and there his most select abode.

But there is yet another reason for his preference; and that is, that " in the house of mirth" *he finds himself countenanced in his neglect of God.* Every man has a secret consciousness that he ought to seek after God in the first place, and to post-pone to that every other duty and enjoyment. But when he sees others as remiss in this duty as himself, he comforts him-self with the thought, that he is no worse than others; and with the hope, that God will never mark with his displeasure what is so generally regarded as innocent and inoffensive. At all events, he finds nothing to reproach him *there.* " In a house of mourning" he would see many things repugnant to his habits; for even a fool *there* puts on, for the time, the semblance of wisdom; and assents to the truth, that the care of the soul is the one thing needful. But " in the house of mirth," all that he either hears or sees bids him to be of good courage, and not to question for a moment the approbation of his Judge.]

I think that the positions in my text are now made sufficiently clear; so that we may with propriety proceed,

II. To point out their bearing on the Christian's life and conversation—

These principles may doubtless be pressed too far: and they are then carried to excess, when they are regarded as prohibiting all friendly intercourse with the ungodly world: for our blessed Saviour himself honoured with his company a wedding feast, and a feast, too, that was provided for him by an ignorant and unhumbled Pharisee. But, taking these different positions with such a latitude as both reason and Scripture will fairly admit, the least that we should learn from them is,

1. To be on our guard against acquiescing too easily in popular opinions—

[From the positions which we have just considered, the carnal mind revolts. Yet, not only are these positions confirmed by our blessed Lord, but they are expressed by him in far stronger terms than by Solomon himself. " Blessed are ye poor : blessed are ye that hunger now : blessed are ye that weep now : blessed are ye when men shall hate you, and when they shall separate you from their company, and shall reproach you, and cast out your name as evil, for the Son of Man's sake. But woe unto you that are rich : woe unto you that are full : woe unto you that laugh now : woe unto you when all men shall speak well of you[g]." It is obvious that light and darkness are scarcely more opposite than these declarations are to the sentiments and habits of the world at large. But are we therefore to question the truth of them, or to refuse submission to them ? No : we are to regard the Scriptures as the only authorized standard of opinion ; and to them must our sentiments be conformed. Even if the whole world combine to reprobate what the Scriptures enjoin, we must not be deterred from following what God prescribes ; but must boldly say, " Let God be true, but every man a liar[h]."]

2. To take eternity into our estimate of present things—

[In the passage just cited from the Sermon on the Mount, we see that every declaration of our blessed Lord is founded on the aspect which our present state has upon the eternal world. And I would ask, What would the Rich Man and Lazarus now think of the condition in which they were severally placed when in this lower world ? Would carnal mirth be commended by the one, or temporal distress be deprecated by the other, in such terms as the spectators of their widely different condition were once wont to use respecting them ? Methinks the enjoyments and sufferings of time would be deemed by them scarcely worthy of a thought ; and eternity would swallow up every other consideration. And so it will be with *us*, ere long. Indeed, even at this present moment, every man's conscience bears witness to this truth, however in the habits of his life he may contradict it. I cannot therefore but entreat all to consider what will be their views of present things, when they shall have left this transient scene ; and to regulate their judgment now by what they believe to be the uniform tenour of God's word, and the full conviction of every creature, whether in heaven or in hell.]

[g] Luke vi. 20—26.   [h] Rom. iii. 4.

3. To examine well the tendencies and inclinations of our hearts—

[In the prospect of death and judgment, men may be led to adopt sentiments which they do not cordially approve, and to follow a conduct in which they have no delight. I ask not, then, what you either say or do under such circumstances. I ask not whether you put a force upon your inclinations, abstaining from indulgences in which you would be glad to revel, and performing services from which you would gladly be excused: I ask, What are the pursuits which *your heart* affects? What is your real and predominant *taste?* and what is the employment in which you chiefly delight? I need not say what would be the taste of an angel, if he were sent to sojourn here; nor need I tell you what was the taste of our blessed Saviour and his holy Apostles: of these things no one of you can entertain a doubt. This, then, I say, Seek now to be, what ere long you will wish you had been: seek to be *in heart*, what you are bound to be *in act*. It is by the inward dispositions of your souls that you will be judged in the last day. What if, like Doeg, you were " detained before the Lord," if yet you had no pleasure in the service of your God? Would your worship be pleasing and acceptable to God? No; "your heart must be right with him," if you would either please him here, or be accepted of him hereafter. To every one of you, therefore, I say, Inquire not where your bodies are, but where your hearts; " for as a man thinketh in his heart, so is he[i]."]

4. To conform ourselves to the suggestions offered in our text—

[Let not any one think them too strong, or that the conduct which they recommend is too self-denying. I have already shewn, that the same things are spoken by Christ himself; and I must further observe, that the whole tenour of God's blessed word suggests and enjoins the same. " Love not the world, neither the things that are in the world: if any man love the world, the love of the Father is not in him: for all that is in the world, the lust of the flesh, the lust of the eye, and the pride of life, is not of the Father, but is of the world[k]." What is there " in the house of mirth " which is not here proscribed? Again: " God forbid that I should glory, save in the cross of our Lord Jesus Christ, by whom (or by which) the world is crucified unto me, and I unto the world[l]." Think at how low a rate the world esteems an object that is crucified, and a man, in the very article of death upon a cross, affects all that the world could give him. Surely, if these and other passages of the same tendency be duly weighed, there will be no difficulty

---

[i] Prov. xxiii. 7.   [k] 1 John ii. 15, 16.   [l] Gal. vi. 14,

in apprehending the true import of my text, nor any doubt upon our minds, which of the two objects before us should be preferred.   Let this preference, then, be seen in the whole of of our life and conversation.   I say not, that we should never *go to* " the house of mirth;" but only that, *our heart should not be there ;* and that, if called there by any peculiar occurrence, we should go, not as those that would be at home there, but as physicians to a hospital, where they desire to do all the good they can, but are glad to come away again, and to breathe a purer atmosphere.

Well do I know that it is not in the power of all to visit the abodes of misery, and to spend their time in administering to the necessities of the poor.   But, where these offices can be performed consistently with the duties of our own peculiar sphere, they are most pleasing in the sight of God, and not a little profitable to our own souls[m] — — — But those who cannot embark to any extent in the office of visiting the afflicted, may yet facilitate the execution of it in others by their liberal contributions[n] — — — And if, from the peculiarity of our engagements, we are so circumstanced that we cannot personally frequent " the house of mourning," let us at least shew that *our hearts are there;* and that we have no occupation more congenial with our minds, than to "rejoice with them that rejoice, and weep with them that weep."]

[m] If this were preached in behalf of *a Benevolent Society*, an appeal might here be made to those engaged in it, whether they have not experienced the truth of Prov. xi. 25. and Isai. lvii. 10, 11.

[n] Here, whether the Institution be of a public or private nature, a statement may be made of the methods pursued, and of the good done.

OUTLINE NO. 834
CONTENTMENT RECOMMENDED.

Eccl. vii. 10.   *Say not thou, What is the cause that the former days were better than these? for thou dost not inquire wisely concerning this.*

IN the writings of Solomon we find many maxims, which, if uttered by an uninspired man, would be controverted; but to which, as suggested by inspiration from God, we submit without gainsaying.   That which is delivered in the passage before us does not, at first sight, carry its own evidence along with it : but the more it is investigated, the more will it appear to be a dictate of sound wisdom, and worthy of universal acceptation.   That we may derive from it the full benefit which it is calculated to impart, let us consider,

I. What is the inquiry which is here discouraged—

It is not *every* comparison of existing circumstances with the past, that is here reprobated—

[In many situations we may, with the utmost propriety, institute an inquiry into the reasons of any change which may have taken place. A man, in relation to *his own temporal concerns*, would be very unwise if he neglected to do so. Suppose, for instance, his business, which was formerly in a very prosperous state, have failed, can we condemn him for inquiring into the occasion of that failure? Should we not think him worthy of severe blame, if he did not labour to find out the cause of this change in his circumstances; in order, if possible, to apply a remedy before it was too late? — — — Nor is all inquiry precluded in relation to *the concerns of the nation.* If there have been a plain and visible decline in the national prosperity, all who are affected by it are entitled, with modesty, to inquire whence that decline has arisen; and to express to those who are in authority their sentiments respecting it; and to point out what they conceive to be the most judicious and effectual means of remedying the existing evils — — — In reference to *the concerns of the soul*, to neglect such inquiries would be the height of folly and wickedness. Suppose a person to have formerly walked with God, and experienced much of His presence in his soul, and now to have become destitute of all spiritual life and comfort; should not he ask, "Wherefore were the former days better than these?" Yes: to examine into this matter is his bounden duty. The Apostle says, "Let a man examine himself:" and the Lord Jesus counsels the Ephesian Church, "when they had left their first love, to remember from whence they had fallen, and to repent, and do their first works[a]." So that it is clear, that the prohibition respecting such inquiries is not universal, but must be limited to such occasions as Solomon had more especially in view.]

The comparisons which are here discouraged, are those which are the mere effusions of discontent—

[In every age, discontented men have been forward to make this inquiry; "What is the cause that the former days were better than these?" They make no endeavour to ascertain the correctness of their sentiments; but, taking for granted that they are right, they demand the reason of so strange a phenomenon. Now it is a curious fact, that this is the habit of discontented men in every age. Those who are now advanced in life, can remember, that, in their early days, the very same clamour was made by discontented men as at this hour: and,

a Rev. ii. 5.

if we go back to every preceding generation, we shall find the same complaints respecting the deterioration of the times : but we shall never arrive at that time, when the people confessed themselves to be in that exalted state in which our imaginations place them. Certainly, if ever there was a time and a place that might be specified as that happy æra when there was no occasion for complaint, it was the state of the Jews in the days of Solomon : for, in respect of peace and prosperity, there never was a nation to be compared with the Jews at that time. Yet, behold, it was *at that time, and under those circumstances*, that the reproof was given : " Say not *thou*, What is the cause that the former times were better than these?" Hence, then, we see what is the inquiry which Solomon discourages : it is that which has no just foundation, and which is the offspring of spleen and discontent.]

These distinctions being duly adverted to, we are prepared to see,

II. Why the making of it is unwise—

I will assign two reasons : it is unwise, because,

1. It is erroneous in its origin—

[It is not true that former times, on a large and extended scale, were better than these. Improvements may have been made in some respects, and matters may have been deteriorated in others; or particular persons and places may be in less favourable circumstances now than formerly : but *times* have been much alike in all ages. There is in every situation a mixture of good and evil. To every man this is a chequered scene. There are no people loaded with unqualified good ; nor are there any oppressed with unmitigated evil. But men know of former times only by report, and by very partial report too : whereas, existing circumstances they know by actual experience ; and they are more observant of one evil, than of a hundred blessings.

In relation to our own times and country, the very reverse of what is here assumed is true. Never did the nation stand higher amidst the nations than at this day[b]. Never was civil liberty held more sacred, or better regulated for the good of the community. Never did religion flourish in a greater extent. Never was there such a combination of all ranks and orders of men to diffuse religion and happiness over the face of the earth. Never were the wants and necessities of human nature provided for in such a variety of forms. There is not a trouble to which humanity is exposed, but societies are formed to prevent or to alleviate its pressure. Never were the blessings of education so widely diffused. In a word, such is the increase

[b] In 1822.

of all that is good amongst us, and such the efforts making to extend it over the face of the whole earth, that, instead of looking to former times as better than our own, we may rather hail the approach of the millennial period, when the Messiah himself shall reign, and diffuse peace and happiness over the face of the whole earth.]

2. It is pernicious in its tendency—

[What is the tendency of this inquiry, but *to hide from our eyes the blessings we enjoy,* to *magnify in our minds the evils we endure,* and to *render us dissatisfied even with God himself?* It is notorious, that they who are most clamorous about the comparative excellence of former times, pass over all our present mercies as unworthy of notice. Nothing has any attraction for them, but some real or supposed evil. And their aim is, to diffuse the same malignant feeling throughout the whole community. And, though in their own immediate purpose they do not intend to complain of God himself, they do so in effect: for it is his providence that they arraign, and his dispensations that they criminate[c]. " There is not evil in the city, any more than good, but God is the doer of it[d] :" and it were far more likely to be rectified through personal humiliation before him, than by intemperate and factious clamours against his instruments. In the midst of such complaints there is not a word to call forth gratitude to God, or even submission to his holy will. There is no recollection of our ill deserts, no admiration of God's tender mercies, no encouragement to praise and thanksgiving. Nothing but murmuring is uttered, nothing but discontent is diffused. Whether, therefore, men consider their own happiness, or the happiness of the community, they will do well to abstain from this invidious inquiry; or, if at any time they feel disposed to make it, to ascertain, in the first instance, that the grounds of their inquiry are just.]

A word of ADVICE shall close the present subject—

1. Instead of complaining of the times, let us all endeavour to make them better—

[Much is in our power, for the improvement of the worst of times. It must be expected, in this distempered world, that troubles of some kind or other will arise: they cannot be wholly averted from individuals, or families, or nations. But, if all ranks of the community would unite, as they might well do, to lighten the burthens of each other, and to contribute, according to their respective abilities, to the happiness of the community, we should have little occasion to complain of present times, and none at all to institute invidious comparisons with former times.]

[c] Exod. xvi. 7.   Numb. xiv. 27.   [d] Amos iii. 6.

2. Let us seek that which will render all times and seasons happy—

[Religion is a cure and antidote to every ill, whether of a public or private nature. Amongst those who were endued with piety in the Apostolic age, you find none who were "murmurers and complainers." Their habit of mind is better expressed by those words of the Apostle, " I have learned, in whatsoever state I am, therewith to be content. I know how to be abased, and I know how to abound: everywhere, and in all things, I am instructed, both to be full and to be hungry, both to abound and to suffer need[e]." Having tasted of redeeming love, they are become comparatively indifferent to every thing else. Whatever they possess, they account an undeserved mercy: whatever they want, they regard as scarcely worthy of a thought. They know that " all things shall eventually work together for their good." " They are hid, in the secret of their Saviour's presence, from the strife of tongues: and whilst the minds of others are agitated with violent and malignant passions, theirs are " kept in perfect peace." This, then, I would earnestly recommend to you: Let your first concern be about your own souls. Seek for reconciliation with your offended God; and endeavour to walk in the light of his countenance. Then, whatever others may do, you may look forward to better times, when all troubles shall have fled away, and your happiness be unalloyed in the bosom of your God.]

[e] Phil. iv. 11, 12.

OUTLINE NO. 835

THE EXCELLENCY OF SPIRITUAL WISDOM.

Eccl. vii. 12. *Wisdom is a defence, and money is a defence : but the excellency of knowledge is, that wisdom giveth life to them that have it.*

TO have our minds well regulated in reference to religion, is most desirable. There is, in reality, no discordance between the duties which we owe to God and to man; or between our callings as men, and our callings as Christians. The things which relate to this world demand our attention, as well as those which relate to a future state. If, on the one hand, our worldly pursuits ought not to thrust out religion; so neither, on the other hand, should our pursuit of heavenly things lead us to neglect any part of our worldly occupations. God has said, " Six days shalt thou labour; but the seventh day thou shalt keep holy to the Lord." This shews, that we then only perform our duty aright, when we comprehend in our daily services a well-regulated devotion to the concerns of time, and to the interests of eternity. The two great objects of general pursuit are, "wisdom, and money." The one is followed only by a select portion of the community; the other is sought by all; but, whichever of the two any man affects, provided he give to heavenly pursuits the chief place, he does right to prosecute it with zeal and diligence; being "not slothful in business, and yet fervent in spirit, serving the Lord[a]." This combination of duties is spoken of in our text: for the elucidation of which, I will shew,

I. The excellency of wisdom above riches—

We are here told, that both wisdom and money are good in their place—

[Both the one and the other of these are "a defence," or, as the word imports, "a shadow." Now, as a shadow affords to persons a protection from the heat of the solar rays, so do wisdom and money screen him from many of the calamities of life; and afford to him many sources of enjoyment, of which those who are not possessed of them are deprived. Money will enable a person to choose his employment in life, whilst the most menial and painful offices are left for those who are not able to choose for themselves. It provides also many comforts, to which the poor are altogether strangers. In a time of sickness, especially, its use is felt: for, by means of it its possessors often obtain relief, for the want of which their poor neighbours are left to sink. So wisdom also brings with it very extensive benefits, in that it elevates the character, and qualifies a man for stations, to which, from birth, he was not entitled to aspire. It provides, also, good occupation for the mind; so that a man possessed of it is never less alone than when alone. Thus it protects him from that state of degradation to which many, for want of it, are reduced; and from that listlessness which induces persons of an uncultivated mind to betake themselves to some evil employment for the sole purpose of getting rid of time.

True, indeed, neither wisdom nor money can protect us from every evil: disease or accident may assault one person as well as another: nor can they afford entire protection under any circumstances, any more than a shadow can altogether remove

[a] Rom. xii. 11.

the heat of the atmosphere. But, as a shadow, they may screen us from much evil, and alleviate many pains which they cannot entirely ward off.]

But wisdom has an excellency far above money—

[Wisdom is *more our own* than money, which soon " makes itself wings and flies away." In many respects, also, has it *a tendency to promote our welfare in life,* beyond money. Riches rather contract the mind than enlarge it; whereas wisdom expands the mind, and dispels that conceit and insolence which characterize a purse-proud man. Money, too, when not combined with wisdom, leads a man into every species of dissipation and folly, and opens to him temptations to every kind of sensual indulgence. But *wisdom provides for his mind such occupations as place him at a distance from temptation,* and especially when his facilities for profuse expenditure are on a contracted scale. And thus the man of wisdom moves in a far safer and happier sphere; his pleasures being more refined, and his employments more innocent. I may further observe, that riches render us a prey to designing men; and subject us to many vexations, to which less opulent persons are but little exposed: whereas *wisdom holds not forth any such baits to dishonest and designing men;* who, if not disposed to join with us in our pursuits, will leave us, without interruption, to prosecute our own. Nor is it the least excellence of wisdom that *it induces thoughtful habits,* which are favourable to sobriety, to meditation, and to a candid investigation of conflicting interests: whilst money rather tends to dissipate thought, and to fix the mind only on present indulgences. In a word, money, without wisdom, tends to the destruction of life; whereas *wisdom, freed from the temptations of wealth, tends rather to the preservation of life,* and to the securing of that equanimity which, to a worldly man, is the main source of comfort in the world.]

Whilst we thus acknowledge that both wisdom and money have, though in different degrees, their respective excellencies, we are constrained to maintain,

II. The excellence of spiritual wisdom above them both—

The benefit ascribed to wisdom in the latter clause of my text necessarily leads our thoughts to a different kind of wisdom from that which is mentioned in the former clause. And we find the same distinction made by the Prophet Jeremiah: " Let not the wise man glory in his wisdom, neither let the mighty man glory in his might: let not the rich man glory in his riches: but let him that glorieth glory in this, that he understandeth and knoweth me, that I am the Lord, which exercise loving-kindness, judgment, and right-eousness in the earth[b]." Here is a spiritual wisdom spoken of, which infinitely exceeds all that the wisest or richest of unenlightened men can possess. To make this clear, let it be remembered,

1. A man may possess all the wisdom and all the riches of the world, and yet be *dead :* but the smallest measure of spiritual wisdom " *giveth life* to them that have it"—

[The manna which God gave by Moses to the Israelites in the wilderness *supported* life, but could not *give* it : whereas our Lord and Saviour, whom that manna typified, *gives* life to all who believe on him[c]. Now spiritual wisdom consists in the knowledge of Christ ; as Christ himself has said, " This is life eternal, to know thee the only true God, and Jesus Christ whom thou hast sent[d]." And if we be but "babes in Christ," still " have we passed from death unto life," and " are become new creatures in Christ Jesus[e]."]

2. Wisdom and riches too frequently lead men to self-confidence and creature-dependence ; whereas spiritual wisdom invariably humbles the soul, and leads it to seek its all in Christ—

[A life of faith upon the Son of God is the very essence of all spiritual wisdom[f]— — —]

3. By carnal wisdom, and by wealth, men are often betrayed into a contempt of all religion ; whereas spiri-tual wisdom brings with it such a love to religion as gradually transforms the soul into the divine image—

[Yes, in truth, faith, if genuine, will "purify the heart[g];" and " he that hath a hope in Christ will purify himself, even as he is pure[h]"— — —]

4. A man possessing wisdom and riches in their utmost extent, may perish ; but a man that is wise towards God, is made " wise unto salvation[i]"—

[Hence it was that St. Paul, who in his unconverted state possessed a very abundant measure of these earthly talents, " considered them all but as dross and dung, in comparison of the excellency of the knowledge of Christ[k]." And hence

[b] Jer. ix. 23, 24.　　[c] John vi. 47—51.　　[d] John xvii. 3.
[e] 2 Cor. v. 17.　　[f] Gal. ii. 20.　　[g] Acts xv. 9.
[h] 1 John iii. 3.　　[i] 2 Tim. iii. 15.　　[k] Phil. iii. 7, 8.

Moses, also, who had attained all the learning of the Egyptians, and was next in power to the king upon the throne, regarded it all as unworthy of a thought, not only for *the crown* of Christ, but in comparison of *his cross;* "esteeming the *reproach* of Christ greater riches than all *the treasures* of Egypt[1]." Yes, spiritual wisdom "has the promise of the life that now is, and of that which is to come[m]:" and fully merits that high encomium which the wisest of men has bestowed upon it[n] — — — "Whoso findeth it, findeth life, and shall to all eternity obtain favour of the Lord[o]."]

Let us then LEARN,

1. To form a correct estimate of all that is before us—

[Earthly things are not to be despised. Religious persons just emerging from darkness unto light, are apt to pour contempt on wealth as if it were good for nothing, and greatly also to undervalue even intellectual attainments. But we should give to every thing its due. Even to money are we indebted for numberless comforts, and to wisdom for much more; because to men's progress in science we owe those very things which money enables us to procure. Doubtless, *in comparison* of spiritual attainments, those which have respect only to the things of time and sense are of but little value. We may say of the moon and stars, that they are of small utility to us in comparison of the sun: but this does not render them of no value in themselves. The heavenly bodies possess great beauty and utility, notwithstanding they are eclipsed by the sun: and the true way to judge of their value to us is, to consider how painful the loss of them would be. So, whilst to heavenly things we ascribe, as we ought to do, a paramount importance, let us remember, that, for the purposes of this life at least, those things which are mainly regarded by the unregenerate, are, in their place, deserving also the attention of the godly. We may say of them, as our blessed Lord does of some other things of subordinate importance, "These things ought ye to do, and not to leave the other undone."]

2. To seek every thing according to its real importance—

[When it is said, "Labour not for the meat that perisheth, but for that which endureth unto everlasting life, we are not to take the expressions absolutely, but only *comparatively;* exactly as when it is said, "I will have mercy, and not sacrifice." I say, then, to those who are engaged in worldly business, Follow it diligently: and to those who are prosecuting

---

[1] Heb. xi. 26.   [m] 1 Tim. iv. 8.
[n] Prov. iii. 13—18.   [o] Prov. viii. 35.

any department of science, Strive to excel in it: " Whatever your hand findeth to do, do it with all your might[p]." The point on which I would entertain a jealousy is, " the placing of your affections on any thing here below; for they are to be reserved exclusively for things above[q]." But I am aware that there is great reason for caution on this head. I well know how easy it is to enter with zeal into earthly pursuits; and how difficult to maintain the same ardour in the prosecution of heavenly things. Let me then remind you, that, whatever importance you may assign to the things of time and sense, they have no real importance, by reason of the superior importance of the things which are spiritual and eternal. These must occupy the whole soul, and engage all its powers. We must "run as in a race;" and "strive as for the mastery;" and "fight" as for our very lives: and we may rest assured, that the crown of victory that shall be awarded to us, will recompense all the labours we have endured, in the prosecution of our duty, and in the service of our God.]

[p] Eccl. ix. 10.   [q] Col. iii. 2.

OUTLINE NO. 836

AGAINST AN OVER-RIGHTEOUS SPIRIT.

Eccles. vii. 16. *Be not righteous overmuch.*

THIS is the sheet-anchor of ungodly men. They hate to see a zeal for God, and therefore endeavour to repress it. From the days of Cain to this hour, they who have been born after the flesh, have persecuted those who have been born after the Spirit[a]. And when they find that neither contempt nor threatenings will avail any thing, they will venture, as Satan before them did[b], to draw their weapons from the very armoury of God.

It must be confessed, that the sense of this passage is not obvious at first sight; and it has been variously interpreted by commentators. Some have thought it to be the speech of an infidel recommending Solomon, in reply to his observation in the preceding verse, to avoid an excess either in religion or in vice. But it is evidently a serious admonition given by Solomon himself. In ver. 15. he mentions two things which had appeared strange to him, namely, Many righteous

[a] Gal. iv. 29.   [b] Matt. iv. 6.

people suffering even unto death for righteousness
sake; and, many wicked people, whose lives were
justly forfeited, eluding, either through force or fraud,
the punishment they deserved. From hence he takes
occasion to caution both the righteous and the wicked;
the righteous, ver. 16, not to bring trouble on themselves by an injudicious way of manifesting their
religion, or to " suffer as evil-doers;" and *the wicked,*
ver. 17, not to presume upon always escaping with
impunity; for that justice will sooner or later surely
overtake them. He then recommends to both of them
to pay strict attention to the advice given them, and
to cultivate the true fear of God, ver. 18, as the best
preservative against wickedness on the one hand, and
indiscretion on the other.

This being the sense of the whole passage, we proceed to the consideration of the text; in illustrating
which we shall,

I. Explain the caution—

The misconstruction put upon the text renders it
necessary to explain,

1. To what the caution does not extend—

[Solomon certainly never intended to caution us against
loving God too much; seeing that we are commanded to " love
him with all our heart, and mind, and soul, and strength[c]:"
nor against *serving the Lord Jesus Christ* too much; since he
" died for us, that we might live to him[d];" and we should be
" willing to be bound or even to die for his sake[e]:" nor against
too much *purity of heart;* for we are required to purify ourselves from all filthiness both of flesh and spirit[f], yea, to purify
ourselves even as he is pure[g]——— Nor could he mean to
caution us against too much *deadness to the world;* for, *provided we conscientiously fulfil the duties of our station,* we
cannot be too much " crucified to the world[h];" we should no
more be of the world than Christ himself was[i]. Nor, lastly,
did he intend to warn us against too much *compassion for
souls;* for, *provided our mode of manifesting that compassion
be discreet,* it would be well if our " head were waters, and
our eyes a fountain of tears, to weep for the ungodly day and
night[k]." These indeed are things in which the world does not

c Mark xii. 30.　　d 2 Cor. v. 15.　　e Acts xxi. 13. Luke xiv. 26.
f 2 Cor. vii. 1.　　g 1 John iii. 3.　　h Gal. vi. 14.
i John xvii. 14, 16.　　　　k Jer. ix. 1.

wish to see us much occupied; they would rather that we should put our light under a bushel. But no inspired writer would ever caution us against excess in such things as these. St. Paul makes the proper distinction between the regard which we should shew to carnal and to spiritual objects: "Be not drunk with wine, *wherein is excess;* but be *filled with* the Spirit;" because therein is no possibility of excess[1].]

2. To what the caution does extend—

[*An intemperate zeal* appears to be the principal thing against which the text is levelled. Too high a conceit of our own wisdom, a hasty persuasion that we are right, and an indiscreet method of fulfilling what we suppose to be our duty, may be found in persons who really mean well. Two apostles, from zeal for their Master, would have called fire from heaven to consume a village that had refused him admission[m]; and a third defended his Master with a sword, to the endangering of his own life, and to the dishonour of the cause he had espoused[n]. Thus do many at this day contend for the truth *in private* in an unbecoming spirit, and go forth to propagate it *in public* to the neglect of their proper duty, and the injury of the Christian cause[o]. *A blind superstition* may also be fitly comprehended in the caution. This obtained in a very great degree among the judaizing Christians; and still prevails over a great part of the Christian world; would to God we could except even Protestants themselves from the charge! How often do we see a most rigorous regard paid to rites that are of human invention, whilst the true spirit and temper of Christianity is sadly neglected! Alas! what fiery and fatal contentions have arisen from this source! There is *a needless scrupulosity* also which ought to be avoided. What schisms has this occasioned in the Church, when, on account of one or two things, in which they could not agree, men have rent the seamless robe of Christ into a thousand pieces! What injury have men done to their bodies by penances of man's device! What trouble and perplexity have they also brought upon their souls by rash vows, and foolish impositions! Such was the spirit against which St. Paul guarded the Christians at Colosse[p]. And Solomon's caution against the same will be useful in every age and place. *A self-justifying dependence* on our own works is nearly allied to the foregoing evils, and is thought by some to be the more immediate object of Solomon's censure. But if we allow it not the first place, we may very properly mention it as another mistaken method of displaying our righteousness. Every person is prone to it; and

[1] Eph. v. 18.   [m] Luke ix. 54.   [n] John xviii. 10.
[o] 1 Cor. vii. 20.   [p] Col. ii. 18—23.

the most upright persons need to be cautioned against it, because there is not any thing more destructive in its issue. It deprives us of all the benefit of whatever good we do; yea, it makes even the death of Christ of no effect[q]: we can never therefore be too strongly guarded against it. We may have much zeal of this kind: but it is a zeal without knowledge. Nor is there any salvation for us, unless, like the holy Apostle, we renounce it utterly[r].]

Having explained at large the import of this caution, we shall,

II. Subjoin some advice—

We fear that, however great occasion there may be to caution sincere people against erroneous methods of exercising their religion, there is far more occasion to exhort the world in general to pay some attention to their duty. Our first advice therefore is,

1. Be *truly* righteous—

[They who are most ready to quote the text, are, for the most part, those who are adverse to the exercise of all religion. And when they exclaim, ' Be not righteous over-much,' their meaning is, ' Be not righteous *at all*.' They would be far better pleased to see all walking in the broad road, than to be put to shame by those who are walking in the narrow path. But let no scoffs keep you from the performance of your duty. If the world set themselves against religion, let not that deter any upright soul. Our Lord has taught us to expect that our " greatest foes would be those of our own household." Let us not be discouraged if we find it so. Let our inquiry be, What is duty? and, having found that, let nothing turn us aside. Let us not be satisfied with the degree of righteousness which the world approves. Let us examine the Scripture to see what God requires. Let us see how the saints of old served God; and let us labour in every thing to " do his will on earth, even as it is done in heaven." This is a conduct which will tend, not to our destruction, but salvation. To act otherwise will issue in our ruin; since " Whosoever doth not righteousness is not of God[s]." But to walk after this rule is to ensure present and everlasting peace.]

2. Be *wisely* righteous—

[" It is good to be zealously affected always in a good thing;" and to " maintain a conscience void of offence towards both God and man." But we are far from recommending a

q Gal. v. 4.   r Phil. iii. 9.   s 1 John iii. 10.

wild inconsiderate regard for religion. We ought to exercise a sound judgment in all things. " I, Wisdom," says Solomon, " dwell with Prudence[t]." There is certainly much room for discretion in the performance of our duty even towards God himself. We may so reprove a fault as to harden those whom we endeavour to reclaim, and, by casting pearls before swine, may cause them to turn again and rend us[u]. We may exercise our Christian liberty so as to cast a stumbling-block before others, and destroy the souls whose salvation we ought to seek to the uttermost[x]. Many things may be " lawful which are not expedient." We should therefore consult times, persons, places, things[y]; and " walk in wisdom toward them that are without." Our determination should be, " I will behave myself wisely in a perfect way[z]." And our prayer should be, " O give me understanding in the way of godliness. In every part of our conduct we should be circumspect, that being " blameless and harmless, the sons of God, without rebuke in the midst of a crooked and perverse generation, we may shine among them as lights in the world." Thus should we unite "the wisdom of the serpent with the harmlessness of the dove[a]." And in so doing we shall both adorn our holy profession, and " put to silence the ignorance of foolish men."]

3. Be righteous *enough*—

[There is more danger of defect than of excess in this pursuit. Indeed whereinsoever you are *truly* righteous it is not possible to be righteous *overmuch*. We are to " walk as Christ himself walked," and to " be perfect even as our Father which is in heaven is perfect. Have you attained much? be thankful for it; but go forward. If you were as holy as St. Paul himself, you must " not think you have already attained, or are already perfect, but, like him, you must forget the things that are behind, and reach forward unto that which is before, and press toward the mark, for the prize of the high calling of God in Christ Jesus." The higher you are in grace, the richer will you be in glory. Begin then, all of you, to " run the race that is set before you." The prize is worth all your care. Lose it not for want of due exertion. But " laying aside every weight, and the sin that doth most easily beset you, run with patience your appointed course, looking unto Jesus the author and finisher of your faith:" and let your constant motto be, *"This one thing I do[b]."* Endeavour, every step you take, to walk in the fear of God. This is the advice of Solomon himself[c]: nor can there be any better preservative against extremes than this.

[t] Prov. viii. 12. [u] Matt. vii. 6. [x] 1 Cor. viii. 11.
[y] Eccl. viii. 5. [z] Ps. ci. 2. [a] Matt. x. 16.
[b] Phil. iii. 13. [c] ver. 18.

By this you will be kept from the undue bias of fleshly wisdom, and from consulting with flesh and blood : by this you will be enabled to maintain your conversation in the world with " simplicity and godly sincerity." Cultivate this, and the path of duty will be clear : cultivate this, and you will never lose the promised reward.]

OUTLINE NO. 837

MAN'S ORIGINAL AND PRESENT STATE.

Eccl. vii. 29. *Lo, this only have I found, that God hath made man upright; but they have sought out many inventions.*

THE whole scope of this book is, to shew the vanity of the world, and all things in it. As in the earth itself there is a visible proof that some great convulsion has taken place ; so, in every thing that is passing upon the earth, there is the clearest evidence imaginable that some great moral change has been effected : for it cannot possibly be, that the world, which still bears such innumerable traces of wisdom and goodness in its first creation, should have proceeded from its Maker's hands in such a state as it now appears. In fact, the whole world is out of course. The very elements are, on many occasions, hostile to man ; and man, in ten thousand instances, is an enemy to himself, to his species, and to his God. And " what is thus crooked, who can make straight[a]?" Who can ward off the effects of all this disorder from his own person or estate ? A monarch is the victim of it, no less than the meanest of his subjects; and the saint, no less than the contemner of all true religion. To what, then, or to whom, shall we ascribe this state of things? The wisest philosophers of Greece and Rome were unable to account for it. But the Holy Scriptures inform us, that the whole creation, as originally formed, was perfect; but sin, entering into the world, effected both a natural and a moral change upon it : so that the man who looks into the Holy Scriptures can solve every difficulty at once, by saying, " Lo, this have I found, that God made man upright; but they have sought out many inventions," and

[a] ver. 13.

thereby reduced the world, and every thing in it, to the state of disorganization in which it now appears.

In illustration of my text, I shall be led to notice both the primitive and the present state of man, and to shew,

I. His uprightness, as formed by God—

We are expressly told, that " God created man after his own image[b]." When, therefore, man came from his Creator's hands, he was perfect,

1. In his intellectual faculties—

[His mind was light: and in him was no darkness at all, in reference to any thing which he was concerned to know. He had a clear knowledge of God, and of his perfections, so far as those perfections were stamped upon the visible creation. The wisdom, the goodness, the power of God, were all apprehended by him, and duly appreciated. He was acquainted also with his own nature, and his obligations to God; seeing the full extent of his duty towards him, as well as all the motives and inducements which he had for the performance of it. Moreover, he saw all these things intuitively, and not by long consideration or rational deduction. They were all stamped upon his very soul, and constantly before his eyes: and he had the same consciousness of them as he had of his own existence.]

2. In his moral dispositions—

[The Law of God was written upon his heart, that he might know it: and, at the same time, the love of it also was engraven there, so that he had not the slightest inclination to violate it in any one particular. It was no difficulty to him to love God with all his heart and mind and soul and strength: it was the very element in which he breathed: the bent of his soul was wholly towards it. Flame did not more naturally ascend in the atmosphere than did his soul, with all its powers, ascend to God. Dear as Eve was to him, she did not rival God in his affections. Every thing was subordinated to his Maker; nor was even a thought entertained in his mind, which had not a direct and immediate tendency to honour him. In a word, he was to God as the impression to the seal: nor was there found one lineament upon his heart which had not been stamped there by God himself.]

Had man continued thus, the whole creation would have retained its original constitution. But man fell; and brought a curse upon the whole world[c]; every thing more or less participating in,

---

[b] Gen. i. 26, 27.   [c] Gen. iii. 17.

II. His obliquity, as deformed by sin—

Man, through the instigation of Satan, desired to be wise as God himself. Not contented with knowing "good," he would know "evil" also[d]; little thinking how impossible it was for light and darkness to exist together. Since that first device, whereby he fell, he has "sought out many inventions;" whereby to remedy, if possible, the first evil which he brought upon himself. Thus his descendants seek,

1. How to rid themselves of all restraint from God—

[They conceive of God, as resident in heaven; and as so remote from this vain world, as scarcely to take any notice of it, or concern himself about it. Besides, from a pretended regard for his glorious Majesty, they conceive it far beneath him to notice the affairs of men: so that the language of their hearts is, "The Lord shall not see, neither will the Almighty regard it[e]." But, as they cannot be certain but that he does inspect their ways, they endeavour to get at as great a distance from him as possible. If at any time, by means of the preached word, or by any remarkable providence, he is brought nigh to them, they endeavour to shut their eyes, and to flee to any thing which may assist them in banishing him from their thoughts. To himself they say in effect, "Depart from us; for we desire not the knowledge of thy ways[f]:" and to his servants they say, "Make the Holy One of Israel to cease from before us[g]." It was thus that our first parents acted, when they strove to "hide themselves from God in the midst of the garden:" and thus do sinners of the present day act, fleeing to business and pleasure and company, and any thing that may serve to drive the remembrance of him from their minds. And he who could contrive any fresh amusement or employ that should have this effect upon their minds, would be accounted one of the greatest benefactors of the human race. That which is, in fact, their heaviest curse, is sought by them as the richest blessing; namely, "to be without God in the world[h]," and "not to have him in all their thoughts[i]."]

2. How to make to themselves gods more suited to their taste—

[Men feel that they must, of necessity, depend on something without them for their happiness, since they have no perennial source of it within themselves. But Jehovah is not one in whom they can find delight: hence, as the Israelites

---

d Gen. iii. 5, 6.   e Ps. xciv. 7.   f Job xxi. 14, 15.
g Isai. xxx. 11.   h Eph. ii. 12.   i Ps. x. 4.

made a golden calf, and worshipped it, so these make to themselves objects of supreme regard, to which in heart and mind they cleave, as sources of satisfaction to their souls. Some, like the ignorant heathen, bow down to stocks and stones, " and say, Ye are our gods[k]:" others, with equal, though less palpable, absurdity, set their affections on the pleasures, riches, and honours of this life, making " a god of their belly[l]," or putting their confidence in gold[m], or " seeking the honour of man, rather than that which cometh of God only[n]." These all, in fact, " forsake the fountain of living waters, and hew out to themselves cisterns, broken cisterns, that can hold no water[o]." All, indeed, have not the same pursuit : but all have some " idol in their hearts[p]," which is to them a god : and all " will walk in the name of that god[q]," looking to it for happiness, and confiding in it for support. This is an " invention," not peculiar to any age or place : it is " sought out," and carried into effect, by every child of man ; there not being a natural man upon the face of the whole earth who does not, in one shape or other, " worship and serve the creature more than the Creator ; who is blessed for evermore[r]."]

3. How to hide from themselves their own deformity—

[One would suppose that the impiety of this conduct should appear at once to every man who is capable of the least reflection. But men contrive, by various arts, to hide it from themselves. They, in the first place, determinately " call evil good, and good evil : they put darkness for light, and light for darkness ; bitter for sweet, and sweet for bitter[s]." Then, not being able to conceal from themselves that they have committed *some* iniquity, they compare themselves, not with the word of God or with the saints of old, but with persons all around them : of these, however, they will select for the purpose those only whom they think not better than themselves : and thus will they satisfy themselves that they are as good as others. If there be some particular evils, of which their consciences accuse them, they will endeavour to find out some good deeds to put into the opposite scale, and to neutralize the effect of them upon their minds : or, if they cannot easily do this, they will satisfy themselves, that, though their actions have been evil, their intentions have been good ; they have injured nobody but themselves ; they have good hearts ; and what they have done amiss, was not so much their own fault, as the fault of human nature in general, and of the temptations to which they were

[k] Hos. xiv. 3. [l] Phil. iii. 19. [m] Col. iii. 5. Job xxxi. 24, 25.
[n] John v. 44. [o] Jer. ii. 13. [p] Ezek. xiv. 4.
[q] Mic. iv. 5. [r] Rom. i. 25. [s] Isai. v. 20.

exposed, and of the persons who were their associates in iniquity. Thus, as our first parents sought " to hide their nakedness by fig-leaves[t]," so do all men by nature strive, by every
device they can think of, to hide from themselves, and from
each other, their real state.]

4. How to persuade themselves that all will issue
well with them at the last—

[They will not believe that eternal punishment can ever
be inflicted on persons for such offences as theirs. God is too
merciful to proceed in such a way. And, if he did, what must
become of the whole world? All who die, are considered as
having gone to their rest; and no one ever once thinks of them
as in a state of misery. Why then should not they, when they
die, go to their rest? or what reason can they have to apprehend that any misery awaits them? But, supposing that God's
threatenings were true, they intend to repent at some convenient season; and have no doubt but that a gracious God
will avert his displeasure from them, in answer to their prayer.
It is possible, indeed, that they may be called away suddenly
(as many are), and not have time to realize their good intentions: but then the suddenness of their removal will plead their
excuse, and their purposes be accepted as though they had been
performed.

Thus, by means of these inventions which men have sought
out, they are kept in a constant state of delusion; wearying
themselves in the pursuit of vanities which elude their grasp,
and filling with vexation both themselves and all around them.]

We may SEE from hence,

1. What is the true intent of the Gospel—

[The Gospel is to remedy all this evil, and to restore man
to the state of holiness and happiness from which he is fallen.
It is to rectify our views of God, and make us see what a great
and holy and gracious God he is. It is to make him known to
us in the person of his Son, and to fill our souls with admiring
and adoring thoughts of his love. It is to bring us also to the
knowledge of ourselves, as lost and utterly undone; and to
engage our whole souls in the service of our God, as his rightful property, his purchased possession.

Beloved Brethren, *this* is an invention of God; sought out
by him; planned in his eternal counsels; and carried into effect
on Mount Calvary: and, if duly received, it will be effectual to
dissipate at once all our " inventions." It will not indeed remove
all the evils that abound in the world: there will yet remain
much that is " crooked, and that cannot be made straight;" but
it will sanctify those evils, and overrule them for our greater

[t] Gen. iii. 7.

good: its operations, however, will be gradual, especially as far as relates to the restoration of the divine image on our souls. We shall be " renewed in knowledge, after the image of Him that created us[u]:" we shall also be " created, after God's image, in righteousness and true holiness[x]:" but then, in both respects, our light will be progressive, advancing like that of the sun, from its earliest dawn to its meridian height[y]. This is the change which the Gospel has wrought on millions of the human race: and that Gospel shall yet be found, by every true Believer, " the power of God to the salvation of his soul."]

2. How we may know whether it has produced its due effect upon us—

[You have heard what it was intended to do; namely, to remove all the obliquity of our fallen nature, and to restore the uprightness in which we were at first created. These are therefore the points for you to inquire into, in order to form a just estimate of your state. Can you say, " *I have found this?*" And can you further say, that the delusions, by which the devil has formerly led you captive, are now dissipated and dispelled? Can you declare yet further, that the intellectual and moral qualities, which man originally possessed, are forming progressively within your souls? Here are marks which may easily be discerned; and which will with great accuracy determine, not only the truth, but also the measure, of the change that has taken place within you. Alas! alas! on far the greater part of us, it is to be feared, no such change as this has ever taken place at all. The greater part of us still live far from God; still have our affections fixed on things below; still are unhumbled before God; and buoying ourselves up with the vain hopes of future happiness, though there is no one lineament of the divine image formed upon our souls. If this be the case with you, my Brethren, deceive yourselves no longer; but " to-day, while it is called to-day, cease to harden your hearts;" and begin to seek the mercy which God has offered you in the Son of his love — — If however, after careful self-examination, you have an evidence of a work of grace upon your souls, then press forward for the attainment of more grace, and for a more perfect restoration to the divine image. If you do this in earnest, then even this present world will be less a scene of confusion to you than it was in your unconverted state; and, in the world to come, the glories of Paradise shall be for ever yours. You shall be admitted into the sweetest intercourse with your God; and " be fully like him, because you shall see him as he is[z]."]

[u] Col. iii. 10. [x] Eph. iv. 24. [y] Prov. iv. 18.
[z] 1 John iii. 2.

OUTLINE NO. 838

MAN'S ABUSE OF GOD'S PATIENCE.

Eccl. viii. 11. *Because sentence against an evil work is not executed speedily, therefore the heart of the sons of men is fully set in them to do evil.*

SIN is in itself an evil of a crimson dye; nevertheless its malignity may be greatly increased by the aggravations with which it is attended. One can scarcely conceive any thing that can enhance its guilt so much, as the committing of it in hopes that God's mercy will pardon it. Yet this is the very ground on which the world indulge themselves in the commission of it. " Because," &c.

I. The extent of man's wickedness—

That sin exists in the world is visible to all; but the degree in which it prevails is very little known. In what way men sin, we may judge from the exceeding depth of colouring which there is in the picture before us. They sin,

1. Habitually—

[All are not equally vicious in their lives, but all forget God, and neglect their own souls. Successive years serve only to confirm this habit. We may all adopt the confession of the church of old [a].]

2. Deliberately—

[It were well if we never sinned, but through ignorance or inadvertence: but what schemes have we formed for the accomplishment of sinful purposes! How often have we seen the sinfulness of our desires, and yet gratified them [b]! The very bent and inclination of our souls has been towards wickedness [c].]

3. Without restraint—

[A regard to our reputation or interests may impose some restraint. A fear of hell may also prevent the gratification of some desires: but few are kept from evil, like Joseph, by the fear of God [d]: that is the only restraint which proves uniformly effectual [e].]

4. Without remorse—

[a] Jer. iii. 25.   [b] Rom. i. 32.   [c] Job xv. 16.
[d] Gen. xxxix. 9.   [e] Jam. ii. 11.

[We must at times have felt some convictions of conscience, but we, for the most part, stifle them by company, amusements, &c. Many attain to dreadful hardness of heart and impenitence [f]. The prophet's description may well be applied to each of us [g].]

Thus are "men's hearts fully set in them to do evil"—

[They walk after the imagination of their own hearts: neither mercies nor judgments can prevail with them to do otherwise.]

If their sins were followed by a visible and immediate punishment, men would not dare to live in this manner; but God defers the execution of his judgments

II. The occasion of it—

God is not an unconcerned spectator of sin. He has appointed a day for the revelation of his righteous judgment. At present he forbears to inflict vengeance. This very forbearance emboldens men to sin—"*because*," "*therefore*." From the delay of punishment men think,

1. That there is but little " evil" in sin—

[God indeed calls sin. "an evil work :" but his forbearance towards sinners is thought to indicate indifference. This however is a fatal delusion. He has marked the evil of sin in many awful instances [h] : he will soon undeceive this blind infatuated world [i].]

2. That there is no "sentence" gone forth against it—

[Men would gladly persuade themselves that they have no cause to fear. The temptation whereby the serpent beguiled Eve is cherished by them [k]. But the wrath of God is indeed denounced against sin [l]. Every species and degree of sin renders us obnoxious to his displeasure [m].]

3. That the sentence (if there be any) will never be " executed"—

[Since God defers punishing, it seems possible that he may decline it altogether. The apparent disproportion between the offence and the punishment seems to countenance this idea. To confirm our hope we are apt to compare God with ourselves [n]. But, however long God delay, he will surely strike at last [o].]

Thus it is that men act in every age—

[f] 1 Tim. iv. 2.   [g] Jer. viii. 5, 6.   [h] 2 Pet. ii. 4—6.
[i] Eph. v. 6.   [k] Gen. iii. 4.   [l] Rom. ii. 8, 9.
[m] Rom. i. 18.   [n] Ps. l. 21.   [o] Eccl. viii. 12, 13.

[David mentions this effect as arising from it in his day [p]. St. Peter foretells the prevalence of this iniquity in the last days [q]. Experience proves how universally it obtains at this hour.]

INFER—

1. How great the folly, as well as wickedness, of unregenerate men!

[If there were only a bare possibility of eternal punishment, how mad were it to continue in sin! But God has pledged himself that he will inflict it on the impenitent [r]. Every moment's continuance in sin increases the condemnation [s]. What extreme folly then is it so to abuse the forbearance of God! May we be ashamed of ourselves, and repent in dust and ashes.]

2. What need have we to be cleansed by the blood and Spirit of Christ!

[What but the blood of Christ can ever expiate the guilt we have contracted? What but the Spirit of Christ can ever deliver us from such habits? That we can never renew our own souls is certain [t]. Let us therefore wash in the fountain opened for us [u]; and let us apply to God for his almighty aid [x].]

3. How dreadful must be the state of those who continue impenitent!

[There is a certain measure of iniquity which sinners are left to fill up [y]: when this is full, nothing can avert the divine vengeance [z]. Already are the arrows of divine justice pointed at them [a]. Eternity itself will be the duration of the punishment [b]. The time is coming when Jerusalem's state will be ours [c]. Let us then tremble lest we exhaust the divine patience [d]. Let us diligently improve this day of salvation [e].]

[p] Ps. lv. 19.	[q] 2 Pet. iii. 3, 4.	[r] Matt. xxv. 46.
[s] Rom. ii. 4, 5.	[t] Jer. xiii. 23.	[u] Zech. xiii. 1.
[x] Lam. v. 21.	[y] Gen. xv. 16.	[z] 1 Thess. ii. 16.
[a] Ps. vii. 11—13.	[b] Mark ix. 43—48.	[c] Luke xix. 42.
[d] Zeph. ii. 2, 3.	[e] 2 Cor. vi. 2.	

OUTLINE NO. 839

THE BLESSEDNESS OF FEARING GOD.

Eccl. viii. 12. *Surely I know that it shall be well with them which fear God.*

NOTHING certain can be determined respecting God's favour from the outward dispensations of his providence [a]. The wicked seem on the whole to

[a] Eccl. ix. 1.

prosper more than others[b]; nevertheless the godly are by far the happier persons[c]. It is of them only that the assertion in the text can be made. We propose to shew,

I. Who they are that fear God—

This, we may suppose, would be a point easy to be determined; but, through self-love and Satan's devices, many mistake respecting it. The characters described in the text may be distinguished by the following marks:

1. They stand in awe of God's judgments—

[Once they disregarded the displeasure of the Almighty[d]: they would not believe that his threatenings would be executed. But now they have learned to tremble at his word[e]. Awakened by his Spirit, they exclaim with the prophet[f]. The Scriptures uniformly represent them in this light[g].]

2. They embrace the salvation offered them—

[In their natural state they felt no need of a physician[h]: they saw no suitableness in the remedy which the Gospel offered them[i]. Their pride would not suffer them to submit to its humiliating terms[k]; but now they gladly embrace Christ as their only Saviour. They flee to him, as the murderers did to a city of refuge. This is the description given of them in the inspired volume[l].]

3. They endeavour to keep all the commandments—

[If ever they obeyed God at all, they served him only to the extent the world would approve. Where the lax habits of mankind forbad their compliance with the divine command, they were afraid to be singular. But they dare not any longer halt between God and Baal: they have determined, through grace, to follow the Lord fully. The language of their hearts is like that of David[m]. This was the very ground on which God concluded that Abraham feared him[n].]

These marks clearly distinguish those who fear God from all others—

[The *formal Pharisee* has never felt his desert of condemnation[o]. The *merely awakened sinner* has never truly embraced

---

[b] Ps. lxxiii. 5, 12.   [c] Ps. lxxiii. 15.   [d] Ps. x. 5.
[e] Isai. lxvi. 2.   [f] Isai. xxxiii. 14.
[g] Acts xvi. 29. and Ps. cxix. 120.   [h] Rev. iii. 17.
[i] 1 Cor. i. 23.   [k] Rom. x. 3.   [l] Heb. vi. 18.
[m] Ps. cxix. 5, 6.   [n] Gen. xxii. 12.   [o] Luke xviii. 11.

the Gospel [p]. The *hypocritical professor* has never mortified his besetting sin [q]. It is *the person* alone, *who fears God*, that unites in his experience a dread of God's wrath, an affiance in Christ, and a love to the commandments.]

Such persons, notwithstanding appearances, are truly blessed.

II. In what respects it shall be well with them—

They are not exempt from the common afflictions of life. They have in addition to them many trials peculiar to themselves; yet it goes well with them,

1. In respect of temporal good—

[They have a peculiar enjoyment of *prosperity*. The ungodly find an emptiness in all their possessions [r]; but the godly have not such gall mixed with their comforts [s]. They have also peculiar supports in a season of *adversity*. The wicked are for the most part miserable in their affliction [t]: if kept from murmuring, it is the summit of their attainments: but the righteous are enabled to glory in tribulation [u], and cordially to approve of God's dispensations towards them [x].]

2. In respect of spiritual good—

[They possess a peace that passeth all understanding. They are filled with a joy utterly unknown to others [y]. The work of sanctification is gradually carried on within them [z]. As they approach towards death they grow in a meetness for heaven, and are serene and happy in the near prospect of eternity [a].]

3. In respect to eternal good—

[Who can set forth their felicity in the eternal world? Who can even conceive the weight of glory preparing for them? How will their faith be lost in sight, and their hope in enjoyment! Then indeed will that truth be seen and felt by them [b].]

These things are far from being " cunningly devised fables."

III. What assurance we have that it shall be thus well with them—

No truth whatever is capable of clearer demonstration. The topics from whence it might be proved are

[p] Acts xxiv. 25, and xxvi. 28.   [q] Acts viii. 23.
[r] Job. xx. 22.   [s] Prov. x. 22.   1 Tim. vi. 17.
[t] Eccl. v. 17.   [u] Rom. v. 3.   [x] 2 Kings xx. 19.
[y] Prov. xiv. 10.   [z] 2 Cor. iv. 16.   [a] Ps. xxxvii. 37.
[b] Ps. cxliv. 15.

innumerable; we shall however confine ourselves to three:

1. The fitness of things requires it—

[No man can seriously think that there is one portion to the righteous and the wicked: there is no well-ordered government on earth where this is the case; much less can we suppose it possible in the divine government. To imagine such a thing, is to strip the Deity of all regard to his own honour. We may be sure that there shall be a distinction made in favour of his servants[c].]

2. The promises of God insure it—

[All *temporal* good is expressly promised to those " who fear God[d]:" all *spiritual* good also is given them as their portion[e]: yea, all *eternal* good is laid up for them as their unalienable inheritance[f]: all the promises are made over to them in one word[g]. Can any one doubt a truth so fully established?]

3. The experience of all that ever feared God attests it—

[Who ever found it unprofitable to serve the Lord[h]? What truly devoted soul was ever forsaken by him[i]? Who ever complained that the means, by which he was brought to fear God, were too severe? Or that any affliction, that increased and confirmed that fear, was too heavy? David indeed did at one time question the position in the text; but on recollection he condemned himself for his rashness and ignorance, and acknowledged that his vile suspicions contradicted the experience of God's children in all ages[k].]

On these grounds we " assuredly know" the truth declared in the text—

[We do not *surmise it as* a thing *possible*. We do not *hope it as* a thing *probable*. We *absolutely know it as infallibly certain*. We are not surer of our existence than we are of this truth. Without hesitation therefore we deliver our message[l]. O that the word may sink deep into all our hearts! And that we might from experience unite our testimony to Solomon's[m].]

We beg leave to ask, whether they who fear *not* God, have any such assurance in their favour?

[We are aware that they will entertain presumptuous hopes; and that, in opposition to God's word, they will expect

c Mal. iii. 18.   d Ps. xxxiv. 9.   e Ps. xxv. 12, 13.
f Ps. ciii. 17.   g 1 Tim. iv. 8.   h Jer. ii. 31.
i Isai. xlix. 15.   k Ps. lxxiii. 12—15, 22.
l Isai. iii. 10, 11.   m Prov. xxviii. 14.

happiness. But does the boldest sinner dare affirm that he *knows* it shall be well with him? His conscience would instantly revolt at such falsehood and blasphemy. Let those then, that fear not God, stand self-condemned. Let them flee unto their God and Saviour with penitence and faith. Let them so live as to preserve the testimony of a good conscience. And then, however enlarged their expectations of good may be, they shall never be disappointed[n].]

n Isai. xlv. 17.

OUTLINE NO. 840

THE WICKEDNESS, MADNESS, AND MISERY OF UNREGENERATE MEN.

Eccl. ix. 3. *The heart of the sons of men is full of evil; and madness is in their heart while they live; and after that, they go to the dead.*

IF we look only on the surface of things, we shall think that all things come alike to all, since all are subject to the same afflictions, and go down to the grave in their appointed season. But the righteous, however afflicted, " are in the hands of God[a]," who ordereth and overruleth every thing for their good; whereas the wicked, however prosperous, are left to run their career of sin, till they fall into the pit of everlasting destruction. The state and end of unregenerated men are awfully declared in the words before us; wherein is depicted,

I. Their wickedness—

[" The hearts of unregenerate men are full of evil." Every species of filthiness, whether fleshly or spiritual[b], abounds within them[c]. They have not a faculty either of body or soul that is not defiled with sin[d]. So full of iniquity are they, that there is no good within them[e]. And this is the state, not of a few only, but of every child of man, till he has been renewed by the Holy Spirit[f].]

II. Their madness—

[It may well be expected that creatures so depraved should manifest their depravity in the whole of their conduct. And in truth they do so: for they are even mad. *They pour contempt upon the greatest good.* Can any thing be compared

a ver. 1. b 2 Cor. vii. 1. c Rom. i. 29—31. d Rom. iii. 10—18.
e Gen. vi. 5. Rom. vii. 18. f John iii. 6. Tit. iii. 3. Jer. xvii. 9.

with the salvation of the soul? And do they not disregard this? And is not such conduct madness? *They also disregard the greatest of all evils,* the wrath of God. And would not this be madness, if there were only a bare *possibility* of their falling under his everlasting displeasure? How much more then, when it is as certain, as that there is a God! Moreover, *they continue in this state,* for the most part, *" as long as they live."* If they acted only through ignorance, or were drawn aside for a little time by temptation, or if they turned from this way, as soon as they came to the full exercise of their reason, yea, if they rectified their conduct as soon as their own consciences condemned it, they would have some shadow of an excuse. But, when they persist, against light and knowledge, against warnings and judgments, yea, against their own vows and resolutions, what is it but madness itself? Let a man act in such a way with respect to *the things of this world,* and no one will hesitate a moment to pronounce him mad[g].]

III. Their misery—

[How pleasant soever the ways of ungodly men appear, they will soon terminate in death[h]. But the righteous also must go the grave: no doubt therefore it is another death that is here spoken of, even " the second death in the lake that burneth with fire and brimstone." This is affirmed by God in the strongest manner[i]; and, however disbelieved by those whom it most concerns, it shall assuredly be found true at the last. Yea, we have even now the consciences of men attesting this awful truth: and if we should say, that the ungodly, after such a life, should "go to" *heaven,* instead of to " the dead," though they might be wicked enough to wish it, they would not be mad enough to believe it. They have a presentiment, in spite of all their reasonings to the contrary, that "their end shall be according to their works[k]."]

INFER—

1. How necessary is it to deal faithfully with the souls of men!

[Should we " prophesy smooth things" unto people who are perishing in their sins, and who before another Sabbath may be " gone to the dead?" Should we, if we beheld a stranded vessel, seek to amuse the sailors, instead of affording them direction and assistance? How much less then if we ourselves were embarked with them, and were partners of their danger? Surely then every time we preach, we should bear in mind that both our hearers and ourselves are dying

---

g Luke xv. 17.   h Job xx. 5—9.
i 1 Cor. vi. 9. Ps. ix. 17.   k 2 Cor. xi. 15.

creatures, and that, if we forbear to warn them, we ruin ourselves for ever[l].]

2. How earnestly should every one seek to be born
again!

[Does the notion of regeneration appear absurd[m]? Let
all hear and understand the grounds of that doctrine. What
must we think of God, if he should fill heaven with sinners
incorrigibly wicked, and incurably mad? Or what happiness
could such sinners find in heaven, even if they were admitted
there? There must be a meetness for the heavenly state[n]:
and that meetness can be obtained only by means of the new
birth[o]. A new heart must be given us[p], and we must be made
"new creatures in Christ Jesus[q]." Let all then seek this
renewal of their hearts[r]: for, unless they be born again, they
shall never enter into God's kingdom[s].]

3. How greatly are all regenerate persons indebted
to the Lord Jesus Christ!

[They were once even as others: if there was any difference, it was only in their *acts*, and not in their *hearts*[t]. But
they are delivered from their sins[u], endued with soundness of
mind[x], and made heirs of everlasting life[y]: and all this they
have received through the atoning blood and prevailing intercession of the Lord Jesus. What a Benefactor then is HE!
And how should the hearts of all be knit to him in love! O
"let them give thanks whom the Lord hath redeemed[z]:" and
let all seek these blessings at the hands of a gracious and
almighty Saviour.]

[l] Ezek. xxxiii. 8.　　[m] John iii. 7, 9.　　[n] Col. i. 12.
[o] John iii. 5, 6.　　[p] Ezek. xxxvi. 25, 26.　　[q] 2 Cor. v. 17
[r] Eph. iv. 22—24.　　[s] John iii. 3.　　[t] Eph. ii. 3.
[u] Rom. vi. 14. and viii. 2.　　[x] 2 Tim. i. 7.　　[y] John v. 24.
[z] Ps. cvii. 1, 2.

OUTLINE NO. 841

EARNESTNESS IN RELIGION RECOMMENDED.

Eccl. ix. 10. *Whatsoever thy hand findeth to do, do it with thy
might; for there is no work, nor device, nor knowledge, nor
wisdom, in the grave whither thou goest.*

THE greater part of mankind imagine, that a continued round of worldliness and pleasure will consist
with religion. But their opinion is contradicted by
the whole tenour of Scripture, which uniformly enjoins
deadness to the world and devotedness to God.

There are however some who err on the other side; and who make religion to consist in penances, and pilgrimages, and mortifications, and a total abstinence from all indulgences, however innocent, not excepting even the comforts and endearments of domestic life. In direct opposition to these are the words of Solomon in all the preceding context. He contends, that neither a cheerful use of the bounties of Providence, nor a prudent participation of the elegancies of life, nor a free enjoyment of conjugal affection, will at all interfere with our " acceptance with God," provided our ardour in the pursuit of heavenly things be not diminished by them[a]. With this St. Paul also agrees: for he says, that " God hath given us all things richly to enjoy;" and, that " godliness is profitable unto all things, having the promise of the life that now is, as well as of that which is to come."

It is not our intention, however, to enter into this general question; but rather to confine ourselves to the direction of Solomon in the text; in which we notice,

I. His advice—

Industry in temporal concerns is doubtless an important duty; and we may certainly understand the words before us as inculcating, and enforcing this duty. But the advice must relate also to spiritual concerns, in transacting which more especially, the utmost zeal is necessary.

Every man has a work to do for his soul—

[*The unconverted* have to get a sense of their guilt and danger, to turn unto their God with the deepest penitence and contrition, and to have their souls renewed after the divine image — — — *The penitent* have also a great work to do. They have only just set out upon their race, and have as yet all the ground before them, over which they are to run. They have to obtain the knowledge of Christ, and get their souls washed in his blood; and, in conformity to his example, to serve God in newness of heart and life — — — *The converted* too, whatever attainments they may have made, have still much which their " hand findeth to do." They have many lusts to mortify, many temptations to withstand, many conflicts to sustain, many graces to exercise, many duties to perform : to their latest hour they will be required to "glorify God with their bodies and their spirits, which are his"— — —]

This work must be " done with all our might"—

[It must be done *speedily, without delay.*—None of us have any time to lose. Whatever be our state at present, we know not how long our lives may be continued. The young and healthy are mortal, as well as the old and diseased: and the sturdy oak may be blown down while the bending rush survives. We should therefore imitate David, who says, " I made haste, and delayed not to keep thy commandments."

It must be done *heartily, without remissness.*—It is not suffi- cient to enter upon this work with indifference, and to prosecute it in a cold lifeless manner. We must "give all diligence to make our calling sure," and " to be found of Christ in peace :" we must " *strive* to enter in at the strait gate, since we may *seek,* and not be able." Even "the righteous are *scarcely* saved," and with great difficulty. If any dream of salvation as a matter easily to be accomplished, they will "perish in their own delusions."

It must be done *perseveringly, without weariness.*—There is no period when we are at liberty to relax our endeavours. While we are in the world, we are still on the field of battle, and surrounded with enemies that are ever ready to take ad- vantage of us. It is not till death that we can " put off the harness:" " till then, there is no discharge in this warfare." We must "not faint, or be weary in well-doing, if ever we would reap;" but must " be steadfast, immoveable, always abounding in the work of the Lord."]

To impress this salutary advice upon our minds, let us proceed to consider,

II. The argument with which it is enforced—

We all are dying creatures, and continually hasten- ing to the grave. Whether we be going to our bu- siness, or our pleasure, or our rest, wherever we are, and whatever we are doing, we are " going to our grave." The precise distance of our grave is hid from us : some arrive at it almost as soon as they set out on their journey : multitudes, when thinking of nothing less, drop into it suddenly, and are seen no more. Those who have walked towards it for a considerable time, have stronger and stronger inti- mations of their approach towards it. Many are seen with one foot already in it: and all, sooner or later, make it their long home.

From hence arise two very powerful arguments for enforcing diligence in the concerns of the soul. In the grave,

1. There is " no work" to be done—

[This life is the time for work: the next life is the time for recompence. The works needful to be done are, to " repent and believe the Gospel:" but in the eternal world there is no opportunity for performing either.

We cannot repent.—A kind of repentance indeed there will be among those who have perished in their sins: they will " weep, and wail, and gnash their teeth" with anguish: they will be sorry, not that they sinned, but that they subjected themselves to misery: sin will appear formidable to them on account of its consequences, but not hateful on account of its malignity. If they were restored to another state of probation, they would in a little time resume their former courses. As now on a bed of sickness they promise to amend their lives, but, when restored to health, become as careless as ever, so it would be with them if they returned even from hell itself: their hearts are unrenewed, and consequently their disposition to " wallow in the mire" of sin would infallibly lead them into their former habits of worldliness and sensuality. They must for ever remain the same obdurate sinners, because the Spirit of God will never descend into their hearts to renew them unto repentance.

We cannot believe in Christ.—Those who have perished will, it is true, believe many things which now they disbelieve: they will believe that Christ is a Saviour, and that he is the only Saviour of sinful men: but they will never believe in him for salvation, because he will never again be offered to them as a Saviour. No tidings of redemption will ever be heard in those dreary mansions. Never will they hear such words as those, " Come unto me, all ye that labour and are heavy laden." No promise of acceptance is given them; and therefore there can be no scope for the exercise of faith: nor, if there were an opportunity to believe, would they be able to embrace it; because " faith is the gift of God;" and they who reject his offers of it in this world, will never have it offered to them in the world to come.

This argument cannot but have the greatest weight with every considerate mind; and the rather, because it is urged by our Lord himself; " Work while it is day; for the night cometh wherein no man can work[b]."]

[b] John ix. 4.

2. There is no remedy to be devised"—

[While we are in this world, our "knowledge and wisdom" may be applied with effect. There is a "device" for the restoration of God's banished people[c]; and, if we be wise enough to adopt it, we cannot fail of obtaining mercy at the last day. But, if we neglect to use the remedy which is now afforded us, no other will remain for us; nothing can ever be devised whereby we may *alter*, or *avoid*, or *mitigate*, or *shorten* our doom.

We cannot *alter* it.—When once the Judge has said, " Go, ye cursed," we can never prevail on him to reverse the sentence, and say, " Come, ye blessed." *Now*, though " we are under condemnation, and the wrath of God abideth on us[d]," yet we may obtain reconciliation through the blood of Jesus, and be made heirs of a heavenly inheritance. But no such change can be effected in the eternal world: " as the tree falleth, so it will lie for ever."

We cannot *avoid* it.—We may " call upon the rocks to fall upon us, and the mountains to cover us from the wrath of the Lamb," but they cannot perform the friendly office. " If we should go up to heaven, or make our bed in hell, or take the wings of the morning and dwell in the uttermost part of the sea, there would God seize us, and thence would he bring us" by his irresistible power, in order that we might suffer the just reward of our deeds.

We cannot *mitigate* it.—*Here* men may flee to business or pleasure: they may drown care in intoxication, and obtain some relief from it in sleep: they may shake it off in a measure by infidelity. But in the eternal world they will find no jovial companions to associate with, nothing to divert their thoughts, nothing to alleviate their pains: " wrath will have come upon them to the uttermost," and their misery will be complete.

We cannot *shorten* it.—Men in this world have one method (as they think) of terminating their miseries, namely, by suicide. A poor and fatal " device" indeed! yet such as it is, they resort to it for relief. But in the future world even this refuge will fail them: " they shall seek death, but shall not find it; and shall desire to die, but death shall flee from them[e]." Eternity will be the duration of their woe: " the smoke of their torment will ascend up for ever and ever."

How forcible then is this argument! If any " device" remained for them, and their " knowledge and wisdom" could be effectual for their relief, then they might be the more indifferent about the improvement of their day of grace. But since " this is the only accepted time, the only day of salvation, surely they should " work out their salvation instantly with fear

[c] Compare 2 Sam. xiv. 14. with Job xxxiii. 24.
[d] John iii. 18, 36.   [e] Rev. ix. 6.

and trembling," and seek " the things belonging to their peace, before they be for ever hid from their eyes."]

ADDRESS—

1. Those who are postponing their work—

[Like those who neglected the rebuilding of the temple, we are apt to say, " The time for this work is not yet come." Youth look forward to adult age; and they who are grown to manhood think that a more advanced period of life will be more favourable for the exercises of religion: and even the aged put off the work from day to day, hoping for some " more convenient season." But how many thousands perish by deferring that work which they acknowledge to be necessary! Sickness and death find them in an unconverted state, and hurry them un-prepared into the presence of God. O that all of us, whether old or young, would guard against these fatal consequences, and turn to God " this day, while it is called To-day."]

2. Those who are trifling with their work—

[There are many who would be offended, if they were thought regardless of religion, who yet by their listlessness and formality shew that they have no real delight in it. They are exact in their attendance on ordinances; but they engage in them with a lukewarm Laodicean spirit: they have " the form of godliness, but not the power." But what can such persons think of the representations which the Scripture gives us of the Christian life? It is there described as a race, a wrestling, a combat; all of which imply the strongest possible exertions. Would to God that this matter were duly considered; and that we called upon " our souls, and all that is within us," to prosecute this great concern. To every thing that might divert our attention from it, we should answer with Nehemiah, " I am doing a great work, and cannot come down[f]." It is in this way only that we shall ever be enabled to adopt the words of our dying Lord, " Father, I have glorified thee on earth, I have finished the work which thou gavest me to do."]

3. Those who are heartily engaged in their work—

[While the greater part of mankind make their worldly duties an excuse for neglecting religion, there are some who run into a contrary extreme, and make their religious duties an excuse for neglecting their worldly concerns. But this will bring great dishonour on religion. We are placed in the world as social beings, and have civil and social, as well as religious, duties to perform. These must be made to harmonize: and all must be attended to in their order. We must " not be slothful in business, though we must be fervent in spirit; for

f Nch. vi. 3, 4.

in both we may serve the Lord." Indeed our relative duties
are, in fact, religious; because they are enjoined by God, and
may be performed as unto God: nor are they less acceptable
unto him in their place than the more spiritual services of prayer
and praise. While therefore we would exhort all to an immediate, earnest, diligent, patient, unremitted attention to the
concerns of their souls, and encourage them to disregard all the
persecutions which they may endure for righteousness sake, we
would entreat them also to " walk wisely in a perfect way;" and
to shew by their conduct that religion is as conducive to the
interests of society, as it is to the welfare of the soul.]

OUTLINE NO. 842

WISDOM NOTIONALLY APPROVED, BUT PRACTICALLY DIS-REGARDED.

Eccl. ix. 14—16. *There was a little city, and few men within
it : and there came a great king against it, and besieged it,
and built great bulwarks against it. Now there was found in
it a poor wise man : and he by his wisdom delivered the city :
yet no man remembered that same poor man. Then said I,
Wisdom is better than strength: nevertheless the poor man's
wisdom is despised, and his words are not heard.*

WHETHER the account here given us was an
actual occurrence, or only a parabolic representation,
we will not undertake to determine : but certainly
the event described may easily be supposed to have
taken place, and to have come to the knowledge of
Solomon. In fact, a precisely similar event had
taken place within the memory of Solomon ; the only
difference being, that the city was saved by " a wise
woman," instead of " a poor wise man." After the
rebellion of Absalom had been suppressed, a man of
Belial, whose name was Sheba, caused the defection
of all the tribes of Israel. David therefore sent an
army to pursue Sheba, and to besiege any city in
which he should have taken refuge. Joab finding
that Sheba was shut up in a city called Abel, went
and " battered the wall of the city, to throw it down."
Then " a wise woman" called to Joab, and remon-
strated with him on the subject of the assault which
he was making ; and undertook, that, if he would
suspend his assault, the object of his indignation

should be sacrificed, and his head be cast over the wall. She then " went to all the people, *in her wisdom,*" and prevailed on them to execute her project; and thus effected by her wisdom the deliverance of the city, and the preservation of all its inhabitants[a]. The minute resemblance which there is between this history and the event mentioned in the text, renders it highly probable, that the passage before us is a parable, founded upon the very fact which is here recorded.

But, whether it be a fact, or a parable, with what view is it mentioned? Some think that it is intended to represent the work of redemption by our Lord Jesus Christ, and the sad neglect with which he is treated, notwithstanding the benefits he has conferred. According to these persons, the interpretation is this. The little city, with a small garrison, is the Church, which confessedly consists of but " a little flock." The great king who comes against it, and besieges it, is Satan, with all his hosts, even all the principalities and powers of hell. The poor wise man is the Lord Jesus Christ, who, by the counsels of eternal Wisdom, has devised a way for the deliverance of his people; yet after the deliverance he has wrought out for them, is by the generality most grievously neglected.

Now though there are parts of this which do not exactly accord with such an interpretation, yet we should not have altogether disapproved of the interpretation, provided Solomon himself had not given us any clew whereby to discover his real meaning: for it is not necessary that a parable should be applicable in all its parts: it is sufficient if in its main scope it be fitted to illustrate the point which it is intended to shadow forth. But we are precluded from affixing to this passage the sense which we have now suggested, because Solomon's own reflection upon the supposed event determines beyond all controversy its precise import. Solomon intended to commend wisdom, as he frequently does in other parts of this book: in one place he exalts wisdom above folly[b];

---

[a] 2 Sam. xx. 1, 2, 6, 15—22. [b] Eccl. ii. 13.

in another, above wealth^c; in another, above soldiers^d, and weapons of war^e. Thus in our text he exalts it above strength; " Then said I, Wisdom is better than strength." Hence the subject for our consideration is two-fold ;

I. The excellency of wisdom—

Wisdom is practical understanding, or knowledge regulated by sound judgment. Now this is greatly superior to physical force, in every point of view :

1. In relation to temporal concerns—

[The particular instance here adduced, the deliverance of a city by some extraordinary devices, will lead us to notice the operations of wisdom in the different departments of civilized life.

In war and politics it prevails far beyond mere bodily strength, however great. It is from superior skill in arms that we, who are so few in number, have been enabled to conquer an immense extent of territory, and by a very small army to keep in subjection eighty millions of people, who have scarcely one feeling, or one sentiment, in common with ourselves. And it is from the wisdom of our Constitution, and of our Governors, that we, under God, have rode out the storm which overwhelmed the rest of Europe, and have been enabled to rescue from their bondage the prostrate nations all around us. Had there been less wisdom at our helm, we, and all the nations of Europe, should probably at this moment have been sunk in the lowest state of degradation and misery.

In arts and manufactures the excellency of wisdom also most eminently appears. See the machinery that is used in every branch of trade ! A few children are enabled to effect in a month what thousands of grown people could not by mere manual labour accomplish in a year.

Nor is the excellency of wisdom less visible *in science and philosophy*. Who can calculate the benefits that have arisen from the study of astronomy, and the invention of the compass ? How light is all human strength when placed in the balance against these products of intellectual research !

In truth, it is wisdom which most elevates us above the beasts; and draws as broad a line of distinction between man and man, as light and darkness do in the material world.]

2. In relation to spiritual affairs—

[Here wisdom is all. See what mere human efforts can effect in heathen lands : what penances, what pilgrimages, what

c Eccl. vii. 12.   d Eccl. vii. 19.   e ver. 18.

sufferings of different kinds, will men have recourse to, in order to obtain peace in their own souls! yet can they never obtain it. They may weary themselves even unto death, yet can they never secure to themselves any spiritual benefit whatever.

But let a man attend to the councils of wisdom given him by our blessed Lord, and all that he can desire is attained at once. Peace will flow into his soul, as soon as ever his conscience is sprinkled with the blood of Christ. His powers are invigorated with preter-natural strength, the moment he by faith apprehends the Lord Jesus: from being so weak as not to be able to do *any* thing, he becomes instantly so strong as to be " able to do *all* things[f]." A new set of energies are developed, and such as Satan is not able to withstand. That enemy, who with assured confidence of success besieged the soul, is constrained, like Sennacherib, to flee with precipitation and disgrace[g]. In a word, the simple device of a "life of faith upon the Son of God" effects every thing, liberating the soul from all its bondage, and making it victorious over all its enemies.]

But from daily observation, we are constrained to lament,

II. The disregard shewn it, notwithstanding its acknowledged worth.

By how few are its dictates attended to as they ought to be! Alas! they are neglected and despised, by the great mass of mankind.

1. By the gay and thoughtless—

[They have no ear for the counsels of Wisdom. They will commend her in general terms; but will have as little as possible to do with her instructions. Let the parent labour ever so much to instil wisdom into the minds of his children, he will find, to his grief, that the enchantments of folly baffle all his efforts. It should seem no difficult task to prevail on them to think before they act, and to regulate their conduct by sound principles: but though he give " line upon line, and precept upon precept," he will have reason to bless himself, if, after all his endeavours, his family do not embitter his days by their faults and follies. The word of God too may be acknowledged by them as good: but not a precept in it is suffered to have an ascendant over their mind. Sabbath after Sabbath are divine instructions poured into their ears; but none are suffered to descend into the heart. In fact, they are despised; and if obtruded upon the mind as principles of action, they are rejected with scorn and contempt.]

[f] John xv. 2. Phil. iv. 13. [g] James iv. 7.

2. By the formal and self-righteous—

[Wisdom's sublimest dictates are by these regarded as the reveries of a heated imagination. The whole life of faith is foolishness in the eyes of a self-righteous Pharisee. He sees no suitableness in it to the end proposed. He thinks that an attendance on ordinances, and a performance of some moral duties, are quite sufficient: Why should he mourn and weep? What is there in faith that can benefit his soul? Why may not his works find acceptance with God? In vain is he told that the Gospel is "the wisdom of God in a mystery;" and that the very angels in heaven are made wiser by the revelation of it to the Church[h]. In vain is he told what the Lord Jesus Christ, that "Wonderful Counsellor," *has done* for the redemption of a ruined world, and *will do* in all who believe in him. No sense of obligation abides upon his mind: no expressions of gratitude flow from his lips: the Benefactor is forgotten, and the benefit despised: and he chooses rather to seek his resources within himself, than to depend for them on the bounty of another.]

3. The backsliding professor—

[The man who has once "professed godliness," has given his testimony to the excellence of wisdom. But when he declines from the way of godliness, he revokes his testimony, and becomes an open advocate for folly: he proclaims to all, that the ways of wisdom are incapable of affording him any solid comfort; or, at all events, that there is more happiness to be found in the vanities of time and sense, than in the service of the living God. Yes, thou backslider, thou "exaltest folly, and praisest the wicked[i]:" and, if thou condemnest, as thou must, the inhabitants of the city that left their benefactor to pine away in poverty and contempt, much more must thou condemn thyself, who hast, by thy declensions, "crucified the Son of God afresh, and put him to an open shame."]

Let me now IMPROVE the subject, by recommending to your adoption,

1. A life of consideration and thoughtfulness—

[The man who has begun to think and to consider, has already got more than half way to heaven. It is inconsideration that ruins the whole world. Would men but inquire from day to day, What have I done? Has it been consonant with the dictates of sound wisdom? Have I proposed to myself the best ends, and have I pursued them by the fittest means? how much evil would they avoid, and how much misery would they escape! O that I might prevail upon you to enter on such a course as

h Eph. iii. 10.   i Prov. xxviii. 4.

this! Admirable is that advice of Solomon, "Prepare thy work without, and make it fit for thyself in the field; and afterwards build thine house [k]." This is what any prudent builder will do, though he is only constructing a temporary habitation for the body: and how much more should *we* do it, who are building for the immortal soul! Adopt this plan then: think what you have to do for God: think by what means you may best advance the interest of your souls; and redeem, as it were, every hour in preparation for eternity. "Walk, not as fools, but as wise, redeeming the time, because the days are evil."]

2. A life of real piety—

[Nothing but this will inspire true wisdom: nothing but this will enable us to counteract with effect the assaults of our great adversary. Let us seek from above "a spirit of wisdom and understanding, a spirit of counsel and of might:" then, whether we be poor or rich, we shall assuredly be victorious. Indeed the poor are for the most part more highly favoured than the rich. The rich are too apt to be self-confident and self-sufficient; whilst the poor accept thankfully the proferred aids of the Gospel. Hence "the things which are hid from the wise and prudent, are frequently revealed to babes;" and hence, whilst the rich are vanquished, the poor are crowned with victory. Let it not be forgotten, that "in the Lord alone we have either righteousness or strength." "Not by might, nor by power, but by my Spirit, saith the Lord of Hosts:" yes, by the Spirit of the living God revealing the Saviour to us, and communicating strength out of his fulness, we shall be "enabled to withstand in the evil day," and shall have that joyful song put into our mouths, "Thanks be to God, who giveth us the victory through our Lord Jesus Christ!"]

[k] Prov. xxiv. 27.

OUTLINE NO. 843

THE DESTRUCTIVE INFLUENCE OF SINNERS.

Eccl. ix. 18. *One sinner destroyeth much good.*

THE influence of every man in his sphere is considerable. Solomon had seen a remarkable instance of a poor man delivering by his wisdom a small and ill-garrisoned city from the besieging army of a very powerful monarch. From hence he was led to consider the superiority of wisdom above wealth or power. On the other hand, he saw that, as a wise and good man might be extremely useful, so a foolish and wicked man might do a great deal of injury, to those around him. Hence, contrasting the two, he observed, " Wisdom is better than weapons of war : but one sinner destroyeth much good."

In illustrating the latter member of the sentence, we shall point out the truth of it,

I. In nations—

[Men of all classes in the community may greatly affect the state to which they belong.

A weak and ambitious monarch, how soon may he involve his people in war, and reduce them to the very brink of ruin! Such was Solomon's only son, who, in the space of a few weeks, goaded ten tribes out of the twelve that he ruled over, to revolt from him, and to establish a separate and independent kingdom[a].

An aspiring subject also may, by exaggerating the people's grievances, and promising them effectual redress, stir up multitudes to insurrection, and involve a nation in all the horrors of civil war. Thus did Absalom[b] : and thus have demagogues in every age, in every state.

What immense evil too may not *a cruel persecutor* effect! How may such an one waste the Church of God and destroy it! One Jezebel could murder a whole host of prophets[c]; and one Saul depopulate the Christian Church[d]. And, in this nation as well as others, time was, when one cruel bigot kindled fires in every part of the country, to extirpate, if possible, those, who would not return to the justly reprobated errors of her religion.

If *a great man* be *conspicuous for impiety and profaneness,* his conduct will be attended with a most baneful influence. Soon will sycophants imitate his example, till irreligion becomes the fashion of the day, and every thing sacred is trampled under foot. What an awful instance of such success have we in Jeroboam ; who, the more effectually to detach from Judah the ten revolted tribes, erected idols in Dan and Bethel, which from that hour became, and ever afterwards remained, the objects of worship through the whole kingdom[e]! Hence he is continually stigmatized with the name of " him who made Israel to sin[f]!"

But indeed *any enormous sinner,* of whatever class, does much to destroy the peace and prosperity of his country. What is it that arms God against a nation, and provokes him

---

[a] 1 Kings xii. 16.   [b] 2 Sam. xv. 2—6, 10—14.
[c] 1 Kings xviii. 13.   [d] Acts ix. 1, 2.
[e] Hos. v. 11.   In this verse is mentioned not his success only, but the evil it brought upon them.   [f] 1 Kings xxii. 52.

to visit it with war, pestilence, and famine? Is it not sin? Every sinner therefore, in proportion as he increases the nation's guilt, contributes also to its punishment. In many instances we know, that the whole kingdom of Israel suffered for the offence of one; not for that of David only, who was the monarch[g]; but for that also of Achan, an obscure individual[h]: nor till the last day will it appear what injury this nation has sustained by means of every one here present.]

II. In families—

[What confusion is brought into any house by *an imperious husband, a contentious wife,* or *an undutiful, stubborn child!* Instead of love and harmony, there is little else than brawling and quarrelling; so that the very sight of each other, which ought to call forth all the tender emotions of their hearts excites nothing but enmity and disgust.

A man addicted to lewdness, gaming, intemperance, evil company, or idleness, to what wretchedness may he soon reduce his family! "God has put a price into the hand of such an one to make his dependents happy, but he knows not how to use it[i]." He might support them in ease and comfort, but brings them to want and desperation. How many instances of this are found in every town and village!

Nor can we easily estimate the good which *a whisperer and a tale-bearer* may destroy. Behold, he comes into a house where friends or relatives are cemented in the strictest bonds of union and amity: but he creates suspicion, and alienates their minds, and kindles feuds, and fills with animosity the bosoms that once glowed with mutual affection[k].

But what shall we say of *the* vile *seducer,* who under the mask of friendship enters the house of his unsuspecting neighbour, and avails himself of the opportunity to decoy his daughter, or to defile his wife? Alas! what incalculable misery does such a man create! For the sake of a momentary gratification, how many hearts does he pierce with the deepest and most lasting sorrow! What disgrace does he bring upon the whole family, involving the innocent with the guilty in irremediable shame, and bowing them down with grief that hurries them to the grave! Would to God that, if such a character exist in this assembly, he might be smitten with remorse, and wounded to his inmost soul!]

III. In the church of God—

[On whom shall we fix our eyes, as hostile to the Church's welfare, so soon as on *the careless minister?* To him God has committed the improvement of sabbaths, and ordinances, and

---

[g] 2 Sam. xxiv. 10, 15.　　[h] Josh. xxii. 20.
[i] Prov. xvii. 16.　　[k] Prov. xvi. 28.

of the sacred oracles. To him he has given souls to be nurtured and disciplined for heaven. But the traitor is intent only on his own gains or pleasures: he performs his weekly task, not caring whether any be edified or not: he wastes the precious opportunities, that can never be recalled; and, in the course of his ministry, leads thousands to destruction. Yes; as far as his influence extends, he makes null and void all the purposes of God's grace, and all the wonders of redeeming love. When, humanly speaking, he might have been a blessing to the world, and an ornament to his profession, he brings his sacred function into reproach, scattering the flock whom he should have gathered, and destroying whom he should have saved. Such an one is Satan's best friend, and the greatest enemy of God and man.

Much good also may be destroyed, especially where men are awake to the concerns of religion, by *a proud disputatious sectary*. I speak not here of those who dissent from the Established Church, but of those who create divisions within the Church by unduly insisting on matters of minor importance, and of doubtful disputation. Though the sentiments of such an one be not fundamentally erroneous, yet if he be laying an undue stress on matters that are comparatively indifferent, and forming parties in the church, he distracts the minds of the simple; he puffs up many with pride; he loosens the bonds of brotherly affection; he weakens the hands of a pious minister, and he causes many to relapse into formality and indifference[1]. Of such a character were Hymeneus[m], and Alexander[n]: and "one such root of bitterness will trouble and defile many[o]:" on which account we should be as studious as possible to stop their growth[p].

There is scarcely any one in the universe who does greater injury to the Church than *the professor who walks dishonourably*. One act of his brings disgrace upon the whole Church of God, and makes religion to stink in the very nostrils of those around him[q]. Instantly do the ungodly begin to triumph[r], to arraign all the people of God as hypocrites, and to represent religion itself as a mask for every thing that is vile[s]. Thus the wicked are hardened, the weak are offended, the saints are dishonoured, and the very name of God is blasphemed in the world[t]. How does God himself complain of this in the case of David[u]! and how incalculable must the evil be, when multitudes are thus offended, and set against the very means of salvation!

[1] Rom. xvi, 17, 18.   [m] 2 Tim. ii. 16—18, 23. and iii. 6, 13.
[n] 2 Tim. iv. 14, 15.
[o] Heb. xii. 15.   See also 1 Cor. v. 2, 6. and Gal. v. 7, 9.
[p] Tit. i. 13, 14. and iii. 9—11.   [q] Gen. xxxiv. 30.
[r] Ps. xxxv. 19, 25.   [s] 2 Pet. ii. 2.   [t] 1 Tim. vi. 1.
[u] 2 Sam. xii. 14.

There is yet one more character that we shall mention, whose conduct indeed is less extensively destructive, but not less injurious to those within his sphere, we mean, *the scoffer.* He brings no disgrace upon religion, because he makes no profession of it. Nor can he greatly impede its progress in the world, because he is not invested with authority or influence. But perhaps there is some relation, some friend, whom he can discourage by sneers and ridicule, if not also by menaces and actual unkindness. Suppose then that, in one single instance, he succeed in breaking the bruised reed and quenching the smoking flax; who shall appreciate the good he has destroyed? to ruin one for whom Christ died; and who, but for such an obstacle, would have got safe to heaven[x]! If the whole world be of no value in comparison of a soul[y], then, in that single act, the scoffer has done more harm than the whole world can recompense.]

APPLICATION—

1. Let us guard against receiving evil from others—

[It was a heathen poet that said, "Evil communications corrupt good manners;" and from him the Apostle quotes it, for the edification of the Church of Christ[z]. Behold then what reason itself, as well as Scripture, teaches us in reference to the subject before us. One person infected with the plague may do us more injury than a hundred healthy persons can do us good. I would earnestly entreat all, therefore, and young persons especially, not to admit to their friendship so much as "one" associate, whose ways are evil. For who can tell to what an extent the principles and conduct of such a man may prevail, to efface the good impressions that have been made upon his mind, and to induce habits that may prove fatal to his soul? If I regarded nothing but your temporal prosperity, I should give this advice: but when I take eternity into the account, I cannot but urge it upon every one here present, and say with the Apostle, "Come out from amongst such persons altogether, and be separate from them, and do not so much as touch the unclean thing" or person that may contaminate your soul.

2. Let us to the utmost of our power repair the evil which we ourselves have done—

[Suppose us ever so free from the more flagrant instances that have been mentioned, there is not one amongst us who has not done much evil by means of his example. We have all lived, like the world around us, in a neglect of God and of our own souls: and, in so doing, have countenanced the same

[x] Rom. xiv. 15.   [y] Matt. xvi. 26.
[z] 1 Cor. xv. 33. It is an Iambic verse from Menander.

conduct in others. Thus, whether we intended it or not, we have confirmed many in their ungodly ways, and have contributed to their eternal ruin. Let us go now, and undo what we have done: alas! we cannot find one half of them : many are not known by us: many are gone to distant parts : many are already in the eternal world : and, if we should attempt to convert those to whom we can get access, they would laugh at us as fools, or despise us as hypocrites. Besides, all of them in their respective spheres have diffused the contagion which they received from us : and thus have put it beyond the reach of man to trace, or even to conceive, the evil we have done. And does not all this call for penitence ? Yes; if our "head were a fountain of tears to run down incessantly" to the latest hour of our lives, it would be no more than the occasion calls for. But with our penitence we must unite our utmost efforts to repair the evil we have done.

To repair it with respect to God, is the work of Christ only. He alone can render satisfaction for our sins; his blood alone can cleanse us from the guilt we have contracted by them. But with respect to man we may do something, though we cannot do all that we could wish. Let us begin with *our example:* this speaks the most forcibly, and the most extensively. Let us, by giving up ourselves to God, shew others what they ought to do : and let our light so shine before men, that they may be constrained to glorify God, and to take shame to themselves. Next, let us use *our influence :* be it small or great, let us not neglect to exert it, that by every means in our power we may counteract our past evils, and stir up others to flee from the wrath to come. Finally, let us be fervent in *our intercessions* at the throne of grace, that God may take to him his great power, and establish his kingdom upon earth. Let us particularly pray for those, whom, in any respect, we may have allured from the path of duty. Thus, like the great Apostle, we shall make some compensation to the world for all the injuries it has sustained by our means, and shew, that, if one sinner can destroy much good, one saint can effect much which shall be a ground of joy and gratitude to all eternity.]

OUTLINE NO. 844

LIBERALITY ENCOURAGED.

Eccl. xi. 1. *Cast thy bread upon the waters: for thou shalt find it after many days.*

WHILST, in the purity of its precepts, the inspired volume exceeds all other books upon the face of the earth, it excels all other compositions in the variety and richness of the images under which it exhibits our duty and urges the performance of it. The image under which liberality is here inculcated is well understood in countries where the heat of the climate, uniting with periodical inundations, enables the husbandman to proceed in a mode of agriculture unknown to us in the colder regions of the globe. In Egypt, for instance, where the Nile overflows the country periodically to a vast extent, it is common for men to cast their seed, their rice especially, upon the waters, whilst yet they are at a considerable depth. This might seem to be folly in the extreme: but experience proves, that, instead of losing their seed, they find it again, after many days, rising into an abundant crop. Such shall be the return which we also shall find to our efforts, if we exert ourselves,

I. For the relief of men's bodily wants—

Liberality to the poor is strongly insisted on in the Holy Scriptures. It is inculcated,

1. In a way of precept—

[Exceedingly clear and strong were the injunctions which God gave on this subject to his people of old[a] — — — So, under the New Testament dispensation, we are enjoined to "labour with our own hands;" and to "lay by us weekly, in proportion as God has prospered us," *for the purpose of relieving others*[b] — — — Nay, so obvious is this duty, that the man who lives not in the practice of it must be an utter stranger to the love of God in his soul[c]: for "if he love not his brother whom he hath seen, how can he love God whom he hath not seen[d]?"]

2. In a way of example—

[The good Samaritan shews us how we ought to exercise generosity, even towards those who, by reason of particular differences and distinctions, may appear to be most remote from us[e]. The widow, in giving her mite, which was all that she possessed, might be thought to have acted a very wild and extravagant part, especially when she gave it for a purpose to which it could bear no proportion, namely, the repairing of the temple: yet is that commended to us, by our Lord himself,

---

[a] See Deut. xv. 7—11. and cite the whole.
[b] Eph. iv. 28. 1 Cor. xvi. 2. [c] 1 John iii. 17.
[d] 1 John iv. 20. [e] Luke x. 33—37.

as an example highly to be admired, and universally to be followed[f]. As for the Macedonians, who were proposed as an example to the Corinthians, their generosity exceeded all belief: for when in *great affliction*, and in a state of *deep poverty*, they *abounded* unto the *riches* of *liberality*, and of their own selves, without any solicitation on the part of the Apostle, besought him with much entreaty to take upon him the distribution of their alms[g]. Nothing can give us a higher idea of the excellence of charity than this.]

3. In a way of encouragement—

[God assures us, that " whatever we give to the poor, we lend unto the Lord; and that he will, in one way or another, repay us again[h]." He will repay us, even *in a way of temporal prosperity* : for the giving of " the first-fruits of all our increase to the poor is the way, not to empty our barns, but to fill them with plenty, and to make our presses burst out with new wine[i]." Still more will he repay us *in a way of spiritual prosperity;* since, " if we draw out our soul to the hungry, and satisfy the afflicted soul, he will satisfy our souls in drought, and make fat our bones, and make us like a watered garden, or like a spring of water, whose waters fail not[k]." Even *with eternal rewards* will he repay us, " recompensing, at the resurrection of the just," the smallest services we have rendered his people[l], and not suffering " even a cup of cold water to be left without its appropriate reward[m]."

I say then, with assured confidence in reference to this matter, " Cast your seed upon the waters; and you shall find it after many days."]

But we may understand our text as encouraging our exertions also,

II. For the advancement of men's mental improvement—

To this the same image is applied by the prophet Isaiah; who gives us this additional information, that persons, previous to their casting of their seed upon the waters, send forth their oxen and their asses to tread the ground with their feet, in order the better to prepare the earth for its reception : " Blessed are ye who sow beside all waters, that send forth thither the feet of the ox and the ass[n]." Now this refers to the publication of the Gospel in every place, however

---

[f] Mark xii. 42, 43.	[g] 2 Cor. viii. 1—4.	[h] Prov. xix. 17.
[i] Prov. iii. 9, 10.	[k] Isai. lviii. 10, 11.	[l] Luke xiv. 14.
[m] Matt. x. 42.	[n] Isai. xxxii. 20.	

untoward the circumstances, or hopeless the appearance. And we can bear witness to the truth of the prophet's observation : for in many places, and on many hearts, where there has been as little prospect of success as could well be conceived, God has given efficacy to the word of his grace ; and the handful of corn sown upon the top of the mountains has sprung up, so that the fruit thereof has shaken like the woods of Lebanon ; and those of the city where it has been cast have flourished like the piles of grass upon the earth°."

To *Infant Schools,* for the promotion of which I now more immediately address you, the text is peculiarly applicable ; since nothing can be supposed more hopeless than any attempt to benefit the rising generation, from the ages of two to five or six. But I must say, that, if you cast your seed upon these waters, you shall find it again, in very abundant benefits conferred on all the poorer classes of society—

[What a relief is it to the mother to have her infants duly attended to through the day ; whilst she, instead of having her hands tied by the care of them, is enabled to earn bread for their support ! What a benefit, too, is it to her elder daughter ; who would otherwise have her time occupied in attending upon her younger brothers and sisters, and be thereby deprived of education for herself, whilst she was discharging that important office ! This is of immense importance, because it secures to all the children of the poor the same advantages ; the elder and the younger being alike partakers of the benefits thus freely accorded to them.

But to the children themselves the benefits are incalculably great. We cannot but have seen, times without number, what depraved habits are contracted by the children of the poor when playing about the streets or lanes of a town without control. At home, for the most part, they see nothing but evil ; and abroad, they practise it in every way with sad proficiency, lying, swearing, quarrelling, the very pests of the neighbourhood wherein they dwell. As for any thing good, they learn it not ; having no good principles instilled into them, and no good examples set before them. But by being brought into a school at the early age of two or three years, they are

° Ps. lxxii. 16. If this be a subject for *Missions*, this idea must be enlarged, and all that follows it be omitted.

kept from all those temptations to which they would otherwise
be exposed ; and have their conduct watched over, their tempers corrected, their habits restrained, their principles improved,
their whole deportment brought into subjection to good instruction and to well-ordered authority.   They are insensibly
taught, by the example of others, what could not have been
infused into them by mere abstract precept ; and they acquire,
by imitation, habits of order and docility, which they could not
by any other method have obtained.   Now, then, who shall
estimate the value of this to the children themselves ? or who
shall say, What benefit shall, in a course of years, arise to the
whole community from such institutions as these, if they be
generally established and well supported?   I have not spoken
respecting religious advantages accruing to the children, because
it may be supposed that they are not at that early age capable
of religious instruction.   But is it nothing, to prevent the soil
being overrun with briars and thorns, and to have it improved
by the infusion of moral principles?   In fact, a child's religion
consists chiefly in the fear of God, and in an habitual regard
to his all-seeing eye : and this is implanted in their minds to
vast advantage, by the entire system of discipline to which they
are subjected, as well as by the distinct instructions which are
given them.   And though it is but too probable that they may
afterwards lose the impressions which are then made upon their
minds, yet they can never forget the general idea, that it was
well with them when they were so disciplined and so instructed.
Nor is the influence which they may carry home into their domestic circles, a trifling matter: for when their parents hear
them giving an account of the lessons they have learned—lessons of meekness and patience, of truth and honesty, of purity
and love—they may themselves be put to shame, and acquire
very important hints for their own improvement.]

I beg leave, then, to RECOMMEND to your support this
      important institution—
   I would recommend it,
   [First, *for the sake of the rising generation,* on whom it
will confer so great a benefit ———— Next, *for the sake of those
who have set on foot this benevolent plan.*   None but persons of
very enlarged minds could ever have devised such means of
benefiting the poor.   To instruct such infants would, to any
common understanding, have appeared as hopeless a task as
that of " casting bread upon the waters."   Yet experience has
proved its vast utility ; and shewn, that if such institutions were
to prevail in every town, a most extensive benefit would be
conferred on the whole community.   Shall, then, persons capable of adorning and instructing the highest ranks in society
not meet with support, when they employ their talents in

contriving means for benefiting the poor? Surely every person ought to bear testimony to the worth and excellence of such designs; and to give them, the best tribute of applause, their active concurrence, and their most liberal support.

Lastly, *for the sake of the Lord Jesus Christ himself*, I would urge upon you the support of this beneficent institution: for he counted not little children beneath his notice; but took them up in his arms, and put his hands upon them and blessed them, and declared that every attention that was paid to such infants would be regarded by him as paid to himself [p]. If, then, you have any love to the Saviour, who himself assumed a state of infancy for you—yea, and died upon the cross for you—shew it by your liberality on this occasion. Let all endeavour to cultivate the ground. Let him that hath an ox, "send forth his ox;" and let him that hath an ass, "send forth his ass." Let every one, according to his ability, contribute to help forward this good work, without intermission and without despondency. To every one amongst you I would say, "In the morning sow thy seed; in the evening withhold not thine hand: for thou knowest not whether shall prosper, either this or that, or whether they both shall be alike good [q]."]

p Matt. xviii. 2, 5.   q ver. 6.

OUTLINE NO. 845

YOUTH WARNED OF THE FUTURE JUDGMENT.

Eccl. xi. 9. *Rejoice, O young man, in thy youth; and let thy heart cheer thee in the days of thy youth, and walk in the ways of thine heart, and in the sight of thine eyes: but know thou, that for all these things, God will bring thee into judgment.*

EARTHLY pleasure is doubtless gratifying to flesh and blood: hence it is more or less an object of desire to all: but there are two considerations which may well abate our ardour in the pursuit, namely, that its gratifications will soon come to an end; and that there is an approaching judgment, at which we must give an account of all that we have ever done in the body, and receive from God's mouth a sentence corresponding with the tenour of our past life. In the verses preceding our text, the former consideration is urged; and we are told, that, however protracted our pleasures may be, they are but like a winter's sun, which will soon set in darkness, and be followed by a long and dreary night. Such a night is not far off, even from those who are in the very morning of life. It may be hastened prematurely, as it were, by sickness, and care, and unavoidable misfortunes; and it must come at last through the infirmities of age, which, if our life be prolonged, will make it but " labour and sorrow." The latter consideration is suggested in the text, which contains two things:

I. A keen remonstrance.

The address here made to youth, though it appears like a concession, is not really so—

[It has been thought by some to be a concession, recommending youth to enjoy themselves in the world; only to do it in such a way as not to endanger their happiness in a future life. And it is certain that there are in this book many concessions to that effect[a]— — — Such passages as these may indeed be easily pressed too far: but, on the other hand, they are not in general understood by the religious world. Religious people are apt to imagine, that Christianity requires an utter abandonment of those things which the carnal mind affects; and that a pious person who possesses any considerable measure of earthly comforts, is necessarily inconsistent in his conduct. But this is a mistake, and a mistake which greatly needs to be rectified; because it occasions many unjust censures, and uncharitable reflections. " God has given us all things richly to enjoy[b]:" and, provided we do not spend an undue portion of our substance on earthly indulgences, or set our affections upon them, there is nothing in Christianity which prohibits a reasonable use, and a temperate enjoyment of them. If only we sit loose to them in our hearts, and enjoy God in them, they are perfectly lawful; yea, " they are sanctified to us by the word of God and prayer[c]."

But it is not in this sense that the address before us is to be understood:]

It is, on the contrary, a just and severe remonstrance—

[The terms here used are such as cannot well be taken in a good sense. To "walk in the ways of our own heart, and in the sight of our own eyes," is equivalent to walking in the ways of *criminal* self-indulgence. This is the import of these expressions in other passages of Scripture[d]— — — and so they must be taken here; as is evident from the awful judgments

---

[a] Eccl. ii. 24. and iii. 12, 13. and v. 18, 19.　　[b] 1 Tim. vi. 17.
[c] 1 Tim. iv. 4, 5.　　[d] Numb. xv. 39.　Deut. xxix. 19.

with which such indulgences are menaced in our text. The text is, in fact, an ironical remonstrance, similar to that which Elijah uttered, when he condemned the worshippers of Baal; "Cry aloud; for he is a God[e]:" and that by which Micaiah reproved the impolicy of Ahab; "Go up to Ramoth-Gilead, and prosper[f]." By this kind of irony Solomon intended to convey an idea, that young men are *bent on* such indulgences; that they *promise themselves security* in the midst of them; and that they *will not be prevailed on by more temperate reproof*: and, in this view, his words may be thus paraphrased: ' You will, notwithstanding all that I can say to dissuade you from it, go on in the ways of sin, persuading yourselves that nothing but happiness awaits you: and therefore go on; and follow the bent of your own inclinations: but know, that in the end you will find yourselves grievously disappointed.' Severe as such a remonstrance is, it is perfectly just: for, who that considers what the great end of our being is, can doubt the wickedness of living to the world and to the flesh? or who that sees how contrary such conduct is to that of Christ and his apostles, can doubt what the issue of such a life shall be? Verily, "if we mind earthly things, we are enemies to the cross of Christ, and our end will be destruction[g];" for, whatever may be said or thought to the contrary, "to be carnally-minded is death[h]."]

To this is annexed,

II. A solemn warning—

There is a day of judgment fast approaching—

[God will most assuredly "judge the world in righteousness by that man whom he hath ordained, even by his Son, Jesus Christ." Before his tribunal we must all appear: the young, as well as the old, shall then give up their account to him; and the things which we did in the earlier part of life shall be brought forth for judgment, as well as those which were done at a more advanced age. The book of God's remembrance shall be opened; and every thing that was recorded in it, from the first moment of our existence to the latest breath we drew, shall be adduced as illustrative of our true character, and as the ground of God's final sentence.]

Then shall the things which are now done receive their proper reward—

[The judgment of God will not then be regulated by our views, but by his own unerring wisdom. We may palliate a life of vanity and worldliness now; but he will view it as

---

[e] 1 Kings xviii. 27. [f] 1 Kings xxii. 15.
[g] Phil. iii. 18, 19. [h] Rom. viii. 6.

indeed it is, as a life of rebellion against him. It argues a total alienation of heart from him : it shews that we lived to please ourselves rather than him, and that we were in reality a god unto ourselves. He had told us plainly, "If ye live after the flesh, ye shall die :" but we would not believe it. He had told us, that "the broad road, in which the many are walking, leadeth to destruction ; and that the narrow way alone leadeth unto life :" but we would not be persuaded that such an awful declaration should ever be verified. Nevertheless so it will be found in the last day : and of this we may be perfectly assured : for it stands on the word of God, which is as immutable as God himself : "Know thou, that for all these things God will call thee into judgment."]

ADDRESS—

1. Those who seek their happiness in earthly things—

[Say not, You commit no gross sin, and therefore have no cause to fear. The question simply is, Do you walk after the way of your own heart? If you do, it matters little what path you choose, whether it be that of open, or secret sin: you are equally living without God in the world, and are equally obnoxious to his heavy displeasure. I mean not by this to say, that all sins are alike, or that gross immoralities will not augment your guilt and condemnation in the last day. But this is an undoubted truth, that he only who gives up himself to God in this world, can ever dwell with him in the world to come : for "if we sow to the flesh, we shall of the flesh reap corruption: and it is only from sowing to the Spirit, that we can hope to reap life everlasting." Knowing therefore the terror of the Lord, we would persuade you, whilst yet we may avert from you the impending storm : we would persuade thee in particular, O young man, that thou mayest not any longer deceive thy soul, and dream of happiness in another world, when thou art only "treasuring up wrath against the day of wrath."]

2. Those who are seeking happiness in the ways of God—

[Say whether thou hast not found more solid joy in the ways of God, than ever thou foundest in the vanities of the world? Say whether thou hast not found it better to "mortify thy members upon earth," than to indulge them ; and to live to God, rather than to live unto thyself? The joy thou now hast is legitimate : it is such as prophets and apostles had before thee ; and such as God has freely conceded to thee, to the utmost extent of all thy wishes : "Let the children of Zion be joyful in their King." Indeed thy present joys are the gift of God to thy soul. Go on then "rejoicing in the Lord always:"

yea, rejoice, if so it may be, "with a joy that is unspeakable and glorified." These joys will never make the future judgment formidable; on the contrary, they will help to prepare thee for it, inasmuch as they are themselves an earnest of thine everlasting inheritance.]

OUTLINE NO. 846

REMEMBERING GOD IN OUR YOUTH.

Eccl. xii. 1. *Remember now thy Creator in the days of thy youth, while the evil days come not, nor the years draw nigh, when thou shalt say, I have no pleasure in them.*

INSTRUCTION may profitably be given in a variety of ways: indeed, in order to be effectual, it must be accommodated in some measure to the dispositions and habits of the persons addressed. To one who is wayward and self-willed, the pungency of irony may be well applied; whilst with the tractable and docile, the more simple and direct way of affectionate exhortation may be of more avail. Both these methods are adopted by Solomon in the passage before us. In the verses immediately preceding our text, he addresses a young man whom he supposes to be bent on the prosecution of his evil ways: "Rejoice, O young man, in thy youth, and let thy heart cheer thee in the days of thy youth, and walk in the ways of thine heart, and in the sight of thine eyes: but know thou, that for all these things God will call thee into judgment." Then, after a serious admonition to avoid the evils which ungovernable passions will bring upon him, he affectionately exhorts him to devote his early life to the exercises of true piety.

It is observed by some, that the word which in our text is rendered "thy Creator," is, in the original, in the plural number, "thy Creators:" and the passage in that view is supposed to mark the concurrence of the three Persons in the ever-blessed Trinity, in the formation of man; according to what is written in the book of Genesis, "Let us make man in our image[a]." But without drawing your attention to any

---

[a] Gen. i. 26.

observations of a critical nature, I shall endeavour simply to shew you,

I. What is implied in "remembering our Creator"—

Of course, it cannot be supposed that it is a mere act of the memory which is here recommended, but such a remembrance as befits the relation in which we stand to him as his creatures. We should remember then,

1. His authority over us—

[As the work of his hands, we have received from him all our powers, whether of mind or body. It is of his bounty alone that we have been endowed with the faculty of reason, which elevates us above all the rest of this lower world, and brings us into a near conformity with that higher order of created intelligences, the holy angels. But for what purpose has he thus distinguished us, but that we might render him services worthy both of our present state, and our future destinies? "He has formed us for himself, that we might shew forth his praise." This is the end for which we are to live: nor is any thing on earth to divert us from the course which HE has marked out for us. Obedience, it is true, is due to our parents, and to all others whom the providence of God has placed over us: but the authority of the creature must always be regarded as subordinate to that of our Creator; and, if at any time the will of man stand opposed to the will of God, we must then reply, "Whether it be right to hearken unto you more than unto God, judge ye." Whatever solicitations we may have from without or from within to violate any part of God's revealed will, we must withstand them manfully, and resist them even unto death. Knowing that "we are not our own, but God's, we must glorify him with our bodies and our spirits, which are his."]

2. The commands he has given us—

[We will not here enter into the different commandments of the law, but draw your attention rather to that great commandment of the Gospel to believe in Christ: "This is his commandment," says St. John, "that ye believe in the name of his Son Jesus Christ[b]." This command should be had in constant remembrance. It is addressed to every child of man. There is no one so innocent, as not to need a Saviour; nor any one so guilty, but that he may, through penitence and faith, obtain an interest in that Saviour, whom God has provided for a ruined world. Do not imagine, my young friends, that you are not concerned in this, or that it will be time

[b] 1 John iii. 23.

enough for you to attend to it, when you shall feel a greater need of mercy. You all are sinners: you all have a consciousness within yourselves that you have done many things which you ought not, and left undone many things which you ought to have done: you therefore have in your own bosoms a witness that you need a Saviour: and as in the presence of the Most High God, I declare unto you, that there is no mercy for the young, any more than for the old, but in the name, and through the mediation, of Jesus Christ: "there is no other name under heaven given among men whereby we can be saved, but the name of Jesus Christ." Go then to this Saviour, and implore mercy at his hands. Look to him as dying for your sins, and "as reconciling you to God by the blood of his cross." Let every one of you from day to day wash in the fountain of his blood, and clothe yourselves with the robe of his unspotted righteousness, and live altogether upon "his fulness, receiving out of it" continual supplies of all needful grace.]

3. His continual presence with us—

["God is in every place, beholding the evil and the good.' and wherever you are, you should see, as it were, this inscription written, "Thou God seest me^c." This is a point which you should never forget for one single moment: for it is only by bearing this in mind that you will be kept from the indulgence of secret sins. When no human eye is upon us, we are apt to think that we may give a greater latitude to our conduct: but we should remember that the darkness is no darkness with God, but the night and the day to him are both alike: "there is no darkness nor shadow of death where the workers of iniquity may hide themselves." Oh, if you bear this in remembrance, you will never do what you know to be wrong, nor utter what you know to be false: you will act in all things as in the immediate presence of your God, and will do nothing but what you believe to be good and acceptable in his sight.]

4. His determination to judge us in the last day—

[God "has appointed a day wherein he will judge the world in righteousness by that man whom he has ordained, even by his Son Jesus Christ." In that day all shall be summoned to his judgment-seat, the old and the young, the rich and the poor: not one that has ever been born into the world shall then be absent: the child that died in the birth, as well as the man of a hundred years old, shall be summoned to receive his everlasting doom, according to what they have done in the body, whether it be good or evil. To those who die before they have attained the knowledge of good and evil, we doubt not but that the mercy of God will be

^c Gen. xvi. 13.

extended: but to those who have lived to your age, judgment or mercy will be dispensed according as you have remembered or forgotten God.   Most awful is that declaration of the Psalmist, "The wicked shall be turned into hell, and all the nations that *forget* God[d]." If you have forgotten his authority over you, and especially his command to believe in his Son Jesus Christ; if you have forgotten that his eye was always upon you, inspecting your most secret thoughts, and noting them down in order to his future judgment; and if you have lived without any concern about the sentence that shall then be passed upon you; it will indeed be an awful day to you, a commencement of such misery as no words can describe, no imagination can conceive.   Remember then that God marks down in the book of his remembrance your every act, and every word, and every thought; and that it is your wisdom so to live, that, whether called at an earlier or later period of life, you may give up your account to him with joy, and not with grief.]

Such is the duty of all without exception : but the text requires me more particularly to shew,

II. Why we should thus remember him in early life—

It were easy to accumulate reasons on so plain a point: but we shall content ourselves with assigning a few of the most obvious;

1. This is the most favourable time—

[It is of the nature of sin to harden the heart and to sear the conscience : and therefore the less we have been habituated to sin, the more hope there is that a good impression may be made upon our minds.   We cannot agree with those who represent the hearts of youth as a sheet of white paper, on which you may write either good or evil: for, alas! there is evil, not merely written, but inscribed there in a most abundant measure, and in characters that are almost indelible : but we cordially accede to this truth, that the young are as yet only like plants sprouting from the earth, pliable and easy to be trained; whilst at a more advanced age they become like trees, which retain their form, unyielding, and unmoved.   From the very employments too of men in more advanced life, there arise many disadvantages: being drawn to a more vigorous pursuit of earthly things, they are, not unfrequently, so oppressed with "the cares of this world, and the deceitfulness of riches, and the lust of other things, that the good seed which has been sown in them, cannot grow up unto perfection."   But from these things young people are comparatively free.   Besides, at this season they have an express promise from God, which they cannot plead in future life[e]: and therefore in a variety of views

d Ps. ix. 17.   e Prov. viii. 17.

they may well consider this as " the most convenient season"
for piety that can ever occur.]

2. It may, for aught we know, be the only time
that shall be allotted us—

[The youngest and the healthiest amongst us may be
speedily removed. Let any one survey the monuments that
surround him, and he will see that multitudes have been cut
off at his age, though once they appeared as likely to live as
any who have survived him. And what if disease or accident
arrest you before you have truly devoted yourselves to God?
Will you have any opportunity to repair your error in the
grave? " Is there any work or device there," by which you can
accomplish what here was left undone? No: " as the tree
falleth, so it lieth:" and as you die, in a converted or unconverted state, so you must remain for ever. "To-day then, while
it is called to-day, harden not your hearts," as the generality,
alas! are but too prone to do.]

3. No other thing in the universe can so contribute
to our present happiness—

[It is quite a mistake to imagine that happiness can be
found in the vanities of time and sense. From infallible authority we can declare that every thing under the sun is mere
" vanity and vexation of spirit." But in the service of God
there is real joy: his ways are all, without exception, " ways
of pleasantness and peace:" and " in keeping his commandments there is great reward." Ask any one whether he ever
regretted that he had given himself up to God too soon? We
have heard of men, even of good men, as Job and Jeremiah,
cursing the day of their *birth:* but who ever cursed the day
of his *new birth?* At every period of life this is a subject that
will bear reflection and impart delight: and in proportion as
we grow in piety will our joy in God be increased.]

4. There will certainly come a time when we shall
wish we had sought the Lord in early life—

[The text speaks of " evil days as coming;" and sooner
or later they are coming to all. There is *a time of sickness* or
old age coming, " wherein we shall have no pleasure" in earthly
things: and shall we not then wish, that we had sought the
Lord in our youth? Shall we then look back with pleasure
on the sins that we have committed, or on the vanities that have
kept us from God? Nothing but the consolations of God will
then be of any avail to make us happy amidst the evils, which,
from pain or debility, we shall have to sustain. But there is
a time of death also which we must meet: and what will be our
thoughts at that period? Then it will be of little moment to
us what joys or sorrows we have met with in our former life.

All our anxiety will be about the future. Oh! with what force will that question press upon the mind, " Am I ready? Am I prepared to meet my God?" How different will our feelings then be, according as we have given up ourselves to God in our early youth, or put off the work of our souls to a dying hour! and what an unfit season will that be to *begin* that work! Go one step farther: follow the soul into the eternal world: view it standing *at the judgment-seat of Christ:* What will be its feelings at *that day?* I need not say: your own consciences will tell you. At this moment, even though you choose not to live *the life* of the righteous, you are saying inwardly in your hearts, " Let me die *the death* of the righteous, and let my *last end* be like his." Then, as these times must come, let us work while it is day, knowing assuredly, that the night is coming when no man can work, and when we shall bitterly lament, that ever we lost this day of our visitation, and neglected the things belonging to our everlasting peace.]

ADDRESS—

1. **The younger part of our audience—**

[You are now going to take upon you the vows that were made in your behalf in baptism[f]. " *Now*" therefore more particularly " remember God." Remember, that he sees the way in which you perform this duty: he sees whether you endeavour truly to approve yourselves to him, or whether you only mock him by a thoughtless compliance with an established form. Go to him, and surrender up yourselves wholly to him, as " the first-fruits of his creatures," and you will have reason to bless God to all eternity that ever you were called to perform this solemn service. But, if you go without any sincere desire to devote yourselves to him, you will only harden your own hearts, and increase the guilt you have already contracted. " Let me however hope better things of you, and things that accompany salvation, though we thus speak." Yes, dearly Beloved, we will hope, respecting some of you at least, that we " have not bestowed upon you labour in vain."]

2. **To those who have grown to man's estate—**

[Every argument used with the young, presses with additional weight on you, and says, with greatly augmented force, " Remember NOW thy Creator." If in your earlier days you were led to comply with this advice, I will venture to ask, Do you repent of having done so? Is not the chief matter of your regret, that you did not give yourselves up to him at a yet earlier period, and that you have not adhered more steadfastly to the engagements you entered into? If you have, on the contrary, advanced in the Divine life, and grown from babes to young men, or from young men to fathers, does not that afford

                    f Confirmation.

you matter of very exalted joy? Go on then, "forgetting what is behind, and reaching forward to that which is before:" and know that, "when the days arrive in which you shall say, you have no pleasure in *them*," you shall experience "a joy with which the stranger intermeddleth not;" which this world can neither give nor take away; and which shall be to you a pledge and earnest of everlasting felicity in the bosom of your God.]

OUTLINE NO. 847
THE SUM OF ALL TRUE RELIGION.

Eccl. xii. 13, 14. *Let us hear the conclusion of the whole matter; Fear God, and keep his commandments: for this is the whole duty of man. For God shall bring every work into judgment, with every secret thing, whether it be good, or whether it be evil.*

IN this book are many things difficult to be understood, and capable of being perverted by any one who desires to justify himself in an undue attachment to the world. But a reference to the condition of the author will enable us to explain the whole in a satisfactory and consistent manner. Solomon was possessed of all that this world could afford; and he rendered every object, and every employment, subservient to his own comfort. In all this he sinned not. It was not in the *use* of God's creatures that he sinned, but in the *abuse* of them. And we also may both possess and enjoy all that God in his providence has allotted to us, if only we enjoy God in the creature, and have earth subordinated to heaven. What the real drift of all his observations was, is told us in the words which we have just read, and which give us a clew to all that he has before spoken. In them we see,

I. The sum of all moral and religious instructions—

Many things we have to say both on the subject of morals and of religion; but they are all comprehended in this one saying, "Fear God, and keep his commandments."

In this is contained the whole substance of religion—

[By the fear of God we understand, not a slavish dread of him, but a holy filial regard, arising from a sense of his relation to us as a reconciled God and Father. And in "keeping his commandments" we include a due attention to that great commandment of the Gospel, the believing in our Lord Jesus Christ for salvation[a]. We must distinguish carefully between a legal and an evangelical interpretation of these terms, lest we confound the Gospel with the Law: we must guard especially against a reliance on our obedience, as if it could in any way, or in any degree, purchase salvation for us. But, if we be duly jealous on these points, we need never be afraid of asserting, that all true religion is comprehended in the duties inculcated in our text. Every thing else is subservient to these things: the most important principles are of little use, except as they conduce to this end. It was for this that the Lord Jesus Christ undertook and executed the whole work of redemption: " To this end Christ both died and rose and revived, that he might be the Lord both of the dead and living[b]," and " purify unto himself a peculiar people zealous of good works[c]." All the promises of the Gospel are given to us for this end, to " make us partakers of the Divine nature[d]," that we may, under their gracious influence, " cleanse ourselves from all filthiness both of flesh and spirit, and perfect holiness in the fear of God[e]." In a word, it is this which is the scope and end of all our ministrations; we are sent " to turn men from darkness unto light, and from the power of Satan unto God[f]."]

In this all is contained that deserves the attention of a rational being—

[It is of very small consequence whether we have more or less of this world: its pleasures, riches, honours, are but for a moment. What enjoyment has the Rich Man now of all his sumptuous fare? or what sense has Lazarus of all his former wants? All is passed away; and nothing remains of all the good or evil that befell them in this world, but a responsibility for the use they made of it. The period allotted for the enjoyment of earthly things is but a day, an hour, a moment. What does it signify to a man acting a play, whether he performs the part of a king or a beggar? Whatever his real character be, that he assumes, and that he retains, as soon as the last scene has ended. So the only thing that is of importance to us is, What is that character which we shall sustain to all eternity? Have we been rebellious and disobedient? or have we feared God and wrought righteousness? Those are the points that will determine our future destinies; and therefore they are the only points deserving of any serious regard.]

But this leads us more particularly to notice,

[a] 1 John iii. 23.   [b] Rom. xiv. 9.   [c] Tit. ii. 14.
[d] 2 Pet. i. 4.   [e] 2 Cor. vii. 1.   [f] Acts xxvi. 18.

II. The consideration that gives to it all its weight and importance—

This will be the one point of inquiry at the last day—

[God will come to judge the world : and, when examining the state of every individual, he will not ask, What sect we were of; or, What our sentiments and professions were; but, What our practice was, and What the habit of our minds towards him? I may even say, that that which passes under the name of Christian *experience*, will be of no account, as distinct from the duties inculcated in our text. It is radical and universal holiness alone, that God values: and, if that be right in its principle and end, it is the only thing which will be regarded in God's estimate of our character. In a word, it is "the whole of man;" it is his whole *duty*, and his whole *happiness :* his whole *duty*, as comprehending universal holiness; and his whole *happiness*, as being really a foretaste of heaven itself.]

According to this will our eternal state be fixed—

[Some of this will appear in our external conduct, but some will be found only in the internal habit of the mind; because there is very rarely scope for discovering in outward act all that the grace of God will form in the heart. "Every secret thing" therefore, every secret desire, purpose, inclination, appetite, affection, will go to the forming of God's estimate, and the determining the measure of our future recompence. If these have been evil, the best acts will have lost their value: but if these have been good, the smallest acts that can possibly have been performed, the widow's mite, or a cup of cold water given to a disciple, will be ranked amongst the most acceptable services, and be acknowledged as such by God himself. If we have really had "the fear of God in our hearts," and "walked in his fear all the day long," and, under the influence of that principle, laboured to approve ourselves to him in all things, we shall assuredly hear him say to us in that day, "Well done, good and faithful servants, enter ye into the joy of your Lord."]

This subject will be of the greatest use,

1. To correct the errors of those who affect superior light—

[Many there are who leave out all practical godliness from their system. They can think of nothing but God's eternal decrees, and of the finished work of Christ *for* us ; forgetting that there still remains a work for him to accomplish *in* us. They would account all such views as have been presented to you, *legal*, and unfit to be offered to a Christian auditory. What Solomon accounted "the conclusion of the whole matter," and "the whole of man," they account as nothing. But so did not Peter, who says, that "in every nation, he that feareth God and worketh righteousness, is accepted of him[g]." Nor was Paul of their opinion; for he has declared (and in the very epistle where he most enlarges on the decrees of God), that it is "by patient continuance in well-doing we must attain to glory and honour and immortality[h]." And we do not hesitate to say, that if an angel from heaven were to be sent to preach the Gospel, the statements before given would constitute a very principal part of his ministrations. St. John in his visions saw an angel flying through the whole world, to carry the everlasting Gospel to people of all nations and tongues: and the words in which he addressed the whole human race were like those of our text, "Fear God, and give glory to him; for the hour of his judgment is come[i]." Here is the very exhortation of Solomon, enforced with the identical consideration which he urges; and it is expressly called, "The everlasting Gospel." Let those who affect a higher and superior tone be convinced of their mistake. Let them bring forward all the sublimest truths of Christianity in their place; but let "this be the conclusion of the whole matter;" for, whether they will believe it or not, this is "the one thing needful," and "the whole of man."]

2. To dispel the fears of those whose knowledge is yet dim—

[As there are many who delight in nothing but the deepest mysteries of our religion, so there are many who make those mysteries an occasion of continual disquietude. The doctrines of predestination and election are ever present with their minds, as grounds of terror and despondency: they cannot see that they are of the number of God's elect; and therefore they imagine that all exertions on their part are in vain. But the fears of this people are such as ought no longer to be indulged: for there is no man in the universe that is authorized to consider himself as one of God's elect, any farther than he has "the spot of God's children" upon him. It is by his fear of God, and his obedience to God's commandments, that he must judge of his state before God: and to judge of his election by any other standard, is only to deceive his own soul. If then those who distress themselves about the doctrines of election would dismiss those subjects from their minds, and contemplate only what is more within the sphere of their comprehension, they would do well. Let me recommend this plan to all. Look not at God's decrees, which you can never explore, but at the visible effects of his grace upon your souls: and, if you can find "the works of faith, and labours of love,

[g] Acts x. 35.   [h] Rom. ii. 7. with 2 Cor. v. 10, 11.
             [i] Rev. xiv. 6, 7.

and patience of hope" evidenced in your conduct, you may from thence assuredly infer " your election of God[k];" since those are indisputably the fruits of his grace; and his grace has been communicated according to his purpose, which " he purposed in Christ Jesus before the world began[l]."]

3. To regulate the conduct of those whose views are scriptural and just—

[" The fear of the Lord is the beginning of wisdom[m]:" and to get this in a more uniform and abiding exercise, is to be the one object of our lives. It is the beginning and " the conclusion of the whole matter." O that this were better understood amongst us! An old writer observes, that religion consists not in *N*otions, but *M*otions: and the observation, though quaint, is true. The difference is not always visible at first sight: and the one is often mistaken for the other; but, if separated, they are as wide asunder as heaven and hell. Let it never be forgotten, that holiness of heart and life is that which constitutes our meetness for heaven; and that it is only by growth in that, that we can ever honour God on earth, or secure the enjoyment of him in a better world.]

[k] 1 Thess. i. 3, 4.   [l] 2 Tim. i. 9.   Jer. xxxi. 3
      [m] Ps. cxi. 10.

CANTICLES.

OUTLINE NO. 848

THE CHURCH'S LOVE TO CHRIST.

Cant. i. 3, 4. *Thy name is as ointment poured forth ; therefore do the virgins love thee. Draw me : we will run after thee.*

THIS divine song was admitted into the sacred canon soon after the Babylonish captivity (most probably by Ezra,) and has been admitted both by Jews and Christians from that time as constituting an important part of the inspired volume. It is called the Song of Songs, because of its peculiar excellence, there being no other to be compared with it, as delineating and describing the love which subsists between Christ and his Church. There are indeed similar images used in other parts of holy writ, and particularly in the 45th Psalm ; but there is a richness and variety in this, by which it is pre-eminently distinguished. True it is, that the representations contained in it render it unfit for the carnal eye, which would be more likely to be injured by it, through the influence of a polluted imagination, than to derive from it the good which to a spiritually enlightened mind it is calculated to convey. Many of the expressions, which, at the time they were written, were clear and intelligible, are, for want of a more intimate knowledge of the various circumstances which would elucidate them, inexplicable to us : but the general purport of the whole is evident enough : it is a kind of allegory written in the form of a pastoral poem, in which different persons are introduced, and bear a part, relieving, as it were, occasionally, the dialogue betwixt Christ and his Church ; the one under the character of a Bridegroom ; and the other, of a Bride, espoused to him in this world, and waiting for the consummation of her nuptials in the world to come.

The abruptness with which the poem opens is very remarkable. The spouse, having her mind full of her Beloved, breaks forth without any mention of his name, " Let him kiss me with the kisses of his mouth." She is ready to think that the minds of all must of necessity be occupied with *his* excellencies, and must therefore of necessity know to whom she refers. She then commends " his love, as better," and more exhilarating, " than wine, because of the savour of his good ointments[a];" and assigns this as *the reason of her love towards him,* and *her ardent desire after him.*

These are the two points for our consideration at this time :

I. The reason of the Church's love to Christ—

" His name is as ointment poured forth"—

[A rich ointment poured forth will fill a whole house with its odour[b], so that all who are within it shall be refreshed with its fragrance: and such is the delight which the whole Church derives from the mention of the name of her Beloved.

Consider his name, " Emmanuel :" it was a name given him eight hundred years before he came into the world : and the interpretation of that name is given us by the sacred historian, that we may know all the riches of grace and love contained in it. Its import is, " God with us[c]." Wonderful name ! God, " the mighty God," with us, worms of the earth ; with us, who have been all our days rebels against his Divine Majesty, and who might well have expected to have been made everlasting monuments of his righteous indignation. In some respect indeed he might bear that name, even in the regions of darkness and misery : since he is there by his power inflicting his heavy judgments on all who inhabit those dreary mansions: but he is with *us* by his love ; yea, he is with *us* in our very nature ; " bone of our bone, flesh of our flesh ;" God and man in one person ! Stupendous mystery ! Can it be so ? Is it true, that the God of heaven and earth has so condescended to assume our nature, and to sojourn upon earth, that he might commend himself to us as our Beloved ? Say, ye who have any spiritual senses, does not a fragrance go forth at this name Emmanuel, sufficient to fill the whole universe with its odours?

But take another name, the name of " Jesus." This was

[a] That seems the more proper place for the stop.
[b] John xii 3.   [c] Matt. i. 23.

given him by the Angel, when he was conceived in the womb ;
and the giving it was considered as a completion of the prophecy that assigned to him the name Emmanuel [d].   And a
fulfilment of the prophecy it was ; for "Jesus" is *Jah Hosea,*
or *Divine Saviour.*   Here, in addition to his Godhead, as
united to the manhood, we have the end of his incarnation
plainly announced : it was, to *save* a ruined world : yes, " he
came, not to *condemn* the world, but that through him," even
through his meritorious blood and righteousness, " the world
might be *saved.*" Think of this, ye who have destroyed your own
souls, and are trembling for fear of the Divine judgments :
your God has become a man, on purpose that he might fulfil
the law which you have broken, and endure the curse which
you have merited ; and by this substitution of himself in your
place, might deliver you from death and hell, and make you
partakers of his own eternal kingdom and glory.   Does not
this name refresh and animate your souls ?   Can you hear it
without receiving from it sensations which it is not in the power
of language to express ?

Consider yet one other name, that name whereby we
are particularly instructed to call him, " The Lord our
Righteousness [e]."   Here you have the same blessed intimations
as in the former names, respecting his Godhead, and the gracious
ends of his incarnation ; with this additional suggestion, that
his righteousness was wrought out for you, yea, that he himself
is your Righteousness.   A creature's righteousness would not
have sufficed for you : you needed the righteousness of God
himself : and God himself has become a man, that in your nature
he might work out a righteousness, that should be imputed to
you, and put upon you, and constitute your justifying righteousness at the bar of judgment.   Tell me, Brethren, can you
hear this unmoved ?   What spiritual perception can you have,
if you are not even ravished with delight at the sound of such a
name as this ?   Surely it is the out-pouring of this ointment
that makes heaven to be the place it is : yea, to be within the
reach of this atmosphere, is heaven.

We forbear to mention any other of his glorious names
lest we distract your attention by the variety [f] : sufficient have
been mentioned to justify the Church's attachment to this
adorable Saviour.]

On account of the fragrance diffused by his name,
" the virgins love him"—

[By " the virgins" we understand, all that are " pure in
heart," and have been betrothed to him in righteousness and
truth [g]."   Of all such the Apostle says, " I have espoused you

---

[d] Matt. i. 21—23.   [e] Jer. xxiii. 6.   [f] See Isai. ix. 6.
[g] Hos. ii. 19, 20.

to one husband, that I may present you as a chaste virgin to Christ[h]." These all love the Lord Jesus Christ. In the eyes of others, this adorable Being has " no beauty or comeliness for which to be desired[i]:" but in the eyes of the Church " he is truly precious[k]," " fairer than ten thousand," and " altogether lovely:" and the one desire of her heart is, to be able to say, " This is my Friend and my Beloved[l]." In comparison of him, all other suitors are utterly despised. The whole universe presents no other object to her view that deserves a thought : the constant state of her soul towards him is, " How great is thy goodness! how great is thy beauty[m]!" " Whom have I in heaven but thee? and there is none upon earth that I desire beside thee[n]." Sweet as created excellencies once appeared to her, she has now no eye to see them, no taste to enjoy them. She is altogether occupied with the savour of her Beloved's name, the perfume of which makes every other odour worthless at least, if not nauseous and offensive. In a word, so entirely does this beloved object fill her soul, that with him a dungeon would be heaven ; and without him, heaven itself would be a dungeon or a desert.]

From hence naturally follows,

II. Her ardent desire after him—

Conscious that his gifts are his own, and that without his gracious assistance she can do nothing, she presents before him,

1. Her supplication—

[Our blessed Lord himself has said, " No man can come unto me, except the Father, who hath sent me, draw him[o]." And this total insufficiency for every thing that is good, the Church confesses in this short but ardent petition, " Draw me!" None but Jesus himself can open for us the box in which this ointment is contained, or give the spiritual perception whereby alone its fragrance can be discovered. How many, in the days of his flesh, were rather incensed against him, than drawn to him, by all the wonders of his love! and how many at this day are like the idols which they worship! " they have eyes, and see not; ears, and hear not; noses, and smell not[p]." But these have had spiritual senses given unto them ; and therefore they pant after communion with their blessed Lord.

Observe, it is not the carnal unregenerate man alone that needs to offer this petition: it is here offered by " the virgins," " the upright[q]," who already love their Lord; and it is necessary

---

[h] 2 Cor. xi. 2.   [i] Isai. liii. 2.   [k] 1 Pet. ii. 7.
[l] Cant. v. 10, 16.   [m] Zech. ix. 17.   [n] Ps. lxxiii. 25.
[o] John vi. 44.   [p] Ps. cxv. 5—8.   [q] See the close of ver. 4.

to be offered by all, as long as they continue in the body.
There are times and seasons when the most favoured of mankind
are comparatively dead and dull: even " the Wise Virgins," as
well as the Foolish ones, for a time " slumbered and slept."
Again and again does every member of the Church need to be
awakened, and to have his sluggishness overcome by fresh
communications of divine grace, and fresh manifestations of the
Saviour's love.   Continually do we need to be " drawn with
the cords of a man, and with the bands of love[r]:" and therefore we must continually renew the same petition as the Church
offers in our text.]

2. Her resolution—

[It is no reluctant service which the Bride will render,
when once she feels the attractions of the Bridegroom's love.
No: she will " run after him:" she will run with all her might:
she will regard no obstacles without; she will yield to no im-
pediments within : she " will run and not be weary ; she will
press forward, and not faint[s]."   The space she has already
passed, she will account nothing; " forgetting the things that
are behind, she will press forward for that which is before, if
by any means she may apprehend that, for which she has been
apprehended of God in Christ Jesus[t]."

The change of *person* also is here remarkable : " Draw *me*,
and *we* will run after thee."   Not only will the Church summon all the powers of her soul, and unite them all in the service of her Lord, but she will bring all she can along with her.
When once she feels the constraining influence of Christ's
love, she will not be content to come alone : she would impress every creature that she beholds, with the same love which
she herself feels, and would bring all others into the very same
union with him which she herself affects.   And herein her love
differs from that which is here used to set it forth: the love
which is felt towards an earthly object, admits not of participation with others: it would engross all the affections of its
beloved object, and not endure a rival : but the Church's love
to Christ is enhanced by the most extended communication of
the blessings which she herself enjoys.   She would have all
the earth to know, and love him.   Just as Andrew and Philip,
as soon as they found the Messiah, invited Peter and Nathanael
to come and participate their joy, so does every member of the
Church of Christ: he will, like Abraham, " command his
household" to fear and love his Lord, and will use all possible
means to extend the kingdom of his Redeemer throughout
all the earth.]

From this subject we may LEARN,

---

[r] Hos. xi. 4.   [s] Isai. xl. 29—31.   [t] Phil. iii. 12—14.

1. What reason we have to seek the knowledge of Christ—

[Who is there that has such a title to our affections as he? Who is there so excellent in himself, or such a source of blessedness to them that love him? Go through the universe; survey every thing that stands in competition with him; and see what it can do for your souls. Take that highest of earthly bliss, which is here used to shadow forth the blessedness of union with Christ: how often have they been disappointed who have most passionately sought, and fondly hoped that they had attained, the summit of human happiness! And where it has been enjoyed in its utmost perfection, how soon has it been cut short by the hand of death! But nothing can damp, and nothing can terminate, the blessedness of those who are united to Christ. On the contrary, in the midst of the deepest distresses, his love will fill you with the richest consolation. When a fainting fit has come upon the body, a strong and pungent odour will revive it: and so will the fragrance of Jesus' name refresh the soul, when nothing else under heaven will reach, and resuscitate, its languid powers. O let every one of you seek this union, and never rest till you can say, " My Beloved is mine, and I am his[u]!"

Yet let me remind you of a most important distinction that must ever be made between *the knowledge* of Christ, and *"the savour* of the knowledge of him[x]." That which resides in the head will be of no avail, as bringing you into union with him: it is that only which diffuses a fragrance through the whole soul, that will terminate in the everlasting enjoyment of him in heaven.]

2. In what way we should testify our regard for him—

[Seek him continually, and with your whole hearts; and whenever you find sluggishness creeping upon you, renew your cry to him, " Draw me, draw me!" Your "hearts are bent to backslide from him," yea, prone too to alienate from him the affections that should centre in him alone: but strive that you may be able at all times to say with David, " My soul followeth hard after thee:" and if at any time you are enabled to lay hold on your Beloved, let him not go, but "cleave to him with full purpose of heart."

At the same time see what you can do in your families, in your neighbourhood, and in the world at large, to bring others also to him. Commend him to them: endeavour to bring them into the assemblies, where he manifests his presence: entreat him to extend his attractive influences to them also, even as he

u Cant. ii. 16.   x 2 Cor. ii. 14.

has done to you: and labour that, if possible, all the world may behold his beauty, and be comforted with his love.

As for yourselves, look to the final consummation of your love in a better world, when your fruition of him shall be more intimate than it can be in this world, and shall continue without intermission or alloy through all eternity.]

OUTLINE NO. 849

THE CHURCH'S FELLOWSHIP WITH CHRIST.

Cant. ii. 1—3. *I am the rose of Sharon, and the lily of the valleys. As the lily among thorns, so is my love among the daughters. As the apple-tree among the trees of the wood, so is my beloved among the sons. I sat down under his shadow with great delight; and his fruit was sweet to my taste.*

FROM the general scope of this whole poem, we can have no hesitation in saying, that the words which we have read are a part of a dialogue between Christ and his Church; the former part containing his testimony respecting her; and the latter, her testimony respecting him. It is a kind of pastoral song, as the images used by both the parties shew; and, though exceeding difficult of interpretation in some parts, it is very intelligible and instructive in others. We must bear in mind, that Christ speaks as the Bridegroom of his Church; and the Church, as his Spouse: whilst the " sons" and " daughters" mentioned in our text, are those children of Adam who yet lie in darkness and the shadow of death, or, at best, have only " the form of godliness, without the power." As for the " daughters of Jerusalem," who occasionally bear a part in the dialogue, they are professors of religion, who, though friendly on the whole, are not yet brought into this near relation to Christ, nor made partakers of his saving benefits.

In discoursing on the words before us, we shall consider,

I. Christ's testimony respecting his Church—

The commendation bestowed upon her is the highest she could possibly receive: it is, that she, according to the measure of grace given to her, resembles him. In order to point out the resemblance,

He first declares his own character—

[" I am the rose of Sharon, and the lily of the valleys."
Whatever is most excellent in the universe, is brought forward
from time to time, to designate and illustrate the character of
our Lord. Of the heavenly bodies he is the Sun, " the Sun
of Righteousness." Of inferior creatures, he is the Lion, " the
Lion of the tribe of Judah." Even the plants and flowers yield
him honour also: as the rose is exceeded by none in fragrance,
and the lily is pre-eminent in beauty, he is a Rose, " the Rose
of Sharon," whose excellence was proverbial[a]; and a Lily, " the
Lily of the valleys," to which Solomon in all his glory was not
worthy to be compared[b]. Infinitely diversified are his perfections. In whatever point of view we consider him, his *person*,
his *offices*, his *relations*, we shall be fully convinced, that to him
alone pertain the garments which were " made for *glory* and
beauty[c]." In *his person* are united all the attributes of the
Deity, and all the grace of humanity in their highest possible
perfection — — — In *his offices*, nothing is wanting that could
contribute to the welfare of his Church and people. As their
High-priest, he has made a full and all-sufficient atonement for
them: as their *Prophet*, he instructs them by his word and
Spirit; and as their *King*, he rules over them, and in them;
and puts all their enemies under their feet — — — As for *his
relations*, there is no relation that can inspire us with hope and
confidence, which he does not bear towards his believing people.
He is our Shepherd, our Brother, and our Friend. Whether
viewed in his exaltation, as God; or in his humiliation, as
Man; or in his mediatorial state, as " Emmanuel, God with
us," he is infinitely great and glorious, " fairer than ten thousand, and altogether lovely."]

He then acknowledges her resemblance to him—
[To the glories of his Godhead no creature can bear any
true resemblance; so infinitely is he above all: but in his humiliation he was a pattern both of lowliness and purity, to which
his believing people are conformed: yea moreover, as he in this
respect infinitely excels the highest of his creatures, so does his
Church excel all others of " the daughters" of men: she is, like
him, " a lily;" like him also, " a lily among thorns;" no others
bearing any more comparison with her, than a thorn or brier
with the lily. Mark the lowliness of the true Christian: he
boweth down his head with a sense of his own unworthiness,
and manifold infirmities: yet is he " pure," at least in purpose
and desire, " even as God is pure." " The very same mind is
in him that was in Christ Jesus:" yea, " being joined to the
Lord, he is one spirit with him;" " a partaker of his holiness,"
" a partaker of his very nature[d]," " created anew after his image

---

[a] Isai. xxxv. 2.   [b] Matt. vi. 29.   [c] Exod. xxviii. 40.
[d] 2 Pet. i. 4.

in righteousness and true holiness." Compare the Church with others, and they are no better than " thorns" before her; so superior is she to them in all her principles, her purposes, her attainments. The one have no higher aim or end than self: the other disdains to act but from the love of God, and for the glory of his name. The one leave God out even from the most sacred exercises; the other brings him into the most common acts and offices of life[e]. The one have no life but what they received from nature: the other has Christ himself living in her; yea, " Christ himself is her life[f]." True it is, that by nature the Believer was not at all different from others, but grace has made the difference; according to that prophetic declaration; " Instead of the thorn shall come up the fir-tree, and instead of the brier shall grow up the myrtle-tree; and it shall be to the Lord for a name, and for an everlasting sign, that shall not be cut off[g]." Thus is that amply verified which was spoken by Solomon, " The righteous is more excellent than his neighbour[h]."]

In reply to this commendation, the Church proclaims,

II. Her testimony respecting him—

This she bears,

1. From her knowledge of his excellencies—

[Christ is " as the apple tree among the trees of the wood." Other trees can afford shadow only; whilst to those who take refuge under him, he administers the most refreshing and satisfying food. Under them, the soul that continues to abide, must perish: but the soul that abides in him, shall live for ever. All that it can want or desire is found in him. He is " the tree of life, that bears twelve manner of fruits[i];" one for every season, every situation, every circumstance of life. " The very leaves of that tree are for the healing of the nations." The law appeared to offer a salutary retreat: but it could never satisfy the hungry soul, or " make a man perfect as pertaining to the conscience." But what not all the trees of that forest could do, Christ has done[k]; and does continually for all who seek repose under the shadow of his wings. And they who have the clearest views of his excellency, " determine to know nothing but him, even him crucified."]

2. From her experience of his love—

[The Church here says, in fact, " What my eyes have seen, my ears have heard, and my hands have handled of the word of life, the same declare I unto you." In fact, no other

[e] 1 Cor. x. 31.   [f] Col. iii. 4.   [g] Isai. lv. 13.
[h] Prov. xii. 26.   [i] Rev. xxii. 2.   [k] Rom. viii. 2.

knowledge than that which has been wrought into our own experience, is of any use; at least, not for the Christian's own benefit. Hear then the Church's happy experience; "I sat down under his shadow with great delight; and his fruit was sweet unto my taste." The Believer has come to Christ weary and heavy-laden with a sense of his sins, and has found rest unto his soul. Like the traveller fainting beneath the intense heat of a vertical sun, he has sought the shade in Christ Jesus, who has approved himself all-sufficient, even like " the shadow of a great rock in a weary land[1]." Of his fruits too does the Believer eat in a rich abundance. O! how sweet is his pardoning love to the soul, when he says, "Thy sins are forgiven thee; go in peace!" Who can describe the blessedness of that peace which proceeds from him; from Him who said, "My peace I give unto you?" Truly it is " a peace that passeth all understanding. As for the joy with which these manifestations are accompanied, it is " unspeakable and glorified." How can a soul feel any thing but exquisite " delight," when thus favoured with " the spirit of adoption," yea, " the witness of the Spirit" also attesting its relation to Christ, " sealing it unto the day of redemption," and giving it even now " an earnest" and a foretaste " of its heavenly inheritance?" Such are the fruits of which every one shall eat, who sits under the shadow of the Lord Jesus; and " sweet shall they be unto his taste," even " sweeter than honey or the honey-comb."]

Having no fear that either of these testimonies shall ever be set aside, we ground upon them a word of EXHORTATION—

1. Let us contemplate the excellencies of the Lord Jesus—

[There is not any thing in the world which may not serve to illustrate his beauty : for, in fact, all created excellencies are but rays of his glory, and stars twinkling with his reflected splendour. We do not think enough of HIM : we can admire beauty in the creature, but have no eyes to behold it in Him who is the centre and source of all. Did we but duly reflect on him, we should pant after an union with him; and despise every thing else in comparison of him. " All other knowledge would be to us but as dross and dung." Truly " his name is as ointment poured forth; and therefore do the virgins love him[m]." Say, Believer, Is he not " precious" to thy soul[n]? O that every one amongst us would be persuaded to go into this garden, and compare the fragrance of this " rose," and the purity of this " lily," with all that ever his eyes beheld, or his most

---

[1] Isai. xxv. 4. and xxxii. 2.   [m] Cant. i. 3.   [n] 1 Pet. ii. 7.

impassioned sense experienced! O that all might "behold his glory, the glory as of the only-begotten of the Father;" "the brightness of whose glory he is, and the express image of his person[o]!" The effect of such a sight cannot be conceived by those who never yet beheld it: for we should be constrained by it to cry out, "How great is his goodness! how great is his beauty[p]!" and, whilst beholding his glory, we should be "changed into his image, from glory to glory, by the Spirit of our God[q]." Go, beloved, into the holy mount, and converse with him; and you shall come down, like Moses, irradiated with the beams of his glory. Be conversant with this "lily," and ye shall become "lilies" yourselves.]

2. Let us receive kindly his overtures—

[We have before shewn, that this is a dialogue between Christ as a Bridegroom, and the Church as his Spouse. Into this relation Christ is desirous to bring us all. We come in his name, to invite you all to unite yourselves with him; we come, that we may "present every soul among you as a chaste virgin to Christ[r]." Hear the invitation given, as it were, from his own lips: "I will betroth thee unto me for ever: yea, I will betroth thee unto me in righteousness, and in judgment, and in loving-kindness, and in mercies: I will betroth thee unto me in faithfulness, and thou shalt know the Lord[s]." Beloved Brethren, Who is there that has such a title to your affections as He? Who can make you so happy as He? Have not all other sources of comfort proved as "broken cisterns, that can hold no water?" Why then will ye not "come to the fountain of living waters?"

Say not, "I am unworthy of this high honour." Who is not unworthy? Who could ever have obtained it by any worthiness of his own? Every creature that was ever united to him was first a wretched, helpless outcast, like thyself[t]: and, if thou desire an union with him, be assured that "he will never cast thee out." Only "come to his banqueting-house, and his banner over thee shall be love[u]."]

3. Let us duly estimate our privileges—

[The happiness of the soul that is united unto Christ, no words can declare, no imagination can conceive. Only hear the terms in which He and his Spouse speak of each other: her he calls, "My Love:" and of him she speaks in that endearing term, "My Beloved." Think, for a moment, what immense, what inconceivable privileges are implied in these terms, whether as applied by him to us, or by us to him! Whatever he *is*, he is for you: whatever he *has*, he possesses for

---

[o] John i. 14. Heb. i. 3.   [p] Zech. ix. 17.   [q] 2 Cor. iii. 18.
[r] 2 Cor. xi. 2.   [s] Hos. ii. 19, 20.   [t] Ezek. xvi. 4—8.   [u] ver. 4.

you: whatever he *does*, he does for you; whatever he *enjoys*, he enjoys as your Head, your Representative, your Forerunner: "The glory which his Father has given him, *He* has given you." You may enjoy earthly sweets, and they will cloy; yea, the most fragrant rose will fade. Not so "the Rose of Sharon:" its fragrance will be undiminished to all eternity. You may sit under the shadow of other trees, and their foliage shall fail; yea, like Jonah's gourd, they may wither in a night: but not so "the apple-tree that grows in the midst of the Paradise of God:" there is no worm at the root of that: its benign influence shall endure for ever: and its delicious fruits be ever new. Make then these things your own, by "apprehending Christ," and giving yourselves up to him: for "all things are yours, if ye be Christ's." Only "taste, and see, how gracious the Lord is:" and having once "tasted that the Lord is gracious, you will never rest till you can say "My Beloved is mine, and I am his."]

4. Let us walk worthy of our high relation—

[If one be brought into union with an earthly monarch, she feels an obligation to conduct herself henceforth in a way suited to her high calling. And shall not we, when united to "the King of kings?" Yes: we must resemble him, and exhibit, according to the measure of the grace conferred upon us, the mind that was in him. Let us especially resemble him in his humility and purity. We are not indeed to "bow down our heads as a bulrush," as if we were in a pitiable and disconsolate state: but to bow our heads as "the lily," is our beauty and our excellence. Never does the Christian look so beautiful as when he is "low in his own eyes." Surely whatever may have been done for us, and in us, we must still to our latest hour "walk humbly with God." We must also be pure and spotless as the lily; yea, "blameless and harmless as the sons of God." We must not be contented with low attainments; but must seek to "walk worthy of the Lord himself," "whose we are, and whom we profess to serve." Let this be the one object of our ambition: and, as we profess to surpass every flower of the field in fragrance and beauty, let us so live, that we may not fear a comparison with any of the sons of men. Let us not be found vain boasters of privileges that are merely ideal: but, whilst we profess to enjoy so much in and through the Lord Jesus, let it be seen, that, "having this hope, we do indeed purify ourselves, even as he is pure[x]."]

x 1 John iii. 3.

OUTLINE NO. 850

PERSEVERANCE CROWNED WITH SUCCESS.

Cant. iii. 1—4. *By night on my bed I sought him whom my soul loveth; I sought him, but I found him not. I will rise now, and go about the city in the streets, and in the broad ways I will seek him whom my soul loveth: I sought him, but I found him not. The watchmen that go about the city found me: to whom I said, Saw ye him whom my soul loveth? It was but a little that I passed from them, but I found him whom my soul loveth: I held him, and would not let him go, until I had brought him into my mother's house, and into the chamber of her that conceived me.*

ONE peculiar excellence of the Song of Solomon is, that it delineates with admirable beauty and precision the workings of the believer's soul under all the varieties of Christian experience. In the first conversion of the soul, God communicates his blessings unsolicited, unsought; so that it may be justly said, " He is found of them that sought him not[a]:" but in our subsequent walk with God, we may sometimes find occasion to complain, " I sought him, but I found him not." Thus it was with the Bride in the passage before us: and her conduct under these circumstances is instructive, as the issue of it is encouraging to the Church of God in all ages. In our remarks on the Bride's experience, we shall notice,

1. Her persevering exertions—

When it is said, " By night on my bed I sought him," we are not to take the words in a *literal*, but *figurative* sense, as expressing the cold and listless way in which the Bride had sought her Beloved: and it is no wonder that, when sought in such a way, he did not vouchsafe to manifest himself unto her. Disappointed in her hopes, " she rose, and went about the city, seeking him in the streets and broad ways," accounting no time unseasonable, no labour too great, for the attainment of an object so dear to her as a sight of her Beloved. Still however her labour was in vain: " she sought him, but found him not." And

a Isai. lxv. 1.

thus the Lord Jesus Christ still frequently for a season suspends the manifestations of his love, and leaves in darkness the soul that seeks him. This he does,

1. To correct our lukewarmness—

[Lukewarmness in his people is most offensive to him[b]; and, when indulged, "grieves his Spirit," and provokes him to hide his face from us. He has told us in the Prophets, that we must not expect to "find him, unless we seek him with our whole hearts[c]." How solemn is that warning which he has given in his Gospel; "*Strive* to enter in at the strait gate : for many shall *seek* to enter in, and shall not be able[d]." What wonder is it therefore if he punish our sloth by a long suspension of his visits, and make us to eat of the bitter fruit of our own ways? By such a dispensation he plainly says to us, "Hast thou not procured this unto thyself, in that thou hast forsaken me, when I led thee by the way? Thine own wickedness shall correct thee, and thy backslidings shall reprove thee: know therefore and see that it is an evil and bitter thing that thou hast forsaken the Lord thy God[e]."]

2. To stimulate our desires after him—

[Our souls ought to "pant after him, as the hart after the water-brooks;" yea, they should "break for the very fervent desire which we have towards him[f]." But if a listless and inoperative wish would suffice, we should never exert ourselves as we ought. Had the Bride succeeded by seeking her Beloved on her bed, she would never have risen to seek him in the streets of the city : and, if we could attain in a way of self-indulgence the rewards of self-denying exertion, we should be too ready to say to our souls, " Soul, take thine ease." But our Lord has told us, that his favour is not to be sought in such a way as that : he has said, that "the kingdom of heaven suffereth violence; and that the violent must take it by force:" and he withholds from us the manifestations of his love, on purpose that he may quicken us in our pursuit of him, and stimulate us to put forth into activity the devoutest energies of our souls[g].]

3. To endear his presence to us—

[To the temporary loss which the Bride had sustained must be ascribed the zeal with which she afterwards held fast her Beloved : and we well know how the Courts of the Lord were endeared to David by his long banishment from them, under the persecutions of Saul, and during the rebellion of Absalom. And, no doubt, in proportion as we are led into

---

[b] Rev. iii. 16.   [c] Jer. xxix. 12, 13.   [d] Luke xiii. 94.
[e] Jer. ii. 17, 19.   [f] Ps. cxix. 20.   [g] Hos. v. 15.

deep waters, will be our gratitude for deliverance from them[h]: in proportion as we have passed through the afflictive scenes of David, — — — will be the zeal and ardour with which we shall henceforth make boast of our great Deliverer: " Who is so great a God as our God[i]?" When we feel that we have " had much forgiven us, we shall love much."]

The Bride however used not her exertions in vain; as we see by,

II. The successful issue of them—

[In her search after her Beloved, she inquired of the watchmen, whether they had seen him, or could give her any intelligence respecting him. And, soon after she had parted with them, she found him. By "the watchmen," we understand the ministers of God, who "watch for souls," whose special commission is, to "strengthen the weak hands, and confirm the feeble knees, and to say to the fearful heart, Fear not; your God will come and save you[k]." And it should seem that it was in following her directions she attained her end. But, however this might be, we see clearly from her example, that persevering endeavours shall be crowned with success.]

This is expressly promised by God himself—

[Exceeding strong is that declaration of our blessed Lord; " Ask, and ye shall have; seek, and ye shall find; knock, and it shall be opened unto you: for every one that asketh, receiveth; and he that seeketh, findeth; and to him that knocketh it shall be opened[l]." It is not said indeed that the answer shall be given, as it was to Daniel, in the very act of prayer: but it is secured from the first moment that we ask in faith; and it shall be given in the best manner, and at the fittest time; according as the Prophet Hosea has said; "Then shall ye know, if ye follow on to know the Lord: his going forth is prepared as the morning; and he shall come unto us as the rain, as the latter and the former rain, unto the earth[m]." " The vision is for an appointed time: and if we wait for it, it shall come, and not tarry an instant beyond the time" fixed in the counsels of unerring wisdom[n].]

It is also confirmed by actual experience—

[The poor Canaanitess who was so urgent in her supplications to Christ to come and heal her daughter, met with a denial; and such a denial as seemed to preclude any hope of ultimate success; " He answered her not a word." The Disciples then interceded for her, and requested, that she might

---

[h] Ps. xl. 1—3.   [i] Ps. lxxvii. 1—4, 13.   [k] Isai. xxxv. 3, 4.
[l] Matt. vii. 7, 8.   [m] Hos. vi. 3.   [n] Hab. ii. 3. and Heb. x. 37.

be dismissed with a favourable answer, if it was only to prevent her from wearying them with her entreaties: yet they also were refused, and in such a manner as effectually to silence them: "I am not sent but unto the lost sheep of the house of Israel." Still however she would not give up all hope, but with deeper prostration than before renewed her petition: but the answer she received was more discouraging than before, in that it blamed her presumption in hoping to participate in any respect the blessings which were designed only for God's peculiar people: "It is not meet to take the children's bread, and cast it unto dogs." Who would believe, that, after all this, she should persevere in her request, and succeed at last? Yet so she did[o]: and such shall be the success of every child of man that "continues instant in prayer." To this effect our Lord assures us, in a parable which was spoken for the express purpose of encouraging persons "to pray and not faint." A poor widow, we are told, obtained redress from an unjust judge through mere dint of her importunity: and from thence we are taught to draw this inference; "And shall not God avenge his own elect who cry day and night unto him, though he bear long with them? I tell you, that he will avenge them speedily[p]." Here then we are warranted in affirming that the Bride's success shall be realized in us, if only, like her, we rise to the occasion, and press through every impediment to the enjoyment of our God. God "never did, nor ever will, say to any, Seek ye my face in vain."]

But that we may profit more fully by the example of the Bride, let us notice,

III. The use she made of her success—

Having found her Beloved, she held him and would not let him go, till she had brought him into her mother's house, where she hoped her communion with him would be more intimate, and free from interruption. And thus should we also,

1. Exert ourselves to retain the Saviour with us—

[There is a holy violence which we are permitted to use, like that of Jacob, who "wrestled all night with the Angel, and said, I will not let thee go, except thou bless me[q]." But how often, for want of this, is our enjoyment of the Saviour short and transient, "like the early dew, or the morning cloud that passeth away!" We should "stir ourselves up to lay hold on him;" and, if he would leave us, we must constrain him, as the disciples at Emmaus did, to take up his abode with

[o] Matt. xv. 22—28.   [p] Luke xviii. 1—8.   [q] Gen. xxxii. 24—28.

us[r]. We should dread nothing so much as the loss of his presence: and knowing what a holy and a jealous God he is, we should strive with all imaginable care to hold him fast, and avoid every thing which may "grieve his Spirit," and provoke him to depart from us.]

2. Seek to enjoy the most intimate communion with him—

[The Church, "which is the Mother of us all[s]," may be considered as the place to which the Bride strove to bring her Beloved. And we also, both in the closet and the Church, should seek such manifestations of his love, as cannot be enjoyed in the noise and bustle of the world. In all the ordinances of his grace, and at his holy table especially, we should labour to ensure his presence; since without him they are only "as wells without water," which "fill with shame and confusion" the thirsty soul[t]. Nor be satisfied with any small communications of his grace and peace: seek the largest possible measure of them, even to "be filled with all the fulness of God." In a word, so "dwell in him, and let him dwell in you;" and so be "one with him, and let him be one with you;" that you may even now, in communion with him, have an earnest of the blessedness of heaven, even of that joy, all "fulness of which is at his right hand for evermore."]

From her example, let us LEARN,

1. To fix our hearts supremely on the Lord Jesus Christ—

[Four times does the Bride designate him by this character, "Him whom my soul loveth." Let him be familiarized to us also under the same endearing name. O let him be in our estimation "fairer than ten thousand, and altogether lovely;" so that, if he interrogate us as he did Peter, Lovest thou me? we may be able to make the same appeal to him as Peter did, "Lord, thou knowest all things; thou knowest that I love thee."]

2. Not to indulge sloth in our pursuit of him—

["The idle soul shall suffer hunger; but the diligent soul shall be made fat." What darkness have many brought upon their souls by their unwatchfulness! Peter was warned by our Lord to "watch and pray, that he might not enter into temptation." But Peter slept; and, though repeatedly awaked and reproved, gave way to sloth again, the instant he was left to himself. What advantage Satan took of him, we all know, and what were the bitter fruits of his supineness. Let *us* "be sober and vigilant." Let us not pray "upon our bed," as regardless whether we are heard or not, but let us "stir up ourselves to

---

[r] Luke xxiv. 28, 29.   [s] Gal. iv. 26.   [t] Jer. xiv. 3.

lay hold on Christ;" and then " cleave unto him with full purpose of heart." If we would succeed in our pursuit of heavenly
joys, we must not only pray, but " watch unto prayer with all
perseverance."]

3. Not to yield to despondency, because we find
him not so present with us as we could wish—

[We are very apt to be impatient under the hidings of his
face, and to conclude, that he has utterly forsaken us. This
was the fault of the Church in the days of old: but God ex-
postulated with her, and reproved her[u] — — — and assured
her, that she was so indelibly engraven on the palms of his
hands, that he could not possibly forget her[x]: he might indeed
" forsake her for a moment, but with everlasting kindness would
he have mercy upon her[y]." If then similar fears arise in your
breast, say as David did, after he had unhappily given way to
them, " This is mine infirmity[z]." Be assured, that God, who
is faithful to his promises, " will never leave you nor forsake
you[a]:" that " if you seek him, he will be found of you[b]:" and
that " in due season you shall reap, if you faint not[c]."]

[u] Isai. xl. 28—31.   [x] Isai. xlix. 14—16.   [y] Isai. liv. 7, 8.
[z] Ps. lxxvii. 7—10.   [a] Heb. xiii. 5, 6.   [b] 2 Chron. xv. 2.
[c] Gal. vi. 9.

OUTLINE NO. 851
SPIRITUAL SLOTH REPROVED.

Cant. v. 2—8. *I sleep, but my heart waketh : it is the voice of
my beloved that knocketh, saying, Open to me my sister, my
love, my dove, my undefiled : for my head is filled with dew,
and my locks with the drops of the night. I have put off my
coat; how shall I put it on? I have washed my feet; how
shall I defile them? My beloved put in his hand by the hole
of the door, and my bowels were moved for him. I rose up to
open to my beloved ; and my hands dropped with myrrh, and
my fingers with sweet-smelling myrrh, upon the handles of
the lock. I opened to my beloved ; but my beloved had withdrawn himself, and was gone : my soul failed when he spake ;
I sought him, but I could not find him ; I called him, but he
gave me no answer. The watchmen that went about the city
found me, they smote me, they wounded me ; the keepers of the
walls took away my veil from me. I charge you, O daughters
of Jerusalem, if ye find my beloved, that ye tell him, that I
am sick of love.*

TWO things we should guard against in reading
the Song of Solomon ; namely, the laying an undue
stress on particular *words*, and the dwelling too

minutely on particular *circumstances*. There is a latitude due to the very species of composition, that may well exempt it from severe criticism, and from an over-strained application of its several parts. No one can have ever read the Holy Scriptures without seeing many expressions, which modern delicacy and refinement constrain us to pass over, as offensive to our ears. These expressions occur both in the Law and in the Prophets; and therefore we cannot wonder if they occur in a composition intended to exhibit the mutual love subsisting between Christ and his Church, and shadowing it forth under the most delicate of all images, the mutual regards of a bridegroom and his bride. Allowance must be made for the customs of different nations: a thing may not be at all improper in one age or country, which in another age and country would be highly indecorous, as not being sanctioned by common usage. Besides, there are many customs which obtained in the days of Solomon, which, if they were known to us, would reflect light on many parts of this poem, which are involved in obscurity because we want the key to the explanation of them. Even what we do know must be touched upon with the greatest delicacy, lest what was written only for the inflaming of our spiritual affections, should become rather an occasion of evil. The true way to profit by this book is to take the general scope of it, rather than its particular images, as the subjects for our reflection. And, if we attend to this rule, we shall find the passage which we have now read, replete with instruction. It informs us of the reproof which the Bride received, for the indifference with which on one occasion she treated her beloved.

Let us distinctly notice,

I. The indolence she indulged—

She was in a state, not of absolute sleep, like the ungodly world, but of slumber, half asleep, and half awake; " I sleep, but my heart waketh."

Moreover, when her beloved came to hold communion with her, she was inattentive to his voice: yea, notwithstanding he addressed her in terms of

most endeared affection, and complained of the incon-
venience he had sustained through her unwatchfulness,
she still gave but little heed to his voice. In hot
countries, "the night dews" are not only strong, but
often very injurious to those who are exposed to them:
yet even this consideration did not operate to produce
in her that activity which the occasion required.

Instead of rising at his call, she urged vain and
foolish excuses to justify her neglect; and in fact told
him, that his visit at that time was unacceptable.
These excuses were only a cloak for her own sloth
and self-indulgence: had her graces been in lively
exercise, the obstacles she complained of would have
vanished in an instant. This conduct gives a striking
picture of what too generally obtains amongst ourselves: it shews,

1. Our slothful habits—

[There is in the very best of men "the flesh yet lusting
against the Spirit, as well as the Spirit striving against the
flesh, so that they cannot do the things they would [a]." Even
St. Paul complained, that, whilst with his mind he served the
law of God, with his flesh he was still in some measure subjected to the law of sin, not indeed as a willing servant, but as
a captive, who in vain sought a perfect deliverance from that
detested enemy [b]. True indeed, where due vigilance is kept
up, "the old man" cannot gain any permanent advantage: but
even when "the spirit is willing, the flesh is too often weak;"
and all in some degree find, that "when they would do good,
evil is present with them." It is indeed greatly to be lamented,
that "the Wise Virgins" should ever so resemble the Foolish
Virgins, as to "slumber and sleep" like them: but so, alas!
it is: and when, by reason of our failures, we are ready to
complain, "Awake, awake, put on strength, O arm of the
Lord!" we need the rebuke which was given to that petition,
"Awake, awake, stand up, O Jerusalem, and put on thy
strength, O Zion [c]!"]

2. Our insensibility to the kindness of our beloved—

[How inexpressibly tender are his addresses to us! See
the invitations, the entreaties, the expostulations that pervade
every part of the sacred volume; and say whether they be not
sufficient to melt the most obdurate heart? "Behold, I stand
at the door and knock: if any man hear my voice, and open

---

[a] Gal. v. 17.   [b] Rom. vii. 14, 18, 22, 23.   [c] Isai. li. 9, 17. and lii. 1.

the door, I will come in to him, and sup with him, and he with me[d]." Yet how long does he stand and knock in vain! His pleadings too, how kind, how gracious, how forcible they are! "Have I been a wilderness to Israel? Wherefore say my people, we will come no more unto thee[e]?" "Turn ye unto me; for I have redeemed you: I am even married unto you[f]:" "Turn ye, turn ye; why will ye die, O House of Israel?" But all his expostulations have been to no purpose with respect to the generality; and even on the best they are far from operating to the extent they ought. St. Paul could say, "The love of Christ constraineth us," or carries us away like a mighty torrent: but how many are the seasons when his attractions are not so felt by us, and when, instead of regarding him as "the chiefest among ten thousand," we see scarcely any "beauty or comeliness in him for which he is to be desired!"]

3. Our vain excuses with which we cloke our sins—

[*Something arising out of our present circumstances* we are ready to plead in extenuation at least, if not in excuse, for our sloth. But, if we would deal faithfully with ourselves, we should see that all our pleas are a mere cloak for self-indulgence: we are called to "crucify the flesh with the affections and lusts," but we do not like self-denial: to "mortify our earthly members" is a work in which we cannot bear to engage: the "cutting off a right hand, and plucking out a right eye" is so painful to us, that we cannot be prevailed upon to put forth the resolution it requires. We promise ourselves a "more convenient season," which in too many instances never comes at all. Like those in the parable, we find some reason for declining the invitations sent us, and return for answer, "I pray thee have me excused" — — —]

A due consideration of her fault will prepare our minds for,

II. The reproof she met with—

At last, beginning to see her error, she rose to open to her beloved: and with such ardour of affection did she open to him, that "myrrh dropped, as it were, from her hands upon the handle of the lock." But behold, he was gone; and though she sought him, she could not find him; and though she called after him, he gave her no answer. The watchmen too reproved her with great severity, as questioning even the sincerity of one who could so treat the beloved of her soul. And such reproof must we all expect, if we give

d Rev. iii. 20.   e Jer. ii. 31.   f Jer. iii. 12, 14.

way to sloth instead of watching unto prayer. We
must expect,

1. That he will depart from us—

[Verily he is " a God who hideth himself," a holy and a
jealous God, that will make us to " eat of the fruit of our own
ways, and to be filled with our own devices." He has warned
us not to " grieve his Holy Spirit," lest he depart from us. I
" will go and return to my place," says he, " till they acknowledge their offence[g]." And oh! how painful are the seasons
when he withdraws from us, and leaves our souls in darkness!
Even he himself, when for our sins he was deserted of his God,
how bitterly did he cry; " My God, my God, why hast thou
forsaken me?" O that we may never provoke him to put that
cup into our hands! How distressing will it be to be reduced
to any measure of that experience which Christ endured for
us; "O my God, why art thou so far from helping me, and
from the voice of my roaring? I cry in the day time, but thou
hearest not; and in the night season, and am not silent[h]!"
See David in this predicament[i]— — —, and " let us be instructed, lest we provoke him to depart from us also."]

2. That the word and ordinances shall be unproductive of any solid comfort to us—

[The "Watchmen" are the ministers, whose office is not
only to instruct and comfort, but also to warn and " rebuke
with all authority." True it is, they may be too hasty and
severe in their reproofs; and may by such indiscreet zeal make
the heart of the righteous sad, when they should rather bind
up the broken heart, and heal the wounded spirit. But it is
possible also, that they may be too lenient, and " speak peace
to persons when there is no peace." But where there is no
fault in their ministrations, God may make their word as a
sword, to enter into the very bones of those who hear it, and
to cut them to the heart. Even the promises, when held forth
in all their fulness and all their freeness, may afford no comfort
to the soul of one who is under the hidings of God's face; but
may add tenfold poignancy to all his griefs. How unhappy
was the state of David, when even the thought of God himself was a source of sorrow and despondency, rather than of
joy and peace ! " He remembered God, and was troubled; and
his soul refused comfort." In like manner, all the wonders of
redeeming love may be made a source of the deepest anguish
to our souls, by the apprehension that we have no part or lot
in them. If then we would not bring these heavy judgments
on our souls, let us " seek the Lord while he may be found,
and call upon him while he is near."]

[g] Hos. v. 15.   [h] Matt. xxii. 1, 2.   [i] Ps. xlii. 3. and lxxvii. 6—9.

ADDRESS—

1. Those who yet enjoy the light of God's countenance—

[Happy, happy are ye, in the possession of this rich mercy: Surely such a state is a foretaste of heaven itself. But do not presume upon it. Do not say, " My mountain stands strong; I shall never be moved;" lest ye cause God to " hide his face from you, and ye be troubled." " Be not high-minded; but fear." Keep upon your watch-tower: " let your loins be girt, and your lamps trimmed;" and watch every moment for the coming of your Lord. " Blessed is that servant, whom his Lord, when he cometh, shall find so doing."]

2. Those who are under the hidings of their Redeemer's face—

[If others are not to presume, so neither are you to despond. " If your sorrow endure for a night, there is joy awaiting you in the morning." This do: imitate the Bride in the passage before us. She desired the prayers and intercessions of the saints, and entreated them, in their seasons of communion with their Lord, to plead her cause: " I charge you, when you shall see him, tell him that I am sick of love." She felt no grief like the absence of her beloved; and could find comfort in nothing but the restoration of his love. Thus let your hearts be fixed on him; even on him only: and suffer nothing to weaken your regards to him. Never entertain hard thoughts of him. Take shame to yourselves, till ye even lothe yourselves in dust and ashes: but relax neither your love to him, nor your confidence in him. Say with yourselves, " Though he slay me, yet will I trust in him." Then will he in due season return to your souls, so that " your light shall rise in obscurity, and your darkness be as the noon-day." Only be content to " go on your way weeping, bearing the precious seed of penitence and faith; and you shall doubtless come again with rejoicing, bringing your sheaves with you."]

OUTLINE NO. 852

TRANSCENDENT EXCELLENCIES OF CHRIST.

Cant. v. 9. *What is thy beloved more than another beloved, O thou fairest among women? What is thy beloved more than another beloved, that thou dost so charge us?*

THOUGH zeal in every earthly pursuit is approved and commended, it is almost universally banished from the concerns of religion. The most temperate exertions are deemed excessive, and a moderate degree of solicitude is called enthusiasm. Even they who profess godliness are too often found ready to damp the ardour, which persons, more active than themselves, may at any time express. Thus the Bride was checked in her inquiries after her beloved. The " daughters of Jerusalem," who keep up the dialogue with the Bride and Bridegroom, seem to be either formal professors of religion, or to have made a very small progress in the divine life. And *they,* when the Bride, under great trouble and anxiety, requested their intercession, reflected on her as manifesting an intemperate and needless zeal. But we will answer their questions, by shewing,

I. The excellencies of our Beloved—

Who the Beloved of the Church is, we need not declare; since it is too manifest to admit a doubt. There is not a member of that body who does not regard *Jesus* with supreme affection. Nor is there any apology needed for such a choice. His excellencies are exceeding great.

[In him are concentrated all the glories of *the Godhead*[a]. Being the brightness of his Father's glory, and the express image of his person, he must of necessity possess all the Divine perfections[b]. To search out these perfections is beyond the ability of any finite being[c]; but to love and adore him on account of them is the duty and privilege of all his people. The excellencies of *his human nature* may be more easily declared. There his glory is veiled, so that we may behold and contemplate it without being blinded by its overwhelming splendour. He was not only holy, but holiness itself, without spot or blemish. His most inveterate enemies, Satan himself not excepted, could not find a flaw in him[d], and God himself has borne testimony, that in him was no sin[e]. *As Mediator,* he united both the Godhead and the Manhood in his own person, and executed an office which he alone was able to sustain. In that character we behold him reconciling God to man, and man to God[f], yea, glorifying all the perfections of the Deity in the salvation of sinners[g]. Well may we, in this view of him, exclaim, "How great is his goodness, how great is his beauty[h]!"]

But the text requires us to speak of him in a comparative view—

a Col. ii. 9. b Heb. i. 3. c Job xi. 7.
d John viii. 46. John xiv. 30. e 1 John iii. 5. f 2 Cor. v. 19.
g Rom. iii. 25, 26. h Zech. ix. 17.

[Surely there is no other object of affection in the universe worthy to be compared with him. *In whom is there such a marvellous combination of excellencies?* As *God*, as *Man*, and as *Mediator*, he not only unites in himself every perfection proper to the Divine and human nature, but exhibits a character peculiar to himself, a character that is and ever must be the admiration of the whole universe. *In whom was there ever found any one excellence in so eminent a degree?* There have been men wise, and virtuous and loving; but in him were hid all the treasures of wisdom and knowledge[i]; and he was not only virtuous, but virtue itself incarnate; and as for his love, its heights and depths can never be explored[k]. Indeed, whatever excellence has at any time beamed forth in the creature, it has been nothing but a ray reflected from this Sun of Righteousness[l]. We may ask yet further, *Whose excellencies were ever so beneficial to us?* Others indeed have profited us by their example; but He, by his obedience, has wrought out a righteousness *for us;* a righteousness wherein the vilest of sinners, if truly penitent, shall stand perfect and complete in the sight of God[m]. Let the contemptuous inquirer then blush for his ignorance; and acknowledge that our Beloved infinitely transcends every thing that can be put in competition with him.]

According to his excellencies must of necessity be,

II. The regard we owe him—

If we look to the example of the Bride, who well knew how to appreciate his worth, we shall see how we ought to manifest our affection towards him.

1. We should esteem him above every thing in the world—

[The Bride has used every simile that the most fertile imagination could suggest, in order to express her sense of his excellency[n]. David esteemed nothing in heaven or earth in comparison of him[o]; and St. Paul counted all things but dung for the knowledge of him[p]. And if *we* do not see a "beauty and comeliness in him for which he is to be desired" infinitely beyond every thing else, our eyes must be altogether blinded by the god of this world. Let us then despise every thing in comparison of him, and take him as our portion, our ALL IN ALL.]

2. We should be exceeding careful that we do not grieve him—

---

[i] Col. ii. 3. [k] Eph. iii. 18, 19. [l] 1 Cor. iv. 7. [m] Rom. v. 18, 19.
[n] Cant. ii. 3. and in ten different particulars, v. 10—16.
[o] Ps. lxxiii. 25. [p] Phil. iii. 8.

[In this also the Bride affords us an excellent example. Frequently does she repeat her tender concern lest by any means he should be provoked to depart from her[q]. Such a holy caution also should *we* continually maintain. He is a holy and jealous God, and will not endure our neglects without manifesting his displeasure[r]. The Bride herself, notwithstanding her care in general, experienced the loss of his presence, when she became remiss[s]. And thus will he also hide himself from us, if by our unwatchfulness we grieve his Holy Spirit. Let us then "walk circumspectly, not as fools, but as wise." Let us "look to him as our Guardian Angel, and beware of him, and obey his voice, and carefully abstain from every species of provocation[t]."]

3. If at any time we have lost a sense of his presence, we should by all possible means immediately exert ourselves to regain it—

[With what contrition did the Bride arise! How did her very soul faint within her, when she found he was departed! With what earnestness did she call after him! How did she instantly inquire after him, applying to those who from their office and character were best fitted to direct her! How did she persist, notwithstanding all the discouragements she met with! And what a solemn charge did she give to her fellow-saints to intercede for her[u]! Such should be our conduct under the hidings of his face. We should not sit down in despondency, but labour with more abundant diligence to obtain renewed expressions of his love and favour[x].]

4. If he vouchsafe to visit us again, we should feel ourselves completely happy in him, and yield up ourselves entirely to his will—

[No sooner were the Bride's endeavours crowned with success, than she redoubled her efforts to retain and enjoy him[y], and earnestly sought to be most intimately, and inseparably united to him[z]. Thus should we seek to "abide in him, and to have him abiding in us[a]." We should "cleave to him with full purpose of heart," and, in the possession of his love, our souls should find all that they can desire[b]. Thrice happy they who are thus influenced by their views of Christ! Their "labour shall never be in vain." They shall enjoy the greatest, the only real good, the light of his countenance[c]; and though in a little wrath he may hide his face from them,

---

[q] Cant. ii. 7. and iii. 5. and viii. 4.

[r] Isai. xlv. 15.   [s] Cant. v. 3—6.   [t] Exod. xxiii. 20, 21

[u] See each distinct step exemplified : Cant. v. 5—8.

[x] Hos. v. 15.   [y] Cant. iii. 2—4.   [z] Cant. viii. 1, 2, 6.

[a] John xv. 4.   [b] 2 Cor. vi. 10.   [c] Ps. iv. 6.

it shall be only for a moment, and with everlasting kindness will he have mercy on them[d].]

It may now be allowed us, not merely to exhort, but to " CHARGE," you all—

[In the name of Almighty God, we " charge" you all to love the Saviour. If the love which Believers bear to him constrains them to be singular, let it be remembered, that *the blame* of singularity does not rest on *them:* as they can " give a reason for the *hope* that is in them," so can they also for their *love* to the Saviour. His transcendent excellencies demand their supreme regard. If they love him with all their heart and soul and mind and strength, it is no more than their bounden duty; yea, their most fervent affections fall infinitely short of his desert. Let all then set their love on *Jesus.* Let them search out his excellencies, till they are ravished with the sight, and let them " cast their idols to the moles and to the bats." Nor let any be ashamed to confess him before men. It is a small matter to bear the taunts of an ignorant and ungodly world. One hour's enjoyment of Christ's presence will more than counterbalance an age of man's contempt; and if on earth, how much more in heaven! Dare then to be singular. Shine, Believers, as becomes your relation to the heavenly Bridegroom. Be " the fairest among women," as your Beloved is among men[e]; and let your union with him be discovered by your conformity to his image.]

[d] Isai. liv. 8.   [e] Ps. xlv. 2—13.

OUTLINE NO. 853

THE EXCELLENCY OF CHRIST.

Cant. v. 16. *He is altogether lovely. This is my Beloved; and this is my Friend, O daughters of Jerusalem.*

WITH many it is a matter of surprise, that truly converted Christians should manifest such zeal in prosecuting their own ways, and in commending religion to all around them. The world see no such excellency in Christ as the true believer does; and therefore, whilst they cannot but acknowledge the superiority of the Christian's walk, they ask, in a tone of self-justifying confidence, " What is thy beloved more than another beloved, that thou dost so charge us[a]?" But, if they beheld the Saviour in his true

[a] ver. 9.

character, so far would they be from wondering that his people loved and served him so ardently, that they would rather wonder at the coldness of their hearts towards him, and at the unprofitableness of their lives. To the above question the Church of old replies, in the words I have read to you: from which I shall take occasion to shew,

I. The excellency of Christ—

This is set forth in highly figurative language; agreeably to the tenour of the whole book, which abounds in allegory from beginning to end. The Church marks, under very sublime images, his beauty in every part—" his head, his locks, his eyes, his cheeks, his lips, his hands, his body, his legs, his countenance, his mouth;" and proclaims him, not only " the chiefest among ten thousand," but " altogether lovely[b]." We will not attempt to follow the particular description here given; for we could never do justice to it. We will rather content ourselves with a general view of Christ, who is altogether lovely,

1. In his person—

[In himself he unites all the perfections of the Godhead, with every grace that can adorn humanity. " In him there was no spot or blemish;" insomuch that his bitterest enemies, after the severest possible scrutiny, were forced to confess, " We find in him no fault at all" — — —]

2. In his offices—

[These were altogether sustained for us, and executed for us; and they are precisely such as our necessities required. Did we need an atonement for our sins? He is our Great High *Priest* who offers that atonement; yea, and offers himself, too, as the sacrifice which alone was sufficient to expiate our guilt. Did we need to be instructed relative to the way in which alone God would accept a returning sinner? He became our *Prophet*, to make known to us the mind and will of God, and to reveal to us inwardly, by his Spirit, what he has outwardly proclaimed to us in his word. Did we need to be delivered from all our spiritual enemies? He yet further assumed the *Kingly* office, that he might rescue us from our bondage, and make us partakers with him of all the glory and felicity of heaven. It is not possible to find in man a want for which provision is not made in him, to the utmost extent of

[b] ver. 9—16.

our necessities; and which he will not supply to all who call upon him — — —]

3. In all his intercourse with his people—

[O, who can conceive the extent of his condescension and grace? How ready is he, at all times, to "draw nigh to those who draw nigh to him;" to "manifest himself to them, as he does not unto the world;" and to impart to them all the consolation and strength which they look for at his hands! "In all the afflictions of his people he is himself afflicted;" and to such a degree is he "touched with the feeling of their infirmities," that every trial of theirs is felt by him as his own. "Whosoever toucheth us, toucheth the apple of his eye." In a word, there is no weakness which he will not succour: no want which he will not supply: nor shall there be any bounds to his communications, except what are fixed by our capacity to receive them — — —]

With this view of Christ's excellency, it is impossible not to connect,

II. The blessedness of those who believe in him—

Between him and his believing people there is the closest union that can be imagined.

1. He stands pre-eminent in their regards—

[So says the Church; "This is my Beloved." It is the Spouse that speaks; and here she claims him as her Divine Husband. Now, conceive a person excelling all others in every endowment, both of body and mind; conceive of whole nations acknowledging him as the Benefactor of the human race; and conceive of him as not only thus lauded for former benefits conferred, but as at the very time scattering in rich profusion all manner of blessings upon millions of mankind: I say, conceive that you behold such an one surrounded by applauding and adoring multitudes; and then think how happy that woman must be who can say, "This is my Beloved;" I have a right in him which no other human being has; all that he is, is mine; and all that he has, is mine. I say, my Brethren, that we cannot conceive of felicity on earth greater than hers. Yet, my Brethren, this is yours, if only you believe in Christ. He is your Beloved; and you may claim precisely the same interest in him as if there were not another, either in heaven or on earth, to claim it with you. What happiness, then, is there to be compared with yours; when it is not a mere man, however excellent, but your incarnate God himself, to whom you stand in this near, this glorious relation?]

2. You also stand high in his regards—

[Yes, the regard is mutual. You might possibly love one in whom there was not a reciprocal attachment. But it is not so in this case. He calls you "The dearly beloved of his soul[c]." As surely therefore as you can say, "This is my Beloved," you may add, with confidence, "This is my Friend." Yes; Jesus himself says, "I call you not servants, but friends." Nor can you imagine any act of friendship which he will not most gladly execute for you. "Abraham was the friend of God." See, then, what God wrought for him! and know, that *that*, yea, and infinitely more, will the Lord Jesus Christ work for you in the time of your necessity. On every occasion will he come to you, to counsel you by his wisdom, to uphold you by his power, and to enrich you with his benefits. We are told, "There is a friend that sticketh closer than a brother:" verily, there is no brother in the universe, that will be so entirely at your command as he. Only apply to him, and spread your wants before him, and you shall never go empty away. On the contrary, "He will do exceeding abundantly for you, above all that you can ask or think."]

Now then let me ASK of you, my Brethren,

1. "What think ye of Christ?"

[This was a question which Christ himself put to his Disciples: and I now put it to you. You know what is said, "To them that believe, he is precious," even *preciousness* itself. Is he viewed in this light by *you?* This will determine whether ye be true Believers, or not: for in every Believer, and in him exclusively, this grace is found. Verily, if you are really his, you will say, "Whom have I in heaven but thee? and there is none upon earth that I desire besides thee" ——— Your sublimest joy on earth must be to say, "My beloved is mine, and I am his[d]."]

2. How are you endeavouring to requite his love?

[If you love Christ, it must be not in word only, but in deed and in truth. Are you then living in the enjoyment of his presence? ——— Are you consecrating yourselves unreservedly to his service? ——— Above all, Are you seeking to grow up into his image, so that he may be as well satisfied with contemplating *your* relation to *him*, as you are in viewing *his* to *you?* See how, in the chapter before my text, Christ views his bride[e]: see how he views her with admiration, as it were, from head to foot[f]; and what a blessed testimony he bears respecting her[g]. Let it be your ambition so to walk before him, that he may testify the same of you; and that the union which has thus been commenced between you on earth, may be consummated in heaven for evermore.]

---

[c] Jer. xii. 7.   [d] Cant. ii. 16. and vi. 3.   [e] Cant. iv. 1.
[f] Cant. iv. 2—6.   [g] Cant. iv. 7.

OUTLINE NO. 854

Cant. viii. 5. *Who is this that cometh up from the wilderness, leaning on her Beloved?*

THERE is an intimate and mysterious union between Christ and his Church. It is often compared, in Scripture, to a marriage union: and in the book before us, the Song of Solomon, there is a figurative representation of the intercourse which subsists between Christ and his Church under this relation. A third description of persons, called " the daughters of Jerusalem," are occasionally introduced, to diversify the dialogue, and to enliven it by bearing their part in it. The words of the text seem to be uttered by *them*. The Church had, in the four preceding verses, expressed her desire after more familiar and abiding fellowship with her divine Husband: and the bystanders, admiring and felicitating her state, exclaim " Who is this?" &c.

I will endeavour briefly,

I. To throw light upon the words thus addressed to the Church—

There does not, indeed, appear any considerable difficulty in them; especially if we bear in mind the passage of the Israelites through the wilderness to the land of Canaan. This world may fitly be represented as " a wilderness"—

[That through which the Israelites passed is called " a waste howling wilderness[a];" " a land of deserts and of pits, a land of drought and of the shadow of death[b];" a land " wherein were fiery serpents and scorpions; and drought, where there was no water[c]." And such, indeed, is this vain world to the weary pilgrim. It affords nothing for the comfort and refreshment of a heavy-laden soul; but furnishes obstructions without number, snares at every step, and enemies filled with the most envenomed hostility — — —]

Through this the Christian is passing, in his way to heaven—

[a] Deut. xxxii. 10.　　　[b] Jer. ii. 6.　　　[c] Deut. viii. 15.

[He has, of necessity, his duties to perform, like other men. But " though in the world, he is not of the world[d]." He regards not this world as his rest; but merely as a country through which he must go, towards " that better country which he is seeking after." He accounts himself a " pilgrim and a stranger upon earth[e];" and advances on his journey with all practicable expedition, " not setting his affections on any thing by the way[f]," but looking forward to the termination of his labours in a better world — — —]

In all his way, " he leans upon his beloved" Saviour for support—

[He feels his insufficiency for the work he has to perform: but " he knows in whom he has believed, that HE is able to sustain him, and to keep that which he has committed to him[g]." No sick or enfeebled traveller places a more entire dependence on one who has undertaken to bear him onward, than the Christian does on Christ, who has engaged to perform this office, saying, " Even to your old age I am He; and even to hoar hairs will I carry you: I have made, and I will bear; even I will carry, and will deliver you[h]." He would account it a most heinous offence if for a moment he should " trust to an arm of flesh[i];" and with a holy indignation at the thought of placing any confidence in the creature, he says, " Ashur shall not save us; we will not ride upon horses; neither will we say any more to the work of our hands, Ye are our gods: for in thee the fatherless findeth mercy[k]." In a word, the whole habit of the Christian's mind, throughout this dreary wilderness, is that which the holy Psalmist addressed to his Lord and Saviour: " Hold thou up my goings in thy paths, that my footsteps slip not:" " hold thou me up, and I shall be safe[l]."]

But my object is, to mark the spirit of my text, and,

II. To point out more particularly the force of the interrogation—

I should say, that, in its strictest sense, it appears to express admiration: but we may very properly consider it as the language,

1. Of inquiry—

[" Who is this?" Is there, amongst ourselves, any one answering to this character? Am I this happy person? Do I so live in this world, that the by-standers notice the peculiarity of my walk, and my entire devotion to the Lord and Saviour

---

[d] John xvii. 6.   [e] Heb. xi. 13.   [f] Col. iii. 2.
[g] 2 Tim. i. 12.   [h] Isai. xlvi. 4.   [i] Jer. xvii. 5.
[k] Hos. xiv. 3.   [l] Ps. xvii. 5.

Jesus Christ? Do I, instead of loving the world, account it a dreary wilderness? Do I renounce, as in my baptismal vows I undertook to do, all the pomps and vanities of this wicked world, and all the sinful lusts of the flesh? and "am I daily dying unto the world," to its cares, its pleasures, its maxims, its habits, its company altogether? Am I " crucified unto the world, and is the world crucified unto me by the cross of Christ," so that I value it no more than a man does who is in the very article of death[m]? And, in my passage through this wilderness, am I leaning constantly on my beloved Saviour, saying, " In the Lord have I righteousness and strength[n]?" This is, indeed, the character of the true Christian; and we are commanded to " examine ourselves, whether we be in the faith, and to prove our own selves[o]." I would entreat you, therefore, to make this a subject of most serious inquiry; and to ask yourselves, Am I the person characterized in the words of our text?]

2. Of admiration—

[This I suppose to be the more immediate feeling expressed in my text. And truly a person so circumstanced as the Bride here was, is one of the greatest wonders upon earth. Conceive yourselves to be that person;—that such *an earthly and sensual creature*, as every one of you must know yourselves to be, should so renounce the world!—that such *a polluted creature* should enjoy such intimacy with the Lord of Glory! that such *a weak creature* should persevere, in despite of so many obstacles both within and without! May not such an one well say, " I am a wonder unto many[p]?" Must he not, above all, be a wonder to himself? " Who am *I* that *I* should be so honoured; whilst the world at large are left to walk after the imaginations of their own evil hearts, and to " live as without God in the world!"]

3. Of congratulation—

[No man in the universe is so to be congratulated, as he who dies to the world, and seeks all his happiness in Christ. Think with yourselves *from what imminent danger he has escaped*. " The whole world is lying in wickedness[q]," and will be condemned at last[r]; but " he has been taken out of the world[s]," and been delivered from it, even as Lot from Sodom. Is not *he* a fit object for congratulation? But consider, further, *to what a glorious place he is hastening;* even to heaven itself, where he shall speedily possess " an inheritance incorruptible and undefiled, and that fadeth not away[t]." Behold, too, *to what a blessed company he is joined!* " He is come to an innumerable company of angels; and to the general assembly and Church

---

[m] Gal. vi. 14.　　　[n] Isai. xlv. 24.　　　[o] 2 Cor. xiii. 5.
[p] Ps. lxxi. 7.　　　[q] 1 John v. 19.　　　[r] 1 Cor. xi. 32.
[s] John xv. 19.　　　[t] 1 Pet. i. 4.

of the first-born, which are written in heaven; and to God, the Judge of all; and to the spirits of the just made perfect; and to Jesus, the Mediator of the new covenant; and to all these, as his everlasting companions." Think, also, *how near he is to all this felicity*, every day and hour bearing him towards it, as fast as the wings of time can carry him. And, above all, *what an all-sufficient support he has in his way thither*, even his beloved Lord, " who is able to keep him from falling, and to present him faultless before the presence of his glory with exceeding joy [u]." Tell me, Who is happy in comparison of him? Who is to be congratulated, if he be not?]

Is there here *a weak believer, who doubts* whether such an one as he can ever attain this blessedness?

[Let him trust in Christ, and not be afraid: for none ever perished, who trusted in Him. As for a man's own weakness and insufficiency, *that* can be no bar to his attainment of this felicity; since the Lord Jesus Christ is " able to save to the uttermost all who come unto God by him [x];" and he has expressly told us, that " he will carry the lambs in his bosom, and gently lead them that are with young [y]." Only take care that he be for you; and then you may hurl defiance at all that are against you.]

But is there any backslider that is turning back to the world?

[O, think what you are doing; and what tremendous evils you are bringing upon your soul! What has this vain world ever done for you, that it should influence you by its attractions? — — — And what has Christ *not* done for you, whilst you sought him, and relied upon him? Hear his complaint against you: " Have I been a wilderness unto Israel; a land of darkness? Wherefore say my people, We are lords; we will come no more unto thee [z]?" The *world* has been a wilderness to you, at all times: but has *Christ* been so? Has he been so at any moment, when you sought your happiness in him? Hear, and tremble at the warning given you by an inspired Apostle: " If, after they have escaped the pollutions of the world through the knowledge of the Lord and Saviour Jesus Christ, they are again entangled therein, and overcome (a case that too frequently occurs), the latter end is worse with them than the beginning. For it had been better for them not to have known the way of righteousness, than, after they have known it, to turn from the holy commandment delivered unto them [a]." And is there one in such an unhappy state as this?

---

[u] Jude ver. 24.　　[x] Heb. vii. 25.　　[y] Isai. xl. 11.
[z] Jer. ii. 31.　　[a] 2 Pet. ii. 20, 21.

"Who is he?" Let every one inquire, "Lord, is it I?" And
whoever he may be, let us all regard him as an object of the
deepest *commiseration*.—The Lord awaken all such ere it be
too late!]

OUTLINE NO. 855

THE CHURCH'S DESIRE OF CHRIST'S LOVE.

Cant. viii. 6, 7. *Set me as a seal upon thine heart, as a seal upon
thine arm: for love is strong as death; jealousy is cruel as the
grave: the coals thereof are coals of fire, which hath a most
vehement flame. Many waters cannot quench love, neither
can the floods drown it: if a man would give all the substance
of his house for love, it would utterly be contemned.*

THE more any person enjoys of Christ, the more
ardent will be his desires after him, and the more
enlarged his petitions for richer communications from
him. The Church, as represented in the song before
us, has already been brought into the closest fellowship with her Beloved; yet this, so far from satisfying
her, serves only for an occasion of soliciting from him
yet further favours, and urging her request with more
powerful pleas: "Set me as a seal upon thine heart,
and upon thine arm; &c." That in this we may be
stirred up to follow her example, let us notice,

I. Her request—

To fix the import of this, we must determine the
precise sense in which the Bride uses the word, "seal."
In the general acceptation of that term in Scripture,
we understand that which is affixed to deeds or cove-
nants of any kind, in order to ratify and confirm
them. Such was that with which Jeremiah's purchase
of a field was confirmed[a]; and in reference to such
was circumcision appointed to Abraham, as the seal
of God's covenant with him, and of the righteousness
which he, by faith in that covenant, already possessed[b]; whilst, on the other hand, God's foreknow-
ledge and fore-ordination of his elect is a seal on his
part, attesting that that covenant stands on a sure
and immoveable foundation[c]. In a similar sense, the
Holy Spirit's work in sanctifying the elect is a seal,

[a] Jer. xxxii. 10, 11, 14.   [b] Rom. iv. 11.   [c] 2 Tim. ii. 19.

whereby he seals them unto the day of redemption, and assures to them their enjoyment of their purchased inheritance[d]. But we apprehend that the use of the term in this place is different; and that it refers to signets which were not uncommonly worn upon the hand or arm, as memorials of persons who were greatly beloved. Such we find mentioned by the Prophet Jeremiah; " As I live, saith the Lord, though Coniah, the son of Jehoiakim King of Judah, were the signet upon my right hand, yet would I pluck thee thence[e]," utterly unmindful of all my former regards. In this view the Church's request is, that her Beloved would *make her the object of his most endeared affections, and of his continual care.* Now,

This is a proper request from every child of man—

[All without exception are invited to come to Christ[f], and to participate freely his richest blessings[g]. Unworthiness on our part is no bar to our acceptance with him; since all, however elevated and ennobled afterwards, are, previously to their union with him, in the lowest state of guilt[h] and degradation[i]. He, and all his benefits, are to be apprehended simply by faith[k]. Whosoever comes to him by faith is united to him, as a branch to the vine[l], and may expect to receive out of his fulness all that has been treasured up in him for our use and benefit[m]. We may ask for the entire affections of his soul, and the unlimited exercise of his power, as if there were no other creature in the universe to share his regards. Less than this we ought not to ask. Less than this would not avail for our eternal happiness. We must have all the love of his heart, and all the power of his arm, if we would be brought through all our difficulties and trials to the everlasting enjoyment of him in his kingdom. Whatever the most beloved Bride may hope for from him to whom she is betrothed, that, and infinitely more, may we expect from our heavenly Bridegroom— — —]

And it shall be fulfilled to all who offer it in spirit and in truth—

[Christ has solemnly pledged himself to this extent by an everlasting covenant[n] — — — And he has fulfilled it to millions of the human race, who were once as guilty, as polluted, and

---

[d] Eph. i. 13. and iv. 30. [e] Jer. xxii. 24. [f] John vi. 37.
[g] Isai. lv. 1. [h] Rom. iii. 19. [i] Ezek. xvi. 3—12
[k] John i. 12. [l] John xv. 1—5. [m] John xv. 7.
[n] Jer. xxxii. 40, 41.

as helpless as we — — — Hence he chides the Church for her doubts, after that he had graven her on the palms of his hands[o] — — — Who can tell the efficacy of fervent and believing prayer? Our God and Saviour could as soon deny himself, as he could withstand it. Instead of rejecting our petitions on account of their being too large, he will approve of them the more, and answer them the sooner, on account of their comprehensiveness and extent: he has said, "Open your mouth wide, and I will fill it[p]:" "Ye may ask what ye will, and it shall be done unto you[q]."]

We shall, however, be more certain of success, if we can follow her in,

II. Her pleas—

Two things in particular she urged on the consideration of her Beloved, in order to prevail on him to grant her request; the one was, that *she could not endure the thought of having a less interest in him than her relation to him required,* yea, that her "jealousy would burn like coals of fire that had a most vehement flame;" and the other was, that *her love to him was supreme and unalterable;* that it was "stronger than death;" that "no waters could quench it, no floods drown it;" and that, if the richest monarch in the universe would "give all the substance of his house" to engage it for himself, "it would be utterly contemned."

Now in these pleas we see

1. What distress is occasioned by a doubt of Christ's love to us—

[To have it a doubtful point whether we be children of God and heirs of heaven, or children of the wicked one and heirs of hell, is a source of unutterable anguish to every man who knows not what "a fearful thing it is to fall into the hands of the living God[r]." How bitterly did Job bewail his condition, whilst he apprehended God to be his enemy! "The arrows of the Almighty are within me, the poison whereof drinketh up my spirit: the terrors of God do set themselves in array against me[s]." David likewise in many of his Psalms pours out similar complaints[t] — — — Careless and ungodly

[o] Isai. xlix. 14—16. [p] Ps. lxxxi. 10. [q] John xiv. 13, 14.
[r] Heb. x. 31. [s] Job vi. 4.
[t] Ps. xlii. 1—3. and lxxvii. 1—4, 7—9. and lxxxviii. 1—7. and cii. 1—6, 9—11.

men can rest satisfied without any inquiries : but an awakened man cannot be so indifferent about his interest in Christ : to him suspense is death : he feels " a jealousy cruel as the grave," (which will never suffer its destined victim to escape,) and devouring, like a flame, which consumes all within its reach.]

2. What consolation arises from a consciousness of our love to him—

[Though there is no *merit* in our love to Christ, it greatly emboldens us in our addresses to him, and gives us a just ground to hope, that he will in due time manifest his love to us, and shed it abroad in our hearts by the Holy Spirit. He has expressly said, " I love them that love me[u];" and has assured us, that, " if we love him, his Father will love us, and come and make his abode with us[x]." The very circumstance of our love to him is of itself, independent of all other evidences, a proof that he does actually love us : for our love to him is the effect of his love to us; " We love him, because he first loved us[y];" yea, " He loved us with an everlasting love; and therefore with loving-kindness hath he drawn us[z]." If then we have within ourselves an evidence, that our love to him is supreme, and that nothing which the world could either offer to us, or inflict upon us, would induce us to surrender our hope in him, we may rest assured, not only that he is ours, but that he will be ours even to the end. We may even make this an argument with him in prayer, as David did, " I am thine : save me[a]!" and as the Church of old did, " Now, O Lord, thou art our father : we are the clay, and thou our potter : and we all are the work of thy hand : Be not wroth very sore, O Lord, neither remember iniquity for ever : behold, see, we beseech thee, we are all thy people[b]." Bearing us, as he does, on his shoulders, and on his breast, in his official capacity as our High Priest within the veil[c], we may be sure that " he will never leave us nor forsake us[d]," nor ever suffer any thing to " separate us from his love[e].]

LEARN from hence,

1. What should be the frame of your minds towards the Lord Jesus Christ—

[Our hearts should be supremely set on him, and we should " count all things but loss for the knowledge of him." So ardent should our love to him be, that no floods of affliction or

---

[u] Prov. viii. 17.   [x] John xiv. 21, 23.

[y] 1 John iv. 10, 19. and xv. 16.   [z] Jer. xxxiii. 3.

[a] Ps. cxix. 94.   [b] Isai. lxiv. 8, 9.

[c] Exod. xxviii. 9—12, 21, 29, 30.   [d] Heb. xiii. 5.

[e] Rom. viii. 35—39.

persecution should ever be able to drown it, nor all that the world can give stand for a moment in competition with it———— Examine yourselves, Brethren, and see whether it be really so? Can ye, in answer to the question put by our Lord to Peter, make the reply that Peter did, " Lord, thou knowest all things; thou knowest that I love thee?"———]

2. What we should daily look for at his hands—

[Your security and happiness depend altogether upon his unchanging love. Were he to withdraw from underneath you his everlasting arms, you would instantly fall and perish. Entreat him then to " carry you in his bosom," and to " bear you still as upon eagles' wings." Plead with him in earnest prayer; and let him not go until he bestow his blessing upon you. " You are not straitened in him: be not straitened in your own bowels:" and let all the fellowship which you enjoy with him here, be regarded by you as a pledge and earnest of still closer fellowship with him in the regions of eternal light and blessedness.]

ISAIAH.

OUTLINE NO. 856

GOD'S COMPLAINT AGAINST HIS PEOPLE.

Isai. i. 2, 3. Hear, O heavens, and give ear, O earth: for the Lord hath spoken, I have nourished and brought up children, and they have rebelled against me. The ox knoweth his owner, and the ass his master's crib: but Israel doth not know, my people doth not consider.

IT is the Lord God Almighty that now speaketh respecting us. Let every ear attend; let every heart be humbled in the dust before him. He hath a controversy with us, and a complaint against us: and he summons both heaven and earth to attest the truth of his charge, and the equity of his judgment. Though he is a Sovereign, and amenable to none, yet he does frequently make his appeal to the whole creation, and constitute his creatures judges between himself and us[a]. In this charge we behold,

I. The evil we have committed—

The charge is doubtless in the first place uttered against the Jews—

[God had truly "nourished them, and brought them up as children." He had chosen them to himself, as his peculiar people; he had brought them up out of Egypt with a mighty hand, and an out-stretched arm: he had fed and supported them forty years in the wilderness; he had given them a revelation of his mind and will; and he had planted them in that good land which he had promised to their fathers. In all this he had acted towards them with all the care and tenderness of a most affectionate Parent[b]———

But how had they requited him for all his kindness? From the very beginning did they show themselves a rebellious and stiff-necked people[c]. They were always murmuring under

[a] Mic. vi. 2.　[b] Deut. i. 31. and xxxii. 9—12.　[c] Deut. ix. 24.

every succeeding trial, and distrusting God in every difficulty, and in heart going back again to the flesh-pots of Egypt. They were often ready to stone those servants of God who had been the instruments of their deliverance; they retained their idols which they had worshipped in Egypt; and even made a golden calf, as the representative, or rather, as the rival and competitor, of Jehovah. In their history we find some seasons of amendment; but, on the whole, they were "a rebellious and gainsaying people."]

But this is no less applicable to ourselves—

[Certainly we are quite as much indebted to the Lord as ever the Jews of old were: for though we have not had such visible interpositions in our favour, we have been no less the objects of his paternal care: and, in that which constituted their "chief advantage," we greatly excel them[d]." "To them were committed the Oracles of God:" but to us is given the Gospel of his dear Son; in comparison of which the Law, glorious as it was, had no glory at all; being eclipsed as a star before the meridian sun[e] — — —

And what has been our conduct towards him? Have we been sensible of the benefits conferred upon us; and have we endeavoured to render to him the recompence that was due? Alas! we have been unmindful of his kindness, and regardless of his authority altogether. It has never entered into our hearts to say, "Come, let us serve the Lord, who hath done such great things for us[f]." Whilst we have violated his holy laws, we have "puffed at his judgments," saying in our hearts, "God seeth not, neither regardeth what we do." If called to obey him, we have replied, in spirit, if not in word, "Who is the Lord, that we should serve him? We know not the Lord, neither will we obey his voice[g]." "Our lips are our own: Who is Lord over us[h]?" In truth, we have lived "without God in the world[i];" and have *practically* said, "There is no God[k]."]

Not content with charging upon us our multiplied rebellions, God proceeds to set forth,

II. The extent of our criminality—

The brute creation demean themselves, for the most part, in a way suited to their several capacities—

[The ox and the ass are amongst the most stupid of the brute creation: yet have they some knowledge of their master, and some sense of their dependence on him. Though fed only

d Rom. iii. 2.   e 2 Cor. iii. 7—11.   f Jer. ii. 5, 6. and v. 23, 24
g Job xxi. 14, 15.   Exod. v. 2.   h Ps. xii. 4.
i Eph. ii. 12.   k Ps. xiv. 1.

for their master's benefit, and used only to subserve his interests, they often express themselves with a kind of grateful acknowledgment towards him.]

But we, notwithstanding our superior advantages, act more irrationally than they—

[We live from year to year on the bounty of our heavenly Father, and yet feel no sense of gratitude towards him. We "do not even consider" our obligations to him. We "do not consider" either *what he has done for us;* (though it is so great, that neither the tongues of men or of angels can ever worthily declare it:) or, *what he requires of us;* (though that should be the subject of our unceasing contemplation:) or, *what return we have hitherto made to him;* (though on that our eternal happiness depends:) or, *what account we shall hereafter give to him;* (though we know not but that before the expiration of another hour we may be summoned into his immediate presence.) In a word, God's testimony respecting us is, that " HE is not in all, or any, of our thoughts[1]." Of the brute creation there are many that act with a degree of foresight and wisdom[m] : but we, who are endued with reason, act a part more irrational than they: and hence are justly reproached by God as more brutish and sottish than even the ox and ass[n]. How humiliating is this view of our state, and especially in relation to persons who have been redeemed by the blood of God's only dear Son! Verily there is not one amongst us who has not reason to blush and be confounded under the accusations that are brought against us.]

In CONCLUSION, we will,

1. Inquire what plea you can offer in your own behalf?

[We know that the young, the old, the rich, the poor, have all their appropriate excuses: but what plea have they that will avail them at the bar of judgment? Will any deny the charge! Alas! alas! Where is there one amongst us that has not been a rebel from the womb? Where is there one amongst us that has ever equalled the ox or ass in their attachment to him who feeds them, and their willing submission to his yoke? We must confess, every one of us, that we have not so much as considered our obligations, or our duties, or our interests, or our true happiness in any respect, unless we have been renewed in our minds by the Spirit of God himself. Let us then put away all our vain pleas and excuses, and adopt, each of us for himself, the language of Agur ; " I am more brutish than any man, and have not the understanding

[1] Ps. x. 4.　m Prov. vi. 6—8. Jer. viii. 7.　n Jer. iv. 22. and v. 21.

of a man°." If we feel not the depth of our depravity, and
refuse to humble ourselves before God, we do in fact "make
God a liar," and provoke him to execute upon us the judgments we have deserved.]

2. Suggest a plea which you may offer with safety
to your souls—

[Vile as we are, Christ died for us; and his death shall
avail even for the chief of sinners. Hear with what confidence
it was pleaded by the Apostle Paul: "Who is he that con-
demneth? It is Christ that died." Does any one imagine that
he is unworthy to hope that this plea shall ever avail for him?
God himself, at the very time that he most fully expatiates on
our guilt, puts this plea into our mouths, and declares that, if
we offer it before him, it shall avail for our justification in the
last day°. Let us then rely simply on the blood and righteousness of the Lord Jesus, and plead his merits at the throne of
grace: then, if heaven and earth do testify our desert of eternal condemnation, they shall testify also our affiance in the
Divine "promises, which in Christ are yea, and in him Amen,
to the everlasting glory of our offended God°."]

° Prov. xxx. 2.   ° Isai. xliii. 22—26.   ° 2 Cor. i. 20.

OUTLINE NO. 857

THE SINFULNESS AND INCORRIGIBLENESS OF THE NATION.

Isai. i. 4, 5. *Ah, sinful nation, a people laden with iniquity,
a seed of evil-doers, children that are corrupters! they have
forsaken the Lord, they have provoked the Holy One of Israel
unto anger, they are gone away backward. Why should ye
be stricken any more? ye will revolt more and more.*

THE end for which God inflicts punishment upon
his people, is, to bring them to repentance, and
thereby prevent the necessity of punishing them in
the eternal world: and when this end is not answered, he leaves them to themselves, to follow the
imaginations of their own hearts, and to bring upon
themselves an accumulated weight of wrath. But
before he utterly abandons them, he sends them
many solemn warnings, if that by any means he may
prevail upon them to turn unto him. Extremely
solemn is the reproof which he gave the Jews in the
passage before us: he summons heaven and earth

to hear his controversy, and to judge between him
and his people : and then, in a way of affectionate
expostulation, he threatens to cease from visiting
them with parental chastisements, and to leave them
to fill up the measure of their iniquities.

The words of our text, accommodated as they may
be to our present circumstances[a], naturally lead us to
set before you,

I. Our sinfulness—

The general description given of the Jews is
equally suitable to us—

[We are a " nation" *extremely* and *universally* " sinful : "
we are "laden with" every species of " iniquity " — — —We
are "a seed of evil-doers:" all ranks and orders of men amongst
us are depraved: the transgressions of individuals are indeed
exceeding various ; but sin of some kind is the delight of all,
yea, it is the very element wherein we live — — — Nor are
we merely corrupt, but " corrupters " of each other, laughing
religion out of the world, and hardening one another in the
commission of sin — — —]

Nor is the particular charge that is brought against
them less applicable to us—

[It is lamentable to see what a general dereliction of religious principle obtains amongst us. Men do not indeed formally
renounce Christianity; but "they forsake the Lord" as unworthy
of their love or confidence ; and, by an inward " apostasy " of
the heart, " provoke the Holy One of Israel to anger." We
might adduce a great variety of charges in confirmation of this;
but we will notice only one, namely, our dependence on our
fleets and armies, rather than on God[b]. This is peculiarly
provoking to the Deity, because it is a virtual denial of his
providence, and an excluding of him from the government of
the world[c]— — —]

But besides these things, there is a further charge
to be brought against us, on account of,

II. Our incorrigibleness—

What improvement have we made of our late
chastisements ?

---

[a] A time of war and of great national calamity.

[b] Instead of this, might be specified, *our not seeing and acknowledging the hand of God in his judgments.*

[c] See Isai. xxii. 8—11. and Jer. xvii. 1

[Almost every kind of plague, as war, famine, and pestilence, has been lately sent us by God[d]; and what are we profited by them? What national sin has been put away? I might almost ask, What unregenerate man has laid to heart his transgressions, and turned to the Lord? Does not sin reign amongst us as much as ever? Are we not like the incorrigible Jews[e]; or rather like King Ahaz, who had a brand of infamy set upon him on this very account, that " he trespassed yet more in his distress[f]?"————]

What reason then have we to hope that our present troubles will be sanctified to our good?

[From past experience we have reason to fear, that we shall still remain a perverse and rebellious people, and only "revolt more and more." And, if God foresee that this will be the case, what can we expect, but that our present troubles should be sent, not for our correction, but for our utter destruction? What can we expect, but that he should execute upon us the vengeance he has threatened[g], and that "his wrath should now come upon us to the uttermost?"]

ADVICE—

1. Let us adore our God for the patience he has long exercised towards us[h] ———

2. Let us tremble at his judgments now impending over us[i] ———

3. Let us take encouragement from his present dealings with us, to turn unto him[k] ———

---

[d] This, of course, must be accommodated to existing circumstances.
[e] Jer. v. 3—5.   [f] 2 Chron. xxviii. 22.   [g] Ezek. xxiv. 13, 14.
[h] 2 Pet. iii. 15.   Rom. ii. 4.
[i] How soon may we find those threatenings fulfilled! Lev. xxvi. 27, 28, 36, 37.
[k] See Jer. xviii. 7, 8. and Judg. x. 15, 16.

===

OUTLINE NO. 858

THE SERVICE WHICH ALONE IS PLEASING TO GOD.

Isai. i. 10—17. *Hear the word of the Lord, ye rulers of Sodom; give ear unto the law of our God, ye people of Gomorrha: To what purpose is the multitude of your sacrifices unto me? saith the Lord: I am full of the burnt-offerings of rams, and the fat of fed beasts; and I delight not in the blood of bullocks, or of lambs, or of he-goats. When ye come to appear before me, who hath required this at your hand, to tread my courts? Bring no more vain oblations: incense is an abomination unto*

me; the new moons and sabbaths, the calling of assemblies,
I cannot away with : it is iniquity, even the solemn meeting.
Your new moons and your appointed feasts my soul hateth :
they are a trouble unto me; I am weary to bear them. And
when ye spread forth your hands, I will hide mine eyes from
you : yea, when ye make many prayers, I will not hear :
your hands are full of blood. Wash you, make you clean;
put away the evil of your doings from before mine eyes;
cease to do evil; learn to do well: seek judgment; relieve
the oppressed; judge the fatherless; plead for the widow.

THOUGH tenderness and compassion are essential
requisites for a Christian minister, yet is fidelity also
indispensable for a due discharge of his duties. If
even a young minister, like Timothy, was to " reprove
and rebuke with all authority," it must become every
servant of God, especially when dealing with hypocritical professors or hardened sinners, to " use great
plainness of speech." It is true, a minister in this
day has not the same license as was given to the
prophets of old : we should not altogether think him
justified in calling his audience " Rulers of Sodom,
and people of Gomorrha:" but, when speaking in
Jehovah's name, we must expostulate with all, even
with the greatest of men, and declare to them, as the
prophet does, *the only way in which they can please*
and serve God. With this view the prophet used the
language in our text; and in prosecution of the same
end, we shall now declare,

I. The inadequacy of ritual observances—

The Jews were prone to rest in a compliance with
the ceremonial law : and our text is, as it were by
anticipation, an answer to their self-justifying remarks.
They are supposed to have said, ' How can you
justly complain of us ? We have served God with
the most commendable zeal : we have offered him
sacrifices—yea many—and of the best kind—and in
the appointed manner—and with great reverence—
and we have abounded in spiritual services also, no
less than in carnal rites.' But, in answer to all this,
God indignantly replies, that, instead of being
pleased with these services, he lothed and abhorred

them; since, in the midst of all their boasted regard
for him, they held fast their besetting sins[a] — — —

The Jewish ritual being abolished, it may be
thought that this address is inapplicable to any of
the present day: but it may justly be applied,

1. To self-righteous formalists—

[There is still, as Solomon expresses it, " a generation
that is pure in their own eyes, but are not washed from their
filthiness." There are many whose whole religion consists in
a performance of outward duties. Among the Papists this is
an acknowledged fact: but it is also true of us Protestants,
though to a less extent than it was a century ago. A regular
attendance on all the public ordinances; a strict observance of
the fasts and feasts of our Church, particularly of the time of
Lent; a daily reading of the Psalms and Lessons for the day,
and a recital of certain prayers; a rigid adherence to some particular forms, with an uncharitable censuring of all who are
not equally strict in their attention to them; these, and other
similar habits, form the ground of their hopes, and of a self-
complacent confidence towards God. But, with all these
apparently religious habits, their views, desires, and pursuits
are altogether earthly: their friends and associates are men of
this world: and vital godliness, together with all who possess
it, is regarded by them with suspicion and dislike.

Now, whatever such persons may think of themselves, they
are by no means in a state acceptable to God. Instead of looking with humility and contrition to the Lord Jesus Christ for
mercy, they are ready to claim heaven as the reward of their
good deeds: and instead of loving, for the Redeemer's sake,
every member of his mystical body, they are among the foremost to despise and persecute his believing people. Whilst
therefore they, in effect, say, " Stand off, I am holier than thou,".
they are, as God declares, " a smoke in his nose[b]."]

2. To many who make a profession of vital god-liness—

[Many there are whose views of the Gospel are correct,
but who are far from experiencing all that it is designed to
teach them. Their zeal for the Gospel is great and ardent:
they will go miles to hear it faithfully proclaimed: they will lose
no opportunity of attending their favourite minister: their very
life seems to be spent as it were in hearing sermons. They
will subscribe largely for building places of worship, especially

---

[a] ver. 10—15. The particular expressions throughout this whole
passage are very emphatical, and worthy of attentive observation
[b] Compare Isai. lxv. 5. with Luke xviii. 9, 14.

for the use of those who are of their own sect and party. They
are fond of prayer-meetings, and religious societies; and perhaps
of shewing forth their own talents too in exposition or prayer.
But, instead of using these things as means to a farther advancement in holiness, they regard them only as sources of present
gratification, and as evidences of a pious mind; while at the
same time they are destitute of all those tempers and dispositions, which are the chief ornament of religion, and the surest
evidences of its existence in the soul. We read of Ezekiel's
hearers, that they attended his ministrations with great delight,
and listened to him as persons fond of music would to a great
proficient in that science; and laid claim to superior piety on
that account: but, "though they heard his words, they would
not do them; for their heart went after their covetousness[c]."
Now this is an exact description of the persons we refer to:
they are conceited of their own knowledge and attainments,
uncharitable towards those who differ from them, contemptuous
towards those who are less instructed than themselves, regardless of the prejudices of others, and indifferent about the effect
of their conduct upon them: they often make religion a cloak
for idleness in their respective callings: they are headstrong
and untractable, and insolent towards their superiors: they
often cannot be depended on, even for truth in their words,
or honesty in their dealings. What shall we say of such professors as these? Are they in a state pleasing unto God? No
verily: they are an offence both to God and man; and their
very best sacrifices are no better than " the cutting off of a
dog's neck, or the offering of swine's blood[d]."]

Whilst our text thus forcibly declares the insufficiency of outward duties to please God, it sets forth
in the strongest terms,

II. The necessity of moral attainments—

In relation to these, two things are required;

1. A renunciation of accustomed sins—

[Every person has some sins which more easily beset him,
and which he is in a more especial manner called to mortify. We
will not speak of gross open sins, as swearing and drunkenness,
and such like: for no man who reflects at all, can suppose it
possible to please God, whilst he is guilty of such flagrant
abominations. But one man is naturally addicted to anger and
passion; another to discontent and envy; another to lewdness
and impurity; another to sloth and idleness; another to covetousness: one is filled with conceit and vanity; another with
scepticism and infidelity; another with unbelieving fears: in a

c Ezek. xxxiii. 31, 32. See also Isai. lviii. 2.   d Isai. lxvi. 2, 3.

word, however the conduct of men may differ as to the immediate line which they pursue, they all, in their natural state,
affect pleasure, or riches, or honour, and feel abundantly more
satisfaction in the things of time and sense, than they do in the
service of their God. Now every man is concerned to find out
what his besetting sin is: for if we must all without exception
become " new creatures in Christ Jesus," if " old things must
pass away, and all things must become new," then is it necessary that we all should experience this change, and have an
evidence of it in our own souls.

Earnestly would we press this thought upon the minds of
those who have been externally blameless in their conduct: for
it is common for persons of this description to be satisfied with
a change in their *sentiments*, when they have never experienced
any change in their *hearts and lives*. We all have, though
certainly in different degrees, a need of that exhortation,
" Wash you, make you clean; put away the evil of your doings
from before mine eyes." It is possible that very little change
can be needed by us that is visible to man; but there is no
natural man under heaven, who does not need to be greatly
changed in the sight of God: and to him it is that we must
approve ourselves, if ever we would be accepted in his sight.]

2. A performance of neglected duties—

[True piety will not consist with any allowed sin, whether
of commission or of omission. But if we look back to our
unregenerate state, how many duties are there, both to God
and man, that we have neglected! By nature we are satisfied
with doing acts of kindness when they come in our way: but
to live for God, and our fellow-creatures, we know not: we do
not search out occasions for the exercise of our benevolence, nor
do we redeem our time in order to effect the greatest good
within our reach. But, if we would please and honour God,
we must imitate him who " went about doing good:" our time,
our talents, our influence must all be put forth for the relief
of the needy, the comfort of the afflicted, the succouring of the
oppressed, and for the spiritual, as well as temporal, benefit of
all. We must also cultivate every kind of grace: not only
putting off what is evil, but putting on what is good. In particular, " as the elect of God, we should put on bowels of mercies, kindness, humbleness of mind, meekness, long-suffering,
forbearing one another and forgiving one another, even as God
for Christ's sake hath forgiven us[e]." These are the things
which God prefers to all the sacrifices that can be offered[f]; and
without these, all that we can possess is in his estimation lighter
than vanity itself[g]."]

[e] Col. iii. 8, 12—14.   [f] Ps. l. 8—14.   Mic. vi. 7, 8.
[g] 1 Cor. xiii. 1—3.

From hence then we may SEE,

1. The nature of true religion—

[That there are many who greatly mistake its nature, is evident from our text : but, when duly received into the heart, it neither insists on spiritual exercises to the neglect of moral virtues, nor on moral virtues to the neglect of communion with God : it has equal respect to both the tables of the Law. Let not any then attempt to put asunder what God has so inseparably joined. Let not any trust to their moral virtues on the one hand, nor to their spiritual exercises on the other ; but let it be the endeavour of all to "have respect unto *all* the commandments," and to stand perfect and complete in *all* the will of God."]

2. The danger of self-deceit—

[We think it evident, that the persons here addressed as "Rulers of Sodom and people of Gomorrha," had by no means formed a just estimate of their own character. And we all see among those around us many who lie under a similar delusion : the conceited professor sees the blindness of the Pharisee, whilst the Pharisee notices with equal clearness his vain conceit. Professors too notice each other's failings, and often, with too much reason, stand in doubt of each other. But all are blind to their own failings : they make far too much allowance for their own evils ; and sometimes glory in them as virtues : and so confident are many, of their own acceptance before God, that they will almost at the bar of judgment challenge heaven as their desert[h]. But, whilst they remain under the power of any allowed sin, " their religion is vain[i]," and their Judge will disclaim all knowledge of them[k] ; yea, their unmortified lust, whatever it be, will plunge their souls into everlasting perdition[l]. We say not this to discourage the sincere, but to put all upon their guard, and especially to bring to self-examination those who are most confident that all is well with them. For it is certain that " the hypocrites in heart heap up wrath," and " fearfulness will surprise them" in the day of judgment[m].]

3. The excellency of the Gospel—

[The Gospel not only teaches us these things[n], but shews us where pardon for all our transgressions may be obtained, and how strength may be acquired for the discharge of all our duties. Even under the law, these views were revealed ; for, in the words following our text, God told his people, that their scarlet sins should, if mourned over and forsaken, " become

---

[h] Matt. xxv. 44.   [i] James i. 26.   [k] Matt. vii. 22, 23.
[l] Matt. v. 29, 30.   [m] Isai. xxxiii. 14   [n] Tit. ii. 11, 12.

white as snow :" and in other places he promised his Spirit to
" write his laws upon their hearts," and to " cause them to keep
his statutes°." But under the Gospel dispensation, the efficacy of the Redeemer's blood to "cleanse from sin," and of his
grace to renew the heart, is declared in the strongest terms[p].
Hence then, when it is said, " Wash you, make you clean,"
there is no room to say, " I cannot ;" for " the grace of Christ
is sufficient" for all, and " we can do all things through Christ
who strengtheneth us[q]." Seek then to be washed in his blood,
and to be sanctified by his Spirit, and then the smallest of your
offerings, even a cup of cold water, shall be an acceptable
sacrifice in the sight of God[r].]

[o] Ezek. xxxvi. 27.　　[p] 1 John i. 7, 9.　　[q] Phil. iv. 13.
[r] 1 Pet. ii. 5.

OUTLINE NO. 859

CRIMSON SINS MADE WHITE.

Isai. i. 18. *Come now, and let us reason together, saith the
Lord : though your sins be as scarlet, they shall be as white
as snow ; though they be red like crimson, they shall be as
wool.*

MAN is a rational being ; and, though prone to
abuse his reason for the vindication of his own evil
ways, is capable of judging, when sound argument is
proposed for his consideration. Hence God addresses
himself to our reason, and makes his appeal to the
whole creation, when our pride or obstinacy prevent
us from acknowledging the truth of his assertions.
The chapter before us exhibits a judicial process :
heaven and earth are called as witnesses against
Israel; the charge against them is opened[a], and their
vindication of themselves is duly considered[b]. Having
convicted them of their iniquities, God invites them

[a] ver. 2, 3.
[b] Their reply is not set down at length ; but it may be gathered
from the answer given to it by God. They plead that they have
offered sacrifices, yea, many, and of the fattest of their flocks ; that
they have done this themselves, before God in the temple, with great
reverence ; that they have presented other offerings also ; that they
have observed the stated feasts ; and that, instead of resting in carnal
ceremonies, they had joined with them the spiritual sacrifices of
prayer and praise. God follows them through their objections, and
leaves them not a word to add, ver. 11—15.

to come and reason with him, and shews them a better way of pleading for themselves.

It is by his ministers that he now condescends to reason with mankind. We therefore propose to you on this occasion in God's stead, and will argue with you upon, the two most important of all points, *the necessity* and *the efficacy* of a religious life:

I. The necessity of a religious life—

The common reasonings of men on this subject are extremely futile and erroneous—

[We are too apt to "confer with flesh and blood," and to be misled by the suggestions of our own evil hearts. The world around us, and our own corrupt nature, unite in asserting, that a life of devotedness to God is *not necessary, not desirable, not practicable.* 'How can it be imagined,' say these objectors, 'that God should require all persons to live in such a holy self-deny-ing way as the first Christians did? It might be proper for them in the infancy of Christianity to set such an example; but it *cannot be necessary* for us in these times to follow it. And to suppose that all who do not give up themselves to God as they did, are doomed to eternal misery, would be to make God a cruel tyrant, and to rob him of his noblest attributes of good-ness and mercy. *Nor is it to be wished,* that religion should operate now as it did then: for how could the affairs of nations be conducted, or the common offices of life be performed? There would be an end to trade, and to all the refinements of civilized society; and men must be brought back again to the simplicity and vacuity of the Patriarchal age ——— In short, it *cannot be effected* now. A few visionaries and enthusiasts may experience something, and pretend to a great deal more: but to eradicate from the breast the love of sin, and to raise the soul above all the things of time and sense, and to bring it into a state of habitual communion with God, is impossible; unless we were all to be set apart to the work of religion, just as the Apostles were, and had nothing else to attend to'———

Such are the reasonings of flesh and blood. But here is little else than mere unfounded assertion, which is contradicted by every page of the Holy Scriptures, and by the actual expe-rience of thousands.]

Let us now, in God's name, reason with you on the same subject—

[*Has not God done enough to merit all the services that you can possibly render him?* Think of what he has done for you in creation and providence, and, above all, in the work of redemption, and then say, whether there "be any thing which he could have done for you more than he has;" or whether, if he had permitted you to ask whatever you would as the price of your services, you could have ventured to have asked a thousandth part of what he has already done for you? Could you have dared to make such a request as that he would give you his dear Son to die for you, and his Holy Spirit to instruct and sanctify you? — — —

Has he not promised you assistance for the performance of every thing he has required of you? We acknowledge your impotency for that which is good: but that is no excuse for your disobedience, while he says, " My grace shall be sufficient for you." If his grace wrought effectually in the saints of old, it cannot but be as sufficient for you as for them — — —

Will not his love and favour amply compensate for all that you can either do or suffer for him? I might ask this question in reference to the tokens of his favour which he would give you *now;* but how much more *hereafter !* Can it be imagined that one saint in glory ever had the thought pass through his mind, that his reward was an inadequate recompence for his former labours? — — —

Will not all of you at a future period wish that you had dedicated yourselves unreservedly to God? Many begin to express that wish on their dying bed; though many are so insensible even to the last, as to feel no regret upon the subject. But what does the soul of every man wish, the very instant it is separated from his body? If we could hear it speak then, we can have no doubt what its language would be. If it had not been convinced before, we have no doubt it is convinced *then*, that former reasonings were vain and delusive — — —

Much more we might easily urge in God's name; but this is sufficient to convince any one who is open to conviction, that an entire surrender of ourselves to God is a good and " reasonable service."]

From the latter clause of the text we are led to reason more especially with you respecting,

II. The efficacy of a religious life—

Men, driven from the false refuges of presumption, are ready to run into the contrary extreme of despondency; and, when convinced of the necessity of a holy life, to doubt, whether any efforts on their part will succeed for the attainment of eternal happiness.

Here, as before, let us briefly consider the reasonings of flesh and blood—

[Many, under a sense of their past transgressions, will say, that it is too late for them to turn to God; that they have

sinned away their day of grace; that they have committed
the sin against the Holy Ghost; and that God has already
sealed them up to final impenitence, and to everlasting condemnation — — —

But here, as in the former instance, is nothing but assertion,
founded on unwarrantable surmises and groundless fears. We
know that such persons will appeal to Scripture: but by what
authority do they apply to themselves passages that have no
real reference to their state, and make use of those passages
to invalidate the plainest assertions of Holy Writ? If only
they desire to come to God, they have an express assurance
from God, that " he will in no wise cast them out."]

Let us again, in God's name, oppose these reasonings by others that are more substantial—

[*Is not God a God of infinite mercy and compassion?*
Search the Scriptures: see the representations which he gives
of himself: how often is it said, " His mercy endureth for
ever!" If then "he delighteth in mercy," who are we that
we should presume to limit him in the exercise of it towards
ourselves? — — —

*Do not his promises extend to all the sins that you have ever
committed?* You know that he hath said, " All manner of sin
and blasphemy shall be forgiven unto men." Moreover, read
the words of our text; and doubt if you can. But, perhaps,
you will reply, that the sin against the Holy Ghost is excepted;
and that that is the sin which you have committed. To that
we answer, that if you desire to repent and turn unto God, it
is not possible that you should have committed it; because, if
you had committed it, you would have arrived at such a degree
of obduracy, that you would glory in your shame, and never
wish to repent at all — — —

*Have not the vilest of sinners already found acceptance with
God?* Look at the character given of the Corinthians; and
see whether you can be in a worse state than they: yet " they
were washed and sanctified and justified in the name of the
Lord Jesus, and by the Spirit of our God[c]." If you are
alarmed about backslidings after conversion, see whether you
have been worse than David and Peter: yet they were restored
to the divine favour as soon as ever they repented themselves
of their iniquities. And myriads of others, once as vile as they,
are at this very moment around the throne of God, rejoicing
and triumphing in redeeming love. What bar then can there
be to your acceptance through "him who loved *them*, and
washed *them* from their sins in his own blood?" — — —

We forbear to urge other considerations, because if you can

[c] 1 Cor. vi. 9—11.

withstand these, there is no hope that any others could be urged with effect.]

ADDRESS—

1. Those who still hold out against God—

[We call heaven and earth to witness against you, that you are most unreasonable creatures. The ox and the ass are indeed more rational than you are in relation to your souls. They seek their true interests, and acknowledge their benefactor: would to God that you might be brought to do the same!]

2. Those who are convinced by his reasonings—

[Beware how you listen to the dictates of flesh and blood. You know how you have been deceived; be on your guard against fresh deceits. Regard not the laughter of a blind infatuated world. They may call you mad; but they, and they only, are "come to themselves," who have been brought to say, "I will return and go to my Father."]

OUTLINE NO. 860

GOD PURIFYING HIS PEOPLE.

Isai. i. 25. *I will turn my hand upon thee, and purely purge away thy dross, and take away all thy tin.*

IN the Holy Scriptures, judgment is often denounced, and mercy promised, with such peculiar force and emphasis, as might lead one to imagine that it was almost a matter of indifference to Jehovah which of the two were called into exercise towards his offending creatures. But we know that "judgment is his strange act," to which he is utterly averse[a]; and that "mercy is the attribute in which he supremely delights[b]." In the passage before us, however, he speaks as if he contemplated vengeance with a degree of pleasure and satisfaction: "Thus saith the Lord, the Lord of Hosts, the Mighty One of Israel; Ah, I will ease me of mine adversaries, and avenge me of mine enemies." On the other hand, in the words which I have just read, he expresses no less satisfaction in the thought of conferring benefits on his chosen remnant, whom he has determined to restore and save.

[a] Isai. xxviii. 21.   [b] Mic. vii. 18.

From them I shall be led to consider,

I. The work which God will accomplish in all his chosen people—

The whole passage primarily refers to the Jews; whom God will, at no distant period, restore to their own land, and elevate in the rank of nations; making them no less conspicuous for piety than in the most favoured seasons of their former prosperity[c]. In the promise made to them, we see what God will do for all his chosen people; cleansing them from their sins, and thereby fitting them,

1. For his service on earth—

[God's people must be " a holy people," dedicated unreservedly to him. He will not accept " a divided heart[d]." He will not behold with satisfaction any one that retains a bosom sin, though it be dear as a right eye, or useful as a right hand[e]. However loud such persons' professions of attachment may be, he will say to them, " Why call ye me Lord, Lord, and do not the things which I say[f]?" The very " prayers of such persons are an abomination to him[g]." The hypocrite is, beyond all other persons, an object of his abhorrence[h]: " He requireth truth in the inward parts[i]:" and, to please him, " we must be Israelites indeed, in whom there is no guile[k]."]

2. For his presence in a better world—

[" God is of purer eyes than to behold evil, or to look upon iniquity[l]:" much less could he admit into his presence in glory any soul that was not purged from its sins[m]: nor, in truth, could a soul that was polluted with sin be happy in heaven, even if he were admitted there. The holiness of God would utterly confound him: nor could he have any communion with the saints and angels that are around the throne. His want of resemblance to them would make his deformity hateful, even in his own eyes; whilst their employment would be so distasteful to him, that he could not join in it for a single hour. Indeed the inhabitants of heaven could not endure the presence of such a hateful being; but would all unite in " thrusting him out[n]." As it is said of King Uzziah: When he was struck with leprosy in the Temple, the priests rose up to thrust him out, " yea, himself also hasted to go out[o]:" so I doubt not but that an unholy soul would of itself hasten out of

c ver. 26, 27. d Hos. x. 2. e Mark ix. 43—48.
f Luke vi. 46. g Prov. xxviii. 9. h Job xxxvi. 13.
i Ps. li. 6. k John i. 47. l Hab. i. 13.
m Eph. v. 5. Rev. xxi. 27. n Luke xiii. 28. o 2 Chron. xxvi. 20

heaven, because of the shame and misery it would feel in a place so unsuited to its dispositions and desires.

Hence, then, God engages for his elect, that he will "turn his hand upon them, purely to purge away their dross, and to take away all their tin;" so that they may be "meet for the inheritance of heaven[p]," and "vessels of honour, meet for their Master's use[q]."]

Nor are we at any loss to declare,

II. The means by which it shall be effected—

God says, "he will turn his hand upon them, to purge them from their dross:" and this he will do,

1. By the visitations of his Providence—

[Gold is put into a furnace, to purge it from its dross: and, in like manner, God has told us that he will subject his people to afflictions, "in order to purify them, that they may offer to him an offering in righteousness[r]." In this way shall God's ancient people be cleansed from their corruptions, and be made holy, "when the Lord shall have washed away the filth of the daughters of Zion, and shall have purged the blood of Jerusalem from the midst thereof by the spirit of judgment, and by the spirit of burning[s]." So also shall his people, in every age, be purified. In truth, the experience of multitudes resembles that of David, when he says, "Before I was afflicted I went astray; but now have I kept thy word[t]." It is by means of affliction that God brings us to consider our ways: by means of it, also, he humbles us before him, and prepares us for the manifestations of his love and mercy to our souls. Hence it is that he promises correction to those who are the objects of his love[u], and teaches us to regard our trials as tokens of his paternal care and tenderness[x]. He will, indeed, accommodate his dispensations to our necessities; "sitting by us as a refiner and purifier of silver," and watching the process for our good. He has told us, that he will "debate with us in measure, staying his rough wind in the day of his east wind: and that by this shall the iniquity of his people be purged; and this shall be the fruit to take away their sin[y]."]

2. By the communications of his grace—

[Affliction, of itself, would only harden; as in the case of Pharaoh; and of those also who gnash their teeth, and blaspheme their God, in hell[z]. But when divine grace is given to accompany and to sanctify the dispensation, then its end is answered, and the afflicted sinner returns in penitential

---

p Col. i. 12.　　　　q 2 Tim. ii. 21.　　　　r Mal. iii. 3—5.
s Isai. iv. 3, 4.　　　　t Ps. cxix. 67.　　　　u Ps. lxxxix. 30—34.
x Heb. xii. 5—11.　　　y Isai. xxvii. 8, 9.　　　z Rev. xvi. 9—11.

sorrow to his God. It was thus that Manasseh's most enormous wickedness was purged: " God took him among the
thorns; and bound him with fetters, and carried him to
Babylon: and when he was in affliction, he besought the Lord
his God, and humbled himself greatly before the God of his
fathers, and prayed unto him: and so God was entreated of
him, and heard his supplication[a]. In fact, " without the grace
of Christ we can do nothing[b]:" it is " by his Spirit alone that
we can mortify the deeds of the body[c]," or " bring forth any
fruits of righteousness to his praise and glory[d]." But to all
his chosen people God will " give more grace[e]," even " grace
sufficient for them[f]," whatever their necessities may be; and
will thus " fulfil in them all the good pleasure of his goodness,
and the work of faith with power[g]."]

Let me now ADDRESS myself,

1. To those who are trembling through fear of
God's displeasure—

[Amongst those whose destruction God contemplated as
a source of ease to his own mind, there was yet a remnant,
towards whom he was " filled with thoughts of love." And
why may not you be amongst that happy number? Certainly,
if you have begun to " tremble at the word of God, that very
circumstance is a proof that " the Spirit of God is striving with
you," and that you are not given over to a reprobate mind.
Peradventure God has already said, " I will turn my hand upon
thee, and purely purge away thy dross, and take away all thy
tin:" and who can tell but that this may be the very hour
fixed, in his divine counsels, for the accomplishment of this
blessed end? Lift up your heart to him; and beg him now to
work effectually upon you, that, being created of him anew,
and transformed into his image, you may serve him worthily on
earth, and participate in his glory in a better world.]

2. To those who are desiring to experience the full
work of God's grace upon their souls—

[Limit not God to any particular mode of acting; but be
as clay in the potter's hands; and let him deal with you as, in
his unerring wisdom, he shall see fit. If he be pleased to put
you into a furnace, complain not of it; but say, ' This he has
done to purge me from my dross.' You cannot but know that
there is an abundance of dross within you. You cannot but
be conscious that every thing which you do is very imperfect;
your very prayers and your praises being little better, for the
most part, than a cold and formal service. Will you not, then,

---

[a] 2 Chron. xxxiii. 11—13.   [b] John xv. 5.   [c] Rom. viii. 13.
[d] Phil. i. 11.   [e] James iv. 6.   [f] 2 Cor. xii. 9.   [g] 2 Thess. i. 11.

have reason to bless his name, if, by any means, he purge you from your corruptions, and assimilate you to his divine image? This, then, I say to you: If God send you any affliction, whether personal or domestic, " hear the rod, and Him that hath appointed it[h]." Entreat of God to shew you what sin it is that he would correct, or what grace it is that he would confirm and perfect within you. In a word, desire not deliverance from affliction, but a sanctified improvement of it to your soul. Thus shall all the purposes of his grace be accomplished; and when the end shall come, it shall be no grief to you, that " through much tribulation you entered into the kingdom of your God."]

[h] Mic. vi. 9.

OUTLINE NO. 861

EXHORTATION TO A HOLY WALK.

Isai. ii. 5.   *O house of Jacob, come ye, and let us walk in the light of the Lord.*

MANY prophecies there are which are not yet accomplished, especially among those which are to be fulfilled " in the last days." The last days were understood even by the Jews themselves as relating to the days of the Messiah; and they comprehend all the time from his first advent in the flesh to the period when his kingdom shall be fully established upon earth. Hence the prophecies relating to that period must have different degrees of accomplishment; being partly fulfilled in the first triumphs of the Gospel, but having a further and more entire accomplishment when all the kingdoms of the world shall become the kingdom of our Lord and Saviour Jesus Christ. Thus it is that we are to understand the ʼprophecy contained in the preceding context. " The mountain of the Lord's House," that is, the Gospel Church, was established on the top of the mountains in the apostolic age, when it triumphed over heathen idolatry and Jewish superstition; and myriads of converts encouraged one another to serve and glorify their God: but we have not yet seen the time when " swords have been beaten into ploughshares, and spears into pruning-hooks, and nations have ceased to learn and practise the art of war." That time however will come: and we should long, and labour to the utmost of our power, to hasten it forward. We should even now anticipate it; yea, we *will* anticipate it: "O house of Jacob, come ye, and let us walk in the light of the Lord!"

Let us walk in the light,

I. Of his truth—

His truth now shines in its meridian splendour—

[" The darkness is indeed past; and the true light now shineth[a]." "The day-star has arisen[b]:" "the day-spring from on high hath visited us[c]:" "the Sun of Righteousness[d]" shineth forth in his brightness: and the way of salvation through a crucified Redeemer is now so plain, that " no wayfaring man, though a fool, can err therein[e]"————— " On the face of Moses there was a veil, that they who received the law should not see its full import: but if the Gospel be hid, it is from those only whom the god of this world hath blinded;" since " we may all with open (that is, *unveiled*) face behold as in a mirror the glory of the Lord[f]"————]

Let us then walk in it—

[Having the light, we should " believe in the light, that we may be the children of light[g]." We should embrace with all thankfulness the way of salvation revealed in the Gospel. We should " *come to Christ*," as the appointed Saviour of a ruined world[h]: we should " *look to him*," as dying upon the cross for us[i]: we should " *build upon him*, as our only foundation[k];" and " *cleave unto him* with full purpose of heart[l];" and " determine to know none but him[m]," and to " glory in nothing but the cross of Christ[n]"————— "Arise then, and *be enlightened*, for the light is come; and the glory of the Lord is risen upon you[o]."]

Whilst confiding in God as reconciled to us by the blood of the cross, we should endeavour to walk in the light,

II. Of his countenance—

This is the privilege of a true believer—

[So it is declared to be, by one who experienced it richly in his own soul[p]. God presents himself to us in the Gospel

---

[a] 1 John ii. 8.   [b] 2 Pet. i. 19.   [c] Luke i. 78, 79.
[d] Mal. iv. 2.   [e] Isai. xxxv. 8.   [f] 2 Cor. iii. 13—18.
[g] John xii. 35, 36.   [h] Matt. xi. 28.   [i] Isai. xlv. 22.
[k] 1 Cor. iii. 11.   [l] Acts xi. 23.   [m] 1 Cor. ii. 2.
[n] Gal. vi. 14.   [o] Isai. lx. 1. *The marginal reading.*
[p] Ps. lxxxix. 15.

under the endearing relations of a Father and a Friend, to whom we may carry every want, every trial, every difficulty; and from whom we may expect a supply according to our need. He will be not only "*our God*," but "*a God unto us*[q]," putting forth all his wisdom, all his love, and all his power, to make us truly blessed. He will engage in this work "with his whole heart and with his whole soul[r];" so that it must be utterly our own fault if we be not as holy, and as happy, as our hearts can wish — — —]

Let us then enjoy our privilege—

[Let us "walk with God," as Enoch did; and "glory in him as the God of our salvation." See what holy joy David found in communion with him[s] — — — and shall we who live under a so much nobler dispensation experience less? Shall not *we*, who have so much clearer views of Christ, "rejoice in him with joy unspeakable and glorified?" O let us "*delight ourselves in God*," and have even now, "in the secret of his presence" and the consolations of his Spirit, an earnest and a foretaste of our heavenly inheritance[t] — — —]

But we shall in vain hope to enjoy his presence, if we walk not also in the light,

III. Of his commandments—

These are given by him "as a light to our feet and a lantern to our paths"—

[Without them we should not "know how to walk and to please God;" but by them we are fully informed in all things that are needful for us to do[u]. They do not indeed descend to every particular circumstance in which we can be placed; but they afford principles which are universally applicable, and which are quite sufficient for our direction when duly applied. The duty of "doing to others as we would be done unto," is so comprehensive as to embrace every part of our social duty, whilst it is so simple that it may be comprehended and applied by every one who desires to please God.]

Let us then make these the one rule of our conduct—

[Let us not attempt to reduce them to the standard of the world, but endeavour rather to raise our conduct to the standard of God's revealed will. Let us treasure up in our minds the most exalted precepts, and "hide God's word in our hearts, that we may not sin against him;" for "then shall

q 1 Chron. xvii. 24.   r Jer. xxxii. 41.
s Ps. lxiii. 1—5. and cxlv. 1—12. and cl.
t Ps. xxxi. 20.   Eph. i. 13, 14.   u Prov. vi. 23.

we not be ashamed, when we have respect unto all God's
commandments"————]

In ADDRESSING " the house of Jacob," we must
speak to,

1. Those who are nominally so—

[It is but too true, that " all are not Israel, who are of
Israel:" and those who are only of the house of Jacob by name
and profession, may know it by their walk and conversation.
Consider, I pray you, in what light you have walked: Is it not
manifest, that the generality who call themselves Christians are
influenced only by the things of time and sense; and that their
principles and pursuits are altogether earthly? Know then,
ye lovers of this present evil world, that, if God's word may
be depended on, you are deluding yourselves to your eternal
ruin[x]. You "sow the wind, and you shall reap the whirlwind[y]." When will you begin to see, that " one thing," and
one thing only, " is needful?" When will you learn to say,
"Whom have I in heaven but thee? and there is none upon
earth that I desire in comparison of thee?" That you should
seek present, as well as eternal, happiness, we grant: but you
should seek it where David did; " Who will shew us any good?
Lord, lift thou up the light of thy countenance upon us; and
that will put more gladness in my heart than any increase of
corn, wine, and oil can ever do[z]."]

2. Those who are really so—

[You have found that God in Christ is "a fountain of
life; and in his light you have seen light[a]." You therefore
are " children of the light and of the day." But if you are so
highly distinguished in your character, think how distinguished
you should also be in our conduct[b]. The eyes of all are upon
you: they will look particularly to see whether religion is such
a source of happiness as you profess. O shew them that "you
need neither the sun to lighten you by day, nor the moon by
night, since the Lord has been a light unto you, and your God
your glory[c]." Shew them that even in the greatest troubles
you have a fountain of consolation to go unto; and that " when
you walk in darkness, the Lord is a light unto you[d]." And,
as it is eminently characteristic of Gospel times to encourage
one another in the ways of God, see that you do so, "speaking
one with another in psalms and hymns and spiritual songs,
singing and making melody in your hearts unto the Lord."

---

[x] Isai. l. 11. [y] Hos. viii. 7. [z] Ps. iv. 6, 7.
[a] Ps. xxxvi. 9. [b] Eph. v. 8. 1 Thess. v. 5, 6.
[c] Isai. lx. 19. [d] Job xxix. 3. Mic. vii. 8.

Then, from enjoying God in his courts below, you shall be taken to serve him in his temple above, where your largest desires shall be satisfied, and your utmost capacities be filled [e].]

e Rev. xxi. 22, 23.   Ps. xvi. 11.

OUTLINE NO. 862

FINAL STATE OF MAN.

Isai. iii. 10, 11. *Say ye to the righteous, that it shall be well with him: for they shall eat the fruit of their doings. Woe unto the wicked; it shall be ill with him: for the reward of his hands shall be given him.*

THE Ministers of the Gospel are " stewards of the mysteries of God," whose office it is " rightly to divide the word of truth," and to " give every one his portion in due season." They are to " take forth the precious from the vile, and to be as God's mouth to all," declaring their true character, and their proper doom. Their commission is sealed in the words before us, and the very message they are to deliver as God's ambassadors, is recorded for their direction to the end of time. In complying with the duty here enjoined, we shall,

I. Describe the characters that are to be addressed—

There are but two classes of men in the world; " the righteous" and " the wicked."

[However diversified men's states may be in some particulars, they all must be ranked under the one or the other of these heads. In distinguishing them, therefore, we must include in the first class, not merely the more eminent saints, but the least and meanest of God's people; seeing that there are in God's household " babes, and young men, as well as fathers [a]." And in the second class we must comprehend all those persons, who, however admired by an undiscerning world, are reputed wicked in the sight of God.

I may say then, they are "righteous" who have been renewed in the spirit of their mind, and are following after universal holiness; and they, on the other hand, are "wicked," who are still in a carnal unregenerate state, and render only a formal and partial obedience to the divine law.

But that I may put this in the clearest possible light, I will

a 1 John ii. 13.

say, They are "righteous," who make religion the great business of life, and prosecute it upon the principles of the Gospel;
and all others without exception must be numbered amongst
"the wicked." Of course, I must not be understood to say
that worldly business is to be neglected. On the contrary, *it
must be attended to with all diligence :* but *it must be followed
in subserviency to the concerns of the soul.* It must occupy,
not the first, but the second place in our esteem. The *heart*
must be God's, and God's alone[b].

Now to these distinct classes does God send a separate message; and therefore it is of great importance that we should
ascertain to which we belong. Let us then, before we proceed
to the consideration of God's message, inquire seriously to
which of these classes we belong?

Can we truly appeal to God, that, in the estimation of our
minds and in the habit of our lives, the salvation of our soul is
regarded as the one thing needful? If our conscience bear
witness to the truth of this, then I must proceed yet further
to ask, whether we prosecute the concerns of the soul upon
the principles of the Gospel? The Pharisees of old engaged
with great ardour in religious duties: but they were not
"righteous" in God's sight, because they sought by their religious observances to establish a righteousness of their own
instead of submitting to the righteousness which God had
provided for them[c]. So it is with the Papists, who observe
with great strictness many religious rites, in the hope of recommending themselves thereby to the Divine favour. But the
religion of the Gospel is altogether different from this. It
requires us to seek for acceptance solely through our Lord Jesus
Christ, and to cleave unto him as "all our salvation, and all
our desire." Say, then, Brethren, whether as before God this
is your experience from day to day? Say whether ye are
washing daily in the fountain of his blood, and clothing yourselves with his unspotted righteousness, and, from a sense of
his redeeming love, endeavouring in all things to fulfil his holy
will? —— —]

This, if carefully inquired into, will give a clear
line of demarcation for us all : and we entreat all to
arrange themselves, as it were, before God in that
particular class to which conscience tells them they
belong; and to attend with solemn awe, while we,

II. Deliver God's message to each of them—

God commands his ministers to "warn the wicked[d],"

---

[b] Prov. xxiii. 26.   [c] Rom. ix. 31, 32. and x. 2—4.
[d] Ezek. xxxiii. 7.

but to "comfort his people^e." In obedience to him we will address,

1. The righteous—

[That I may not "break any bruised reed," or "make sad the heart" of any one that is truly upright, let me say, that in the first stages of the Christian course we must judge rather by our desires than by our actual attainments: not because our attainments should be less the objects of scrutiny than our desires, but because in reference to *our desires* we have a complete *consciousness;* whilst the defectiveness of *our attainments* makes us doubtful of *our real integrity.*

Taking this into consideration, I am aware that some, on account of the smallness of their attainments, may be saying, "I fear it will go ill with me at last." But God says, "It shall be *well* with you:" and, in despite of all your fears (if only you press forward in the ways of righteousness) it shall be well with you, in life, in death, and to all eternity. We cannot promise you affluence, or exemption from pain and trouble; but we can promise, in the name of God, that your trials, whatever they be, shall work for good^f; that your latter end shall be peace^g; and that you shall have a crown of righteousness and glory at the instant of your departure from the body^h.

These are the things which you labour to attain : and you shall surely "eat the fruit of your doings." Dismiss then your unbelieving fears: for this is the word of your faithful God, whom neither the subtlety of Satan can deceive, nor his power be able to withstand.]

2. The wicked—

[Glad should we be, if we could say, It shall be well with you. But if we should dare to deliver such a message, the falsehood of it must immediately appearⁱ———Against you, God sends us to denounce woe: "Woe to the wicked! it shall be ill with him." You, under the influence of presumption, may be saying, "I hope, notwithstanding what is spoken in the Bible, that it will fare well with me at last." But, if there be any truth in God, it must be *ill* with you. Even in the midst of all your boasted enjoyments we defy you to say, that you have any solid peace^k: ———and in your dying hour, if you are not insensible as beasts, you will be full of regret and terror^l ———and, after death, you will lie down in everlasting burnings^m———

Nor is this unjust, since *you reap only what you sowed* ———You chose the world as your portion; and you have

---

^e Isai. xl. 1.   ^f Rom. viii. 28.   ^g Ps. xxxvii. 7.   ^h 2 Tim. iv. 8.
ⁱ Put it into language, and how horrible will it sound.
^k Isai. lvii. 20, 21.   ^l Eccl. v. 17.   ^m Rev. xxi. 8.

nothing beyond it: you "*would* have none of God[n];" and you
have none of him: you said to him, "Depart[o];" and he says
to you, "Depart[p]." In your banishment from God and heaven,
"the reward of your own hands is given to you."

Painful it is to deliver such a message; but we must deliver
it at the peril of our souls[q]: and whether it be credited by
you, or not, it shall be confirmed and ratified in heaven[r].]

We cannot conclude without recommending to your
NOTICE,

1. The equity of the future judgment—

[The decision of the Judge will be grounded entirely on
our works. No man that was righteous in this world, shall
perish; nor shall any man that persisted in his wickedness, be
saved. The reward indeed that will be given to the righteous,
will be *the gift of grace* for Christ's sake: whereas that which
will be given to the wicked, will be *the just wages* of their
iniquity[s]. Still however, the quality of every person's works
will determine his state; and the happiness or misery of each
will be proportioned to his improvement or abuse of the talents
committed to him. You all know, if you see one man industrious, sober, frugal, and another idle, dissipated, extravagant,
what must in process of time be the difference between them.
Each of them is laying up for himself a treasure which in due
season he must reap: nor are you at all surprised when you
see the one enjoying the fruits of his industry, and the other
reaping the bitter fruits of his folly. Such will assuredly be
the issue of our conduct in reference to religion. Let every
person therefore remember, that he is daily and hourly treasuring up for himself that which shall be delivered to him again
at the day of judgment[t]: and that, if he perish for ever, he
will have none to blame for it but himself.]

2. The importance of preparing for our great account—

[If the declarations in the text proceeded from man, they
might well be disregarded. But they are the words of God;
and are as truly spoken to us by him, as if they were now
uttered by an audible voice from heaven. Should we not then
take warning? Should not the wicked inquire how they may
become righteous; and the righteous increase their diligence
to hold on in God's holy ways? Would to God this effect
might now be produced! how gladly should we set Christ
before you as an all-sufficient Saviour! and how joyfully should
we proclaim the promises of God, both to sincere penitents[u],

---

[n] Ps. lxxxi. 11.   [o] Job xxi. 14. and xxii. 17.
[p] Matt. xxv. 41.   [q] Ezek. xxxiii. 8.   [r] Matt. xviii. 18.
[s] Rom. vi. 23.   [t] Gal. vi. 7, 8.   [u] Isai. lv. 7.

and to humble believers[x]! Let all stir themselves up without
delay, and prepare in earnest to meet their God.]

3. The use and benefit of divine ordinances—

[In the world, we may pass days and years, and never
once hear the sentiment, That "it shall go ill with the wicked."
On the contrary, we shall hear ten thousand assertions that
encourage a directly opposite opinion. And, if a friendly monitor attempt to undeceive us, he is accounted rude, harsh, fanatical. But in the house of God we may venture to speak with
plainness, and to declare the determinations of heaven. God
sends us for this very purpose, that we may draw aside the veil
of futurity, and open to your view the things that shall be hereafter. We are to shew you "the righteous shining forth as the
sun in the kingdom of their Father," and the wicked "lifting
up their eyes with unavailing wishes in the torments of hell."
Let the ordinances then be reverenced with humble gratitude,
and improved with unwearied assiduity[y].]

[x] Job xvii. 9.
[y] If this were the subject of an *Assize Sermon*, this third remark
might be to this effect ; *The use and benefit of human judicatories ;*
which are intended to distribute justice, as far as possible, in this
world, as God himself will distribute it in the world to come.

OUTLINE NO. 863

GOD THE PROTECTOR OF HIS CHURCH.

Isai. iv. 5. *The Lord will create upon every dwelling-place of
Mount Zion, and upon her assemblies, a cloud, and smoke by
day, and the shining of a flaming fire by night : for upon all
the glory shall be a defence.*

THE Church of God is frequently represented as
hated both by men and devils, and exposed to their
united assaults. But it is protected by an invisible
and almighty Agent, who keeps it alive, as a spark
in the midst of a tempestuous ocean. His watchful
eye is ever over it for good : He considers it as his
glory, and will therefore himself be its defence. This
is promised to the Church in the words before us;
in which we are told,

I. The Church is God's glory—

Mount Zion is a name given to the Gospel Church[a]:
and a strict attention to the text will shew, that it is

[a] Heb. xii. 22.

here considered as "the glory" of God[b]; by which term its members also are expressly designated by God himself[c].

1. The various "dwelling-places of Mount Zion" are his glory—

[Wherever Christianity has gained its full ascendant over any family, God will most assuredly be worshipped and served by every member of it. The master will say with Joshua, "As for me and my house we will serve the Lord;" and, in order to carry this resolution into effect, he will, like Abraham, command his children, and his household after him[d]. His house will be a temple in which he himself officiates as priest; and, as far as he can prevail, he will cause every heart to be an altar to the Lord, that they may daily offer to him the sacrifices of prayer and praise. Such a family will be like a beautiful garden, filled with "trees of righteousness of the LORD's planting, that HE may be glorified[e];" and while God calls himself "their God," he will dignify them with the exalted appellation of "his people," and "his servants in whom he will be glorified[f]."]

2. The "assemblies of Mount Zion" also are his glory—

[As the Israelites came up thrice every year to worship God at Jerusalem, so on every Sabbath do his people assemble for the exercise of social and public worship. In those holy convocations does every one speak of his glory[g]; and his ministers in particular, who are "the glory of Christ[h]," proclaim the riches of his grace and mercy. In these God vouchsafes his more peculiar presence; for "he loveth the gates of Zion more than all the dwellings of Jacob[i]." "He comes down as in the days of old[k], and fills the place with his glory;" he pours out his Spirit in a more abundant measure; and by communicating the blessings of grace and peace, he "glorifies the house of his glory[l]."]

While they are thus highly esteemed by God, they are favoured with his peculiar care; for,

II. God is his Church's guardian—

The Israelites, when coming out of Egypt, had a cloud with them as a symbol of the Divine presence[m].

---

[b] "The glory" evidently relates to the "dwelling-places," &c. before mentioned.   [c] Isai. xlvi. 13.

[d] Josh. xxix. 15. Gen. xviii. 19.   [e] Isai. lxi. 3.

[f] Jer. xxxi. 1. Isai. xlix. 3.   [g] Ps. xxix. 9.   [h] 2 Cor. viii. 23.

[i] Ps. lxxxvii. 2.   [k] Exod. xl. 34, 35.   2 Chron. vii. 1.

[l] Isai. lx. 7.   [m] Exod. xiii. 21, 22. Neh. ix. 19.

This was intended both to guide them in their journeys, and to protect them from their enemies. And in reference to it God promises to his Church to be,

1. Her guide—

[The cloud went before the people in all their journeys, moving or resting when it was proper for them to move, or rest[n]. Thus will God direct the concerns of his Church. Though he will not interpose in the same *visible* manner, yet he will manifest the same attention to its interests, and guide it with the same unerring hand. Nor is it to the Church at large only that God extends his care; he will regard " the dwelling-places of Mount Zion" no less than " her assemblies;" and consult the welfare of the meanest individual as much as of the largest community[o]. Does any one look up to him for direction? He says, " The meek he will guide in judgment, the meek he will teach his way[p]:" " He shall have an unction of the Holy One that shall teach him all things[q];" and so plainly shall his path be marked, that, " though a fool, he shall not err therein[r]." Is he involved in any peculiar difficulty? He shall hear a voice behind him, saying, " This is the way, walk ye in it[s]." And though his path may often appear dubious, yet he shall find at last that he has been " led in *the right* way to the city of habitation[t]."]

2. Her defence—

[The cloud on one occasion went behind the Israelites, and wore a dark and threatening aspect to their enemies, while it gave light to *them*[u]. Thus will God give salvation for walls and bulwarks to his Church[x]. No weapon that is formed against it shall prosper[y]: God will not only go before it, but be its rear-ward[z]: nor shall the gates of hell ever prevail against it[a]. Never for one moment will he intermit his care[b]: his protection shall be as effectual as that of lofty mountains[c], or an impassable river[d], or a wall of fire[e]. And its preservation shall be seen to be evidently *his* work, as much as the "*creation*" itself; so that all who behold it shall say, This hath GOD wrought[f].]

3. Her glory—

[It was the presence of God with Israel of old that marked them as his peculiar people. They were feared on this account, so that " all the inhabitants of Canaan melted because of them[g];"

[n] Exod. xl. 34—38.	[o] Isai. lxvi. 2.	[p] Ps. xxv. 9.
[q] 1 John ii. 20.	[r] Isai. xxxv. 8.	[s] Isai. xxx. 21.
[t] Ps. cvii. 7.	[u] Exod. xiv. 19, 20.	[x] Isai. xxvi. 1.
[y] Isai. liv. 17.	[z] Isai. lviii. 8.	[a] Matt. xvi. 18.
[b] Isai. xxvii. 3.	[c] Ps. cxxv. 2.	[d] Isai. xxxiii. 21.
[e] Zech. ii. 5.	[f] Job xii. 9. Isai. xli. 4.	[g] Josh. ii 9, 11.

as also terror was diffused through the whole camp of the Philistines[h]. Thus it is with the Church at this time; it is the presence of God in it that renders it the joy of the whole earth[i]. It is God's glory that is seen upon it, which brings kings to the brightness of its rising[k]. There is often a power in the ordinances that evidences the presence of the Deity, and constrains his most inveterate enemies to submit themselves to him, and to unite themselves to his Church[l]. And it will be in consequence of that more abundant manifestation of his presence which shall be vouchsafed to the Church at a future period, that all the nations of the earth shall seek with eagerness an interest in its privileges, and a participation of its blessings[m]. Persons of all ranks, from the lofty "fir-tree" to the humble "box," shall come together to the Church, of which it will be said, "The Lord is thine everlasting light, and *thy God thy glory*[n]."]

To IMPROVE this subject, let me entreat you,

1. To give yourselves up to God as his people—

[The whole of this subject refers, as you have seen, to Israel as God's redeemed people. To such alone were these promises made; and by such alone were they experienced. To the Egyptians the cloud was as darkness, whilst to the Israelites it was a pillar of light: and the sea, which afforded to Israel a path of safety, was to the Egyptians without exception a fatal grave. So to those only who give up themselves to our Lord and Saviour Jesus Christ are the blessings of redemption fully known: to them the Gospel is "a savour of life unto life, whilst to others it is only a savour of death unto death:" to them is Christ a sanctuary, whilst to others he is only a stumbling-block and a rock of offence." What then shall I say unto you? *This* I will say: Imitate the Israelites on the occasion referred to. Cast off your bonds, and put yourselves under the guidance of "that Prophet, whom Jehovah has raised up unto you, like unto Moses." Go forth from Egypt in dependence on your God: rely upon him for every thing during the time of your sojourning in this dreary wilderness: and look forward to your possession of the promised land as your sure and abiding portion. "Follow the Lord fully," as Joshua and Caleb did; and rest assured that, like them, you shall in due season enjoy the promised inheritance.]

2. To glory in God as your God—

[Tell me one promise that ever failed those who trusted fully in their God. If Joshua, after forty years of conflict, could make this a matter of appeal to Israel, be sure that none

[h] 1 Sam. iv. 7.   [i] Ps. xlviii. 2.   [k] Isai. lx. 1—3.
[l] 1 Cor. xiv. 25.   [m] Zech. viii. 23.   [n] Isai. lx. 13—16, 16.

of you shall ever be disappointed of your hope. With Jehovah
for your guide and defence, you have no ground for fear: for
" if God be for you, who can be against you?" Your enemies
may be great in might, and many in number: but " they are
all but bread for you." In your conflicts with them, you may
endure much: but your trials shall be only as " the spirit of
judgment and of burning to purge and to purify you from your
filth°," and to call forth those exertions from God, which he
has promised to you. Whatever difficulty obstruct your way,
say to it as God has taught you, " Who art thou, O great
mountain? Before Zerubbabel thou shalt become a plain."
Only " be strong in faith, giving glory to God." " Only hold
fast your confidence, and the rejoicing of your hope;" and
" not so much as one jot or tittle of God's word shall ever fail."]

° ver. 4.

OUTLINE NO. 864

GOD'S APPEAL TO MAN'S DECISION.

Isai. v. 3—5. *O inhabitants of Jerusalem, and men of Judah,
judge, I pray you, betwixt me and my vineyard. What could
have been done more to my vineyard that I have not done in
it? Wherefore when I looked that it should bring forth
grapes, brought it forth wild grapes? And now go to; I
will tell you what I will do to my vineyard.*

MERCIES are obligations to obedience, and
aggravations of the guilt of disobedience. This is
declared under the similitude of an unfruitful vineyard. The parable in the text foretold the captivity
of the Jews in Babylon. Our Lord applied it in
reference to the approaching dissolution of their
ecclesiastical and civil polity by the Romans[a]. It is
applicable also to the Church of God in all ages. In
this solemn address of God to his Church and people
are contained,

I. His appeal to them—

Many and great are the *temporal* blessings which
we enjoy—

[In our *civil* capacity, we possess civil and religious
liberty. In our *social* relations, our privileges and comforts

[a] Matt. xxi. 33, 41, 45.

are many[b]. In our *personal* concerns, we **may all** find abundant cause for gratitude.]

But our *spiritual* advantages are greater still—

[We have *infallible directions* respecting the way of salvation[c]. We are urged by the *strongest motives* to walk in it[d]. *Sufficient assistance* also is provided for us[e]. We have the *religion* of Christ *established* in the land[f].]

In the name of God then we call you to judge between God and your own souls[g]—

[*What obstructions to our fruitfulness has he not removed? What means of promoting it has he not employed*[h]? We appeal to you, and make you judges in your own cause.]

Happy were it for us, if, while we reflect on the advantages God has favoured us with, which are greater far than those which were enjoyed by his people of old, there were not the same reason as formerly for,

II. His expostulation with them—

[b] If this were the subject of a *Commemoration Sermon*, the peculiar advantages belonging to the Society should be enumerated.

[c] John x. 9. and xiv. 6.   1 Cor. iii. 11.   Acts iv. 12.

[d] Not only our hopes and fears, which are the grand springs of human activity and vigour, are excited, Rom. ii. 6—10, but the love of Christ is set before us as the most irresistible of all motives, 2 Cor. v. 14.

[e] Luke xi. 13.   Every Christian may adopt the apostle's words, Phil. iv. 13.

[f] The *Establishment* has been " the pillar and ground of the truth" ever since the reformation.   Its liturgy is pure and scriptural : its articles and homilies are a barrier against the intrusion of error: and, were its institutions observed as they ought to be, there would be no minister in its communion who was not orthodox in his opinions and holy in his life ; none could undertake the office of a teacher, who was not himself taught of God, and " moved by the Holy Ghost."

[g] See the verse before the text ; which, stripped of the figure, may be considered as comprehending the two questions contained in this bracket.

[h] Could *superstition* obscure the light? its clouds have been dispelled by the revival of literary and religious knowledge.   Could *prejudice* pervert our judgment?   a liberality of sentiment prevails beyond the example of former ages.   Could *guilt* dismay our hearts?   God has sent his own Son to die for us.   Could a sense of our *weakness* discourage us?   God has promised the aid of his Spirit.   Could *persecution* alarm our fears?   we " sit every one under his own vine and fig-tree."   Could *erroneous teachers* misguide us? care has been taken, as far as human foresight could prevail, to exclude them. What, then, has not God done that could be done ?

The fruit which God requires, is suitable to the pains he has bestowed upon us—

[He expects that we *follow his directions,* and live by faith on his dear Son, and that we *feel the influence of the motives* he has set before us, and, that we *go forth against all the enemies of our souls in a humble dependence on his promised aid.*]

But very different is the fruit which the greater part of us have brought forth—

[We have substituted in the place of Christ some self-righteous methods of acceptance with God. We have been actuated chiefly by earthly, carnal, and selfish principles. We have gone on in the strength of our own resolutions, instead of looking up continually for the assistance of the Spirit. Alas! our fruit has been only as "the grapes of Sodom, and clusters of Gomorrha[i]."]

But that God is displeased with our unprofitableness, will appear from,

III. His menace—

Under the figure of "laying waste" a vineyard[k], God warns us what he will do to us if we continue unprofitable servants:

1. He will bestow no more pains upon us—

[He who by "pruning and digging" has laboured incessantly for our good, will abandon us at last to our own hearts' lusts[l]. He who has "commanded the clouds to rain down rain upon us," will cease to guard us by his providence, or assist us by his grace[m].]

2. He will withdraw the advantages we now enjoy—

---

[i] How great the difference between him that produces good fruit, and him that "brings forth only wild grapes!" *The one* makes Christ all his salvation and all his desire; *the other* exalts himself into the place of Christ, and wishes to become, in part at least, his own Saviour : *The one* regards eternal things as a reality; *the other* is scarcely more affected by them than if they were a fiction : *The one* conquers sin and Satan in the strength of Christ; *the other* is, either openly or secretly, led captive by them both. In a word, *the one* is a compound of humility, heavenly-mindedness, and zeal; and *the other* of pride, worldliness, and indifference.

N. B. The notes [f], [h], and [i], are too much compressed, and the subject of them is too remote for a country congregation. To an illiterate auditory, a general and popular statement would be more edifying.

[k] ver. 5, 6.   [l] Hos. iv. 17. Ps. lxxxi. 11, 12.   [m] Gen. vi. 3.

[He will " take away the candlestick" when we exclude or abuse the light[n]. Or if he cause not "a famine of the word," he will make his Gospel " a savour of death to us rather than of life[o]."]

3. He will expose us to the heaviest calamities—

[We may easily conceive how the wild boar of the field will desolate a vineyard, when its fences are all removed ;" and we know, from the instances of Peter and of Judas, what Satan will effect, if he be suffered to execute his will upon us ; yet we can expect nothing but to be " delivered over to Satan for the destruction both of our bodies and souls," if we " bring forth only wild grapes" after all the culture bestowed upon us[p].]

APPLICATION—

What reason have we all to be ashamed of our unfruitfulness, and to tremble lest God should execute upon us his threatened vengeance !

[*No words can more forcibly express his fixed determination to execute it, than the concluding words of our text.* Let us be thankful that the execution of it has been so long delayed; let the "forbearance exercised towards us, lead us to repentance[q];" and let us henceforth seek to resemble the primitive Christians[r].]

And what reason can be assigned that shall justify our bringing forth only " wild grapes" under such circumstances ?

[Has there been any want of care on the part of the husbandman ? Has there been any thing defective in the means he has used ? Could he, consistently with his plans of government, have done more for us than he has done? Can we at all excuse ourselves, and cast with propriety the blame on him? "Judge ye" whether the fault be not entirely in yourselves?]

[n] Luke viii. 18. Rev. ii. 5.   [o] 2 Cor. ii. 16.
[p] Heb. vi. 7, 8. Luke xiii. 7. and John xv. 6.   [q] Rom. ii. 4.
[r] Rom. vi. 22.

OUTLINE NO. 865

THE SINFULNESS OF CONFOUNDING GOOD AND EVIL.

Isaiah v. 20. *Wo unto them that call evil good, and good evil; that put darkness for light, and light for darkness ; that put bitter for sweet, and sweet for bitter.*

THAT man in his present state is a corrupt and sinful creature, is too plain to be denied: the whole

tenour of his conduct proves it beyond a doubt. But
the generality give themselves credit for meaning well
at the very time that they are doing ill. In this,
however, they are mistaken. There is in all a far
greater consciousness of the evil of their conduct than
they are willing to allow. But they wish to quiet
their own minds, and to approve themselves to the
world : and therefore they change the names of things,
" calling good evil, and evil good, putting darkness
for light, and light for darkness, bitter for sweet, and
sweet for bitter." By these means they succeed in
allaying their own fears, and in commending themselves to each other ; but their guilt before God is
thereby greatly increased : for our Lord says, " *This
is the condemnation*, that light is come into the world,
and men loved darkness rather than light, because
their deeds were evil." There is in their hearts a
rooted aversion to what is good, and a consequent
determination to decry it : there is also an inveterate
love of evil, and a consequent desire to justify it.
Hence arises that conduct which is so justly reprobated in the text ; the *prevalence* and *evil* of which we
shall proceed to lay before you.

We will endeavour to point out,

I. The *prevalence* of this conduct—

The more we examine the principles and actions of
men, the more shall we find that this system obtains
among them both in *theory* and *practice*.

Inspect their views of religion ; and it will appear
that they consider it as a *superficial* thing, consisting
in a bare assent to certain notions, and a formal
observance of certain rites. If they have been baptized in their infancy ; if they have some general
views of Christianity, together with a persuasion of
its divine authority ; if they attend regularly on public
worship, and occasionally communicate at the Lord's
supper ; and finally, if they are not guilty of any gross
and scandalous violations of their duty, they think
they have all the religion that they need.

But they substitute the shadow for the substance.

Religion is widely different from this : it is a conversion of the soul to God; it is a resurrection from the dead : it is a new creation. Religion, as it exists in the soul, is a heaven-born principle, that pervades all its powers, and operates in all its faculties. It is to the soul what the soul is to the body. It restrains our passions, corrects our appetites, purifies our affections. It enters into all our motives, and subjects every thing to itself. It will endure no rival : it will make a truce with no enemy : it will reign absolute over the whole man. Its avowed object is to bring man to God as a redeemed sinner, and to restore him to a meetness for that inheritance which he has forfeited by his transgressions : in order to accomplish this, it casts down every high and towering imagination, brings its votary to the foot of the cross, constrains him to walk in the steps of his divine Master, and progressively transforms him into the image of his God.

Compare this with the slight and worthless thing which men in general call religion, and it will appear that they use the term without any just apprehension of its true import.

Again; as religion is esteemed a superficial thing, so it is also deemed a *melancholy* thing. When true religion is described, the generality of men are ready to exclaim against it as incompatible with social happiness : ' If we must repent of our past sins, and enter on a course of mortification and self-denial; if we must renounce the pleasures of sin, and the society of the ungodly; if we must converse familiarly with death and judgment, and spend our lives in preparation for eternity; what remains for us in this world but gloom and melancholy?' So *they* think.

But is this the light in which the Scriptures speak of religion? or are these notions justified by experience? We allow the premises to be correct; but is the conclusion just? Suppose for a moment that the whole life of a person who appeared religious, were a scene of melancholy : must that melancholy be imputed to religion? Must it not rather be imputed

to his former wickedness, and to his present want of
more religion ?   If pain arise to the body during the
cure of an inveterate disorder, is that pain to be imputed to the medicine, or the disease? to the disease,
no doubt: to that therefore must be ascribed all the
pain of sorrow and contrition, even supposing it to be
ever so great, and ever so long continued.   As for
religion itself, we need only ascertain what it is, and
we shall immediately see the absurdity of calling it a
source of misery.   What; is it melancholy to walk
with God, to enjoy God, to glorify God?   Was our
Lord melancholy?   Were his Apostles melancholy?
Are the angels in heaven melancholy ?   *Then* shall *we*
be melancholy in proportion as we resemble *them!*
But if " the ways of religion be ways of pleasantness
and peace," and they who believe in Christ be privileged to " rejoice with joy unspeakable and glorified,"
then are they perverse who deem religion melancholy;
" they call evil good, and good evil, they put darkness for light, and light for darkness, they put bitter
for sweet, and sweet for bitter."

To complete their perverseness, men go farther still,
and actually represent religion as *contemptible*.   What
is there under the sun more despised than this?   With
what opprobrium has it not been stigmatized?   We
appeal to all, whether terms of reproach are not universally assigned to religious characters, and whether
the name given them do not universally convey the
idea of a weak contemptible enthusiast ?   Is not their
very profession considered as a just bar to their pre-
ferment?   Yea, are they not so odious in the eyes of
the world, that none but those infected with their
mania will venture to associate with them, or to
acknowledge them as their friends?   The drunkard, the
whoremonger, the sabbath-breaker, the infidel, shall
find a more favourable reception than they ; and *solely
on account of their religion.*

But does religion deserve this character?   What is
there in it that is so contemptible ?   What is there in
it that to an impartial judge would not appear lovely,
great, and venerable?   Is the subjugation of the

passions a contemptible attainment? Is a superiority to all the pleasures of sense, and the interests of the world, a worthless acquisition? Is there any thing mean in love to God, and benevolence to man? Is the aspiring after heaven a low and pitiful ambition? Viewing at a distance the conduct of the Apostles, we call it magnanimity: but when we see it exhibited before our eyes, we call it preciseness, enthusiasm, hypocrisy. Ah! when will men " cease to pervert the right ways of the Lord," and to brand that with infamy, which he prescribes and approves?

Hitherto we have noticed only men's conduct in respect of *theory;* let us now behold it as it is manifest in their *practice.*

1. In the first place they *magnify* beyond all reasonable bounds *the pursuits of time—*

From our earliest infancy we hear of little but getting forward in the world. To be rich, to be great, to be honourable, this is the chief good of man. All are aspiring after a higher place than they possess, and conceive that they shall catch the phantom of happiness when they have reached a certain point. Moreover, all are applauded in proportion as they succeed in this race; and no period but that of their departure from the body is thought a fit season for prosecuting their eternal interests.

But are the concerns of time really of such importance? When we have got forward in the world, what have we more than food and raiment, which we might have possessed with half the trouble? We do not mean to discourage industry; *that* is truly becoming in every person, and highly advantageous in every state. But if all our time and labour be occupied about this world, and the concerns of the soul be subordinated to those of the body, then is our conduct precisely such as is reprobated in the text.

2. In the next place, men *extenuate sin as venial—*

There are some crimes which degrade human nature, or greatly disturb the happiness of society, which are therefore very generally reprobated and abhorred.

But a forgetfulness of God, a neglect of Christ, a resistance of the Holy Ghost, an indifference about the soul, with ten thousand other sins of omission or of commission, are considered as light and venial, and as affording no ground for sorrow and contrition. If the outward conduct have been decent, it is no matter what has been harboured within, or how much God has been disregarded and despised.

But is this the light in which the Scriptures teach us to regard sin? What was it that cast angels out of heaven? the sin of pride. What drove our first parents from Paradise, and brought a curse on all their posterity? one single transgression; and *that* a breach, not so much of a moral precept, as of a positive institution. Whom is it that according to God's declaration he will cast into hell? " the wicked, and all the nations that forget God." Does sin appear a light matter when we are told, that nothing but the sacrifice of the Son of God could make atonement for it? Or will it appear a light matter to ourselves, when we are suffering the vengeance due to it in the lake that burneth with fire and brimstone? Surely, they are "fools who make a mock at sin," and blind, who doubt of its malignity.

3. To adduce only one instance more, they *persuade themselves that their eternal state is safe*—

Men living in a direct violation of God's commandments, and in a perfect contrast with the example of Christ, imagine that they have nothing to fear: " they have done no harm; and God is very merciful; and if *they* were to perish, what must become of all the world?" *These,* and such like arguments, are considered as sufficient to invalidate every word that God has spoken, and to justify their hopes of eternal happiness.

But darkness and light are not more opposite than these sentiments are to the declarations of God. Where will they find one single passage that will warrant such expectations as these? They must indeed *make* " evil good, and good evil, and must *change* bitter to sweet, and sweet to bitter," before they can have the smallest ground of hope in such a state as theirs.

We might easily prosecute this subject in a great variety of views: but enough has been spoken to elucidate the words before us: and we trust that no doubt can remain upon your minds, but that all who consider religion as *superficial, melancholy,* or *contemptible,* together with all who *magnify the pursuits of time,* and *extenuate sin as venial,* and at the same time *persuade themselves that their eternal state is safe,* are indeed obnoxious to the censure in the text.

We shall pass on therefore to shew,

II. The *evil* of this conduct—

But where shall we find words sufficient to declare its great enormity?

1. It is in the first place, *a contemptuous rejection of God's truth*—

God has clearly marked the difference between good and evil in his word: and if the eyes of our understanding be not blinded by prejudice or passion, we may discern it as easily as we can discern by our bodily senses, light from darkness, or sweet from bitter. But when an appeal is made to the sacred records, their testimony is considered as of no account. Who has not seen the contempt with which God's word is treated, when it is brought forward to oppose some fashionable practice, some favourite lust? One would suppose that its import should be candidly examined, and carefully ascertained. One might expect that they who heard it, should act like mariners sailing by the compass; that they would endeavour to proceed, as much as possible, in the right direction; that they would deliberate, if at any time they had reason to think that they were out of their proper course; that they would be thankful for any information that might tend to rectify their mistakes: above all, they would not madly steer in direct opposition to the compass, and at the same time discard all doubts about their safe arrival at the place of their destination: *that* were a folly of which no man in his senses is capable. Yet this is the very manner in which men act with respect to the Scriptures. There is no other directory than that; and yet they will not only not follow it, but will go on in wilful opposition to it, and still affirm that they are in the way to heaven. Do we speak too harshly of this conduct if we call it a contempt of God's truth? It is the very expression used by our Lord himself; "He that heareth you, heareth me; and he that despiseth you, despiseth me; and he that despiseth me, despiseth him that sent me." Indeed, the inspired writers speak in yet severer terms: they do not hesitate to affirm, that whosoever acts thus, makes God a liar; "he that believeth not God, hath made him a liar." What horrible iniquity is this! If an avowed infidel disregard the admonitions of the Scriptures, he acts consistently, because he does not acknowledge them to be of divine authority. But if *we* despise them, *we* who profess to regard them as inspired of God, *we* who expect to be judged according to them in the last day, what can be said in extenuation of our guilt? Even " Sodom and Gomorrha may well rise up in judgment against us."

2. In the next place their conduct is a *wilful deluding of those around them*—

Every man, whether he design it or not, has a considerable influence on his friends and neighbours. The rich and learned in particular, and more especially they who minister in holy things, are looked up to as examples; and their conduct is pleaded both as a precedent, and as a justification of those who follow it. ' Can such learned men be deceived? Can they who have entered into the service of the sanctuary, and solemnly undertaken to guide us in the way of peace, can *they* be wrong? Can they be " blind, who are leaders of the blind?" If then they, who from their education, their office and profession, ought to understand the Scriptures better than we, if *they* do not approve, either in theory or practice, the things which appear to be enjoined in the Bible, doubtless they have good reasons for their conduct: they would not proceed in a way which they knew to be wrong; we therefore may safely follow them.

By this mode of arguing, all persons lull themselves asleep in their evil ways. Every one upholds his neighbour in the sentiments he has embraced, and in the path he has marked out for himself: and all, instead of condemning themselves for not obeying the divine commands, unite in condemning the obedient as needlessly singular and precise.'

Now we cannot but know that, though an individual has not this extensive influence, the collective body of individuals has ; and that every member of society contributes his share according to the conspicuousness of his station, and the sanctity of his profession. Yet we persist in calling good evil, notwithstanding we know that, by so doing, we encourage others to do the same. And is this no aggravation of our guilt ? Are we not responsible to God for stirring up, according to our ability, an universal rebellion against him; and for contributing thus to the eternal condemnation, not of those only with whom we associate, but of thousands also whom we have not known ?

Doubtless Jeroboam contracted peculiar guilt in " establishing iniquity by a law :" but did not exceeding great guilt attach also to those, who " willingly ran after his commandment ?" Did not every one of them countenance idolatry, and render an adherence to the true God more difficult ? They however might plead obedience to an established law : but there is no law, except the imperious law of fashion, to mislead *us;* and *that* we establish, whilst we follow it : we bind others, while we ourselves yield obedience to it. Would to God that men could consider their conduct in this view, as discouraging, and perhaps turning aside, the weak; as rendering odious the godly ; and as hardening the wicked ! Surely they would not then say, What harm have I done ? but would be ready to confess themselves the very chief of sinners.

III. Lastly, the confounding of good and evil is *an awful trifling with our eternal state—*

We profess to believe that there is " a day appointed of God, wherein he will judge the world in righteousness by that man whom he hath ordained :" and that " every one of us shall stand at the judgment-seat of Christ to receive according to the things done in the body, whether they have been good or evil." Now in that day we shall not be judged by the opinions of men, but by the word of God. It will be no excuse to any one that such or such maxims were generally received, or that such practices were sanctioned by custom: there will be one standard to which every principle and every action will be referred. The sacred volume will be open before the Judge: and every erroneous sentiment be confronted with the dictates of inspiration. The Judge himself will know no other rule of judgment : every thing that accorded with the Scriptures will be approved; and every thing that contradicted them will be condemned. To what end then is it to impose specious names on things, when they will so soon appear in their true light? Will *God* call evil good, and good evil, because *we* have done so? Can we convince *him* that light was darkness, and darkness light, because we persuaded ourselves and others that it was so? What infatuation is it so to trifle with our eternal state! If our error could be pleaded before God in extenuation of our fault, then indeed we might have some reason for persisting in it : but how can we excuse ourselves before him, when we had the means of information in our hands, and followed our own surmises in preference to his commands?

Let us then remember that we are acting now for eternity; and that in a little time every thing will appear, not as we wish it, but as it really is. And, if we think it of any importance what our condition shall be in the invisible world, let us desist from our self-deception, which, however pleasant or fashionable it may be, will most unquestionably issue in our eternal ruin.

Before I conclude, suffer me to address a word of EXHORTATION both to *those who are deceiving their own souls,* and to *those who desire to regulate their conduct according to truth.*

To the former I beg leave to propose one solemn question: God has said, *Woe* unto them that call evil good, &c. Can *you* change that woe into a blessing? Can *you* prevail on God to retract his word? Can *you* make void that sentence, when God shall come to execute it upon you in the last day? Yea, will you not then curse your folly, for using such pains to deceive yourselves and others, and for involving yourselves in everlasting misery, when, if you had not so "rebelled against the light," you might have been heirs of everlasting glory? Permit me then to address you in the words of the Apostle, "Awake, thou that sleepest, and arise from the dead, and Christ shall give thee light." Begin to weigh both sentiments and actions in the balance of the sanctuary. Begin to "judge righteous judgment." Begin to view things, as you will surely view them when you shall stand at the tribunal of Christ. Bear in mind, that in your present state God has denounced a woe against you. Remember too, that it will be small consolation to you to have others involved in the same misery with yourselves: it will rather be a source of more intense misery to all, by reason of their mutual execrations, for having so greatly contributed to each other's ruin. If the word of God be intended for "a light to our feet, and a lantern to our paths," then make use of it; study it, as it were, upon your knees: meditate upon it day and night: and beg of God "to open your understandings that you may understand it," and to sanctify your hearts that you may obey it.

To those who are of a better mind I would say, Be strong, and dare to stem the torrent of iniquity, that would bear down all before it. Be not ashamed to call good and evil by their proper names; and to shew by the whole tenour of your lives, that you know how to distinguish them. Let not too great weight be given to the opinions of men. Bow not to the authority of fashion and custom; but "prove all things, and hold fast that which is good." Bring your advisers to " the law and to the testimony: for if they speak not according to that, there is no light in them." In matters of duty or of discipline indeed you cannot be too diffident, you cannot be too submissive. In those things obedience is your highest honour. But when men presume to *think* for you in the concerns of your souls, it is high time to inquire, whether they will also *perish* for you? If you perish, you must perish for yourselves; and therefore it behoves you to think for yourselves, and to act for yourselves. The self-deceiving world cannot remove the woe from their own souls; much less can they from yours. " Walk not then according to the course of this world:" " follow not a multitude to do evil." Look not at your neighbours, but at Christ and his holy Apostles. Let the Scriptures regulate your every sentiment, your every act. And, without concerning yourselves about the misrepresentations which blind and ungodly men will give of your conduct, " be steadfast, immoveable, always abounding in the work of the Lord, forasmuch as ye know that your labour is not in vain in the Lord."

OUTLINE NO. 866

ISAIAH'S VISION OF CHRIST.

Isai. vi. 5—7. *Then said I, Woe is me! for I am undone; because I am a man of unclean lips, and I dwell in the midst of a people of unclean lips: for mine eyes have seen the King, the Lord of hosts. Then flew one of the seraphims unto me, having a live coal in his hand, which he had taken with the tongs from off the altar; and he laid it upon my mouth, and said, Lo, this hath touched thy lips, and thine iniquity is taken away, and thy sin purged.*

PREVIOUS to the full revelation of himself in the Gospel, God was pleased to communicate his mind and will to men by dreams and visions, which, since the completion of the sacred canon, are no longer to be expected. But we must not therefore imagine that the revelations so made are less interesting to us, than those which proceeded more immediately from the enlightening influence of the Holy Ghost. The same importance must be attached to every thing which God has spoken, so far at least as the instruction which is intended to be conveyed is itself important. For instance, the vision of Isaiah seems to have been a peculiar favour vouchsafed to him: but still it contains many instructive lessons for us: and in this two-fold view we will consider it,

I. As a peculiar favour vouchsafed to him—

That we may have a more distinct view of it, we shall notice in succession,

1. The vision given—

[The place where the prophet was supposed to be, was the outer court of the temple; from whence, the veil which separated it from the sanctuary being drawn aside, he beheld JEHOVAH seated on his throne, and his train, like that of eastern monarchs, filling the temple. Had no additional light been cast on this vision in the New Testament, we should not have thought of inquiring more minutely about the glorious object whom he saw, and who is here so repeatedly designated by titles peculiar to the one supreme God: but we are authorized to declare, that the person whom he saw, was the Lord Jesus Christ, even our " Immanuel, God with us[a]."

Around the throne were " the seraphim," the holy angels, like flames of fire[b], in a posture of devout adoration. Each of them had six wings; with two of which he covered his face, as unworthy to behold the Deity; and with other two, his feet, as unworthy to serve him; whilst with the remaining two he flew with all possible activity to fulfil his will. In themselves they were perfect and spotless creatures: yet, conscious of being as nothing in the sight of a pure and holy God, they were filled with profoundest awe, and served him with reverential fear.

In their worship of him they celebrated, in alternate and responsive songs, *the holiness of his nature,* and *the wonders of his grace.* Whether, in the repetition of the word " holy," there be any reference, as some have thought, to the Three Persons of the Godhead, we undertake not to determine: but they evidently regarded the holiness of the Deity as that attribute, which constitutes the glory and perfection of all the rest: and indeed it is that attribute in which he is more especially glorious[c], and at the remembrance of which the whole universe should give thanks[d]. Together with this glorious subject they evidently combined the wonders of redeeming

[a] John xii. 41.   [b] Ps. civ. 4.   [c] Exod. xv. 11.   [d] Ps. xxx. 4.

love. It is in that view alone that "the *earth*" can be said to be "full of his glory." In the whole creation indeed there is a marvellous display of wisdom and power; but in redemption alone are seen the mercy, and truth, and faithfulness of our God. And though the seraphims are not interested in that work as we are, yet, as exhibiting the full radiance of all the divine perfections in united splendour, they admire it, they sing of it, they glorify the Lord Jesus on account of it[e].

At the sound of their voices the doors of the temple were shaken, and the house was filled with smoke. It is possible that this was designed to express the approbation of the Deity, and his delight in that work which was the subject of their praise[f]. But we rather suppose, that it was intended to intimate the future abolition of the temple worship, when the time should have arrived for the complete establishment of the Christian dispensation[g].]

2. The fear excited—

[In all the manifestations of God to men, the sight of his majesty has excited alarm and terror[h]. A measure of this feeling we behold in the prophet on this occasion. But together with this, there was also a deep sense of humiliation and contrition. As Job, on a similar occasion, was led to exclaim, "I abhor myself, and repent in dust and ashes[i]," so the prophet, viewing himself, and all around him, in the light of God's holiness, accounted himself a leper in the midst of a leprous world. Whatever he might have judged of himself before, he now was dumb; as indeed every human being must be in the presence of a holy God[k]; since "we are all as an unclean thing, and all our righteousnesses are as filthy rags[l]." From the apprehension and terror we are freed by the Gospel: but the humiliation and self-abasement should rather increase in proportion to the more exalted privileges we enjoy[m].]

3. The consolation administered—

[Instantly did one of the seraphim fly to him, to declare, that his iniquities were all blotted out as a morning cloud, through the atoning blood of Christ. This was emblematically represented to him by a coal taken from off the altar of burnt-offering, and applied to his lips. Doubtless the performance of this office was a delightful service to the Seraph, who would willingly forego for a season the more immediate vision of the Deity himself, for the honour of executing his will as a messenger of mercy to sinful man.]

[e] Compare Ps. lxxii. 17—19. where the *same person* is spoken of, and the *same subject* pursued.

[f] 2 Chron. v. 13, 14. and vi. 1.   [g] Amos ix. 1. with Heb. xii. 27.

[h] Judg. xiii. 22. Dan. x. 6—8. Rev. i. 17.   [i] Job xlii. 6.

[k] Rom. iii. 19.   [l] Isai. lxiv. 6.   [m] Ezek. xvi. 63.

But we hasten from this more restricted view of the subject, to consider it,

II. As an instructive lesson to us—

Whilst we acknowledge that such visions are not to be expected by us, we may contemplate this with great advantage to our souls. We may learn from it,

1. That a sight of Christ is the highest privilege we can enjoy—

[What is it that constitutes the felicity of heaven? What is it that is the great source of happiness to the seraphim around the throne? It is a sight of Christ enthroned in his glory. Yet was that sight afforded to the prophet in a vision, and afterwards to St. Paul, by an immediate admission to it in heaven. And is there no such vision to be enjoyed by us? To our bodily eyes indeed there is not; nor to our imaginations will any such view of him be presented: but to the eye of faith the Lord Jesus is clearly visible; and the eyes of every believer may even now "behold the King in his beauty[n]." In the Gospel he is fully revealed to us: there he appears as "the brightness of his Father's glory, and the express image of his person:" and we may " behold his glory, the glory as of the only-begotten of the Father, full of grace and truth." We need not envy the prophet himself; for we may have even brighter views of Jesus than he ever enjoyed. We are told that John was greater than all the prophets; and yet that " the least in the kingdom of heaven," that is, under the Gospel dispensation, " is greater than he[o]." How did *he* excel all others? Others prophesied of Christ; but *he* pointed him out; " Behold the Lamb of God which taketh away the sins of the world!" And wherein do *we* excel him? He beheld Jesus when he came to accomplish our redemption: and *we* behold him after its accomplishment, seated on his throne of glory, and actually applying to millions of his people the full benefits of that redemption. Let those who embrace the Gospel know their high privilege. Let the poor especially rejoice and be glad. It is not to human learning or to strength of intellect that this discovery of Christ is made, but to faith: and if we search the sacred records with a believing eye, then will " God shine into our hearts, to give us the light of the knowledge of the glory of God in the face of Jesus Christ."]

2. That the more lowly we are in our own eyes, the richer communications we shall receive from him—

[Behold how speedily the angel was sent to comfort the mind of the dejected prophet! This was a faithful represen-

---

[n] Isai. xxxiii. 17.   [o] Luke vii. 26—28.

tation of the care which Jesus takes of all his afflicted people, especially when humbled in the dust before him. " He will not break the bruised reed, nor quench the smoking flax, till he bring forth judgment unto victory." Though he is " The High and lofty One that inhabiteth eternity, whose name is Holy, yet will he dwell with him that is of a contrite and humble spirit, to revive the Spirit of the humble, and to revive the heart of the contrite ones P." Does not his word universally attest this blessed truth, that " whilst he who exalteth himself shall be abased, the man that humbleth himself shall be exalted?" Be not afraid then, ye who feel your own unworthiness: give not way to despondency: say not, "Woe is me! I am undone:" follow not the unbelieving example of Peter, saying, " Depart from me; for I am a sinful man, O Lord q." But know that, if you feel yourselves lost, it was precisely such persons that he came to seek and save r; and that, " where sin has abounded, his grace shall much more abound s:" and if, like Mary, you are enabled to go behind him, and wash his feet with your tears, he will ere long say to you, "Thy sins, which are many, are forgiven thee." Indeed it is in this way that he is daily acting by the ministry of his word: he sends his servant to take his promises, and apply them to the hearts and consciences of his people t, and thus to fill them with " a peace that passeth understanding," and with " joy that is unspeakable and glorified."]

3. That a sense of his pardoning love should animate us to an unreserved surrender of ourselves to him—

[See the effect which was instantly produced on the prophet's mind. God designed to send his messages of love and mercy to the Jews, notwithstanding he knew beforehand that they would prove ineffectual for their conversion. To carry such messages was a painful task; but yet, when God asked, " Who will go for us?" the prophet hesitated not one moment to offer his services, saying, " Here am I, send me u." Thus should we also manifest our gratitude to God for all the mercies vouchsafed unto us through the Son of his love. We should not inquire whether the office be pleasant; or, whether it will advance our credit in the world. It should be sufficient for us to know what the will of the Lord is; and then we should account it our honour to do, or suffer it. Especially does this observation apply to those who minister in holy things: if God say, Who will go for me, to carry my Gospel to the heathen? we should not stand to inquire, Whether the office be lucrative or not; or, whether the climate to which we are to go be more or

---

p Isai. lvii. 15. and lxvi. 2.   q Luke v. 8.   r Luke xix. 10.
s Rom. v. 20, 21.   t 1 Thess. i. 5.   u ver. 8.

less salubrious. No: we should stand forth and say, " Here am I; send me." O that we all felt this holy zeal, and that we did not so lamentably "confer with flesh and blood," when, if called to it, we should leave even the vision of God himself, to execute his will towards sinful man! [x]

But, in whatever line of life we move, we should be actuated by the same spirit; and so feel the constraining influence of Christ's love, as to live no longer to ourselves, but altogether unto Him who died for us, and rose again [y].]

[x] This is a fit subject for *Missions*. [y] 2 Cor. v. 14, 15.

OUTLINE NO. 867

A MISSIONARY SPIRIT DESCRIBED.

Isai. vi. 8. *I heard the voice of the Lord, saying, Whom shall I send? and who will go for us? Then said I, Here am I; send me.*

IN former ages, God was well pleased to reveal his will to men, sometimes in dreams, and sometimes in visions, and sometimes by an audible voice, like that of a man conversing with his friend: and these methods were more especially vouchsafed when he was about to devolve on them any particular office, or to employ them on any extraordinary service. It was God's intention to send the Prophet Isaiah on a painful errand; such as, if he consulted his own feelings only, he would be very averse to execute. But to prepare him for it, God vouchsafed to him a vision of the glory and felicity of the heavenly world. The scene of the vision was, the temple, in which Jehovah, Father, Son, and Holy Ghost, was worshipped. An assurance, at the same time, was given him of qualification for his work, and of acceptance in it: and by this he was brought to such a state, that, at the very first proposal from God to send a messenger to his people, he offered himself for the service, willing and desirous to undertake any thing whereby his God might be honoured, and his Saviour glorified.

Respecting the vision itself, I forbear to speak. The points to which I shall call your attention, are,

I. The proposal made —

[In the first instance, the proposal referred solely to a mission which God intended to send to his people. And, in this view, it may justly be applied to any call which may be given to undertake the ministry of the Gospel, either in our own country or in foreign parts [a]— — —

But we may consider the call as given to every one of us, not to undertake the office of the ministry, but to serve God in a way of general obedience : " Who is willing to fulfil my will, and to consecrate himself to me ?" — — — This honour God is ready to confer on all who are willing to accept it : and, if we be really desirous to engage in His service, he will make us lights in the world, and monitors to all around us — — —

Such offers as these are common in the Holy Scriptures — — —and we may suppose it as now made to *us*, in the name, and by the command, of God himself — — —]

To the proposal so made, let us consider,

II. The answer given—

This also we may regard, in the first instance, as an acceptance of the prophetic office. And we cannot but admire the conduct of Isaiah in relation to it, when he offered himself to God *without hesitation* and *without reserve.* Here were no inquiries made, what the particular office was, or what would be the difficulties attending the execution of it. It was sufficient for this holy man that he should be employed in doing the will of God ; and he was willing to devote to that service all his faculties and all his powers [b] — — —

But, taking the proposal as made to us in general to serve our God, we may here see what a spirit we should cultivate. We should offer ourselves to God to serve him,

1. Instantly—

[There should be no delay ; no looking for a more convenient season. We should not be questioning, whether we shall be able to do all that is required of us ; but should

---

[a] Here somewhat of a parallel may be drawn between that particular occasion and any other which presents itself for more especial consideration.

[b] Here, if the subject of *Missions* be treated of, it would be proper to shew, that every Candidate for the office of such a Ministry ought to possess the very disposition which was here evinced.

expect assuredly, that God will enable us to perform whatever we undertake for him, and will give a successful issue to our endeavours — — —]

2. Without reserve—

[We should not draw back from any labour, nor hesitate to make any sacrifice. The loss of life itself should be regarded as no loss, yea, rather as a gain, in such a cause — — — To live for God, or die for God, should be deemed equally desirable, if only God's will may be done in us, and the Lord Jesus Christ be magnified[c]— — —]

But the point to which I would more particularly draw your attention, is,

III. The peculiar obligation which lies on *us* to follow the prophet's example—

You will find in the vision, that the prophet was favoured with a bright manifestation of the glory of Christ: for St. John, referring to it, says, " These things said Esaias, when he saw *his* glory, and spake of *him*[d]," that is, of *Christ*. You will see, also, that assistance in his work was promised him: for the putting of the live coal upon his mouth seems to have been designed to assure him of it[e]. In addition to all this, a sense of God's pardoning love, through the Redeemer's sacrifice, was applied to his soul: for the live coal, being taken from the altar of burnt-offering, marked clearly the connexion between the *atonement offered for* him, and the *pardon vouchsafed unto* him. But in no respect do we fall short of the favours conferred on him: yea, rather, we may be considered as having,

1. More glorious discoveries of Christ—

[Bright as that vision was, it was far inferior to that which is vouchsafed to us in the Gospel. There we behold Christ as " the brightness of his Father's glory, and the express image of his person[f];" yea, we see all "the glory of God shining in the face of Jesus Christ[g]" — — —]

2. More abundant communications of the Spirit—

[Whatever measures of grace were imparted to some highly-favoured individuals under the Law, as to David, Isaiah, Daniel, and others, the effusions of the Holy Spirit were very small and

___

[c] Acts xx. 24.   Phil. i. 20, 21.   [d] John xii. 41.
[e] Compare Jer. i. 9. and Acts ii. 3.   [f] Heb. i. 3.   [g] 2 Cor. iv. 6.

partial in comparison of those which are given to the Christian Church: so that none of us need to draw back from the greatest work; since the weakest of true Believers may say, " I can do all things through Christ, who strengtheneth me[h]."]

3. More certain assurances of the forgiveness of our sins—

[Doubtless the vision, and that one promise given him in it, were sufficient to satisfy his mind. But in the New Testament we have promises without number, " exceeding great and precious promises;" so "great," that they comprehend every possible state that can be imagined; and so " precious," that they bring us into a participation of the divine nature[i], and "fill us with all the fulness of God[k]." I can have no hesitation in saying, that were an alternative offered to any true Christian, to receive for his comfort the *personal* and *particular* promise that was given to the prophet, or to have given him for his dependence the *broad and general promises* of the New Testament, he would do well to rest on those *broad promises*, which engage that " *all manner* of sin shall be forgiven unto men," and that " all who believe shall be justified from all things."]

Say, then, whether *we* be not bound to imitate the prophet, in his surrender of himself to God?

[Doubtless, if mercies vouchsafed are motives to obedience, *we*, who have received such transcendent mercies, ought to " present our whole selves as living sacrifices unto God; which, as it is a holy and an acceptable, is also a most reasonable, service[l]" — — —]

It may be proper, in CONCLUSION, to reply to a question which will probably be asked, *How shall I know whether any particular call to any special service is really from the Lord?*

[I readily grant, that that is a point very difficult to be determined. There is no difficulty at all in determining that we are every one of us called to devote ourselves to God. The difficulty lies in reference to those particular acts which are required only of few. And here I must say, that no rules can be given which shall apply to all cases; nor perhaps any rules that shall be perfectly satisfactory to every mind. And probably, instead of giving *a direct answer* to the question, the best answer will be, to *suggest a caution* against those workings of mind which render the full solution of the case so difficult. Moses, we know, was called to go to Pharaoh, and to bring the Lord's people out of Egypt. Now, in opposition to this call, he urged *his own unworthiness* of such an office[m]; *the impro-*

bability of succeeding in his attempt[n]*; his own utter unfitness* for the work assigned him[o];" and *his desire that it should be transferred to some one else*[p]." Nay, he further adduced *his own experience* of disappointment in less arduous labours, as a certain ground for apprehending that he must of necessity fail in a matter of so much greater difficulty[q]. But what were all these objections? They were, in truth, only *so many excuses, urged to cover his own backwardness to undertake the work.* Had he been in the frame of mind which the prophet manifested in my text, all these difficulties would have vanished; and he would have engaged in his work as Paul did, who was "not disobedient to the heavenly vision," but "preached at once the faith, which, till that moment, he had laboured to destroy." To any one, therefore, who desires an answer to the question that has been proposed, I say, Get your soul filled with love to Christ; and *that* will answer ten thousand difficulties, and constrain you to engage in any thing whereby the kingdom of the Redeemer may be advanced in the world. You will depend on your Lord and Saviour for " grace sufficient for you[r]," and expect that " strength shall be given you according to your day[s]."

As to excuses for withholding or delaying a general surrender of ourselves to God, they are lighter than vanity itself. Think not that they can stand one moment, when you come before your God. To serve God instantly, and with our whole hearts, is the duty of every child of man: and therefore, to the proposal which God at this moment makes by my voice, let every individual amongst you reply, " Here am I; send me."]

[n] Exod. iv. 1.   [o] Exod. iv. 10.   [p] Exod. iv. 13.
[q] Exod. vi. 12.   N.B. Cite all these passages from Exodus, because they are, in fact, the very excuses which *a false humility* invariably suggests.
[r] 2 Cor. xii. 9.   [s] Deut. xxxiii. 25.

OUTLINE NO. 868

GOD THE ONLY PROPER OBJECT OF FEAR.

Isai. viii. 12—14. *Say ye not, A confederacy, to all them to whom this people shall say, A confederacy; neither fear ye their fear, nor be afraid. Sanctify the Lord of hosts himself; and let him be your fear, and let him be your dread: and he shall be for a sanctuary.*

RELIGION, under any circumstances, is of incalculable advantage: but its benefits are most seen and felt when we come into trials of a complicated and

overwhelming nature. Such were the troubles of the
Jewish nation at the time referred to in my text. The
Syrians had entered into a league with the ten tribes
of Israel to dethrone Ahaz, King of Judah, and to
establish a king of their own appointment upon his
throne: and the prospect of this event spread such
dismay amongst the Jewish people, that they were
" all moved by it as trees of the wood before the
wind[a]." But the prophet was sent to shew them
where their strength lay, and to assure them, that, if
they would but trust in God, they had nothing to
fear, since Omnipotence itself would interpose for
their deliverance. In the message which the prophet was instructed to deliver to them, we see,

I. A word of reproof—

To the people of that day was a reproof most justly
due—

[They all were alarmed at the confederacy that had been
formed; and each, by expressing his own fears, helped to
spread a panic through the land. But the prophet was ordered to discountenance this, both by precept and example, not
by any means joining in the general cry, or suffering himself
to participate in the people's fears.

Somewhat of a similar consternation prevailed occasionally
among the Apostolic Churches: on which account St. Peter,
plainly referring to the very words of my text, bade the
Christians of his day not to be troubled about the menaces of
their adversaries, but to follow the advice here given[b].

And are there not many amongst ourselves who give way to
needless fears, on account of the number and inveteracy of their
enemies? "We wrestle, not with flesh and blood only, but with
all the principalities and powers of hell:" and at times our hands
are ready to hang down, and our hearts to faint in utter despondency. It was thus with David when he said, " I shall one
day perish by the hands of Saul." And more especially was it
thus with Asaph, when he questioned with himself, " Will the
Lord cast off for ever? and will he be favourable no more[c]?"
In fact, by the recital of our own doubts and fears, we often
contribute to create the same painful feelings in others, and to
diffuse amongst our brethren apprehensions, which ought rather
to be discountenanced and withstood. We know what discouragement the spies occasioned through the whole camp of

a Isai. vii. 1, 2, 6.   b 1 Pet. iii. 14, 15.   c Ps. lxxvii. 7—9.

Israel by their representations of the promised land, and of the difficulties which must be overcome, before it should be possessed[d]. We know also the commendations given to Caleb and to Joshua for their manly opposition to such degrading fears[e]. This shews us of what spirit *we* should be, whatever confederacies may be formed against us, or whatever difficulties we may have to encounter: we should dismiss all fear from our own hearts, and strengthen to the uttermost the hands of our timid and desponding brethren.]

To his reproof the prophet adds,

II. A word of counsel—

[Surely it became the Jews, whose whole history was one continued record of miraculous interpositions, to " encourage themselves in the Lord their God," and to expect at his hands all needful support. But more particularly were they taught in this place to look unto their Messiah, whose advent had just been predicted in express connexion with these very events[f]. That HE is the person here designated by " the Lord of Hosts himself," is evident; because, whilst he is spoken of as "a Sanctuary" to some, it is declared that he shall be " A stone of stumbling and a rock of offence" to others[g]. Now, says the prophet, " Sanctify HIM in your hearts, and let HIM be your fear, and let him be your dread." And precisely the same advice does the Apostle Peter give to timid and desponding Christians in his day, " Be not afraid of their terror, neither be troubled; but sanctify the Lord God in your hearts[h]." To " sanctify the Lord Jesus Christ in our hearts," is, to regard him as possessing all power in heaven and in earth, and as exercising it for his people's good. This is the true antidote to all distressing fears, from whatever quarter they may arise. For, supposing a confederacy of all the men on earth and all the devils in hell, what device can prevail against infinite wisdom, or what efforts against Almighty power ? If " the Lord's eye be over us for good," it matters not what eye is upon us for evil. " No weapon formed against us can prosper," when both the smith who formed it, and the man who holds it, were created by him and are under his controul[i]. Protected by this Saviour, we can have no cause for fear. Our minds may be *peaceful* in the midst of the most troublous scenes;[k] *confident*, though menaced by the most inveterate foes[l]; and *assured*, though in circumstances, in which no power less than that which is infinite could uphold us[m]. This then is the counsel which I

[d] Numb. xiii. 28—33. and xiv. 1.　　[e] Numb. xxxii. 10—12.
[f] Isai. vii. 7—14.　　[g] Compare ver. 14. with Rom. ix. 33.
[h] 1 Pet. iii. 14, 15.　　[i] Isai. liv. 15—17.　　[k] Ps. xlvi. 1—3.
[l] Ps. xxvii. 3—5.　　[m] Rom. viii. 35—39.

would give to every drooping and desponding soul: "Fear none except the Lord of Hosts himself." HIM you can never fear too much: "Let HIM therefore be your fear and your dread." But, having him for your Protector, you need fear none else: for "if He be for you, who can be against you?"]

Hear ye then as from God himself,

III. A word of encouragement—

[To his people of old this adorable Saviour was "a Sanctuary:" and such he will be to *us*. You remember that when the Man-slayer had once got within the city of refuge, he was safe: the pursuer of blood could not touch him. So, when once you "have fled to Christ for refuge," you are out of the reach of every enemy; "Your life is hid with Christ in God:" nor can all the powers of darkness ever destroy it. It is not by *power* only that you are protected, but by *love*, and *truth*, and *faithfulness*. The Lord Jesus Christ has pledged his word, that none shall ever pluck you out of his hands[n]:" yea, and Jehovah has "confirmed his word with an oath, on purpose that by two immutable things, in which it is impossible for God to lie, you may have the stronger consolation[o]." What then have you to do but to repose your confidence in him, assured, that "heaven and earth shall sooner pass away, than one jot or tittle of his word shall fail?" Know ye then for your comfort, that "the name of the Lord is a strong tower; and that if you run to, and take refuge in it, you are safe[p]," safe from every enemy that would assault you; safe in time, and safe in eternity.]

And now I APPEAL to you whether the true believer be not the happiest person upon earth?

[I grant, he may be an object of the most inveterate hostility both to men and devils. But he has "horses of fire and chariots of fire all around him[q];" yea, "the Lord Jehovah is himself a wall of fire round about him[r]," for his protection. Compare the state of Ahaz and all his people at this time with that of those who believed the prophet's word. Who were the happier, those who feared the confederacy, or those who feared the Lord? See also the state of Hezekiah's mind at the time of Sennacherib's invasion: "The virgin, the daughter of Israel, hath laughed thee to scorn[s]" —— —— "The Lord will put a hook in thy nose, and a bridle in thy jaws, and turn thee back by the way by which thou camest[t]." This is the effect of a realizing sense of God's providence. The man who fears the

n John x. 28, 29.   o Heb. vi. 17, 18.   p Prov. xviii. 10.
q 2 Kings vi. 14—17.   r Zech. ii. 5.   s Isai. xxxvii. 22.
t Isai. xxxvii. 29.

Lord has nothing else to fear: and the man who "sanctifies the Lord," may be assured, that under all circumstances God will preserve him even as the apple of his eye. But take eternity into the account, and how happy is the Believer *then*. O what a sanctuary is the Lord to him from the terrors of a guilty conscience, and from the fears of God's wrath! The Believer, and he alone, understands the true import of these words, "I will keep him in perfect peace whose mind is staid on me, because he trusteth in me[u]." Yes, even at the day of judgment may the Believer stand before the Lord with great boldness[x], whilst the unbelieving world are "crying to the rocks and to the hills to fall upon them, and to hide them from his wrath." Make then the Lord Jesus your sanctuary here, and he will be your portion for evermore.]

[u] Isai. xxvi. 3.   [x] 1 John iii. 21. and iv. 17.

OUTLINE NO. 869

BELIEVERS ARE FOR SIGNS AND WONDERS.

Isai. viii. 18. *Behold, I, and the children whom the Lord hath given me, are for signs and for wonders in Israel, from the Lord of hosts which dwelleth in Mount Zion.*

FROM the time of Cain and Abel to the present moment, there have existed upon earth two classes of men, essentially distinct from each other, and indeed opposed to each other, even as light and darkness: the one of these consists of men "born after the flesh only; the other, of persons born after the Spirit also." Unhappily, it is to the former of these classes that the great majority of mankind have at all times belonged: the latter class has been composed of only a small remnant, who, on that account, have been, to all the rest of the world, objects of reproach and contempt. The Prophet Isaiah complains of this, in his day: and from his complaint I shall take occasion,

I. To confirm his statement—

There is, in the special case before us, a reference probably to the prophet's own family at that time—

[The prophet had two sons; to whom, by God's special direction, he gave very peculiar names. The name of one was "Shear-jashub[a];" the name of the other was "Maher-shalal-hash-baz[b]." These names were given for the purpose of

[a] Isai. vii. 3.   [b] Isai. viii. 3.

declaring to that people God's intentions respecting them; and the children were therefore both *signs* of what God had purposed respecting the land, and *pledges* that he would carry that purpose into effect. The ungodly people of that day, not believing the purposes of God, turned both the prophet and his children into objects of contempt and ridicule. And *this* seems to be the *literal* import of our text.]

But the prophet had some followers also, who, having been converted by his ministry, were regarded by him as " his children"—

[These also, as being witnesses for God against their ungodly neighbours, were, together with the prophet, regarded as objects of popular reproach.

These, too, were honoured by the Lord as his peculiar friends and favourites; or, rather, as *his own* children, to whom he stood in the relation of a Father. In this respect the prophet was a type of the Messiah; who, being the spiritual Parent of these persons, acknowledged them as members of his mystical body; yea, as "members of his body, of his flesh, and of his bones[c]."

Now this rendered them still more obnoxious to the ungodly world; who always hate the saints, in proportion as they bear the divine image, and appear to be objects of God's peculiar love[d]. And *this* I conceive to be the precise import of the prophet's words. He has, in the first place, an oblique reference to his own sons; but he more especially alludes to his pious followers, whom, through the instrumentality of his word, the Lord himself had brought into the nearest possible union with himself. Of these he says, that they were "for signs and for wonders in Israel."]

In the same light have the saints in all ages been regarded—

[In the days of the Apostles, the children of God were looked upon " as the filth of the world, and the off-scouring of all things[e]:" and to this very hour are they, as the prophet Zechariah expresses it, "men wondered at[f]." There is no one thing which will render persons more universally despised than a profession of real godliness. Every description of men, the moral and the immoral, the proud Pharisee and the scoffing Infidel, are alike hostile to the true Christian. The whole world will hate a follower of Christ. To the whole world, he himself was a butt of contradiction[g]: and all who designated him Beelzebub, will be sure to find some name sufficiently

---

c Heb. ii. 13. with Eph. v. 30.   d John xv. 19.   e 1 Cor. iv. 13.
f Zech. iii. 8.   g Luke ii. 34. The Greek.

opprobrious, for the purpose of characterizing his faithful disciples.]

This statement being still as true as in the prophet's days, I will proceed,

II. To point out its aspect on the parties concerned—

Truly its aspect is very different,

1. On those who account the saints to be " for signs and for wonders"—

[They, alas! only betray their own ignorance. Methinks, if they exercised any sound judgment, they would rather account themselves " signs and wonders;" and stand amazed that ever they should have been capable of acting so irrational a part as they have, throughout their whole lives. What! " gaze strangely at persons, and speak evil of them, merely because they will not run to the same excess of riot" as the ungodly world are pursuing[h]! Is this consistent—I will not say, with piety, but with common sense? But, in fact, these very persons, in the midst of all their profane jests or acrimonious proceedings, cannot help venerating, in their hearts, the servants of Christ, and wishing at least to " die their death," even though they will not endeavour to live their life. And assuredly the time is coming, when they will condemn their present conduct as bitterly as now they inveigh against the conduct of the Lord's people. Now they call the saints " the troublers of Israel;" and complain of them, as wishing " to turn the world upside down:" but in a little time their voice will be changed; and they will bemoan themselves, saying, " We fools accounted their life madness, and their end to be without honour: but now, how are they numbered among the children of God, and their lot is among the saints! Therefore have we erred from the way of truth . . . . but as for the way of the Lord, we have not known it[i]."]

2. On those who are so accounted—

[Be it so, that ye are and must be, despised and " hated, of all men, for Christ's sake." But shall I condole with you on this account? No: I will rather congratulate you; for the whole tenour of Scripture pronounces this to be a ground of joy[k]— — — Is it a ground of joy, that " the Spirit of glory and of God resteth upon you? and that you are conformed to your Saviour's image? and that he is glorified in you[l]? Then I bid you rejoice. Again; Is it a ground of joy that the work of God's grace is advanced in you[m], and an accumulated

[h] 1 Pet. iv. 4. The Greek.   [i] Wisd. v. 4—7.
[k] Matt. v. 10—12.   [l] 1 Pet. iv. 12—14.   [m] 1 Pet. i. 7

weight of glory is preparing for you[n]? Then, again I say,
Rejoice. But particularly bear in mind what was **before**
spoken respecting our blessed Saviour's acknowledgment of
those who thus serve him with fidelity : even in the presence
of his Father will he confess them, as partakers of his nature,
and as heirs of his glory[o]. I say, then, be content to be signs
and wonders for a little season; that ye may answer the
designs of God respecting you in this world, and be partakers
of his glory for ever in the world to come.]

n 2 Cor. iv. 17.   o Heb. ii. 13.

OUTLINE NO. 870
SEEKING AFTER GOD.

Isai. viii. 19. *Should not a people seek unto their God?*[a]

THE appeals which God makes to men in the inspired volume are exceeding forcible: they make men
judges in their own cause; and cannot fail to carry
conviction to every mind. Who could resist the appeal
of Nehemiah to the usurious and oppressive Israelites:
"Ought ye not to walk in the fear of God[b]?" So I
doubt not but that all of you will readily acknowledge
the obligation which lies upon you, whilst I,

I. Make the appeal to you—

Nothing can be conceived more just or simple
than the question here proposed for your consideration. For,

1. Who amongst us does not stand in need of help ?

[Who has not many sins to be forgiven?———and many
wants, temporal as well as spiritual, to be supplied?———]

2. Who but God can supply our wants?

[We have " not in ourselves a sufficiency even for a good
thought[c]"——— nor is there a creature in the universe able
to render us any effectual assistance[d]———]

3. Is not God both able and willing to do for you
all that you can possibly desire?

[Suppose your sins to be as great as those of Manasseh,
can he not pardon them[e]? or your necessities to be as great

a The extreme simplicity of this subject renders any further
elucidation of it superfluous.   b Neh. v. 9.
  c 2 Cor. iii. 5.   d Ps. xlix. 7.   e 2 Chron. xxxiii. 12, 13.

as those of Israel in the wilderness, can he not supply them[f]?
Search the annals of the world, and find one, if you can, " who
ever sought his face in vain[g]"————]

4. Will it not, hereafter, be to you a ground of
bitter self-reproach, if you neglect to seek him?

[Our Lord will surely say to you at the last day, "How
often would I have gathered you, even as a hen gathereth her
chickens under her wings, and *ye would not*[h]!" The fault is all
your own : " *ye would not* come to me, that ye might have life[i]."
And the conviction of this will be the bitterest ingredient of
that cup which shall then be given you to drink to all eternity.]

Assured that you cannot but have felt the force of
this appeal, I will,

II. Found upon it some suitable advice—

What shall I say? Seek the Lord :

1. With understanding—

[You must seek God as reconciled to you in Christ Jesus[k].
In Himself he is " a consuming fire[l]." It is in Christ alone that
any sinner in the universe can gain access to him[m] ———]

2. With earnestness—

[It is not by any formal services that you can hope to
succeed. You must " not only seek but strive[n]." " The kingdom of heaven suffereth violence ; and the violent must take
it by force[o]" ———]

3. With speed—

[There may come a time, even in this life, when God may
give you over to a reprobate mind, and heaven may be shut
against you for ever[p] ——— At all events, death may quickly
terminate all your hopes. In the eternal world, however loudly
you may cry, you will " not be able to obtain one drop of water
to cool your tongue."]

4. With constancy—

[To the latest hour of your life must you continue to seek
help from God, as much as at the present moment. If at any
period you draw back from him, you will " draw back unto
perdition[q]." You must not " be weary in well-doing;" for
" he only who endures to the end shall be saved[r]."]

[f] Ps. lxxviii. 12—16. Eph. iii. 20.   [g] Isai. xlv. 19.
[h] Matt. xxiii. 37.   [i] John v. 40.   [k] 2 Cor. v. 19—21.
[l] Heb. xii. 29.   [m] John xiv. 6. Heb. x. 19—22.
[n] Luke xiii. 24.   [o] Matt. xi. 12.
[p] Ps. lxxxi. 10—12. Rom. i. 28. Isai. lv. 6.
[q] Heb. x. 38, 39.   [r] Matt. x. 22.

OUTLINE NO. 871

BLESSINGS IMPARTED BY THE GOSPEL.

Isai. ix. 2—4. *The people that walked in darkness have seen a great light: they that dwell in the land of the shadow of death, upon them hath the light shined. Thou hast multiplied the nation, and not increased the joy: they joy before thee according to the joy in harvest, and as men rejoice when they divide the spoil. For thou hast broken the yoke of his burden, and the staff of his shoulder, the rod of his oppressor, as in the day of Midian.*

THE dispensations of God in this world are never so afflictive, but there are some alleviating and consolatory circumstances to cheer us under them. The judgments with which he threatened to punish his apostate people were very tremendous[a]: yet he comforted them in the mean time with prospects of the Messiah's advent. Whatever reference the words of my text may have to the deliverance of the Jews from Sennacherib's army, we are sure that they refer to Christ, and to the blessings that should issue from the ministration of his Gospel. St. Matthew quotes them in this view[b]; and the very words themselves are far more suited to a spiritual subject than to any temporal occurrence[c].

We notice then in the text three rich blessings resulting from the ministry of Christ, and of his servants in all ages; namely, *light, joy,* and *victory.* The first which the Christian receives, is,

I. Light—

Men are everywhere " sitting in darkness and the shadow of death"—

[a] Isai. viii. 19—22.　　　[b] Matt. iv. 12—16.

[c] The first verse of the chapter is inexplicable, according to our version. Bishop Lowth translates it differently, and thereby makes the sense of the whole passage clear. " There shall not hereafter be darkness in the land which was distressed. He formerly debased the land of Zebulon and Naphthali, but in the latter time he hath made it glorious, even the way of the sea, beyond Jordan, Galilee of the Gentiles. [For] the people, &c." The meaning is, that as the northern part of Galilee had been particularly afflicted by the incursions of the Assyrians, so it should be particularly honoured by the ministry of Christ.

[This was the case with the Jews, notwithstanding they were God's professing people, and had continual access to the word and ordinances of God. And it is the case with us, notwithstanding we are called Christians, and have the word and sacraments administered amongst us. We are like persons immured in a dungeon, or bereft of sight: light is shining all around us, but we see it not: we are as much in darkness as if there were no light at all. The Scriptures uniformly represent us thus; and experience abundantly confirms their testimony. How ignorant are men of their own hearts; of God; of the way of acceptance with him; and indeed of the whole circle of divine truth! Nor is this ignorance confined to the illiterate: it obtains as much among the great and learned, as among the poorest and meanest of mankind.]

But by the Gospel the eyes of their understanding are opened—

[All were not enlightened by the preaching of Christ and his apostles; nor are *all* instructed now by the word they hear: but they whose eyes are opened, do attain by the Gospel a wonderful insight into "the truth as it is in Jesus:" they discover the depth of their own depravity: they behold "the glory of God in the face of Jesus Christ:" a thousand other things, "which the natural man cannot receive," are open to their view: "they are brought out of darkness into marvellous light[d]:" "neither do they from thenceforth walk any more in darkness, because they have the light of life[e]."]

Together with light, the Christian is filled with,

II. Joy—

That which in the text we read "Thou hast *not* increased the joy," is in the margin translated, "Thou hast increased *to it* the joy," namely, to the nation of saints that are multiplied. This seems to be the more proper rendering of the words, and to agree best with the context; for all who are illuminated with divine truth, have,

1. A sacred joy—

[Whatever joy a carnal man partakes of, let him only be brought into the divine presence, and it vanishes at once. To speak to him of God and heaven and hell, is to make him melancholy. But the Christian's joy is a holy sacred joy: "he joys before God." It was appointed under the Law that the people at the beginning and end of harvest should bring their first-fruits and their tithes to the temple, and, feasting upon them

---

[d] 1 Pet. ii. 9.   [e] John viii. 12

with their friends, rejoice before God[f]. Thus the Christian brings his temporal comforts into the divine presence, that he may enjoy God both in and with them. By religion, all his joys are greatly enhanced; nor does he ever enjoy his food or his friends or any blessing in life so much, as when he is led to God by them, and glorifies his God in them. But the most delightful seasons are those wherein he can go to his God in secret, and pour out his soul before him. One hour spent in communion with his Lord is more to him than a whole life of carnal joy: it is a feast of fat things, an antepast of heaven.]

2. An exalted joy—

[The Christian's joy is compared to that of a successful husbandman, and a victorious warrior. In every age, the in-gathering of the harvest has been an occasion of joy[g]: the seizing also of the spoil from a vanquished enemy has ever been considered as a ground of triumph. There is indeed on both these occasions too much of what is merely carnal: still however the spirits of the people are raised far beyond their usual pitch. In this respect the Christian's joy resembles theirs. When he begins to see the fruit of his painful labours and his dubious conflicts, he cannot but rejoice that he has not laboured in vain, or fought in vain. Yes, his soul is joyful in his God, and " he rejoices with a joy that is unspeakable and glorified."]

To this the Gospel contributes, by crowning its converts with,

III. Victory—

As natural men are blind, so are they also under sore bondage—

[The Egyptian or Babylonish yoke was light in comparison of that which Satan has imposed on all the human race. He holds them fast in his chains, and " leads them captive at his will"— — —]

But through the Gospel they are effectually delivered from it—

[When the Jewish nation was oppressed by the Midianites, God raised up Gideon to effect its deliverance. But how was the deliverance wrought? by arms? No: God would not suffer him to employ the army he had raised, but first released all of them except ten thousand, and then dismissed all of those except three hundred. And how were those three hundred armed? with sword and spear? No: but with earthen pitchers, and lamps, and trumpets: and with this little army so

[f] Deut. xvi. 9—15.   [g] Isai. xvi. 9, 10.

accoutred, he put to flight the whole host of Midian: they brake
their pitchers, held forth their lamps, and blew 'tneir trumpets; and the enemies were put to flight[h]. Thus, precisely
thus, does the Christian triumph over his enemies: unable to
accomplish any thing by his own arm, he, by the mere light
and sound of the Gospel, vanquishes his foes. When indeed
the rout commences, he summons all his powers to destroy
them; nor ceases from the pursuit, till he has effectually subdued them all. Behold a man who was lately enslaved by the
world, the flesh, and the devil; see him at once throw off the
yoke, behold him trampling on the world, crucifying the flesh,
and bruising Satan under his feet! Is this a dream? No;
it is a reality, that may be seen now as much as it was on the
day of Pentecost, or on the day that the blood-thirsty Saul
became a preacher of the faith he had once destroyed. " Such
is the heritage of the servants of the Lord:" they all are conquerors, and " more than conquerors, through Him that loved
them."]

INFER,

1. How strangely do men misconceive of the nature and operation of the Gospel!

[That which Christ and his apostles preached, is deemed
fanaticism, and is supposed to lead to melancholy and licentiousness. But how opposite is this sentiment to that which
is contained in the text! Only let the Gospel be searched into
with candour and diligence, and we will venture to affirm that
it shall approve itself as *light*, and become a source of *joy*, and
lead to certain *victory*. Whatever remains of darkness, grief,
or bondage, shall be gradually banished, and the felicity of
heaven be enjoyed, in proportion as the soul is subjected to
the dominion of Christ.]

2. How much do the saints of God live below their privileges!

[If we look at the first converts, we shall be ready to think
that they were of a different species from us; so far are we below
them in spiritual attainments. But is not the Gospel the same
as it was in their day? Does it not require as much of us as
it did of them? And will it not operate as powerfully on our
hearts as it did on theirs? O let us not be satisfied with such
indistinct views of the mysteries of God: let us not be contented
with such scanty measures of joy and triumph: let us not 'think
it enough to gain some small advantages over our spiritual
enemies: let us look for greater things, and expect more
signal displays of the Divine power and goodness! We are not
straitened in God, but in ourselves: let us only be strong in
faith; and " according to our faith it shall be unto us."]

[h] Judg. vii. 19—21.

OUTLINE NO. 872

CHRIST'S INCARNATION AND CHARACTER.

Isai. ix. 6. *Unto us a child is born, unto us a Son is given: and the government shall be upon his shoulder: and his name shall be called Wonderful, Counsellor, The mighty God, The everlasting Father, The Prince of Peace.*

THERE is no true peace or happiness in the world except that which arises from the Gospel of Christ; for God himself testifies that there is no peace to the wicked. But where the Gospel truly prevails, peace and joy immediately spring up as its proper fruits. Such a change as this the prophet describes in the preceding context; and then, in the words before us, traces it to its real source. From the words themselves we shall be led to consider,

I. The advent of Christ to take the charge of his kingdom—

Though given to us by God, he came in an obscure and humble form—

[He was a little "child, born" in as helpless a state as others, and subject to all the sinless infirmities of our nature. He was indeed in a more especial manner *the gift* of the Father's love[a]; the most invaluable gift that God himself could bestow. He was *the* Child, and *the* Son, of whom all the prophets spake, the offspring of a virgin, "Emmanuel, God with us." But as the end of his coming was to redeem our fallen race, he came in such a way, as was best suited to the accomplishment of his own eternal purpose and grace.]

Yet, notwithstanding his mean appearance, he came to assume the government of the Church—

[As the Creator of the universe, he must of necessity have also been the governor of it before his incarnation. But now he came to administer the government *as mediator;* for all judgment was committed to him, not only *as* the Son of man, but *because he was* the Son of man[b]. The Church, in a more especial manner, is subjected to him in this view; and he is the head of it, as well for the purpose of communicating his influence to the members, as of managing its concerns[c]. And so entirely is every thing under his controul, that not so much as a hair falls from the head of any of his people without either his express command, or righteous permission. As in the days

a John iii. 16.   b John v. 27.   c Eph. i. 22.

of his flesh he exercised the most unlimited authority over diseases, devils, and the very elements, so now every thing, whether designedly, or against its will, fulfils his unerring counsels.]

We shall the less wonder at his elevation to a throne, if we consider,

II. His qualifications for the regal office—

His being called by any name, imports that He really is what he is called. He is therefore,

1. A wonderful Counsellor[d]—

[He, in concert with the Father, formed the stupendous plan of man's redemption, a plan in which are contained all the treasures of wisdom and knowledge[e]. Moreover in executing this plan, he has not only defeated all the plots and devices of Satan, but has invariably overruled them for the accomplishment of his own designs. His people too he endues with " wisdom from above," enabling them to discern things hidden from the carnal eye, and guiding them in the way to heaven, so that a wayfaring man, though a fool, shall not err therein[f]. Who that has known ever so small a part of his ways, must not exclaim with amazement, How unsearchable are his judgments, and his ways past finding out!]

2. The mighty God—

[Angels and magistrates are sometimes called gods in a subordinate sense; but He is " The mighty God," " God with us," even " God over all, blessed for ever." The dispensations, both of his providence and grace, manifest him to be a " God, wonderful in counsel, and excellent in working." Indeed, if he were not God, he never could bear upon his shoulder the government of the universe. He must be omnipresent, omniscient, omnipotent, or else he never could hear the supplications, and supply the wants, of all his people at the same instant. However strange therefore it may seem, He who was a little child, was at the same time the mighty God; it was " the Lord of glory that was crucified;" it was " God who purchased the Church with his own blood[g]."]

3. The everlasting Father—

[This title respects not his relation to the Deity (for with respect to *that*, he is the Son and not the Father) but rather his relation to his spiritual seed, whom he has begotten by his word and Spirit. But perhaps the words should rather have

---

[d] These are by many considered as two distinct titles ; but, if we unite them, each title will have its proper attribute.

[e] Col. ii. 3. ἐν ᾧ scil. μυστηρίω.　　　　[f] Isai. xxxv. 8.

[g] 1 Cor. ii. 8. Acts xx. 28.

been translated, " The Father of the everlasting age." The
Jewish dispensation was intended to continue but for a limited
time; but the Christian dispensation was never to be succeeded
by any other: hence it is called " the last times;" and may
be considered as " the everlasting age." Of this Christ is the
author; it owes its existence to him as its parent; it is preserved by his guardian care; and the whole family in heaven
and earth who participate its blessings, both bear his image,
and inherit his glory.]

4. The Prince of Peace—

[In all which Christ has done, whether in planning or
executing the work of redemption, he has consulted the peace
and welfare of his people. It was to purchase their peace that
he became incarnate and died upon the cross. It was to bestow
on them the blessings of peace, that he assumed the reins
of government, and undertook to manage all their concerns.
Peace was the legacy which he left to his Church when he was
just departing from the world; and, on his ascension, he poured
it down like a river on myriads of his blood-thirsty enemies:
yea, at this very hour does he dispense it according to his own
sovereign will, and impart it, with royal munificence, to all the
subjects of his kingdom.]

This SUBJECT furnishes us with abundant reason,

1. For admiration—

[If all heaven was filled with wonder at the sight of their
incarnate God, and if the " Angels yet desire to look into" that
" great mystery of godliness," how marvellous should it appear
in our eyes! Let us then adore with reverence what we cannot
comprehend; and exclaim with profoundest wonder, " Thanks
be to God for his unspeakable gift[h]."]

2. For gratitude—

[Has the mighty God become a little child for us, and shall
we regard his condescension with indifference? Is he governing and overruling every thing for our good, and shall we feel
no sense of his kindness? Let us rather say, What shall I
render to the Lord for all the benefits he has done unto me?]

3. For devotedness to God—

[If the government be upon his shoulder, we should shew
ourselves willing to have it there, and submit ourselves cheer-
fully to his authority. In vain shall we regard him as the
source and foundation of our peace, unless we yield ourselves
to him as the governor of our lives.]

h 2 Cor. ix. 15.

OUTLINE NO. 873

OUR IMPENITENCE UNDER THE DIVINE CHASTISEMENTS.

Isai. ix. 13. *The people turneth not unto him that smiteth them,*
neither do they seek the Lord of hosts.

RICH as God is in mercy to repenting sinners, he
is full of indignation against the impenitent. Hence
his most gracious invitations and promises are often
intermixed with the most awful threatenings[a]. He
had just before declared his intention of sending the
Messiah to his chosen people. He now threatens
them with utter excision for their impenitence[b]. The
grounds of his displeasure are no less visible amongst
ourselves than amongst the Jews. We are at this
time suffering under his chastising hand. But few, if
any, of us are suitably affected with his judgments.

The solemnity of this day[c] leads us to inquire,

I. What is the end for which God chastises us?

He does not ever afflict his people willingly and
without a cause. Sin is the ground of the controversy
that he has with us. It is for the removal of this that
he sends afflictions,

1. Upon individuals—

[His most highly favoured people are not exempt from
chastisement : while they have any sin unmortified, God will
not leave them altogether unpunished[d]. Even the upright
Job had much dross which was to be purged in the furnace of
affliction[e]. David also found much benefit arising from his
trials[f]; and acknowledged them to have been tokens of God's
love and faithfulness[g]. Under the New Testament dispensation God has had the same end in view : He " delivered the
incestuous man to Satan for the destruction of his flesh, that
his spirit might be saved in the day of the Lord Jesus[h];" and
visited with bodily sickness many of those who had profaned
the Lord's supper, in order that they might not perish with
the ungodly world[i]. Nor can we doubt but that *our* troubles
are sent for the same benevolent purpose; of whatever kind
they be, they are intended to purge away our sin, and bring us
nearer unto God[k].]

[a] Matt. xi. 20, 21, 28.   [b] Compare ver. 6, 7. with ver. 11—15.
[c] The Fast-day, March 1798.   [d] Jer. xxx. 11.
[e] Job xxiii. 10.   [f] Ps. cxix. 71.   [g] Ps. cxix. 72.
[h] 1 Cor. v. 5.   [i] 1 Cor. xi. 30, 32.   [k] Heb. xii. 10.

2. Upon nations—

[When a nation is altogether ripe for ruin, God executes vengeance without any view to their reformation; but till then he will continue to correct them with much long-suffering and forbearance. The ten successive plagues of Egypt were sent to overcome their obstinacy. The Israelites, both in the wilderness and in Canaan, were continually informed of the distinct offences for which their various punishments were inflicted; and even their captivity in Babylon was intended *for their good*[1]. We cannot precisely say what are the peculiar enormities by which we have provoked the Majesty of heaven. But it is certain that God is visiting us for sin: the calamities we this day deplore, are tokens of his displeasure[m]; nor can we expect a removal of them, till the end, for which they are sent us, is accomplished.]

It should be the business of this day to inquire—

II. What effect his chastisements have produced upon us?

The rod, which is now held over us, has a voice, if we have ears to hear it[n]. It calls us to repent of all our evil ways. But what change has hitherto been produced,

1. In the nation?

[Every reform is talked of, except a reform of our hearts and lives. What order of men amongst us has duly improved this awful crisis? Is not dissipation as prevalent among the higher ranks as ever? Is there a reformation begun among those who ought above all to be examples to the flock[o]? Are the watchmen, whose office it is to warn others, as earnest and faithful as the occasion requires[p]? Are evils of any kind put away from amongst us? Or is there, even at this hour, any serious appearance of turning unto God? Are not our very fasts a mere formal and hypocritical lip-service? May they not even be numbered amongst our greatest sins? Alas! what shall the end of these things be? The generality are altogether regardless of God's displeasure: because they do not feel in their own persons the stroke of his rod, they are indifferent about the calamities of others[q]. Many, like Ahaz, have even increased in their iniquities since the commencement of our present troubles[r]. They have hardened their hearts and refused

---

[1] Jer. xxiv. 5.   [m] Isai. xlii. 24, 25.   [n] Mic. vi. 9.

[o] Those whom God particularly notices in the text, are "the ancient and honourable, and the prophet that teaches lies."

[p] Ezek. xxxiii. 6—8.   [q] Isai. lvii. 10.   [r] 2 Chron. xxviii. 22.

to receive correction; nor will they cry when God binds them[s]. Nor is this peculiar to any one order of people more than another[t]: some are presumptuously boasting of our power to withstand the arm of God[u]; others, of whom better things might have been hoped, refuse to unite even in the outward services of this day. (Have these men never done any thing to increase our national guilt, that they refuse to deprecate our national judgments? Or have they no occasion to implore mercy for themselves?) To none was the prophet's complaint ever more applicable than to ourselves at this juncture[x].]

2. In individuals?

[Some there are, we trust, who "weep between the porch and the altar." Some are "grieved for the affliction of Joseph[y], but these are few in number; nor are *they* by any means so deeply affected as they ought to be. But where shall we find any that have been humbled under the divine chastisements? Who amongst us is truly "turning unto him that smiteth us?" Who is "seeking the Lord of hosts?" Who have been mourning over their sins this day in secret? Who have put from them their idols and their abominations[z]? Who have cried for mercy as perishing sinners? Or stood in the gap to intercede for their distressed country? Happy they whose *personal* troubles have wrought this blessed change! But we fear that few, if any, have so laid to heart the *public* calamities, as to have experienced from them such a salutary effect.]

We shall conclude our inquiries with some suitable and important OBSERVATIONS—

1. God will surely overcome at last—

[He is now maintaining a controversy with us. Nor can we expect that he should lay aside his rod till it has accomplished his will. If we continue to walk contrary to him, no doubt he will continue to walk contrary to us. If the scourging us with rods will not suffice, he will scourge us with scorpions[a]. He will repay us seven-fold more for our sins[b]. *Four* times are we warned that his hand is stretched out still[c]. Let us then cease from the unequal combat[d], and turn to him, before the measure of our iniquities be completely filled.]

2. If we turn to God with our whole hearts, he will cease from his anger—

---

[s] Job xxxvi. 13.   [t] Jer. v. 1, 4, 5.   [u] ver. 10.
[x] Isai. i. 4—6.   [y] Amos vi. 6.   [z] Ezek. xx. 7.
[a] 1 Kings xii. 11.   [b] Lev. xxvi. 21, 27, 28.
[c] Isai. ix. 12, 17 ˙21. and x. 4.   [d] Ezek. xxii. 14. Isai. x. 3.

[We have most abundant evidence of this delightful truth. The repentance of Nineveh is a standing encouragement for all nations.[e] Even the temporary humiliation of Ahab prevailed to defer the impending judgments[f]. What then should not be effected if this whole nation turned to God in sincerity? God would sooner send an angel to deliver us, or open a passage for us through the sea, than suffer our enemies to prevail against us[g]. His promise to this effect is absolute[h]. Let this consideration lead us to repentance ; and let the prophet's advice to mourn, and fast, and weep, be followed without delay[i].]

3. If we return not to God, our present miseries will be only an earnest of far greater miseries in another world—

[God punishes men in this world in their national capacity ; but in the future world every individual shall answer for his own sins. Nor are we left to doubt what will be the doom of the impenitent[k]. In comparison of that, temporal calamities are of no account. Oh! who can dwell with everlasting burnings[l]? Let me beseech you then by the terrors of the Lord. It would be terrible indeed to fall into the hands of man ; but woe be to those who fall into the hands of the living *God*[m]. Let the exhortation of Christ then sink deep into your hearts, " Fear not man, who can only kill the body, but God, who can destroy both body and soul in hell. I say unto you all, Fear HIM[n]."]

[e] Jonah iii. 10.   [f] 1 Kings xxi. 29.
[g] Exod. xiv. 22. with Isai. li. 10. and 2 Kings xix. 35. with Ps. xxxiv. 7.
[h] Jer. xviii. 8.   [i] Joel ii. 12, 13.   [k] Luke xiii. 3.
[l] Isai. xxxiii. 14.   [m] Heb. x. 31.   [n] Luke xii. 5.

OUTLINE NO. 874

PRIDE AND DOWNFALL OF THE ASSYRIAN MONARCH.

Isai. x. 12—17. *It shall come to pass, that, when the Lord hath performed his whole work upon Mount Zion and on Jerusalem, I will punish the fruit of the stout heart of the King of Assyria, and the glory of his high looks: for he saith, By the strength of my hand I have done it, and by my wisdom; for I am prudent: and I have removed the bounds of the people, and have robbed their treasures, and I have put down the inhabitants like a valiant man : and my hand hath found as a nest the riches of the people : and as one gathereth eggs that are left, have I gathered all the earth; and there was none that moved the wing, or opened the mouth, or peeped. Shall*

the axe boast itself against him that heweth therewith? or
shall the saw magnify itself against him that shaketh it? as
if the rod should shake itself against them that lift it up, or
as if the staff should lift up itself, as if it were no wood.
Therefore shall the Lord, the Lord of hosts, send among his
fat ones leanness; and under his glory he shall kindle a burn-
ing, like the burning of a fire: and the light of Israel shall
be for a fire, and his Holy One for a flame: and it shall burn
and devour his thorns and his briers in one day.

THE doctrine of an all-disposing Providence is
most consolatory to the mind of man. If every
thing were left to chance, or were at the disposal of
mortal men, we should have nothing to cheer us in
adversity, or to moderate our overweening conceit in
prosperity. But the thought, that all things are
directed by an all-wise Being, who " does according
to his will in the armies of heaven and among the
inhabitants of the earth," and " whose counsel," whatever the designs of men may be, " shall surely stand,"
preserves our minds composed and equable, in every
situation, and in every condition. The situation of
Jerusalem at the time when the prophet wrote this
was very afflictive: but by God's command he addressed
them thus, in a few verses following our text: " O my
people that dwellest in Zion, be not afraid of the
Assyrian: he shall smite thee with a rod, and shall
lift up his staff against thee, after the manner of
Egypt (at the Red Sea): for yet a very little while,
and (as in the case of Pharaoh and his host) the
indignation shall cease, and mine anger in their
destruction[a]." To the same effect does he speak also
in the text itself; which we shall consider,

I. As fulfilled in Sennacherib—

Sennacherib was a proud and haughty monarch—

[The Assyrian empire was the most powerful at that time
existing in the world: and Sennacherib was dignified with the
title of, THE GREAT KING[b]. He himself too conceived that he
was omnipotent, a rival of Jehovah, or rather, his superior[c].

Strange it is that mortal man should entertain such wild
conceits: but such is frequently the effect of power: it

a ver. 24, 25.   b 2 Kings xviii. 19, 28.
c 2 Kings xviii. 33—35. with Isai. xiv. 13, 14.

altogether intoxicates us worms of the earth, and makes us forget that we are men [d].]

But God brought him down in a most awful manner—

[In one single night was his power broken by the sword of a destroying angel, who slew 185,000 of his troops: and, not very long after, was he himself assassinated by two of his sons, whilst worshipping in the house of Nisroch his god [e]. And thus it is that God has often humbled his proud blaspheming creatures [f]: yea, and more such instances of vengeance yet remain to be accomplished [g].]

This subject, so interesting of itself, is yet far more interesting,

II. As illustrated at this time [h]—

The resemblance between Sennacherib, and that powerful enemy with whom we have been contending now so many years, is very striking. We will point it out in a few particulars:

1. His unconscious agency—

[The great object of Sennacherib's ambition was, to subdue as many nations as he could, and bring them under subjection to himself. This was his object in warring against Judah. But God had another object in view. God raised him up to punish his offending people the Jews, and thereby to bring them to repentance. No such thought as this entered into the mind of Sennacherib. He went on with a view to his own aggrandizement; but God made use of him as " the rod of his anger, and the staff of his indignation [i]."

Thus it has been with *him* who has for so long a period desolated every part of Europe [k]. He has been instigated only by his own ambition, and a desire after universal empire: but God has been using him to punish the nations, who, though " naming the name of Christ, had scarcely any thing of Christianity except the name!" As God's instrument he has effected a very great change in Europe: he has given a death-blow to Popery, and has liberated the minds of men from those shackles with which they were held in a worse than Egyptian bondage. He has also, though quite unintentionally on his part, rooted out those principles of infidelity towards God, and of insubordination towards man, which were the means of placing him on his high eminence, and which he himself laboured as much as

---

d Ezek. xxviii. 2. and 2 Thess. ii. 3, 4.   e 2 Kings xix. 35—37.

f Ezek. xxviii. 3—10.   g 2 Thess. ii. 8.

h Thanksgiving-day, Jan. 13, 1814.   i ver. 5—7.

k Bonaparte, Jan. 13, 1814.

any one to disseminate. Nay more, by the very miseries which
he has inflicted on the human race, he has occasioned a spirit
of humiliation and of piety, which, unless at the Reformation
and in the apostolic age, never before obtained in Europe to
the extent it now does. True it is, " he never meant these
things, nor did they ever enter into his mind;" but still he has
been an instrument in God's hand of effecting them.]

2. His great success—

[Nothing could stand before Sennacherib[1]: and till lately,
nothing has been able to withstand this proud oppressor, whom
we are comparing with him. Nation after nation has he sub-
jugated; so that what Sennacherib said may be justly said by
him also, " Are not my princes altogether kings[m]?" Whilst he
raised his generals to the rank of kings, he made the old established kings his vassals. And truly one part of Sennacherib's
commission he executed to perfection: if he had believed himself " *charged* by God, to take the spoil, and to take the prey,
and to tread men down like mire in the streets[n]," he could not
have fulfilled his mission with more fidelity or with less remorse.
He truly regarded the wealth of all the countries which he
invaded, as " eggs found in a nest;" and he transported to
his own capital every thing that was valuable, that the seat of
his empire might become the centre of all that was great and
glorious in the world. Yea, not content with acting thus towards
the nations that opposed him, he exercised the same rapacity
towards neutral and unoffending states[o]; and, whilst he was
" gathering all the earth, there was none that moved the wing,
or opened the mouth, or peeped[p]," or dared even to remon-
strate with him, and much less to oppose by force, his tyrannical
proceedings. In a word, he " removed the bounds of nations,"
apportioning them according to his own pleasure, and " robbed
their treasures[q]," compelling all of them to augment and support his armies; and, with the exception of our favoured land,
he exercised in every country a most despotic sway ; and, if he
could but have placed any bounds to his tyranny, and been
content with consolidating instead of extending his dominions,
he would have been the uncontrolled governor of Europe at
this hour.]

3. His atheistic pride—

[The Assyrian monarch took to himself all the glory of
his conquests : " By the strength of my hand I have done it,
and by my wisdom; for I am prudent[r]." And how astonish-
ingly striking is the resemblance between our great enemy

[1] ver. 9—11.   [m] ver. 8.   [n] ver. 6.
[o] The Hanse Towns especially.   [p] ver. 14.
[q] ver. 13.   [r] ver. 13

and him in this particular! His official reports have been one continued boast from beginning to end. Never once has God been acknowledged by him as the disposer of the different events. We wonder not that a heathen should vaunt himself in this manner: but that a man professing himself a *Christian* should do it, and that too in the face of the whole *Christian* world, only shews to what a height his pride and impiety have risen. Well is the folly, as well as the impiety of such conduct exposed in our text: it is, in fact, "the axe boasting itself against him that heweth with it; and the saw magnifying itself against him that shaketh it: it is the rod shaking itself against him that lifts it up, and the staff lifting itself up against its Master[s]." Presumptuous man! "Know that the Lord is greater than all gods; and that whereinsoever they deal proudly, he is, and will be, above them[t]."]

His sudden fall—

[In one single night was Sennacherib overthrown. So completely was that prediction verified, "The Light of Israel shall be for a fire, and his Holy One for a flame; and it shall burn and devour his thorns and his briers in one day." And taking the day for a prophetic day, it has been almost as literally accomplished in our great adversary. It was very little more than a year, between the time when he was in the plenitude of his power, and the time when he was reduced to his present state of weakness and degradation. There is a remarkable correspondence too in the very terms in which the destruction of the Assyrian monarch was foretold, and the means by which the destruction of the modern Sennacherib was effected. "God himself was for a fire and a flame," to burn him out of that city, where he had hoped to rest his army during the winter season. God put it into the heart of the people themselves to reduce their own houses to ashes, rather than to let them prove an asylum to their barbarous invader. This it was that necessitated him to measure back his steps "*by the way he had come*[u];" and this retreat was attended with the loss of all his army. Another desperate effort has he made to retrieve his fortunes; but that also was defeated in one single battle; which has left him more naked and destitute than Sennacherib himself; his own more immediate territory, which he had proudly deemed inviolable, being now invaded on every side, and his regal power being probably near the close of its existence. We pretend not ourselves to prophesy: but the time is probably very near at hand, when Ezekiel's description of the *character* and *end* of the Tyrian monarch will be accomplished in him in all its parts: "Will he then say before him that slayeth him, I am God?

[s] ver. 15.   [t] Exod. xviii. 11.   [u] 2 Kings xviii. 28, 33.

No: he will be a man, and not God, in the hand of him that slayeth him ˣ."]

Our text is yet further worthy of attention,

III. As speaking to men in all ages—

Divested of all those particular circumstances which give it more than ordinary interest at this time, it suggests many lessons of great, and general, and perpetual utility. It teaches us,

1. To receive afflictions as from the hand of God—

[The Jews probably ascribed their troubles to the insatiable ambition of the Assyrian monarch; as we also have traced ours to the ruler of France. But God has told us, that, in the triumphs of Sennacherib, he himself was " performing a gracious work upon Mount Zion, and on Jerusalem:" and we know that Nebuchadnezzar also, and Cyrus, in their victories, were nothing more than " God's sword" and " battle-axe ʸ." In this light then we should view all our *public* calamities. By whomsoever they may be occasioned, they come from God himself, and are sent by him for our good. As the Jews were sent by him into captivity in Babylon " for their good ᶻ," so are our severest losses and defeats intended to humble us, and to bring us to the footstool of our God. The same may be said also of our *personal* afflictions. When the Chaldeans and Sabeans plundered all the property of Job, and the elements conspired to augment and complete his misery, Job saw in every part of his trials the hand of God: " The *Lord* gave, and the *Lord* hath taken away: blessed be the name of the *Lord* ᵃ." And afterwards he prayed, " Shew me wherefore thou contendest with me ᵇ." This is precisely what the text teaches us also to do in every affliction. We should receive it as from God; and, having done so, we should " hear the rod, and him that appointed it." Were we but attentive to God's voice in afflictive dispensations, we should say to the instruments of our trouble, as Joseph did to his brethren, " It was not you that sent me hither, but God:" and, instead of quarrelling with second causes, we should kiss the hand that smote us, and say, " I will bear the indignation of the Lord, because I have sinned against him."]

2. To acknowledge God in our successes—

[Certainly the interposition of God in the destruction of Sennacherib could admit of no doubt: it was as clear as that of Pharaoh, who was brought into the Red Sea for that very

---

ˣ Ezek. xxviii. 3—10.

ʸ Jer. xxv. 9. Isai. xli. 25. and xlv. 1. with Jer. li. 20.

ᶻ Jer. xxiv. 5.　　　ᵃ Job i. 13—21.　　　ᵇ Job x. 2

purpose[c]. And scarcely less visible was his agency in the destruction of our great adversary. God allured him into the heart of the Russian empire, and inclined him to continue there, till his retreat was become impracticable : and to a still further infatuation did he give him up; for, instead of retreating with his forces entire to the confines of his own kingdom, where he might, humanly speaking, have defied all the efforts of the allies, he madly retained an untenable position, till he was reduced to the necessity of risking all upon a single battle.   In these errors of his we see him given up to judicial blindness in order to his destruction, precisely as the enemies of Zion were in the days of old : " Many nations," says the prophet Micah, " are gathered against thee, that say, Let her be defiled, and let our eye look upon Zion.   But *they know not the thoughts of the Lord,* neither understand they his counsel: for he shall GATHER THEM AS SHEAVES INTO THE FLOOR. *Arise and thresh, O daughter of Zion*[d]!" Indeed, notwithstanding the backwardness of men to " consider the operation of God's hands," there is scarcely a thoughtful person to be found, who does not see it, and acknowledge in the present instance, that HE *gathered them together* in both those places *as sheaves into the floor.*

But we must not think that God interposes only in great concerns, such as the fate of empires : he equally interests himself in all the events that are daily and hourly occurring : and from him does our success flow, even in the most trivial matters. Have we succeeded in business?   It is " he that has given us power to get wealth[e]."   Have our agricultural labours been followed with an abundant increase?   Not the abundance only, but the skill we exercised, was altogether from " God, who is wonderful in counsel and excellent in working[f]." Have we prospered in our spiritual course, and gained the victory over our spiritual adversaries?   We must say with Paul, " He that hath wrought us to the self-same thing is God[g]:" " Thanks be to God, who giveth us the victory through our Lord Jesus Christ[h]!"   Whatever evil we escape, or whatever good we enjoy, God must be regarded as the true, the only source of all.   " In him are all our fresh springs[i];" and " of him is our fruit found[k]:"   and all the glory must be his alone[l].]

3. To look to the final issue of every thing—

[Who that saw the issue of Sennacherib's invasion, would not prefer the salutary trials of Jerusalem before the short-lived triumphs of the proud Assyrian? and who that considers

[c] ver. 24. with Exod. xiv. 17.   [d] Mic. iv. 11—13.
[e] Deut. viii. 17, 18.   [f] Isai. xxviii. 23—29.
[g] 2 Cor. v. 5.   [h] 1 Cor. xv. 57. and 2 Cor. ii. 14.
[i] Ps. lxxxvii. 7.   [k] Hos. xiv. 8.   [l] Isai. xlv. 5—7.

aright, does not now congratulate the yet bleeding countries of Europe, especially those who have derived spiritual benefit from their afflictions, and look with pity on the fallen oppressor, laden as he must be with an intolerable load of conscious guilt, and the curses and execrations of half the human race? We may have been stumbled for awhile, just as David was, at the sight of prosperous wickedness; but, if with him we enter into the sanctuary, and contemplate the end of these men, or if we look at their end as exemplified in our fallen adversary, we shall know how to judge of such mysterious dispensations [m]. In like manner we may learn how to judge of every thing, whether prosperous or adverse, in our own affairs. Let us look to the final issue. What will prosperity benefit us, if it draws us from God, and leads us, like the rich fool, to fix our happiness on things below? On the other hand, what reason can we have to complain of afflictions, if they be sanctified to our spiritual and eternal good? Has the stone reason to complain that it receives many strokes, when it is thereby fitted for a conspicuous place in the Temple of the Lord? or the vine, even granting it to be fruitful, that it is " pruned, when it is made thereby to bring forth more fruit?" or the vessel, that it is put into the furnace, when it is thereby rendered meet for the Master's use? Be not then so much concerned to get rid of present trials, as to have them made subservient to the good of your souls. Only beg of God, that " his whole work may be performed upon you;" and leave the means of accomplishing that work to Him, who ordereth every thing with unerring wisdom and unbounded love. You will then see, ere long, that " he hath abounded towards you with all wisdom and prudence;" and in all future trials you will say, " Though he slay me, yet will I trust in him."]

[m] Ps. lxxiii. 3—14, 16—20.

OUTLINE NO. 875

CHRIST'S QUALIFICATIONS FOR HIS OFFICE.

Isai. xi. 2, 3. *And the Spirit of the Lord shall rest upon him, the spirit of wisdom and understanding, the spirit of counsel and might, the spirit of knowledge, and of the fear of the Lord; and shall make him of quick understanding in the fear of the Lord.*

THE richest promises which God has given to the Church, are generally introduced after some awful threatening denounced against his enemies. The prophet has been predicting the utter ruin of the

Assyrians, as of a tree cut down to the very stump. He then contrasts the state of the Church, to which the Messiah should come, springing like a tender sucker from the root of Jesse, after that his family should have been reduced to the lowest state of degradation. He then, in reference perhaps to what he had before spoken respecting " the anointing[a]," shews who this anointed person should be, and what was that unction with which he should be consecrated to his office.

From the words of the text, which beyond all doubt refer to Christ, the Son of David, we shall be led to consider,

I. His qualifications for his office—

The same Spirit that formed Christ's body in the virgin's womb[b], endowed also his soul with all the faculties requisite for the discharge of his high office—

[Jesus Christ, *as a man*, needed to have his mind enlightened, and his heart sanctified, even as other men : nor could he have been qualified for his *mediatorial* work, if he had not been anointed in a superabundant measure, by the Holy Ghost[c]. God therefore anointed him[d], and caused the Spirit to rest upon him[e], not merely for a time, and for a limited purpose, as he had done to others[f], but in an immeasurable fulness[g], and for every end for which he could possibly need it[h].

The Spirit came upon him as a " Spirit of *wisdom and understanding*[i]." He gave to Jesus a full and comprehensive view of all the mysteries which from eternity had been hid in the bosom of the Father[k]; and enabled him also to discern the most secret recesses of men's hearts[l]: so that nothing, either in heaven or in earth, was concealed from him[m].

The Spirit, as "a spirit *of counsel and might*," instructed him how to conduct himself in all those situations of difficulty and danger into which he was continually brought; and endued him with such undaunted courage, unwearied activity, and

[a] Isai. x. 27.   [b] Matt. i. 18, 20.   [c] Ps. xlv. 7.
[d] Acts x. 38.   [e] John i. 32.   [f] Numb. xi. 25, 26.
[g] John iii. 34.   [h] Luke iv. 18, 19.

[i] Vitringa thinks that the *sevenfold* gifts of the Spirit are here enumerated. See Rev. i. 4. and v. 6. but we rather suppose that each *couplet* (not each *expression*) is to be taken separately, as declaring, in a comprehensive manner, the operations of the Holy Spirit.

[k] John viii. 28.   [l] Matt. ix. 4.   [m] John xxi. 17.

invincible patience, that through the whole course of his ministry he never yielded to discouragement, or erred by inadvertence[n].

The Spirit further enriched his soul with "*the knowledge* (or
rather, with *the love*[o]) *and fear of God.*" Through his incessant operations, he was enabled to maintain a continual sense
of the divine presence[p], and to act in all things with a view to
his Father's glory[q]. Under the influence of this divine principle He was carried on in one steady course, like the sun in
its orbit, causing its light to shine with unclouded splendour
through the whole period of his sojourning on earth[r].]

By these means Jesus attained the most consummate holiness—

[The terms whereby the prophet expresses the quickness
of Christ's spiritual perceptions, are taken from that power of
smelling, which some animals possess, and which admirably
represents the exquisite sensibility which our Lord possessed
with respect to every thing that was right and fitting to be said
or done. His enemies of every description, Herodians, Pharisees, and Sadducees, endeavoured to ensnare him. Sometimes
they tempted him with questions, which, in whatever way they
should be answered, would give them occasion against him:
but he invariably replied with such consummate wisdom as
defeated their purposes, and filled them with admiration[s].
Sometimes they sought opportunity to entrap him by means
of his actions: but still he was proof against their malice, and
always turned their efforts to their own confusion[t]. He knew
on all occasions how to vary his conduct, so as ultimately to
answer best the purposes of his mission. And so nice was his
discernment, so unsearchable his skill, that, whether he denounced judgments or proclaimed mercy, whether he maintained
silence or "witnessed a good confession," he invariably combined majesty with meekness, and fidelity with love.

Nor (to carry on the metaphor) was he less earnest in following, than he was acute in discerning, the path of duty. If he
had spent the night in prayer, he still prosecuted by day his
labours of love, till he was exhausted with fatigue, and his
friends declared that his zeal transported him beyond the bounds
of reason[u]: so fully was that prophecy accomplished in him,
"The zeal of thine house hath even consumed me[x]."]

[n] Isai. xlii. 2, 4, 6. and l. 4, 7.   [o] See Vitringa in loc.
[p] John viii. 29.   [q] John vii. 18. and viii. 50.
[r] John viii. 46. and xvii. 4.
[s] Matt. xxii. 16—21, 23—33, 34—40.
[t] John viii. 3—9. Luke vi. 6—11.   [u] Mark iii. 21.
[x] John ii. 17.

Such being his qualifications, let us consider,

II. Our interest in them—

This is by no means a speculative subject, since it serves to shew us,

1. Christ's sufficiency for his work—

[The work which Christ had to do *for us*, was exceeding arduous. He was to obey the law without deviating from it in the smallest point, in thought, word, or deed. If therefore he had been turned aside by any obstacle, or had erred through any inadvertence, or fallen short through any weakness, or exceeded through any temptation, he would have been a violator of the law; and, instead of being a Saviour to us, would have needed a saviour for himself. But by these rich endowments which were communicated to him by the Holy Ghost he was enabled to maintain an unspotted purity even to the last: and, having fulfilled the law in its utmost extent, he has " brought in an everlasting righteousness," which " shall be unto all and upon all them that believe."

Besides this, he has a work to do *in us*. He is exalted to be " head over all things to the church[y]," in order that he may instruct his people in divine knowledge, and counsel them in their difficulties, and strengthen them in their trials, and maintain in them a superlative regard for God. And how should he effect all this, if he himself did not possess an inexhaustible treasure, out of which he might impart to every needy suppliant? But we need not fear, since we are assured, that in him all fulness dwells[z], and that out of his fulness we may all receive, even grace for grace[a]. We may therefore safely glory in him as made unto us wisdom, and righteousness, and sanctification, and complete redemption[b].]

2. The blessings we expect at his hands—

That holy oil which was poured upon the head of our great High-priest, was to descend to the skirts of his clothing, and to the very meanest of his members[c]. Nor are his people called Christians merely as being followers of him, but also as being partakers of the same divine unction[d]. As soon as he was seated on his throne of glory he poured out his Spirit upon his waiting disciples for the very ends and purposes for which he himself had received it[e]. Instantly they were filled with a "wisdom and understanding," which exceeded that of the greatest philosophers. They were endued with such " counsel and might," that none could withstand their words, or shake

[y] Eph. i. 22, 23. [z] Col. i. 19. [a] John i. 16.
[b] 1 Cor. i. 30. [c] Ps. cxxxiii. 2. [d] 1 John ii. 20, 27.
[e] Acts ii. 33. Gal. v. 22.

their resolution. And to such a degree were their hearts filled
with the "love and fear of God," that all sublunary things were
divested both of charms and terrors, and the service of God became, as it were, the very element in which they breathed.

Thus may the most ignorant amongst us have "the eyes of
his understanding enlightened" by him: to every one of us
will he approve himself a "wonderful counsellor[f]:" he will
"strengthen us with might in our inward man:" he will fill
us with a most affectionate and reverential regard for God: he
will give us both an exquisite discernment of what is right, and
a supreme delight in it[g]: and, in a word, he will "transform
us into his own image in righteousness and true holiness[h]."
However different these gifts may appear, and however unequal the capacities of those who are to receive them[i], they shall
be imparted to all according to their measure of faith[k]; and the
Spirit that Jesus will bestow, shall work them all, and in all[l].]

APPLICATION—

[It has been seen that Christ "ascended up on high on
purpose that he might fill all things[m]:" moreover he has assured
us that, if we ask for the gift of his Spirit, we shall not ask in
vain[n]. Now we cannot but acknowledge that we need the influences of the Holy Spirit in all the preceding particulars. In
consequence of our not habitually weighing all existing circumstances with due care and impartiality, we are extremely apt
to err, and, by injudicious conduct, to give offence[o]. But it is
both our duty and our privilege to "walk wisely before God in
a perfect way." The Holy Spirit is promised to us for this
very end. Let all then direct their eyes unto him. Let the
ignorant, the doubting, the weak, and all who desire to have
the divine life carried on and perfected in their souls, apply to
him. Nor let any rest satisfied with low attainments, since
Christ is both able and willing to enlarge our faculties, and to
increase our sanctity, and to bring us to the measure of his own
perfect stature.[p]]

[f] Isai. ix. 6.   [g] Col. i. 9—11.   [h] Eph. iv. 24.
[i] Matt. xi. 25. Isai. xxxv. 8.   [k] Eph. iv. 7. Matt. ix. 29.
[l] 1 Cor. xii. 4, 11.   [m] Eph. iv. 10.   [n] Luke xi. 13.
[o] I wish religious professors to pay particular attention to this hint.
[p] Eph. iv. 13.

OUTLINE NO. 876

THE CHANGE TO BE WROUGHT BY THE GOSPEL IN THE
LATTER DAY.

Isai. xi. 6—9. *The wolf also shall dwell with the lamb, and
the leopard shall lie down with the kid; and the calf and the*

young lion and the fatling together; and a little child shall lead them. And the cow and the bear shall feed; their young ones shall lie down together: and the lion shall eat straw like the ox. And the sucking child shall play on the hole of the asp, and the weaned child shall put his hand on the cockatrice' den. They shall not hurt nor destroy in all my holy mountain: for the earth shall be full of the knowledge of the Lord, as the waters cover the sea.

THE happiness and prosperity of kingdoms depend much on the wisdom and equity of those who govern. Yet the best of rulers cannot always secure their people either from the turbulence of faction, or from assaults of foreign enemies. Thus it is with the kingdom of Christ on earth. He, the Lord and Governor of all, is endowed with every qualification for the discharge of his regal office[a], and executes that office with consummate equity and wisdom[b]: yet, through the infirmities of his subjects, and the malice of his adversaries, his kingdom is far from enjoying the full advantages of his administration. There will, however, be a time, when his dominion shall be extended over all the earth, and perfect peace shall reign throughout all his empire.

The prophecy on which this observation is grounded, will naturally lead us to shew,

I. The change that shall be wrought on men in the latter day—

Men in their intercourse with each other too much resemble the brute creation—

[It is indeed humiliating to compare men with venomous and ferocious beasts: but there is scarcely any beast, however savage, to which God himself has not compared us[c]. Nor is it by figurative representation only, but by plain and express declarations, that God has marked the evil dispositions of our fallen nature[d]. And if we either look around us, or within us, we shall see that his descriptions are by no means exaggerated. Let any one observe the proud and envious, the wrathful and

---

[a] ver. 1—4.   [b] ver. 5.

[c] He likens us to foxes, Cant. ii. 15 ; serpents and vipers, Matt. iii. 7. and xxiii. 33 ; wolves, Matt. x. 16 ; wild asses, Jer. ii. 24 ; wild boars, Ps. lxxx. 13 ; wild bulls, Isai. li. 20, &c.

[d] Rom. i. 29—31. 2 Tim. iii. 2—4.

malicious, the selfish and covetous workings of the heart, and
he shall soon perceive that, if man were unrestrained by human
laws, he would prey upon his fellow-man with as much ferocity
as the beasts themselves.]

But in the latter day universal harmony shall prevail—

[Then this beautiful description shall be fully realized.
Men shall dwell together as the beasts in the ark, none at-
tempting to hurt or destroy another: or rather, they shall dwell
together as the beasts in Paradise; none having so much as a
disposition to hurt; but all filled with gentleness and love.
This event is foretold in other passages of Holy Writ[e]; and
it shall surely be accomplished at the appointed season: "The
zeal of the Lord of Hosts will do this."]

To confirm our expectation of this universal
change, let us consider,

II. The means by which it shall be effected—

It is beyond the power of any human efforts to
accomplish it—

[However civilization may have changed the manners of
men, it is but too evident that their hearts are the same as ever.
In proof of this we need only appeal to the bloody wars which
nations wage with each other; to the duels which are fought
on account of the most trifling injuries or insults; and to the
execrable traffic in slaves, which, to the disgrace of the Christian
name, yea, to the disgrace of humanity itself, is justified and
carried on amongst us, in spite of all the efforts that have been
made for its abolition. If further proof were necessary, we
may all find it very abundantly in the various circles in which
we move: for there is scarcely a society, or even a single family,
in which feuds, dissensions, quarrels, do not frequently arise:
yea, the very relatives most interested in cultivating love and
harmony, are often most at variance. Does not this shew how
untamed we are, notwithstanding the restraints of wholesome
laws, and the instructions given us in the word of God?]

But the Gospel of Christ, when universally received,
shall soon effect it—

[Men continue like wild beasts, because "they know not
the Lord[f]." The knowledge of Christ, and of his salvation,
would produce a wonderful change on their spirit and conduct.
Behold, what it wrought as soon as ever the Gospel was
preached! Thousands of blood-thirsty murderers were transformed into the most lovely and loving of the human race[g].

---

[e] Isai. lxv. 25.   [f] 1 Sam. ii. 12.   [g] Acts iv. 32.

And, wherever it is received, its tendency is the same. It is the rod of God's strength, which brings down every adverse power, and accomplishes for man the salvation of his soul[h]. It renews all after the same image[i]; brings all into the same family[k]; unites all in the same interests[l]; and forms all into one mystical body[m]: how then can it fail of producing harmony and love? This knowledge shall at a future period be universally diffused[n]: and these effects shall as universally result from it[o].]

Let us LEARN from this subject,

1. The nature of true conversion—

[Conversion does not consist in embracing any tenets, however scriptural, or important. The knowledge of Christ is indeed, as has been before observed, *the means* of converting us; but conversion itself consists in a thorough change in all our tempers, dispositions, and conduct, and in a renewal of our souls after the divine image[p]. The lion must become a lamb: we must "become as little children, if ever we would enter into the kingdom of heaven[q]."]

2. The excellency of the Gospel—

[In vain is the moral fitness of things insisted on; yea, in vain are the demands of the law and the terrors of hell displayed, for the conversion of men: nothing but the knowledge of Christ crucified can ever operate on the soul of man, so as to produce in it a radical and universal change[r]. But, where Christ is known aright, there the whole man will assume a new character: and in proportion as his glory is seen by us, we shall be assimilated to his image[s]. Let not the Gospel then be despised as fanatical, or be defamed as licentious; but let it be revered and embraced with our whole hearts.]

3. The blessedness of those who know the Lord—

[It is to be lamented that the knowledge of Christ does not produce in these days the *full* effects that were visible in the Apostles. But the fault is in *us*, and not in the Gospel. Nevertheless there are many, who, even in this age of vice and infidelity, are monuments of the power and grace of Christ; and who, from having been as despiteful towards each other as Jews and Gentiles, are living in the sweetest communion with each other, and with their God. Happy they, whose views are thus rectified, whose passions are thus subdued, and

---

[h] Ps. cx. 2.   2 Cor. x. 4, 5.   Rom. i. 16.   [i] Col. iii. 10.
[k] Eph. ii. 19.   2 Cor. vi. 18.   [l] Eph. iv. 4, 5.
[m] 1 Cor. xii. 20, 21, 25, 27.   [n] Hab. ii. 14.
[o] Isai. ii. 4. and Tit. ii. 11, 12.   [p] 2 Cor. v. 17. Eph. iv. 22—24
[q] Matt. xviii. 3.   [r] Rom. viii. 3.   [s] 2 Cor. iii. 18.

whose lives are thus regulated by the Gospel of Christ[t]!
They have indeed a paradise below; and shall soon enjoy un-
interrupted harmony in heaven[u].]

[t] Deut. xxxiii. 29.   [u] 1 John i. 3. and iv. 16, 17.

OUTLINE NO. 877

THE MILLENNIUM.

Isai. xi. 9. *The earth shall be full of the knowledge of the Lord,
as the waters cover the sea.*

THE generality of mankind ascribe a far greater
degree of moral influence to civilization, than the
state of the heathen world in its most refined ages
will justify. We are willing however to admit, that
some good effects are to be traced to this cause. But
to renew and sanctify the heart is far beyond its
power : this is the province of religion, even of that
religion which is revealed to us in the Gospel. The
prophet has been describing in most beautiful language the change that shall one day be wrought on
the face of the earth ; and he traces it to the propa-
gation of the Gospel, and the extension of divine
knowledge, as its true and only source; " The wolf
shall dwell with the lamb," &c. *for* " the earth shall
be full of the knowledge of the Lord."

In these words he shews us,

I. Wherein true religion consists—

It cannot be more justly or comprehensively described than in these words, " the knowledge of the
Lord"—

[Many indeed, even of those who call themselves Christians, suppose that religion is altogether comprehended in doing
to others as we would be done unto. But, though it must be
acknowledged that this is an important branch, yet it is far from
being the whole, since it relates only to the duties of the second
table, and leaves out all the duties which we owe to God. We
must rather say, that the knowledge of God in Christ Jesus is
the sum and substance of religion : because in this is contained
that vital energy which puts forth itself in all the fruits of
righteousness. It is in this light that the scriptures continually represent it. The Prophet Isaiah says, " By his knowledge shall my righteous servant justify many[a]." Jeremiah

[a] Isai. liii. 11.

cautions us against " glorying in any thing, but in the understanding and knowing of God " as displaying justice and mercy
in the person of Christ[b]. Our Lord himself affirms that, " to
know God, and Jesus Christ as sent by him, is life eternal[c]."
And St. Paul, in his nervous mode of expression, " counts all
things but loss for the excellency of the knowledge of Christ
Jesus his Lord[d]."]

But by " the knowledge of the Lord" we must
of necessity understand a *practical* and *experimental*
knowledge of him—

[Were a speculative knowledge sufficient, Balaam, and even
the devils themselves, might vindicate their claim to religion;
since *he* could boast, that he " knew the knowledge of the
Almighty," and .indeed prophesied of Christ in very exalted
terms[e]; and *they* could say to Christ, "We know thee who
thou art, the Holy One of God[f]." But the only knowledge
that can be considered as constituting religion, is that which
the apostle so emphatically described and so earnestly desired;
" I count all things but dung, that I may win Christ, and know
him in the power of his resurrection, in the fellowship of his
sufferings, and in a conformity to his death[g]." St. John, with
a simplicity peculiar to himself, confirms this truth, saying,
" Hereby do we know that we know him, if we keep his commandments : he that saith, I know him, and keepeth not his
commandments, is a liar, and the truth is not in him[h]."]

Painful as the general want of this religion is at
present, we shall be comforted in considering,

II. In what manner it shall hereafter prevail—

The comparison, which the prophet makes between
the diffusion of true religion and the waters of the
unfathomable and boundless ocean, leads us naturally
to observe, that the knowledge of the Lord in that
day will be,

1. Universal in its extent—

[Improbable as this event may appear, there is scarcely any
other so frequently and so plainly foretold in the prophetic
writings as this. David, in a Psalm where he not only speaks
of Christ, but even personates him, says, " All the ends of the
earth shall remember themselves and turn unto the Lord, and
all the kindreds of the nations shall worship before him; for
the kingdom is the Lord's, and he is the governor among the

---

[b] Jer. ix. 23, 24.   [c] John xvii. 1.   [d] Phil. iii. 8.
[e] Numb. xxiv. 16, 17.   [f] Luke iv. 34.   [g] Phil iii. 10.
[h] 1 John ii. 3, 4.

nations[i]:" and, in another Psalm, which is altogether on this subject, he says, " Christ shall have dominion from sea to sea: all kings shall fall down before him; all nations shall serve him[k]." To cite what Isaiah speaks to this effect, would be to repeat whole chapters[l]. Jeremiah, confirming at the same time the truth we have before insisted on, that true religion consists in the knowledge of the Lord, says, " In that day they shall no more teach every man his neighbour, saying, Know the Lord; for they shall all know me, from the least to the greatest of them, saith the Lord[m]." Daniel assures us, that " the kingdom which God himself will then erect, shall break in pieces all adverse powers, and fill the whole earth[n]." Zechariah tells us, that " Holiness to the Lord shall be written upon the very bells of the horses; that the most common things in every place shall be consecrated, as it were, to God in their daily use: and that there shall then be no more the Canaanite in the house of the Lord of Hosts[o]." The apostles also, and our Lord himself, add their testimony; St. Paul affirms, not only that " the fulness of the Gentiles shall be brought in," but that " the Jews shall be again engrafted on their own olive-tree[p];" and our Lord says, that all, Jews and Gentiles, " shall be one fold under one shepherd[q]:" and St. John, passing over the intermediate space of time, represents the angels in heaven as already rejoicing in the accomplishment of this event, and saying, " The kingdoms of the world are become the kingdoms of the Lord, and of his Christ; and he shall reign for ever and ever[r]."]

2. Deep in its degree—

[The knowledge which the Jews enjoyed was very contracted: ours, since the completion of the canon of Scripture, is considerably enlarged; insomuch that the least of true Christians is, in respect of knowledge, greater than even John the Baptist, who was himself the greatest of all the prophets[s]. But in that day the light will shine far brighter; and the knowledge of all true converts will be, in comparison of ours, as the ocean's depth to a shallow stream. This also is declared with very abundant evidence in the prophetic writings. " The veil that is spread over all nations, is then to be taken away[t]." Nor are any, whose eyes are opened, to have an indistinct view of the truth: the Prophet Isaiah says, " the eyes of them that see shall not be dim, and the ears of them that hear shall hearken; the heart also of the rash shall understand knowledge, and the tongue of the stammerers shall be ready to

[i] Ps. xxii. 27.   [k] Ps. lxxii. 8, 11, 17.   [l] See Isai. xlix. and lx.
[m] Jer. xxxi. 34.   [n] Dan. ii. 44.   [o] Zech. xiv. 20, 21,
[p] Rom. xi. 24, 25.   [q] John x. 16.   [r] Rev. xi. 15.
[s] Matt. xi. 11.   [t] Isai. xxv. 7.

speak plainly[u]." In another place the prophet supposes men
to have received a stroke or wound upon their eyes, and
that, by the healing of that wound, a vast increase of light
shall shine into their minds; " The light of the moon shall be
as the light of the sun, and the light of the sun shall be seven-
fold, as the light of seven days, in the day that the Lord bindeth
up the breach of his people, and healeth the stroke of their
wound[x]." To mention no more passages, the same prophet
represents the saints in that day as seeing Christ, not as in a
shadow, like the Jews, nor as in a mirror, like us, but eye to
eye, and face to face; " Then shall they see eye to eye, when
the Lord shall bring again Zion[y]."]

INFER,

1. What a glorious period will the millennium be!

[The time referred to in the text is often called the mil-
lennium, because it is to last a thousand years. And how blessed
will be the state of the world during that period! How will the
whole face of the earth be changed! The description of it in
the preceding context, figurative as it is, will be almost literally
accomplished: men, savage as the most ferocious animals, will
be transformed into meek and lowly followers of the Lamb.
No more wars, no more enslaving of our fellow-creatures, no
more public feuds or private animosities; all will be love;
" there will be none to hurt or destroy in all God's holy mountain[z]." O that the day were already come! O that " God
would hasten it in his time!" But, if we cannot be privileged
to see it, let us at least help it forward by every means in our
power: let us diffuse the savour of the knowledge of Christ in
every place; and exert all our influence to send the light of the
Gospel to the heathen world, till " Ethiopia herself shall stretch
out her hands unto God."]

2. How thankful should we be for that little know-
ledge, with which God, in his mercy, has favoured us!

[Surely God has not left himself without witness amongst
us, but " has given testimony to the word of his grace," and
evinced its quickening, transforming efficacy. Doubtless there
are some amongst us, whose dispositions and habits were once
as adverse to the Gospel, as the wolf is to a lamb, or the leopard
to a kid, who now harmoniously unite with the saints of God,
and approve themselves to the world as new creatures. Till they
knew the Lord, nothing could effectually tame their spirits, much
less transform them into the divine image: but since the light
of divine truth has shined into their hearts, they have enjoyed
the peace, and exercised the love, and maintained the purity

---

u Isai. xxxii. 3, 4.　　x Isai. xxx. 26.
y Isai. lii. 8.　　z ver. 6—9.

of God's dear children. Let such then be thankful for the distinguished mercies vouchsafed unto them: let them remember that " all things, which pertain unto life and godliness, are communicated to us through the knowledge of Christ[a];" and let them seek to " grow both in grace and knowledge," till from " beholding Christ only as in a glass darkly," they shall " see him as they are seen, and know him as they are known[b]."]

a 2 Pet. i. 3.　　　　b 1 Cor. xiii. 12.

OUTLINE NO. 878

CHRIST A STANDARD FOR THE GENTILES.

Isai. xi. 10. *In that day there shall be a root of Jesse, which shall stand for an ensign of the people; to it shall the Gentiles seek: and his rest shall be glorious.*

IN the Scriptures, you frequently see a particular period referred to under the designation of " that day." This term very generally marks the season of the Messiah's advent; of which season the prophet speaks in the words before us. In the preceding chapter he has predicted the total destruction of the Assyrian empire, which, having already brought into captivity the ten tribes, now menaced, with every prospect of success, the other two tribes, which had been reduced to the lowest ebb of weakness and misery: " The Lord, the Lord of hosts shall lop the bough with terror; and the high ones of stature shall be hewn down, and the haughty shall be humbled: and he shall cut down the thickets of the forest with iron; and Lebanon shall fall by a mighty one." Then, in the beginning of this chapter, he declares, that, whilst Assyria should be destroyed to rise no more, the Messiah should rise from the family of David, when it should have sunk to a state of utter insignificance: " And there shall come forth a rod out of the stem of Jesse, and a branch shall grow out of his roots." He mentions the stem of *Jesse*, rather than of David; because David was a powerful monarch; whereas Jesse, his father, was but a private individual of low rank. Then, in my text, he repeats that same prophecy, saying, " In that day there shall be a root of *Jesse*, which shall stand for an ensign of the people; to it shall the Gentiles seek; and his rest shall be glorious." Now that this refers to Christ there can be no doubt; since an inspired Apostle, speaking of Christ as having come in order "that the Gentiles should glorify God for his mercy," quotes this very passage; "Again Esaias saith, There shall be a root of Jesse, and he that shall rise to reign over the Gentiles; in him shall the Gentiles trust[a]."

With this inspired explanation of my text for our guidance, we may proceed to consider,

I. The advent of Christ as here announced—

We are told, that "He shall stand for an ensign of the people." Now what is "an ensign?" It is a standard raised by the authority of a monarch, inviting his subjects to flock unto it, and to fight under his guidance against his enemies.

Now such an occasion existed before Christ came into the world, and still exists in every quarter of the globe—

[Behold, the whole universe has risen up in rebellion against "the Lord and his Christ." I confidently ask, Who amongst you has not been a rebel against God? Who has not trampled on his laws, and set at defiance his authority?———— Who has not said, respecting the Lord Jesus Christ in particular, "We will not have this man to reign over us?" Who has not ranged himself under the banners of Beelzebub, and executed *his* will in direct opposition to Christ's? It is not for nought that Satan is called "The god of this world;" for "he works in all the children of disobedience," and "leads them captive at his will"————]

To meet that occasion, Christ is come into the world—

[He "comes to effect deliverance for the captives." He erects his standard in the world. He bids us to throw down the weapons of our rebellion, and to join his ranks against the common enemy. He gives us armour from head to foot; and offers to discipline us for the warfare; and assures us of final victory. Nor is it to those only who are in full vigour of life, and amongst the lower ranks of society, that He sends his invitation; but to those of every rank, and every age. There is with him no preference of age or sex: all are equally called to fight his battles; and are assured of ultimate success. Nor is it

[a] Rom. xv. 12.

in this, as in common warfare, that they who fight endanger
their lives; and they who stay at home consult their safety:
on the contrary, they who fight shall both conquer and live for
ever; but they who decline the combat shall assuredly and
eternally perish.]

Though Christ's advent, in this view of it, appears
formidable, we shall rejoice in it, if we consider,

II. The blessedness arising from it—

To all who view it aright, shall this blessedness be
sooner or later vouchsafed. For,

1. The whole Gentile world shall in due time be
subdued before him—

["To him shall the Gentiles seek." Thousands and millions
were converted to him in the apostolic age. The whole Roman
empire was, within the space of a few years, filled with those
who had flocked to his standard. And still is his kingdom
advancing in the world. In the very place where we are, I
trust, there are not a few whom "God has brought from the
kingdom of darkness, and translated into the kingdom of his
dear Son." But the time is near at hand when "all kings shall
fall down before our Lord, and all nations shall serve him;"
yes, "all the kingdoms of the world will be subdued to him,"
and become a part of his universal empire. *Now* there are
kings many and lords many: but "*in that day* there shall be but
one Lord to all the earth, and his name One."

Only then contemplate the change which has taken place in
any one regenerate soul, and then say, whether this reign of
Christ over the whole race of man be not an event greatly to
be desired———]

2. "His rest" after all these conflicts shall be
"glorious"—

[Here is no change of metaphor, as a superficial observer
would imagine. When this Mighty Warrior went to deliver
his people from their captivity in Egypt, he "brought them
forth with a mighty hand and a stretched-out arm." And, when
he subdued their enemies in Canaan, he abode by the ark (the
symbol of his presence) even for five hundred years, "between
curtains" in the tabernacle, moving about from place to place.
But David then prepared for him a settled habitation on Mount
Zion, and said, in reference to it, "Arise, O Lord, into thy *rest*,
thou and the ark of thy strength. For the Lord, having chosen
Zion, and desired it for his habitation, hath said, that is *my rest*
for ever: here will I dwell; for I have desired it[b]." Such was

---

[b] Ps. cxxxii. 8, 13, 14.

David's testimony: and similar expressions did Solomon also use, when he had deposited the ark in the sanctuary of his temple[c]. But since Christ has come, he has a far nobler *rest*, even in the bosoms of his obedient people; a rest, in comparison of which the temple of Solomon in all its glory was perfectly contemptible[d]. Truly *this rest* is glorious indeed: for *here* he vouchsafes far brighter manifestations of his glory, and incomparably richer communications of his grace. The glory that filled the temple, so that the priests could no longer stand to minister there, infinitely excelled all that the temple itself contained: but, in comparison of the discoveries which God vouchsafes to his believing people, it was darkness itself. See the Lord Jesus as " the brightness of his Father's glory, and the express image of his person;" see the glory of God beaming in his face, and all the divine perfections shining with harmonious and united splendour in the work he has accomplished, and you will readily perceive, how far brighter are the discoveries of Christ now made to the believing soul, than all that ever were vouchsafed to men before his advent. The grace, the mercy, the peace, the joy, the strength, which animated some highly favoured souls before this time, were indeed very abundant: but *as a general communication to his Church of old*, these gifts were but as a drop before the shower: for " the Spirit was not then given, because that Jesus was not then glorified." So truly does he now " glorify the house of his glory, and make the place of his feet glorious[e]."]

We may SEE from hence,

1. What improvement we should make of the preached Gospel—

[The preaching of the Gospel is, in fact, the raising of this standard before the eyes of men: it is the setting forth of Christ crucified, and the calling of men to enlist under his banners. What then have we to do, but to flock around him; to give up our names to him, that they may be inscribed on his list; and to gird ourselves for the combat at his command? Let us then vie with each other in zeal for his service: and let us willingly " endure hardness as good soldiers of Jesus Christ," that, being more than conquerors, we may receive a crown of righteousness at the hands of our righteous Judge[f].]

2. The blessedness of those who improve it aright—

[Whoever complies with the invitations of the Gospel, and unites himself to the army of saints, the Church of God, he instantly becomes a distinguished favourite of heaven; his heart is the temple of the Deity; he is God's residence, he is God's

---

[c] 2 Chron. vi. 41.   [d] Isai. lvii. 17. and lxvi. 1, 2.
[e] Isai. lx. 7, 13.   [f] 2 Tim. iv. 8.

rest: and more glorious is he, than if all earthly dignities were centered in him: more happy, than a combination of all earthly comforts could make him.   Let us then aspire after " the good of God's chosen, that we may rejoice in the gladness of his nation, and glory with his inheritance ^g."]

g Ps. cvi. 5.

<hr>

OUTLINE NO. 879

THE BELIEVER'S SONG.

Isai. xii. 1, 2. *In that day thou shalt say, O Lord, I will praise thee: though thou wast angry with me, thine anger is turned away, and thou comfortedst me. Behold, God is my salvation; I will trust, and not be afraid: for the Lord Jehovah is my strength and my song; he also is become my salvation.*

GLORIOUS prospects are open to our poor benighted world.   The time is coming, and we trust it is not far distant, when " all the kingdoms of the world, whether of Jews or Gentiles, shall become the kingdom of our Lord, and of his Christ."   " The Root of Jesse," the Lord Jesus Christ, does already " stand as an ensign to the Gentiles;" and though but few, comparatively, have flocked to his standard yet, he shall " gather to him all nations" ere long, and " his rest shall be glorious^a."   His ancient people, too, shall return to him, and experience at his hands mercies similar to those with which they were favoured in the day that they came forth out of the land of Egypt^b. For them all, and especially for the latter, is this song prepared; and it shall be sung by them with most exalted joy.   But we need not wait till that day: for every redeemed soul is authorized to adopt it, as expressing his own feelings in the contemplation of the blessings vouchsafed unto him.

To assist you in the attainment of this heavenly frame, I will shew,

I. That praise is the proper employment of the whole intelligent creation—

[When God first called forth the universe into existence, he made every thing for the glory of his own great name: and

a Isai. xi. 10.   b Isai. xi. 11—16.

to this hour " the heavens declare the glory of God, and the firmament sheweth his handy-work." Whilst these inferior works unconsciously proclaim his praise, his intelligent creatures more especially engage in this delightful work ; and, so far as they are restored to their original state, account it their highest happiness to glorify their God[c]. Conceive of our first parents in Paradise : how, may we suppose, were their minds occupied, whilst they retained their primeval innocency ? No doubt they contemplated, with incessant admiration, the perfections of Him to whom they owed their existence, and the obligations conferred upon them above all the rest of the creation, the angels alone excepted. Now, what reason is there why our employment should not accord with theirs ? Be it granted, that we have cares and labours, to which they, in their state of innocence, were strangers : after their fall, they were no strangers either to the one or to the other : yet we cannot doubt but that they endeavoured to blend these holy feelings with their daily occupations ; and, instead of complaining of religion as a task, they found in the exercise of it their richest solace and support. In this, all the most eminent saints have resembled them. David, especially, was in the habit of praising God, as it were, " all the day long," and of putting forth all the powers of his soul in that holy exercise[d]. Doubtless it is necessary for us to pour out also our supplications before the Most High : yea, we should " pray without ceasing:" but yet should we also "in every thing give thanks; for this also is the will of God in Christ Jesus concerning us[e]." The perfections of God are still the same as ever, and our obligations to him are the same; or rather, they are infinitely increased ; inasmuch as the gift of his only dear Son to die for us, is, in comparison of all other gifts, as the radiance of the sun when compared with the twinkling of a star. I say not then too much, when I affirm, that " praise is comely for the upright[f];" and that it is no less our happiness than our duty to abound in it, every day, and all the day long. In truth, this is the felicity of heaven : for all the hosts, whether of saints or angels, are engaged continually in this one employment of singing praises unto God : the one, for for all the wonders of redeeming love ; and the other, for the blessed experience which they have of it in their own souls[g].]

That you may enter upon this blessed work without delay, I proceed to shew,

II. What abundant occasion for it there is to the redeemed soul—

[c] Ps. cxlv. 10.   [d] Ps. xxxv. 28. and ciii. 1, 2.
[e] 1 Thess. v. 17, 18.   [f] Ps. xxxiii. 1.   [g] Rev. v. 8—13.

The mercies vouchsafed to every true convert are here set forth,

1. In a way of simple acknowledgment—

[With every soul of man has God been angry, seeing that there is not one of all the human race that has not violated his holy laws — — — But, when we seek for mercy at his hands in his Son's name, " he turns away from us his anger," and " sheds abroad in our hearts a sense of his love" — — —

Say now, whether one so " comforted" has not reason to bless and adore his God? See the soul when trembling through dread of his displeasure: see it when first the light of God's reconciled countenance is lifted up upon it: see it when the Holy Ghost, the Comforter, is sent forth to dwell in it as his temple, and to manifest unto it all the riches of redeeming grace—Has such an one no ground for praise and joy? Verily, " if he should hold his peace, the very stones would cry out against him."]

2. In a way of exultation and triumph—

[" Behold, God is my salvation!" says the believing soul. How wonderful a truth! Methinks, if it were not uttered by the voice of inspiration, one would be almost ready to call it blasphemy. What! Is God, even the Most High God, our salvation? Yes; and not our Saviour only, but salvation itself; inasmuch as He dwells in us, and abides in us, and " works all our works in us." Hence the believing soul further adds, " The Lord Jehovah is my strength and my song; He also is become my salvation." This is a blessing not future, but present; not hoped for, but actually possessed. The Lord God, Almighty himself has undertaken for us. Yes, our Saviour is no other than the Deity incarnate, " God with us," " God manifest in the flesh," and " purchasing the Church with his own blood." Every thing that was necessary for our reconciliation with God, He wrought for us on the cross: and every thing that is necessary to make us meet for our inheritance He works in us, by his Holy Spirit: so that, whilst he is " our strength, he is also our song" from day to day.

I ask then, Is here no cause to praise our God? The wonder is, that any person, thus favoured, can find time for any other employment, or have any inclination to utter a word which has not a direct reference to these mercies.]

In our text, we further see,

III. What is that frame of mind with which our praise should ever be accompanied—

Many will be the trials of a Christian, notwithstanding all that he is privileged to enjoy—

[Still will he have many conflicts with his in-dwelling corruptions ; and be constrained, at times, to cry, " O wretched
man that I am! who shall deliver me?"———— Satan, too,
that great and subtle adversary of God and man, will doubtless
assault him with all manner of temptations; insomuch, that, if
God were not to uphold him, he could never stand————
Nor will he find light difficulties even from his fellow-creatures,
who will exert themselves to the uttermost, both by fraud and
violence, to obstruct his way————]

But, in the midst of all, his heart will be stayed
upon the Lord—

[" I will trust, and not be afraid," is the continued language of his soul. He knows in whom he has believed; and
that his God is " *able* to keep that which he has committed to
him;" yea, and *pledged* also, to " save to the uttermost all that
come to him in his Son's name." Hence he says, " The Lord
is my strength and my salvation; whom shall I fear? The
Lord is the strength of my life; of whom then shall I be
afraid[h]?" " If God be for me, who can be against me?"
Thus is " his heart fixed, trusting in the Lord;" and he goes
forth to his daily conflicts assured of victory, yea, assured that
he shall be " more than conqueror through him that loved him."]

And now let me,

1. Take up a lamentation over those who have
never yet seen this day—

[How many of us are there who are not even sensible
that God is angry with them, or that, consequently, have never
cried to him in earnest to turn away his displeasure? Let
each consult the records of his own heart, and say whether this
be not his unhappy condition? Yes, verily, there are many
amongst us, it is to be feared, who have never, in their whole
lives, shed one tear for their sins, nor ever uttered one cry to
God for the remission of them. And what must I say to you?
I have no wish to lay upon you more guilt than you have contracted: but you all are sinners before God, and as sinners, are
obnoxious to his wrath. You all therefore need to repent of
your sins, and to implore mercy at the hands of your offended
God, in the name and through the mediation of the Lord Jesus
Christ: and if you have not done this in sincerity and truth,
you are at this moment " under condemnation, and the wrath
of God abideth on you[i]." As to the consolations of God's
Spirit, you are as much strangers to them as if no such blessings ever were vouchsafed to mortal man. Were you to hear
one speaking of the manifestations of God's presence to his soul,

[h] Ps. xxvii. 1.   [i] John iii. 18, 36.

and of a sense of God's love shed abroad in his heart, you would account it all enthusiasm and delusion. Say, then, whether you be not in a most deplorable condition? For, if God's anger be not turned away from you *here*, do you suppose it shall be in the eternal world? No, indeed: you will there have to endure his frowns to all eternity, and to " drink of the cup of his indignation for ever and ever." The Lord avert from every one of you this fearful doom! But remember, that till your experience accord in good measure with that described in my text, you have not any scriptural hope of happiness in the realms of bliss. It is in vain to think that you shall spend eternity in songs of praise, when you have never had your hearts tuned to them in this present life.]

2. Offer my congratulations to those with whom this day has commenced—

[Though, as far as respects God's ancient people and the world at large, this day is yet distant, to the real Christian it is already come; as many of you, I trust, can attest. And what terms can I find sufficient to express the congratulations due to you? Carnal friends will congratulate you on the acquisition of wealth and honour: but if crowns and kingdoms had been given you, I should account them of no value in comparison of the blessings which you enjoy. Pardon of sin, peace with God, the consolations of his Spirit, and the prospect of his glory—what on earth can be added to you? The things of this world, in comparison of all this, are but as the small dust upon the balance. I ask not, whether you possess any earthly comfort: if God be yours, what can you want? If " God be your strength, your song, and your salvation," truly you have heaven already begun in your souls. Know, then, your blessedness, and estimate it aright: and not only " *say*, O Lord, I will praise thee," but *do* it: *do* it with your whole hearts; *do* it with your whole souls; and do it, not only with your lips, but in your lives; by giving up yourselves to His service, and by walking before him in righteousness and holiness, without ceasing, and without reserve.]

OUTLINE NO. 880

THE WELLS OF SALVATION.

Isai. xii. 3.   *With joy shall we draw water out of the wells of salvation.*

WE wonder not that the Scriptures are read with so little interest by the generality: for, till persons know somewhat of their lost estate, and of the way

of salvation provided for them, the Bible is to them
a sealed book. But let them once experience a taste
of the Redeemer's love, and instantly they will find
in the inspired volume mines of wealth. Such a
storehouse is that blessed book to the godly in this
day : and such will it be to the Jewish Church, when
once they shall be converted to the faith of Christ.
" *In that day* they will say, O Lord, I will praise
thee : though thou wast angry with me, thine anger
is turned away, and thou comfortedst me." (Such
will be the reflections at the time of their first discoveries of God's mercy to them in Christ Jesus.
Then they will advance farther to express their full
confidence in God.) " Behold, God is my salvation!
I will trust, and not be afraid : for the Lord Jehovah
is my strength and my song; he also is become my
salvation." (Then will they be fully prepared to
derive the richest benefit from the Scriptures : and)
" *therefore* shall they draw water with joy out of the
wells of salvation."

That we may form a just estimate of their privilege,
let us consider,

I. The character by which the Scriptures are here
　　　designated—

The expression, " wells of salvation," is supposed
by many to be spoken of Christ : and doubtless it
may be very fitly applied to him. But I rather
understand it of the Scriptures, from whence, as from
an inexhaustible fountain, all true comfort flows.
They eminently deserve that name,

1. As containing in themselves all the blessings of
salvation—

[The whole of salvation, as planned in the Divine counsels
from all eternity, as executed for us by the Lord Jesus Christ
in his incarnate state, as still carrying on by him at the right
hand of his Father, and as offered through him to every child
of man, is there fully contained. " This mystery of Godliness
was indeed kept secret since the world began; but now it is
made manifest; and by the Scriptures of the prophets, according to the commandment of the everlasting God, is made
known to all nations for the obedience of faith[a]."

[a] Rom. xvi. 25, 26.

Now let any one contemplate this mystery, and endeavour to explore the *wisdom*, the *love*, the *mercy*, and the *grace* contained in it: how surpassing all finite comprehension will they be found! Verily, the breadth, and length, and depth, and height of this mystery, and of the wonders contained in it, are utterly unsearchable; and the blessings flowing from it are a plenteous and perennial spring, for the refreshment of all on earth, and of all in heaven.]

2. As revealing them for our use—

[In the whole world besides, there is not to be found one drop of water to satisfy a thirsty soul. Where can one look that is oppressed with a sense of guilt? Where, one who is mourning over the corruptions of his nature? Go to those who have not the Scriptures: go to even the wisest philosophers of Greece and Rome; and see how vain were all their expedients for pacifying a guilty soul, or purifying a polluted soul. But in the Scriptures we find all that a sinner can desire; an atonement sufficient for the sins of the whole world; and an Almighty Agent ready to dwell in the hearts of all who seek him, and engaged to transform into the divine image all who commit their souls to him. In them are promises suited to every condition incident to our fallen nature; as suited to refresh the soul, as water is to allay our thirst. Conceive of every want with which a sinner can be oppressed, and the appropriate relief will there be found.]

3. As actually imparting them to our souls—

[As a spring pours forth its waters, so do the Scriptures impart life, and peace, and strength, to all who go to them as God's appointed channel of communication to their souls. They have within themselves a life-giving virtue[b]; so that, when brought home and applied by the Spirit of God, they quicken the dead, and give a vital energy to all our powers. They are able, not only to "make men wise unto salvation[c]," but to impart salvation itself; being "like fire" to consume dross, and "a hammer to break the rock in pieces[d]," and "a two-edged sword to pierce the very inmost soul[e]," and "a weapon to destroy every enemy[f]." They have a power to enlighten the darkest mind[g], and to sanctify all on whom they operate aright[h]; and so to sanctify them, as to prepare them for the perfect fruition of their God[i].]

Think then of,

II. The blessedness of having access to them—

b John iv. 10.   c 2 Tim. iii. 15.   d Jer. xxiii. 29.
e Heb. iv. 12.   f 2 Cor. x. 4, 5.   g Ps. xix. 7, 8.
h John xv. 3. and xvii. 19.   i Eph. v. 26, 27.

Truly we should never contemplate them but with joy, on account of,

1. The freeness with which we may approach them—

[There is no prohibition to any creature under heaven. About wells that have been dug for a supply of common water, there have been the fiercest contentions[k] : but these are public property, and equally accessible to all : none have to " pay for this water," as Israel had[l] : it is to be had " without money and without price[m]." True indeed it is that there are many, protestants as well as papists, who would bar our access to them : but God has given to all an equal right to come to them : for his invitation is, " Let him that is athirst come ; and whosoever will, let him come and take of the water of life freely[n]."]

2. The ease with which we may draw from them—

[There are those who think it in vain for the poor to come to them, seeing that " the wells are deep, and they have nothing to draw with[o]." But be it known, that however valuable learning may be for the attaining of a *critical* acquaintance with the Holy Scriptures, it is not at all necessary for a *spiritual* perception of their truths. It is faith, and not learning, that is wanting for *that* end. All the learning in the universe will not impart to us a spiritual discernment, any more than it will furnish us with any corporeal organs. It is faith alone that will avail us here. That discerns the things which are not visible to mortal eyes ; and will go to the very bottom of these wells, and draw from thence the most refreshing consolations.]

3. The abundance that we may receive out of them—

[When the rock was struck by Moses, the waters gushed out in such abundance, that the whole camp of Israel, with all their cattle, could drink thereof. And, if all the sinners in the universe will go to these wells, they shall find no lack for the supply of their most enlarged necessities. Our Lord says, " If any man thirst, let him come unto me and drink ; and out of his belly shall flow rivers of living water[p]." Indeed, the more intense and ardent your thirst is, the more abundant shall be the blessings which you shall derive from them — — —]

4. The perfect satisfaction that we may find in them—

[" Whoever drinks of other waters will thirst again : but whoever drinks of these wells, will never thirst : for the water

k Gen. xxvi. 18—21.   l Numb. xx. 19.   m Isai. lv. 1.
n Rev. xxii. 17.   o John iv. 11.   p John vii. 37, 38.

which he has received will be in him as a well of water spring-ing up into everlasting life[q]." I may appeal to all, whether the most copious draughts of carnal pleasure ever satisfied? Solomon, who drank as deep of it as a human being could do, pronounced it all to be vanity and vexation of spirit. "The eye was never yet satisfied with seeing, nor the ear with hear-ing." But he who has obtained the knowledge of Christ, and drunk deep of the promises of the Gospel, has no longer any relish for earthly vanities, nor any desire after them. Give him all the world, and he feels empty: give him the presence of God, and he desires no more.]

ADDRESS—

1. Those who are going to broken cisterns—

[What is the creature but "a broken cistern that can hold no water?" ——— And will you for this forsake "the fountain of living waters[r]?" Let me prevail on every one of you to go to God as your reconciled God in Christ Jesus, and to say with David, "All my fresh springs are in thee[s].]

2. Those who are drinking from "the fountain of life[t]"—

[Say whether you have not "a joy with which the stranger intermeddleth not?" Say whether the fountains do not richly supply you; and whether, even on the highest places, which, according to human apprehension, are inaccessible to rivers, the rivers do not follow you[u]? Yes, till you arrive at heaven itself, the streams shall never fail; and even there shall they run beside you for your comfort to eternal ages[x].]

[q] John iv. 13, 14. Isai. xlix. 9, 10.   [r] Jer. ii. 13.
[s] Ps. lxxxvii. 7.   [t] Ps. xxxvi. 9.   [u] Isai. xli. 17, 18.
[x] Rev. vii. 17.

OUTLINE NO. 881

THE BELIEVER'S SONG.

Isai. xii. 3—6. *With joy shall ye draw water out of the wells of salvation. And in that day shall ye say, Praise the Lord, call upon his name, declare his doings among the people, make mention that his name is exalted. Sing unto the Lord; for he hath done excellent things: this is known in all the earth. Cry out and shout, thou inhabitant of Zion; for great is the Holy One of Israel in the midst of thee.*

THE restoration of the Jews, and their union with the Gentiles under one head, the Lord Jesus Christ is foretold so plainly by the inspired writers, that we have no doubt at all but that it shall be accomplished in due season. The prediction contained in the foregoing chapter is peculiarly full and express. It relates not to Judah only, but to the ten tribes also; who shall be brought from Assyria, as the other two tribes once were from Babylon. The ensign to which they will flock, is that of the Son of Jesse, the Lord Jesus[a]: and the joy excited in their breasts will be like that which their fathers felt at their deliverance from Egypt, when they beheld all their enemies dead upon the sea-shore.

The chapter before us is a song, which shall be sung on that occasion by the whole assembly of the Lord's people : and in it we see,

I. Their high privilege—

The learned prelate to whom the world is so much indebted for his translation of the Prophecies of Isaiah, renders the first verse of our text, not, " *Therefore* ye shall draw," but, " *When* ye shall draw ;" which all will do in the day to which our text refers. But,

There are wells of salvation now open unto us—

[Often is our blessed Lord and Saviour represented under the image of a well or fountain[b] — — — And he himself, in his conversation with the Samaritan woman, assumed, as it were, that title[c]. Moreover, the very passage from whence our text is taken was applied by him to himself.

At the feast of Tabernacles a custom obtained, which will fully illustrate our text. The people on the last day of that feast used to go in procession, and draw water from the pool of Siloam, and then to mix it with wine, and pour it on the sacrifices. There was no direction for this in the law of Moses ; but the custom was instituted by the Jews themselves after their return from the Babylonish captivity, with a reference to this prophecy which we are now considering. On the day of this ceremony, Jesus stood in the place where the procession was passing, and cried, " If any man thirst, let him

---

[a] Isai. xi. 10, 12.

[b] Ps. xxxvi. 9. Zech. xiii. 1. Another view of the subject is here taken, different from that in the preceding discourse. As the precise import of the " wells " is not determined in Scripture, it may be taken either way.   [c] John iv. 6—14.

come unto ME, and drink [d]:" as if he had said, 'I am the person spoken of by the Prophet, and the person whom ye profess to expect: and, if you will believe in me, I will give you my Holy Spirit in such abundance, as shall be effectual for your present peace, and your everlasting salvation.' Indeed, his person, (as God-man,) his work, (even his whole obedience unto death,) his offices, (as our Great High Priest that makes atonement for us, our King that rules over us and in us, and our Prophet that guides us into all truth,) may all be considered as so many wells from whence our salvation flows — — — Yea, his word also, and ordinances, may be considered in the same light, because from them we draw all the instruction, the grace, the consolation, that we stand in need of.]

From these we may draw water with joy—

[Truly there is nothing which can conduce to our salvation, which is not to be found in Christ. The water that he will give us will cleanse us at once from all the guilt and defilement of sin: it will purify our very nature, so that we shall be renewed after the Divine image in righteousness and true holiness." From him *all* may draw. Not a sinner in the universe is so unworthy, but that he may come to Christ, and by faith receive from him whatsoever he stands in need of. The invitation is given to "all who thirst:" no qualification is required on their part, except an earnest desire, and a humble faith: they may take as much as they can wish freely, "without money and without price[e]." They are not in the situation of Hagar, who when she relieved her son's thirst from the small vessel that she had taken, grudged, as it were, every drop that was expended, because she knew not where to obtain enough to satisfy his returning wants, which would speedily arise: they may come and draw "with joy," knowing that the supply is inexhaustible, and perfectly commensurate with all their wants. The very first taste of this water shall so invigorate their souls, that they shall feel "like a giant refreshed with wine:" and every successive draught shall "strengthen them with might in their inner man," and "fill them, as it were, with all the fulness of God[f]."]

But the true virtue of this fountain will be best seen in,

II. Their heavenly employment—

There is a remarkable difference between the two parts of this divine song: in that which precedes our text, the expressions relate entirely to the case of the individual himself; but, in the text, the individual

---

[d] John vii. 37—40.   [e] Isai. lv. 1.   [f] Eph. iii. 19.

rises to the concerns of others, and becomes, as it were, a preacher to all around him. Hence then we see the employment of all true Christians:

1. They glorify God themselves—

[The first thought of their hearts is that of *humble gratitude* for the unspeakable mercy of reconciliation with God. They look back, and see the innumerable offences whereby they have excited the displeasure of Almighty God, and how justly they might have been made monuments of his wrathful indignation. They contemplate the state of those who have died in their sins, and wonder that they themselves are not now taking their portion with them. They then contrast the happy state to which they themselves are brought through the atoning sacrifice of the Lord Jesus: they behold God as reconciled to them through the blood of his cross; and with inexpressible comfort are enabled to address him by the endearing name of Father. In the view of these things they exclaim with profoundest adoration, " O Lord, I will praise thee: for though thou wast angry with me, thine anger is turned away, and thou comfortest me."

From thence they proceed to glory in God with *unshaken* affiance: for, What can *they* want, who have God himself for their salvation? "If God be for them, who can be against them?" " JEHOVAH himself is their strength," " dwelling in them," " working in them mightily," and " enabling them always to triumph in Christ." Shall he not then be " their *Song?*" Yes; " they know in whom they have believed:" they know his power, and love; his faithfulness and truth: and therefore, though on the field of battle, they assure themselves of victory, and anticipate with joy unspeakable the final issue of their conflicts. Not that they are blind to the difficulties which they have to encounter, or ignorant of the enemies they have to contend with: but they see Jehovah himself engaged for them by covenant and by oath; and in the confidence that he will never leave them nor forsake them, they say, " I will trust and not be afraid;" " being confident of this very thing, that he who hath begun a good work in me will perform it until the day of Jesus Christ [g]."]

2. They stir up others to glorify him also—

[Having a light kindled in their souls, they " do not put it under a bushel, but set it on a candlestick," that others may see their light. They burn with zeal for God, and would gladly extend the knowledge of him to the ends of the earth. They are filled with love also to their fellow-creatures; and would not have one to perish, if by any means they might be

[g] Phil. i 6

instrumental to the salvation of his soul.   Towards the household of faith in particular they feel an ardent desire to promote
their advancement in all that is " lovely and of good report."
Hence they exhort one another to abound in praise and thanksgiving to their common Lord and Saviour : they urge one
another to " call upon him," to " declare his name," to make
known his love, to commend him to the whole world.   They
would have all to " sing unto Him " " with thanksgiving and
the voice of melody."   They cannot endure the thought that
" an inhabitant of Zion" should be silent; they would have
every believer to cry out and shout," so that, were it possible,
the whole universe might hear.

They remind each other of the great things which the Saviour
has done, and is yet doing, for his Church and people.   They
delight to speak of " the excellent things" which he has done,
in assuming our nature, and dying in our stead, and working
out for us a free and full salvation : and they rejoice no less to
contemplate, how " great the Holy One of Israel is in the
midst of them," and how certainly he will put down all their
enemies, and " bruise Satan himself under their feet."

These are things which are the daily subject of their thoughts,
their conversation, and their praise : and in proportion as any
are endued with his grace, they will infallibly abound in these
holy exercises.]

LEARN then from hence,

1. How great a matter is the salvation of the soul—

[Many think of it as a matter of course — — — but not
so the person who has been taught of God : *he* sees that it is
a miracle of mercy that any child of man is saved.   That he
himself has obtained mercy, is to the true Christian a source of
wonder and amazement.   That God should ever look upon
him, and pardon *him*, and save *him!* he knows not how to express his sense of such amazing love.   He would have " the
rocks and hills to break forth into singing, and all the trees of
the wood to clap their hands with joy."   And if we have never
thus been penetrated with a sense of God's unbounded love, we
are yet strangers to the salvation he has wrought out for us.]

2. How precious is Christ to all who know him—

[Mere nominal Christians can think and speak of him
without emotion ; but not so the persons who " have tasted of
his grace:" they can never find words whereby to express their
love and gratitude to their adorable Benefactor.   They are
ashamed that they can ever think or speak of any thing else.
" To them *indeed* he is precious ;" and, if they could have their
desire, they would love him, and serve him, and glorify him,
on earth, even as the glorified saints are doing it in heaven.   Is

this your experience, my beloved Brethren? Does the whole universe appear to you but " as a broken cistern," and is Christ the only fountain from whence you desire to draw? O that you may be able more and more to say, " All my fresh springs are in thee[h]!"]

3. How happy is the Christian's state—

[Doubtless there is a great diversity in men's attainments: there are babes, and young men, and fathers in the family of Christ. But in this there is a resemblance among them all: they are full of gratitude to their incarnate God: and all their hope is in his power and grace. They are also active in diffusing the knowledge of him. They will not spend their time in disputing about matters of doubtful disputation, whether relating to doctrines, or to sects and parties, but will labour to promote the glory of their God. Whether they be ministers or not, they will all be priests in their own families, and all be anxious to guide their friends and neighbours to the knowledge of the truth. Having experienced the life-giving virtue of that fountain, will they see their neighbours perishing with thirst, and not point it out? No: they will desire that others should " receive out of the fulness that is in Christ," and would have " all flesh to see the salvation of God."]

[h] Ps. lxxxvii. 7.

OUTLINE NO. 882

THE CHRISTIAN WARFARE.

Isai. xiv. 2. *They shall take them captives whose captives they were, and they shall rule over their oppressors.*

IN the midst of the prophecies relating to the deliverance of the Jews from Babylon, we shall find many expressions which necessitate us to look forward to some other event for their full accomplishment. The destruction of Babylon is undoubtedly the subject of this and of the preceding chapter. The whole forms one prophecy, abounding with the most beautiful imagery, and, in point of composition, equalling, if not excelling, the most admired poems of antiquity. But if we could confine the preceding part of this verse, and the verse before it, to that event, (which yet we cannot with any propriety,) what must we do with the words before us? *they* were never accomplished at that period: the Jews did not carry the

Babylonians into captivity; nor at any subsequent period did they rule over them. But if we understand these words as looking forward to another redemption, then will they be easy; and their accomplishment will be seen, not only in the Church at large, but in every individual member of it. The grace of Christ triumphed over all its opponents in the apostolic age; and will, in a yet more extensive manner, in the millennial period. The peculiar way in which his grace triumphs, is a subject worthy of our more particular attention: and the words of our text afford us a fit occasion for setting it before you. We shall,

I. Trace a work of grace on the souls of men—

Taking such a view of it as is suggested by our text, there are four distinct states in which the Christian will successively be found:—a state,

1. Of captivity—

[This is the state of every man, before the grace of God enters into his heart. The Jews in Babylon were not more enslaved than we are by nature. Our principles and actions are altogether in bondage to *the world*. Nothing appears so free as the mind: yet, in our natural state, we are so shackled with prejudice, that we cannot exercise it aright: we cannot apprehend truth, when it is proposed to us: "the things of the Spirit of God appear even foolishness to us; neither can we receive them," because our faculties are pre-occupied by the current sentiments of the world. Our ways too are under the same constraint. Custom has prescribed the paths in which we shall walk; and we dare not violate its arbitrary laws. Let us even see the light of a bright example set before us, we feel not ourselves at liberty to follow it. As far as fashion authorizes a holy life, we will go: we may perform a round of religious duties; but to cultivate real piety is contrary to our inclination, and beyond our power.

As the world by its maxims, so *sin* by its allurements, fetters and controuls us. So interwoven with all our faculties is sin, that we cannot resist its influence. Sooner might an Ethiopian change his complexion, or a leopard his spots, than the natural man break forth from the dominion of sin. Though he do not yield to it in a gross and shameless way, yet his thoughts and desires are altogether vitiated by it; nor is so much as one inclination or affection free from its malignant taint. A principle of evil resides within him, and dictates every imagination of his heart[a].

[a] Gen. vi. 5.

We may observe also, that *Satan* maintains a tyrannic sway over the natural man, as over his rightful vassal. How he works upon our minds, we cannot exactly say : (for we know not how our own spirit operates upon our material body; and therefore we must not wonder if we cannot declare how that wicked spirit operates on our spirits:) but he certainly does " work in all the children of disobedience," and " lead them captive at his will." And when the grace of God first comes into the soul, it finds us altogether under the power of " that strong man armed."]

2. Of conflict—

[The first entrance of grace into the soul stirs it up immediately to break its bonds, and assert its liberty. The person who is once enlightened to see what masters he has served, and what will be his recompence, is filled with indignation against himself for so long submitting to such ignominious bondage. He first probably begins with efforts made in his own strength : but when he finds how unavailing they are, he will betake himself to prayer, and implore help from above. Now the sins to which he once addicted himself are resisted ; and the very inclinations to them are bitterly bewailed. Now he cannot be satisfied with taking his notions of sin and duty from the world, or with conforming himself to the standard which the world approves : he inquires what God's will is, and determines to renounce whatever is inconsistent with it. Difficulties he meets with, innumerable difficulties, in his new course : his indwelling corruptions, like a stream obstructed by a dam, threaten to bear down all before them : and Satan exerts himself, by various wiles and devices, to divert him from his purpose : and the world, Satan's best advocate and co-adjutor, labours, by menaces or allurements, to keep him under its dominion : but he gathers strength from opposition, and courage from defeat ; and resolves, that nothing but victory or death shall put an end to his warfare.]

3. Of victory—

[No person will long continue to oppose his spiritual enemies, without reaping the fruit of his exertions in victory and triumph. After he has once learned to use the armour which God has prepared for him, he finds, to his unspeakable comfort, that none of his enemies can stand before him. The world, that was once so formidable, has lost its power : and neither sin nor Satan can deceive him, as they once did. The grace of Christ is now found sufficient for him : and though he still is violently assaulted with various temptations, he is enabled to repel them " by the shield of faith and the sword of the Spirit." Sometimes indeed he is ready to exclaim, " O wretched man that I am ! who shall deliver me ?" but soon he recollects himself, and adds, " I thank God through Jesus Christ our Lord."]

4. Of dominion—

[This is that state of which the text particularly speaks: and doubtless it is a state to which many attain. That the warfare will ever cease in this world, we have no reason to expect; but that our progress will be more easy, and our victory more certain, in proportion as we become habituated to the contest, there can be no doubt. As there are babes, young men, and fathers in the family of Christ, so are there amongst his army some, who have not only gained the victory, but are dividing the spoil. The world is crucified to them; sin is mortified, and Satan bruised under their feet. They are filled with a peace that passeth all understanding, and a joy that is unspeakable and glorified. The prize is, by anticipation at least, already in their hands. They enjoy already the earnest of heaven in their souls; and they are looking forward with delight to the happy hour, when they shall cease from their warfare altogether, and rest for ever in the bosom of their Lord.]

Though doubtless many variations will be found in the duration or degree in which the different parts of this experience exist in different persons, yet this, on the whole, is the experience of every true believer, he emerges from his natural bondage, and comes forth into the liberty of God's children. Such, I say, is the work of divine grace in the soul; and we shall now proceed to,

II. Make some observations upon it—

We remark then that this work is,

1. A stupendous work—

[None but God is equal to it. None but an Almighty Being could have created the universe out of nothing: nor can any other Being create anew the souls of men. Every good soldier of Jesus Christ must say, " He that hath wrought us to self-same thing, is God." The power exercised in this work is compared, by St. Paul, with that which was put forth in the resurrection of Christ, and his establishment on his throne, above all the principalities of heaven or hell[b]. Let all then who have within themselves an evidence that they are the subjects of it, rejoice: let them magnify their God in the energetic language of the Psalmist[c]: and let them " go forth, and shew what great things the Lord has done for them."]

2. An effectual work—

[b] Eph. i. 19—21.   [c] Ps. xxxv. 10.

[We wish not to discourage those who find difficulties in their warfare: but yet we must say, that God does not do his work by halves (if we may so express it). If he begin a good work in any soul, he will not suffer Satan to defeat his purpose. "He will give more and more grace," till it prove effectual to the end for which it is given. Grace that is not sufficient, (I mean, that does not finally prevail,) is not true grace. We know, that if a judgment be formed from the actual attainments of the religious world, we shall be ready to think that piety and carnality, and victory and bondage, can consist together. But they cannot; and those who with a religious profession unite an habitual subjection to any one sin, will feel themselves grievously disappointed in the issue. " They may dream of plaudits from their Judge; but he will say to them, " I never knew you, ye workers of iniquity." " The weapons of our warfare are sufficiently powerful to cast down all the strong-holds of Satan," and to bring even " our thoughts into captivity to the obedience of Christ:" the soldier therefore that yields to any one of his spiritual enemies, betrays his Lord; and for submitting to the chains of sin, will be bound " in chains of everlasting darkness."]

3. A work of which none need despair—

[A more desperate state than that described in the text, can scarcely be conceived: they were captives, and captives in a state of grievous oppression: yet they are not only delivered, but made to "rule over their very oppressors." Who then has any reason to despair? We may say perhaps, that our enemies are more powerful than those of others; that by our own consent they have acquired an indisputable right over us; and that therefore *we* cannot hope for deliverance. But God states, and answers, this very case[d]. And, not content with this, he makes his readiness to relieve such persons a prominent feature in his own character: as if he were especially to be known by it[e]. He makes his promises too to this very description of persons[f], as though he counted himself most glorified, when the weakness of his people has given the most scope for the exercise of his almighty power[g]. To the weakest then, and to the most desponding, we would say with the prophet, that though " without God the strongest of men should bow down under the prisoners, and fall under the slain[h]," yet " with him you shall be able to do all things[i]:" even " the lame shall take the prey[k]," and " the feet of the poor and of the needy shall tread down their mightiest enemies[l]."]

d Isai. xlix. 24—26.   e Amos. v. 9.   f Ps. lxxii. 4, 12, 13.
g 2 Cor. xii. 9.   h Isai. x. 4. Jer. xxxvii. 10.
i Phil. iv. 13.   k Isai. xxxiii. 23.   l Isai. xxvi. 5, 6.

OUTLINE NO. 883

IMMUTABILITY OF GOD'S COUNSELS.

Isai. xiv. 27. *The Lord of hosts hath purposed, and who shall disannul it? and his hand is stretched out, and who shall turn it back?*

IT is common with the Lord, when predicting distant events, to confirm men in the expectation of them by the accomplishment of something near at hand. Thus when God foretold the incarnation of his own Son by the Prophet Isaiah, he foretold also the speedy destruction of the ten tribes, that the fulfilment of the one might excite in their minds an expectation of the other[a]: and when to Hezekiah he promised an addition of fifteen years to his life, he caused the shadow on the sun-dial of Ahaz to recede ten degrees, as a sign that his life should certainly be prolonged to the period that had been fixed[b]. Thus, in the chapter from whence our text is taken, and in that which precedes it, a very full and minute prophecy of the destruction of Babylon, and of the consequent restoration of the Jews to their own land, is given two hundred years before it was to be accomplished. But there was another event of great importance speedily to take place, namely, the destruction of the Assyrian army before Jerusalem : this therefore is introduced, not merely as an independent prophecy, but as a near event, which would assure to them the accomplishment of those which were more remote. It is in reference to all these events that the immutability of God's purpose is so strongly declared in our text, but more especially to those events which constitute the main subject of the prophecy.

The immutability of God's decrees is confessedly a very deep and mysterious subject, which we would not enter upon but with fear and trembling. We do not approve of bringing it forward on every occasion, and making it, as some do, the great subject of our ministrations: but we do not feel at liberty to pass

[a] Isai. vii. 14—16.   [b] Isai. xxxviii. 7, 8.

it over as if we were afraid of it, or as if we thought the inspired writers had erred in ever bringing it before our eyes. Now that it lies clearly in our way, we will proceed to give it the attention it deserves. We will consider it,

I. In a general view—

The Scripture continually represents God as having ordained every thing from before the foundation of the world—

[St. James, before the whole college of apostles at Jerusalem, declared this as a truth unquestionably acknowledged by them all; "Known unto God are all his works, from the beginning of the world[c]." But, if they were known to him, they must be certain: and, if they were certain, it must be because he had ordained them so to be. Hence even the salvation of his people is said to be in consequence of his having elected them in Christ Jesus before the foundation of the world, and predestinated them to the adoption of children by Jesus Christ to himself. In this he is represented as acting solely according to his own sovereign will, for the praise of the glory of his own grace, in conformity with his own eternal counsels: and all who finally obtain an inheritance in heaven, are said to have been " predestinated according to the purpose of him who worketh all things after the counsel of his own will, that they should be to the praise of his glory[d]."

Now to conceal, or to explain away, such expressions as these, is certainly not right. That they involve many difficulties, is true; but there are difficulties also on that side of the question which denies the existence of God's decrees: and it is far safer and better to receive with humility the declarations of God which we cannot fully comprehend, than to set ourselves determinately against them, and to impose on them a sense which they were obviously not intended to bear. The man that receives them with childlike simplicity, cannot doubt their general import, though he may doubt respecting inferences which may appear to be deducible from them.]

His decrees, to whatever they relate, are unchangeable—

[This also is plainly and strongly declared in the Holy Scriptures. He has confirmed his word with an oath, on purpose that " *the immutability of his counsel* may be known[e]." If his purposes were changed, it must be either through the inward operation of his own mind, or through the outward operation of something else upon him: but in his own mind he

[c] Acts xv. 18.   [d] Eph. i. 4, 5, 6, 9, 11, 12.   [e] Heb. vi. 17.

is altogether unchangeable ; as he has said, " I the Lord change not[f]:" and St. James says, that " with him is no variableness, neither shadow of turning[g]" Nor can he be wrought upon by any thing from without : he cannot be deceived by subtlety ; for " there is no wisdom, nor understanding, nor counsel against the Lord[h]:" nor can he be constrained by force ; for " he doeth according to his will in the armies of heaven, and among the inhabitants of the earth ; nor can any stay his hand, or say unto him, what doest thou[i]?" In a word, " He is not a man that he should lie, or the son of man that he should repent : hath he said, and shall he not do it ? hath he spoken, and shall he not make it good[k]?" Yes, " His counsel shall stand ; and he will do all his pleasure[l]:" " He is in one mind, and who can turn him[m]?" "His counsel standeth for ever, and the thoughts of his heart to all generations[n]."]

Whatever difference of opinion may exist about the abstract question of the immutability of God's decrees, there will be found little difference about it,

II. In reference to the particular points specified in the context—

It is *the practical use* of this subject that renders it so interesting to the Church of God : and it is *in that view only* that we wish to impress it on our minds. It is introduced by the prophet in reference to two points :

1. The deliverance of God's people—

[The state of the Jews in Babylon was as hopeless as could well be conceived : but God foretold their deliverance from it, and their restoration to their own land ; and that, though captives, and grievously oppressed, "they should take them captives whose captives they were, and should rule over their oppressors[o]." This God declared to be irreversibly decreed.

Now the same is true respecting the deliverance and salvation of all the Lord's people, in every age and quarter of the world. As the Jews were his elect, so is there now " a remnant according to the election of grace[p];" a people whom he has given to his Son[q], and to whom, as viewed in him, he gave a " promise of eternal life, before the world began[r]." Now these he will search out, wherever they are, even amongst the remotest Gentiles[s]: and in due time he will call them by

---

f Mal. iii. 6.   g Jam. i. 17.   h Prov. xxi. 30.
i Dan. iv. 35.   k Numb. xxiii. 19.   l Isai. xlvi. 10.
m Job xxiii. 13.   n Ps. xxxiii. 11.   o ver. 1, 2.
p Rom. xi. 6.   q John xvii. 6, 9.   r Tit. i. 2.
s John x. 16.

his grace[t], and bring them to the saving knowledge of his truth[u]. These also will he keep, and not suffer so much as one of them ever to be lost[x]. For their full and complete salvation God has made abundant provision in his word. If ever they should perish, it must be through their own departure from him, or through their being wrested out of his hands, or by his casting them off: but on all these heads he has revealed his immutable purpose and decree. Is it apprehended that they will depart from him? He will " put his fear in their hearts, that they may not do so[y]." Is it feared that either men or devils may wrest them from him? He assures us that " none shall pluck them out of his hands[z]," or " separate them from his love[a]." Is it supposed possible that he himself may cast them off and forsake them? He gives the fullest possible assurance to them all, that he will not do so[b]; that " not one of his little ones shall perish[c];" and that, however sifted, " not the smallest grain among them shall ever fall to the ground[d]." Their state may appear distressing, and even desperate, for a time; but God will not abandon them to themselves[e]; for " all his promises to them are yea and Amen in Christ Jesus[f]."]

2. The destruction of his enemies—

[Babylon, just previous to its destruction, seemed capable of defying all its enemies: but it was destroyed, precisely at the time, and in the manner, and by the person, that had been foretold two hundred years before. Thus, how secure soever God's enemies at this day may think themselves, they shall assuredly perish at the appointed time.

Of the people of God we have spoken as God's elect: but we are not therefore to imagine of God's enemies, that they have from eternity been doomed to destruction. No: though we maintain, and have not a doubt about, the doctrine of election, we do not believe the doctrine of absolute reprobation. It is true, we do not know where to draw the line so as to answer all the questions that may be asked. We acknowledge that we are ignorant, and contentedly ignorant, of many things relating to this mysterious subject: but, in our apprehension, God's *oath*, " that he willeth not the death of any sinner, but rather that he should turn and live," is a satisfactory proof, that he has " not ordained any to wrath," except as the fruit and consequence of their own wickedness. We apprehend that the true distinction between the elect and non-elect is marked with admirable precision by the Apostle Peter; who speaks of

[t] Ezek. xxxiv. 11—13.   [u] Isai. lxv. 1.   [x] John xvii. 12.
[y] Jer. xxxii. 40.   [z] John x. 27—29.
[a] Rom. viii. 33—39.
[b] 1 Sam. xii. 22. Heb. xiii. 5, 6. The Greek.   [c] Matt. xviii. 14.
[d] Amos ix. 9.   [e] Isai. liv. 7—10.   [f] 2 Cor. i. 20.

the elect, as saved purely in consequence of God's eternal
choice; but of others, as perishing purely through their own
obstinate unbelief, to which God has irreversibly decreed a
sentence of eternal condemnation[g]. This is sufficiently plain,
that, if God be true, the unrighteous, and unregenerate, can
never enter into the kingdom of heaven[h]. We are ready to
think, that God will rescind his decrees in relation to this
matter; but he will not: he will not from pity; for however
we may knock, and cry, " Lord, Lord, open to us!" he will not
open the door; nor, when " weeping and wailing and gnashing
our teeth" with anguish, will he grant us so much as " a drop
of water at our request to cool our tongue." Nor shall any be
able to resist his will: for when he shall say, " Depart from
me, ye cursed, into everlasting fire," we cannot maintain our
ground one moment; nor, if we call on the rocks and mountains
to fall upon us, can they afford us the desired aid. Even in this
life the infliction of punishment is sometimes irreversibly decreed; and much more shall it be in that day, when God will
only laugh at our calamity, and execute upon us all the judgments which he has denounced against us[i].]

REFLECTIONS—

1. On what a slender foundation are the hopes of the generality fixed!

[A strange idea pervades the great mass of the Christian
world, that God will relax somewhat of his demands, and forbear to act agreeably to the strict tenour of his word: and, when
we urge upon their consciences the strictness of his precepts,
or the awfulness of his threatenings, they reply, ' God is too
merciful to act thus; we have no fear, but that he will relax
somewhat of these things in the day of judgment.' Thus they
hope that God's purposes shall change; and they contentedly
rest their everlasting salvation on this ground. What an
amazing infatuation is this! O, beloved, think well, ere you
determine to venture your everlasting happiness on such a presumption as this. Know that, in so doing, you absolutely bar
heaven against yourselves; and render it impossible for God
himself to save you. True, he can work faith in your hearts;
but he can never save you in unbelief: " he cannot deny himself;" and if you will not seek him in his appointed way of faith

---

[g] 1 Pet. ii. 7—9. The words in italics, ver. 8. should be omitted,
and the word Οἱ be translated *These*. Then the contrast observable
in that whole passage will be complete. There is a double antithesis :
Ὑμῖν οὖν πιστεύουσιν—ἀπειθοῦσι δὲ — — — οἱ προσκόπτουσι—ὑμεῖς
δὲ — —. See Doddridge's note on the place.

[h] 1 Cor. vi. 9. John iii. 3, 5. [i] Prov. i. 24—31. Ezek. xxiv. 13, 14.

and holiness, there " remains nothing for you but a fearful looking for of judgment and fiery indignation, to consume you[k]."]

2. On what an immoveable foundation does the believer stand;

[You are fixed upon a rock, against which the gates of
hell shall never prevail. We suppose indeed that you are not
affecting to trust in God, whilst you are negligent in the use
of his appointed means: (*that* would be to trust, not *in God,
but in a presumptuous unfounded conceit of your own:*) but,
if you are " fleeing to Christ for refuge," then are you safe in
God's everlasting arms; and he desires that you should be
assured of this: yea, it is for this very end that he has confirmed his promise with an oath, even that you might be
assured of the immutability of his counsel, and be filled with
the stronger and richer consolation[l]. If a sense of your own
weakness and unworthiness discourage you; then know that
" God is able to perform all that he has promised," and that
the consideration of his power and faithfulness is the very
antidote which he himself has provided for all your fears[m].]

[k] Heb. x. 26, 27.   [l] Heb. vi. 17.   [m] Isai. xlix. 24, 25.

OUTLINE NO. 884

GOD'S CHURCH AND PEOPLE SECURE.

Isai. xiv. 32. *What shall one then answer the messengers of the
nation? That the Lord hath founded Zion, and the poor of
his people shall trust in it.*

GOD is for the most part overlooked in the
government of the world: and hence arise an over-
confidence among some, and an undue timidity
amongst others. But, if we viewed God as ordering
and overruling every thing, even to the falling of a
sparrow, we should undertake nothing ourselves
without a direct reference to him; nor fear what was
undertaken by others, whilst we had him for our protector. This is the great lesson which we are taught
in the passage which we have now read. The context
contains a prophecy respecting the fate of Palestine.
The Philistines had been invaded and conquered by
King Uzziah[a]; but in the days of Ahaz, Uzziah's son,

[a] 2 Chron. xxvi. 6.

they had regained their cities, and made reprisals on the provinces of the Jewish monarch[b]. At the accession of Hezekiah to the throne of Judah, they hoped to make yet further inroads on the Jewish territory: and the Prophet Isaiah was inspired to foretell, that they should not only fail in their attempts, but be utterly vanquished by him, whom they so fondly thought to subdue and subjugate.

Read the passage in this view, and the whole address will appear extremely spirited and beautiful. " Rejoice not thou, whole Palestina, because the rod of him that smote thee is broken;" (i. e. because thou hast triumphed over Uzziah's son:) " for out of the serpent's root shall come forth a cockatrice, or adder; and his fruit shall be a fiery flying serpent." (Uzziah bit thee only as a common serpent: but his grandson Hezekiah shall inflict a wound as fatal as an adder; and prove as irresistible as a fiery flying serpent.) " And the first-born of the poor (Jews, whom thou hast so oppressed) shall feed, and the needy (whom thou hast so terrified) shall lie down in safety: whilst thy root shall be destroyed by famine, and thy remnant with the sword." (Instead then of rejoicing, " Howl, O gate; cry, O city; thou whole Palestina art dissolved: for there shall come from the north (Judea) a smoke (and dust of an army in full march:) and none shall be alone (or decline serving in this army) at the appointed time." (In the mean time,) " what shall one then answer the messengers of the nation," (when they come, full of alarm and terror[c], announcing thy preparations to invade the land of Judah?) Answer, " that the Lord hath founded Zion: and the poor of his people shall trust in it;" and that no weapon ever formed against them shall prosper.

The words thus explained we shall consider as proclaiming,

[b] 2 Chron. xxviii. 18.

[c] The general interpretation of their being *foreign ambassadors sent to congratulate* Hezekiah, enervates the whole force of the passage, and is in opposition to the text itself, which speaks of them as the messengers of *the nation*, and not of foreign nations.

I. An unquestionable fact—

" God has founded Zion "—

[He has founded it *in his eternal counsels;* and he has founded it also *in his covenant engagements.* He determined from all eternity that he would have a Church and People from amongst the sinners of mankind ; and that he would get glory to himself from the introduction of sin into this lower world. For this end he entered into covenant with his co-equal, co-eternal Son; and engaged, that if he would become a man, and " make his own soul an offering for sin," he should have from amongst our fallen race, a people, who should be his purchased possession, and should for ever shew forth his praise[d]. This covenant being made, he gave to his Son " a multitude, whom no man can number, out of all nations, and kindreds, and people, and tongues ;" and agreed to accomplish in them all his good pleasure, and to bring them in due season to the full possession of that glory, which by their transgressions they had lost. To this the Lord Jesus Christ repeatedly refers, declaring, that he was invested with " power to give eternal life to as many as the Father had *given him*[e]:" and *under this character* the Lord Jesus Christ prayed for them[f], and committed them into the Father's hands to be kept for him[g], and declared his assured expectation of having them, in due time, as the trophies of his grace, and the partners of his glory[h].]

" The poor of his people also shall trust in it"—

[God never leaves his chosen people to trust in themselves : he never has done it : he never will do it. From the beginning he has made them to feel their need of a Saviour; and has caused them to build on " that foundation which he has laid in Zion." The institution of sacrifices even in Paradise (for we doubt not but that the beasts, with the skins of which our first parents were clothed by God himself, had been offered in sacrifice to God) taught them from the beginning to rely, not on themselves, but on a sacrifice which should in due time be offered : and his grace has invariably wrought to the production of this one effect, according to that declaration of the prophet, " Behold, I lay in Zion for a foundation, a stone, a tried stone, a precious corner-stone, a sure foundation; and he that believeth shall not make haste, or, as St. Paul interprets it, shall not be ashamed[i]."]

But in the text there is also contained,

II. An instructive lesson—

It teaches us,

[d] Isai. liii. 10.   [e] John xvii. 2.   [f] John xvii. 9.   [g] John xvii. 11.
[h] John xvii. 24.   [i] Isai. xviii. 16. with Rom. ix. 33.

1. That our trust must be on God alone—

[To none can we look, but to our Covenant God and Saviour. There is no other foundation, but that which God has laid[k]; nor any other name whereby a human being can be saved, but the name of Jesus Christ[l]. Hence his invitation, " Look unto ME, and be ye saved, all the ends of the earth[m]." Hence also that solemn declaration, " I am the way, the truth, and the life: no man cometh unto the Father, but by me[n]." To confide in the creature, is to entail only a curse upon ourselves[o] Whence was it that the Jews, with all their earnestness in following after righteousness, could never attain it? It was, because they would rely upon themselves, and not seek it by a simple exercise of faith on the Lord Jesus Christ[p]. So it will be with us also, if our reliance be not altogether on the providence and grace of God: for what God said to his people respecting the Egyptians, he says to us; " The creature shall help in vain, and to no purpose: therefore have I cried concerning this, Their strength is to sit still[q]."]

2. That confidence in him shall never be disappointed—

[When it is said in our text, " The poor of his people shall trust in it," the meaning evidently is, that by so doing they shall be secure. And certain it is, that " the name of the Lord is a strong tower; and that the righteous runneth to it and is safe." Find in the whole annals of the world one person who, when trusting in God, was disappointed of his hope. Did Manasseh rely on *the mercy* of God? He, even he, obtained pardon. Did Asa, or Jehoshaphat, or Hezekiah, rely on *the power* of God? No enemy could withstand them. Did Abraham believe in *the truth and faithfulness* of God? The long-expected seed was given to him, that became " as the stars of heaven for number, and as the sands upon the sea-shore innumerable." Thus shall every one be blessed who putteth his trust in God: " he shall be firm, and immoveable as Mount Zion itself, which cannot be removed, but abideth for ever[r]." The question, " Who ever put his trust in God and was confounded?" never has been, and never can be answered, but in a way of universal negation.]

The text should be yet further viewed as,

III. A consoling truth—

It is unspeakably consoling,

1. In reference to the Church at large—

k 1 Cor. iii. 11.   l Acts iv. 12.   m Isai. xlv. 22.
n John xiv. 6.   o Jer. xvii. 5.   p Rom. ix. 30—32.
q Isai. xxx. 7.   r Ps. cxxv. 1.

[Many are the enemies of the Church at this day, as well as in former times: nor were the Philistines half so envious at the prosperity of Zion, as millions of Christians, so called, are at this very hour. But when the Church was in its infancy, and had all the power and policy both of Jews and Gentiles combined against it, it stood as a rock, that defies all the efforts of the tempestuous ocean. The waves that menace its existence are dashed in pieces at its feet. So shall it still be to the end of time: whatever confederacies are formed against the Church shall come to nought: for " it is founded on a rock; and the gates of hell shall not prevail against it."]

2. In reference to the poorest and weakest of its members—

[The chief of its members are characterized as "a poor and afflicted people, who trust in the name of the Lord[s]: and their conscious weakness often proves to them a source of great discouragement. But how consoling is the truth, that *they* are pre-eminently destined to receive the benefits of Christ's heavenly mission[t], and to be the objects of his peculiar care[u]! It is under the very character of persons poor and weak and destitute, that they are designated as triumphing over all their enemies; (" the foot shall tread them down, even the feet of the poor, and the steps of the needy[x]:") and their weakness is described as carried to the utmost extent than can be imagined, even as resembling that of persons wounded, and captive, and dead: and yet in that very state is success insured to them; for " though lame, they shall take the prey[y];" " though captives, they shall take those captive whose captives they were, and shall rule over their oppressors[z];" and though slain, they shall rise and overcome, and " their enemies shall fall under the slain[a]." Hence the weakest amongst them all, " knowing in whom he has believed," may adopt the triumphant language of the prophet, " The Lord God will help me; therefore shall I not be confounded: therefore have I set my face like a flint, and I know that I shall not be ashamed. He is near that justifieth me: who will contend with me? Let us stand together: who is mine adversary? let him come near to me. Behold, the Lord God will help me: who is he that shall condemn me? lo, they all shall wax old as doth a garment; the moth shall eat them up[b]."]

APPLICATION—

[Look then, Brethren, to the Scriptures, to see what God has done in former ages — — — See what instruction is to be

[s] Zeph. iii. 12.	[t] Isai. lxi. 1—3.	[u] Isai. xl. 11.
[x] Isai. xxvi. 6	[y] Isai. xxxiii. 23.	[z] Isai. xiv. 2.
[a] Isai. x. 4.	[b] Isai. l. 7—9.	

gathered from those records, for your own conduct — — —
And know, that God is as ready to "perfect his own strength
in your weakness," as he has been in any instance from the
foundation of the world — — — Only realize the thought of
his universal agency in the government of the world, and of his
watchful care over the interests of his peculiar people ; and
then "you need not fear, though the earth be moved, and the
mountains be carried into the midst of the sea[c]." See David's
composure amidst such troubles as drove his friends to despair:
"In the Lord," says he, "put I my trust: how say ye then to
my soul, Flee as a bird to your mountain; for, lo! the wicked
bend their bow; they make ready their arrow upon the string,
that they may privily shoot at the upright in heart; and, if the
foundations be destroyed, what can the righteous do?" What?
"The Lord is in his holy temple: the Lord's throne is in
heaven:" and *that* is ample security for me[d]. Such composure may you also, even the least and weakest of you, enjoy, if
you confide in God: for "there is no wisdom nor counsel
against the Lord[e];" but "*his* counsel shall stand; and he will
do all his will[f]."]

[c] Ps. xlvi. 2.	[d] Ps. xi. 1—4.
[e] Prov. xxi. 30.	[f] Isai. xlvi. 10.

OUTLINE NO. 885

CHRIST A GREAT SAVIOUR.

Isai. xix. 20. *They shall cry unto the Lord because of the
oppressors, and He shall send them a Saviour, and a great
One, and he shall deliver them.*

GOD usually vouchsafes his mercies when we are
reduced to the greatest straits. This is manifest in
his most remarkable dispensations of providence and
of grace. In the greatest extremity God promised to
send a deliverer to Egypt[a]. But there is a further
reference to Christ as the Saviour of the Gentile

[a] In this view it seems applicable to the angel who slew 185,000
of Sennacherib's army : for, though that deliverance was more immediately vouchsafed to the Jews under Hezekiah, yet in its consequences it extended to Egypt. Sennacherib had before conquered
and ravaged Egypt ; and it was most probable that if he had taken
Jerusalem he would have again proceeded thither with his victorious
army, and reduced that already desolated kingdom to the lowest ebb
of misery. But perhaps there may be a further reference to some
other deliverers.

world[b]; and it is in seasons of heavy dejection that He reveals himself to them: to him therefore we must look as the Saviour foretold in the text.

I. In what respects He is " a great Saviour"—

It is justly said by the Psalmist that " his greatness is unsearchable[c]; nevertheless we may, not unprofitably, endeavour to illustrate it.

He is great when considered *in his own person*—

[He has a name above every name either on earth or in heaven. He is exalted to be a Prince that can give repentance and remission of sins[d]. The voice of inspiration calls him, " the great God and our Saviour[e]." He speaks of himself in terms of similar import[f]; nor can any thing be more glorious than the description given of him by the prophet[g]. This Saviour, " though a man, thinks it not robbery to be equal with God[h]." He is " God manifest in the flesh[i]," even "God over all blessed for ever[k]."]

He is also great in respect of *the salvation he has wrought out for us*—

[Who can count the number of the sins from which he has delivered us? ——— or estimate the misery from which he has redeemed us? ——— Through our whole lives we have been heaping up treasures of wrath[l]. Yet is there no condemnation to us if we be interested in him[m]; besides, he has purchased for us an eternal inheritance in heaven. Who can estimate all that is there enjoyed? ——— We must know all the glories of heaven and the horrors of hell, before we can fully appreciate the greatness of his salvation.]

But before we speak peace to ourselves, it becomes us to inquire,

II. For whose deliverance he is sent—

Great as his mercy is, it will not indiscriminately extend to all. They, for whose relief he comes, are " oppressed" with the burthen of sin—

[The generality, alas! are well contented with their bondage. If he should offer to deliver them, they would thrust him from them, as the Israelites of old did their saviour Moses[n].

---

b This appears from the whole context, ver. 18—25.
c Ps. cxlv. 3.   d Acts v. 31.   e Tit. ii. 13.
f Isai. xlv. 22.   g Isai. ix. 6.   h Phil. ii. 6.
i 1 Tim. iii. 16.   k Rom. ix. 5.   l Rom. ii. 5.
m Rom. viii. 1.   n Acts vii. 37, 39.

But there are some who mourn like the saints of old[o]. They desire nothing so much as to be delivered from their corruptions———For these Jesus came down from heaven, and died upon the cross———Nor, though they be lawful captives, will he leave them in the hand of their enemies[p].]

They at the same time "cry earnestly to the Lord" for deliverance—

[There are some, it must be confessed, who are uneasy in their sins, yet do not with fervour and constancy implore his mercy[q]———Such therefore, notwithstanding their uneasiness, obtain no help from him. His mercy is promised to those alone who seek it with importunity[r]. But humble and believing suppliants shall never be rejected by him——— They shall find him a great, compassionate, and all-sufficient Saviour———]

APPLICATION—

[Are any among you *unconcerned about their sins?* O! reflect on your state. Would God have sent you *such* a Saviour, if your condition had not required it? Or, will you take occasion from this stupendous grace, to live more securely in your sins? O! consider that your cries, however available now, will soon, if delayed, become of no effect[s].

Are others of you *conflicting with sin and Satan?* Lift up your heads with joy. However desperate your state may seem, your redemption draweth nigh, nor shall all the powers of darkness rescue you from your Redeemer's hands[t].

Are there here any *who have experienced deliverance?* Adore your Lord, and go on, "strong in the grace that is in Christ Jesus." Only commit yourselves entirely to him, and you shall join in eternal Hallelujahs to God and to the Lamb.]

[o] Isai. vi. 5. Rom. vii. 24.   [p] Isai. xlix. 24, 25.
[q] Ps. xxxii. 3, 4. Hos. vii. 14.   [r] Matt. vii. 7. Ezek. xxxvi. 37.
[s] Luke xvi. 24, 25.   [t] John x. 28.

OUTLINE NO. 886

THE CONVERSION OF JEWS AND GENTILES.

Isai. xix. 24, 25. *In that day shall Israel be the third with Egypt and with Assyria, even a blessing in the midst of the land; whom the Lord of hosts shall bless, saying, Blessed be Egypt my people, and Assyria the work of my hands, and Israel mine inheritance.*

THERE is among God's ancient people an idea, that, so far from their nation being converted to Christianity, the whole world is, in due season, to be converted to Judaism. Nor do we wonder much that this error should obtain amongst them; since, in the prophetic writings, the change which is to be wrought upon the Gentiles is very generally described in terms taken from the Jewish Law. This is peculiarly observable in the passage before us, where Assyria and Egypt, the representatives of God's enemies in all ages, are spoken of as " raising an altar to the Lord," and " offering sacrifices thereon;" and " making vows unto the Lord," and " swearing by his name;" and as " raising up to him a pillar," such as the Israelites formed after their passage through Jordan, " to be a sign and a witness to the Lord" that they were his redeemed people, and that he alone was their God[a]. But a more thorough knowledge of their prophecies would convince them, that they are to enjoy a far different dispensation · from that of Moses—a dispensation, not of works, but of grace; a dispensation, suited not to one small nation only, but to Egyptians and Assyrians, and to every people under heaven. In fact, though legal terms are here used to express the piety which shall characterize the latter day, it is of that day that my text speaks, when " all the kingdoms of the world shall become the kingdom of our Lord and of his Christ;" and it is in this view that God expresses such satisfaction in it.

Let us consider,

I. The event in which God expresses such delight—

It is the conversion of the whole world to God—

[Egypt and Assyria, and the whole Gentile world, when the Lord Jesus Christ shall be erected as a standard in the midst of them, shall flock to it from every quarter; and, together with the outcasts of Israel, and the dispersed of Judah, form one universal Church, " one fold under one Shepherd[b]." " With Assyria and Egypt shall Israel be a third, even a blessing in the midst of the land." Hitherto, " the Israelites have only been a curse in the different countries over which they have been dispersed[c]:" for whilst they have been universally

---

[a] See these different expressions, ver. 18—21.
[b] Compare ver. 23, 24. with xi. 10—12, 15, 16.
[c] Zech. viii. 13.

execrated, they have been a snare to their enemies, and an occasion of greatly aggravating their guilt. But "in that day
will they prove a blessing" to all amongst whom they dwell:
they will prove a blessing, *as examples* "whose conversion will
be as life from the dead to the whole world [d]:" they will prove
a blessing, too, *as instruments*, who, being themselves converted, "will declare God's glory amongst the Gentiles," and,
like the priests of old, present thousands and millions of them
as free-will offerings upon God's altar [e]. We all know of what
use the showers are which descend upon the face of the earth,
wheresoever God is pleased to send them: and precisely that
office are the Jews, now dispersed over the earth, in due season
destined to perform [f]. The whole process is well described by
the Prophet Zechariah, who says, that "many people and
strong nations shall come to seek the Lord of Hosts in Jerusalem, every one of them taking hold of the skirt of him that
is a Jew, saying, We will go with you; for we have heard that
God is with you [g]."]

In this event God will greatly rejoice—
[To this effect he has said, " I create Jerusalem a rejoicing, and her people a joy: and *I will rejoice in Jerusalem, and
joy in my people* [h]." The expressions in my text are peculiarly
striking to this effect: " The Lord of Hosts shall bless all his
converts, saying, Blessed be Egypt my people, and Assyria
the work of my hands, and Israel mine inheritance." All will
be regarded by him with peculiar affection, whilst yet his people
Israel shall possess their original and distinctive honour, as
" his peculiar people," the lot of his inheritance [i]." But
when God pronounces these "blessed," he makes them so:
he makes them blessed by the richest communications of
his grace, his mercy, and his peace: and in due season he
will consummate their blessedness in the fullest possible enjoyment of his presence and glory. Such is the blessedness
prepared for all who believe in Christ, whatever may have
been their former state. We may have been as hostile to
Christ as the superstitious Jews, or as far from him as the
idolatrous Gentiles; and yet, if we embrace and obey the
Gospel, this blessedness shall be ours.]

And is this event now fast approaching? Let us
then consider,
II. The effect which the prospect of it should produce
on us—
Surely we should not be insensible to it. No: it
should prevail,

[d] Rom. xi. 12, 15.   [e] Isai. lxvi. 19, 20, 21.   [f] Mic. v. 7.
[g] Zech. viii. 20—23.   [h] Isai. lxv. 18, 19.   [i] Deut. xxxii. 9.

1. To enlarge our philanthropy—

[We are, for the most part, very narrow and contracted in our regards for our fellow men. Rarely do we feel much for any, except our own immediate neighbours, or those in whose welfare we have some personal interest. And even then, it is for their temporal, rather than their spiritual welfare that we are chiefly concerned. But we ought to extend our regards to the whole family of man dispersed throughout the earth; and, above all, to feel for their eternal interests. Behold how Jehovah expresses himself in our text. One would have thought that the great oppressors of his people, Egypt and Assyria, might have been excepted from his benevolent regards; but we find he contemplates their return to him with the utmost complacency and delight. Thus, then, should it be with you. You should be like-minded with God in this holy feeling. The whole world, whether Jews or Gentiles, should be objects of your deepest solicitude. To see them ignorant of God and his Christ, should fill you with pain: and to have a prospect of their conversion, should excite in you the liveliest joy. Let me not be mistaken: I would not have your neighbours overlooked, either in relation to their temporal or their eternal interests: but I would have your hearts expanded, even as God's is, to embrace the whole family of man: and, as the conversion of their souls to God is, beyond all comparison, the most important object, I would have *that* to occupy the chief place in your minds.]

2. To raise our expectations—

[We think it almost impossible to enlighten the minds of the idolatrous Gentiles; and we quite ridicule the idea of converting the bigoted and superstitious Jews. But the work shall be done: for the prophet says, "If this be marvellous in your eyes, should it also be marvellous in mine eyes? saith the Lord of Hosts[k]." Beloved Brethren, not only is this event certain, but it is also near. Between two and three thousand years ago, the Prophet Isaiah had such clear views of it, that he saw it through this long vista, exhibited as it were before his eyes: "Lift up thine eyes round about, and behold: all these gather themselves together, and come to thee. As I live, saith the Lord, thou shalt surely clothe thee with them all as with an ornament, and bind them on thee as a bride doth . . . . Thou shalt say in thine heart, Who hath begotten me these, seeing I have lost my children, and am desolate, a captive, and removing to and fro? and who hath brought up these? Behold, I was left alone: these, where had they been[l]?" "Who are these that fly as doves to their windows[m]?" Now,

---

[k] Zech. viii. 6.   [l] Isai. xlix. 18, 21.   [m] Isai. lx. 8.

did the prophet in his day see it realized before his eyes, and shall not we, now that the time is so nearly come? Dear Brethren, you may already see " a stir among the dry bones, through the whole valley of vision: and it is yet but a very little time, and the Spirit of God shall breathe upon them, and they shall live, a whole army[n]." Yes, I can confidently say, " It is now but a very little while, and Lebanon shall be turned into a fruitful field, and the fruitful field shall be esteemed as a forest[o]."]

3. To quicken our exertions—

[In every age has God carried on his work, through the instrumentality of men. What were the Prophets or the Apostles, but Ministers, by whom he accomplished the purposes of his grace? And so, at this time, he appeals to us respecting the ignorant and ungodly world, " How shall they hear without a preacher[p]?" You will say, perhaps, " We cannot all be preachers." True; but there is much which may be done by every one amongst us. We may all comply with that direction of the prophet, " Lift up thy prayer for the remnant that is left." Yes, we may all "pray for the peace and welfare of Jerusalem." In fact, we are commanded, not only to pray, but to give God no rest, till he establish and make Jerusalem a praise in the earth[q]." We may also contribute, each according to his ability, to further those means which are employed, of circulating through the world the Scriptures of truth, and of sending Missionaries also to instruct mankind. The command given by our Lord was, " to go forth into all the world, and to preach the Gospel to every creature." But how can persons go at their own cost? If a warfare against a hostile nation be determined, we never think of men going to maintain it at their own cost. Nor is it to be supposed that now persons should wage war against all the powers of darkness, and go forth to rescue the millions whom they hold in bondage, if they be not aided in their efforts by the contributions of their brethren. In this way, then, all may exert themselves in the common cause: and if our blessed Lord gave up himself to the most cruel death for the salvation of the world, methinks we, who have been partakers of his mercy, should use our efforts, in every possible way, to extend the knowledge of Him through the world; and never to rest, till " all shall know Him, from the least to the greatest," and " all flesh shall see the salvation of God."]

[n] Ezek. xxxvii. 7—10. [o] Isai. xxix. 17.
[p] Rom. x. 14. [q] Isai. lxii. 6, 7.

OUTLINE NO. 887

PROFANE SCOFFERS INSTRUCTED.

Isai. xxi. 11, 12. *The burden of Dumah. He calleth to me out of Seir, Watchman, what of the night? Watchman, what of the night? The watchman said, The morning cometh, and also the night. If ye will inquire, inquire ye: return, come.*

THIS portion of holy writ is justly considered as very obscure; and the more so, because we are not aware of any records of history that will reflect light upon it. The learned Vitringa conceives the scope of the prophecy to be this: that, on occasion of some heavy calamity inflicted either on the Assyrians or Chaldeans in common with the Jews, an inhabitant of Edom inquired of the prophet what the duration of the trouble should be: and then he supposes the prophet to answer, that, as far as respected the Jews, a morning of relief was at hand: but that to Edom there was coming a night of long and heavy affliction. But on such an interpretation, the severe answer of the prophet seems uncalled for. I should rather confine the whole subject to Idumea: and then the question of the Edomite, and the answer of the prophet, will be natural, and perfectly consistent. It is well known that the Prophet Isaiah foretold the fate of Edom, as well as of all the other nations around Judea; and that he predicted the heaviest calamities to them all. Now, I suppose an Edomite unbelievingly and contemptuously to ask, " Watchman, what of the night? Watchman, what of the night?" that is, ' You, as placed on a watch-tower, presume to declare what shall befall our nation: tell me how long is it before these calamities, which you predict, shall come upon us?' To this question the prophet answers, ' You will have yet a " morning" of prosperity: but, I can assure you, it shall be succeeded by a long "night" of heavy adversity. If you really desire to be informed, in order to avert, by penitence, the threatened calamity, follow up your inquiries in a becoming spirit: " return" to God, whom you have forsaken; and " come"

to Him, from whom you have deeply revolted. Then
there may yet be hope both concerning you and your
nation.'

In this view of the prophecy, we see,

I. In what way men treat the Divine testimony—

The spirit shewn by the inquiring Edomite is precisely that which has obtained in every age, and which
the Apostle Peter teaches us to expect as still more
prevalent in the latter days: " There shall come, in
the last days, scoffers, walking after their own lusts,
and saying, Where is the promise of his coming? for
since the fathers fell asleep, all things continue as they
were from the beginning of the creation[a]." This, I
apprehend, was the way in which the predictions of
Noah relative to the deluge were treated by the
scoffers in the antediluvian world: and persons of a
similar spirit abounded in Isaiah's days; whom he
describes as teeming with atheistical defiance, and
saying, " Let him make speed, and hasten his work,
that we may see it; and let the counsel of the Holy
One of Israel draw nigh and come, that we may know
it[b]." To such an extent did this impiety prevail in
the time of Ezekiel, that God speaks of it as actually
passed into a proverb: " Son of man, what is that
proverb that ye have in the land of Israel, saying,
The days are prolonged, and every vision faileth?"
And it is worthy of particular observation, that the
answer which Ezekiel was commanded to give to the
scoffers of Israel, is precisely to the same effect with
that which Isaiah had given to the Idumean inquirer:
" Tell them, thus saith the Lord God; I will make
this proverb to cease; and they shall no more use it
as a proverb in Israel: but say unto them, The days
are at hand, and the effect of every vision[c]."

Thus it is that men treat the Divine testimony at
this day: they speak of it,

1. With unbelieving indifference—

[As God's ambassadors to a guilty world, we are constrained
to denounce his judgments against impenitent transgressors

---

[a] 2 Pet. iii. 3, 4.　　[b] Isai. v. 19.　　[c] Ezek. xii. 22, 23.

— — — But how is our testimony received by them? Have
we not reason to take up the lamentation which was first uttered
by the Prophet Isaiah, and was afterwards repeated both by the
Lord Jesus Christ and his servant Paul, " Who hath believed
our report? and to whom hath the arm of the Lord been revealed[d]?" It is in vain that we bring forth either the declarations of Jehovah, or positive instances of their accomplishment:
the prevailing idea is, that men, however they may live, have
nothing to fear; for that God is too merciful to inflict punishment on them, and especially the punishment of everlasting
torments, which no actions of ours can be reasonably supposed
to merit. Full of this erroneous conceit, they become settled on
their lees, and say, in their hearts at least, if not also with their
lips, " The Lord will not do good, neither will he do evil[e]."]

2. With contemptuous levity—

[This, I apprehend, was the real feeling expressed in those
interrogations, " Watchman, what of the night? Watchman,
what of the night?" In the same manner was the Apostle Paul
regarded as a " babbler," unworthy of any thing but derision.
His discourse, which almost converted King Agrippa to the
faith, brought to Festus no other conviction than this: " Paul,
thou art beside thyself; much learning doth make thee mad[f]".
And even the Lord Jesus Christ himself, who " spake as never
man spake," was considered as unfit for any person of respec-
tability to hear: " He hath a devil, and is mad: why hear ye
him[g]?" Is it to be wondered at, then, if those who faithfully
preach the Gospel be still at this day branded with opprobrious
names, and their message be considered only as " a cunningly
devised fable?" It must be so, as long as there shall be a
carnal man on earth: for " the things of the Spirit are foolishness to him;" and those who live only to proclaim and propagate those things, can appear to him in no other light than fools.
If, like Ezekiel, we have boldness to deliver God's messages to
men, we shall be sure to have applied to our ministrations the
same contemptuous observation as was made on his, " Ah!
Lord God, doth he not speak parables[h]?"]

The prophet's answer to his scoffing inquirers
shews us,

II. In what way they themselves should be treated—

It is good, in many cases, to " answer a fool according to his folly." But there are cases (and particularly
where the eternal interests of men are at stake,) in
which we should " not answer a fool according to his

---

[d] Isai. liii. 1. John xii. 37, 38. Rom. x. 16.   [e] Zeph. i. 12.
[f] Acts xxvi. 24.   [g] John x. 20.   [h] Ezek. xx. 49.

folly[i]," but should give him such counsel and admonition as his necessities require. Mark the conduct of the prophet on this occasion:

1. His admonition—

[He tells the inquirer, that, though his countrymen should yet have a season of prosperity, a night of fearful adversity awaited them. And this is the answer which I must make to the profane scoffer, or the careless unbeliever: ' You may go on prosperously for a season; you may have riches in the world; you may account yourselves happy, and be so accounted by all your carnal friends: but, though your day may be bright and long, as in the height of summer, a night, a long and fearful night, will come at last. O! how terrible will be that night, which shall never be irradiated with so much as a single gleam of hope! Yet such is the state that awaits you: for, for you " is reserved the blackness of darkness for ever[k]."' It may seem at present to be at a great distance; but every day and hour brings it nearer to you; and at the appointed hour it will commence. Yes: St. Peter tells us, that " now of a long time your judgment lingereth not, and your damnation slumbereth not[l]." Whilst men " refuse to turn, God whets his sword, and bends his bow, and ordains his arrows against them" for their destruction[m]. And the very interval that is allowed them is only given that they may " fill up the measure of their iniquities," and have " his wrath come upon them to the uttermost." Their present prosperity is only like the rich pasture to flocks and herds, whereby " they are nourished for the day of slaughter[n]." Happy, happy is the brute creation, which, if taken in an unexpected hour, survives not the stroke that takes them hence! But let us reflect a moment on that hour when a profane scoffer, or a careless unbeliever, shall open his eyes in the eternal world. He has buoyed himself up with the hope that he should see the face of his God in peace: but how will he shrink back at the sight of an angry God! What a shriek will he utter, that shall be heard through the vast expanse of hell; when, instead of a listless and unobservant Deity, as he had pictured to himself, he shall see a holy God filled with wrath and fiery indignation, and prepared to execute all the judgments which he had denounced against him! I must, I must warn you, my beloved Brethren, that these are indeed the true sayings of God; and, whether believed or not, they shall be verified ere long: for " God will be true; and every man," that contradicts him, " will be found a liar."]

2. His counsel—

[i] Prov. xxvi. 4, 5. [k] Jude, ver. 13. [l] 2 Pet. ii. 8.
[m] Ps. vii. 12, 13. [n] Jam. v. 5.

[Not even the scoffer should be dismissed without such counsel, as, if duly received, may operate a saving change upon his soul. The prophet here says to the inquiring Edomites, " If ye will inquire seriously, inquire ye; returning" from your evil ways, and " coming" humbly and believingly to your God. So say I to you. If there be amongst you any who really desire to know the purposes of heaven, come; and, as God's watchman, I will, to the best of my power, instruct you. And this in particular will I declare to you, that if only you will return to God, your past iniquities shall not be your ruin." Hear what God himself said to the Prophet Jeremiah : " Go, and proclaim these words toward the north, and say, Return, thou backsliding Israel; and I will not cause my anger to fall upon you . . . . Turn unto me; for I am married unto you . . . . Return, ye backsliding children, and I will heal your backslidings." And the very instant that they replied, " Behold, we come unto thee; for thou art the Lord our God;" the prophet was commanded to say, " If thou wilt return, O Israel, saith the Lord, return unto me°." This fully explains the words, " Return, come." In all the Scriptures there is not a single word that tends to the discouragement of a returning sinner. No : the whole sacred volume says, Come, come, come : "The Spirit and the Bride say, Come : and let him that heareth say, Come : and whosoever will, let him come, and take of the water of life freely." And lest we should suppose that any sin whatever shall prove a bar to the acceptance of a returning penitent, our blessed Saviour expressly says, " Him that cometh unto me, I will in no wise cast out." This counsel, then, I would affectionately give to you, " Inquire ; Return; Come."]

But that this counsel may be better understood, I will now, in CONCLUSION, address you more at length.

1. Be serious in your inquiries into the truth of God—

[Inquire after nothing in a light, contemptuous manner : " Be ye not mockers, lest your bands be made strong." Nor make any inquiry with indifference; like Pilate, when he asked of our Lord, " What is truth ?" and never waited to receive an answer. But set yourselves diligently to " search the Scriptures;" for in them alone will you find the whole truth, without any mixture of error. Inquire, too, into the state of your souls before God. Bring them to the true and proper touchstone, the word of God : examine yourselves by it ; and beg of God to search and try you; that, if there be any hidden evil in your heart, it may be disclosed to you, and be purged away by the blood and Spirit of Christ — — —]

° Jer. iii. 12, 14, 22. and iv. 1.

2. Be assured that God's word shall take effect—

[Presume not to sit in judgment on it, or condemn it. You are not called to judge, but to submit. If you see not the reason of God's declarations, do not therefore conclude that they are not founded in wisdom or goodness or truth: but say, " What I know not now, I shall know hereafter." If the word of God hold forth a threatening, tremble at it, and beg of God that it may never be executed upon you. If, on the contrary, it set forth a promise, lay hold of it, and rest upon it, and expect the accomplishment of it to your soul. And be fully satisfied in your minds, that the final states of the whole world shall be in exact agreement with it, and happiness or misery be awarded to all according to its unerring dictates.]

3. Let the final issue of things be the great object of your concern—

[It matters little whether your present portion resemble morning or night. If you enjoy all the prosperity that the world can afford, of what value will it be when night cometh? On the other hand, if you experience here one continued night of affliction, it will soon pass away, and no more be remembered, when once the bright morn of everlasting day shall have arisen upon you. Learn then to despise the pleasures of sense, and to endure with fortitude the troubles of life. Fear not to make sacrifices, or to sustain any afflictions, in the cause of Christ, " in whose favour is life, and whose loving-kindness is better than life itself." Set eternity before you, and keep it ever in your view: and then, though your night be long, the day shall soon arise upon you, when " your sun shall no more go down;" but " the Lord shall be an everlasting light unto you, and your God your glory."]

OUTLINE NO. 888

THE UNCONCERN OF MEN AMIDST GOD'S CALLS TO REPENTANCE.

Isai. xxii. 12—14. *In that day did the Lord God of hosts call to weeping, and to mourning, and to baldness, and to girding with sackcloth: and behold, joy and gladness, slaying oxen, and killing sheep, eating flesh, and drinking wine: let us eat and drink; for to-morrow we shall die. And it was revealed in mine ears by the Lord of hosts, Surely this iniquity shall not be purged from you, till ye die, saith the Lord God of hosts.*

TRUE religion is equally abhorrent from an atheistical contempt of God's providence, and a presumptuous reliance on it. It teaches us neither to " trust in lying words, saying, The temple of the Lord, the temple of the Lord, the temple of the Lord are we[a];" nor, on the other hand, to trust in human devices, to the neglect of him, who "worketh all things after the counsel of his own will."

It was for the latter of these sins, that the Jews were reproved in the words before us. The Assyrians had invaded their country, and were coming against Jerusalem itself: and the Jews, instead of crying to God for help, contented themselves with fortifying their city; and lived as securely as if no danger were at hand. This greatly incensed God, and caused him to denounce against them his heaviest judgments.

The words before us will lead us to consider,

I. The duty to which God calls us—

The terms used in the text were intended to express repentance—

[The shaving of the head, and cutting of the beard, and putting on of sackcloth, were used among the Jews as indications of sorrow[b]. Of themselves indeed, neither those nor any other actions, however significant, had any value before God: they were even hateful to him, if used without correspondent dispositions of heart[c]: but, when accompanied with inward contrition, they were pleasing and acceptable in his sight[d].]

This is the duty to which God calls us at this time—

[He spake to the Jewish nation by the dispensations of his providence[e], and the voice of his prophets[f]. And is he not calling us to repentance at this time, by the calamities of the nation, by the command of our rulers, and by the voice of all his faithful ministers[g]? Yes; he says aloud, "Turn ye to me with all your heart, and with fasting, and with weeping, and with mourning[h]."]

But how little attention we pay to him will appear, if we consider,

II. The state in which we continue—

---

[a] Jer. vii. 4.　　　　　　[b] Ezek. xxvii. 30, 31.
[c] Isai. i. 13, 14. and lxvi. 3.　　[d] 1 Kings xxi. 27—29.
[e] Mic. vi. 9. Awful visitations were always considered in that view, Judg. xx. 25, 26.
[f] Joel, Isaiah, &c.
[g] The particular circumstances of the nation should be here stated.
[h] Joel ii. 12.

The evils of which the prophet complained, are, alas! too descriptive of our state:

1. We confide in our own preparations without looking to God—

[So often has God prospered our naval exertions, that we almost universally overlook his providence, and ascribe our success to our own superior skill and valour. Our hopes also of future conquests are founded wholly on our own prowess. We are active enough in making preparations; but are as unmindful of God, as if we needed not his aid, nor were at all dependent on his will. For the truth of this assertion we appeal to the public prints, and to the expressions of all with whom we converse[i].]

2. We still live in our wonted habits of conviviality and dissipation—

[It is not intemperance and excess that is the object of the prophet's reprehension, but an unsuitable gaiety of mind, at a time when it became them to be humbling themselves in dust and ashes. And is not this the case with us amongst all ranks and orders of the community? Doubtless the pressure of the public burthens must impose restraints on many: but still the change in them is not the effect of a voluntary humiliation, but the reluctant fruit of irresistible necessity.]

3. We, in too many instances, turn the very warnings of Jehovah into contempt and ridicule—

[The Jews were warned of the *near approach* of their destruction: and they, to ridicule the idea, said, "Let us eat and drink, for *to-morrow* we shall die." We indeed, having no information from God respecting the issue of public affairs, cannot imitate, with respect to them, the impiety of the Jews. But, in relation to infinitely more important matters, there is as much profane scoffing amongst us, as amongst them: the declarations of God's word are set at nought; and they, who most faithfully denounce God's judgments against sin and sinners, are, for the most part, regarded either as hypocrites or fanatics.]

Let us then, as it becomes us, proceed with all fidelity to shew,

III. The evil and danger of such a state—

What can be more *unsuitable to our condition?*

---

[i] This statement must of course be adjusted to the existing circumstances, but with a clear reference to the preceding context, ver. 7—11.

[What should we think of a child or servant that should manifest such a spirit under our rebukes? Does such conduct then become us towards God, when he is contending with us, and chastising us for our sins? Yea, are we not as devoid of humanity as of piety, while we feel no sympathy with the thousands of our suffering fellow-creatures? Well says the prophet on a similar occasion, "Should we *then* make mirth[k]?" Surely it becomes us rather to " cry and howl " for the miseries that are come upon us, or at least impending over us.]

What can be more *offensive to God?*

[The word "surely" is equivalent to an oath[l]: and is it a light thing which causes Jehovah to swear by his own life and immortal perfections? Is it a small matter that causes " the Lord God of hosts[m] " to shut up his tender mercies, and to swear that the guilt of such or such an action shall " never be purged away?" Must not that be beyond measure offensive to him, that can fill his breast with such "fiery indignation?" The sins that have brought down his chastisements are doubtless great; but an obstinacy under those chastisements which are intended to reform us, is but too probably a forerunner of our utter excision[n],]

What can be more *destructive in its consequences?*

[The nation cannot be delivered but by means of a national repentance: nor can any individual escape the eternal wrath of God, but by means of his own personal repentance[o]. If there be only one impenitent transgressor in the whole kingdom, " God will search him out with candles," in order to punish him[p]." Even in his present dispensations God will put a difference between those who mourn for sin, and those who are at ease in Zion[q]; but much more in his decisions at the day of judgment[r]. Whether therefore we consider our national or our personal danger, it becomes us instantly to put away our unbelief and impenitence, and to turn to God with the deepest contrition.]

ADDRESS—

[It may be thought that the injunctions given to the Jews, had respect to *them* rather than to ourselves. Let an apostle then be heard in confirmation of the prophet; and let us depart

---

[k] Ezek. xxi. 9, 10, 12.   [l] Heb. vi. 13, 14.

[m] This title, being thrice repeated, is very emphatical.

[n] Jer. vii. 12—16. Such also is the import of that threatening, Amos iv. 12. the ground of which is *five* times repeated from ver. 6 to 11.

[o] Luke xiii. 3.   [p] Zeph. i. 12.

[q] Amos vi. 1, 3—7. Ezek. ix. 4, 5.

[r] Isai. v. 11, 12. and lxv. 12—14.

with a determination through grace to obey his voice; " Be afflicted, and mourn, and weep; let your laughter be turned into mourning, and your joy into heaviness: humble yourselves under the mighty hand of God; and he shall lift you up [s]." The very Gospel itself, with all that Christ has done and suffered for us, will do us no good, if we remain impenitent. The command is, " Repent, and believe the gospel." We must " sow in tears, if ever we would reap in joy."]

[s] Jam. iv. 9, 10.

OUTLINE NO. 889

ELIAKIM A TYPE OF CHRIST.

Isai. xxii. 24.   *They shall hang upon him all the glory of his Father's house.*

IN the various changes that take place in human governments, or in the persons who are to be entrusted with the supreme authority, the hand of God ought to be continually acknowledged : whoever be the instruments, or whatever be the means, of effecting those changes, we must look through the second causes to God, as the first great Cause, who ordereth all things after the counsel of his own will, and makes use of men as his agents, to convey blessings to a nation, or to inflict his just judgments upon it. But, in his dispensations towards the Jews, there was often some mystery concealed, where we should have observed nothing but an ordinary occurrence. This was the case with respect to the deposition of Shebna, and the substitution of Eliakim in his place, as first minister of state under Hezekiah. Eliakim seems to have been raised as a type of Christ: the agreement between him and Christ is strongly marked in the passage before us,

I. In the authority committed to him—

[The appointment of both was of God [a]. Shebna was a proud, vain-glorious man, far more intent on aggrandizing himself and his family, than on executing the arduous duties of his station. God therefore moved Hezekiah to dismiss him, and inspired Isaiah, not only to predict his degradation, but to

[a] To put the audience in full possession of the subject, read distinctly from ver. 15. to the end ; and observe that ver. 25. refers, not to Eliakim, but to Shebna.

foretel the elevation of *Eliakim to his post and office*. Thus was our Lord appointed to succeed the governors of the Jewish nation, who, both in the civil and ecclesiastical departments, had abused their trust, and rendered themselves unworthy to be continued in it. Humiliating in the extreme are the descriptions which the prophet gives of the rulers both in church and state[b]: and the time was coming, when God would fulfil his word, in "raising up in their place a faithful priest, who should do all his will, and another king who should reign over the house of David for ever[c]." "With their robe was He to be clothed, and with their girdle was he to be strengthened; and their government was to be committed into his hands[d];" and *this* too, not only according to the commandment of God, but by the immediate agency of his overruling Providence[e].]

The authority with which they were invested was supreme—

[To mark his office, Eliakim was to have "the key of the house of David laid upon his shoulder, and then to exercise the the most unlimited authority:" nor was he ever to be removed, like Shebna; (whose boasted security would soon fail him;) but he was to be "a nail fastened in a sure place."

Now our blessed Lord applies to himself the very words here used in reference to Eliakim[f]; thereby shewing that Eliakim was indeed a type of him; and that what was spoken of Eliakim only in a figure, was really, and in the strictest sense, applicable to himself; the power of both being *uncontrollable* and *unalterable*. "All power in heaven and in earth is committed unto Christ[g]:" in every thing that relates to the kingdom of nature or of grace, "he openeth and no man shutteth, and shutteth, and no man openeth." None are exalted, or disgraced, either in this world, or the world to come, but agreeably to the orders which he issues: nor can any, even in the smallest degree, resist his will: "He doeth according to his will in the armies of heaven and among the inhabitants of the earth; nor can any stay his hand, or say to him, What doest thou?" Nor will the lapse of ages effect any change on him: "He is the same yesterday, to-day, and for ever[h]:" "He is a nail fastened in a sure place." Seated on his holy hill of Zion, He laughs at the impotent combinations of men and devils, and has all his

---

[b] Isai. i. 5. and lvi. 10—12.

[c] 1 Sam. ii. 30, 35. and Jer. xxiii. 2, 5.

[d] Compare ver. 21. with Rev. i. 13. Isai. xi. 5. and ix. 6.

[e] As this was marked in the case of Eliakim, (ver. 19—21.) so in that of Christ by the raising him from the dead, and utterly destroying the Jewish polity.

[f] Rev. iii. 7.   [g] Matt. xxviii. 18.   [h] Heb. xiii. 8.

enemies in derision[i]. " His dominion is an everlasting dominion, and his kingdom that which shall not be destroyed[k]."]

II. In the benefits resulting from his administration—

[A wise and righteous governor is a rich blessing, as well
to the prince who appoints him, as to the people whom he
governs. Such was Eliakim; who was most probably of the
royal seed; since it would not otherwise have been any virtue
in him to seek with so much diligence the exaltation of his
father's house.

But in what an infinitely higher degree do the benefits of
Christ's administration appear!

Was Eliakim " a father to the inhabitants of Jerusalem,
and to the house of Judah?" What a blessing is Christ also
to the world at large! As, in a state, all are benefited by a
wise administration, though many are insensible to the blessings they enjoy; so the world is much indebted to the revelation which Christ has given us, and to his wise government
of the universe, though they deny his providence, and despise
his grace — — —

Was Eliakim " a nail, on which all the vessels of his father's
house hung " in safety? What security does Christ afford *to
his dependants in particular!* The various orders and degrees
of Christians are elsewhere compared to vessels of various
kinds[l]; and every one of them, from the greatest to the least,
hangs upon him : were HE to fall, they would perish; but as
long as HE stands, they shall be upheld : " because HE liveth
they shall live also[m]"— — —

Was Eliakim " a glorious throne to his father's house?"
Jesus also, by his righteous administration, advances the glory
of *his heavenly Father.* In ascribing to Jesus the power and
dominion over all, we do not derogate from the Father's honour,
but add to it[n]. His mediatorial office he holds from the Father,
and improves it, in every instance, for his glory. Whether he
open or shut, whether he kill or save alive, every perfection of
the Deity receives brighter lustre from the dispensation— — —
and gives reason for unbounded thankfulness to God, for having
" committed all judgment to his Son," and " laid our help upon
One so Mighty[o]."]

We cannot IMPROVE this subject better, than by learning
    from it,

1. To renounce all creature-dependence—

[Great as the power of Shebna was, both he, and all his
dependants, were brought down in God's appointed time; and

[i] Ps. ii. 1—4.   [k] Dan. vii. 14.   [l] 2 Tim. ii. 20, 21.
[m] John xiv. 19.   [n] Phil. ii. 11.   [o] Ps. lxxxix. 19.

the vanities in which he had gloried, became monuments of his shame, and means of perpetuating his disgrace[p]. Thus will it be with all who trust in an arm of flesh. God has denounced a curse against them[q]; and though, through the forbearance of God, it may be awhile delayed, it will surely come at last; and all, wherein we trusted, will turn to our confusion: our wisdom will become folly; our strength, weakness; our righteousness, as filthy rags[r]. We may dream of being "as a nail fastened in a sure place;" but if we rely on any thing of our own, our hopes will be disappointed, and our expectations will perish. Let us not then lean to our own understanding, or depend on our own strength, or trust in our own righteousness: we must be empty in ourselves, if we would be filled by God; for it is "the hungry alone whom he filleth with good things; the full and the rich he will send empty away:" "He will resist the proud; and give grace only to the humble[s]."]

2. To trust in the Lord with our whole hearts—

[Jesus is indeed "a nail fastened in a sure place;" and able to bear the weight of the whole universe. He is exalted by the hand of God himself on purpose that He may "be a Prince and a Saviour" unto us. And, if we rely on him, he is "able to save us to the uttermost." Only let our trust in him be entire, (exactly like that of a vessel on a nail,) and we may rest assured, that all, who *so* hang on him, shall be "the glory of his Father's house." As there is no other support for sinful man, so neither is there any fear of disappointment to those who trust in him. Let none then imagine themselves so great as not to need his support; or deem themselves so insignificant, that they shall not obtain it; or think themselves in such perilous circumstances, that He cannot uphold them. "Every vessel, from the largest flagon to the smallest cup," must owe its preservation to him alone; and by him shall all be saved, if they do but "cleave to him with full purpose of heart."]

[p] ver. 18.　　[q] Jer. xvii. 5.　　[r] 1 Cor. i. 19. Isai. lxiv. 6.
[s] Luke i. 52, 53. Jam. iv. 6.

OUTLINE NO. 890

THE REIGN OF CHRIST GLORIOUS.

Isai. xxiv. 23. *Then the moon shall be confounded, and the sun ashamed, when the Lord of hosts shall reign in Mount Zion, and in Jerusalem, and before his antients, gloriously.*

THE chapter before us seems to refer to the destruction of the Jewish Church and polity by the

Chaldeans. But it looks forward, also, to their restoration, and to the establishment of the Messiah's empire consequent upon it. Of that period it is delightful to speak: for, in fact, the glory of it far exceeds all that language can express, or the most enlarged imagination can conceive.

To give you some idea of the Messiah's advent, as it is here described, I will endeavour to set before you,

I. The nature of his kingdom—

[It differs widely from all other kingdoms. Other kings have dominion over the persons and the property of their subjects; but his empire is over their souls — — — The laws of other kingdoms are almost entirely restrictive: *his*, however restrictively expressed, are not prohibitory only, but preceptive; and intended to call forth into exercise every power of the soul. The substance of them all is contained in these two sayings, " Thou shalt love the Lord thy God with all thy heart, and with all thy mind, and with all thy soul, and with all thy strength; and thy neighbour as thyself." Nor does any one *fully* approve himself to him as a faithful subject, unless " every thought of his heart be brought into captivity to the obedience of Christ[a]."]

II. The extent of his dominion—

[Never was there a kingdom like unto His. At present, indeed, His is very limited: but, at the period mentioned in my text, it will be absolutely universal: " All kings shall bow down before him, all nations shall serve him[b]," and " the utmost ends of the earth shall be his possession[c]." " There will then be but one Lord over the face of the whole world, and his name one[d]." Nor will there be any who yield him only a forced or partial obedience; for in that day " all will be righteous[e]:" " nor will there be any more a Canaanite in the land of the Lord of Hosts[f]."]

III. The happiness of his subjects—

[If the happiness of a people be estimated by their honours, their wealth, their enjoyments, never was there a kingdom to be compared with His. The most exalted person in any other kingdom is but a child of man: whereas the least and meanest of his subjects is a child of the living God. " Israel," says Jehovah, " is my son, my first-born[g]." The wealth of earthly monarchs, however great, may be counted: that which is owned

[a] 2 Cor. x. 5.   [b] Ps. lxxii. 11.   [c] Ps. ii. 8.
[d] Zech. xiv. 9.   [e] Isai. lx. 21.   [f] Zech. xiv. 21.
[g] Exod. iv. 22

by the poorest of his subjects is " unsearchable[h]." " Though
he have nothing (of an earthly nature), he actually possesses
all things[i]." In earthly kingdoms, a few only, and those of
the higher ranks, have access to their king; and that only for
a short season, on some particular occasions. But in Christ's
kingdom, every one of his subjects has access to him at all times;
yea, and has liberty to " ask whatsoever he will;" with an absolute certainty, that (provided the gift will be beneficial to his
soul) he shall obtain it[k]. In other kingdoms, the subjects are
only subjects: but in Christ's kingdom every subject is himself
a king[l], having a throne[m], a crown[n], a kingdom[o], for his unalienable and everlasting possession. The subjects of other
kingdoms have their pleasures and their joys; but the subjects
of Christ are " full of joy and peace in believing[p]," yea, " of joy
unspeakable and glorified[q]." Well might Moses say, " Happy
art thou, O Israel, O people saved by the Lord, who is the shield
of thy help, and who is the sword of thine excellency[r]!"]

IV. The glory of his reign—

[Truly, never did there exist among men such a kingdom
as this. In this there will not be found one enemy unsubdued;
ar one subject of the realm debased, or destitute, or unholy, or
unhappy. Even at present, so far as Christ really reigns in the
heart, this is found a truth: but in that day, when his power
will be universally operative and effectual, it will be productive
of these effects in every place and in every bosom. But, as
the crown and summit of all, every soul will refer to Christ as
the life, the peace, the strength, the joy, the glory of his whole
Church. There will be stars differing from each other in splendour; but all will acknowledge him as the sun, from whence
all their lustre is derived, and to whom alone all the glory must
be ascribed. In the reign of Solomon, so great was the prosperity of the Jewish people, that " silver was common as the
stones," and " of no account" in the public estimation[s]. But
that was poverty itself, in comparison of what shall be the portion of God's people in the millennial age: for then the very
poorest amongst them shall be able to say, " All things are
mine; for I am Christ's[t]."

That there may be trials then, as well as now, I do not deny:
but they will all be made subservient to the advancement of
the people's happiness: seeing, that " as their tribulations
abound, their consolations also by Christ shall much more
abound[u]."]

[h] Eph. iii. 8.	[i] 2 Cor. vi. 10.
[k] John xiv. 13, 14. and xv. 7.	[l] Rev. i. 6.
[m] Rev. iii. 21.　　[n] 2 Tim. iv. 8.	[o] Luke xxii. 29.
[p] Rom. xv. 13.　　[q] 1 Pet. i. 8.	[r] Deut. xxxiii. 29.
[s] 1 Kings x. 21, 27.　　[t] 1 Cor. iii. 22, 23.	[u] 2 Cor. i. 5.

See then, Brethren,

1. What you should affect on earth—

[The sun and moon may well be considered as emblems of all that is great and glorious upon earth: but "glorious as they are, they have no glory, by reason of the glory that excelleth." Before the superior lustre of the Redeemer's kingdom they must hide their diminished heads, "ashamed and confounded," as unworthy of regard, in comparison of Christ, and of the felicity that is enjoyed through him. Let this, then, be the one object of your desire, to become subjects of his kingdom. Verily, "to be a door-keeper in his house, is better than to dwell in the most magnificent and richly furnished tents of the ungodly[x]." Seek to be able to say, "My Beloved is mine, and I am his[y];" and you can have no richer bliss out of heaven.]

2. What blessedness awaits you in the eternal world—

[There you will "behold the King in his beauty[z]," yea, in the full effulgence of his majesty and glory. There, too, will you yourselves be freed from all your present infirmities: for there "the spirits of the just are made perfect[a]." There your powers will be enlarged, beyond all that you can now conceive; and you will be filled with bliss, to the utmost extent of your capacity to contain it. And what will you think of earthly honours and enjoyments *then?* Verily you will wonder how it was ever possible for you to be so enchanted with them as you once were. The sight of Christ "face to face[b]" will swallow up every inferior object, even as the meridian sun eclipses and banishes the stars: and then your bliss will be complete, because there will no longer remain any object to distract your mind, or so much as a thought that does not emanate from, and centre in, your Saviour and your King. Methinks, in the anticipation of that day, I hear you already saying, "Allelujah; for the Lord God omnipotent reigneth[c]!"]

x Ps. lxxxiv. 10.   y Cant. ii. 16.   z Isai. xxxiii. 17.
a Heb. xii. 23.   b 1 Cor. xiii. 12.   c Rev. xix. 6.

OUTLINE NO. 891

CHRIST A SUITABLE AND ALL SUFFICIENT HELP.

Isai. xxv. 4. *Thou hast been a strength to the poor, a strength to the needy in his distress, a refuge from the storm, a shadow from the heat, when the blast of the terrible ones is as a storm against the wall.*

IT is generally thought that no great comfort can arise from meditating upon God: and this is true, as far as it respects those who are determined to live in sin : but to those who desire to serve and enjoy God, there cannot be a richer source of consolation : a view of his attributes, as displayed in the works of his providence and grace, would soon elevate our minds, and turn our fears and sorrows into " thanksgiving and the voice of melody." We find the prophet breaking forth into rapture, " O Lord, thou art my God ; I will exalt thee ; I will praise thy name :" but what was the foundation of this joy ? It was, as he adds, " for thou hast done wonderful things[a] :" and what those wonders were, he informs us in the words which we are about to consider, in which we may see,

I. What is here supposed respecting the Lord's people—

We forbear to mention the temporal calamities which God's people are called to suffer, because they are common to the wicked as well as to the righteous. But there are many and severe afflictions peculiar to the godly. They are often in great distress,

1. From a sense of guilt and danger—

[When persons first begin to turn to God, they are often filled with horror at the sight of their past iniquities, and terrified with apprehensions of the wrath they have so justly merited. However " stout-hearted " any man may have been in the days of his ignorance, he no sooner sees what transgressions he has committed, and what a God he has defied, than, like Belshazzar at the sight of the hand-writing on the wall, his loins are loosed with fear, and his knees, as it were, smite one against the other[b]. The jailor, it should seem, from his treatment of Paul and Silas, was of a very ferocious disposition ; but, when God smote him with a sense of sin, how was his heart appalled! he " sprang in with trembling, and cried out before his prisoners, Sirs, What must I do to be saved[c] ?" Thus it is, in a greater or less degree, with all : and many in this state have even envied the beasts the privilege of annihilation.]

2. From the persecutions of an ungodly world—

[From the days of Cain, even to this present hour, they who have been born after the flesh have persecuted those who were born after the Spirit[d]. And the more eminent any have

---

a ver. 1.　　　　　　　b Dan. v. 5, 6.
c Acts xvi. 29, 30.　　　　d Gal. iv. 29. 1 John iii. 12.

been for piety, the more have they been the objects of the world's hatred and contempt. With what astonishing cruelty were the saints of old treated! They, of whom God says, the world was not worthy, were made as the filth of the world, and the off-scouring of all things[e]. What though the same violence does not rage at present? is the enmity of the carnal heart slain? Does not the same aversion to religion exist now as in former times? and is it not still found in many instances that our "greatest foes are those of our own household?" Yes; and in many instances is this a source of deep affliction, even as "a terrible blast, and as a wintry storm."]

3. From the temptations of Satan—

["Whoever will set himself to seek the Lord must prepare his soul for temptation." Satan will not lose any of his vassals without endeavouring to reduce them to their former state of subjection. For this end he will harass the soul with his temptations, which, as fiery darts, will inflame it with evil passions, and with a "venom will even drink up the spirits[f]." How inexpressibly grievous these are to a child of God, may be seen by the bitter complaints of Paul respecting that thorn in his flesh, and his entreaties for deliverance from the buffetings of Satan[g]. Never does a saint feel himself more "needy and distressed" than in circumstances like these; nor could any endure this "conflict with the principalities and powers of darkness," if not upheld by an invisible and almighty arm.]

4. From the hidings of God's face—

[God oftentimes, for wise and gracious ends, withdraws himself from his people, and suffers them to "walk in darkness for a season, and without light. And this is incomparably the most distressing of all the trials that can be endured in this world. Our blessed Lord, who never complained of the cruelties exercised upon his body, cried out with inexpressible anguish, by reason of the dereliction he experienced in his soul, "My God, my God! why hast thou forsaken me[h]?" Many too of his dearest children have mourned like him, and been ready to conclude that God had forsaken and forgotten them[i]. To estimate aright the greatness of this affliction, it must be felt; for neither words can express, nor imagination conceive, the gloom and misery of a deserted soul.]

Were we to view them in this light only, we should dread, rather than desire, to be of their number. But in the text, we see,

[e] Heb. xi. 36—38. 1 Cor. iv. 13.
[f] Eph. vi. 16. Job. vi. 4.   [g] 2 Cor. xii. 7, 8.
[h] Matt. xxvii. 46.   [i] Isai. xlix. 14. Ps. lxxvii. 7—9

II. God's compassionate regard towards them—

God is never more concerned about his people than when they are "in heaviness through manifold temptations:" nor will he merely afford them succour, but will himself be to them,

1. A suitable help—

[As the trials of the saints are various, so, of course, must their necessities be also: but whatever it be that they need, they shall surely receive it out of the Redeemer's fulness. Is it a sense of guilt that oppresses them? God will "apply to their lips a live coal from the altar, and say, Thine iniquity is taken away, and thy sin purged[k]." Are they bowed down under a weight of persecution, and destitute of human aid? He will strengthen them in their inward man, that they shall even rejoice in being counted worthy to suffer for his sake[l]. Are they buffeted by Satan? He will clothe them with armour, whereby they shall be enabled to resist him manfully, and to bruise him under their feet[m]. And has he himself forsaken them? It shall be but for a little moment[n], that they may learn when in darkness to stay themselves on him[o], and rejoice with more exalted joy in the renewed expressions of his love. Thus it is intimated in the text itself, that whether it be strength or protection, or whatever else, that we want, he will surely impart it to us.]

2. A seasonable help—

[God may suffer his people to lie a considerable time under their afflictions: but in the very instant that he sees it best to interpose, he will come to their support. This is not only intimated in the parable of the Importunate Widow, but absolutely promised, as a deduction from that parable; "Shall not God avenge his own elect, who cry day and night unto him, *though he bear long with them?* Verily I say unto you that he will avenge them *speedily*[p]," that is, in the very best and fittest season. And how remarkably was this exemplified in his conduct towards Abraham! That holy patriarch was made to go three days' journey to the mountain where he was to slay his son: he was permitted to take the wood, the fire, the knife, for the execution of the divine command; he was even suffered to bind his son, and lift up the knife that was instantly to inflict the fatal wound; and then it was that God stopped him by a voice from heaven. Thus in ten thousand other instances has that proverb been verified, In the mount of

[k] Isai. vi. 6, 7. [l] Acts v. 41. 2 Tim. iv. 17. [m] Eph. vi. 11.
[n] Isai. liv. 7, 8. [o] Isai. l. 10. [p] Luke xviii. 7, 8.

the Lord it shall be seen[q]. And it is remarkable that the poor illiterate fishermen, who followed our Lord, were even ordered not to think beforehand what they should say, when summoned before their rulers, but to expect that the Holy Ghost should suggest to them at the moment what they ought to speak[r]; and though their example does not justify a want of foresight and premeditation in *us*, yet the promise made to them warrants us to look to God as *a help*, a *present*, "a *very* present help in the time of trouble[s];" and to expect his interposition *then*, when "the storm" would otherwise overwhelm us.]

3. A sufficient help—

[However "needy and distressed" we be, God is able to support and deliver us. Though we be as "worms, yet will he enable us to thresh the mountains[t]." And though earth and hell conspire against us, yet will he make us "more than conquerors." Our weakness is no ground of discouragement: for "his strength shall be perfected in our weakness[u]." He has undertaken for us, and he will perform his engagements: and, sooner than not make us triumph over our enemies, he would cause "the very stars in their courses to fight for us[x]," or the earth to open and swallow up our adversaries. Never has a child of God yet failed for want of his effectual aid; nor shall any one to all eternity: sooner shall heaven and earth pass away than "one of his little ones shall perish[y]."]

From this subject we may clearly SEE,

1. The true nature of *experimental* religion—

[The acknowledging of these things to be true does not constitute real piety: it is the experience of them in the soul that is the foundation, and indeed the very essence, of vital godliness. Our blessed Lord has said, "Come unto me, all ye that are weary and heavy-laden, and I will give you rest[z]:" and this comprehends all the whole work of God's grace upon the soul. To be heavy-laden with a sense of sin; to seek rest in Christ; and to be brought by the Lord Jesus to an entire rest in God as our Father and our Friend; *this*, I say, is true religion: and the experience of this on earth will lead assuredly to the everlasting experience of it in heaven[a] — — —]

2. The true nature of *practical* religion—

["A form of godliness" may easily exist "without any of its power." Then only do we serve the Lord Jesus aright, when we are conformed to the image of Christ, and have

---

[q] Gen. xxii. 14.   [r] Matt. x. 19, 20.   [s] Ps. xlvi. 1.
[t] Isai. xli. 14, 15. Deut. xxxiii. 25.   [u] 2 Cor. xii. 9.
[x] Judg. v. 20.   [y] Matt. xviii. 14.   [z] Matt. xi. 28.
[a] Rev. i. 5, 6.

learned to walk as he walked." "Love is the very fulfilling of
the law!" and this love of Christ to us is the true pattern for
our love to each other[b]. This is what becomes us "as the
elect of God[c]:" and this will be the test of our obedience in
the day of judgment[d]. "Let the same mind then be in you,
as was in Christ Jesus[e]" —— —— And let this be the habitual
exercise of it as far as your circumstances will admit[f]—— —— ——]

[b] Eph. v. 2.   [c] Col. iii. 12—14.   [d] Matt. xxv. 34—36.
[e] Phil. ii. 5.

[f] If this be the subject of a *Charity Sermon*, this will be the place
for opening the peculiar nature of the charity.

OUTLINE NO. 892

THE GOSPEL A SOURCE OF RICHEST BLESSINGS.

Isai. xxv. 6—8. *In this mountain shall the Lord of hosts make
unto all people a feast of fat things, a feast of wines on the
lees : of fat things full of marrow, of wines on the lees well
refined. And he will destroy in this mountain the face of the
covering cast over all people, and the veil that is spread over
all nations. He will swallow up death in victory; and the
Lord God will wipe away tears from off all faces; and the
rebuke of his people shall he take away from off all the earth:
for the Lord hath spoken it.*

MANY passages of Scripture, which, from the language, might be supposed to belong to the Jewish
dispensation only, will be found to refer in a more
especial manner to the times of the Gospel. The
" mountain" so frequently mentioned in this place
was Mount Zion, which was distinguished above all
other mountains by being the peculiar residence of
the Deity: and it should seem that all the great things
which God promised to the world, were to be transacted upon that spot. But Mount Zion was a type
of the Gospel Church, wherein God yet more eminently dwells: and it is in the Church of Christ that
he bestows the blessings which are here promised.
The Gospel, which is here promulgated, affords,

I. Food to the hungry—

The Gospel calls us to a luxurious feast—

[The terms in which this feast is expressed, are evidently
intended to raise in our minds the highest possible conceptions
of its excellency. "A feast" is far more than a common meal,

and conveys an idea of costliness and abundance : a feast " of
fat things " imports that the choicest provisions are set forth :
and the fat things being " full of marrow," suggests, that no
expense is spared in procuring whatever can provoke the
appetite of the guests, or afford them pleasure. But " wines "
are also added ; wines that have contracted a delicious flavour
by being long kept " upon the lees ;" and wines " well refined,"
that are bright as a ruby, that " sparkle in the glass," and that
delight the eye whilst they gratify the palate. What are we
to understand from this accumulation of ideas, but that, as the
choicest viands administer nourishment and comfort to the
body, so the Gospel provides every thing which can exhilarate
and support the soul. After all, this representation falls very
far short of the truth : for the promises of the Gospel are
infinitely sweeter to the hungering and thirsting soul than the
most exquisite food can be to our taste. Let but a sinner,
who pants after pardon, be enabled to apply to his soul that
promise of Jehovah, That " crimson sins shall be made white
as snow," or that word of Christ, That " whosoever cometh to
him he will in no wise cast out ;" what transports of joy will
he not feel ! how will he be " filled as with marrow and fatness,
while he praises his God with joyful lips !" What strength did
that word, " My grace is sufficient for thee," administer to
Paul under the buffetings of Satan ! In the strength of that
one meal he was enabled to go on, not for forty days only, but
to the latest hour of his life[a]. And such is the Gospel to all
who cordially embrace it.]

This feast has God himself prepared for all people—

[It is none other than " the Lord of hosts " who has
spread this table at his own expense. And he invites " all
people," not of the Jews only, but of the Gentiles also ; yea,
the very vilest of the human race. He sends out his servants
into the highways and hedges, to call the halt, the lame, and
the blind, and orders them to take no refusal, but to compel
them to come in[b]." Yea, though in every succeeding age there
have been myriads of guests brought in, yet his message to *us*
is, that " yet there is room."]

But, as this feast can be of no use to those who feel
not their need of it, nor discern its excellency, the
Gospel suits itself to our necessities, and offers,

II. Light to the blind—

There is a thick, impenetrable " veil " over the hearts
of men—

---

[a] In allusion to Elijah, 1 Kings xix. 7, 8.
[b] Matt. xxii. 4. Luke xiv. 17, 21, 22.

[The lusts and prejudices of men cast a film over their eyes, and incapacitate them from discerning spiritual things: and Satan by his subtle devices confirms their blindness[c]. As the Jews, even while Moses was read to them every Sabbath day, were unable, by reason of the veil that was upon their hearts, to comprehend the great ends and purposes of the Mosaic dispensation[d], so thousands who live under the light of the Gospel are total strangers to its fundamental truths; or admit them only in theory, while they are destitute of any experimental knowledge of them in their hearts. "They have eyes, but see not; ears, but hear not; hearts, but understand not."]

But God by his Gospel removes this veil—

[" He who commanded light to shine out of darkness will shine into the hearts" of those who seek him. " The things which flesh and blood could never have discovered, he will reveal unto them[e]." He will shew them the evil of sin, the depravity of their hearts, the fulness and suitableness of Christ, the stability of the covenant, together with every thing else which they need to know. He will not merely turn aside the veil, and give them a transient view of the holy of holies, but will "destroy" the veil, and "rend it in pieces from the top to the bottom." It is true, this clear knowledge of divine truth will not be imparted all at once; but it shall gradually increase, till they " see as they are seen, and know as they are known."]

To complete the happiness of his people, God further promises,

III. Victory to the oppressed—

The former part of the text refers to the apostolic and millennial periods; but the latter will not be accomplished till the day of judgment. To that season in particular St. Paul applies the words before us[f]. Taking him for our guide, we are in no danger of misinterpreting their import, whilst we say, that God will rescue us from,

1. The power of death—

[Death is even now disarmed of its sting; and the king of terrors is made our friend. They who through the Gospel are enabled to live unto Christ, may justly account it "gain to die:" not life only, but even death itself, is numbered among their treasures[g]. Such is their victory over it, that it is an

c 2 Cor. iv. 4.   d 2 Cor. iii. 14, 15.   e Matt. xvi. 17.
f 1 Cor. xv 54.   g Phil. i. 21. 1 Cor. iii. 22.

object of hope and desire rather than of terror and aversion[h]: and when it comes, they are not so properly said to die, as to "fall asleep in Jesus." Nor will its apparent triumphs be of long duration; for that which swallowed up mankind with insatiable avidity, shall itself "be swallowed up in victory," and not a vestige of it ever again be found among the saints of God.]

2. The sorrows of sin—

[Whilst we continue in the body there will be occasion for us to "go on our way weeping." But even now the sorrows of believers are widely different from the sorrows of the world: instead of corroding the heart, they bring a peace along with them; and the persons who are most affected with them, so far from wishing to get rid of them, desire to have them more deep and abiding. But ere long they shall sully the face no more; but shall be "wiped away" by the hand of a compassionate Father, and be followed by a harvest of eternal joy[i].]

3. The reproaches of the world—

[There is scarcely any thing which an ungodly world will not say or do, to asperse the character of the godly, and to destroy their peace. But God in this world so far "takes away their rebuke," as often to manifest himself to them, and to interpose visibly on their behalf[k]. But in a little time "He will bring forth their righteousness as the noon day;" and they who were regarded "as the filth of the world and the off-scouring of all things," shall be openly acknowledged as the children of the living God.]

ADDRESS—

1. To those who are living at a distance from God —

[Whatever you may promise yourselves from the enjoyment of this world, you in reality are feeding only on husks; and however you may boast of attainments in philosophy, there is a veil on your hearts that hides from you all spiritual knowledge. Besides, whatever satisfaction you feel, or whatever reputation you enjoy, death will speedily swallow up both you and it, and will consign you over to everlasting shame and misery. Say, then, whether you have not made a wretched choice, and whether the mourning and despised Christian be not in a far happier state than you? It is not however too late for you to repent: the invitations of the Gospel are sent to you as well as to others; and if you put away your vain excuses, and return to God as prodigals, you shall find a cordial welcome, and feast this very hour on the fatted calf. O

[h] Phil. i. 23.   [i] Rev. xxi. 4. and vii. 16, 17.
[k] Ex. gr. Joseph, Daniel, the Hebrew Youths, &c.

that the " scales may fall from your eyes;" and that, being
" brought from darkness unto light, you may be turned from
the power of Satan unto God!"]

2. To those who are come to God's holy mountain—

[You find that the promises of the Gospel have not
disappointed you. If you are not " satisfied with the plente-
ousness of God's house," it is not because the provisions are
withheld from you, but because you want a better appetite for
them. " Be not straitened in yourselves;" and be sure you
never shall be straitened in your God: " open your mouth
wide, and he will fill it." Above all things remember to feed
continually on " the body and blood of your beloved Lord ;
for his flesh is meat indeed, and his blood is drink indeed[1]."
And soon you shall be called to the banquet above, where
" your Lord shall gird himself and come forth to serve you."
Then shall these promises receive their full accomplishment;
and you shall possess that " fulness of joy which is at God's
right hand for evermore."]

[1] John vi. 54, 55.

OUTLINE NO. 893

CHRIST'S ADVENT A GROUND OF JOY.

Isai. xxv. 9. *It shall be said in that day, Lo, this is our God ;
we have waited for him, and he will save us : this is the Lord;
we have waited for him, we will be glad and rejoice in his
salvation.*

IF the benefits of Christianity were duly estimated
by us, there would be no bounds to our attachment
to it, or our delight in it. What an assemblage of
images have we in the verses immediately preceding
my text, to display the excellence of our holy religion!
In truth, the human mind is scarcely capable of com-
bining such a variety of ideas as are here presented
to us, so as to reduce them to one common focus,
and at one view to comprehend them all. But the
common result of all will doubtless be that which is
declared in my text. The whole Church of God, and
every individual member of it, will be impressed alike
with wonder and admiration at a discovery of our
redeeming God, and will exclaim, " This is our God;
we have waited for him, and he will save us : this is

the Lord; we have waited for him; we will be glad and rejoice in his salvation!"

Let us, then, consider this,

I. As the language of the Church at large—

The time spoken of in Scripture as " that day" sometimes refers to one period, and sometimes to another; and frequently comprehends several distinct periods, in which the things predicted shall receive a partial and progressive accomplishment. In the passage before us, the prophet may be considered as comprehending in his view,

1. The apostolic age—

[For many hundred years had the Jews been waiting for the Messiah's advent: and at that precise time, when Jesus came, were they " expecting him, as the consolation of Israel," and " looking for redemption in Jerusalem." And no sooner was he born into the world, than an angel appeared to certain shepherds, to announce his advent; saying, " Behold, we bring you good tidings of great joy, which shall be to all people: for unto you is born, this day, a Saviour, which is Christ the Lord[a]." As for the joy which these tidings excited, we may judge of it, not only from the exultation of the shepherds, but from the expressions of that aged saint, who, on taking the infant Saviour in his arms, exclaimed, " Lord, now lettest thou thy servant depart in peace, for mine eyes have seen thy salvation[b]!"]

2. The millennial period—

[The Church is now expecting a second advent of our Lord, when he shall take to him his great power, and reign over the face of the whole earth. We verily believe that the time is near at hand, when " all kings shall bow down before him, and all nations shall serve him," and " all the kingdoms of the world become his undivided empire." And oh! what joy will his advent diffuse throughout the whole intelligent creation, both of Jews and Gentiles! Of that time the Prophet Isaiah speaks, when he says, " Rejoice ye with Jerusalem, and be glad with her, all ye that love her: rejoice for joy with her, all ye that mourn for her: for thus saith the Lord, Behold, I will extend peace to her like a river, and the glory of the Gentiles like a flowing stream. And when ye see this, your heart shall rejoice, and your bones shall flourish like a herb[c]." And in the book of Revelation, the same event is thus

---

[a] Luke ii. 10. 11.   [b] Luke ii. 25—30.   [c] Isai. lxvi. 10—14.

announced: " I heard as it were the voice of a great multitude, and as the voice of many waters, and as the voice of mighty thunderings; saying, Alleluia: for the Lord God omnipotent reigneth. Let us be glad and rejoice, and give honour to him: for the marriage of the Lamb is come, and his wife hath made herself ready[d]."

But there will be yet a further accomplishment of our text at,]

3. The day of judgment—

[All that are in the graves are waiting for the Saviour's advent: and when we consign any saint to the silent tomb, we do it in an assured expectation that, at the appointed hour, he shall rise again to "meet the Lord in the air." The very spirits that are before the throne of God are also waiting for that blessed day, when, by their re-union with the body, their bliss shall be complete, and their felicity entire. To that period we may conceive the Apostle refers, when he says, "The whole creation groaneth and travaileth in pain together until now. And not only they, but ourselves also, who have the firstfruits of the Spirit, even we ourselves groan within ourselves, waiting for the adoption, to wit, the redemption of our body[e]." At all events, we are sure that it is that period which " the grace of God " teaches us to be " looking for, even for that blessed hope, and the glorious appearing of the great God and our Saviour Jesus Christ[f]." How will every saint, even from Adam to that very hour, then say, " Lo, this is our God; we have waited for him; this is the Lord; we have waited for him: we will be glad and rejoice in his salvation!" Then, indeed, will " death be swallowed up in victory, and all tears be wiped from off all faces[g]," and the Saviour's advent be celebrated in this universal song.]

But we need not wait for any distant seasons; for even now may our text be taken,

II. As the language of every individual believer—

Yes, now, at this present moment, does the believer thus express himself,

1. In the recollection of what is past—

[Long has he waited upon God, that he might obtain mercy to his soul. To " win Christ, and be found in him," has been the supreme object of his desire. For this he has wept, and prayed, and laboured, if by any means he might obtain it. And now, at last, Christ has revealed himself to him, as an able and all-sufficient Saviour. Now, then, with

---

[d] Rev. xix. 6, 7. [e] Rom. viii. 22, 23.
[f] Tit. ii. 13. [g] ver. 7, 8.

grateful surprise, he exclaims, ' Lo, this is my God, for whom
I have waited and prayed! this is my Lord, whom alone, and
above all things, I have desired to behold. I once thought the
time long; but now I regret not the troubles which I endured
whilst seeking after him: had they been ten times as pungent,
or had I endured them ten times as long, I should not now
repine: one view of him as reconciled to me, and one hour
spent in communion with him, is sufficient to repay me for a
whole life of sorrow and suspense.' I will appeal to all, whether any man, who can say, "He hath taken me out of the
horrible pit, and out of the miry clay," does not find occasion
also to add, "He hath put a new song into my mouth, even
thanksgiving to our God[h]"?]

2. In the anticipation of what is yet future—

[Doubtless he looks forward to many conflicts with sin
and Satan: he sees a host of enemies arrayed against him,
enemies with whom he would be utterly unable to cope: but
he knows in whom he has believed; and, in dependence on the
Saviour, he defies every adversary, saying, "In the Lord put I
my trust: I will not fear what either men or devils can do
against me[i]." In answer to the remonstrances of a guilty conscience, he replies, "My Lord will *save* me:" and, if the
number or power of his enemies be urged against him, he answers with confidence, "This Saviour is my *God:* and if HE
be for me, who can be against me?" This is HE for whom I
have waited; and HE will save me. "In his name I set up
my banners;" and in reliance upon HIM, I know that no enemy
shall prevail against me, or "ever pluck me out of his hands."
I give loose therefore to joy: yea, "I will be glad, and rejoice
in his salvation[k];" and though I "see my Saviour no otherwise than by faith, I will rejoice in him with joy unspeakable
and full of glory."]

APPLICATION—

What now shall I say, to commend this Saviour to
you?

1. Let your expectations from him be enlarged—

[It is not possible for you to expect too much. If your
sins were numerous as the sands upon the sea-shore, you might
expect that he would "blot them all out as a morning cloud,"
or "cast them behind him into the depths of the sea." If he
who has undertaken to save you be "God," what have you to
fear? And if he have promised to be "a God unto you," it is
not possible that you should ever want. You may stretch your

---

[h] Ps. xl. 1—3.   [i] Ps. xxvii. 1.   [k] Ps. xx. 5.

requests to the utmost bounds of human language to express, or of human ingenuity to conceive, and they shall fall infinitely short of what you shall surely realize, if he himself be yours. " All things are yours, if ye be Christ's[1]."]

2. Let your joy in him abound—

[Doubtless, whilst you are in the body, you will have more or less cause for sorrow. But methinks, if you were out of the body, you could scarcely have more ground for joy. Only reflect on him who has undertaken to save you, or on the salvation which he has engaged to bestow upon you; and your whole life will be one continued scene of joyful exultation and of holy triumph. It will be, in short, a very heaven upon earth.]

[1] Adopt the language of David, Ps. lxii. 5—8.

OUTLINE NO. 894

TRUST IN GOD RECOMMENDED.

Isai. xxvi. 3, 4. *Thou wilt keep him in perfect peace, whose mind is stayed on thee; because he trusteth in thee. Trust ye in the Lord for ever: for in the Lord* JEHOVAH *is everlasting strength.*

IT was designed of God that under the Gospel dispensation his people should enjoy a state of very exalted happiness. The Jews had a spirit of bondage, as servants: we have a spirit of adoption, as sons. In conformity with this idea, the prophet, in the preceding chapter, speaks of the Lord as spreading a rich luxurious feast for all nations[a]; and, in the chapter before us, records " A song which should be sung" by all the guests[b]. And well indeed may *they* sing, who are enabled to make such an appeal to God, as that which we have just read : well may they sing, who have the Lord JEHOVAH himself engaged to keep them in perfect peace.

May our hearts be tuned to join in this Divine anthem, while we,

I. Shew what blessedness God will confer on his believing people—

It is said by the voice of inspiration, " The faithful man shall abound with blessings[c]:" and again, " God will bless his people with peace[d]."

[a] Isai. xxv. 6.   [b] ver. 1.   [c] Prov. xxviii. 20.   [d] Ps. xxix. 11.

The unbeliever is an utter stranger to peace—

[He may be stupid and insensible as a beast; but he can know nothing of real peace: even his apathy vanishes when once he begins to think of death and judgment. As his serenity resembles that of the irrational creation; so it arises from a similar source, a want of foresight or reflection in reference to the concerns of his soul. If he thinks of God, he is troubled, and will gladly have recourse to any thing to banish such uneasy reflections from his mind. This is his state, even when in the midst of all that the world accounts good and great: but how utterly devoid of peace is he, when once he is awakened to a sense of his real condition! Then he is full of terror, like the three thousand on the day of Pentecost; and, if he do not think of suicide, like the affrighted Jailor, he would gladly exchange condition with the beasts, if only the dissolution of the animal life might put an eternal period to his existence.

We speak not of the tumultuous passions by which the ungodly are agitated; because there are some who by the mere force of philosophy are enabled in a very great degree to moderate their feelings. But none can reflect on an eternity beyond the grave, without being appalled at the thought of the doom that awaits them, if they are unprepared to meet their God: so true is that which is spoken by the prophet, "The wicked are like the troubled sea, that cannot rest: there is no peace, saith my God, to the wicked[e]."]

But God promises this blessing to the believer—

[" The man whose mind is stayed on God, shall be kept in perfect peace." He shall have peace *in relation to his pardon and acceptance with God*. Often in the day of his flesh did our Lord assure persons that their sins, though numerous, were forgiven[f]: and will he be less gracious to his people now? Though he will not give us that assurance by any audible voice, he will by the inward witness of his Spirit[g]. As once he sent " a Seraph to take a live coal from off his altar, and to touch with it the prophet's lips, and to say to him, Thine iniquity *is* taken away, and thy sin *is* purged[h]," so will he now send his Holy Spirit, as a Spirit of promise, to apply the promises to our souls, and to be within us a pledge and earnest of our heavenly inheritance[i].

The Believer shall have peace also *in relation to his perseverance in the divine life*. He " knows in whom he has believed, and that he is able to keep that which has been committed to him[k]." He knows that his Lord and Saviour is " able to keep

---

[e] Isai. lvii. 20, 21.   [f] Matt. ix. 2. Luke vii. 47.
[g] Rom. viii. 16.   [h] Isai. vi. 6, 7.   [i] Eph. i. 13, 14.
[k] 2 Tim. i. 12.

him from falling, and to present him faultless before the presence
of his glory with exceeding joy[1]:" and whilst he contemplates
heaven as an " inheritance reserved for him, he has the comfort
of reflecting that he also is kept for it, even by the power of
God through faith unto everlasting salvation[m]." Persuaded as
he is that "He is faithful who hath promised[n]," and " able also
to perform" his word[o], he is " confident of this very thing, that
He who hath begun a good work in him will perform it until
the day of Christ[p]," and " will preserve him blameless unto his
heavenly kingdom[q]."

He shall have peace also *in relation to every thing that may
occur in his way to heaven.* Numberless things arise of a temporal or spiritual nature to disturb the minds of those who are
weak in faith : but when once " the mind is stayed on God,"
all these distractions cease. God is acknowledged as the
author of all that is done, whether good or evil : not a sparrow,
or a hair of our heads, falls to the ground, but by his special
permission : and from whatever quarter trials arise, whether
from voluntary agents, or unconscious elements, he is regarded
as their true and proper source[r], and that consideration reconciles the soul to the dispensation[s]; yea, he acquiesces in it,
assured that " all things shall work together for his good[t]."
He is careful for nothing, because he " casts all his care on
God[u];" and in humble prayer commits every thing to his
all-wise disposal : and thus in a measure enjoys as much tranquillity, in relation to future events, as the birds of the air, or
the lilies of the field[x].]

This blessing God will bestow upon him, *" because*
he putteth his trust in him"—

[There is nothing *meritorious* in faith, any more than in
other graces : but there is in faith a *power* peculiar to itself :
it engages the Most High God, and, if we might dare to use
such an expression, we would almost say, binds him to exert
himself in our behalf. When we lay hold on his word by faith,
he feels his own honour pledged to fulfil our desire, and not to
suffer us to be disappointed of our hope. Indeed, inasmuch as
faith pre-eminently honours him, he delights to honour it : and
to such a degree would he honour it, that, " if we had faith only
as a grain of mustard-seed," that figure should be realized in
our experience ; we should be rooted up from this world, as a
sycamore-tree from the earth ; and though liable in ourselves
to be tossed about by every wave, we should be fixed immove-
ably amidst the most tempestuous billows[y]. This is strongly

---

[1] Jude, ver. 24.   [m] 1 Pet. i. 4, 5.   [n] Heb. x. 23.
[o] Rom. iv. 21.   [p] Phil. i. 6.   [q] 2 Tim. iv. 18.
[r] Job i. 14—21.   [s] Ps. xxxix. 9.   [t] Rom. viii. 28.
[u] 1 Pet. v. 7.   [x] Matt. vi. 25—34.   [y] Luke xvii. 6.

intimated in the very words of our text, where the literal expression, as pointed out in the margin, is, " Thou wilt keep
him in *peace, peace*," that is, in peace indubitably *certain*, unin-
terruptedly *abiding*, and richly *abundant*. If only we cherished
an " earnest expectation and hope" in God, verily " we should
never be ashamed or confounded world without end[z]."]

Having thus shewn what God has prepared for
them that love him, we would,

II. Urge you to seek that blessedness in God's ap-
pointed way—

God calls us all to trust in him :

1. Consider what a God we have to trust in—

[*Consider what " exceeding great and precious promises he
has given to us.*" There is not a situation or a circumstance
wherein we can be placed, but God has given us promises
exactly suited to it. It would be a highly profitable employment to extract from the Scriptures for ourselves the various
promises contained in them, and especially those which apply
more particularly to our own case; and then to spread them
from time to time before our God in prayer. What sweet
encouragement would this afford us, in all our addresses at the
throne of grace; and what holy confidence would it create in
us! If we have only a promise from a man like ourselves, it
tends exceedingly to compose our minds : but how much more
would this effect arise from apprehending the promises of a
faithful God!

But *consider also how able God is to perform all that he has
promised to us.* Truly " with him is everlasting strength :"
" There is nothing impossible with him." " It is alike with
him to save by many or by few." He can save with means, or
without means, or against means. As for our weakness, or
the strength of our enemies, it makes no difference to him. In
the words following our text, it is said, " He will bring down
them that dwell on high : the lofty city, he layeth it low; he
layeth it low, even to the ground; he bringeth it even to the
dust." Is it asked, By whom he will do this? it is added,
" The foot shall tread it down, even the feet of the poor, and
the steps of the needy[a] :" yes, " He will strengthen the spoiler
against the strong, so that the spoiled shall come against the
fortress[b]." The weaker we are in our own apprehension, the
more strong we are in reality; because " his power shall rest
upon us," and " his strength be perfected in our weakness[c]."]

Let us trust in him with our whole hearts—

z Phil. i. 20. Isai. xlv. 17.   a ver. 5, 6. See also ch. xiv. 2.
b Amos v. 9.   c 2 Cor. xii. 9, 10.

[There are persons who imagine they trust in God, when, in fact, they are trusting only in their own delusions[d]. There must be an express renunciation of every other hope[e], and an actual committing of our way to him in prayer[f]. There must be a direct exercise of faith in him, as able, and willing to effect whatsoever our necessities require; and a firm persuasion that he will do that which shall in the issue be best for us. This is implied in having "the mind stayed on him." We have a fine description of this state of mind contained in the prophecies of Isaiah: it is primarily indeed applicable to the Messiah; but is proper also to be realized in the experience of all the saints; since "all who fear the Lord" are exhorted in seasons of the deepest darkness and distress to set it before them as a model, and, after his example, to stay themselves upon their God[g] ——— How important this duty is, may be inferred from the *reiterated* injunctions given us respecting it[h]. Let us then "trust in God *at all times.*" In times of ease and security, let us remember that we are in his hands, and not be saying with ourselves, "My mountain standeth strong; I shall not be moved[i]." In times of trouble and distress, let us "not stagger at the promises through unbelief, but be strong in faith, giving glory to God." Let us, after the example of David, say, "My soul, wait thou only upon God; for my expectation is from him. He only is my rock and my salvation; he is my defence; I shall not be moved. In God is my salvation, and my glory: the rock of my strength, and my refuge, is in God[k]."

This is the kind of trust to which alone the promise is made. "If our faith waver, we shall receive nothing of the Lord[l]:" but if we commit our every concern to him, "our very thoughts," the most fluctuating of all things, "shall be established[m]," and "the peace of God which passeth all understanding shall keep (the affections of) our hearts and (the imaginations of) our minds, through Christ Jesus[n]."]

ADDRESS—

1. Those who know nothing of this blessedness—

[Do not suppose that this peace is merely ideal; and that, because you do not experience it, it has no existence in the Believer's mind: for it is the legacy of Christ to all his people: "Peace I leave with you; MY peace I give unto you[o]:" and it is indeed "a peace *that passeth all* understanding." It is not a mere absence of feeling, but a positive sense of reconciliation with God, a sweet consciousness of being under

d Isai. xlviii. 1, 2.   e Prov. iii. 5, 6.   f Ps. lxii. 8.
g Isai. l. 7—10.   h Ps. cxv. 9—11.   i Ps. xxx. 7.
k Ps. lxii. 5—7.   l Jam. i. 6, 7.   m Prov. xvi. 3.
n Phil. iv. 6, 7. See the Greek.   o John xiv. 27

his protecting care, and a humble, yet confident, expectation, that he will order every thing for our eternal good. We cannot give a juster picture of it, than by referring you to the description given of it by the sweet singer of Israel[p]. Nothing alarms him, or disturbs his rest, because he knows that "his God is for him, and that therefore none can, with any effect, be against him[q]." "His God gives him quietness; Who then can make trouble[r]?"

And will you be content to continue ignorant of this happiness? Why should you do so? Christ has purchased it for "those who are afar off, as well as those who are near[s];" and he will confer it in rich abundance on all who call upon him[t].]

2. Those who through the weakness of their faith do not yet partake of it—

[How dishonourable is your conduct, and injurious to that God who redeemed you by the blood of his only dear Son! Whom has he ever deceived, that you cannot rely upon his promises? In what instance has he ever shewn himself deficient, either in faithfulness or power? What enemies also are you to your own happiness, at the time that you are so dishonouring him! "Has he not said to you, that, if you would believe, you should see the glory of God[u]?" "Believe in the Lord, so shall ye be established; believe his prophets, so shall ye prosper[x]:" but, "if ye will not believe, surely ye shall not be established[y]."]

3. Those who profess to enjoy that peace—

[Well may we say with David, "O Lord of Hosts, blessed is the man that trusteth in thee[z];" blessed is the man who with humble confidence can approach thee, saying, "O God, thou art my God." And are any of you brought to this happy state? O "cast not away your confidence, which has such great recompence of reward[a]:" for then, and then only, "are we partakers of Christ, if we hold fast the beginning of our confidence steadfast unto the end[b]." But, on the other hand, beware lest you abuse that confidence, and walk unworthy of your high calling: for, "if God has spoken peace" unto your souls, he especially enjoins you "never more to return to folly[c]." Let it be seen then what is the genuine effect of saving faith: and, if you call yourselves sons of God, and profess to have your portion with him in the world to come, then remember, that "every one that hath this hope in him, purifieth himself even as He is pure[d]."]

[p] Ps. xxiii.   [q] Rom. viii. 31.   [r] Job xxxiv. 29.
[s] Eph. ii. 17.   [t] Rom. x. 11—13.   [u] John xi. 40.
[x] 2 Chron. xx. 20.   [y] Isai. vii. 9.   [z] Ps. lxxxiv. 12.
[a] Heb. x. 35.   [b] Heb. iii. 14.   [c] Ps. lxxxv. 8.
[d] 1 John iii. 2, 3.

OUTLINE NO. 895

HUMILIATION WITH ZEAL.

Isai. xxvi. 13.   O Lord our God, other lords besides thee have had dominion over us : but by thee only will we make mention of thy name.

MANY devout songs are composed in Scripture for the use of God's Church and people in the latter day. But, amidst their praises for mercies vouchsafed untc them, care is taken to keep up in their minds a remembrance of their former sins, and a sense of those duties which they owe to their heavenly Benefactor. On a review of the past, they are taught to acknowledge the evil of their ways ; and in a prospect of the future, to consecrate themselves, with all due solemnity, to the service of their God.   Now, at this season[a], I cannot do better than recommend to your adoption,

I. Their retrospective acknowledgment—

It is probable, that, in the words before us, respect is had to the *civil* bondage to which that nation had again and again been reduced on account of their iniquities[b] — — — But, considering for what period the song is prepared, we cannot doubt but that there is a reference also to the *moral* bondage in which they have been held by their corruptions.   And in this sense, the acknowledgment well becomes us at this day; since we are told by an inspired Apostle, that " to whomsoever we yield ourselves servants to obey, his servants we are to whom we obey[c]."   And what has been our conduct through life ?

The greater part of us have " served only our own lusts and pleasures[d]"—

[Look at all around you: or, rather, look within your own bosoms ; and say, to whom have your lives been devoted, to God, or Mammon? — — — Verily, there is but too much reason to confess, that " God has not been in all our thoughts[e]" — — —]

Of those who have had *some* respect to God, still must this acknowledgment be required—

---

[a] *New Year's Day.*   [b] 2 Chron. xxviii. 5, 6. Neh. ix. 36, 37
[c] Rom. vi. 16.   [d] Tit. iii. 3.   [e] Ps. x. 4.

["Other lords *besides God*, have had dominion over you. The lip and the knee perhaps you have devoted to Jehovah in the observance of outward duties, both in the public assemblies of the Church, and in your own closets; but where has been *the heart*[f]? You "have had *the form* of godliness perhaps, but where has been *the power*[g]? Call to mind your prayers and your praises, how cold have they been! Have they not even frozen, as it were, upon your very lips? On the other hand, see with what ardour and delight you have followed your earthly pursuits, whether intellectual or corporeal, and whether for pleasure or honour or emolument ———— But God says, "Give ME thine heart;" and in the want of this, all the services you have rendered him are no better than "the cutting off a dog's neck for sacrifice, or the offering of swine's blood[h]" ———]

Whilst I recommend the deepest humiliation before God in the review of your past lives, I cannot but urge for your adoption what is here suggested for,

II. Their prospective determination—

The Israelites were forbidden to make mention of the name of any of the gods which were worshipped in the land of Canaan[i]. By them no other name than that of Jehovah was to be uttered; because He, and he alone, was God. Hence "the making mention of his name was equivalent to an acknowledgment of him as the only true God, and was therefore considered as a just description of his peculiar people[k]. But this must be done in sincerity and truth; else it would be regarded only as an act of hypocrisy and profaneness[l]. It must comprehend all that attachment which is due to the supreme God, who is the only proper object of fear, or love, or confidence ———

Now, then, I recommend this to you,

1. As your duty—

[Who else is entitled to any of these regards, except in entire subordination and subserviency to Him? ———]

2. As your interest—

[Who can so recompense your services, or so avenge the want of them? ———]

[f] Isai. xxix. 13. [g] 2 Tim. iii. 5. [h] Isai. lxvi. 3.
[i] Exod. xxiii. 13. Josh. xxiii. 7. [k] Isai. lxii. 6.
[l] Isai. xlviii. 1.

3. As your happiness—

[Ask the most successful votaries of this world what they have ever gained? Ask them what solid satisfaction they have ever found in all that the world could give them? Then ask the servants of the living God, whether they have not found his service to be perfect freedom, and " his ways to be ways of pleasantness and peace?" As to the eternal world, it is almost superfluous for me to speak: for there are none so ignorant as not to know, that the pleasures of sense all " perish with the using," and that those only who seek their happiness in God can ever enjoy " the pleasures which are at his right hand for evermore"——— I therefore confidently say to all of you without exception, Let this be the determination of you all, that henceforth you will make no mention of any name in a way of fear, or love, or confidence, but " the name of Jehovah only."]

Thus far I have spoken to you *as men* only. But what shall I say to you as Christians?

[Tell me, whether, as "bought with the precious blood of Christ," you have any duty, any interest, any happiness, worthy of a moment's consideration, in comparison of *his* service, *his* honour, *his* glory[m]?——————]

Let me, in conclusion, submit to your consideration the following QUESTIONS—

1. Who amongst you does not need to make this retrospective acknowledgment?———

2. What will the acknowledgment avail you, if you do not make, and carry into effect, the prospective determination?———

3. To what purpose will it be to begin well, if you ever " become weary in well-doing[n]?"

[You must maintain " a patient continuance in well-doing, if ever you would attain eternal life[o]." If ever you draw back, whatever your attainments for a season may have been, " you will draw back unto perdition:" for " God's soul can have no pleasure in you[p]"————]

I must not, however, dismiss you without one most important and necessary CAUTION—

[The resolution which I have recommended must not be made in your own strength, but entirely in dependence upon God. *This is very particularly intimated in my text:* " By thee only will we make mention of thy name." In the very words before the text is it said, " Thou hast wrought all our works in us." Yes, " our sufficiency is of God alone[q]." The Apostle

---

[m] 1 Cor. vi. 20.   [n] Gal. vi. 9.   [o] Rom. ii. 7.
[p] Heb. x. 38, 39.   [q] 2 Cor. iii. 5.

Paul himself was constrained to say, " By the grace of God I
am what I am[r]:" and if any of you confide for one moment in
your own strength, you will fall[s].   On the other hand, if you
trust in the Lord Jesus Christ, you are assured, in this very
Song, that your "strength shall be according to your day[t]."
" Be strong, then, in the Lord, and in the power of his
might[u]:" and then let the Psalmist's resolution be yours, and
his song be yours ; " My mouth shall shew forth thy righteousness and thy salvation all the day ; for I know not the numbers
thereof. *I will go in the strength of the Lord God : I will make
mention of thy righteousness, even of thine only[x].*"]

[r] 1 Cor. xv. 10.   [s] Prov. xxviii. 26.
[t] Compare ver. 3, 4. with Jude, ver. 24.   [u] Eph. vi. 10.
[x] Ps. lxxi. 15, 16.

OUTLINE NO. 896

THE ONLY REFUGE OF SINNERS.

Isai. xxvi. 20, 21. *Come, my people, enter thou into thy chambers, and shut thy doors about thee : hide thyself as it were
for a little moment, until the indignation be overpast.   For
behold, the Lord cometh out of his place to punish the inhabitants of the earth for their iniquity.*

GOD has been pleased to manifest at all times such
a tender concern for the welfare of his people, that
he has scarcely ever done any thing of importance,
which he has not revealed to them beforehand by his
servants the prophets[a].   Did he determine to destroy
the earth with a flood ? he instructed Noah first to
build an ark for the preservation of himself and his
family[b].   Was he about to rain fire and brimstone
upon Sodom and Gomorrha ? he could not execute
his vengeance till righteous Lot had retired to a place
of safety[c].   Had he decreed to bring on Jerusalem
such judgments as the world had never before seen ?
he warns his people to escape from it, and provides
them a retreat in the neighbouring mountains[d].   Thus
he had decreed the destruction of Babylon ; and the
preceding part of the chapter contains a hymn of
triumph, which should be sung by his people on that
occasion.   But, as there would be great danger of

[a] Amos iii. 7.   [b] Gen. vi. 13, 14.
[c] Gen. xix. 22.   [d] Luke xxi. 21, 22.

their being involved in the common calamity, he apprises them of his intention, and exhorts them to hide themselves, till the danger should be overpast It is not, however, necessary to confine the words to this sense; because there are many other occasions on which God comes forth to punish mankind; and because the advice given, is suitable to all such occasions.

In discoursing on this passage, we shall call your attention to,

I. The warning here given—

Heaven is the habitation of God's holiness and glory[e]. And from thence he is said to " come forth," when he manifests himself in any signal manner upon earth[f]. And, alas! how often do the iniquities of men necessitate him to come down and visit them with his sore judgments[g]! But there is one period in particular, when God shall come, not to punish one particular nation only, but all who shall have lived and died in sin, from the foundation of the world.

[The day of judgment is called " the day of wrath," "the day of vengeance," " the day of the revelation of God's righteous judgments," " the day of the perdition of ungodly men[h]." In that day the Lord Jesus Christ, "whom the heavens have received till the time of the restitution of all things[i]," " shall come in power and great glory:" and the express end of his coming will be "to reveal his wrath against all ungodliness and unrighteousness of men[k]."

Now he winks, as it were, at men's iniquities[l]; and endures with much patience and longsuffering the vessels of wrath that are fitting themselves for destruction[m]: yea, to such a degree does he exercise forbearance towards them, that scoffers are ready to say, Where is the promise of his coming[n]? But soon the time fixed for the exercise of his grace, shall come to an end, and all the dead shall be summoned to his tribunal, to receive at his hands according to their works[o].

---

[e] Isai. lvii. 15. and lxiii. 15.   [f] Mic. i. 3.

[g] If this were the subject of a *Fast Sermon*, the particular judgments that are deprecated, should be specified here as the tokens of God's displeasure, and should be dwelt upon at some length.

[h] Rom. ii. 5. 2 Pet. iii. 7.   [i] Acts iii. 21.   [k] Rom. i. 18.

[l] Acts xvii. 30.   [m] Rom. ix. 22.   [n] 2 Pet. iii. 3, 4.

[o] Rev. xx. 12, 13.

Nor let any one think that gross iniquities only shall be noticed in that day; for God will "manifest even the counsels of men's hearts," and "bring every secret thing into judgment[p]:" then a forgetfulness of God, or a rejection of his Gospel, shall as surely be punished with everlasting destruction, as any of those sins which are more reprobated and condemned by the world[q].]

The warning being of such universal and infinite importance, let us consider,

II. The advice accompanying it—

[The exhortation in the text may simply import, that we should retire to our chambers to commune with our own hearts, and with our God[r]. In this view it recommends the duty, the indispensably necessary duty of secret prayer.

But by "chambers" we may understand GOD himself, who is often spoken of in this light[s], and who is the sure refuge of all that flee unto him. Every perfection of his forms, as it were, a hiding-place whereto we may run for safety. His wisdom would be our guide, his power our defence, "his faithfulness and truth our shield and buckler."

To us, who are taught to view God in the person of Christ, the word "chambers" may convey a more immediate intimation respecting Christ himself, who is our refuge[t], and whom this very prophet describes as "an hiding-place from the wind, and a covert from the storm[u]." His person, work, and offices are a security to his people, that "they shall never perish, but shall have eternal life."

To him therefore we should flee by faith, and hide ourselves from the impending judgments. As Noah entered into the ark[x], which was the appointed mean of delivering him from the deluge, and as the Israelites shut themselves up in their houses to escape the sword of the destroying angel[y], so are we to take refuge, as it were, in Christ, that the sword of divine justice may not slay, or the deluge of God's wrath overwhelm us.]

While we listen to the voice of God, we must not overlook,

III. The particular manner in which the advice is given—

[Almost every word of this exhortation contains an argument for our compliance with it.

[p] 1 Cor. iv. 5.
[q] Ps. ix. 17.   2 Thess. i. 7, 8.
[r] Ps. iv. 4. Matt. vi. 6.
[s] Ps. xc. 1. and lvii. 1.
[t] Heb. vi. 18.
[u] Isai. xxxii. 2.
[x] Gen. vii. 7.
[y] Exod. xii. 22, 28.

If we were bidden to hide ourselves in a pit or a dungeon, methinks, any place should be a welcome hiding-place from the wrath of God. But it is to our own "chamber," where every thing is provided for our rest and comfort; yea, it is a pavilion[z], surrounded by guards, and furnished with royal dainties; it is even to the tabernacle [a] wherein God himself dwells, and where we shall have most intimate communion with him, that we are told to flee. Shall we need any inducement to yield to such advice?

If we cannot endure confinement (though surely we can have no reason to complain of that in such a retreat) we are told it is to be only for "a moment," yea, lest that should appear too long, it is said to be only for "a little moment." Did the Israelites think a single night too long, when they were to be screened from the destroying angel? and shall we think a moment, a little moment (for such in truth is the present life), too long to abide in Christ, that we may escape the wrath of an incensed God?

The certainty of success is another argument which may well induce us to follow this advice. Were there only a distant probability of obtaining deliverance from such unspeakable miseries, it were a very sufficient reason for our trying the experiment: but when success, as the text intimates, is certain to attend our efforts, shall we need any persuasion to exert ourselves?

On the other hand, the certainty that God's indignation must fall upon us, if we be not found in Christ, ought to operate powerfully on our hearts: for "who can stand before his indignation? who can abide the fierceness of his anger[b]?" The fate of those who despised the warnings of Moses, and sought not shelter from the storms of hail, shews us what we must expect, if we seek not refuge in Christ Jesus[c].

Above all, the earnestness of the exhortation should overcome the reluctance of our hearts. To enter fully into its spirit, we should conceive a parent, seeing a savage beast running towards his heedless and unprotected child in order to destroy him. The affrighted father calls to him in the agony of his mind; " Come, my son, run into the house, shut the door, hide yourself till the danger be overpast." Thus, precisely thus, does God himself cry to each of us. He knows our danger; he sees our inadvertence; and, with all the anxiety of a parent, he calls to us. Must we not be more deaf than adders, more obdurate than rocks, if we will not obey his voice?

But there is one thing yet, which must on no account be overlooked. The language is intentionally changed from the plural to the singular; " Come, my people, enter *thou*," &c.

z Ps. xxvii. 5.   a Ps. xxvii. 5.
b Nahum i. 6.   c Exod. ix. 19, 25.

One is ready to think, that he has no need to fear the indignation of God : *another* thinks he is too unworthy to be admitted into the chamber to which others have fled. But God addresses both the one and the other of them ; "Enter *thou;*" for, however secure thou mayest think thyself, there is no security but in Christ ; and "*thou;*" for unworthy as thou art, it is "*thy*" chamber; it was erected for such as thee ; and the more unworthy thou art in thy own estimation, the more ready admittance shalt thou find there ; the more certainly also shalt thou enjoy in it everlasting security[d].

Thus whether we consider the chamber to which we are to flee, the time we are to abide in it, the certainty of success, the danger of delay, or the earnest manner in which God addresses every one of us in particular, we should without hesitation follow the advice, and seek deliverance in Christ our Lord. None of us should indulge security ; none of us should give way to desponding fears. But, rejoicing that the chamber is not yet barred against us, we should all hide ourselves in it ; nor venture out of it one single moment, till the danger be for ever past.]

[d] This section might not improperly form the basis of a particular *application* to the self-righteous Pharisee, and the self-condemning penitent.

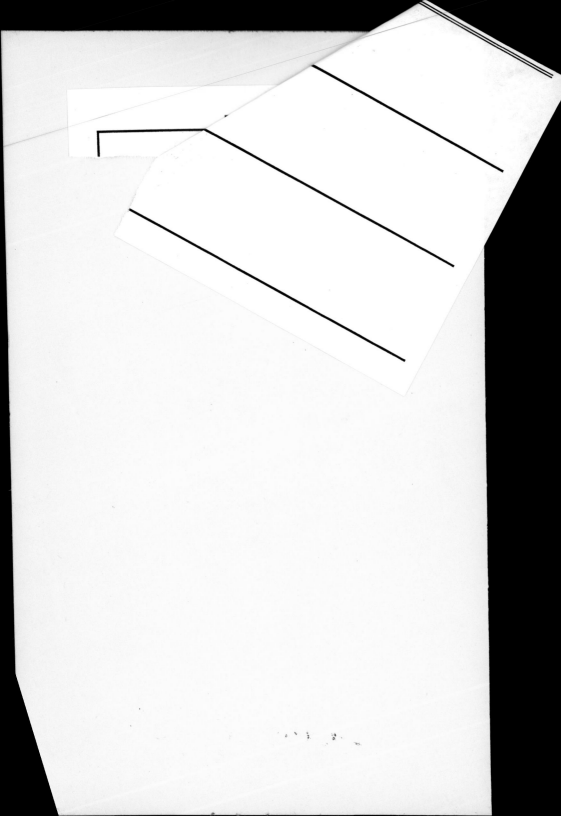